AF781234

Inter-Organizational Information Systems and Business Management:

Theories for Researchers

Kishor Vaidya
University of Canberra, Australia & University of Southern Queensland, Australia

BUSINESS SCIENCE
Reference

Managing Director:	Lindsay Johnston
Senior Editorial Director:	Heather Probst
Book Production Manager:	Sean Woznicki
Development Manager:	Joel Gamon
Development Editor:	Hannah Abelbeck
Acquisitions Editor:	Erika Gallagher
Typesetters:	Mackenzie Snader, Chris Shearer
Print Coordinator:	Jamie Snavely
Cover Design:	Nick Newcomer

Published in the United States of America by
Business Science Reference (an imprint of IGI Global)
701 E. Chocolate Avenue
Hershey PA 17033
Tel: 717-533-8845
Fax: 717-533-8661
E-mail: cust@igi-global.com
Web site: http://www.igi-global.com

Copyright © 2012 by IGI Global. All rights reserved. No part of this publication may be reproduced, stored or distributed in any form or by any means, electronic or mechanical, including photocopying, without written permission from the publisher. Product or company names used in this set are for identification purposes only. Inclusion of the names of the products or companies does not indicate a claim of ownership by IGI Global of the trademark or registered trademark.

Library of Congress Cataloging-in-Publication Data

Inter-organizational information systems and business management: theories for researchers / Kishor Vaidya, editor.
p. cm.
Includes bibliographical references and index.
Summary: "This book highlights the most influential organizational theories and their applications in Inter-Organizational Information Systems, providing theories that have been consistently tested and proven to be valid over time"--Provided by publisher.
ISBN 978-1-60960-768-5 (hbk.: alk. paper) -- ISBN 978-1-60960-769-2 (ebook : alk. paper) -- ISBN 978-1-60960-770-8 (print & perpetual access: alk. paper) 1. Information technology--Management. 2. Management information systems. 3. Communication in organizations. 4. Interorganizational relations. I. Vaidya, Kishor, 1967-
HD30.2.I5594 2012
658.4'038011--dc23

2011041789

British Cataloguing in Publication Data
A Cataloguing in Publication record for this book is available from the British Library.

All work contributed to this book is new, previously-unpublished material. The views expressed in this book are those of the authors, but not necessarily of the publisher.

Editorial Advisory Board

Michael Essig, *Bundeswehr University, Germany*
Robert Fichman, *Boston College, USA*
Angappa Gunasekaran, *University of Massachusetts, USA*
Micky Hyde, *Indiana University of Pennsylvania, USA*
Dharmendra Sharma, *University of Canberra, Australia*
Jeffrey Soar, *University of Southern Queensland, Australia*

List of Reviewers

John Campbell, *University of Canberra, Australia*
Michael Essig, *Bundeswehr University, Germany*
Robert Fichman, *Boston College, USA*
Scott Gardner, *Murdoch University, Australia*
Andrea Genovese, *University of Naples "Federico II", Italy*
Micky Hyde, *Indiana University of Pennsylvania, USA*
Robert B. Johnston, *University College Dublin, Ireland*
Ik-Whan G. Kwon, *St. Louis University, USA*
Maria Madlberger, *Webster University, Austria*
Anne Rouse, *Deakin University, Australia*
Jeffrey Soar, *University of Southern Queensland, Australia*
Khi V. Thai, *Florida Atlantic University, USA*
Shiro Uesugi, *Matsuyama University, Japan*
Jim Underwood, *University of Technology, Sydney, Australia*
Kishor Vaidya, *University of Canberra, Australia*
Marilyn Wells, *CQ University, Australia*

Table of Contents

Detailed Table of Contents

While some organizations have benefited significantly by effectively using inter-organizational information systems (IOIS), other organizations with IOIS deployment have struggled to gain expected business value of IOIS, and yet other trading partners have resisted the participation in IOIS. This paper asserts that academic theories provide means to form meaningful conclusions to understand the underlying causes of these phenomena. Against this background, this chapter presents a research framework to study IOIS and business management related issues. It identifies the key constructs and variables for each research domain of the framework. A brief description of over 30 theories has been provided and the entities named in the theory are expected to predict the outcome of the theory-governed occurrences. An attempt has been made to link each domain of the IOIS and business management framework to key relevant theories. It is expected that understanding of various antecedents that influence IOIS and its impact on inter-organizational processes and organizational effectiveness in light of these theories can help organize and guide academic research efforts as well as offer insights to research practitioners on IOIS and business management.

are social exchange theory and embeddedness theory (organization theories), transaction cost theory and agency theory (economics-related theories), the resource-based view of the firm and network theory (strategic management approaches), and game theory. The findings and the resulting framework imply that all these theories lead to similar recommendations on the use of IOIS although they have very diverse assumptions and lines of argumentation. The chapter stresses that the investigated theories supplement rather than contradict each other.

Transaction Cost Economics (TCE) was once described as "revolutionary" in economic theory. Even though this seems to be a bit excessive, TCE is a major approach to combining the rigorous instruments of microeconomic analysis with the practical relevance of incomplete markets. Instead of comparing "relevance versus rigor," TCE offers the opportunity to combine both aspects through scientific research that combines a sound theoretical basis with concrete implications for management. The fact that transaction costs occur both within companies and among companies in a market make TCE an ideal approach for inter-organizational (information) systems. Additionally, as a microeconomic-based approach, it can also be used for managerial purposes. In this chapter, we have determined an inter-organizational approach by using the perspective of a company using (and buying) outside resources, which means a concentration of supply management activities.

The foundation of efficient and effective supply chain management rests on collaborative efforts by all parties involved in executing the supply chain optimization process. Every partner in the chain has to exercise its best effort to achieve the most efficient and effective results. Research indicates that transaction cost can be reduced if partners practice trust-based collaborative supply chain operations. Studies also show that cooperation among and between potential supply chain partners sometimes can lead to collaboration if partners see an opportunity for mutual value creation. Collaboration may foster an environment conducive to building trust and form the basis for the first step toward making a tangible business commitment. As the level of trust within and outside an organization increases, speed of decision making increases, and subsequently, transaction costs decrease. The inverse is also true. Accordingly, trust and information sharing are central tenets of supply chains in reducing the transaction cost. As transaction cost decreases, total supply chain cost may also decrease making operations more competitive in the global market. This chapter describes the relationship between trust and transaction cost in supply chain operations. Empirical findings from several research studies on trust and transaction cost in supply chain operations will be presented in support of the argument for managing transaction cost in supply chain management. A suggested future research agenda on this topic is also provided.

Inter-organizational information systems depend at least as much on collaboration across organizational cultures as on the development of technical infrastructure for their success. Actor-network theory (ANT) is a useful approach for bringing together social and technical considerations. In this chapter we discuss key features of ANT and show how it might be applied to a particular case of IOIS adoption; this ANT approach is compared to co-evolutionary theory which was originally applied to this case. Some possible extensions to ANT are contemplated, and we offer advice to those attempting ANT-based research. We also give advice, based on ANT, to those undertaking IOIS development.

This chapter reports on the development of the technology acceptance model from 1986 when Davis investigated technology acceptance from an individual's view as to the ease of use and perceived usefulness of a system. Since then, many variations have been presented in attempts to explain how and what influences a computer system user's uptake of new technology within an organisation. Whilst all variations were developed explicitly to predict users' acceptance or rejection of new technology, these variations are in essence predictors of acceptance or rejection of change. Factors such as the organisational change environment and informal communication (rumours), together with social influence as exercised by colleagues should be considered major contributors to the perceptions of new technology and therefore acceptance. This chapter extends the original model to include the variations and proposes that rather than look at technology acceptance in isolation, acceptance of new technology should be viewed as acceptance of change. The author proposes the model Social Influence and Change Acceptance (SICAM) to reflect the inclusion of TAM's variations in an organizational change context.

Outsourcing of IT-supported business processes (systems development; customer relationship management; helpdesk, etc.) has become increasingly common in Western economies since the late 1990s. Such outsourcing is totally dependent on the provision of inter-organizational information systems (IOSs), which act as the "glue" to link vendor(s) and client(s). Hence understanding the importance of IOSs, and conversely, the downsides or risks they embody, is a critical part of ensuring that outsourcing arrangements are successful. In this chapter the theory behind outsourcing is unpacked, and readers are alerted to sometimes-overlooked aspects of the IOSs on which outsourcing depends. These raise the risks, and reduce the benefits, of outsourcing if they are not well thought through. Decision makers are advised to explicitly include the notion of risk in their outsourcing business cases, including those risks associated with the IOSs that support outsourcing arrangements.

In the late 1970s, a new approach to the management of operations was developed by Goldratt. Now known as the theory of constraints (TOC), it provides a coherent management theory for running an organisation. It has two major components: a philosophy which underpins the working principle of on-going improvement and a generic approach for investigating, analyzing, and creating solutions to problems, called the "thinking process" (TP). Several books, numerous articles, and a few journal special issues have been published on TOC. This chapter provides a comprehensive review of TOC concepts, philosophy, and working principles.

Merger and acquisition (M&A) activity has many strategic and operational objectives. One operational objective is to develop common and efficient information systems that can be the source of creating significant cost savings for the joined companies. In combining the IS divisions of the acquiring firm with that of the acquired firm there are many hurdles when the technical and social system are to be integrated. Exactly how this process will evolve and exactly what results can be achieved is hard to determine. This chapter identifies some of the major factors associated with the integration process and proposes Agent Based Simulation as a possible methodology to study this phenomenon.

Information is very important throughout the government budgetary process, which consists of budget preparation, budget appropriations, budget execution, and auditing and evaluation. When their budgets are prepared, agencies need financial data including those related to all types of government revenues and expenditures, economic conditions, agency needs, et cetera. When budgets are in the appropriation phase, the legislative branch also needs similar information, although information can be interpreted in different ways depending on each legislator's perception.

The following chapter provides an overview of sociotechnical theories that can be used to understand, design, implement, and evaluate clinical information systems in health care settings. The sociotechnical approach is one that seeks to identify the dynamics between technology and the social, professional, and cultural environment in which it is used. Theories and models covered include: the technology and information technology acceptance models; a multi-level integration framework approach; social cognition theory; theories that propose a fit between individuals, tasks and the technology; diffusion of innovation theory, and a contextual implementation model. The frameworks presented in this chapter are not exhaustive but are most relevant to the complexity of information and communication technology use in health care settings.

This chapter argues that diffusion theory models like the technology acceptance model (TAM) need to be rethought of in light of contextual factors that are becoming increasingly important in modern inter-organisational settings. This is due to the growing complexity of organizations with respect to different organisational types, contexts, and political structures that have been shown in research literature to hinder information systems acceptance. The chapter looks at possible contextual factors that are ignored by TAM by critiquing its parent diffusion theory (diffusion of innovations). This approach was considered best as there are many variations of TAM, but the diffusion of innovations (DOI) theory underlies all these variations. The chapter also recommends a way forward for research into inter-organisational information systems by examining an example situation of Feral Information Systems (FIS) to illustrate the problem. The chapter concludes with a discussion about future research directions.

Today most e-government and e-procurement research and discussion are done in a quite utilitarian and technical way. This follows the worldwide positivist and utilitarian approach to research that neglects the social, organizational, cultural, and political aspects of social life. Therefore, most research initiatives are based on a market-driven and utilitarian approach in which technology is treated as a mere tool. So, under the use of a traditional top-down model or the "tool-approach," information and communication technologies (ICTs) have been implemented in developing countries detached from their social and

and other procurement related documents between organisations and their suppliers. Although some literature exists on the adoption of e-procurement systems within the government sector, relatively little has been focused on the outcomes of these systems particularly within the Australian local government context. Furthermore, much of the attention of the existing eProcurement literature is on understanding adoption decisions of these systems from the perspective of senior management, and few research efforts have been made to examine how employees who actually use these systems perceive the benefits arising from these systems. In addition, although the role of demographic characteristics of users is recognised in the innovation adoption and broader IS/IT adoption literatures, it is not clearly known how the demographic characteristics of employees (who interact with such systems) may influence their perceptions about eProcurement benefits. To address this gap in the literature, we analyse the views captured from sixty employees working in three large city councils located in the state of Victoria, Australia. The findings indicate that the outcomes of eProcurement systems adoption were largely seen in a positive light as the employees reported favourably about the attainment of benefits from their use of these systems. More specifically, efficiency improvement and establishing control were perceived as the two most important benefits. However, except user type, popular demographic characteristics of employees (e.g. gender, job role, working experience at councils) were not related to their perceptions of eProcurement benefits. These findings offer limited support for the views expressed in the existing innovations and IS/IT adoption literatures. The implications of these findings are discussed, and future directions of research are proposed.

Compilation of References 309

About the Contributors 342

Index 351

Foreword

The discipline of Information Systems has long struggled with its identity. Many in the discipline argue that for information systems to be gauged as a discipline then it needs it own set of theories. Such theories seem not to be easily developed and information systems academics continue to search for theories that assist in defining the discipline's scope. In the meantime academics in the discipline, and their research students, need theoretical bases for their research. Without theory, research studies lack the depth and breadth of intellectual rigour and value that they can and should espouse. If research students of information systems topics are not aware of theory or do not use appropriate theory in their research then their efforts are likely to fall on fallow ground, particularly from dissertation examination and publication perspectives. I cannot remember the number of times that I have reviewed research papers for journals and conferences and asked the question "but where is the theory, what theory does this research address or consider?"

Collections of articles that provide exemplars of the use of theory are particularly valuable for research students. This book is one attempt to provide a significant coverage of theory in a form that shows how various theories can be applied in the context of inter-organisational information systems and business management. Often a multitude of theories are well known to research students but their application in the students' own research domain is less well established or understood. As such this book is a welcome addition to the literature and it could form a valuable resource to research students and indeed their research advisors.

The contributors to this book are respected academics from many countries throughout the world including from most continents: Asia, Australia, Europe, North America and South America. In developing the material the editors have been careful to consider articles relevant to the information systems discipline so that relevance to the potential audience, most notably research students (PhD, Masters and Honours) and research practitioners, is sharp.

I commend the book to you and hope that it not only guides you in your consideration of existing theories for your research but also makes you think about discovery or development of new theories and in particular theories that the information systems discipline might one day call its own.

Mark Toleman
University of Southern Queensland, Australia
President, Australian Council of Professors and Heads of Information Systems

Mark Toleman *is Professor and Head of the School of Information Systems, and Chair, Academic Board at the University of Southern Queensland. Professor Toleman has a MSc in mathematics from James Cook University and a PhD in computer science from the University of Queensland. He has published over 130 peer reviewed articles in areas ranging from information systems development methodologies to human-computer interaction to agricultural science. His current research interests include community support information systems, IT service management, IT governance, and systems development methodologies. Professor Toleman is currently President of the Australian Council of Professors and Heads of Information Systems.*

Preface

Research in Information Systems (IS) is concerned with the development and use of information systems to achieve improved organizational performance including business value. Information systems are mainly based on information and communication technology (ICT) and today they increasingly cross organization boundaries to facilitate the exchange of products and services among the organizations and their stakeholders. Such information systems, traditionally called as Inter-organizational Information Systems (IOIS), are obviously more complex than typical information systems and have thus greater impact on business management of the organizations.

Recent studies indicate that the assimilation of web-based IOIS into the mainstream business is occurring at a much slower than expected pace and its implementation and use of have not been smooth with business press reporting a number of failures of IOIS initiatives in public and private sector agencies. While in some cases this may be due to various technology and business process risks, most often the reasons are rooted in social and contextual issues including internal and external business risks. Although technological issues are important and the disruption of IOIS even for a short period of time would cause big problems for business operations and management, most of the research studies in IOIS report concern over the managerial and business issues. It is important for IOIS and business management researchers that such issues are identified and understood, and risks mitigated in order to increase efficiency, effectiveness, and other measures of organizational performance.

As with other disciplines, research projects in the areas of inter-organizational systems and business management always begin with a problem statement or research questions. Whether the questions themselves are worth asking can only be considered against the state of knowledge, as presented in relevant theories in the field at the time (Truex et al., 2006). Theoretical foundations are in fact a prerequisite to critically take stock of developments from various perspectives and understand the fundamentals of a particular problem (Pikot and Baumann, 2009). Weber (2003) argues that the field of Information Systems is significantly dependent on theories borrowed and adapted from other disciplines and thus calls for an increased awareness of the role of theory in our research. Lyytinen and King (2004) further argue that intellectual shortcomings are haunting the IS field more than other fields. According to Lyytinen and King, a better theory is likely to contribute to stronger results; however, the relative lack of core theories is a key problem in IS research. Truex et al., (2006) highlight the importance of theory. They contend that a researcher always approaches a topic from some theoretical point of view - if it remains an implicit and unstated set of assumptions it may actually hinder the study of the phenomena at hand. In fact, collecting data without theory is not research but observation or reporting (Dubin, 1978). As such, IS researchers need to be aware of the core theories in the field and link the results of their research back to theories in a cumulative manner (Kuhn 1970).

The study of IOIS is multidisciplinary in nature as it draws inspiration from a wide variety of other fields of study and imports theories from other references disciplines. The multidisciplinary nature of IOIS requires that researchers use concepts and perspectives from multiple theories from reference disciplines such as social science, economics, management, and organization science simultaneously as appropriate in order to devise and implement effective solutions. However, although the focus of IOIS is primarily technology, Picot and Baumann (2009) argue that little attention has been paid to theoretical insight from other disciplines. The authors recommend that multiple theories be used to define a set of agreed upon key terms and thus avoid the risk of blindly following a trend and the subsequent haphazard application of technology.

THE CONTEXT AND THE REVIEW PROCESS

The editorial idea for this book was conceived when I was a research student myself about ten years ago. I decided on a research topic in the area of IOIS for my PhD thesis but struggled a lot in search of suitable theories to guide me to study the topic. Even after consulting a number of publications for a particular theory, I would get little idea about the theoretical variables of interest. I had to thus go through hundreds of papers on various theories in the process of developing my research model and coming up with the most relevant variables from different theoretical perspectives. I wished I had been able to read a single book containing all those most influential theories, which would significantly save my time and also guide me through the conceptual model development and operationalization process. Seeing that no significant effort had been made to publish such a book even after ten years, I accepted the invitation from the IGI Global to edit the book.

Against this context, an editorial advisory board was formed and, in mutual agreement with the publisher, the 'call for chapter proposals' process was initiated. In the course of that quest, a number of 2-3 page chapter proposals clearly explaining the mission and concerns of proposed chapter were summoned for peer reviewing. The core criteria for inviting the authors to submit a contribution was the adherence with the book theme and the quality of the proposed chapter. The 'call for chapter' obviously generated a great interest among the IOIS and Business Management scholars. While over 40 such proposals were accepted, only 28 of them were found to be compliant with the book theme and seemed interesting enough to proceed to the next process step which was the submission of the full chapters.

The chapters were then sent to peers/reviewers for a blind review. After almost six months of reviewing and enhancing the chapters with the invaluable help of the body of reviewers, a set of 16 long chapters dealing with application/development of theories in IOIS and business management were accepted, while others were rejected upon the recommendation of the reviewers.

OBJECTIVE OF THE BOOK AND TARGET AUDIENCE

This edited book aims to provide relevant theoretical frameworks and the latest empirical research findings in the area. An understanding of IOIS and related organizational theories is important to the work of all business and IT professionals including executive managers who determine the organisation's strategic direction, information professionals who design and deliver new information services, and business managers who use information systems for change management and business reporting.

Various organizational theories have been developed, which try to explain the relevant behaviors and activities within the organizations adopting or using various information systems. However, only some of the theories have been consistently tested to be valid and influential over time, and as argued by Chatterjee and Ravinchandran (2004), IOIS have been inadequately operationalized in the existing literature. The purpose of this book is to highlight the most influential organizational theories and their applications in IOIS and Business Management. It seeks to guide the research scholars and members of faculty working in this area to get a quick glimpse of the most influential theories and current research issues in IOIS and business management.

The target audience of this edited book is composed of professionals and researchers working in the field of IOIS and business management in various disciplines, e.g. information technology, information and communication sciences, administrative sciences and management, supply chain/logistics management, public procurement, customer relationship management, knowledge management, and e-Business/e-Government. It has been specifically written for research students and their supervisors who are always in search of relevant theories to carry out their research, and for practitioners who want to improve their understanding of information systems and their impact on business performance.

BOOK STRUCTURE AND CONTRIBUTIONS

Most chapters of this book provide discussion of particular theoretical framework/s and a few last chapters have been organized to provide the results of empirical application of the theories. While the publication of some later chapters would better the need of a journal, they have been included in the book so as to provide the readers with the theoretical concepts as well the examples of their application in the context of IOIS and business management.

Introduction

The introductory chapter argues that while some organizations have benefited significantly by effectively using inter-organizational information systems (IOIS), other organizations with IOIS deployment have struggled to gain expected business value of IOIS, and yet other trading partners have resisted the participation in IOIS. This chapter asserts that academic theories provide means to form meaningful conclusions to understand the underlying causes of these phenomena. Against this background, this chapter presents a research framework to study IOIS and business management related issues. It identifies the key constructs and variables for each research domain of the framework. A brief description of over 30 theories has been provided and the entities named in the theory are expected to predict the outcome of the theory-governed occurrences.

An attempt has been made to link each domain of the IOIS and business management framework to key relevant theories. It is expected that understanding of various antecedents that influence IOIS and its impact on inter-organizational processes and organizational effectiveness in light of these theories can help organize and guide academic research efforts as well as offer insights to research practitioners on IOIS and business management.

Chapter 1

Chapter 1 (*Evolution of Inter-Organizational Information Systems on Long Timescales: A Practice Theory Approach*), by Kai Reimers, Robert Johnson and Stefan Klein, presents a theory of IOIS in which the on-going use and evolution of IOIS is treated as a practical and socio-material accomplishment of communities through boundary practices and structures. The authors draw on the structure/action reproduction paradigm of Structuration Theory to account for the persistence of these systems, and thus explain their structure, while using the embodiment of action from Practice Theory to treat the material nature of these systems. The authors distinguish three dimensions of structure - material, normative, and ideational - and we also distinguish patterns of actions (along these three dimensions) from constraining and enabling structures.

Chapter 2

Chapter 2 (*Assimilation of Inter-Organizational Information Systems: Insight from the Change Resistance Theory in Public Electronic Procurement*), by Kishor Vaidya, John Campbell, Jeffrey Soar, and Scott Gardener, is primarily built upon theoretical work in the IOIS diffusion area, and in particular on theories of technology assimilation. Stages of the assimilation process and the aggregation strategy have been explained in the context of public electronic procurement. Resistance theory is also discussed. The authors have argued that understanding both change resistance variables and relevant change management interventions or moderators can be very useful in determining the extent of public e-procurement assimilation.

Chapter 3

Chapter 3 *(Theoretical Foundations of Inter-Organizational Information Systems: Towards a Framework Grounded on Seven Theories*), by Maria Madlberger, analyses and compares seven theories. This chapter argues that research on inter-organizational information systems (IOIS) provided many insights, which, however, are very fragmented in terms of applied theories. This results in a quite isolated understanding of single aspects of IOIS rather than a comprising approach to the research subject. To address these shortcomings, the chapter investigates seven theories in respect of their explanation of IOIS adoption and use, its drivers, IOIS-based collaboration between firms, and benefits and costs of IOIS. The applied theories are social exchange theory and embeddedness theory (organization theories), transaction cost theory and agency theory (economics-related theories), the resource-based view of the firm and network theory (strategic management approaches), and game theory. The findings and the resulting framework imply that all these theories lead to recommendations on the use of IOIS although they have very diverse assumptions and lines of argumentation. The chapter stresses that the investigated theories supplement rather than contradict each other.

Chapter 4

Chapter 4 (*Transaction Costs in Inter-Organizational Systems: Theory and Selected Examples in Supply Management*), by Michael Essig and Raphael Boerner, suggests that the transaction costs which occur both in companies and when crossing the company's border to exchange with other market partners, make it an ideal approach for inter-organizational information systems. As a microeconomics-based approach, the authors further suggest that such inter-organizational approach can be used to manage supply management activities by using the perspective of a company using (and buying) outside resources. The authors argue that it should be then possible to combine the rigor instruments of microeconomic analysis with the practical relevance of incomplete markets. Instead of playing "relevance versus rigor," the authors suggest that Transaction Cost Economics can offer the chance to combine both aspects in the sense of scientific research, which combines a sound theoretical basis with concrete implications for management.

Chapter 5

Chapter 5 (*Trust and Transaction Cost in Supply Chain Cost Optimization: An Exploratory Study*), by Ik-Whan G. Kwon, John H. Hamilton, and Seock-Jin Hong, suggests that the foundation of efficient and effective supply chain management rests on collaborative efforts by all parties involved in executing the supply chain optimization process. Because of complexities in global supply chain networks coupled with ever increasing use of just-in-time techniques, lean applications, and global outsourcing, the authors warn that the threat of supply chain disruptions always exists in operations. Based on this argument, the authors conclude that there is no single management theory/tool that resolves such complex issues; however, trust and communication can be central tenets of supply chains in cost reduction efforts. As such, this chapter describes the relationship between trust and transaction cost in supply chain operations. Empirical findings from several research studies on trust and transaction cost in supply chain operations are presented in this chapter in support of the argument for managing transaction cost in supply chain management.

Chapter 6

Chapter 6 (*Using Actor-Network Theory to Research the Adoption of Inter-Organizational Information Systems*), by Jim Underwood and Bruce McCabe, argues that Inter-organizational information systems depend for their success at least as much on collaboration across organizational cultures as on the development of technical infrastructure. The authors suggest Actor-network theory (ANT) as a useful approach for bringing together social and technical considerations. They then discuss key features of ANT and show how it might be applied to a particular case of IOIS adoption. This chapter also compares the ANT approach to co-evolutionary theory which was originally applied to this case. Some possible extensions to ANT are contemplated in this chapter, and the authors offer advice to those attempting ANT-based research. They also offer advice, based on ANT, to those undertaking IOIS development.

Chapter 7

Chapter 7 (*Organisational Change and Acceptance: Perspectives of the Technology Acceptance Model*), by Marilyn Wells, reports on the development of the technology acceptance model from 1986 when Davis investigated technology acceptance from an individual's view as to the ease of use and perceived usefulness of a system. The author suggests that many variations have been presented in attempts to explain how and what influences a computer system user's uptake of new technology within an organization since then. The author argues that whilst all variations were developed explicitly to predict users' acceptance or rejection of new technology, these variations are in essence predictors of acceptance or rejection of change. According to the author, factors such as the organisational change environment and informal communication (rumours), together with social influence as exercised by colleagues should be considered major contributors to the perceptions of new technology and therefore acceptance. This chapter then extends the original model to include the variations and proposes that rather than looking at technology acceptance in isolation, acceptance of new technology should be viewed as acceptance of change. Based on these proposals, the author proposes the model Social Influence and Change Acceptance (SICAM) to reflect the inclusion of TAM's variations in an organizational change context.

Chapter 8

Chapter 8 (*Business Case Development Risks in On and Offshore IT Outsourcing: Unpacking the Theories*), by Anne C. Rouse, observes that outsourcing of IT-supported business processes (systems development; IT service delivery; customer relationship management; helpdesk, etc.) has become increasingly common in western economies since the late 1980s. The author argues that such outsourcing is totally dependent on the provision of inter-organizational information systems (IOSs), which act as the "glue" to link vendor(s) and client(s). The author makes the point that it is critical to understand the importance of IOIS to ensure that outsourcing arrangements are successful. This chapter, therefore, unpacks the theory behind outsourcing and alerts the readers to aspects of IOIS that raise the risks of outsourcing if they are not well thought through. This chapter concludes by offering advice to decision makers to explicitly include the notion of risk in their outsourcing business cases, including those risks associated with the IOSs that support outsourcing arrangements.

Chapter 9

Chapter 9 (*The Theory of Constraints: A Management Philosophy*), by Shams Rahman, explains the philosophy behind the theory of constrains (TOC). The author suggests that TOC has two major components: a philosophy which underpins the working principle of on-going improvement and a generic approach for investigating, analysing and creating solutions to problems, called the 'thinking process' (TP). While several books, numerous articles, and a few journal special issues have been published on TOC, this chapter provides a comprehensive review of TOC concepts, philosophy, and working principles.

Chapter 10

Chapter 10 (*The Effect of Merger and Acquisitions on the IS Function: An Overview and a Potential Agent-Based Approach*), by Andrea Genovese, Sebastian Titz, Khole Gwebu, Barry Shore, Jing Wang, and Venky Venkatachalam, discusses various strategic and operational objectives of merger and acquisition (M&A) activity. The authors of this chapter note that the objective of developing common and efficient information systems that can be the source of creating significant cost savings for the joined companies in the inter-organizational setting can be especially challenging. The authors caution the readers that in combining the IS divisions of the acquiring firm with that of the acquired firm there are many hurdles when the technical and social system are to be integrated. The authors then note that exactly how this process evolves and exactly what results can be achieved is hard to determine. To help address this challenge, this chapter identifies some of the major factors associated with the integration process and proposes Agent Based Simulation as a possible methodology to study this phenomenon.

Chapter 11

Chapter 11 (*Information Management for Public Budget Decision Making: Insights from Organization and Budget Theories*), by Yaotai Lu and Khi V. Thai, makes the point that budget agencies are faced with a great number of uncertainties and constraints because of bounded rationality and uncontrollable factors in the environment. The authors of this chapter suggest that information management intends to reduce these uncertainties and risks in the budgetary process so that budget decision making will be more rational; thus public resources are expended efficiently, effectively, and equitably. The authors argue that organization theories and budget theories together produce considerable impacts on practice of public budgetary decision making and relevant information management. This chapter attaches importance to appropriate combination of theoretic function and budget formats and goals in the budget process in the inter-organizational context.

Chapter 12

Chapter 12 (*The Value of Sociotechnical Theories for Implementation of Clinical Information Systems*), by Joanne Callen, Andew Georgiou, Julie Li, and Johanna Westbrook, provides an overview of socio-technical theories which can be used to understand, design, implement, and evaluate clinical information systems in health care settings. The authors suggest that the sociotechnical approach is one which seeks to identify the dynamics between technology and the social, professional, and cultural environment in which it is used. Theories and models covered in the chapter include: the technology and information technology acceptance models; a multi-level integration framework approach; social cognition theory; theories which propose a fit between individuals, tasks, and the technology; diffusion of innovation theory, and a contextual implementation model. The authors conclude that the frameworks presented in this chapter may not be exhaustive but most relevant to the complexity of information and communication technology use in inter-organisational health care settings.

Chapter 13

Chapter 13 (*Diffusion of Innovation Theory and the Problem of Context for Inter-Organisational Information Systems: The Example of Feral Information Systems*), by Luke Houghton and Don Kerr, argues that diffusion theory models like the technology acceptance model (TAM) need to be rethought in light of contextual factors that are becoming increasingly important in modern inter-organisational settings. This is due to the growing complexity of organizations with respect to different organisational types, contexts, and political structures that have been shown in research literature to hinder information systems acceptance. The chapter looks at possible contextual factors that are ignored by TAM by critiquing its parent diffusion theory (diffusion of innovations). The authors suggest that such approach can be considered as the best as there are many variations of TAM, but the diffusion of innovations (DOI) theory underlies all these variations. The chapter also recommends a way forward for research into inter-organisational information systems by examining an example situation of Feral Information Systems (FIS) to illustrate the problem. The chapter concludes with a discussion about future research directions.

Chapter 14

Chapter 14 (*Public E-Procurement Implementation: Insights from the Structuration Theory*), by José Rodrigues Filho and Flavio Perazzo Babosa Mota, argues that although public e-procurement has similarities with the private sector, it also has some special characteristics that make it different. As it is not clear to which extent recent decisions on public e-procurement have been optimal, the author attempts to show how qualitative research traditions like structuration theory (specifically from the perspective of "dialectic of control") and qualitative research analysis can be used in the analysis of e-procurement in Brazil, leading to results that differ substantially from the mainstream positivist research that does not always touch the barriers and challenges that can constrain the adoption and implementation of public e-procurement projects in the specific country context.

Chapter 15

Chapter 15 (*The Technology Acceptance Model: A 'Localized' Version to Predict Purchasing Behavior in Internet Shopping*) by Kanokwan Atchariyachanvanich, Hitoshi Okada, and Shiro Uesugi examines the factors affecting consumer purchasing behavior in Internet shopping. Multiple group analysis and structural equation modeling are applied in this chapter to investigate whether the existing model of Consumer Acceptance of Virtual Stores is able to identify those factors in Japan and South Korea. The authors report that the results of online questionnaires filled out by 1,111 Japanese online customers and by 998 Korean online customers revealed that the model failed to do so. Therefore, the localized models for Japan and South Korea were conducted by the authors. According to the localized model, perceived trust is the most important factor affecting purchasing behavior of Japanese customers. In South Korea, purchasing behavior is highly related to perceived usefulness and perceived service quality. The authors hope that the differences between online customer nationalities regarding their perceptions of purchasing through the Internet offers insights that can help e-commerce vendors increase the number of customers in different world market segments.

Chapter 16

Chapter 16 (*Perceived Benefits from a Local Government Public Procurement Initiative: A Diffusion of Innovation Perspective*), by Md Mahbubur Rahim and Adarsh P. Bantwal, notes that much of the attention of the existing e-Procurement literature is on understanding adoption decisions of e-Procurement systems from the perspective of senior management, and little research efforts have been made to examine how employees who actually use these systems perceive the benefits arising from these systems. According to the authors, although the role of demographic characteristics of users is recognised in the innovation adoption and broader IS/IT adoption literatures, it is not clearly known how the demographic characteristics of employees (who interact with such systems) may influence their perceptions about e-Procurement benefits. To address this gap in the literature, this chapter analyses the views captured from sixty employees working in three large city councils located in the state of Victoria, Australia. The findings indicate that the outcomes of e-Procurement systems adoption were largely seen in a positive light as the employees reported favourably about the attainment of benefits from their use of these systems. However, except user type, popular demographic characteristics of employees (e.g. gender, job role, working experience at councils) were not related to their perceptions of e-Procurement benefits.

Based on the results of this study, the chapter discusses the implications of these findings and proposes future directions of research.

CONCLUDING REMARKS

The theoretical approaches presented in above chapters are by no means exhaustive and prescriptive, but rather they provide examples of various frameworks and derived theoretical variables in a given context to guide a researcher. Obviously, the more knowledge researchers have of multiple theories, the greater will be their capacity to choose appropriate theory to study IOIS phenomena of interest. The chapters in this book are thus intended as an invitation to further exploration of relevant theories to study IOIS and business management.

While each of the theories discussed above has individually received attention in prior innovation/IOIS literature, they have not yet been collectively brought together into a single book. We believe that each of the chapters in this book offers its own focus and explanation, predictive power, and frameworks for the study of IOIS from multiple perspectives. Furthermore, a set of these theories when integrated and adapted in a given context can provide a systematic frame of reference for investigating the assimilation of IOIS.

REFERENCES

Chatterjee, D., & Ravinchandran, T. (2004). Inter-organizational Information Systems research: A critical review and an integrative framework. *Proceedings of the 37th Hawaii International Conference on System Sciences*.

Dubin, R. (1978). *Theory development*. New York, NY: Free Press.

King, J. L., & Lyytien, L. (2004). Reach and grasp. *Management Information Systems Quarterly*, *28*(4).

Kuhn, T. S. (1970). *The structure of scientific revolutions* (2nd ed.). Chicago, IL: Univ. of Chicago Press.

Picot, A., & Baumann, O. (2009). The relevance of organization theory of the field of business and information systems engineering. *Business Information Engineering*, *1*(1), 62–69.

Truex, D., Holmostrom, J., & Keil, M. (2006)... *Journal of the Association for Information Systems*, *7*(12), 797–821.

Webber, R. (2003). Editor's comments. Still desperately seeking the IT artefact. *Management Information Systems Quarterly*, *27*(2), iii–xi.

Acknowledgment

Each chapter in this book has been prepared by eminent professors and research scholars from Australia, the USA, Europe, Latin America, and Asia involved IS/IOIS and business management research. Many thanks for their valuable contribution. I would also like to thank the reviewers (most of them were the contributors of the chapters themselves) for their time to contribute to the blind review process and offer valuable feedback to the authors of the chapters. I am very grateful to all of them – without their contributions and support this book project would not have been successful. My sincere thanks also go to the members of the Editorial Advisory Board who kindly accepted to serve as the members of the board and offered advice on numerous occasions.

I thank Ms. Jan Travers, Director of Intellectual Property Rights and Contracts, IGI Global, Ms. Kristin Klinger, Director of Editorial Content, and Hannah Abelbeck, Editorial Assistant, for their support and guidance throughout the editing and publication process.

Kishor Vaidya
University of Canberra, Australia

Introduction
Inter-Organizational Information Systems and Business Management:
A Research Framework and an Overview of Key Theories

Kishor Vaidya
University of Canberra, Australia & University of Southern Queensland, Australia

ABSTRACT

While some organizations have benefited significantly by effectively using inter-organizational information systems (IOIS), other organizations with IOIS deployment have struggled to gain expected business value of IOIS, and yet other trading partners have resisted the participation in IOIS. This paper asserts that academic theories provide means to form meaningful conclusions to understand the underlying causes of these phenomena. Against this background, this chapter presents a research framework to study IOIS and business management related issues. It identifies the key constructs and variables for each research domain of the framework. A brief description of over 30 theories has been provided and the entities named in the theory are expected to predict the outcome of the theory-governed occurrences. An attempt has been made to link each domain of the IOIS and business management framework to key relevant theories. It is expected that understanding of various antecedents that influence IOIS and its impact on inter-organizational processes and organizational effectiveness in light of these theories can help organize and guide academic research efforts as well as offer insights to research practitioners on IOIS and business management.

DOI: 10.4018/978-1-60960-768-5.ch000

Copyright © 2012, IGI Global. Copying or distributing in print or electronic forms without written permission of IGI Global is prohibited.

1. INTRODUCTION AND BACKGROUND

This decade has seen fundamental changes in the way organizations manage business. In today's networked business environment, the focus of business management is shifting from individual organizations to inter-organizations, and consequently from managing traditional information systems (IS) to managing inter-organisational information systems (IOIS). Obviously, managing IOIS and business in inter-organizational environment has introduced more significant opportunities and challenges than managing IS in individual organizational environment and is certainly worth of further study. One of the most important challenges is how to best utilize IOIS to support inter-organisational governance, relationships, and business processes and practices in order to achieve business goals of the organization.

Effective use and assimilation of IOIS enables organizations to transform their processes and build capabilities. Various antecedents including cooperation, collaboration, integration and flexibility are needed to support inter-organizational relations and business processes. IOIS can enhance this, which in turn, can help improve the organizational performance. While there are many operational and strategic benefits that can be achieved from using IOIS, challenges are that IOIS can also alter the balance of power between trading partners and other change management requirements may need to be addressed. Obviously, in today's inter-organizational business environment, understanding the most important antecedents influencing the use and assimilation of IOIS and its impact on inter-organizational business process is more important than ever.

In fact, the deployment of IOIS has experienced explosive growth in some organizations while other trading partners have resisted its participation and assimilation (Vaidya & Hyde, 2011). Similarly, while some organizations have benefited significantly by effectively deploying IOIS, other organizations with IOIS deployment have struggled to gain much benefits (Saeed et al., 2011). Besides, IOIS are expensive undertakings and the level of investment is significant for most organizations. Despite the potential benefits, organizations differ in the level with which they assimilate IOIS and in the level with which they realize improvement in business performance. New trading partners, especially, are struggling to make sense of how to use IOIS.

This has raised several questions that deserve answering in relation to the use/assimilation of IOIS and its impact on business performance. What are the antecedents that could lead towards the successful assimilation of IOIS, and its impact on inter-organizational governance, processes and practices, and the resulting organizational effectiveness? Which theory or a combination of theories can best explain them? How can business managers influence and manage IOIS and business management in light of these theories? Without a solid understanding of antecedents that influence the use and assimilation of IOIS and its impact on business performance, organizations involved are at a disadvantage in knowing how best to use IOIS so that they will provide operational and strategic benefits to their owners.

1.1 What is an IOIS?

Rose (1999) describes an information system (IS) in structurational terms as a social system (information practice), supported by material resources (information technologies), which are designed and managed by a further social system. IS literature uses various terms including inter-organizational information sharing system, inter-organizational system, and net-worked based information system to refer to inter-organizational information system (IOIS).

While most definitions use similar approach to IOIS as an automated information systems shared by two or more companies as defined by Cash and Konsynksi (1986), the most recent definition by

Table 1. Definitions of IOIS over time

Definition of IOIS	Source
systems that involve resources shared between two or more organizations	Barrett & Konsynski (1982)
automated information systems shared by two or more companies	Cash and Konsynski (1986)
information system that links one or more firms to their customers or their suppliers, and facilitates the exchange of products and services	Bakos (1991)
information and communication technology that transcends organizational boundaries	Kumar and van Dissel (1996)
infrastructure which constitutes of a large number of application and/or organisation-wide information systems, spans over at least two organisations, and is designed to inform.	Kanellis and Paul (1997)
a network-based IS that extends beyond traditional enterprise boundaries... permitting information access to other organizations.	Hong (2002)
Information systems that facilitates the exchange of products, services and information between firms	Han et. al. (2008)
a set of practices residing in separate organizations but connected through a special type of material boundary object.	Reimers et al. (2010)

Reimers et al. (2010), who consider that an IOIS is in ongoing use, differs from others. Based on the concept of Communities of Practices as informed by the Practice Theory, Reimers et al. (2010) define an IOIS as "a set of practices residing in separate organizations but connected through a special type of material boundary object". Table 1 provides definitions of IOIS over time to help establish the perspective of IOIS.

Diverse types of IOIS have been distinguished including electronic data inter-changes, extranets, shared databases, B2B/B2G or G2G/G2B electronic commerce systems, and XML-based messaging and web services with more recent IOIS based on open standards. IOIS have been increasingly employed to provide pooled information resources and allow partners in a network to collaborate by exchanging both structured and unstructured data stored in repositories (Robey et al., 2008). Obviously, IOIS are increasingly used to coordinate and manage inter-organizational business activities. It has been argued that the distinction between different IOIS over time is far from trivial and has not yet been addressed properly by IS scholars (Schellhammer, 2010).

While the literature discussed in this chapter considers both traditional (e.g. EDI) and new (e.g. web-based) IOIS, Subramaniam (2002) contends that the scope of web-based IOIS is very expanded as it not only reduces transaction costs dramatically but also supports coordination and collaboration mechanisms. The author summarizes the key differences between EDI-based and web-based IOIS. Some of characteristics of web-based IOIS include: i) it supports many-to-many electronic networks, ii) uses open standards and platform independent applications, iii) it handles processes of varying complexities, iv) its rich-media interface allows exchange of complex images and drawings and enhances collaboration between business partners.

An IOIS is by definition a relational system (Schellhammer, 2010). Robey et al. (2008) note that IOIS can be treated as many other innovations. In fact, the IOIS does not only interconnect users residing in different organizations but it may be used as well inside one of these (Schellhammer, 2008). It means that the theories which have been applied to study organizational information systems can also be used to study IOIS when looking IOIS at a given point in time. However, Reimers et al. (2010) argue that some of prior assumptions may not hold true when looking at IOIS in large time scales.

1.2 Why Theories

Robey et al. (2008) note that IOIS is an area in which numerous theories have been used and where no single theory has dominated. The authors advise researchers to theorize the IOIS artifact and to focus on theory in order to maintain the IS field's inherent diversity and also to establish a more distinct identity. As Moody et al., (2011) state:

The intellectual core of any research field is its theories: more than anything else, the core theories of a field define its distinct identity...All researchers, regardless of their speciality, should know what the core theories are and have a working knowledge of them. They should be an integral part of the educational curriculum at all levels.

According to Doty and Glick (1994), a theory must meet three primary criteria that constructs must be identified; relationships among these constructs must be specified; and these relationships must be able to be tested. Gregor (2006) notes that the nature of theory in IS are different from that found in other disciplinary areas as a characteristic that distinguishes IS from other fields is that it concerns the use of artifacts in human-machine systems. The four primary goals of theory as identified by Gregor (2006, p.619) are that the theory:

- provides a description of the phenomena of interest, analysis of relationships among the constructs.
- provides an explanation of how, why, and when things happened, relying on varying views of causality and methods for argumentation.
- states what will happen in the future if certain preconditions hold.
- provides a description of the method or structure or both for the construction of an artifact.

Why to use academic theories as frames of reference? Leibenstein (1976) asserts that academic theories provide means to form meaningful conclusions to understand the underlying causes of phenomena. Leibenstein (1976) further explains that the entities named in the theory predict the outcome of the theory-governed occurrences.

It would be certainly easier and more manageable to study the problem under the single theoretical framework. However, force-fitting the study of IOIS and business management research issues into a single theoretical paradigm may not adequately capture the variety of IOIS research domains and constructs/variables presented in this chapter. To this end, Truex at al. (2006) sought to generate increased awareness of the issues that one might consider when adapting theories from other domains to research in the IS field. Accordingly, they offered four recommendations for theory adaptation: (1) consider the fit between selected theory and phenomenon of interest, (2) consider the theory's historical context, (3) consider how the theory impacts the choice of research method, and (4) consider the contribution of theorizing to cumulative theory.

Against this background, this chapter has been organised in 4 Sections. In Section 2, a research framework to study IOIS and business management related issues has been presented. The 12 research domains (themes) of the framework have been briefly discussed. This Section also identifies key constructs and variables for each research domain. Section 3 provides brief descriptions of over 30 theories and the constructs/variables suggested by the theories are also presented. More importantly, an attempt has been made to link the domains/sub-domains of the IOIS and business management framework to relevant theories in

Figure 1. IOIS and Business Management: A Research Framework

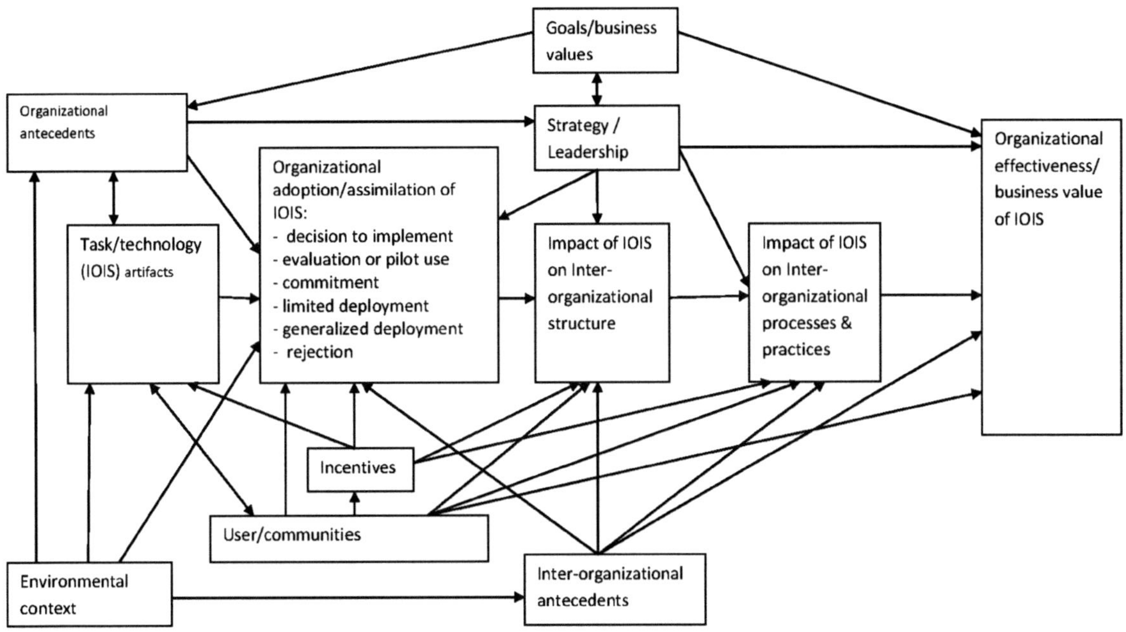

Section 4, which is the theme of this book. Although not fully developed yet, the expectation is that the research framework and matching its domains with key theories will further allow researchers to consider the relevant theory or a set of theories to study particular phenomena of their interest within the domain of the framework.

2. IOIS AND BUSINESS MANAGEMENT: THE RESEARCH FRAMEWORK

The process by which a firm adopts and implements technological innovations is influenced by the technological context, the organizational context, and the environmental context (Tornatzky and Fleisher 1990). Following the work of Rainey (2009) on organizational analysis and using Tornatzky and Fleisher's work (1990) on technology-organization-organization framework as a base, the section below puts the research framework (Figure 1) in perspective as follows:

Inter-organizational information systems (IOIS) are information systems shared by several organizations or connected across organizations to pursue a business goal stated in their strategies. Organizations do so by attaining resources from their environment. They seek to transform those resources by accomplishing tasks to achieve organizational effectiveness/business value of IOIS, thereby attaining additional resources. They deal with the many challenges and opportunities presented by the environments, task/technologies, inter-organizational antecedents, and their own antecedents by managing (organizing, coordinating etc.) their IOIS and business activities, all leading to higher use/assimilation of IOIS. IOIS and business management also involves leadership processes, through which leaders guide the development of inter-organizational strategies for achieving goals and the development of inter-

organizational structures and processes/practices to support those strategies in light of the impact of IOIS use/assimilation. Within these evolving structures and processes, users and communities respond to incentives presented to them, contributing to higher use/assimilation of IOIS that further impacts the inter-organizational structures and processes/practices, and ultimately results in achieving higher organizational effectiveness/business value of IOIS.

While there could be other ways to depict the perspective on IOIS and business management, various components of this framework are meant to mainly set forth the research domains/themes for IOIS and business management researchers. As one of many such frameworks to organize the research issues around IOIS and business management, it is our expectation that this framework guides research efforts as well as offers insights to academic researchers and practitioners.

It should be noted that while the Figure 1 serves our purpose to set forth the topics and indicate the casual relationships among the constructs, it may be a complex endeavour to study all the relationships in a single empirical study. Moreover, over the long time scale, many of the relationships included in the Figure may become two-way, for example, the environmental contingencies may begin to be affected by the organisational antecedents.

2.1 Domains of IOIS and Business Management Research Framework

2.1.1 Goals/Values

Inter-organizational information systems (IOIS) are information systems shared by several organizations or connected across organizations to pursue a business goal stated in their strategies. According to organizational learning theory, organizations must change their goals and actions to reach those goals in order to be competitive in a changing environment. In the IOIS context, it is important to manage the inter-organizational relationships towards achievement of strategic goals. Based on the analysis of principal economic, social and behavioural theories, Barringer and Harrison (2000) conclude that inter-organizational partners can be motivated by specific goals and efficiencies that would be enhanced by establishing inter-organizational relationships. Cha et al. (2008) emphasise on the need to align business goals and business values to be achieved by the use of IOIS.

2.1.2 Leadership/Strategy

Leadership and strategy is provided by the senior management. Armstrong and Sambamurthy (1999) define senior management as the organisational collective consisting of the organisation's CEO, CFO, CIO, and other senior managers/specialists and project managers who are formal members of the top management team. For example, to build confidence IOIS use and assimilation, the development of performance measures and compliance verification schemes should be promoted. It is also essential to plan and monitor legal, institutional and organizational changes at many levels.

Senior management also can participate in establishing operational and management controls and undertakes benchmarking exercises. Leadership needs to act strategically and estimate not only the strategic and operational benefits of using IOIS but also perceived costs and perceived risks. Studies in the field of IOIS have shown the importance of the often underestimated critical role which 'politics' play in the implementation of new technology (Avgerou, 2000) which can easily overpower the rational and planned economic and technical efforts made during the introduction of technology in an organization.

The resource-based perspective provides guidance for IOIS researchers to evaluate and review how IOIS effect the organizational strategy and business performance. More recently, management fashion theory has been used by IS researchers to understand and explain how the academics and other entrepreneurs consultants, business gurus, technology vendors generate demand for the innovation and promote it as being on the leading edge of managerial practice.

2.1.3 Environmental Context

IOIS are a phenomenon that is difficult to separate from its environment and thus very difficult to bound (Reimers et al., 2010). As noted by Reekers & Smithson (1995), environmental variables not only affect the structure of inter-organiztional relationships but also the coordination of activities. According to authors, the principal source of uncertainty is the variability of resources and they conceptualise the environment as a dynamic reality without well-defined shape, size or elements. It can be said that business trends including outsourcing and globalization are such dynamic realities which resulted because of environmental forces.

Institutional theories have been used to explain the environmental factors that may influence the diffusion of IOIS. While Teo et al. (2003) discuss the mimetic, coercive, and normative institutional pressures at organizational, industry, and institutional levels. competitive pressure has been found to be the main source of external pressure influencing the diffusion of innovation (Premkumar et al., 1997). In fact, the changing environment forces organizations to change and innovate new ways of value creation with the use of IOIS. For example, participating in the Electronic Marketplaces is one of the ways that can allow organizations to survive in new conditions. Supplier demand can also be one of the external pressures. Suppliers may favour the buying organizations that participate in the e-Marketplaces. Similarly, pressures from the government and industry and legitimacy concerns have been identified in a field survey by (Grewal et al., 2001).

Teo et al. (2003) discussed the positive effect of mimetic, coercive, and normative institutional pressures on the intention to adopt EDI. Normative pressures can potentially hasten IOIS assimilation, depending on the specific kinds of pressures exercised by entities within the business environment. For example, as argued by Grewal et al. (2001), institutional pressures play a role in inducing upstream suppliers and downstream channel members to embrace socially accepted norms and behaviours.

2.1.4 Organizational Antecedents

Organizational readiness in the context of IOIS refers to both the organization's internal resources required leading to the higher assimilation of IOIS. Lack of organizational (internal) readiness has been shown to inhibit IOIS assimilation in organizations where readiness is defined as the availability of needed organizational resources (Baura et al., 2005). Robey et al. (2008) have identified organizational readiness variables as financial resources, IT sophistication, top management support, trading partner readiness, and elapsed time since adoption.

The availability of the infrastructure also facilitates higher technical knowledge, which in turn increases assimilation of an innovation (Damanpour 1992). Successful assimilation of IOIS depends not only on the advancement of the adopted technology, but also on organizational readiness to support the technology.

The organization should also be concerned with the readiness of suppliers, since the success of an organization's net initiatives is likely to be influenced by its partners' ability to conduct business electronically (Iacovou, 1995). Barua et al. (2005) argue that supplier readiness should be considered as an enabler that requires a proactive commitment of an organisation's resources even though it is regarded as an external to the organization.

2.1.5 Inter-Organizational Antecedents

Inter-organizational antecedents include inter-organizational trust, relationship, interdependency, and coordination. Mayer, Davis, and Schoorman (1995, p. 712) defined trust as "the willingness of a party to be vulnerable to the actions of another party based on the expectation that the other will perform a particular action important to the trustor, irrespective of the ability to monitor or control that other party." Inter-organizational trust is established when a trading partner employs impersonal structures such as perceived monitoring, perceived legal bonds, perceived accreditation, perceived feedback, and perceived cooperative norms that facilitate transactions (Robey et al., 2008).

According to Thompson (1967), the level of interdependence is determined in terms of coordination, mutual adjustments, ongoing communications and decision making in an inter-organizational relationship. Reekers & Smithson (1995) argue that the scope and intensity of IOIS use is largely determined by the needs of inter-organizational coordination requiring inputs from their trading partners, and it in turn affects the efficiency and interdependency of relations. Reekers & Smithson (1995) measure interdependence through the importance of relationships with particular trading partners, the dependence on products and the importance of logistics.

2.1.6 Task/Technology (IOIS) Artifacts

Information and Communications Technology (ICT) has been instrumental for the development of IOIS. A number of research studies have identified key technological capabilities of an IOIS. According to Kumar and van Dissel (1996), the technical capabilities such as authentication, security, system integrity, and mature and stable standards, data communication, and database technologies can be considered as critical elements in IOIS assimilation. In the IOIS environment, interoperability, standardisation and security are key capabilities, which enable exchange of data between trading partners. Robey et al. (2008) have identified infrastructure design, supporting features as system capabilities of IOIS, and asset specificity, complexity of product description, transaction frequency and market & environmental uncertainty as transaction characteristics. IOIS affects several of these attributes by reducing product complexity, lowering external search costs, and reducing asset specificity, thereby permitting a greater use of market-based mechanisms with its application integration, data compatibility, analytic ability, evaluation ability, and alertness capabilities (Saeed et al., 2011).

Kwon & Zmud (1987) regard compatibility of an innovation as the organizational fit of the system introduced. According to the authors, it is the degree to which the innovation is perceived as being consistent with existing financial and accounting systems, procurement practices and the IT strategy and business policies and guidelines of the organization. According to Premkumar and Ramamurthy (1995), compatibility of the new system with existing work procedures increases the likelihood of higher use. The use of the Internet, the open standard, and the web technologies are such strengths of IOIS that contribute to its interoperability. This result in lower total cost of procurement, higher return on investment, scalability, flexibility, risk reduction, and faster implementation, which are among the widely reported benefits of IOIS. Numerous research studies show that various perceived operational and strategic benefits greatly contribute to higher use/assimilation of IOIS.

2.1.7 User/Communities

Individual or group user characteristics that can contribute to higher level of IOIS use/assimilation include age, gender, voluntariness, self-Efficacy, attitude, and subjective norm (Venkatesh et. al., 2003). User must be satisfied to achieve higher level IOIS assimilation. User satisfaction is the degree to which a user is satisfied with using IOIS and it can be an important means of measuring users' opinions about the overall success of IOIS.

It's not only individual user but also the groups or communities that have a role to play in the success of IOIS. According to Lave and Wenger (1991), learning always occurs in communities which they call Communities of Practice (CoP). Coakes (2004) argues that groups and communities of practices (CoPs) arise from special social relationships and are made by individuals, which are motivated to participation by common sets of interests and are willing to develop and share both tacit and explicit knowledge.

Nambisan & Wang (2000) argue that the degree of complexity and risk in using an Internet technology can create "knowledge barriers" among the managers and employees because they may lack skills or knowledge. The inhibitors may be perceived in the application and integration processes, which may negatively influence the IOIS assimilation. In fact, the use and assimilation of IOIS is so significant that it changes an organization's shape, the nature of its jobs, its processes and routines. If the user and community groups consider such changes negative, it is highly likely that members will resist these changes (Krovi, 1993).

2.1.8 Incentives

The incentive for trading partners to engage in IOIS grows stronger with the volume and number of transactions that the individual institutions make on an annual basis. The higher volume and number of transactions enables the trading partners and the communities to make better return on investment. Barua et al. (2005) suggest the organizations to design certain incentive mechanisms such as subsidy or guaranteed business to encourage business partners to get connected. According to Bakos and Nault (1997), the incentive to invest in IOIS depends on the respective ownership levels, and their relative levels of indispensability.

Resistance theories can help understand the incentive issues concerning the use and assimilation of IOIS. Resistance may, for example, manifest itself as a result of shifting power relationships. A well-designed system, for example, might be resisted by those who fear it might take away some of their power or social stature in the organization. The real reasons for resistance are users' perceived values and social content gain or loss before/after system implementation (Markus, 1983). Recent research has supported these findings adding that other reasons for resistance are loss of status, alternation in interpersonal relationships, loss of power, and uncertainty, unfamiliarity and misinformation (Jiang et al., 2000). As it follows, an appropriate incentive mechanism motivates the user and community groups to use IOIS.

2.1.9 Adoption and Assimilation of IOIS

Meyer and Goes (1988) first applied the concept of IT assimilation, thus proposing a nine-stage assimilation model to study medical innovations. They assessed breadth and depth of the innovations and their impact on processes, structures, and culture of the organization. Prescott & Conger (1995) developed a typology of IT innovations that on the IS unit impact, intra-organizational impact, and inter-organizational impact employing a four-stage assimilation process that includes adoption, implementation, and routinization.

The process of assimilation of a complex technological innovation "rarely unfolds in a smooth and predictable fashion" (Fichman and Kemerer, 1999). In addition to being complex, IOIS assimilation is a multi-dimensional and multi-stage process (Swanson and Ramiller, 2003). Most IS researchers now agree IT assimilation process occurs in stages. The assimilation process that includes adoption, implementation and routinization (Kwon and Zmud, 1987), (Prescott and Conger, 1995) has been modelled as containing the six stages of (i) intention to implement, (ii) evaluation or pilot use, (iii) commitment, (iv) limited deployment, (v) generalized deployment, and (vi) rejection (Fichman and Kemerer, 1997; Ramiller and Swanson, 2003). Theories of technology assimilation also recognise the concept of an aggregate strategy in order for the study findings of various classes of technologies to be more robust and generalizable (Fichman and Kemerer, 2001). The authors believe that such strategy facilitates the identification of antecedents with consistent characteristics across the class of technology.

While prior studies in MIS (e.g. Cooper and Zmud, 1990) have also utilized this approach, it was Fichman's (2001) study on software process innovations that provided a conceptual evaluation of aggregated measures (conditions). The conditions include (i) the primary objective of the research, (ii) the validity of generalization across assimilation stages, (iii) the effects of organization characteristics, (iv) the effects of innovation characteristics (v) the effects of innovation substitutes and complement, and (vi) the effects of reporting errors.

Reekers & Smithson (1995) suggest various indicators of scope of IOIS use. They include the implementation status and level of integration into internal planning and control systems, which is related to overall level of IT applications in an organization, and the total number of trading partners, and the number of different messages and intensity of interaction through IOIS.

More recently, Reimers et al. (2010) argue that a condition for the existence of an IOIS is that it is in ongoing use, i.e. an IOIS is never adopted or implemented in traditional sense – for an IOIS to be said to exist it must be already implemented. In fact, the authors argue that it is possible to explain the evolution of IOIS in terms of post adoption phenomena such as routinization, drift, adaptation to changing circumstances. However, as IOIS can be treated as many other innovations Robey et al. (2008) and that it may also be used as an internal system (Schellhammer, 2008) and at a given point in time (Reimers et al., 2010), there certainly is scope to apply the theories of technology adoption/assimilation and other theories to study IOIS.

2.1.10 IOIS Impact on Inter-Organizational Structure

According to Reekers & Smithson (1995), inter-organizational structural dimensions are shaped by environmental forces and the choice of co-ordination mechanisms. In terms of IOIS, they have identified relevant variables including the centrality and size, and the proportion of business covered through IOIS. They also consider the connectivity as well as the number and intensity of transactions and the range of message types and multiplexity.

According to Malone and Crowston (1994), 'coordination is managing dependencies'. Several mechanisms have been identified in the literature to manage inter-organizational dependencies. The impact of IOIS on the coordination structures in a given situation depends on several aspects of the goods or services being produced and supplied. The relationships between the trading partners can be associated with different perspectives such as dyads, chains, industries, and networks (Malone and Crowston, 1994). Coordination structures can be classified into decentralized and centralized structures and their aspects as dominated or neutral takeing into account the power of setting prices and rules (Malone & Crowston, 1994).

IOIS can have a positive impact on coordination and coordination structures can become more centralized because of IOIS. IOIS can also have a significant supportive role to formalize the co-operative relationship. According to Williamson (1985), the use of IOIS enables trading partners to shape coordination in terms of more effective and more efficient coordination processes, and new coordination structures, and also increased outsourcing as the use of ICT can facilitate an increase in the number of organizations involved. Accordingly, in an inter-organizational outsourcing relationship, transaction cost factors such as bounded rationality, opportunism and risk are argued to influence governance structures (i.e., adoption decision, screening, and monitoring (Williamson, 1985). IOIS also provides the possibility to change the coordination structure to a more market-like structure (Malone & Crowston, 1994). Although an IOIS lowers coordination costs, it can also increases the complexity of coordination in terms of more communication activities and more information to be taken into account when making a decision (Hengst & Sol, 2001).

Hengst & Sol (2001) have identified the six aspects that influence the way in which inter-organizational coordination can be carried out: homogeneity, specificity, time pressure, value, frequency, and uncertainty. The authors argue that another aspect should be considered important is the relationship of trust. Similarly, the five critical factors to explain the different inter-organizational relationships have been identified by Oliver (1990). They are: asymmetry, reciprocity, efficiency, stability and legitimacy. Her study also identified the six types of relationships as trade associations, voluntary agency federations, joint ventures, joint programs, corporate-financial interlocks, and agency-sponsor linkages.

2.1.11 IOIS Impact on Inter-Organizational Processes and Practices

Increasing change in underlying inter-organizational processes and practices requires more learning and effort on the part of users. Consequently, more attention should be given to inter-organizational learning. To this end, Vaidya et al. (2006) assert that as the process of assimilation of IOIS demands exchange of information within and among trading partners, the organization must have capacity to exercise inter-organizational learning and information sharing. Hart and Saunders (1998) view IOIS as a convenient means of information sharing across boundaries to improve supply chain management by coordinating order taking and fulfilment activities.

Inter-organizational learning is defined as learning by the individual organizations in the context of groups or pairs of organizations (Knight, 2002). According to Knight, inter-organizational learning starts from the individual and ends to inter-organizational level depending on the level of learner and the context of learning. To ensure effective inter-organizational learning, the concept of absorptive capacity captures the similarity and specialities of innovation patterns, in terms of knowledge bases, inter-organizational structures and policies, knowledge processing style and commercial objectives (Dyer & Singh, 1998).

An IOIS, by definition, changes the way trading partners conduct inter-organizational business processes. It can be said that changes required supporting business processes are directly related to the speed of use/assimilation of IOIS. As the inter-organizational business partners are required to create values jointly, a certain level of ongoing coordination and adjustments is expected.

It is also important to note that standards are particularly important in inter-organizational business processes with a significant exchange of business document and electronic integration. In the IOIS context, electronic integration has been defined as "the strategic choices made by a firm to exploit ICT to transform business processes and relationships, and business networks" (Kambil and Short 1994). In fact, the aim of dynamic capabilities approach (Dyer & Singh, 1998) is to integrate complementary capabilities to enhance the use of IOIS through identifying the capabilities and critical resources to engage trading partners in innovative practices.

Based on practice theory (Wenger, 2002), a practice has been defined as a common enterprise of a group of people which mutually engage with one another and interact/negotiate to build trust and relationships. The interacting parties in an IOIS are negotiating about the meaning of things important to their interaction (Schellhammer, 2010). Reimers et al. (2010) state that practices are linked through brokers if one person is a member in several communities of practice. The authors then propose that ongoing existence (i.e. persistence) of an IOIS requires frequent brokering actions and/or encounters. This concept of IOIS persistence is complemented by resilience which refers to the ability of constituent practices of an IOIS to absorb environmental changes such as introduction of new rules, technologies, or business models (Reimers et al., 2010).

2.1.12 Organizational Effectiveness/ Business Value of IOIS

Robey et al., (2008) note that studies of IOIS use a broad array of theories to study the business value of using IOIS. These include the resource-based view of the firm, organizational information processing, resource dependence, social network theory, organizational learning, institutional theory, and structuration theory.

IOIS can lead to a fall in transaction costs along the supply chain (Reekers & Smithson (1995) and thus increase the operational efficiency. Strategic impacts refer to the effects of IOS on the mission and scope of organizations, including the opening of new markets and development of new products and services (Robey et al. 2008). According to resource-based view (RBV), organizations possess resources and subsets of which enable them to achieve competitive advantage and lead to strategic organizational performance (Barney, 1991).

Current research on organizational effectiveness of IOIS focuses on strategic, operational, and social impacts on organizations using IOS (Robey et al., 2008). According to authors, strategic impacts include the opening of new markets and development of new products and services, which are the effects of IOIS on the goals and values of the organizations. While operational impacts of IOIS include improved ordering, delivery, productivity, and control leading to more efficient operations; social impacts of IOIS refer to organizational change leading to better inter-organizational relationship quality between trading partners.

3. IOIS RESEARCH FRAMEWORK: KEY CONSTRUCTS AND VARIABLES

Having broadly discussed the 12 domains of the IOIS research framework developed for this chapter, we now identify the most relevant constructs/variables for each domain. While not rigorous and comprehensive as intended, it is our expectation that Table 2 will help the IOIS and business management researchers identify the constructs and associated variables in their chosen research domain.

4. IOIS AND BUSINESS MANAGEMENT: KEY THEORIES

Given that there have been few theoretical generalizations developed despite the interest and volume of research, and no single theory is sufficient to explain the different forms of inter-organizational arrangements, (Chatterjee and Ravichandran, 2004). The authors also suggest that typologies of IOIS used are inadequate to identify the relevant and important dimensions of IOIS.

For the purpose of selecting theories for this chapter, we made use of the scholarly journals database provided by ProQuest. The search for the phrase was restricted to occurrences of all of the keywords Business Information System appearing in the abstracts covering the period of 2001-2011. Total of 1433 scholarly journal articles thus retrieved were further refined using the key words inter-organizational, information systems, and theory and 606 articles were finally selected as the analysis sample. As this sample also contained quite irrelevant articles, the abstracts of these journal articles were individually scrutinized and manually analysed in order to come up with

Table 2. Key constructs and variables

IOIS research domain	Constructs/variables	Source/s
Goals/values	• Goal alignment • Organizational effectiveness/business value of IOIS	Cha et al., 2008; Barringer and Harrison (2000)
Leadership/strategy	• Competitive/collaborative (business/IT) strategy • Top management support • Innovativeness and responsiveness • Policy, compliance and legislation • Cost/risk-sharing strategy	Grover, 1993; Avgerou, 2000; Armstrong and Sambamurthy, 1999; Kumar & van Dissel, 1996;
Environmental context	• Network externality • Environmental uncertainty/ turbulence, complexity, competition • Isomorphic pressures: normative pressure, coercive pressure, mimetic pressure • Business trends (globalization, outsourcing) • Regularities issues • Industry characteristics and market structure • Dynamism (rapid change versus slow change in environment) • Country/regional characteristics • Cultural forces	Reimers et al., 2010; Teo et al., 2003; Premkumar et al., 1997; Grewal et al., 2001; Christiaanse & Huigen, 1997 Robey et al., 2008)
Organizational antecedents	• Organizational size, scale, structure, centralization, formalization, culture • Organizational skills, knowledge/ability/awareness, slack • Absorptive capacity • Organizational readiness - financial resources, - IT sophistication, - trading partner readiness, and - elapsed time since adoption	Robey et al., 2008; Baura et al., 2005; Damanpour, 1992; Iacovou, 1995
Inter-organizational antecedents	• Inter-organizational dependence • Inter-organizational trust • Inter-organizational information sharing • Inter-organizational relationships, relationship quality/ specificity • Frequency of transactions • Potential/exercised power • Inter-organizational tasks: search, processing, monitoring & control, coordination	Robey et al., 2008; Reekers & Smithson; 1995; Mayer et al., 1995, Thompson, 1967
Task/technology (IOIS) artifacts	• IOIS capabilities: configurations, interoperability/standards, security, network speed, reliability • IOIS type, reach, scope, focus, location • IOIS characteristics: application integration, data compatibility, analytic ability, evaluation ability, and alertness. • IOIS structure: breadth, multiplicity, depth, formality, centrality/governance • Relative advantage/strategic benefits • Compatibility/task-technology-fit • Complexity • Trust in technology • Perceived benefits/cost	Kumar and van Dissel, 1996; Robey et al., 2008; Reimers et al., 2010; Kwon & Zmud, 1987; Premkumar and Ramamurthy, 1995; Saeed et al., 2011
User/communities	• Individual characteristics (gender, age, education, experience, voluntariness) • Group characteristics (skills and expertise as a group) • Community of practice characteristics (shared interest, culture, collaboration) • User acceptance	Markus, 1983; Venkatesh et. al., 2003; Coakes, 2004; Lave and Wenger, 1991; Nambisan & Wang, 2000; Krovi, 1993

continued on the following page

Table 2. Continued

IOIS research domain	Constructs/variables	Source/s
Incentive	• User satisfaction • Job satisfaction • Perceived need • Related training • Job security	Joshi, 1991; Markus, 1983; Barua et al., 2005; Bakos and Nault, 1997; Jiang et al., 2000;
Adoption/assimilation of IOIS	• Stages of assimilation - intention to implement, - evaluation or pilot use, - commitment, - limited deployment, - generalized deployment, - rejection • Assimilation gap • Time since adoption • Persistence and resilience • IOIS use: diversity, breadth, volume, depth	Mayer and Goes, 1988; Purvis et al., 2001; Prescott & Conger 1995; Kwon and Zmud, 1987; Fichman and Kemerer, 2001; Swanson and Ramiller, 2003; Reimers et al., 2010; Ramamurthy et al., 1999.
Impact on inter-organizational structure	• Co-ordination structure • Relationship structure • Power structure • Governance structure (market, organizational) • Transaction structure • Network structure	Robey et al., 2008; Markus, 1983; Clemons et al., 1993; Williamson, 1981; Malone, 1987
Impact on inter-organizational processes and practices	• Inter-organizational learning • Electronic/business process integration/reengineering • Change management • Negotiation/decision making (IOIS investment, outsourcing • Inter-organizational information integration/exchange/sharing • Inter-organizational relationship/contract management	Robey et al., 2008; Vaidya et al., 2006; Hart and Saunders, 1998; Knight, 2002 Dyer & Singh, 1998; Kambil and Short, 1994; Wenger, 2002; Schellhammer, 2010; Reimers et al., 2010
Organizational performance / business value of IOIS	• Relationship quality • Organizational change • Operational impacts • Strategic impacts	Robey et al., 2008; Barney, 1991; Reekers & Smithson, 1995; Icovou et al., 1995; Ramamurthy et al., 1999.

some relevant and influential inter-organizational information systems and business management theories.

We are aware of the limitations of this rather less systematic approach to come up with a list of theories for discussion. However, as our goal was only to generally identify the most relevant inter-organizational information systems and business management theories using a convenient approach for a book chapter (as opposed to a journal paper), a rigorous statistical analysis of the search output (e.g. count and percent data for various theories and associated variables) was not conducted.

While beyond the scope of this chapter, we believe such a rigorous statistical approach would reveal very illuminating results relating to the use of theories in terms of ranking of journals and categorisation of disciplines and research fields in inter-organizational information systems and business management. The theories identified in the sections below have not been ranked for importance/use and are thus in no order.

4.1 Institutional Theory

Institutional forces guide strategic changes in the organizations. Institutional theory suggests organizations adopt rules and practices that may not necessarily increase technical efficiency, but increase legitimacy in external stakeholders' eyes (DiMaggio and Powell 1983). According to authors, increase in the number of organisations that adopt and implement an innovation, creates pressure on the remaining organizations and trading partners and manipulate their decisions. Another central element in institutional theory is the concept of organizational legitimacy. It refers to the acceptance of an organization by its external environment (Deephouse 1996; DiMaggio and Powell 1983). Organizations achieve this legitimacy through adopting processes, structures, and strategies that others have already taken (Deephouse 1996; DiMaggio and Powell 1983). Organizational legitimacy in the case of IOIS use and assimilation depends upon the pressure exerted by trading partners and stakeholders (Abrahamson and Fairchild, 1999).

DiMaggio and Powell (1983) posit that managers have limited predictive capability hence the adoption decision taken at other organizations become critical to make a decision. Adoption by other organizations may provide indications that the concerned IOIS is beneficial. If a significant proportion of an organization's stakeholders – buyers, suppliers, competitor and other trading partners in the industry – use the IOIS, then the firm may get pressured into adopting the technology.

From an institutional theory perspective, the level of IOIS adoption and use depends on the organisations' legitimization needs and resulting isomorphic pressures (Dimaggio and Powell, 1983). IOIS can be viewed as organizational innovation, which are explained by three forces recognized by the institutional theory, namely mimetic, coercive and normative pressure. Institutional factors have a strong influence on the type of IOIS being developed and the IOIS *diffusion path* (Teo et al., 2003). Reimers et al. (2010) argue that while institutional theory can explain ongoing use of certain type of IOIS as a specific instance of organizational form, it does not provide explicit indications regarding their descriptions.

4.2 Diffusion of Innovation Theory

Substantial literature exists that investigates Inter-organizational information systems (IOIS), and IT adoption, diffusion and use (e.g. Cohen et al., 2003; Iacovou et al., 1995). Obviously, innovation diffusion theory (IDT) (Rogers, 1983; 1995) can be used to understand IOIS adoption and use as the theory has been extensively used recently as a fundamental theoretical base of innovation adoption research in the field of IOIS. Although the attributes suggested by IDT include relative advantage, compatibility, complexity, trialability, and observability (Rogers, 1983; 1995), only two variables – relative advantage (i.e. degree to which an innovation is perceived as being better than the idea it supersedes) and compatibility (of an innovation with existing practices and values) have been consistently found to be positively related and only one variable – complexity (i.e. degree to which an innovation is perceived as relatively difficult to understand and use) - has been consistently found to be negatively related to adoption of innovation (Iacovou et al.; 1995, Cohen et al., 2003). For details on Diffusion of Innovation theory, please refer to Chapters 13 and 16 of this book.

4.3 Structuration Theory

Structurational Theory of Technology Use (Orlikowski et al., 1995) is a dominant theory in the IOIS literature. This framework allows a better understanding of the emergence of information technologies in use as people interact within certain structural properties of the system. Johnston and Gregor (2000) argue that an organization's decision to adopt an IOIS is enabled and constrained by industry structure. As such, the authors recommend tracing relationships that define the structure and studying constraining and enabling effects of such structure.

Studies that have taken a structurational perspective on technology seem to be promising as they emphasize the emergent view on technology (Schellhammer (2010). In their study of Web technologies, Chatterjee et al. (2002) see the need to learn from a range of experiences with the assimilation of such technologies and investigate how organisations can encourage managerial activities in order to further enhance the levels of technology assimilation. Drawing upon the ideas in the structurational theory of technology use (Orlikowski et al. 1995), Chatterjee et al. (2002) propose that the organisational assimilation of Web technologies in e-Commerce initiatives is a cumulative consequence of the actions of managers and departments across the organisation and these actions are stimulated by an organisational milieu of norms, values and rules.

According to Orlikowski et al. (1995), individual cognition and behaviours are influenced by the three institutional structures of significance, legitimisation, and domination and individuals utilise these structures to make sense of the technology and undertake the improvisational actions (referred to as "structuring actions"). These structures are reproduced through actions and they can be manipulated by the senior management, who influence the structuring actions indirectly (referred to as "metastructuring actions") (Orlikowski et al. 1995).

Structuration theory views IOIS as the constructs of structure and action. As such, this theory helps identify structural aspects of IOIS, and also to identify patterns of behaviours and flows of materials and information resulting from actions (Reimers et al. 2010). Since Structuration theory is not very clear on how reproduction occurs, Reimers et al. (2010) draw on Practice Theory which they argue that enables them to explain the reproduction process empirically. For further details on structuration theory, please refer to Chapter 14 of this book.

4.4 Practice Theory

Practice theory (Wenger, 2002) views IOIS as groups of aligned practices connected by a specific type of boundary structures which are reproduced in communities of practice (CoP). Reimers et al., (2010) argue that such a practice view of IOIS is appropriate for describing IOIS at evolutionary timescales as socio-technical systems. According to authors, the key concepts to describe a practice are structures and patterns of practitioner's actions. Reimers et al., (2010) used practice theory to define the IOIS as a set of CoPs located in separate organizations which are connected through specific material IOIS boundary structures such as a shared data processing application, including a shared database. For details on practice theory, please refer to Chapter 1.

4.5 User Resistance Theory

According to the resistance theories (Markus, 1983), the system accepted by the users in one organisational setting may be rejected by the users in a different organisational setting.

Markus (1983) argues that resistance to change can be either person-centric (people resist because of their own internal factors), or system-centric (users resist the poor design of the system), or political (where interaction with the system and the organization context cause resistance). Markus also offers recommendations to address the resistance. For example, she suggests educating and participating the user in the design of the system to address person-centric resistance; focusing on improving human factors and re-engineering the system to address system-centric resistance; and finally restructuring incentive systems and relationships to address political resistance. For details on resistance theory, please refer to Chapter 2.

4.6 The DeLone and McLean Information Systems Success Model

The performance of information systems has been measured by using the original DeLone & McLean Information Systems Success model (DeLone & McLean, 1992) over a past decade. DeLone and McLean proposed a taxonomy and an interactive model as frameworks for conceptualizing and operationalizing IS success. The model is claimed to be based on both process and causal considerations and the dimensions of success are proposed to be interrelated rather than independent.

In evaluating information systems success, DeLone and McLean proposed an updated model in 2004, which was considered very significant in contributing towards a universal model. Finally, in 2004, DeLone and McLean further argued that new metrics were needed to address the success of such new technological developments as e-Commerce where decision makers now include both internal and external customers in the e-Commerce environment. According to the authors, the new model has been improved by the addition of two constructs – Service Quality to address the demand of customers for support (services) from their service providers; and Net Benefits – to address the issues such as "what qualifies as a 'benefit'? for whom? and at what level of analysis"?

The updated DeLone and McLean Information Systems Success Model can be a suitable framework to match the multiple metrics to the six dimensions – Information Quality, System Quality, Service Quality, Use, User Satisfaction, and Net Benefits. The model is interpreted in the following way: Systems Quality, Service Quality and Information Quality singularly and jointly affect both Use and User Satisfaction. Additionally, the amount of Use can affect the degree of User Satisfaction - positively or negatively (and vice versa). And lastly, Use and User Satisfaction are direct antecedents of Net Benefits (DeLone and MaClean, 1992, 2004).

4.7 Transaction Cost Theory

Transaction cost theory views IOIS as governance structures and asset specificity. The key characteristics of transactions are (Williamson, 1981): (i) the degree of uncertainty surrounding the transaction; (ii) the degree of asset specificity; and (iii) the frequency of the transactions. The literature on transaction costs divides them into three main classifications: information costs, negotiation costs, and monitoring (or enforcement) costs (Williamson, 1981). The theory explains the ability of IOIS to explain different governance structures and asset specificity, which prevent the one party from exploiting the other by threatening to break up the relationship. Transaction cost theory can be used for describing IOIS only on the level of a bilateral business relationship, not on the level of collectives (Reimers et al., 2010). For details on transaction cost theory, please refer to Chapters 4 and 5 of this book.

Transaction cost theory can also be used to analyse the impacts of IOIS on transaction structure. Various studies show that transaction economies of scale and learning curve effects of IOIS can not only decrease external and internal coordination costs and increase operational efficiency but also increase the level of explicit coordination and reduce transaction risks, thus affecting the governance structure of inter-organizational relationships (Malone, 1987; Clemons et al., 1993). However, transaction cost theory has some limitations (Reekers & Smithson, 1995): it takes little account of organizations' strategic choices and their abilities to use IOIS; it neglects the political aspects of inter-organizational relationships, and there are weaknesses in operationalizing the concepts of transaction and transaction costs.

4.8 Socio-Technical Theory

An IOIS is a socio-technical system. Bostrom and Heinen (1977) promoted the use of a socio-technical system (STS) approach as a MIS design methodology. This approach, which was pioneered by research in the 1950s and 1960s, was thought to assist in the solution of many of the problems associated with new applications of IT in order to reduce the number of IT-related failures. STS is a method of viewing organisations that emphasizes the interrelatedness of the functioning of the social and technical dimensions (Bostrom and Heinen, 1977). Although this sort of perspective could be used to explain the resulting success or failure of less complex information systems, it appears that STS can predict other important assimilation determinants of a complex IOIS which can exhibit different properties in different organizations.

According to socio-technical theory, two sub-systems - the technical sub-system and the social sub-system, are present in every organization. While the technical subsystem converts system inputs into system outputs, the social sub-system entails a revision of the jobs and of the corresponding social roles of the individuals and the groups which impact the technical sub-system (Watson, 2004). More recently, the importance of the consideration of the leading role for communities of practices (CoP) to explain consistency and resilience of IOIS has been recognized (Reimiers et al., 2009). For details, please refer to Chapter 12.

4.9 Technology Acceptance Model (TAM)

Another popular perspective is presented by Davis et al. (1989) who modified a widely studied model in social psychology, the Theory of Reasoned Action (TRA) to construct and test a model, Technology Acceptance Model (TAM), in the IS context. The researchers found the significant and positive relationship between intentionality, usefulness, and perceived ease of use.

The focus of this theory is on IOIS characteristics. According to TAM, perceived usefulness and perceived ease of use determine an individual's intention to use an IOIS, and perceived ease of use directly impacts the perceived usefulness. IOIS researchers have attempted to simplify and extend TAM by removing the attitude construct found in theory of reasoned action from the current specification, and by introducing factors from related models. Additional constructs include experience, voluntariness, job relevance and result demonstrability (Venkatesh et. al., 2003). For details, please refer to Chapter 7.

4.10 Task-Technology-Fit Model

The task-technology-fit model was proposed in the mid nineties. It argued that information systems including systems, policies, and IS staff have a positive influence on organisational performance provided there is fit between the functionalities of the technologies and the task requirements of the users (Goodhue, 1998). As argued by the propagator of this theory, "the strongest link between information systems and performance impacts will be due to a correspondence between task needs and system functionality". Thus the fit between tasks and technology can be explained with the help of task-technology fit theory which defines task-technology fit as the "degree to which a technology assists an individual in performing his/her portfolio of tasks" (Goodhue, 1998). However, like the DeLone and McLean IS success model (2004), task-technology-fit model has been criticized for overemphasis on 'task' rather than on the assimilation process of the IOIS from other perspectives. Another criticism about this theory is that it ignores the dynamics between organizational factors and the technology (Chwelos et al., 2001).

4.11 Network Externality Theory

The diffusion of IOIS has also been explained by utilizing network extrnality theory (also known as critical mass theory) which looks at the system requiring collective action and collaboration among potential participants (such as suppliers) for any adopter to use the innovation effectively (Bouchard, 1993). According to Bouchard (1993), an organization's adoption of innovation is dependent on the number of organizations that have already adopted or are planning to adopt the innovation, who these adopters are and their level of participation and contribution, rather than on the characteristics of the technology.

The success of an IOIS normally depends on a "critical mass" of users accepting and making proper use of the application. Critical mass theorists believe in the creation of positive network externalities which arise as a direct function of the number of current adopters. Fichman and Kemerer (1999) argue that performance outcomes of adoption also depend on size of the network of adopters because organizations benefit from increasing returns on adoption as the network keeps increasing. Network externality theory ignores this size factor and also other factors in the social or environmental networks and is heavily focused on technological networks. Network externalities are the effects on a product user of other users consuming the same product, thereby expanding the analysis of diffusion beyond individual firms to the surrounding network of firms (Robey et al. 2008).

4.12 Resource Dependence Theory

Resource dependence theory posits that organizations try to respond to uncertainty and dependence by establishing inter-organizational relationship and co-specialization with the environment or a party that possesses critical resources necessary (Dyer, 1996). The level of such relationship varies according to decision-making for investment on transaction-specific assets. According to the theory, such transaction-specific assets can enhance the competitive advantage once investment on transaction-specific assets is implemented to further enhance the mutual dependence between transaction parties. However, this leads to increase in cost to suspend the existing transaction as well as the cost for any new transaction with an alternative partner (Williamson, 1979; Dyer, 1996).

According to Thompson (1967), organizational dependence is determined by the organization's requirement for specific resources and the availability of other inter-organizational partners to meet their needs. This inter-organizational dependence is influenced by the importance of a resource, the extent to which the organization has discretion over the resource allocation and use, and the extent of concentration of resource control (Pfeffer and Salancik, 1978).

Resource dependence theory views IOIS as devices of organizations to increase/decrease the dependence on other organizations (Reekers & Smithson, 1995). The authors note that many of the weaknesses of transaction cost theory are the strengths of resource dependence theory, which focuses on the political and behavioural aspects of inter-organizational relationships. The authors also note that its emphasis on process complements transaction cost's emphasis on structure. However, like transaction cost theory, it is based on dyadic relationships between two organizations.

Power is a key concept in resource dependence theory. Five sources of power have been identified (Thorelli, 1986): economic power, technological power, expertise or knowledge power, trust and legitimacy, and three forms of power have been distinguished (Reve & Stern, 1979): potential power, enacted power and perceived power.

4.13 Theory of Constraints

The purpose of Theory of Constraints (TOC) (Goldratt, 1990) is to identify the weak link (constraint) within the system and to strengthen this link to the point where it is no longer the limiting factor in determining the strength of the system. Based on TOC, the five focusing steps have been developed to ensure that managers direct attention to things essential to successful management (Noreen et al., 1995). The TOC approach to the management of change involves answering three basic questions: what to change, what to change to, and how to cause the change (Goldratt, 1990).

The TOC Thinking Process (TP) advocates the use of a framework to help managers better understand key relationships associated with improving the system. The Thinking Processes are intended as a set of structured steps that lead decision-makers to identify the root cause of "undesirable effects," to identify the faulty and/or incomplete logic regarding the root cause and to develop an improved logic regarding the root cause that, in turn, leads to more desirable effects (Noreen et al., 1995). The TP methodology addresses policy constraints and creates breakthrough solutions using common sense, intuitive knowledge and logic. The TOC thinking process relies on five basis logic diagrams to understand, analyse, and improve the existing asset management system to proactively determine and correct any unwanted consequences of change (Cox et al, 2003). For details on this theory, please refer to Chapter 9 of this book.

4.14 Incomplete Contract Theory

While transaction cost theory addresses the type of inter-firm relationship based on financial benefits such as cost efficiency, Incomplete Contact Theory emphasizes on the improvement of non-financial aspects such as quality, responsiveness, defect rate, innovation, technology, acquisition, reliability and information sharing. The theory posits that a certain level of investment is required by suppliers in order to improve such non-financial factors, which may be difficult to accurately specify in a contract (Milgrom and Roberts, 1990). The authors content that buyers should derive the investment on non-financial (i.e. non-contractible) factors from suppliers by providing incentives for the investment in order to respond to the uncertain environment.

Bakos and Brynjolfsson (1993) further explain the Incomplete Contract Theory by arguing that the number of suppliers is inversely proportional to supplier's incentives for investment on non-contractible factors. This further implies that the investment on non-contractible factors can be considered as a key antecedent for the decision of an optimal number of suppliers with transaction costs and relationship-specific assets.

4.15 Resource-Based View

The resource-based perspective can be used to distinguish between different forms of IOIS resources and capabilities. It also provides guidance for IOIS researchers to evaluate and review how IOIS affect the organizational strategy and business performance. According to resource-based view (RBV), organizations possess resources and subsets of which enable them to achieve competitive advantage and lead to strategic organizational performance (Barney, 1991). Resources that are valuable and rare can lead to the creation of competitive advantage. That advantage can be sustained over longer time periods to the extent that the firm is able to protect against resource imitation, transfer, or substitution (Barney, 1991).

Empirical studies within IOIS using RBV have strongly supported the resource-based view. IOIS researchers can use RBV of the firm to understand technology strategy perspective, which is primarily concerned with understanding the conditions that lead to sustained competitive advantage (Barney, 1991). While the resource-based view focuses on unique resources and contextual conditions in the IOIS context, more generic organizational characteristics are considered in the prior IS literature.

4.16 Bounded Rationality Theory

Bounded rationality means the limited extent to which rational calculation can direct human behaviour. Bounded rationality theory sees human beings as objective information processors, who make decisions rationally. While they make decisions by weighing the consequences of adopting each alternative course of action where one stage uses the outputs of the previous stage, they have cognitive limitations which constrain the amount of information they can absorb (Simon, 1960). These limitations lead to high levels of uncertainty, to which humans respond by developing a simplified model of the real situation by reducing, constraining and bounding the problem until it becomes sufficiently well-defined to be resolved (Gasson, 2005).

Human beings then evaluate alternative solutions until an alternative is identified which satisfies a set of criteria for a satisfactory solution of the problem. Bounded rationality theory introduced the concept of satisficing - the outcome achieved by this process of bounded rationality is not optimal, but satisficing, in that it satisfies a minimal, rather than optimal set of solution criteria (Simon, 1960).

IOIS researchers can use this theory to study the use of IOIS to enhance inter-organizational relationships with trading partners, especially in making outsourcing decisions and also to design and develop/integrate appropriate applications.

4.17 Collective Action Theory

Theories of collective action explain some aspects of human behaviour. Collective action has been defined as "a set of social practices (i) involving simultaneously a number of individuals and groups, (ii) exhibiting similar morphological characteristics in contiguity of time and space, (iii) implying a social field of relationships and (iv) the capacity of the people involved of making sense of what they are doing." (Melucci, 1996, p.20). The theory basically classifies standard-setting consortia (implementation consortia, application consortia, and proof-of-technology consortia) and defines the role of consortia in the standards development process (Weiss and Cargill, 1992).

In IOIS context, Bimber et al. (2005) has proposed some modifications to this theory, which redefines collective action as a phenomenon of boundary crossing between private and public domain. The authors identify the problem of "free riding" and the importance of formal organization as one means to overcome it. They further note that as IOIS provides novel affordances to those seeking public goods, and as the frequency, intensity, breadth, and depth of interdependence increases, the importance of understanding the dynamics of collective action becomes greater than ever before.

4.18 Public Goods Theory

The public goods theory describes how public goods are produced and used (Marwell and Oliver, 1993). According to the authors, "actions taken by two or more people in pursuit of the same collective good" (p.4) usually result in public good which can be used in *nonrivalrous* and *nonexcludable* way. The authors further clarify that once public goods are available, no one can be excluded from their benefits and one individual's consumption does not decrease the amount of the good left to be consumed by other public.

According to Fulk et al. (1996), IOIS can generate two kinds of public goods namely connectivity and communality. With the advent of the Internet, the information and communication public goods offer the trading partners who participate in IOIS various collective benefits. As the IOIS provide various operational and strategic benefits to those seeking public goods, and as the frequency of transactions, inter-organizational dependence, inter-organizational information sharing and learning greatly increases with the use of IOIS, the importance of understanding the dynamics of collective action becomes greater than ever before.

4.19 Dynamic Capabilities Theory

Teece et al. (1997) define dynamic capabilities as 'the ability to integrate, build, and reconfigure internal and external competencies to address rapidly-changing environments'. The dynamic capabilities concept overcomes a weakness of the resource-based view of the firm. The RBV has been criticized for ignoring factors associated with resources, for example, how resources are developed, how they are integrated within trading partner organizations and how they are released. Dynamic capabilities attempt to fill these shortcomings by acting as a buffer between organization resources and the changing business environment. While the RBV emphasizes the selecting of appropriate resources for competitive advantage, dynamic capabilities emphasize resource development and renewal (Teece et al., 1997).

According to dynamic capability theory, it is more important for organizations to mobilize resources than to control them because resources create the most value when they are reconfigured in response to competitive conditions (Newbert, 2007). Because critical resources may be embedded in inter-organizational processes IOIS can be considered to be boundary-spanning capabilities that can be dynamically reconfigured with other resources for greater competitive advantage (Dyer and Singh, 1998).

In fact, IOIS capabilities possess many of the attributes of dynamic capabilities. According to Wade & Hullan (2004), IOIS resources and capabilities can produce greater value and can lead to a sustainable competitive advantage when they are combined with other resources (Wade & Hullan, 2004). Morgan (2000) suggests that trading partners need to properly combine their resources into desirable capabilities to add superior value to business and to differentiate their products and services making them difficult for competitors to replicate.

4.20 Path Dependency Theory

The theory of path dependency explains processes of IOIS diffusion and answers why in spite of an efficient market an inferior technology reigns (David, 2001). According to David, organizations and their trading partners are part of institutions that structure and channel their behavioral standards and activities along established paths. These paths are determined by their values, standards and rules) and public policies determined by past actions that impose constraints on institutional development. This is because once a path is chosen, change management is constrained because the processes become institutionalized and are reinforced over time.

Some IOIS studies show that path dependencies resulting from prior learning, investment and experience give organizations preferential advantages in treating real options, and thus enhance option value (Sambamurthy *et al.* 2003). The theory of path dependency puts the sequence of events in history into the focus of the researcher. Recent literature has applied the path dependency theory to explain the stability of IOIS (Schellhammer, 2008).

4.21 General Systems Theory

IOIS researchers can use systems theory to focuses on the arrangement of and relations between various elements of the IOIS which connect them into the system. Systems concepts include system-environment boundary, input, output, process, state, hierarchy, goal-directedness, and information (Ludwig von Bertalanffy, 1962). General systems theory also appears to be useful for IOIS researchers when developing hypotheses about which elements are required for a properly functioning IOIS, how those elements should interact, their strength of influence on overall IOIS effectiveness, and how to manage the relationships towards achievement of strategic goals (Weick, 1979).

4.22 Management Fashion Theory

Innovations are traditionally assumed to provide economic benefits to adopters. However, according to management fashion theory (Abrahamson and Fairchild, 1999), organizations imitate innovation models promoted by "fashion-setting organizations" and that the diffusion of technically inefficient innovations cannot be fully explained under conditions of uncertainty. Abrahamson and Fairchild (1999, p. 709) define management fashion as "relatively transitory collective beliefs, disseminated by the discourse of management-knowledge entrepreneurs, that a management technique resides at the forefront of rational management progress."

Fichman (2004) identifies four key features of this definition: first, fashions are transient rather than enduring; second, the fashion itself is not some real world thing, but rather, collective beliefs about a thing; third, the focus rests on management fashion setters as the mechanism by which fashions are disseminated; and fourth, the technique is viewed as beneficial and progressive.

The theory also discusses how the marketing and media campaigns help to produce a self-reinforcing adoption bandwagon among the managers, directors and business partners and thus diffuse the innovation even in the absence of any systematic evidence of the innovation's efficacy. Fichman (2004) further suggests that the theory can be used to examine the following general research questions: (1) why do *fashion waves* arise when they do? (2) what characterizes the typical patterns of discourse *intensity* surrounding *transient fashions*, (3) what patterns exist in the *content* of this discourse? (4) what intervention characteristics or macro-level environmental factors might correlate with patterns of discourse intensity?

4.23 Actor-Network Theory

Actor network theory views IOIS as embracing not only the human actors but also the physical artifacts and the concept to which to actors related and helps understand all the heterogenous elements of a network (Latour, 2005). According to this theory, any actor, whether an individual or communities, object (including IOIS infrastructure), or organization and its trading partners, is equally important to a social network. For more information on ANT, please refer to Chapter 6 of this book.

4.24 Real Options Theory

Real options theory allows the IOIS researchers to quantify the value of management flexibility and to assess the strategic value of investment in IOIS. The five types of real options include waiting-to-invest option, growth option, flexibility option, exit option and learning option (Black and Scholes, 1973). The Black-Scholes model calculates option value based on (1) the projected value of the project, (2) the variability of projected value, (3) the cost of the project, (4) the risk-free rate of return, and (5) the time until expiration.

Fichman (2004a) notes that it can be difficult for managers to decide which IOIS to use, when to use them, and how to manage the assimilation process in order to realize business value. Fichman further notes that as traditional methods have been criticized for failing to accurately capture the economic value of investments in a changing environment, the real options theory can be used for the valuation and management of IOIS investments.

The challenge for IOIS researchers, according to Fichman (2004a), is that they are equipped to understand where real options are most warranted on theoretical grounds, and which factors drive option value in IOIS investments.

4.25 Organizational Information Processing Theory

IOIS has been viewed as tool for increasing information processing capability in order to decrease uncertainty and increase inter-organizational coordination in inter-organizational relationships. As such, three concepts of the organizational information processing theory: information processing needs, information processing capability, and the fit between the two to obtain optimal performance provide the constructs to explain interorganizational cooperation (Premkumar, Ramamutrhy, and Saunders, 2005).

Bensaou and Venkatraman (1995) argue that a cooperative interorganisational relationship is dependent upon the ways the trading partners address uncertainties, and with the information capabilities they develop. The authors identify three types of uncertainty in the interorganisational relationships: environmental uncertainty, task uncertainty, and partnership uncertainty, and again three mechanisms that effect information processing capabilities: structural capabilities, process capabilities, and information technology capabilities. They conclude that interorganizational cooperation is determined by the fit between these uncertainties and mechanisms. This conclusion is supported by Premkumar, Ramamurthy and Saunders (2005) who suggest that organizations can develop buffers to reduce the effect of uncertainty, and implement structural mechanisms and information processing capability to enhance the information flow and thereby reduce uncertainty.

4.26 Unified Theory of Acceptance and Use of Technology

According to Unified theory of acceptance and use of technology, performance expectancy, effort expectancy, social influence, and facilitating conditions directly determine the determinants of usage intention and behaviour whereas gender, age, experience, and voluntariness of use moderate their impact (Venkatesh et. al., 2003). Performance expectancy is based on beliefs about perceived usefulness, interactivity and flexibility. Effort expectancy is based on beliefs about ease of learning, perceived ease of use and self-efficacy. Social influence is based on subjective norm and image. The unified model claims to have integrated significant elements across eight user acceptance models and formulates a unique measure with core determinants of user behavioral intention and usage.

4.27 Theory of Technology Dominance

Theory of technology dominance posits that dependency on an intelligent decision aid can create a long-term, de-skilling effect in the user as well as deter that user's development of knowledge and advancement in his or her domain (Arnold & Sutton, 1998). When the expertise of the user and intelligent decision aid are mismatched, there is a negative relationship between the user's expertise level and the risk of poor decision making). By the same token, when the expertise level of the user and intelligent decision aid are matched, there is a positive relationship between reliance on the aid and improved decision making (Arnold & Sutton, 1998)

IOIS researchers can use this theory to analyse the usefulness of analytic and evaluation capabilities of IOIS for a decision maker. The theory enables to identify (i) the factors that determine the likelihood of relying on IOIS, (ii) conditions under which a decision maker using IOIS is susceptible to dominance by the technology, and (iii) long-term impact of IOIS use on de-skilling domain experts.

4.28 Organizational Learning Theory

Organizational learning theory emphasizes the importance of organizational learning and suggests that the organizations must consciously link decisions and actions to outcomes. The core concept of the theory is organizational effectiveness, which has been defined as the degree to which expected outcomes match actual outcomes in a given environmental conditions. The degree to which they do not match is called performance gap (Cha et al., 2008). According to this theory, learning occurs in three stages: data acquisition, data interpretation, and adaptation/action and a continual and iterative feedback process takes place at all stages of the process (Cha et al., 2008).

IOIS researchers can apply this theory to study the organizational effectiveness/performance of using IOIS. In fact, there is a great scope for IOIS researchers to use this theory to study most of the domains of the IOIS research framework suggested in this chapter. For example, the theory guides to assess the impact of using IOIS on inter-organizational processes and practices including inter-organizational learning in terms of its type, level and the process.

4.29 Game Theory

Game theory uses applied mathematical models to study interactions with formalized incentive structures taking into account the decisions that are made in an environment where various players interact strategically. Game theory concerns with the predicted and actual behaviour of individuals in games, as well as optimal strategies.

IOIS views game theory in the context of inter-organizational information sharing between trading partners that can be enhanced with its use. The theory can help assess the investment decisions and situations under which inter-organizational cooperation can provide more effective intended consequences than isolated action (Chu & Lee, 2006). Chu & Lee (2006) have used game theory to show that investment in IOIS can increase inter-organizational information sharing between trading partners resulting in cost/transaction savings and improved business performance (Chu & Lee, 2006).

4.30 Adaptive Structuration Theory

Adaptive Structuration Theory (AST) is the adapted version of Anthony Giddens' structuration theory (ST) to study the interaction of groups and the role of advanced information technologies in organisational change. According to DeSanctis and Poole, 'AST provides a model that describes the interplay between advanced information technologies, social structures, and human interaction' (DeSanctis et al., 1994, p. 125).

AST views IOIS as being comprised of 'structural features' (rules, resources and capabilities of the system) and the 'spirit' of the technology (DeSanctis and Poole, 1994). While structural features bring meaning and control to group interaction, the spirit is the intention of these features. The spirit acts as a means of signification in helping the groups interpret their meaning, add value to processes of domination and provides legitimation by supplying normative frames with regard to appropriate behaviours (DeSanctis and Poole, 1994). The authors further explain that as the technology structures are applied in group interaction, new forms of social structure emerge which may then be reproduced and institutionalized over time.

AST is a more theory to study IOIS issues than ST in the sense that ST focuses on changes in social practices in general, while AST focuses on changes that occur when advanced technologies are introduced. Understanding the spirit and features of the IOIS as well as the characteristics of the organizational environment may help IOIS researchers in predicting and explaining the degree of 'fit' as well as potential appropriation and the business value of IOIS.

4.31 Principal-Agency Theory

Also known as agency theory, principal-agent theory suggests that principal-agent relationships should reflect efficient organization of information and risk-bearing costs, specifically focusing on the trade-off between the costs of measuring the agent's behavior and the costs of measuring the outcomes (Eisenhardt, 1989). When a principal hires an agent, his interdependence and relationship with the agent is mainly based on the trust and cooperation of the agent. The principal should be able to bear the risks/costs in that the agent may not be able to monitor the agent's behaviour and progress with the project (moral hazard), and to ensure that the agent has the ability to deliver as contracted (adverse selection). Agency theory suggests that incomplete contracts and asymmetric information between the principal and agent, and opportunism are three causes (risks) of principal-agent dysfunction. Various mechanisms may be used to mitigate the risks including piece rates/commissions, profit sharing, efficiency wages, the agent posting a bond, or fear of firing.

IOIS researches have the opportunity to use agency theory to assess the impact of IOIS on inter-organizational information sharing or information asymmetry problems in inter-organizational relationships. For example, IOIS applications such as public e-Procurement have the capability to enhance transparency and accountability and thus mitigate the asymmetric information problem by increasing information sharing with the agents. Public e-procurement can minimise the agent's opportunities for arbitrary actions by reducing discretion, and thus can reduce the chances of corruption in public procurement (Vaidya, 2006). In fact, agency theory can provide a much needed theoretical support to IOIS researchers to assess the anti-corruption capabilities of IOIS and the resulting business value of IOIS.

4.32 Social-Exchange Theory

Social exchange theory provides the theoretical foundation for the study of relationships between non-profit making inter-organizational transactions. The main focus of this theory is that inter-organizational relationship does not necessarily need to be directly related to any economic/transactional outcomes. According to social exchange theory, the outcomes of an organization's behaviour are based on the responsive behaviour of trading partners within the relationship (Premkumar and Ramamurthy, 1995).

IOIS researchers have used social exchange theory as the theoretical background to examine various aspects of inter-organizational information sharing through a lens of non-economic aspects including power, trust, and interdependency (Premkumar and Ramamurthy 1995). Trust and power have been identified as key elements for IOIS that impact interdependency between trading partners (Hart and Saunders 1997). According to Bakos and Brynjolfson (1993), trust leads to communication openness and information sharing, commitment between organizations, and therefore increases cooperation. This in turn, results in trading partners' satisfaction, long-term return on investment, and reputation. Similarly, IOIS researchers have studied the role of power in inter-organizational relationships in terms of interdependencies between trading partners to achieve business value of IOIS (Hart and Saunders 1997).

While we briefly presented the description of 32 theories, there are also other key theories which look useful to study IOIS-related issues. They include contingency theory, network theory, Porter's competitive strategy, theory of planned behaviour, theory of reasoned action, work systems theory, interaction theory, theory of human needs and motivation, user involvement theory, industrial organization theory, theory of referent organization, and industrial life cycle theory.

5. KEY THEORIES AND THE MAIN CONCEPTS/CONSTRUCTS

We briefly described the key theories and discussed how they have been applied in prior IS literature or how they can be applied to study various IOIS issues. IOIS and business management researchers often need to invest lots of time and resources to identify the most relevant key theories and the associated constructs/concepts to conduct their research. Considering this, the following table (Table 3) provides the main concepts/constructs and level of analysis for each identified theory for this chapter. It is our expectation that the table will provide the IOIS and business management researchers a much needed tool to generally visualize the theory or theories of interest and associated

Table 3. Key theories and the main constructs/variables

Theory	Main concepts/constructs	Level of analysis	IS/IOIS literature that discusses/uses the theory
Institutional theory	Institutional emergence, conformity/legitimacy; conflict, change, isomorphism, schemas, rules, norms and routines, external pressure, competitive pressure, dependence, exercised power, government policies;	Group Organization Industry	Premkumar, Ramamurthy, and Crum, 1997; Teo et al., 2003
Diffusion of Innovation Theory	Implementation success/technology diffusion, relative advantage, compatibility, complexity	Group Organization Industry	Rogers, 1995; Iacovou et al., 1995
Structuration theory	Structures of signification, domination, and legitimation; social system, resources, norms or rules, interactions (communications, power), consciousness/knowledgeability	Individual, system/ structure	Orlikowski et al. (1995), Chatterjee et al. (2002); Reimers et al., 2010
Practice Theory	Structures, patterns, actions	Group	Wenger, 2002 Reimers et al., 2010
Transaction cost theory	Governance structure, degree of outsourcing, outsourcing success, inter-organizational coordination/collaboration, coordination costs, transaction/ opportunity costs, operational risk, asset specificity, uncertainty, trust, frequency of transactions	Organization	Williamson, 1981; Reimers et al., 2010; Malone, 1987; Clemons et al., 1993; Reekers & Smithson, 1995
Socio-technical theory	Organization, individual, environment, technical sub-system and the social sub-system, system inputs into system outputs, revision of the jobs and of the corresponding social roles, design process	Individual, system, tasks	Bostrom and Heinen, 1977; Watson, 2004
Technology Acceptance Model	Behavioral intention to use, System usage, Perceived usefulness, Perceived ease of use	Individual	Davis et al. (1989) Venkatesh et. al., 2003).
Task-technology-fit model	Individual performance, system utilization, task characteristics, technology characteristics	Individual	Goodhue, 1998; Chwelos et al., 2001
Network externality theory	collective action and collaboration; network externalities	Network	Robey et al. 2008); Bouchard, 1993; Fichman and Kemerer (1999)
Resource Dependence Theory	Sources/forms of power, dependence, resource, inter-organizational relationships; specificity (site specificity, physical asset specificity, human asset specificity)	Organisation	Dyer, 1996; Thompson (1967), Thorelli, 1986; Reve & Stern, 1979
Resistance theory	User involvement, user resistance/acceptance, technical factor, organizational factor, user's factor, job threatening factor	Individual	Markus, 1983; Alderfer, 1969; Ives, 1984; Jiang et al., 2000
DeLone & McLean Information Systems Success model	Information Quality, System Quality, Service Quality, Use, User Satisfaction, and Net Benefits.	Individual, Organization	DeLone and MaClean, 1992, 2004;
Theory of Constraints	Thinking Processes undesirable effects common sense, intuitive knowledge and logic policy constraints	Individual, process	Goldratt, 1990; Cox et al, 2003; Noreen et al., 1995
Incomplete Contract Theory	Quality, responsiveness, defect rate, innovation, technology, acquisition, reliability and information sharing	Organization, individual, group	Milgrom and Roberts, 1990 Bakos and Brynjolfsson (1993
Resource-based view	Competitive advantage, organizational performance, rents, assets, capabilities, resources	Organization	Barney, 1986; Penrose, (1959
Bounded rationality theory	non-rationality, decision making	Individual	Simon, 1960; Gasson, 2005

continued on the following page

Table 3. Continued

Theory	Main concepts/constructs	Level of analysis	IS/IOIS literature that discusses/uses the theory
Principal agent theory	Self interest, Bounded rationality, Risk aversion, Information asymmetry, power, trust, efficiency, goal conflict	Individual, group	Eisenhardt, M, K. (1989); Raghu et al. (2004
Collective action theory	Interdependence, mutual interests, coordinated action, free riding, formal organization, human behaviour	Individual, group	Bimber et al. 2005
Public goods theory	Collective good, connectivity and communality, resources, costs and gain related to participants' contributions, the group, interdependence, social network.	Individual, group	Marwell and Oliver, 1993; Fulk et al., 1996;
Dynamic capabilities theory	Competitive value relationships, resources, reconfiguration, value creation, capabilities, absorptive capacity, environmental turbulence,	Organization	Newbert, 2007). Dyer and Singh, 1998; Wade and Hulland, 2004;
Path dependency theory	Potential inefficiency, path dependent processes, outcomes, dependence institutional values, standards and rules public policies	Organization	David, 1997; Ackermann, 2001;
General Systems theory	system-environment boundary, output, input, process, hierarchy, goals, relationships, throughput, feedback, control,	System	Weick, 1979 Bertalanffy in 1962
Management fashion theory	Adoption of management innovations, status of fashion setters, sources of discourse, external pressures for organisational change (competition, economic factors,, efficacy)	Organization, Group, Industry, Society	Abrahamson & Fairchild, 1999; Fichman, 2004; Baskerville & Myers, 2009
Actor network theory	Human actors, physical artifacts, social network	Organization Individual, communities,	Latour, 2005
Real options theory	Option value, management flexibility, IT investment/cash flow, adjusted risk factors, uncertainty, volatility, types of real options	Decision	Black and Scholes, 1973; Fichman, 2010
Socio-technical theory	Task/technology, environment/society	Organization, user/ employee	Bostrom and Heinen, 1977; Watson, 2004
Organizational information processing theory	Information processing performance, information processing needs, information processing capability, inter-organizational cooperation/relationships	Organization	Bensaou and Venkatraman, 1995; Premkumar, Ramamutrhy, and Saunders, 2005
Unified theory of acceptance and use of technology	Performance expectancy, effort expectancy, attitude toward using technology, social influence, facilitating conditions, self-efficacy, anxiety, gender, age, experience, voluntariness of use	Individual	Venkatesh et. al., 2003
Theory of technology dominance	Reliance, dominance, task complexity, task experience, decision aid familiarity, cognitive fit	Individual	Arnold & Sutton, 1998
Organizational learning theory	Organizational effectiveness, levels/types of learning, learning process, complexity of environment, degree of organizational change, dynamism of external environment, stress, organizational strategic focus, structure of organization, organizational environment	Organization	Cha et al., 2008

continued on the following page

Table 3. Continued

Theory	Main concepts/constructs	Level of analysis	IS/IOIS literature that discusses/uses the theory
Game theory	Cost /benefit of option/decision made, incentive	Individual, Group, Organization, Industry	Chu & Lee, 2006
Adaptive Structuration Theory	Decision outcomes (efficiency, quality, consensus, commitment), social structures (rules, resources), structure of advanced information technology (structural features, spirit, task, organizational context), group's internal system.	Group	DeSanctis and Poole (1994)
Principal-agent theory	Efficiency, alignment of interests, risk sharing, successful contracting, information asymmetry, contract, moral hazard, trust, power	Individual, group	Eisenhardt, 1989; Vaidya, 2007;
Social exchange theory	Value and utility, profit, rewards, approval, status, reputation, flexibility, trust, exchange relation, dependency, power	Individual, Group, Organization,	Premkumar and Ramamurthy, 1995; Bakos and Brynjolfson (1993); Hart and Saunders, 1997

constructs and consider their suitability to study a particular issue of interest.

6. LINKING THE THEORIES TO RESEARCH DOMAINS

Table 3 presented the key theories and the main constructs/variables for this chapter. The table could be useful if the researcher is confident about using a particular theory to investigate a particular issue, that is, the researcher already knows about the theory and the research questions that can be explained with the help of this theory. However, the researcher may want to ask which research domain/s can be explained by which set of theories? That is, we have research questions that are likely to be explained by multiple theories. To help with this situation, the table below (Table 4) presents matrix of theories versus research domains. While the research domains have been matched with the theories based on the broad descriptions of the theories and the subjective interpretation of the constructs/variables as suggested by theories, it is our expectation that such approach greatly helps the IOIS and business management researchers identify an appropriate set of theories to study the IOIS issue/s of their interest. Please note that '**X**' means that the theory listed in the first column can be matched to explain one or more constructs/variables of the research domain and 'x' means that whether or not the theory can be matched with the domain depends upon a certain interpretation of the theory and the research issue/s of interest.

7. CONCLUDING REMARKS

Having set the background and discussed the need for academic theories for IOIS and business management researchers, this chapter first presented the research framework to depict the perspective on IOIS and business management. The twelve components of the framework set forth the research domains/themes for IOIS and business management researchers. The extant literature was briefly reviewed to describe each research domain.

Second, informed by the review/description of each domain, the chapter then identified the most relevant constructs/variables for each domain. While not rigorous and comprehensive as

Table 4. Matching the theories with research framework domains

	Goals, values	Strategy / Leadership	Environmental context	Task, technology artifacts	Organizational antecedents	User, communities characteristics	Incentives	Inter-organisational antecedents	Organizational use / assimilation of IOIS	Impact of IOIS on Inter-organizational structure	Impact of IOIS on Inter-organizational processes & practices	Organizational effectiveness/ business value of IOIS
Institutional theory		x	X		x			x			X	X
Diffusion of innovation theory				x	x				X			x
Structuration theory	x	x	x	x	x	x		x		X	x	X
Practice theory				x		X				x	X	
Resistance theories			x	x	x	X	X					x
DeLone & McLean Information Systems Success model	X			X		x	x		X			X
Transaction cost theory			x	x	x			x		X	X	x
Socio-technical theory			x	X	x	x	x				x	
Technology acceptance model				x		X	x		X			
Task technology fit model				X		X			x			
Network externalities theory				x	x	X		x				
Resource dependence theory			x		x			X		x		X
Theory of constraints	x	x	x		x	x					X	x
Incomplete contract theory			x		x			x			X	x
Resource-based view		x	x	x	X			x				X
Bounded rationality theory	X	X		x		x			x	x	X	
Collective action theory					X	x		x			X	
Public goods theory			x	X		x		x			x	

continued on the following page

Table 4. Continued

	Goals, values	Strategy / Leadership	Environmental context	Task, technology artifacts	Organizational antecedents	User, communities characteristics	Incentives	Inter-organisational antecedents	Organizational use / assimilation of IOIS	Impact of IOIS on Inter-organizational structure	Impact of IOIS on Inter-organizational processes & practices	Organizational effectiveness/ business value of IOIS
Dynamic capability theory			x	X	x			x	x			x
Path dependency theory		x	x		x			x	X		x	x
General systems theory	X		x					x			x	x
Management fashion theory		x	X		x			x				
Actor-network theory	X			x	x	X		x		x		
Real options theory	x	x	x		x						X	x
Organizational Information Processing Theory			x	X	x			X		x	x	x
Unified theory of acceptance and use of technology				x		X	X		X			x
Theory of Technology Dominance			x	X		x						
Organizational learning theory		x	x		x	x	x	x		x	X	X
Game theory	x	X	x			x	X	x	x		x	X
Adaptive structuration theory			x	X	x	X					x	x
Principal-agent theory			x		x			x		x		X
Social exchange theory			x		x		x	x		x		X

intended, the tool (Table 2) should help to identify the domain of the problem and narrow it down to the issue/s of interest (associated constructs/variables) in the chosen domain of the research framework.

Third, this chapter identified over thirty influential key theories and briefly described them in the context of IOIS and business management. The methodology to come up with the theories was briefly explained. While not a very scientific/rigorous selection, we believe that most relevant/influential theories have been identified for consideration by the IOIS and business management researchers.

Fourth, this chapter listed the main concepts/constructs and level of analysis for each identified theory for this chapter. With this, the IOIS and business management researchers will be able to generally visualize the theory or theories of interest and associated constructs and consider their suitability to study a particular issue of interest.

Finally, to deal with the situation of answering the research questions that are likely to be explained by multiple theories, this chapter presented matrix of theories versus research domains. It is our expectation that such approach greatly helps the IOIS and business management researchers identify an appropriate set of theories to study the IOIS phenomena of their interest.

This chapter is not without its limitations, and as such, offers opportunities for further study in this area. First, the IOIS and business management framework was specifically developed to set forth topics for this chapter and there is a scope for its further development. IOIS and business management researchers are suggested to exercise caution in that it may be a complex endeavour to attempt to empirically test all the relationships between constructs in a single study. It is rather suggested that researches can select one or several domains of their interest and identify appropriate constructs/variables to investigate. Second, the examples of key constructs/variables in relation to both the framework and the theories are not exhaustive – researchers may be able to identify other constructs/variables more important depending on the focus of their research context. Third, an attempt has been made to generally and briefly present the key theories and it has not been deemed practicable to provide detailed description of the theories in a single chapter. Researchers are suggested to refer to other chapters of this book for details of some key theories. Again, researchers may find other theories more important to investigate their particular research problem. Finally, researchers are suggested to exercise caution when matching the theories with research domains. While an attempt has been made to guide researchers to choose outcome and explanatory variables within the domain, they should be mindful of the fact that the appropriate fit always depends upon the certain contextual interpretation of the theory and the research issue/s of interest.

Understanding the relevant theories may then help an organization develop its future IOIS and business strategies and understand where their future efforts need to be focused in order to successfully manage IOIS assimilation. However, practitioners should understand that unsystematic pursuit of IOIS; especially without taking into account the critical antecedents and theory-based evidence, may not deliver intended results. It should be noted that the process of IOIS adoption and assimilation can be tricky, but offers great rewards for those who use it successfully.

Despite some limitations, the contributions from this chapter, especially the relevant constructs/variables derived from various theories, should provide researchers and practitioners with a greater ability to make more intelligent and informed decisions regarding the IOIS and business management, for example, to make decision as to whether or not to invest/participate in IOIS. By understanding the key constructs and their interactions relating to IOIS, and more importantly the theories behind them, practitioners will be in a better position to design appropriate strategies to deal with them and consequently improve organizational effectiveness. Practitioners can now look at IOIS with more concrete antecedents and relevant theories in mind to influence and manage their inter-organizational processes and practices. We hope that the research framework presented in this chapter helps organize and guide academic research efforts as well as offer insights to research practitioners on IOIS and business management.

ACKNOWLEDGMENT

The author would like to thank Professor Kai Reimers of RWTH Aachen University, Germany; and Associate Professor Robert Fichman of Carroll School of Management at Boston College, USA for their comments on some parts of the earlier version of this chapter.

REFERENCES

Abrahamson, E., & Fairchild, G. (1999). Management fashion: Lifecycles, triggers, and collective learning processes. *Administrative Science Quarterly*, *4*(44), 708–740. doi:10.2307/2667053

Arnold, V., & Sutton, S. G. (1998). The theory of technology dominance: understanding the impact of intelligent decision aids on decision makers' judgments. *Advances in Accounting Behavioral Research*, *1*, 175–194.

Bakos, J. Y. (1991). A strategic analysis of electronic marketplaces. *Management Information Systems Quarterly*, *15*, 295–310. doi:10.2307/249641

Bakos, J. Y., & Brynjolfsson, E. (1993). From Vendors to Partners: Information technology and incomplete contracts in buyer-supplier relationships. *Journal of Organizational Computing*, *3*(3), 301–328. doi:10.1080/10919399309540206

Bakos, Y., & Nault, B. (1997). Ownership and Investment in Electronic Networks. *Information Systems Research*, *8*(4). doi:10.1287/isre.8.4.321

Barret, S., & Konsynski, B. R. (1982). Interorganizational Information sharing systems. *Management Information Systems Quarterly*, *6*(special issue), 93–105. doi:10.2307/248993

Bensaou, M. and Venkatraman, N. "Configurations of Interorganizational Relationships: A Comparison between U.S. and Japanese Supplier Relations," *Management Science* (41:9), pp. 1471-1492.

Bertalanffy, L. V. (1962). General system theory - A Critical Review. *General Systems*, *7*, 1–20.

Bimber, B., Flanagin, A. J., & Stohl, C. (2005). Reconceptualizing Collective Action in the Contemporary Media Environment. *Communication Theory*, *15*(4), 365–388. doi:10.1111/j.1468-2885.2005.tb00340.x

Black, Fischer and Myron Scholes, "The Pricing of Options and Corporate Liabilities," Journal of Political Economy, 81:3, 1973, pp. 637-654.

Bostrom, R., & Heinen, S. (1977). MIS Problems and Failures: A Sociotechnical Perspective. *Management Information Systems Quarterly*, (September): 17–32. doi:10.2307/248710

Bouchard, L. 1993): *Decision Criteria in the Adoption of EDI*, "International Conference in Information Systems," Orlando, Florida, pp. 365-376.

Cash, J.I. and Konsynski, B.R.(1986). "IS redraws competitive boundaries", Harvard Business Review, March-April 1985, pp. 134-42.

Cha, H. S., Pingry, D. E., and Thatcher, M. E.. (2008). "Managing the Knowledge Supply Chain: An Organizational Learning Model of Information Technology Offshore Outsourcing," MIS Quarterly (32:2), June, pp. 281-306.

Chatterjee, D., Grewal, R., & Sambamurthy, V. (2002). Shaping Up For e-Commerce: Institutional Enablers of the Organisational Assimilation of Web Technologies. *Management Information Systems Quarterly*, *26*(2), 65–89. doi:10.2307/4132321

Chatterjee, D., & Ravichandran, T. (2004). Inter-organizational information systems research: a critical review and an integrative framework. In the 37th Hawaii International Conference on System Sciences (Sprague Jr., R.H. Ed) pp. 164-173, Hawaii.

Chu, W. H. J., & Lee, C. C. (2006). Strategic information sharing in a supply chain. *European Journal of Operational Research*, *174*(3), 1567–1579. doi:10.1016/j.ejor.2005.02.053

Chwelos, P., Benbasat, I., & Dexter, A. S. (2001). Research report: Empirical test of an EDI adoption model. *Information Systems Research*, *12*(3), 304–321. doi:10.1287/isre.12.3.304.9708

Cohen, J., Cohen, P., West, S. G., & Aiken, L. S. (2003). *Applied multiple regression/correlation analysis for the behavioral sciences* (3rd ed.). Hillsdale, N.J.: L. Erlbaum Associates.

Cooper, R. B., & Zmud, R. W. (1990). Information Technology implementation research: A technological diffusion approach. *Management Science*, *36*(2), 123–139. doi:10.1287/mnsc.36.2.123

Cox, J. F., Blackstone, J. H., & Schleier, J. G. (2003). *Managing Operations: A Focus on Excellence*. Great Barrington, MA: North River Press.

Davis, F. D. 1989. "Perceived Usefulness, Perceived Ease of Use, and User Acceptance of Information Technology," *MIS Quarterly*, v. 13, i. 3, pp. 319-339.

Deephouse, D. L. (1996). Does isomorphism legitimate? *Academy of Management Journal*, *39*(4), 1024–1039. doi:10.2307/256722

DeLone, W. and E. R. McLean. 1992. Information Systems Success: The Quest for the Dependent Variable, *Information Systems Research*, v. 3, i. 1, pp. 60-95.

DeLone, W. H., & McLean, E. R. (2004). Measuring e-Commerce Success: Applying the DeLone & McLean Information Systems Success Model. *International Journal of Electronic Commerce*, *9*(1).

DeSanctis, Geradine & Poole, Scott, M. (1994). Capturing the complexity in advanced technology use: Adaptive structuration theory. *Organization Science*, *5*(2), 121. doi:10.1287/orsc.5.2.121

DiMaggio, P., & Powell, W. (1983). The iron cage revisited: Institutional isomorphism and collective rationality in organizational fields. *American Sociological Review*, *2*, 147–160. doi:10.2307/2095101

Doty, D. H., & Glick, W. H. (1994). Typologies as a Unique Form of Theory Building: Towards Improved Understanding and Modeling. *Academy of Management Review*, *19*(2), 230–251.

Dyer, J. H. (1996). Specialized Supplier Networks as a Competitive Advantage: Evidence from the Auto Industry. *Strategic Management Journal*, *17*, 271–291. doi:10.1002/(SICI)1097-0266(199604)17:4<271::AID-SMJ807>3.0.CO;2-Y

Dyer J.H., Singh H. 1998. The relational view: cooperative strategies and sources of interorganizational competitive advantage. *Academy of Management Review* 23(4), 660–679.

Eisenhardt, M, K. (1989). Agency theory: An assessment and review. *Academy of Management Review*, *14*(1), 57.

Fichman, R. G. (2004). Going Beyond the Dominant Paradigm for IT Innovation Research: Emerging Concepts and Methods. *Journal of the Association for Information Systems*, *5*(8).

Fichman, R. G. (2004a). Real Options and IT Platform Adoption: Implications for Theory and Practice. *Information Systems Research*, *15*(2), 132–154. doi:10.1287/isre.1040.0021

Fichman, R. G., & Kemerer, C. F. (1999). The Illusory Diffusion of Innovations: An Examination of Assimilation Gaps. *Information Systems Research*, *10*(3), 255–275. doi:10.1287/isre.10.3.255

Fulk, J., Flanagin, A. J., Kalman, M. E., Monge, P. R., & Ryan, T. (1996). Connective and Communal Public Goods in Interactive Communications Systems. *Communication Theory*, *6*, 60–87. doi:10.1111/j.1468-2885.1996.tb00120.x

Gasson, S. 2005. A Brief History of Information System Design. Working paper, College of Information Science & Technology, Drexel University

Goldratt, E. M. (1990). *Theory of Constraints*. N.Y.: North River Press, Croton-on-Hudson.

Goodhue, D. L. (1998). Development and Measurement of Validity of a Task-Technology Fit Instrument for User Evaluations of Information Systems. *Decision Sciences*, *29*(1), 105–138. doi:10.1111/j.1540-5915.1998.tb01346.x

Gregor, S. (2006). The Nature of Theory in Information Systems. *Management Information Systems Quarterly*, *30*(3), 611–642.

Gulati, R., & Singh, H. (1998). The Architecture of Cooperation: Managing Coordination Costs and Appropriation Concerns in Strategic Alliances. *Administrative Science Quarterly*, *43*, 781–814. doi:10.2307/2393616

Hagen, J. M. and S. Choe, "Trust in Japanese Interfirm Relations: Institutional Sanctions Matter," Academy of Management Review. 23, 3, (1998), 589-600.

Hengst, M., & Sol, H. (2001). The Impact of Information and Communication. Special Series on *Information Exchange in Electronic Markets*, Volume 4 No 3, Hong I.B. (2002). "A new framework for Interorganizational Systems based on the likage of participant's roles. *Information & Management*, *39*(4), 261–270.

Huber, G. P. (1991). Organizational learning: the contributing processes and the literatures. *Organization Science*, *2*(1), 88–115. doi:10.1287/orsc.2.1.88

Iacovou, C., & Benbasat, I. Dexter A. 1995. EDI and Small Organizations: Adoption and Impact of Technology, *MIS Quarterly*, December, pp. 465-485.

Johnston, R. B., & Gregor, S. (2000). A Theory of Industry-Level Activity for Understanding the Adoption of Interorganizational Systems. *European Journal of Information Systems*, *9*, 243–251. doi:10.1057/palgrave/ejis/3000375

Joshi, K. (1991). A Model of User's Perspective on Change: The Case of Information Systems Technology Implementation. *Management Information Systems Quarterly*, *15*(2), 229–242. doi:10.2307/249384

Kanellis, P., & Paul, R. (1997). On the Nature of Inter-Organisational Information Systems and the Issue of Adaptability. *Proceedings of The Thirtieth Annual Hawwaii International Conference on System Sciences*.

Knight, L. (2002). Network learning: Exploring learning by inter-organizational networks. *Human Relations*, *55*(4), 427–454.

Kumar, K. and van Dissel, H. G. (1996). "Sustainable Collaboration: Managing Conflict and Cooperation in Interorganizational Systems,"

Kwon, T. H., & Zmud, R. W. 1987. Unifying the fragmented models of information systems implementation. J. R. Boland, & R. A. Hirschheim (Eds.), *Critical issues in information systems research* (pp. 227-251). New York: John Wiley.

Lane, P. J., & Lubatkin, M. (1998). Relative absorptive capacity and interorganizational learning. *Strategic Management Journal*, *19*(5), 461–477. doi:10.1002/(SICI)1097-0266(199805)19:5<461::AID-SMJ953>3.0.CO;2-L

Latour, B. (2005). *Reassembling the social: an introduction to actor-network theory*. USA: Oxford University Press.

Malone, T. W., & Crowston, K. (1994). 'The Interdisciplinary Study of Coordination'. *ACM Computing Surveys*, *26*(1), 87–119. doi:10.1145/174666.174668

Markus, M. L. (1983). Power, Politics and MIS Implementation. *Communications of the ACM*, *26*(6), 430–444. doi:10.1145/358141.358148

Marwell, G. And P. Oliver (1993), *The Critical Mass in Collective Action: A Micro-social Theory*, New York: Cambridge University Press.

Mayer, R. C, J. H. Davis, and F. D. Schoorman, "An Integrative Model of Organizational Trust," Academy of Management Review, 20, 3, 1995, 709-734.

Melucci, A. (1996). *Challenging Codes – Collective Action in the Information Age*. Cambridge: Cambridge University Press. doi:10.1017/CBO9780511520891

Meyer, A.D., and Goes, J.B. 1988. Organizational Assimilation of Innovations: A multilevel Contextual Analysis, *Academy of Management Journal* (31:4), pp. 897-923.

Milgrom, P. And J. Roberts. (1990). The Economics of Modern Manufacturing: Technology, Strategy, and Organization. *The American Economic Review*, *80*(3), 511–528.

Moody, D. L., Iacob, M. E., & Chintan, A. (2011). In Search of Paradigms: Identifying the Theoretical Foundations of the Information Systems Field. 18th European Conference on Information Systems.

Noreen, E., Smith, D. A., & Mackey, J. T. (1995). *The Theory of Constraints and its Implications for Management Accounting*. Great Barrington, MA: The North River Press Publishing Corporation.

Orlikowski, W. J., Yates, J., Okamura, K., & Fujimoto, M. (1995). *"Shaping Electronic Communication: The Metastructuring of Technology in the context of Use," Organization Science*. July/August.

Ostrom, Elinor, (1987). "The Implications of the Logic of Collective Inaction for Administrative Theory".

Premkumar, G., Ramamurthy, K., & Saunders, C. S. (2005). Information processing view of organizations: An exploratory examination of fit in the context of interorganizational relationships. *Journal of Management Information Systems*, *22*(1), 257–294.

Prescott, M. B., & Conger, S. A. (1995). Information Technology Innovations - a Classification by IT Locus of Impact and Research Approach. *The Data Base for Advances in Information Systems*, *26*(2-3), 20–41.

Purvis, R. L., Sambamurthy, V., & Zmud, R. W. (2001). The Assimilation of Knowledge Platforms in Organizations: An Empirical Investigation. *Organization Science*, *12*(2), 117–135. doi:10.1287/orsc.12.2.117.10115

Rainey, H. G. (2009). *Understanding and Managing Public Organizations* (4th ed.). Jossey Bass.

Reekers, N., & Smithson, S. (1995). *The Impact of Electronic Data Interchange on Interorganizational Relationships: Integrating the Theoretical Perspectives*. Proceedings of the 28th Hawaii International Conference on System Sciences.

Reimers, K., Johnston, R. B., & Klein, S. (2010). Toward a Theory of IOIS Variance: A New Framework for Studying Inter-Organisational Information Systems. *International Journal of Strategic Information Technology and Applications*, *1*(3), 36–56. doi:10.4018/jsita.2010070104

Robey, D. Im, G.; Wareham, Jonathan D. (2008): Theoretical Foundations of Empirical Research on Interorganizational Systems: Assessing Past Contributions and Guiding Future Directions. In: Journal of the Association for Information Systems, Vol. 9, No. 9, pp. 497-518.

Rogers, E. M. (1995). *Diffusion of Innovations*. New York: Free Press.

Rose, J. (1999). "Frameworks for practice – structurational theories of IS," *Proc of 6th European Conference on Information Systems*, pp. 640-655, Granada.

Saeed, K. A., Malhotra, M. K., & Grover, V. (2011). Interorganizational System Characterstics and Supply Chain Integration: An Empirical Assessment. *Decision Sciences*, *42*(1), 7–40. doi:10.1111/j.1540-5915.2010.00300.x

Schellhammer, S. (2008). *Accounting or stability of interorganizational information systems*. Germany: Traingular Graduate Confernce. University of Munster.

Schellhammer, S. (2010). "Theorizing the IT-Artifact in Inter-Organizational Information Systems: An Identity Perspective," *Sprouts: Working Papers on Information Systems*, 10(4).

Subramaniam, C., & Shaw, M. (2002). A study of the Value of B2B E-Commerce: The Case of Web-based Procurement. *International Journal of Electronic Commerce*, *6*(6), 19–40.

Thompson, J. D. (1967). *Organizations in Action: Social Science Bases of Administration*. New York: McGraw-Hill.

Vaidya, K. Sajeev, A.S.M., and Callender, G. 2006. Critical Factors that Influence e-Procurement Implementation Success in the Public Sector. *Journal of Public Procurement,* Volume 6, Issues 1 & 3, pp.70-99.

Vaidya, K., & Hyde, M. (2011). Inter-organisational information systems assimilation: an empirical evaluation in light of the diffusion of innovation theory. *International Journal of Business Information Systems*, *7*(3), 247–268. doi:10.1504/IJBIS.2011.039330

Venkatesh, V., Morris, M. G., Davis, G. B., & Davis, F. D. (2003). User Acceptance of Weick, Karl. (1979). Cognitive processes in organizations. In Staw, B. (Ed.), *Research in organizational behavior* (pp. 41–74). Greenwich, CT: JAI Press.

Williamson, O. E. (1979). Transaction cost economics: The governance of contractual relations. *The Journal of Law & Economics*, *22*, 3–61. doi:10.1086/466942

Chapter 1
Evolution of Inter-Organizational Information Systems on Long Timescales:
A Practice Theory Approach

Kai Reimers
RWTH Aachen University, Germany

Robert Johnston
University College Dublin, Ireland

Stefan Klein
University of Muenster, Germany

ABSTRACT

Inter-Organizational Information Systems (IOIS) are computer-based systems shared by, or connecting, several organizations. The on-going use and evolution on long timescales of these large-scale socio-technical systems so far cannot be satisfactorily explained on the basis of existing theories of IS adoption, implementation, and use. In this chapter, we present a theory of IOIS in which the on-going use and evolution of IOIS is treated as a practical and socio-material accomplishment of communities through boundary practices and structures. We draw on the structure/action reproduction paradigm of Structuration Theory to account for the persistence of these systems, and thus explain their structure, while using the embodiment of action from Practice Theory to treat the material nature of these systems. We distinguish three dimensions of structure—material, normative, and ideational—and we also distinguish patterns of actions (along these three dimensions) from constraining and enabling structures. However, we attempt to treat these three structural dimensions and their reproduction processes symmetrically throughout. This symmetrical treatment leads us to propose that these action/structure dimensions are not reproduced in isolation but rather undergo an intimate mixing, or mangling, in the process, which in turn suggests a new kind of two-way causal accommodation between the various aspects of structure that we term "resonance."

DOI: 10.4018/978-1-60960-768-5.ch001

Copyright © 2012, IGI Global. Copying or distributing in print or electronic forms without written permission of IGI Global is prohibited.

INTRODUCTION

Many countries engage in building ICT infrastructures in areas as diverse as customs clearance, electronic patient records or collection of road tolls. These infrastructures are by design multi-stakeholder enterprises, and many of them cross the boundaries between the private and public sector. These infrastructures are broad in scale and scope; they affect the life of individuals, are likely to change the landscape of industries, and are claimed to have transformative power. They are also instances of Inter-Organizational Information Systems (IOIS). As IOIS are evolving to become infrastructures for industries or even across industries, they need to be studied at that level.

In this paper, we argue that while the extant literature has largely succeeded in explaining success and failure of IOIS initiatives on the timescale of particular projects and at levels of analysis of single organizations, dyads and a little higher, it does not provide a theoretical framework for addressing the evolution of IOIS over long timescales and at the scale of industries within nations, an issue that has been identified as a significant gap in the literature. Specifically, in a review of research on Electronic Data Interchange (EDI, a key IOIS technology), Elgarah et al. (2005) find that "most studies reviewed in this research … employed the technological imperative to understand the short-term benefits and shortcomings of data exchange" (p. 19). In addition the time frame of the majority of studies was categorized as "cross sectional single snapshot" (p. 16).

By contrast, when we take a view of IOIS on longer timescales than these, and at units of analysis larger than organizations or dyads, different phenomena become visible that are both challenging and important. Many significant IOIS, such as computerized airline reservation systems (Copeland and McKenny, 1988) and electronic ordering systems in pharmaceutical distribution (Short and Venkatraman, 1992; Klein et al., 2008), have persisted for several decades with a recognizably persistent identity despite changing material form and institutional embedding. The traditional theoretical themes of IOIS research that, according to a recent survey by Robey et al. (2008), are adoption, governance and organizational consequences, do not capture the nature of this phenomenon. Beyond adoption we need to be able to explain post-adoption phenomena such as routinization, drift, adaptation to changing circumstances, in short, the evolution of IOIS. Beyond the usual conceptualization of governance in terms of hierarchies and markets (Robey et. al., 2008) the role and governance of IOIS as shared, and possibly contested, infrastructure comes into view. Beyond organizational consequences the issue of how to conceptualise the role of Information and Communication Technologies (ICT) in the transformation of whole supply chains, industries and institutions needs to be dealt with. In addition to managers, policy makers in governmental organizations, trade associations and the like become addressees of recommendations developed by the IS discipline.

Explaining and modelling these phenomena requires theoretical tools that are different from those employed by IOIS research at the firm or network level of analysis dominant in the literature. In this paper we put forward a new theory of IOIS consisting of a set of concepts and relations between concepts, which, as we will argue in detail, are both required by the nature of this phenomenon and form a coherent framework for theorising IOIS in a way appropriate to this new timeframe and scale.

Development of a theory that operates on this level of analysis poses a significant challenge as any such theory has to resolve an issue that still puzzles many researchers, namely the way that technology, as a material structure, interacts with organizational and institutional forces (Orlikowski and Scott, 2008). Specifically, focusing on IOIS evolution on long timescales implies that we treat technology, as materiality, symmetrically with regard to other social forces such as norms and ideas since, over long periods of time, these forces mutually influence one another. Additionally, none of these influences can be considered to be a purely passive element, nor as an external determining force that is beyond the reach of possible feedback loops. Symmetrical treatment of material and other social influences requires that we come to grips with the complex two-way causality implied by such a symmetrical treatment, which we have done by developing a new concept referred to as resonance and dissonance. To make contact with the materiality of IOIS as technologies we have elaborated Structuration Theory (Giddens, 1984) with ideas drawn from Practice Theory (Wenger, 2002; Reckwitz, 2002) to include a material dimension along with normative and ideational dimensions to the structure-action-duality.

The theory we present here is the outcome of an extended comparative study of evolution of IOIS in the pharmaceutical wholesale supply chains of four countries, which iterated between theory development and empirical work that extended over five years (Reimers and Li, 2008; Klein et al., 2008; Reimers et al., 2008; Reimers et al., 2009). Rather than developing a theoretical model that, supposedly, applies to all types of information and communication technology, we focus our theory on IOIS. While we do not want to argue that it is in principle impossible to develop a comprehensive theoretical concept of technology as an integral part of social theory, we submit that often disagreement on the proper role of technology in social science can be traced to incompatible concepts of technology that refer to different levels of analysis (e.g. infrastructure vs. specific applications), allow for different degrees of physical manifestation (machines vs. technological knowledge), or imply different levels of 'systemness' (program code vs. information systems), to name just a few dimensions along which—often implicit—definitions of technology can vary in fundamental ways (Leonardi and Barley, 2008). Conversely, we decided not to further restrict the scope of our study object—e.g. by focusing on IOIS supporting only certain system functions—because one of the phenomena we observe at the evolutionary timescale is change in the very function and scope of IOIS (see, for example, the evolution of an IOIS described in Reimers et al., 2008).

We set out by developing our theoretical model in a step by step fashion. Subsequently, we will discuss our theory in view of previous calls for creating better and more explicit theoretical bases for IS research and outline how our theory can be used to generate new and promising questions for IS research. The conclusions summarize the main ideas and contributions of the paper.

A PRACTICE THEORY OF IOIS

Technology is a material structure that, in social systems, is intertwined with other dimensions of structure that jointly enable and constrain action (Orlikowski, 2000). In order to understand the role technology plays in shaping social systems it is necessary to understand the nature of this association between technology and other dimensions of structure. At the same time, structure (including technology) does not exist independent of action in social systems (Giddens, 1984). Therefore, understanding the evolution of social systems (and the role played by technology in that evolutionary process) also requires an understanding of the relationship between structure (including technology) and action.

While there have been multiple approaches towards theorizing the relationship between technology and other dimensions of structure on the one hand and between structure and action on the other hand, only relatively recently have scholars attempted to consider these constructs in a symmetrical way (Orlikowski, 1992 and 2000, Orlikowski and Scott, 2008). To our knowledge, however, there are no models that achieve symmetrical treatment of both the relationship between structure and action as well as that between technology and other dimensions of structure. By invoking the term "symmetry" we refer to a theoretical treatment that does not, per se, privilege one theoretical entity as a causal factor. In this paper, we introduce a theory-based model that aims at such a symmetrical treatment.

We draw on several theoretical concepts developed in different but related literatures from which we build a new model that allows us to describe IOIS in a standardized way and to explain persistence, resilience and evolution of IOIS. We begin with a definition of social practices and then explain how social practices are learned in so-called Communities of Practice that we also view as the mechanism of structural reproduction.[1] We continue by demonstrating a novel way in which materiality can be incorporated into a practice-based model of information systems and conclude by synthesizing these concepts into our IOIS model and by showing how this model can be used to understand evolution of IOIS. At each point we indicate why the theoretical elements are required by the phenomenon (evolution of IOIS) modelled.

Social Practices

Reckwitz (2002) characterizes a practice as "routinized bodily activities" (p. 251). Bodily activity here is intended to encompass mental and emotional activities, use of things, and talking, reading and writing (discourse), in addition to other (routinized) movements of the body. However, mental and emotional activities are bodily activities only on a "certain level" (p. 251) and go beyond bodily activities in that they are routinized ways of understanding (knowledge) and desiring (motivation).

This notion of practice contains elements that can be used for empirically identifying a practice, namely the repeated (routine) performance of a specific body movement, routine patterns of discourse and use of things. One cannot capture actions of a non-routine kind by this method, of course, that are also enabled and constrained by structure. This disadvantage, however, seems to be minor in the context of the study of IOIS since the operational nature of most IOIS implies a focus on routine action. Meanwhile, the huge advantage of basing a theory of IOIS evolution on the concept of practice is that practices are, by their very definition, ongoing phenomena that do not necessarily rely on conscious decision making for their explanation. For IOIS research on adoption of technology for specific instrumental purposes a focus on strategic decision-oriented modes of action is often appropriate. However, when discussing the persistence, evolution and resilience of socio-technical practices on timescales greater than single projects, a good account of the dynamics of routinized modes of action is essential.

Communities of Practice and Structural Reproduction

While Reckwitz (2002) provides a useful description of social practices as "the product of training the body in a certain way" (p. 251), it remains open how this learning process comes about. In addition, to understand IOIS evolution we need a formulation of social practices that allows us to describe practices as part of organizational (and cross-organizational) phenomena. We draw on Lave and Wenger (1991) and Wenger (2002) to obtain a description of this learning process and, at the same time, of practices as organizational phenomena. According to Lave and Wenger, learning always occurs in communities that they call Communities of Practice (CoPs). As we describe the process of becoming competent in a practice we are also describing the process by which participation in the practice creates the conditions for is reproduction, and thus its durability. We will refer to the durable elements of the practice as its structure and distinguish several dimensions of this structure. The essential elements of our account of structure and structural reproduction derive from Structuration Theory (Giddens, 1984).[2]

New members to a CoP become attuned to a practice through apprenticeship, i.e. by observing the behaviour of experienced members and their responses to their own engagement in action. New members try to identify patterns of behaviour, attempt to make sense of these observed patterns, sense possible structures that could have enabled/constrained the actions resulting in the observed patterns, and then tentatively engage in their own actions, thus continuously validating (or invalidating) their sense-making regarding rules and affordances. As such behaviour is repeated, parts of it become routine and automatic, i.e. some parts of behaviour are relegated to "body memory" (a "trained body" according to Reckwitz) that makes use of the affordances of the physical environment, including technology. Actors also develop a "moral sense" that helps them to distinguish right from wrong actions without the need for cognitive processing of information. Finally, actors learn how to rationalize their actions in view of ideas that are discursively reproduced in that CoP. Figure 1 summarizes the ideas presented thus far.

The three dimensions of the structure of practices that emerge through these distinctions (material, normative, ideational structure) have a counterpart in corresponding patterns, namely patterns of flows of physical things (including movements of the human body), sanctioning patterns and discursive patterns. Actors may accidentally, consciously or strategically change these patterns, which may affect the reproduction of structures; in addition, actors may change their perceptions of patterns, which could also affect the reproduction of structures (Giddens, 1984). Thus, the process of structural reproduction allows for changes while structures cannot be changed arbitrarily. We further propose that, within a Community of Practice, the three dimensions of structure tend to be mangled together in the reproduction process. That is, material structure is not reproduced in isolation through movement patterns but rather, actions and perceptions always involve bodily movements, sanctioning patterns and, generally, the exchange of arguments through discourses. This mangling together stabilizes the

Figure 1. A proposed model of practice

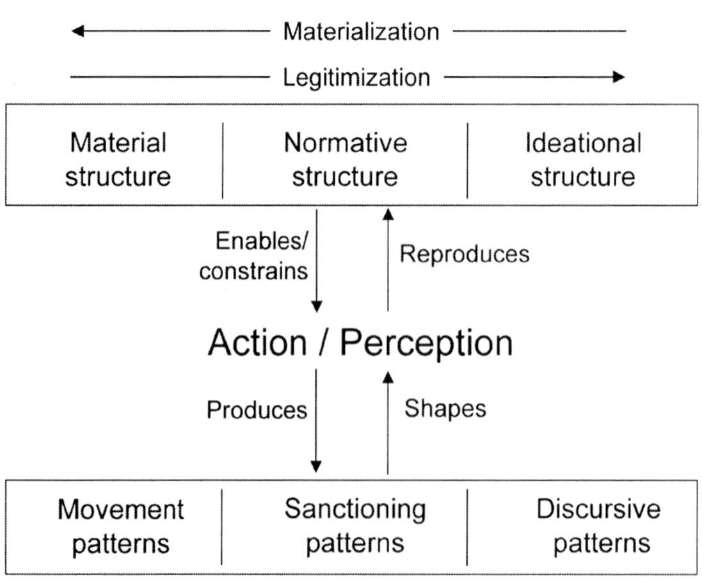

reproduction process through processes of materialization and legitimization.[3] We will expand on this idea below.

This formulation of the reproduction process, based on the CoP concept, is useful to us as it provides a way to empirically identify practices, namely by making sense of observed patterns just as new members to a CoP would. However, we recognize that our formulation is also an extension of Structuration Theory, albeit theoretically compatible with it. According to Giddens (1984), structural change occurs through "reflexive monitoring of action" (p. 191). In so far as one monitors the actions of others, reflexive monitoring of action becomes a social process. Through perception of patterns of behaviours actors can sense the structural properties that have supposedly guided the actions of others. This 'reconstruction' (the reproduction of structure) thus takes place in and through the process of perception by observers who then use these structures to guide their own actions (that will be observed by others, and so on). The theory of social practices, as formulated by Lave and Wenger (1991), views the reproduction of structure as a process of participation in which actors perceive and imitate each other because they are mutually engaged in a common endeavour; this process (social learning) is viewed as "a source of social structure" (Wenger, 2002, p. 96). Note that the concept of 'perception' does not necessarily or even generally imply a process of intentional thought; rather, the process of perception can be automatic in the sense that certain observed events result in certain actions through a learnt reaction template (cf. Michaels and Carello, 1981). This is a big advantage over rational theories of action often employed in research on adoption of particular IOIS projects that implicitly assume that relevant action (strategic decision) is reasoned, but that cannot capture important aspects of routinization of system use in post-adoption phases and over longer timescales (see Smith et al., 2007); this is especially true in the context of operational information systems that are characterized by dominance of routine actions.

The two-way causal relationship between structure and patterns of action depicted in Figure 1 is an essential ingredient of our theory of IOIS evolution. When studying IOIS phenomena at smaller units of analysis, such as adoption of specific IOIS technologies in organizations or dyads, it is reasonable to view cause and effect in a linear mode, for instance, as certain factors determining project outcomes. It is also reasonable to view action against a substantially fixed context external to the focal organizational actor. However, when modelling evolution of IOIS practices in larger units (supply chains and national industries) we must acknowledge that the contexts in which actions take place are substantially created and reproduced by those action themselves (Johnston and Gregor, 2000; Kurnia and Johnston, 2000). Consequently, the arc of causation linking structure and action is necessarily two-way while the constructs of structure and action are not independent but mutually constitutive. This is what is depicted by the vertical elements of Figure 1.

Material Aspects

It has been noted that often IS studies fail to specify the role or the place of information technology as a material artefact in their conceptual frameworks (Orlikowski and Iacono, 2001). This is also true for earlier attempts to apply Structuration Theory to the study of information systems (Orlikowski, 2000). Integrating the materiality of information technology into the conceptual apparatus of IS studies is important for our purpose as we need to treat information technology on par with organizational and other social forces in order to be able to address IOIS evolution. IOIS consist of material as well as organizational and other social elements that jointly affect each other and in this mutual interaction bring about continuous change. In order to overcome this weakness of Structuration Theory when applying it to our framework we draw on a proposal by Child (2000) who developed a framework for studying organizations across national cultures. Child, in turn, based his framework on a distinction between material and ideational forces introduced by Max Weber (1964) and suggests that these two forces influence institutions that then constrain and enable social action. The main idea of this framework is that cultural factors affect institutions through ideational forces while material forces represent some economic and thus universalistic constraints.

Child suggests that both ideational and material forces have an indirect and a direct effect on action; indirectly, they affect action through shaping institutions while also directly affecting action through task contingencies—in the case of material forces—and value preferences—in the case of ideational forces. Earlier attempts to apply Structuration Theory have struggled with the idea that rules become 'inscribed' in technologies (Orlikowski, 2000). Application of Child's framework allows for viewing rules as a separate category of structure that is not 'hard-wired' into technology while still being able to conceptualize material structure as constraining and enabling action. This can be illustrated by integrating Child's ideas into the model of practices developed above.

We are concerned here with the direct effects referred to by Child (while much of the literature that discusses technology from a structuration perspective is concerned with what Child (2002) would term indirect effects such as "embodiment" or "inscription" of social rules in technology). These direct effects could be understood, in the context of Reckwitz' practice concept, as..." stable relations between agents (body/minds) and things within certain practices ..." (p. 253) that are reproduced in practices. Reckwitz claims that these relations are social structures in exactly the same way as other social structures such as norms that involve relations between agents (ibid).

In the context of our extended practice model described above, the reproduction of material structure in the same way as social structure can be illustrated as follows. Observation of moving bodies and things not only makes material structures visible but also informs about their affordances. For instance, when a driver observes other cars racing by on a winter day, he/she might (possibly wrongly) conclude that the street is not slippery. Another example is people moving along a hardly visible path indicating where exactly the path runs. Thus, observation of moving things indicates existence and properties of material structures that then enable/constrain action. That is, reproduction of material structure does not refer to their maintenance from a planner's or operator's point of view, but to the perception of the material properties of an actor's environment that guide that actor's behaviour. This is strictly similar to how normative and ideational structures are reproduced. For example, observation of discursive patterns reveals to the socially knowledgeable actor valid cause-effect or means-ends relationships that then guide his or her actions. Again, reproduction here refers to the perception of socially mediated ideational structures reproduced through—possibly reflective—monitoring of discursive patterns, rather than to reproduction of some form of objective, externally existing natural law. Note that we explicitly refer to material properties, as opposed to physical properties, because the term emphasizes the world as it is encountered by the body, rather than the physicality of the world that is viewed by scientist (things, properties, atoms, etc).

Inter-Organizational Information Systems

So far we have only considered reproduction of a practice within a single community. To make the connection to IOIS we must now consider how multiple distinct practices can become and remain aligned. In addition, to come to grips with persistent alignment of IOIS on long timescales over which even the material form of the systems may change, we tackle this problem in a way quite distinct from the standard IOIS literature, using Practice Theory notions. Different kinds of practices are distinguished by the differing enterprises in which the members of the communities engage and around which they form their identities. Examples from our empirical context are the product ordering (procuring) practice and product provision (supply) practice. These are distinct Communities of Practices with separate procedures, objectives, legal restraints, languages, stories, norms, and operating methods; in addition, these Communities of Practice are often—but not necessarily—located in separate commercial organizations, as is the case for a supply chain. However, the differing enterprises of these communities are necessarily connected through the "product" that must be passed from one to the other effectively if they are to fulfil their respective enterprises. Consequently, the connected communities must achieve some alignment of their practices that must be maintained over time in addition to the separate reproduction of these practices in each community. When these practices are located in different organizations, maintaining this alignment is problematic because the individual practices will tend to drift to accommodate changing circumstances in the particular organizations (Ciborra, 2000). Some possibilities for maintenance of such an alignment are discussed by Wenger (2002), and range from the brokering actions of individuals to full-blown separate practices whose enterprise is such an alignment.

According to the three dimensions of structure described above, several communities of practice can be connected through patterns of sanctioning behaviour and discursive patterns in addition to patterned movements of things (such as products). As things, sanctions and discourses cross from one CoP into another, they contribute to the reproduction of structure in both communities. For our study of IOIS, the case of practices that are connected through flows of things is the most relevant one. These things are primarily goods, money and data. We call flows of things across practices a transaction.

The material structures reproduced through transactions can be viewed as one type of boundary object (Gal et al., 2008; Wenger, 2002; Star and Griesemer, 1989). Bowker and Star (2000) describe a boundary object as an interface between different communities of practice; more specifically, they describe it as an entity that is shared by different communities of practice but viewed or used differently in each of them; this property, we argue, enables connections between the several practices through transactions. A product file assigning standardised product codes to product descriptions can be such a boundary object: for the buyers the standardised product file facilitates splitting of orders across a number of suppliers while it enables suppliers to reach a large constituency of buyers who are adhering to the standard. According to Star and Griesemer (1989), boundary objects should posses a high degree of interpretive flexibility, i.e. they may be interpreted differently and thus lessen the degree of requisite alignment between practices in cases of transactions. However, in the context of information systems, boundary objects tend to lack interpretive flexibility when automated data processing is involved. While boundary objects can be material, normative, and ideational structures (Wenger, 2002), we focus on material boundary objects as, for the specific case of IOIS, we are interested in understanding how communities of practice are connected through data flows.

Patterned flows of things within a practice are, according to our theory, mangled together with the reproduction of norms and ideas. In contrast, if two practices are connected only by material flows, these horizontal stabilization processes of materialization and legitimization will be lacking. One could also say they are overly rigid or "brittle" as they concern only the material dimension. This brittle nature of material connections between practices—if not compensated—would lead one to predict that any resulting alignment will not be stable. Structures reproduced in the separate practices may become inconsistent and, with no accompanying flows of discursive and sanctioning patterns that would make these material flows more plastic, they will not adjust to these changed structures. Consequently, in order to explain persistence and evolution of alignment in IOIS on long timescales we must consider how this brittleness is overcome as an on-going practical achievement rather than a rigid technical link.

Since purely material boundary structures are brittle, maintaining connections through transactions frequently requires additional effort to make sense of transactions. Such effort could consist of translation, coordination, or alignment actions (Wenger, 2002). Wenger describes such activities as brokering and encounters. Brokering is a unilateral activity, involving a member of one practice participating in the reproduction process of another practice through negotiation, translation, and coordination activities while encounters refer to a bilateral action in which "delegates" of two practices meet. We prefer to subsume both concepts under the more established notion of boundary spanning (Thompson, 1967). Boundary spanning can evolve into a separate practice (Levina and Vaast, 2005) that would be called a boundary practice (Wenger, 2002). The enterprise of a boundary practice is the alignment between the connected practices through manipulation of the boundary object. While actions performed as part of a boundary practice cannot directly affect the reproduction process of the boundary object (as structure) as it is manifested in the connected practices, they can modify the boundary object (as an artefact) in view of the knowledge of these reproduction processes. Such actions include facilitation of negotiations and translations. In the following, we use the term 'boundary object' in relation to boundary practices but speak of a boundary structure when we refer to the practices that are connected through it.[4]

Thus, we define an inter-organizational information system as a set of CoPs located in separate organizations that are connected through specific technological (i.e. material) boundary structures so as to facilitate transactions between these CoPs. IOIS boundary structures can be either shared definitions of data to be exchanged between data processing applications or shared databases that connect data processing applications maintained in separate practices. This rather unusual definition of, and perspective on, IOIS has been necessitated by the phenomenon we wish to model. A particular IOIS can then be characterized by the identity and constellation of practices (including boundary practices) that are aligned with each other as well as by the structural properties of each involved practice. Evolution of an IOIS can be described as changes in the structural properties of involved practices and as changes of the identity and constellation of practices forming the IOIS. Figure 2 illustrates our definition of an IOIS.

Evolution of IOIS

In order to understand the way the structural constitution of practices change, the horizontal relationships among structural dimensions need to be analyzed more explicitly. As proposed above, structural dimensions are not reproduced in isolation; rather, the reproduction process mangles together the several dimensions, thus creating a mechanism through which structural dimensions interact with one another. For example, as one uses an ATM for withdrawing cash, one may be reminded of the efficiency and convenience with which transactions in small-scale shopping are possible using cash payments; thus, the idea that using cash for shopping is (still) efficient "resonates" with the experience of (successfully and quickly) obtaining cash from ATMs. In terms of our practice model, (successfully) using an ATM not only reproduces the material structure that we call an ATM but also contributes to the reproduction of the idea that cash-based payments for small-scale shopping are (still) efficient. We call such mutual confirmation or reinforcement of structures "resonance." It occurs because structures, under the right circumstance, can

Figure 2. Conception of an IOIS in our practice theory-model. Practices share an IOIS boundary structure. Alignment of the practices through the boundary structure requires either ad-hoc boundary spanning activity or a full-blown boundary practice (that views the boundary structure as a boundary object).

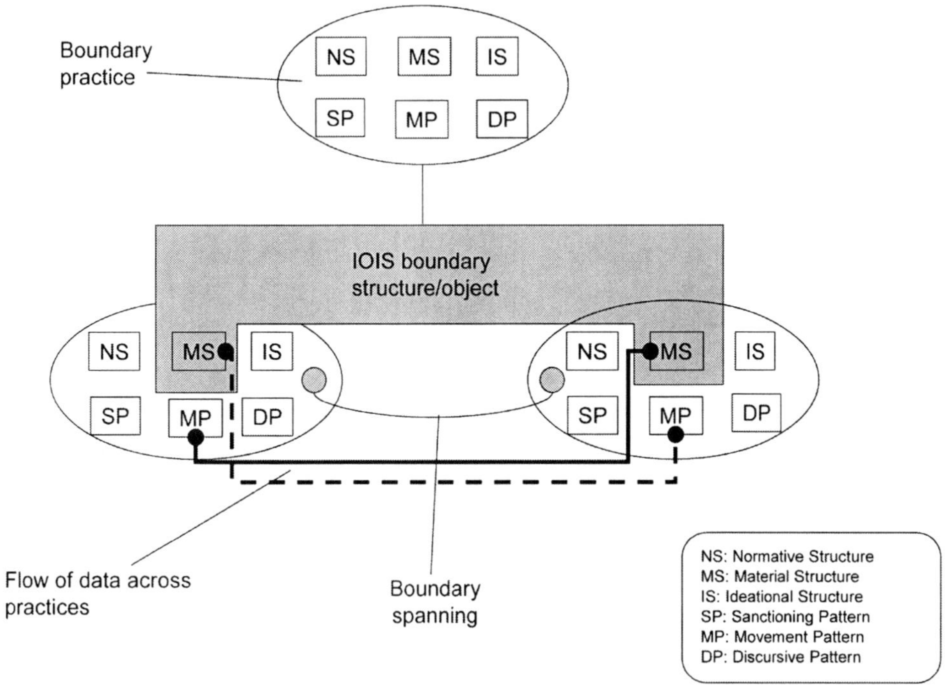

be co-reproduced. Co-reproduction is possible, in turn, because the structural dimensions are mangled together in their reproduction rather than being reproduced in isolation. In sum, mangling is the process that, under the right circumstance, leads to co-reproduction, which we call resonance. Conversely, the mangling can also lead to dissonance if reproduction of structure in one dimension disadvantages reproduction of structure in another dimension.

The development and implementation of an IOIS can then be re-conceptualized at our level of analysis as a process of embedding IOIS boundary objects in existing practices. "Embedding" means that boundary objects are modified so as to resonate with existing structures in the several practices. Dedicated boundary practices may evolve that are concerned with maintaining and adjusting boundary objects. An example would be the boundary practice of a retailer association to maintain product codes that are used in the ordering and delivery practices of retailers and wholesalers respectively. Alternatively, boundary spanning activities may occur that affect the reproduction of a boundary object as it manifests itself in the several connected practices. Over the lifetime of an IOIS, individual instances of (material, normative, ideational) structure may be replaced, added, or removed from the practices that—together—constitute the IOIS.

This conceptualization of technological change contrasts with standard alternatives such as technological determinism (e.g. Chandler, 1980) and social shaping (e.g. Williams and Edge, 1996). From a technology determinist perspective, material structure would be considered to be privileged in explaining the development of an IOIS; for example, the initial technical features of the IOIS might be considered to have a determining influence on its further evolution. A social shaping perspective would privilege some other structural aspects (such as supply chain power structures) in explaining the development of an IOIS (we recognize, though, that social shaping theorists generally avoid any reference to the notion of structure in their explanations). From a rational perspective (such as economics) explanation of IOIS evolution would rely on the influence of some ideas, especially of improved efficiency through standardisation. None of these privileged determinisms is viable in explaining the phenomenon of evolution of socio-technical systems at long timescales. In contrast, based on our model we explain the evolution of an IOIS as processes of adding, removing and replacing instances of structure through reproduction processes in individual practices connected by boundary structures and/or in boundary practices. Agents within these practices are constantly trying to appropriate and manipulate structures to extend their influence while at the same time relying on the stability of structure to be able to act at all (for instance to keep transactions happening).

DISCUSSION

In an influential paper, Markus and Robey (1988) distinguish three dimensions of causal structure in organizational theory, namely causal agency, logical structure, and levels of analysis, and suggest that "[b]y carefully considering each of the[se] dimensions of causal structure ..., researchers should be able to construct sounder theories to guide more fruitful research." (p. 596). We have adapted and extended their theoretical meta-categories to contrast our approach with the conventional approach found in much of the current IOIS literature (Robey et al., 2008) as depicted in Figure 3.

Rather than attempting to accurately synthesize the existing IOIS literature into a single characterization we have created a stylized characterization that we believe captures the majority of the

Figure 3. Characteristics of our theoretical approach relative to the majority of the current IOIS literature

Research Entity	Stylized IOIS theory	Our IOIS theory
Level of analysis*	Organisations or dyads Single layer	Supply chains, industries within nations Multilayer
Causal agency* (Mode of explanation)	Input/output Factors/conditions => outcomes	Two-way causality Emergence
Logical structure* (Theoretical paradigm)	Preceding event causes or conditions subsequent event	Duality of structure and action (simultaneous mutual conditioning)
Theory type**	Predictive, normative, descriptive	Explanatory
Unit of analysis	Episodes of organisational use of technical system	Time extended trajectory of sociotechnical practice
Phenomenon to be explained	Success/failure Use/non-use	Persistence Plasticity/resilience
Empirical data	Org. cases at present time	Historical cases
Relation of people to technology	People use technology Technology is tool	People and technology make constituting practices

* Category defined by Markus and Robey (1988)
** Category defined by Gregor (2006)

literature without claiming to be comprehensive, for the purpose of juxtaposing our approach and thus highlighting its novelty and possible contribution. The first three dimensions of this characterization are taken from Markus and Robey (1988) while the fourth draws on Gregor (2006). We have added another four dimensions that we believe bring out the novelty of our approach.

The IOIS literature predominantly studies single organizations adopting some type of technology used for building inter-organizational information systems or dyads of such organizations. Only relatively recently have researchers moved to higher levels of analysis such as a whole industry (Rodon et al., 2008; Steinfield et al., 2005; Reimers et al., 2004; Damsgaard and Lyytinen, 2001; Johnston and Gregor, 2000). Our model extends across the organizational and the network level, specifically through the concept of boundary structures and boundary practices linking the constituent practices of the IOIS.

While the IOIS literature predominantly relies on case research methodology and thus does not fall into the category of 'variance theories' (that require statistical sampling), the causal structure employed in explanations is nevertheless unidirectional, whether the causal agent is modelled as a factor or, more cautiously, as a condition or pre-condition. In contrast, our model of causality—resonance—is two-way, implying that events are not caused but emergent.

The dimension of logical structure relates to issues of causal agency. The dominant position in the IOIS literature views events as unfolding sequentially in time; this, in our opinion, is also the reason why recent attempts to apply Structuration Theory in the IS field (Leonardi and Barley, 2008; de Vaujany, 2008; Volkoff et al., 2007; Dobson, 2001) rely on an episodic approach such that time is divided into periods in which unidirectional causality can be assumed. In contrast, our model attempts to achieve a treatment of theoretical entities such that simultaneous mutual conditioning can be captured.

In terms of Gregor's (2006) categories most models in the IOIS literature can be described as predictive, normative or descriptive in the sense that these theories do not describe an abstract mechanism that would explain observed events and outcomes. In contrast, the concepts of legitimization, materialization, and reproduction that figure prominently in our model can be viewed as abstract, "generative mechanisms" (Mingers, 2004) that explain observed events and outcomes while we also acknowledge that, given the inherent openness of agency, precise prediction is untenable.

Clearly, the distinctions made thus far transcend the often made distinction between variance and process theories. In fact, we would view both, variance and process theories as mostly converging on the left-hand side of our stylized spectrum of theories. This point is underscored by the main motive driving both many variance as well as process theory-type studies, namely an interest in explaining success and failure or use and non-use of IOIS at the system project level. In contrast, our main interest is in explaining the phenomenon of persistence and resilience of IOIS that appeared on our radar once we started to look at IOIS over extended periods of time, through the use of historical case studies, not just single episodes of system adoption, implementation or use. That different unit of analysis (extended trajectories of socio-technical practice) itself came into focus as a result of our different conceptualization of causal agency. Thus, along with our model emerged a new way of looking at the phenomenon, which we propose will stimulate new, interesting and relevant research questions. For example, the literature on system failure or non-use often views such phenomena as resistance to change and increasingly relies on political causal agents for explanation (Doolin, 2004; Dhillon, 2004; Silva and Blackhouse, 2003; Levine and Rossmoore, 1995). While researchers are often sympathetic with users who resist using new technology, they still view this as a problematic outcome that needs to be amended, albeit by methods more sensitive to the interests of users. In contrast, we would view such outcomes as instances of resilience of existing socio-technical practices, i.e. as something that may also be seen as positive. Attention then converges on the issue of how amenable to change practices are and questions may be asked such as how to lever existing degrees of plasticity or resilience for organizational purposes. Another significant difference in terms of the research questions emanating from our model is that adoption and implementation would fade into the background on these timescales as research topics. Rather, evolution of existing practices, including technologies that are always a constituting element of practice, would come to the fore. Thus, rather than asking whether users/organization will adopt certain new technologies or whether certain new systems will be implemented successfully, the very distinction between existing and new technology would seem to be problematic and researchers would rather focus on understanding how technology, as material structure, is evolving and changing along with the other dimensions of structure. The concepts of plasticity and resilience may then be extended and built upon in order to address questions of immediate organizational relevance, such as how an organization can build new capabilities or adapt to changing environments.

Finally, technology is viewed differently. It is less a tool that can be used for certain individual or organizational purposes. It is rather seen as a specific type of structure that becomes an integral aspect of the very phenomenon of human organization. Organizational theory is, as has been pointed out several times in the literature (Orlikowski and Barley, 2001; Orlikowski and Scott, 2008) largely void of technology as if humans could build an organization entirely without technology and then, selectively and for specific purposes, amend organizational capabilities by adopting certain technologies. In contrast, our model suggests that the phenomenon of human organization is fundamentally intertwined with the development and use of technology and therefore becomes a constituting element of organization theory. Thus, our model suggests that the study of organizations necessarily has to include technology as a constituent of organizational phenomena. We anticipate that such an approach would reinvigorate both the organizational as well as the information systems literatures that, so far, have largely maintained separate scholarly identities.

CONCLUSION

We have presented a new practice theoretical perspective on IOIS for the purpose of explaining their evolution. We have argued that, as IOIS are evolving into the information infrastructure of whole industries, this change of perspective becomes necessary from both an academic and a practitioner's point of view. Our theoretical model allows us to identify and describe IOIS in a standardized way; as our model is theory based, it also allows us to describe possible influences on the evolution of IOIS as these factors are implicated in the processes that explain the very existence of IOIS, namely structural reproduction and materialization and legitimization.

The paper contributes to theory in the information systems discipline by presenting a theory of IOIS in which the on-going persistence and change of these large-scale systems is treated as a practical and socio-material accomplishment of communities of practice. The information technology and system component is modelled in terms of boundary practices and structures. The approach is novel and contrasts with existing rational theories of "adoption" as a decision and technological determinist theories emphasising the technological manifestation of these systems at the expense of human interpretation and appropriation.

We have also made contributions to the social theory approach to information technology adoption and use. We draw on structuration-style reproduction and embodiment of practices to propose a symmetrical treatment of three dimensions of structure—material, normative and ideational—and associated patterns of actions. Recognition that material structures (as opposed to physical entities) are the experienced durable complement of bodily actions is an important and novel step that allows a material/bodily-action duality to be treated on a par with social and ideational structure/action dualities. This symmetrical treatment of structure/action reproduction leads us to propose that these action/structure dimensions are not reproduced in isolation but rather undergo an intimate mixing, or mangling, in the process, which in turn suggests a new kind of two-way causal accommodation between the various aspects of structure that we term "resonance." We believe they have wider applicability in the study of the use and evolution of use of technologies in general.

In the course of our theory development we have introduced extensions to Practice Theory—as elaborated by Structuration Theory—to show how meso-level social systems can be modelled from this orientation, using inter-organizational information systems as a specific case. We propose that this approach could be fruitfully extended to develop a fresh theoretical perspective on meso-level organizational phenomena such as supply networks or large, divisionalized and multi-site firms. Practice Theory provides us with conceptual tools to specifically address inter-organizational issues and elaborate different ways in which Communities of Practice can be linked to each other.

ACKNOWLEDGMENT

The first and the last author would like to acknowledge support by the Deutsche Forschungsgemeinschaft (grant number 1328/2-2)

REFERENCES

Bowker, G., & Star, S. L. (2000). *Sorting things out: Classification and its consequences*. Cambridge, MA: MIT Press.

Chandler, A. D. (1980). *The visible hand: The managerial revolution in American business*. Boston, MA: Harvard University Press.

Child, J. (2000). Theorizing about organization cross-nationality. In Chen, J. L. C., & Peterson, R. B. (Eds.), *Advances in International Comparative Management, 13* (pp. 27–75). Greenwich, CT: JAI Press.

Ciborra, C. U. (2000). *From control to drift: The dynamics of global information infrastructures*. Oxford, UK: Oxford University Press.

Copeland, D. G., & McKenney, J. L. (1988). Airline reservation systems - Lessons from history. *Management Information Systems Quarterly*, (September): 353–370. doi:10.2307/249202

Damsgaard, J., & Lyytinen, K. J. (2001). The role of intermediating institutions in the diffusion of Electronic Data Interchange (EDI). How industry associations in the grocery sector intervened in Hong Kong, Finland, and Denmark. *The Information Society*, *17*(3), 195–210. doi:10.1080/01972240152493056

de Vaujany, F. (2008). Capturing reflexivity modes in IS: A critical realist approach. *Information and Organization*, *18*(1), 51–72. doi:10.1016/j.infoandorg.2007.11.001

Dhillon, G. (2004). Dimensions of power and IS implementation. *Information & Management*, *41*(5), 635–644. doi:10.1016/j.im.2003.02.001

Dobson, P. J. (2001). The philosophy of critical realism-An opportunity for Information Systems research. *Information Systems Frontiers*, *3*(2), 199–210. doi:10.1023/A:1011495424958

Doolin, B. (2004). Power and resistance in the implementation of a medical management Information System. *Information Systems Journal*, *14*(4), 343–362. doi:10.1111/j.1365-2575.2004.00176.x

Elgarah, W., Falaleeva, N., Saunders, C. S., Ilie, V., Shim, J. T., & Courtney, J. F. (2005). Data exchange in interorganizational relationships: Review through multiple conceptual lenses. *The Data Base for Advances in Information Systems*, *36*(1), 8–29.

Gal, U., Lyytinen, K., & Yoo, Y. (2008). The dynamics of IT boundary objects, information infrastructures, and organisational identities: The introduction of 3D modelling technologies into the architecture, engineering, and construction industry. *European Journal of Information Systems*, *17*, 290–304. doi:10.1057/ejis.2008.13

Gherardi, S. (2009). Introduction: The critical power of the practice lens. *Management Learning*, *40*(2), 115–128. doi:10.1177/1350507608101225

Giddens, A. (1984). *The constitution of society-Outline of the theory of structuration*. Berkley, CA: University of California Press.

Gregor, S. (2006). The nature of theory in Information Systems. *Management Information Systems Quarterly*, *30*(3), 611–642.

Johnston, R. B., & Gregor, S. (2000). A theory of industry-level activity for understanding the adoption of interorganizational systems. *European Journal of Information Systems*, *9*(4), 243–251. doi:10.1057/palgrave/ejis/3000375

Klein, S., Schellhammer, S., Reimers, K., & Riemer, K. (2008). *Evolutionary paths of Inter-organizational Information Systems (IOIS)*. Paper presented at the 12th Annual Conference of the International Society for New Institutional Economics (ISNIE 2008), June 20-21 2008, Rotman School of Management, University of Toronto, Canada.

Kurnia, S., & Johnston, R. B. (2000). The need for a processual view of Interorganizational Systems. *The Journal of Strategic Information Systems*, *9*(4), 295–319. doi:10.1016/S0963-8687(00)00050-0

Lave, J., & Wenger, E. (1991). *Situated learning - Legitimate peripheral participation*. Cambridge, UK: Cambridge University Press.

Leonardi, P. M., & Barley, S. R. (2008). Materiality and change: Challenges to building better theory about technology and organizing. *Information and Organization*, *18*(3), 159–176. doi:10.1016/j.infoandorg.2008.03.001

Levina, N., & Vaast, E. (2005). The emergence of boundary spanning competence in practice: Implications for implementation and use of Information Systems. *Management Information Systems Quarterly*, *29*(2), 335–363.

Levine, H. G., & Rossmoore, D. (1995). Politics and the function of power in a case study of IT-implementation. *Journal of Management Information Systems*, *11*(3), 115–133.

Markus, M. L., & Robey, D. (1988). Information Technology and organizational change: Causal structure in theory and research. *Management Science*, *34*(5), 583–599. doi:10.1287/mnsc.34.5.583

Michaels, C. F., & Carello, C. (1981). *Direct perception*. Englewood Cliffs, NJ: Prentice-Hall.

Mingers, J. (2004). Realizing Information Systems: Critical realism as an underpinning philosophy for Information Systems. *Information and Organization*, *14*, 87–103. doi:10.1016/j.infoandorg.2003.06.001

Orlikowski, W. J. (1992). The duality of technology: Rethinking the concept of technology in organizations. *Organization Science*, *3*(3), 398–427. doi:10.1287/orsc.3.3.398

Orlikowski, W. J. (2000). Using technology and constituting structures: A practice lens for studying technology in organizations. *Organization Science*, *11*(4), 404–428. doi:10.1287/orsc.11.4.404.14600

Orlikowski, W. J., & Barley, S. R. (2001). Technology and institutions: What can research on Information Technology and research on organizations learn from each other? *Management Information Systems Quarterly*, *25*(2). doi:10.2307/3250927

Orlikowski, W. J., & Iacono, C. S. (2001). Research commentary: Desperately seeking the "IT" in IT research - A call to theorizing the IT artifact. *Information Systems Research*, *12*(2), 121–134. doi:10.1287/isre.12.2.121.9700

Orlikowski, W. J., & Scott, S. V. (2008). *The entangling of technology and work in organizations.* Working Paper, Department of Management, Information Systems and Innovation Group, London School of Economics, February 2008.

Reckwitz, A. (2002). Toward a theory of social practice - A development in culturalist theorizing. *European Journal of Social Theory*, *5*(2), 243–263. doi:10.1177/13684310222225432

Reimers, K., Johnston, R. B., & Klein, S. (2004). The shaping of inter-organisational Information Systems: Main design considerations of an international comparative research project. In *Proceedings of the 17th Bled eCommerce Conference "eGlobal"*, June 21-23 2004, Bled, Slovenia.

Reimers, K., Johnston, R. B., & Klein, S. (2009). Understanding resilience and evolution of IOIS in the Australian pharmaceutical distribution industry. In *Proceedings of the Thirtieth International Conference on Information Systems*, December 16-18 2009, Phoenix.

Reimers, K., Johnston, R. B., Klein, S., Wagner, T., & Schellhammer, S. (2008). *Beyond mutual shaping - Rethinking symmetry and causality in the treatment of socio-material systems.* Paper presented at the Joint Conference of the Society for Social Studies of Science (4S) and the European Association for the Study of Science and Technology (EASST), August 20-23 2008, Rotterdam, The Netherlands.

Reimers, K., & Li, M. (2008). Interaction of technological and institutional change in the development of an electronic commerce system in China's pharmaceutical distribution chain - A transaction cost perspective. In *Proceedings of the International Conference on Health Informatics (HEALTHINF)*, January 28-31 2008, Funchal, Portugal.

Robey, D., Im, G., & Wareham, J. D. (2008). Theoretical foundations of empirical research on Interorganizational Systems: Assessing past contributions and guiding future directions. *Journal of the Association for Information Systems*, *9*(9), 497–518.

Rodon, J., Pastor, J. A., Sesé, F., & Christiaanse, E. (2008). Unraveling the dynamics of IOIS implementation: An actor-network study of an IOIS in the Seaport of Barcelona. *Journal of Information Technology*, *23*, 97–108. doi:10.1057/palgrave.jit.2000131

Sewell, W. H. (2005). *Logics of history – Social theory and social transformation*. Chicago, IL: The University of Chicago Press.

Short, J. E., & Venkatraman, N. (1992). Beyond business process redesign: Redefining Baxter's business network. *Sloan Management Review*, *34*(1), 7–21.

Silva, L., & Backhouse, J. (2003). The Circuits-of-power framework for studying power in institutionalization of Information Systems. *Journal of the AIS*, *4*(6), 294–336.

Smith, S. P., Johnston, R. B., Shanks, G., & Rahim, M. M. (2007). *From intention to motivation: Developing a motivation-based model of IOS implementation.* Paper presented on the Twenty Eighth International Conference on Information Systems, Montreal, Canada.

Star, S. L., & Griesemer, J. R. (1989). Institutional ecology, translations and boundary objects: Amateurs and professionals in Berkeley's Museum of Vertebrate Zoology, 1907-39. *Social Studies of Science*, *19*(3), 387–420. doi:10.1177/030631289019003001

Steinfield, C. W., Markus, M. L., & Wigand, R. T. (2005). Exploring interorganizational systems at the industry level of analysis: Evidence from the US home mortgage industry. *Journal of Information Technology*, *20*(4), 224–233. doi:10.1057/palgrave.jit.2000051

Thompson, J. D. (1967). *Organizations in action - Social science bases of administrative theory.* New York, NY: McGraw-Hill.

Volkoff, O., Strong, D. M., & Elmes, M. B. (2007). Technological embeddedness and organizational change. *Organization Science*, *18*(5), 832–848. doi:10.1287/orsc.1070.0288

Weber, M. (1964). *The theory of social and economic organization (Trans. A.M. Henderson & T. Parsons).* New York, NY: Free Press.

Wenger, E. (2002). *Communities of practice - Learning, meaning, and identity.* Cambridge, UK: Cambridge University Press.

Williams, R., & Edge, D. (1996). The social shaping of technology. *Research Policy*, *25*(5), 865–899. doi:10.1016/0048-7333(96)00885-2

ENDNOTES

1 In contrast to the literature that has been characterized as Practice-Based Studies (Gherardi, 2009), we use Practice Theory for the purpose of building explanatory theory rather than for critiquing managerial practices. Both uses of Practice Theory are recognized in the literature (ibid.).

2 While Reckwitz draws, among others, on Giddens and Bourdieu, he claims that structure is not confined either to the minds of actors nor to the patterns created by their behaviour, which may be interpreted to constitute a deviation from Giddens; Wenger (2002), in his exposition of the concept of *communities of practice*, emphasizes the emergent nature of structures and positions his concept relatively closer to Giddens' than to Bourdieau's notion of structure (p. 96). Below, we will make a proposal how to reconcile the slightly inconsistent notions of structure in practice theory and in Structuration Theory.

3 In a similar way Sewell (2005) conceives the character of structure as "composed simultaneously of schemas, which are virtual, and or resources, which are actual. ... if resources are instantiations or embodiments of schemas, they therefore inculcate or justify the schemas as well.“ (p. 136); note, however, that we would not conceptualize material structure as "embodiment" of ideational structure while we also register concerns regarding the distinction between virtual and actual structure.

4 Our distinction between boundary object and boundary structure corresponds to that by Orlikowski (2000) between technology-in-practice and technology-as-artefact.

Chapter 2
Assimilation of Inter-Organizational Information Systems:
Insight from Change Resistance Theory in Public Electronic Procurement

Kishor Vaidya
University of Canberra, Australia & University of Southern Queensland, Australia

John Campbell
University of Canberra, Australia

Jeffrey Soar
University of Southern Queensland, Australia

Scott Gardner
Murdoch University, Australia

ABSTRACT

Public electronic procurement is an Internet-based inter-organizational information system (IOIS) that is intended to facilitate government-to-business (G2B) or government-to-government (G2G) electronic communication, information exchange and transaction support through web access or value-added network. This chapter is primarily built upon theoretical work in the IOIS adoption and diffusion area, and in particular on theories of technology assimilation. Stages of the assimilation process and the aggregation strategy have been explained in the context of public electronic procurement. Resistance theory is also discussed. We have argued that understanding both resistance variables and relevant change management interventions or moderators can be very useful in determining the extent of public e-procurement assimilation.

DOI: 10.4018/978-1-60960-768-5.ch002

Copyright © 2012, IGI Global. Copying or distributing in print or electronic forms without written permission of IGI Global is prohibited.

INTRODUCTION AND BACKGROUND

An Inter-organizational Information System (IOIS) is an infrastructure of computers and communication crossing organization boundaries and permitting information sharing (Cash and Konsynski, 1985). A more straightforward definition was provided by Hyde (2002) who defined inter-organizational systems as information and communication technology-based systems that are shared by two or more organizations for performing revenue-generating transactions. The Internet, as an enabler of organizational collaboration, can be regarded as the ultimate inter-organizational system (Hyde, 2002). The Internet is an extremely important technology for IOIS and provides better opportunities for organizations to establish distinctive strategic positions than older generations of IT (Porter, 2001). Along with Porter, McGhee (2003) and more recently Waldman (2010) have also observed that the internet offers significant economies of scale and scope for organizations based on low cost access to global markets and disintermediation of suppliers across the e-value chain.

The conceptual background underlying our research draws upon theories of technology assimilation (Tornatzky and Klein 1982, Mayer and Goes, 1988; Cooper and Zmud 1990; Fichman and Kemerer 1997). Mayer and Goes (1988) define technology assimilation as an organizational process that (1) commences when individuals within an organization first become aware of a new innovation, (2) which can then lead to the organization acquiring the innovation, and (3) if suitable, the technology may then be fully accepted, utilized, and institutionlized. Starting from this conceptual position, Purvis et al. (2001) further defined assimilation as the extent to which the use of a technology diffuses across organisational projects and work processes, and becomes routinised in the activities of those projects and processes.

It is important to note that Theories of Technology Assimilation distinguish assimilation from the concept of adoption. Adoption is a dichotomous variable and indicates whether the organisation has reached a decision of whether to utilise an IOIS or not, whereas assimilation is the extent of collective outcomes of activities by individuals and departments within the organization. Also while there has been much research undertaken on the issues of technology adoption, very little empirical work has been done on assimilation issues

This chapter is primarily built upon theoretical work in the IOIS diffusion area, particularly the theories of technology assimilation, in the context of public electronic procurement (e-procurement). Public e-procurement is an Internet-based inter-organizational information system that is intended to facilitate government-to-business (G2B) or government-to-government (G2G) electronic communication, information exchange and transaction support through a web access or value-added network. The existing literature on IOIS, particularly, electronic commerce innovation has contributed significantly to our understanding of e-procurement assimilation. However, this literaturehas limited applicability for investigating the extent of organizational e-procurement assimilation in the public sector. Web based procurement is relatively new, and the transactional characteristics of the Internet differ significantly from other technologies such as EDI (Electronic Document Interchange) examined in prior literature (Subramaniam and Shaw, 2002)

There has been an increase in popularity of e-procurement systems in governments in advanced and emerging economies alike. Consequently, governments around the world are implementing e-procurement initiatives as part of their Electronic Government (e-Government) agendas. During the last decade the implementation of e-procurement has shown explosive growth in some organizations while others seem to have resisted its assimilation (Vaidya and Hyde, 2011). These paradoxical results raise questions about the likely success of e-procurement systems being implemented by various government agencies (Vaidya, Sajeev, and Callender, 2006). It has been suggested that if e-procurement were to be fully assimilated, it could save governments up to 5% on expenditure and up to 50-80% on transaction costs (CEC, 2004). The reluctance of organizations to utilize e-procurement technologies despite their substantive benefits indicates a need to thoroughly study resistance to change and the management factors influencing e-procurement assimilation. These factors will be explored in this chapter in relation to the IT assimilation process. We also explore moderatingchange management interventions employed to reduce resistance and improve alignment with the management systems, culture, and performance metrics of the organisation.

Against this background, this chapter provides an overview of IOIS adoption and diffusion concepts related to IOIS assimilation. Theories of technology assimilation including the stages of the assimilation process and the concept of aggregation strategy will be explained in the context of public e-procurement. Resistance Theory is discussed in this chapter with reference to change management interventions which may be used to support assimilation of Information Technologies (IT) and web enabled Information and Communication Technologies (ICT) including e-procurement systems.

Based on this analysis the authors conclude that assimilation of IOIS takes place at many levels and that it is possible to increase the assimilation level by taking into account both the change resistance antecedents and the use of change management and benefits realisation interventions methodologies. These conclusions are supported with reference to precedents in the literature where change interventions and benefits realisation methods have been used to reduce resistance, build support from stakeholders, and improve outcomes for e-procurement systems in business and government in Australia and internationally. Relevant work includes that of Gardner and Ash (2003), Burn and Robins (2003), Fink (2003), and Erwin and Garman (2010).

ADOPTION AND DIFFUSION OF IOIS: AN OVERVIEW

An IOIS is defined as a computer and communication infrastructure crossing company boundaries to enable information sharing (Cash and Konsynski, 1985). Most commonly used examples of IOIS are EDI (Electronic Ddata Interchange) and B2B (Business to Business), B2G (Business to Government), G2G (Government to Government) or G2B (Government to Business) electronic commerce systems. While this chapter considers both traditional (e.g. EDI) and new (e.g. web-based) IOIS, Subramaniam (2002) contends that the scope of web-based IOIS has greatly expanded as it not only reduces transaction costs dramatically but also supports coordination and collaboration mechanisms. The author summarizes the key differences between EDI-based and web-based IOIS. Some of the characteristics of a web-based IOIS includes: i) supports many-to-many electronic networks; ii) uses open standards and platform independent applications; iii) handles processes of varying complexity; iv) a rich-media interface which allows exchange of complex images and drawings and enhances collaboration between business partners.

IT innovation researchers have sought to identify the factors that promote or hinder the assimilation of IT innovations (Fichman 2000, Swanson and Ramiller 2004). It is thus important to review IOIS diffusion literature before attempting to identify the change resistance antecedents and change management moderators that may influence the assimilation process of public e-procurement. As such, this chapter reviews existing theories relevant to this research and how they inform our understanding of the change resistance antecedents of IOIS assimilation. The subject of technology adoption and implementation is well explored in MIS research. Most of the studies are focused on EDI (e.g. Chwelos et al., 2001, Slacovou et al., 1995; Ramamurthy et al., 1999), MRP (Material Requirements Planning) (Cooper

& Zmud, 1995), and the B2B applications (Premkumar & Ramamurthy, 1995, Premkumar et al., 1994; Ranganathan et al., 2001), which discuss the influence of various external, internal and technical factors. Premkumar et al. (1994) identified the major barriers to IOIS implementation. They found compatibility of hardware/software between trading partners, differences in data formats between participating organizations, lack of willingness among the trading partners, difficulty in justifying ROI, resistance to change, and lack of technical knowledge as the main barriers.

Armstrong and Sambamurthy (1999) discuss three factors that influence the assimilation of IT in organizations. Their focus was on quality of senior leadership, sophistication of IT infrastructure, and organizational characteristics. Beatty et al. (2001) introduced a website adoption framework taking into account five factors: perceived benefits, organizational compatibility, technical compatibility, complexity, and management support.

Building on the critical mass theory, innovation diffusion theory, and power theory, Chwelos et al. (2001) used a survey method to examine organizational readiness, perceived benefits, and external pressure as EDI adoption intention determinants. Their important conclusion was that since IOIS spans organizational boundaries, both the organization and its partners must be ready to adopt the IOIS. The work of Iacovou et al. (1995) looked at an EDI adoption and integration model. They found perceived benefits, organizational readiness, and external pressure as significant determinants that impacted on EDI adoption and integration. Similarly, Premkumar and Ramamurthy (1995) investigated the impact of inter-organizational and organizational factors on IOIS adoption. Their study suggested antecedents such as competitive pressure, exercised power, internal needs, and top management support as critical determinants of IOIS adoption.

Employing a mixed method of literature review, interviews and a survey, Ranganathan et al. (2001) developed list of factors that facilitate and inhibit B2B application deployment. The authors' measurements included improvement in customer service, better inventory control, lower marketing and distribution costs, reduced cycle time, better supplier relationships, increased competitive advantage, and reduced operation costs. Using a field survey of eighty-three firms in the motor carriers industry, Ramamurthy et al. (1999) investigated interorganizational (customer support, customer expertise, and competitive pressure) and organizational (internal support, benefit potential, compatibility, and resource intensity) variables' effect on EDI diffusion. The authors constructed EDI diffusion, (the dependent variable), as external and internal integration. They found that while compatibility positively influenced external integration, resource intensity negatively affected external integration. They also identified the influence of competitive pressure as a significant determinant of EDI diffusion.

The study of innovation diffusion has a long history as a multi-disciplinary field (Rogers, 1995), with contributions from sociologists, communication researchers, economists, organizational researchers, IT researchers, and many others. Nevertheless, no single theory of innovation exists, nor does it seem likely that one will emerge (Fichman, 1999). The absence of a general theory of innovation suggests that researchers should develop theories of the middle range, that is, theories tailored to specific classes of technologies, and/ or to particular adoption contexts. The distinctive characteristics of IT innovations have motivated much of the recent theoretical work related to IT adoption and diffusion. In addition, since there are theoretical overlaps among the existing studies, future research should work towards combining multiple theoretical streams into a more integrated view of IT innovation (Fichman, 1999).

THEORIES OF TECHNOLOGY ASSIMILATION

Meyer and Goes (1988) first applied the concept of IT assimilation in proposing a nine-stage assimilation model to study medical innovations. They assessed the breadth and depth of the innovations and their impact on processes, structures, and culture of the organization. Prescott & Conger (1995) developed a typology of IT innovations focused on the Information Systems (IS) impact, intra-organizational impact, and inter-organizational impact employing a four-stage assimilation process that includes adoption, implementation, and routinization. Fichman and Kemerer (1997) extended the concept to study software process innovations. Their contribution was to assess organizational learning factors to explain the assimilation of the innovations.

Purvis et al. (2001) conducted an empirical investigation to understand the assimilation of knowledge management systems in organizations. Their empirical examination identified the impact of institutional antecedents on the assimilation of CASE (Computer Aided Software Engineering) technologies in systems development projects in organizations. The authors argue that IT assimilation is a result of structuring and meta-structuring actions of individuals. A similar argument was proposed by Chatterjee et al. (2002) in their study on Web assimilation. They found that top management support was a significant antecedent for a successful IT assimilation. Burn and Robins (2003) reported similar findings identifying the crucial role of change leaders and champions in their study on assimilation of e-government technologies in Western Australia.

Research in Management Information Systems (MIS) indicates that, more often than not, an assimilation gap (Fichman & Kemerer, 1997) occurs between adoption and implementation for complex projects. In other words, regardless of the widespread initial adoption, an innovation may still not be thoroughly deployed among the organisations that acquire the innovation. This concept has special significance in our study's context. As e-procurement is primarily meant for improving procurement performance, studying adoption alone does not make much sense. Adopting and even implementing e-procurement does not guarantee its assimilation. There are various antecedents at play that may influence the successful assimilation of e-procurement. It is for this reason; this research focuses on the process of e-procurement assimilation as a dependent variable rather than only adoption or intention to implement.

ORGANIZATIONAL ASSIMILATION OF PUBLIC E-PROCUREMENT

E-procurement is a fast moving set of technologies and therefore much of the information available on public e-procurement is in the practitioner literature, especially government reports rather than independent evaluations. Consequently much of the literature may be biased in favour of adoption and implementation successes because of the likely hesitation of governments to publicize their failures. In addition there is no clear agreement with respect to what public e-procurement is and what its main characteristics are (Vaidya et al., 2003, World Bank 2002).

A definition of public e-procurement that is useful for academic research and for public procurement practices, must take into account at least these four elements: The Internet/e-commerce (enabler); Process automation and integration (action); The practice of public procurement (process): and Value for money principles (objective) (Vaidya, 2007). As such, public electronic procurement has been defined as the use of any Internet-based Inter-organizational Information System, which automates and integrates any part of the procurement process in order to improve efficiency and quality in public procurement, and promote transparency and accountability in the wider public sector (Vaidya, 2007). As argued by Vaidya this definition accommodates most of the theoretical elements found in the practitioner and academic literature.

Popular e-procurement technologies include: electronic tendering; e-catalogue management systems; and electronic marketplace. E-Tendering is the complete web-based tendering process from the advertising of the requirement through to the placing of the contract, including exchange of all relevant documents in electronic format. While e-catalogues are the web-based representations of supplier information, e-marketplaces are web-based applications that bring multiple buyers and suppliers together in one central virtual marketplace and facilitate the electronic trade between buyers and suppliers at a dynamic price that is determined in accordance with the rules of the exchanges.

E-procurement assimilation has been defined as the extent to which the organisational use of e-procurement technologies diffuses across the procurement process and becomes standard business practice in facilitating transactional and strategic procurement activities associated with that process (Vaidya, 2007). It is conceptualized as an important construct in the casual chain of influence from the organizational adoption of e-procurement to the evidence of its impact on procurement performance. The author argues that this definition is consistent with the theories of technology assimilation which regard organisations as innovation systems for attaining differential levels of technology assimilation successes (Chatterjee, et al. 2002, Fichman 2001, Jarvenpaa and Ives, 1990).

Stages of the Assimilation Process

Meyer and Goes (1988) conceptualized the assimilation process as the penetration of the technology through the various stages such as awareness, evaluation, utilization, and institutionalization. The broader IT assimilation process captures each of these stages. Drawing on the work of Meyer and Goes and a range of other key authors in the field of IT studies including: Fichman & Kemerer, 1997; Ramiller and Swanson, 2003; Kwon and Zmud, 1987; Prescott and Conger, 1995; Fichman and Kemerer, 1997; Ramiller and Swanson, 2003) we have modelled the e-procurement assimilation process across the following six stages-

1. Intention to implement (the organization has an e-procurement strategy in place or is preparing concrete plans to investigate e-procurement within the next 12 months or in the near future);
2. Evaluation or pilot use (the organization has purchased 'trial' capabilities or implemented 'pilot' projects and is currently evaluating the possible use of e-procurement);
3. Commitment (the organization has specific plans and made formal commitments to utilise e-procurement);
4. Limited deployment (the organization has established a programme of regular but limited use of e-procurement);
5. Generalized deployment (the organization has deployed one or more forms of e-procurement and in its generalized capacity as integrated e-procurement in the majority of information systems); and
6. Rejection (the organization has evaluated and rejected the use of e-procurement).

The sixth stage can be justified by our arguments that the implementation of an innovation cannot be considered successful even if it survives through the deployment stage, as the innovation may ultimately be rejected by its users (Ramiller and Swanson, 2003). Organizations are diverse and the assimilation of e-procurement may also depend on other unique variables such as: the assimilation gap, the aggregated stage of the assimilation and the size of the organization (Fichman and Kremerer, 2001). Further variables in the e-procurement context include the percentage of procurement spending through e-procurement, the number of e-procurement technologies utilized, and the type of e-procurement technologies utilized.

An Aggregated Strategy

An aggregate strategy has been chosen to represent the various dimensions of e-procurement technologies in order for the findings to be more robust and generalizable (Fichman and Kemerer, 2001). Fichman and Kemerer believe that such strategy facilitates the identification of antecedents with consistent characteristics across the class of technology (e.g. e-procurement). While prior studies in MIS (e.g. Cooper and Zmud, 1990) have also utilized this approach, it was Fichman's (2001) study on software process innovations that provided a conceptual evaluation of aggregated measures (conditions). The conditions include: (i) the primary objective of the research; (ii) the validity of generalization across assimilation stages; (iii) the effects of organization characteristics; (iv) the effects of innovation characteristics; (v) the effects of innovation substitutes and complement; and (vi) the effects of reporting errors. The following are six conditions that favour aggregation of e-procurement technologies in the context of this research.

1. Our main interest in this chapter is to develop a model that generalizes the e-procurement class, as opposed to a specific e-procurement technology such as e-Marketplace. We expect to generalize our conceptual model of e-procurement assimilation across the assimilation stages.
2. Antecedents are posited to have effects in the same direction in the assimilation stages of a number of e-procurement technologies. We expect that the antecedents of technologies do not have different directional effects across the assimilation stages.
3. Characteristics of organizations can be treated as constant across the e-procurement initiatives within the public sector. As most of the public sector is serviced-based and mostly procure indirect goods and services, this condition should not be problem.
4. E-procurement characteristics cannot be treated as constant across Australian public sector agencies. Although the primary characteristics of e-procurement are related to the characteristics of the Internet (i.e. ubiquity and connectivity, immediacy and interactivity, multimedia and universal interface and ease of use", (Ware et. al, 1998)), this study considers the secondary characteristics of various e-procurement technologies. The innovation in this study (i.e., e-procurement) can include substitutes or moderate complements. An Idiosyncratic characteristic of e-procurement, as argued by Kalling & Caderskold (2004), is that e-procurement will not replace old procurement systems. Instead the new technology will complement other technologies. Organizations can choose to implement one or more e-procurement technologies that may complement each other to meet their procurement requirements.
5. Sources of noise in assessing the impact of antecedents on e-procurement assimilation and, in turn, its impact on measurement of the procurement performance may be present in the study of single innovation research design. Instead, we expect to minimize this noise by studying a class of technology and adopting the aggregate strategy.

As such, e-procurement assimilation can be aggregated across various technologies in order to identify the change resistance antecedents that influence the assimilation. We believe that such aggregated strategy will enable to undertake a dimensional-level analysis on each e-procurement technology implemented in an organization.

While we have explained the e-procurement assimilation as the dependent variable, it is important to identify and understand the antecedents (i.e. independent variables) that impact the assimilation, and it makes sense to seek theoretical support from resistance theory to identify the most important antecedents relating to change resistance. Why? Leibenstein (1976) asserts that academic theories provide means to form meaningful conclusions to understand the underlying causes of phenomena. Leibenstein (1976) further explains that the entities named in the theory predict the outcome of the theory-governed occurrences. As such, we believe that the resistance theory offers its own focus and explanation, predictive power and framework for the study of e-procurement assimilation from a change management perspective. The following section discusses resistance theory and attempts to identify the antecedents suggested by the theory which influence the assimilation of IOIS such as public e-procurement. These antecedents are discussed in relation to interventions identified in the change management and benefits realisation literature, that may be used to moderate between resistance antecedent and levels of assimilation of e-procurement within and across government agencies and departments.

Political Variant of the Interaction Theory

According to Political variant of the Interaction Theory, system resistance is caused by an interaction between organizational participants and the system concerned. According to Markus (1983), the system accepted by the users in one organisational setting may be rejected by the users in a different organisational setting. Resistance is viewed as the product of the interaction of the system's design features with the inter-organisational distribution of power. People who perceive they have lost power are more likely to resist the system and those who believe they have gained power are more likely to accept the system (Vaughan, 2000). Nevertheless, resistance should not be understood as an irrational response or a misguided and selfish reaction to an innovation (Jiang et al., 2000). Reasons for resistance depend on differences in the intended purpose of the system, the unique characteristics of its targeted users and broader network of salient stakeholders.

USER RESISTANCE THEORY

Change management in the context of the IOIS has been defined as "...a planned approach to integrating technological change. This includes formal processes for assessing the impact of the change on both the people it affects and on the way they do their jobs. It also uses techniques to get users to accept a change caused by technology and to change their behaviour to take advantage of the new IT functionality" (Goff, 2000, n.p.) As with other IT/e-Commerce implementations, issues that are likely to be encountered in an e-procurement environment can be broadly related on change management strategies, objectives and stakeholder communication processes.

Organizational resistance to change relating to the assimilation of a new technology can be influenced by the unique characteristics of the organization, its maker and product expertise, customer and supplier relationships (Chircu & Kauffman, 2000). Whilst an understanding of the unique local conditions is an important factor in determining the success of IT assimilation and informing the design of project implementation and communication process, useful lessons in IT change management and resistance reduction can be gleaned from different organisational contexts.

In this regard, Lin (1994) has identified the organizational and political factors including organisational climate, organisational commitment to change, power and control redistribution, and conflicts among organizational subunits. As such, Dickson & Wetherbe (1985) has identified the technical factors including ease of use, cost and time, system response and reliability, previous system experience, and data problem. Similarly, the author identified the personal factors as age of user, educational level of user, perceived need, communication and feedback channel, related training, degree of expected use of IOIS, and control of change.

User Involvement Theory

According to Ives and Olson (1984), user involvement theory refers to participation in the system development process by the target user group. Participative decision making, and planned organisational change have been identified as the two areas of organizational behaviour relevant to user involvement.

Burns and Robbin's (2003) study of e-government assimilation in a large Western Australian government department identified the crucial role of committed leadership with a clear vision, engagement of both line managers and cross functional teams for reducing resistance to change. These measures also increased the level of support for embedding e-government systems into day to day work routines. This is consistent with the findings of Gardner and Ash (2003) who explored ICT adoption and implementation practices in a UK bank and in the Norwegian operations of US petroleum services multinational. In the findings from the two cases and their '*Dynamic model for change in ICT Networks*', they stress the importance of early and ongoing engagement of line managers and other cross-functional stakeholders with throughout the ICT implementation process. The model also highlights the importance of senior managers, line managers, IT and HR specialists as internal change agents or moderators to reduce employee resistance and any tension between the imperatives of the ICT system, the business model and key performance metrics of the organisation.

The implementation of new technology is so significant that it changes an organization's shape, the nature of its jobs, its processes and routines. If organization members consider such changes negative, it is highly likely that members will resist these changes (Krovi, 1993). What could be the reasons behind the resistance? Markus (1983) contends that the reasons for resistance may differ depending on differences in the intended purpose of the system and the characteristics of its target set of users. Resistance may, for example, manifest itself as a result of shifting power relationships. A well-designed system, for example, might be resisted by those who fear it might take away some of their power or social stature in the organization. The real reasons for resistance are users' perceived values, and social content gain or loss before and after the system implementation (Markus, 1983). Waddell, Cummings and Worley (2011) cite a study of sources of resistance by Del Val and Fuentes (2003) which identified a range of factors such as implicit assumptions that are not discussed, communication barriers, past failures, deep rooted values and emotional loyalty as significant contributors to change resistance.

Other sources of resistance to change identified in the literature include uncertainty concerning jobs and skills, a lack of felt needs, a potential distribution of power and resources, a lack of organizational validity, and a lack of management support (Hirschhenim & Newman, 1988). Past research studies have found that the change in job content and decision-making approach could be the main reasons why managers oppose system implementations (Kotter and Schlesinger, 1979; Krovi, 1993). Recent research has supported these findings adding that other reasons for resistance are loss of status, alternation in interpersonal relationships, loss of power, and uncertainty, unfamiliarity and misinformation (Jiang et al., 2000).

Markus (1983) argues that resistance to change can be either person-centric (people resist because of their own internal factors), or system-centric (users resist the poor design of the system), or political (where interaction with the system and the organization context cause resistance). Markus also offers recommendations to address the resistance. For example, she suggests educating and participating the user in the design of the system to address person-centric resistance; focusing on improving human factors and re-engineering the system to address system-centric resistance; and finally restructuring incentive systems and relationships to address political resistance. However, if resistance is because of both internal and external factors, "neither changing the individuals involved with the system nor changing the technical features of the system itself will reduce the resistance", notes Vaughan (2000).

Understanding the unique characteristics of different organisational contexts and local conditions is crucial to the success of IT assimilation and reduction of resistance to change. Organisational leaders must analyse their current situation, identify factors that will facilitate or exhibit change, proceed with necessary changes, then implement a system that supports the revised organisational situation based on stakeholder feedback and constant alignment of IT and business or organisational critical success factors and performance measures.

Table 1 lists the literature reference that has used the various variables suggested by Resistance Theories.

Impact of Change Resistance Antecedents on e-Procurement Assimilation

Technical issues in e-procurement are often less complicated compared to people issues. That was the conclusion of a study on critical success factors by Vaidya, Sajeev and Callender (2006). An e-procurement system, by definition, changes the way people conduct procurement. It can be said that changes required supporting business processes are directly related to the speed of adoption of e-procurement. Change management issues become more substantial as stakeholder needs increase (CGEC, 2002). The UK based Office of Government Commerce (OGC, 2002) recommends that increasing change in underlying processes requires more learning and effort on the part of users. Consequently, the OGC suggests giving more attention to change management issues, citing three ways to achieve successful change management for e-procurement assimilation: consultation, communication, and issue resolution (OGC, 2002). The World Bank Report cautions that while change management may be the least expensive aspect of an e-procurement project, a

Table 1. Variables suggested by resistance theories

Change resistance variable	Studies which used the variable/s
Political/cultural factors (change in decision making approach, implicit assumptions and deep values, cultural fit)	Hirschhenim & Newman, 1988; Kotter and Schlesinger, 1979; Krovi, 1993; Jiang et al., 2000; Waddell, Cummings and Worley 2011; Del Val and Fuentes 2003
Organisational factors (organisational climate, organisational commitment to change, power and control redistribution, and conflicts among organizational subunits)	Lin, 1994; Kotter and Schlesinger, 1979; Robey and Boundreau, 1999;
Job threatening factors (loss of status, job security, change in job content, Uncertainty, unfamiliarity and misinformation)	Jiang et al., 2000; Vaughan, 2000; Soete and Weehuizen, 2003; Kotter and Schlesinger, 1979; Krovi, 1993;
Personal factors (age of user, educational level of user, perceived need, communication and feedback channel, related training, degree of expected use of IOIS, and control of change)	Jiang et al., 2000; Chircu & Kauffman, 2000; Dickson & Wetherbe (1985)
Technical/process factors (ease of use, cost and time, system response and reliability, previous system experience, and data problem)	Chircu & Kauffman, 2000; Jehn, 1997; Vaughan, 2000; Robey and Boundreau, 1999; Dickson & Wetherbe (1985)

lack of it can be a leading cause of project failure (World Bank, 2003).

Soete and Weehuizen (2003) further support this notion that public sector organizations often lack innovation and are resistant to change – they tend to emphasize conformity and defend status quo instead of focusing on creativity, improvement and change. This is especially evident when implementing innovative information technologies such as e-procurement systems. Vaidya et al. (2005) assert that as the process of assimilation of e-procurement in the public sector demands exchange of information within and among users (specialist-users and end-users) and suppliers (large suppliers and local/regional SMEs), the procurement organization must have capacity to exercise organizational learning and share the lessons learnt. This has been supported by AGIMO (2006) which suggests identifying inhibitors of e-procurement implementation and incorporating them into the communications plans and training programs. So, it can be concluded that the antecedent of e-procurement of assimilation not only involves user and technological factors but also power and political actions.

The importance of user uptake has been highlighted in recent e-procurement literature. Vaidya and Hopkins (2004) analyzed the puzzle of "we built it but they haven't come yet…" in the case of New South Wales (NSW) Government's e-Marketplace (smartbuy®) in reference to the theories of resistance. The authors noted that they (the client agencies) did not participate in the e-Marketplace because of factors unique to the individual rather than common to the entire group (internal factors). Otherwise they did not participate because of the factors inherent in the e-procurement system being implemented (external factors). The authors conclude that they did not participate because of both internal factors (people) and external factors (systems) in combination.

In this regard, Jehn (1997) researched the types of conflicts in organizations and defined three types: task conflict, relationship conflict and process conflict. In the context of e-procurement, the task conflict may arise out of the variation of changing from the traditional procurement system to e-procurement system. Although e-procurement will save considerable time and pays for itself after a certain time period, if the buyer is not computer literate he or she will resist the change.

Markus (1983) describes the above mentioned effect as "resistance effect", a phenomenon where systems are used in different ways from what was intended by the system designers, in terms of organizational resistance, which builds on the lack of understanding of the interaction between organisational and technological variables. Vaidya and Hopkins (2006) highlight the lack of interaction between organizational and technological variables in their study of the smartbuy® e-marketplace system. The authors contend that organisations might not have been motivated enough to join smartbuy® for their perceived efficiency reasons or their inability to do so.

As changes required in supporting business processes are directly related to the speed of assimilation of e-procurement, change management issues become more substantial as the number of stakeholder groups and variety of stakeholder needs increase (CGEC, 2003). Other information systems researchers have also contributed to this area of literature. Robey and Boundreau's research (1999) on organizational change highlight the importance of empirically identifying the opposing forces, exploring contradictory hypothesis and exploring process research while researching the area of resistance to change. This view is echoed in the more recent work on the future of (soft) organisational development change interventions supporting the technological innovation in globally networked, (ICT enabled) organisations (Waddell, Cummings and Worley, 2011). Based on these views and the variables suggested by Resistance Theory (Table 1), Figure 1 depicts

Figure 1. Conceptual model

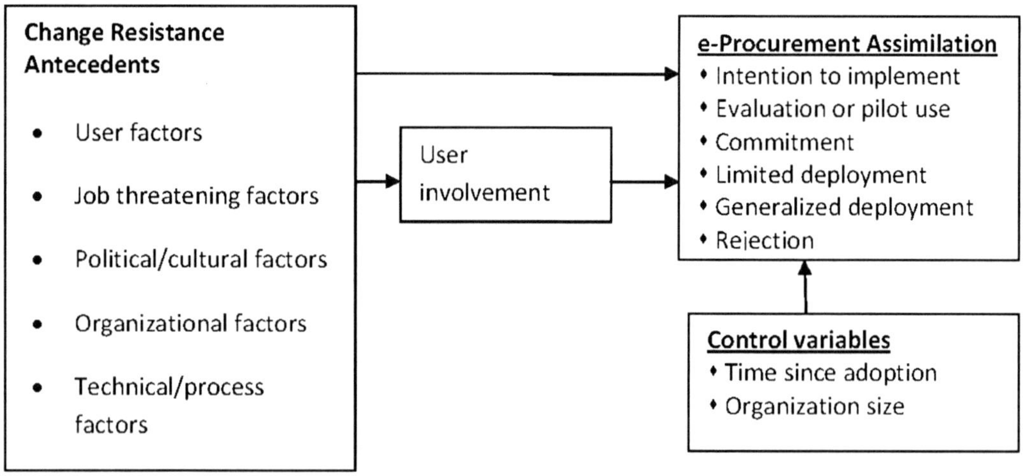

the impact of change resistance antecedents on e-procurement assimilation.

LIMITATIONS, FUTURE RESEARCH DIRECTIONS AND CONCLUSIONS

In this chapter we reviewed the IOIS adoption and diffusion literature and discussed several traditional theoretical frameworks that were likely to explain the IT assimilation process. The main contribution of this chapter is to show managers that the assimilation of IOIS takes place at many levels and that it is possible to increase the assimilation level by taking into account change resistance antecedents and relevant change management moderators Most research focuses on antecedents that influence the 'adoption decision' of e-Procurement. This is one of few research studies that moved beyond this adoption paradigm. Based on our extensive review of the relevant literature on IOIS assimilation, e-procurement and resistance theory this is one of the very first studies to include the 'rejection' stage in the process of IOIS assimilation. The discussion in this chapter will assist the practitioners to understand: what change resistance conditions they may face; why these conditions will often arise while managing an IOIS assimilation process; and what change management actions or interventions may be appropriate to address or pre-empt resistance.

This study is focused on public electronic procurement as an example of IOIS. As such, the study should also be applied to other sectors and industries, and to other contexts of IOIS. Furthermore, Resistance Theory provides only one view of the possible antecedents influencing IOIS assimilation. There is great scope to identify and integrate other relevant theories and the variables suggested by them which may influence IOIS assimilation. We believe that a further expanded integrated framework, supported by relevant theoretical bases, should provide a much improved foundation to better understand the processes involved in IOIS assimilation..

The findings from this study allow practitioners to view IOIS with change resistance-related antecedents in mind so as to affect greater influence and better manage the assimilation process. The discussion of IOIS based on theories of technology assimilation should provide both researchers and practitioners with a greater ability to make more intelligent and informed decisions regarding the management of IOIS assimilation leading to greater success and realisation of benefits.

REFERENCES

Armstrong, C.P. & V. Sambamurthy. (1999). Information Technology Assimilation in Firms: The Influence of Senior Leadership and IT Infrastructures, *Information Systems Research*, v. 10, i. 4, pp. 304-327.

Australian Government Information Management Office. (2006). *Strategic Guide to e-Procurement, Commonwealth of Australia*. AGIMO.

Burn, J., & Robins, G. (2003). Moving towards e-government: A case study of organisational change processes. *Logistics Information Management*, *16*(2), 25–36. doi:10.1108/09576050310453714

Cash, J. I. J., & Konsynski, B. R. (1985). IS redraws competitive boundaries. *Harvard Business Review*, *63*(2), 134–142.

Chatterjee, D., Grewal, R., & Sambamurthy, V. (2002). Shaping Up For e-Commerce: Institutional Enablers of the Organisational Assimilation of Web Technologies. *Management Information Systems Quarterly*, *26*(2), 65–89. doi:10.2307/4132321

Chircu, A. M., and Kauffman, R. J. (2000). Reintermediation Strategies in Business-to-Business Electronic Commerce, *International Journal of Electronic Commerce*, 4, 4, Summer, pp. 7-42.

Consortium for Global Electronic Commerce. (2002). *Measuring and Improving Value of E-procurement Initiatives*. Madison, WI: University of Wisconsin-Madison, Consortium for Global Electronic Commerce (CGEC).

Cooper, R. B., & Zmud, R. W. (1990). Information Technology implementation research: A technological diffusion approach. *Management Science*, *36*(2), 123–139. doi:10.1287/mnsc.36.2.123

Del Val, P., & Fuentes, C. M. (2003). Resistance to change; A literature review and empirical study, *Management Decision*: *Vol. 41. No2 in Waddell, D.M Cummings, T.G and Worley C.G. (2011) Organisational change, development and transformation. Asia Pacific* (4th ed., pp. 100–106). Cengage Learning Australia.

Dickson, G. W. (1985). *And Wetherbe, J.* New York: The Management of Information Systems, McGraw Hill.

Erwin, D. G., & Garman, A. N. (2010). Resistance to organizational change: linking research to practice. *Leadership &Development Journal*, *31*(1), 39–56. doi:10.1108/01437731011010371

Fichman, R. G., & Kemerer, C. F. (1997). The Assimilation of Software Process Innovations: an Organizational Learning Perspective. *Management Science*, *43*(10), 1345–1363. doi:10.1287/mnsc.43.10.1345

Fichman, R. G., & Kemerer, C. F. (1999). The Illusory Diffusion of Innovations: An Examination of Assimilation Gaps. *Information Systems Research*, *10*(3), 255–275. doi:10.1287/isre.10.3.255

Gardner, R. S., & Ash, C. G. (2003). ICT enabled organisations: a model for change management. *Logistics Information Management*, *16*(2), 18–25. doi:10.1108/09576050310453705

Hyde, M. (2002). *An Empirical Examination of Inhibitors Affecting Web-Based Interorganizational Applications*. PhD Dissertation (Unpublished), Southern Illinois University at Carbondale, USA

Iacovou, C., & Benbasat, I. Dexter A. (1995). EDI and Small Organizations: Adoption and Impact of Technology, *MIS Quarterly*, December, pp. 465-485.

Ives, B. (1984). And Olson, M. H. "User Involvement and MIS Success: A Review of Research. *Management Science*, *30*(5), 586–603. doi:10.1287/mnsc.30.5.586

Jarvenpaa, S. L., & Ives, B. (1990). Executive Involvement and Participation in the Management of Information Technology. *Management Information Systems Quarterly*, *15*(2), 205–227. doi:10.2307/249382

Jehn, K. A. (1997). A Qualitative Analysis of Conflict Types and Dimensions in Organizational Groups. *Administrative Science Quarterly*, (42): 530–557. doi:10.2307/2393737

Jiang, J. J., Muhanna, W. A., & Klein, G. (2000). User resistance and strategies for promoting acceptance across system types. *Information & Management*, *37*, 25–36. doi:10.1016/S0378-7206(99)00032-4

Kotter, J. A., & Schlesinger, L. A. (1979). Choosing strategies for change. *Harvard Business Review*, *57*(2), 106–114.

Krovi, R. (1993). Identifying the causes of resistance to IS implementation. *Information & Management*, *25*, 327–335. doi:10.1016/0378-7206(93)90082-5

Leibenstein, H. (1976). *Beyond Economic Man: A New Foundation for Microeconomics*. Cambridge, MA: Harvard University Press.

Lin, T. (1994). An Integrated Model for User Resistance to Information Systems – The Taiwa Case. *Journal of Information Technology Management*, *V*(3).

Markus, M. L. (1983). Power, Politics and MIS Implementation. *Communications of the ACM*, *26*(6), 430–444. doi:10.1145/358141.358148

McGhee, J. (2003) Strategy as orchestrating knowledge in Cummings and Wilson (eds) *Images of Strategy*, Blackwell UK, pp 136-163.

Meyer, A.D., and Goes, J.B. Organizational Assimilation of Innovations: A multilevel Contextual Analysis, *Academy of Management Journal* (31:4), pp. 897-923.

Premkumar, G., & Ramamurthy, K. (1995). The role of interorganizational and organizational factors on the decision mode for adoption on interorganizational systems. *Decision Sciences*, *26*, 303–336. doi:10.1111/j.1540-5915.1995.tb01431.x

Purvis, R. L., Sambamurthy, V., & Zmud, R. W. (2001). The Assimilation of Knowledge Platforms in Organizations: An Empirical Investigation. *Organization Science*, *12*(2), 117–135. doi:10.1287/orsc.12.2.117.10115

Ramiller, N. C., & Swanson, E. B. (2003. Whether, When, and How to Innovate with Information Technology: What do Empirical Studies Tell Us? *Information Systems Working Paper 2-03*, The Anderson School at UCLA, March.

Ranganathan, C., Teo, T. S. H., Dhaliwal, J. S., Ang, J. S. K., & Hyde, M. 2001. *Facilitators and inhibitors for deploying business-to-business e-Commerce applications: A multi-method, cross-cultural study*. Proceedings of the 22nd Annual International Conference on Information Systems. New Orleans, LA, 593- 600.

Robey, D. and Boudreau, S. 1999. "Accounting for the Contradictory Organizational Consequences of Information Technology: Theoretical Direction and Methodological Implications." *Information Systems Research* (10:2), pp. 167-185.

Soete, L., & Weehuizen, R. (2004). The Economics of e-Government: A Bird's eye view. *International Journal of Communications Law and Policy, Issue*, *8*(Winter).

Subramaniam, C., & Shaw, M. (2002). A study of the Value of B2B E-Commerce: The Case of Web-based Procurement. *International Journal of Electronic Commerce*, *6*(6), 19–40.

Vaidya, K. (2007). Electronic Procurement in the Australian Public Sector: Organisational Assimilation and its Impacts on Public Procurement Performance (PhD thesis). The Univesity of New England, NSW Australia.

Vaidya, K., & Hopkins, P. (2006). The Case of 'smartbuy®' e-Marketplace in the NSW Public Sector: Constraints and Lessons Learnt. Proceedings of the 8th Collaborative Electronic Commerce Technology and Research international conference, December 8-9, Adelaide, Australia.

Vaidya, K., Sajeev, A. S. M., & Callender, G. (2006). e-Procurement Initiatives in the Public Sector: Critical Success Factors that Influence Implementation Success. *Journal of Public Procurement*, *5*(Issue 4/5), 70–99.

Vaughan, P. J. (2000). *System Implementation Success Factors: It's not just the Technology*. University of Colorado at Boulder.

Waddell, D. M., Cummings, T. G., & Worley, C. G. (2011). *Organisational change, development and transformation. Asia Pacific* (4th ed.). Cengage Learning Australia.

Waldman, S. (2010). *Creative disruption: What you need to do to shake up your business in a digital world*. Financial Times, UK: Prentice Hall.

World Bank. 2003. *Electronic Government Procurement (e-GP): World Bank Draft Strategy*. Washington, DC (WB).

Chapter 3
Theoretical Foundations of Inter-Organizational Information Systems:
Towards a Framework Grounded on Seven Theories

Maria Madlberger
Webster University Vienna, Austria

ABSTRACT

Research on Inter-Organizational Information Systems (IOIS) provided many insights, which, however, are very fragmented in terms of applied theories. This results in a quite isolated understanding of single aspects of IOIS rather than a comprising approach to the research subject. To address these shortcomings, the chapter investigates seven theories in respect of their explanation of IOIS adoption and use, its drivers, IOIS-based collaboration between firms, and benefits and costs of IOIS. The applied theories are social exchange theory and embeddedness theory (organization theories), transaction cost theory and agency theory (economics-related theories), the resource-based view of the firm and network theory (strategic management approaches), and game theory. The findings and the resulting framework imply that all these theories lead to similar recommendations on the use of IOIS although they have very diverse assumptions and lines of argumentation. The chapter stresses that the investigated theories supplement rather than contradict each other.

INTRODUCTION

Inter-Organizational Information Systems (IOIS) have largely affected the way of doing business in many ways. In particular, IOIS are enablers and drivers of various forms of inter-organizational coordination and collaboration. Based on the fact that IOIS-based collaboration is related to a variety of business contexts, research efforts in this field are by nature spanning across business administration and information systems research. As a result, research in the context of IOIS relies on multiple theoretic approaches. For example, a literature review conducted by Madlberger &

DOI: 10.4018/978-1-60960-768-5.ch003

Copyright © 2012, IGI Global. Copying or distributing in print or electronic forms without written permission of IGI Global is prohibited.

Roztocki (2008) revealed that not less than 23 theories were applied in 80 information systems (IS) research papers on IOIS-based collaboration.

The existing large body of research on IOIS provides a rich source of knowledge about IOIS use, its benefits, and risks. At the same time, the available knowledge about IOIS misses a common theoretical understanding and is therefore highly scattered and unstructured which limits its value to researchers as well as practitioners. Especially the large diversity of underlying theories that are used to explain the impact of IOIS often leads to results that seem to be contradictory. A comprehensive theoretical framework for IOIS research could provide substantial benefits to researchers and practitioners. For IS researchers it can help to identify research gaps, address contradictory facts, further develop theories, and draw conclusions for related issues, such as implications for research on collaboration, social and sociological issues and technical requirements for IOIS based on key tasks performed by them. Benefits to practice are a more consistent approach of business and management problems and a possibly more aggregated and comprising view. Thus a framework of IOIS-related theories can provide business practice with a bird's eye view instead of focusing on theoretic details. Furthermore, the framework can serve as a basis for empirical work which can benefit practice considerably.

One useful step to move towards a more comprising theoretical viewpoint is the discussion and comparison of theories that were used by IS researchers to analyze IOIS. Such a comparison should highlight the different foci and backgrounds of the theories and allow identifying what these theories have in common and what differentiates them in terms of their contribution to investigating IOIS issues.

The proposed approach considers the analysis of theories that were applied by IS researchers in the IOIS context. As a starting point, the main focus lies on theories that contribute to an understanding of the organizational behavior related to IOIS use as well as the impacts that are achieved through IOIS. Thus this analysis is related to the business administration and economics viewpoint on IOIS. Therefore it does not cover theories outside this discipline, for example theories stemming from IS research and sociology as well as social sciences which would provide further insights in a wider analysis.

As a conceptual background the systematics of (Osborn & Hagedoorn, 1997) is applied. Osborn & Hagedoorn (1997) investigate theories related to interorganizational alliances and thus focus specifically on the interfirm collaboration. Following their approach, the author starts her analysis within the following conceptual research streams: organization theories, economics-based theories, and strategic management theories. These approaches are supplemented with an analysis of game-theory. The latter research stream is highly related to economics and contributes much to the understanding of drivers and benefits of information sharing, which is tightly connected to IOIS use and impacts. These four theoretical streams cover large areas of IOIS use and IOIS-based collaboration. Within these approaches seven theories are examined. Each of them is analyzed with regards of organizations' adoption and usage behavior of IOIS as well as IOIS-related benefits and costs. The discussed theories are the following:

1. **Organization theories approach:** social exchange theory and theory of embeddedness,
2. **Economics-based approach:** transaction cost theory and agency theory,
3. **Strategic management approach:** resource-based view of the firm and network theory, and
4. **Game-theoretic approaches.**

Research on IOIS covers many different aspects that need to be understood in order to analyze theories' implications for IOIS. For analyzing theories in respect of their contribution to research on IOIS, particularly behavioral and organizational issues are considered relevant. Therefore for this analysis the following IOIS-related issues are addressed: (1) the adoption and use of IOIS, (2) the drivers of IOIS adoption and use, (3) IOIS-based relationships, coordination, and collaboration with trading partners, and (4) the impacts of IOIS on performance, i.e. strategic and operational benefits and costs of IOIS.

The findings indicate that despite the different assumptions and conceptual backgrounds all theories have surprisingly similar implications for IOIS use as well as IOIS benefits and costs. The analyzed theories largely supplement rather than contradict each other although they do this based on largely different assumptions. This analysis thus demonstrates how different theories can lead to similar results. The following sections discuss each of the selected theories in terms of their general assumptions as well as their contribution to IOIS research. Following that, the theories are compared and an initial framework for a more unified understanding of IOIS application and benefits/costs is proposed. The chapter ends with concluding remarks on a further extension of the framework.

ORGANIZATION THEORIES

Organization theories have their background in business and management. They investigate organizational issues inside and between companies, thus including interorganizational collaboration. Interorganizational relationships can either be based on equity or contractual agreements. Of particular interest in this approach are strategic alliances that are characterized by (1) an independence of the involved organizations, (2) shared benefits among the involved organizations, and (3) ongoing participation in one or several key strategic areas, such as information technology, products or markets (Yoshino & Rangan, 1995). Alliances can have varying levels of intensity, ranging from highly integrated forms with strong linkages between the engaged organizations (e.g., joint ventures) to loose forms that do not share equity and have little control built in (Gulati & Singh, 1998). As opportunistic behavior can occur in such a relationship, uncertainty is an important factor that might impede interorganizational relationships. These uncertainties can be reduced in various ways, especially by increased information transparency and knowledge; a context in which IOIS can contribute value.

Within organization theories, two approaches particularly contribute to the explanation of IOIS and related collaboration. These approaches are social exchange theory and embeddedness theory.

Social Exchange Theory

Social exchange theory is based upon the sociological perspective and seeks to explain a human behavior that is related to do others a favor without a clear expectation of the exact future return (Kankanhalli, Tan, & Wei, 2005). This implies the existence of a long-term relationship which is opposed to loose, arms-length interactions. In respect of the relationship between trading partners long-term relationships can be differentiated from arms-length transactions by various contractual elements which cover situational and process characteristics and involves high interdependency between trading partners (Dwyer, Schurr, & Oh, 1987). Arms-length and discrete transactions imply a very loose coupling between the organizations.

Key cornerstones of many research efforts on interorganizational relationships with a social exchange theory background are trust, commitment, and power. These streams of research were further put forward with the emergence of IOIS. The role of IOIS in social exchange theories is twofold: (1) the role IOIS as a means to establish trust and commitment as prerequisites of interorganizational relationships and (2) the use of IOIS as a result of trust, commitment, and power between trading partners.

Trust is defined as an optimistic anticipated behavior of others (Hart & Saunders, 1997). As there is some uncertainty about this behavior, trust involves risk taking and a willingness to rely on the other partner (Kwon & Suh, 2005). As Mayer, Davis, & Schoorman (1995) point out, trust implies the "willingness to be vulnerable to the actions of another party" (p. 712). If trust exists between trading partners, it may ease the conditions of doing business together. First, trust reduces the necessity to set up formal agreements on any potential happening in the business relationship that might occur. As Bakos & Brynjolfsson (1993) point out, contractual agreements are incomplete as it is not possible to account for the total variety of possible future scenarios. If such agreements can be replaced with trust, the transaction costs can be lowered considerably. Second, trust can indirectly be a source of benefits. If firms are less concerned about opportunistic behavior by their trading partners, they may be willing to a larger extent to collaborate with these partners which can yield benefits (Kwon & Suh, 2005).

Several studies in IS research imply that trust is an important antecedent of IOIS use (e.g., Hart & Saunders, 1997). Trust in a relationship can result in a double-sided impact: first, it can create a transaction climate in which firms have more incentive to make investments in IOIS as a relationship-specific asset. Second, the availability of IOIS in a relationship can stimulate mutual information sharing, which further increases trust. As Morgan & Hunt (1994) point out, trust is highly interrelated with commitment.

Commitment is understood as a trading partner's belief that an ongoing relationship with the partner is highly important so that it deserves a maximum of efforts at maintaining it (Morgan & Hunt, 1994). Therefore commitment is both or all parties' interest in an ongoing relationship that is not intended to be terminated. Sharing of common goals as well as information is an important element. In the absence of commitment interorganizational relationships become vulnerable and fragile (Kwon & Suh, 2005). Kingshott (2006) posits that an appropriate climate and atmosphere in the relationship is a prerequisite which enables confidence in the partner. The relationship commitment consists of disclosing, signaling, and initiating behavior (Leuthesser & Kohli, 1995). It implies that a firm is willing to communicate sensitive information about itself, its products, and prices and attempts to understand its trading partner (Kingshott, 2006). This behavior is opposed to opportunism which is characterized by information distortion and reneging on commitments by shirking or failing to fulfill promises. An important antecedent of relational commitment is trust.

IOIS can be a means to establish, support and demonstrate commitment in a relationship. A company that uses IOIS signals that it invests money in improving the communication and intends to exchange information with it trading partners. The more relationship-specific this IOIS is, the higher is the demonstrated commitment to the relationship. Termination of the relationship would make specific assets, such as customized IOIS, useless and would turn into sunk costs.

Power theory has its roots in the social exchange theory where relationships between firms are explained by asymmetries in dependency between them (Premkumar & Ramamurthy, 1995). It is defined as the "ability to evoke a change in another's behavior" (Gaski & Nevin, 1985, p. 13) As firms within a supply chain are likely to be faced with different conditions and different competitive positions, power theory can be an appropriate theoretical basis for understanding the use of IOIS in supply chains.

A well-known classification of power concepts was developed by French & Raven (1959) who distinguish (1) reward power, i.e., a firm's ability to reward its trading partner, (2) coercive power, i.e., a firm's ability to punish its trading partner, (3) expert power, i.e., a firm's perceived expertise in a particular area, (4) referent power, i.e., a firm's perceived reputation, and (5) legitimate power, i.e.

a firm's perceived formal right to determine what to do. Power can be exercised by persuasion or coercion. Persuasion involves various incentives, such as training, cost sharing, information sharing, or IT support. Often, persuasion can be more effective than enforcement because a better relationship with the trading partner can be achieved, a reason why many firms in practice prefer persuasion. Coercion implies that the influencer threatens with punishment to force its trading partner to follow its direction. Typical instruments are the threat to pass processing costs onto the trading partner or terminate business with it. Such measures can only be undertaken if negative consequences for the influencer are low (Hart & Saunders, 1997).

As IOIS are by nature applied between different trading partners, power theory can help explain why and how firms apply IOIS in their business relationships. Literature identified three main settings within which the impact of power on IOIS use can be analyzed: First, exercised power to enforce the adoption of a certain IOIS technology (e.g., Premkumar & Ramamurthy, 1995): As large firms are more likely to benefit from IOIS due to their large volume of information involved they are also more likely to use IOIS. Due to the interorganizational nature of IOIS, however, these firms have to apply these systems jointly with their trading partners, thus powerful firms will use their strong position in order to have their trading partners adopt the technology as well. For smaller firms, their trading partners' power is a strong incentive to use IOIS which is, however, rather related to avoid negative consequences than achieving benefits.

Second, exercised power to enforce the achievement of a certain level of an IOIS technology (e.g., Massetti & Zmud, 1996; Nguyen & Harrison, 2004): Firms can try to induce trading partners not only to adopt an IOIS technology, but also to achieve certain levels of IOIS implementation, e.g. volume, diversity, breath, and depth of IOIS (Massetti & Zmud, 1996) or infrastructure, types of information, B2B applications, and integration with other applications (Nguyen & Harrison, 2004). As the benefits obtained by an IOIS implementation depend on the degree of integration in the trading partners' internal information systems it is likely that strong trading partners are interested in advanced levels of IOIS integration. Furthermore, large firms will tend to aim at homogenous IOIS levels with a majority of their trading partners in order to avoid too many parallel systems and interfaces.

Third, potential power which induces the influencee to fulfill the perceived wishes of the trading partner in advance (e.g., Hart & Saunders, 1997): weaker firms can try to fulfill their trading partner's wishes before the latter starts to exert power. This behavior could enable the adopting firms to be more flexible in their choice of IOIS as well as becoming familiar with the technology earlier, which can turn into a competitive advantage later.

Generally speaking, with few exceptions (e.g., reported by Clark, Croson, & Schiano, 2001), a firm's power tends to enforce the adoption of IOIS as powerful firms (1) largely benefit from IOIS and (2) have the capability of having their trading partners use IOIS as well.

Embeddedness Theory

The embeddedness theory analyzes what different kinds of interfirm relationships can occur and how they determine the way firms do business. The concept has its origin in sociology where it was introduced by Granovetter (1985). It was put into an organizational context by combining organization theory with social exchange theory. The pioneer work in this respect was done by Uzzi (1997) who made the basic assumption that the quality of social ties between organizations impacts their economic action, e.g. interorganizational collaboration.

The theory assumes that interorganizational relationships can differ considerably on a continuum between loose, arms-length relationships with little coordination and embedded relationships with a high degree of ongoing interpersonal relationships. Embedded relationships show a high level of mutual trust and positive experiences and allow firms to handle many problem areas without formal contracts (Chatfield & Yetton, 2000). A high degree of embeddedness is characterized by three basic elements (Uzzi, 1997): (1) an exchange of sensitive information, (2) joint problem-solving arrangements, and (3) trust. The information exchange is related to proprietary and partly tacit information which is highly referred to the organizations and is more difficult to be transferred to other organizations. Joint problem solving arrangements denote the willingness of firms to collaborate on certain problem areas, thus allowing them to unify their forces for problem solving and facing challenges. Like in social exchange theory, trust plays an important role in embeddedness theory as it shows a moderating effect on information exchange and joint problem solving by providing an appropriate environment.

The embeddedness theory can be used to explain under what conditions IOIS can be successfully used. Chatfield & Yetton (2000) discuss the role of fit between companies' strategies, structures, management processes, individual roles and skills, and technologies and their embeddedness of relationship. In such a relationship IOIS are a key element to achieve the fit, which is characterized by an IOIS-supported exchange of information, well-aligned joint economic action, and trust between the trading partners. Embeddedness can increase the diffusion of information between firms by enhancing trust, reputation, and the exchange of information (Lin 2006). The largest benefits are supposed to be obtained in relationships where trading partners are in a similar structural position, e.g. when power is balanced.

ECONOMICS-RELATED APPROACHES

In many economics-related theories information plays a key role. New institutional economics investigates how players interact with each other and coordinate buying and selling processes. One major factor is uncertainty which results from a lack of information. Among economics-oriented approaches, there are two theories that are particularly relevant for the investigation of information exchange and therefore IOIS. These theories are the institutional economics-based transaction cost theory and the information economics-based agency theory.

Transaction Cost Theory

IOIS-related research used transaction cost theory very frequently to analyze the adoption and use of IOIS as well as its drivers and results. The theory seeks to explain the formation of two main coordination mechanisms which are based on asset specificity and uncertainty: markets and hierarchies (Williamson, 1975). Uncertainty is due to bounded rationality and opportunism. Bounded rationality is a result of limited ability to process information without errors. Opportunism is individuals' self-interest which can lead to unfair behavior. Efforts to reduce uncertainty and opportunism increase the transaction costs (Grover & Malhotra, 2003).

According to transaction cost theory, in a market the coordination of supply and demand takes place between independent, loosely related partners. Parameters such as prices, quantities, and delivery schedules are determined by market forces. In contrast, hierarchies coordinate the flow of goods by an explicit control mechanism, i.e. management. Hence, attributes like prices, quantities or delivery schedules are subject to managerial decisions. This leads either to an intensive coordination with few trading partners or even vertical integration.

The theory assumes that firms seek to benefit from economies of scale as well as efficiency pressure. Both can occur if there is market coordination, i.e. several firms are specializing in certain goods, thus achieving economies of scale, and are competing with each other, which raises efficiency pressure. Both mechanisms decrease the costs of the goods. However, a market causes considerable transaction costs, i.e. locating a reliable supplier, establishing, monitoring, and enforcing a contract, and coordination with the market partner for the duration of cooperation. If a certain good involves significant investments in transaction-specific capital resources, so-called asset specificity, the number of firms offering these goods becomes smaller and competition among firms diminishes. Those few firms providing these goods recognize their importance and tend to act more opportunistically. This further increases the transaction costs to prevent opportunistic behavior (Lin, Huang, & Lin, 2002). Simultaneously, their economies of scale and efficiency pressure may be lower, which increases the costs of the good. Under such circumstances, a firm will tend to prefer hierarchies over markets, because transaction costs are reduced and the savings on the costs of goods are limited in market coordination.

IOIS significantly support the exchange of information both in markets and hierarchies. In particular, IOIS decrease transaction costs as they reduce bounded rationality by facilitating information exchange and allowing more information transparency. In literature, there are different opinions about the impact of IOIS on governance mechanisms. Malone, Yates, & Benjamin (1987) distinguish two effects: The electronic brokerage effect provides an electronic intermediary between trading partners, thus favoring markets. The electronic integration effect denotes the intensification of the business processes between trading partners, which results in a tendency toward hierarchies. While electronic marketplaces were less successful in practice than anticipated, the electronic integration between firms gained importance. The majority of researchers in this field conclude that IOIS rather favor hierarchy-based coordination (e. g., Malone, Yates, & Benjamin, 1987; Holland, 1997) which is also reflected in practice.

Agency Theory

Agency theory was used extensively to investigate different interorganizational phenomena. Its origin lies in information economics (Eisenhardt, 1989). The theory investigates to what extent contractual agreements between organizations contribute to efficient outcomes with accounting for varying levels of outcome uncertainty, risk aversion, and amount of information. An agency relationship is characterized by a principal who delegates work to the agent. The principal depends on the cooperation of the agent. The latter has "an information advantage" (Kleinaltenkamp & Jakob, 2002, p. 151) as the principal cannot be sure about the way the task is carried out by the agent. In interorganizational relationships, it is likely that there is a mutual interdependence. The risk sharing problem is addressed in agency theory by analyzing scenarios in which it is difficult or expensive for the principal to get to know what the agent is doing and whether is behaves appropriately. The theory seeks to elaborate maximum efficient contracts for governing the relationship.

Within agency theory, the principal-agent theory (in contrast to the positivist stream) is appropriate for analyzing interorganizational relationships (Eisenhardt, 1989). Of particular interest is information asymmetry between the principal and the agent which raises two problems: moral hazard and adverse selection. Moral hazard is the principal's inability to verify whether the agent undertakes the necessary effort or whether it is shirking. Adverse selection implies that the principal does not know totally whether the agent has the skills it claims to have. Both problems result in the principal's risk that the agent's behavior is unobservable. The principal may either apply information systems to unveil the agent's behavior or determine it by contractual agreements. Therefore central to agency theory is the trade-off between the costs of measuring the agent's behavior and the costs of measuring the outcomes (Eisenhardt, 1989).

Information asymmetries can be further distinguished into (1) hidden attributes which are not known when the contract is set up but become revealed later during task fulfillment, (2) hidden intention that refers to secret freedoms of the agent to change its behavior later, and (3) hidden action which is the agent's opportunistic behavior that can never be revealed by the principal (Kleinaltenkamp & Jakob, 2002). The key role of information asymmetry makes agency theory a particularly useful theoretical lens for investigating IOIS use. IOIS and the interorganizational information flow may impact these agency problems in two opposite directions:

On the one hand, the information flow may contribute to a lower information asymmetry as the information transparency between the trading partners is higher. Therefore the information flow can strengthen the principal's position by providing it with more control opportunities. At least moral hazard may be detected earlier if information is shared intensively. Thus, IOIS are an incentive for the principal to continue relationships with agents. For the agent, the increased information transparency, facilitated by IOIS, may be an incentive not to support the use of IOIS as this could weaken its position.

On the other hand, the information flow itself is part of the agency relationship. If the partners exchange information, they make themselves more vulnerable to their trading partner. A firm that disseminates information exposes itself to the risk of being cheated. The information shared may be abused in an opportunistic manner by the trading partner. For the principal, dissemination of information may further increase the information asymmetry, whereas information dissemination of the agent can reduce it. Thus, depending on how information sharing takes place between the principal and the agent, it may improve or weaken the relationship between the principal and the agent.

STRATEGIC MANAGEMENT APPROACHES

Research on IOIS in the field of strategic management seeks to explain different types of interorganizational relationships from a strategic point of view. Of particular interest are the strategic impact and opportunities that arise from such relationships (Kanter, 1994). A prominent approach is the resource-based view of the firm. In IS research it was applied extensively for explaining the benefits of information systems in organizations. The second strategic management approach discussed is network theory (Gulati, Nohria, & Zaheer, 2000). This approach investigates why and how independent organizations enter into network-kind relationships and particularly accounts for interorganizational relationships that comprise more than two involved organizations.

Resource-Based View of the Firm

The resource-based view of the firm (Barney, 1991) assumes that each firm possesses resources which enable it to achieve competitive advantages and long-term performance gains. Therefore an organization's resources are of key importance. Resources can be competencies, skills, assets, and stocks (Wade & Hulland, 2004). Several IS researchers argue that IS can be regarded as resources (Jarvenpaa & Leidner, 1998; Wade & Hulland, 2004) in the sense of the resource-based view. Some studies divide IS resources into *IS assets* (technology-based) and *IS capabilities* (systems-based). While IS assets can easily be copied by other firms, IS capabilities are more difficult to copy and can therefore better ensure sustainable advantages (Day, 1994).

When it comes to IOIS, one key assumption in the resource-based view has to be made: The theory implies that firms should rather protect, not share, resources with other companies. As a consequence, the theory does not point at advantages that arise from sharing of asset, knowledge, or information. Hence, at a first glance the theory seems to be inappropriate for explaining the strategic value of IOIS as such systems are by nature spanning across companies. If, however, the observed entity in the theory is not one single organization but a partnership or network of collaborating firms, it can be extended to an interorganizational context (Dyer & Singh, 1998; Dovev, 2002) and therefore also to IOIS. Within this approach that considers interorganizational relationships as unit of analysis competitive advantages can be achieved by (1) investments in relationship-specific assets, (2) information and knowledge sharing routines, (3) the combination of complementary, but scarce, resources or capabilities with resulting joint creation of unique new products, services or technologies, and (4) lower transaction costs than competing relationships due to more effective governance mechanisms.

IOIS are applicable to support the interorganizational relationship at all four levels: they substantially support information and knowledge-sharing routines as well as drastically reduce transaction costs. Besides that, IOIS can be customized to become a relation-specific asset, and they allow a joint creation of new products, services, or technologies.

Network Theory

The previously mentioned theories mainly focus on single organizations as the unit of analysis. Some researches also apply suppler-customer dyads as the unit of analysis. In contrast, research on interorganizational networks highlights the relevance of long-term networks consisting of more than two organizations. The establishment of networks is a significant strategic management decision (Gulati, Nohria, & Zaheer, 2000). Network theory seeks to answer the following questions (Amit & Zott, 2001): (1) why and how are networks formed? (2) What interfirm relationships allow a firm to compete successfully in the market? (3) How is value created in a network? (4) How do firms' positions and relationships in networks impact their performance?

In a network, organizations are nodes which are linked with others and fulfill the role of actors. The whole network is influenced by its environment (Poulymenakou & Klein, 2006). The concept of strategic networks was particularly raised because traditional approaches that focused on single organizations lacked in accounting for the tight relationships between an organization and its surroundings (Gulati, Nohria, & Zaheer, 2000). Network theory allows extending the coordination mechanisms of transaction cost theory to hybrid coordination mechanisms between markets and hierarchies. It also adds trust as an impact factor. Networks combine key characteristics of both coordination mechanisms: specialization of functions, efficiency pressure, opportunism, and information isles (markets) and function integration, protection from market pressure, trust, and information integration (hierarchies). Networks are supposed to combine the advantageous elements of both coordination mechanisms, i.e. the function specialization and efficiency pressure as market elements and trust and information integration as hierarchy-related, which makes the whole network more competitive (Corsten & Gössinger, 2008).

IOIS are key enablers of interfirm networks as they create the necessary prerequisites of regular information exchange (Reimers & Klein, 2006). By facilitating ongoing information exchange, IOIS can increase trust in a network. But IOIS can also be a driver, if firms establish networks to create joint IOIS. IOIS play a crucial role for the formation of networks in three ways (Poulymenakou & Klein, 2006): (1) IOIS provide information and communication channels which enable the coordination between the members in the network, (2) IOIS are often used as necessary devices for information partnerships, i.e. a collaboration based on an extensive sharing of information among organizations (Konsynski & McFarlan, 1990), and (3) IOIS are an enabler for innovative business and collaboration models.

The application of IOIS in networks is also referred to as business networking (Österle, Fleisch, & Alt, 2001). The strategic perspective refers to the long-term collaboration agreement with trading partners. However, the mere availability of IOIS does not guarantee that a company is able to conduct interfirm collaboration. Instead, a certain level of "networkability" is required (Alt & Fleisch, 2001) that depends on the adoption and use of IOIS, the availability of internal IS, and an alignment of IT and business processes. Business networking can take place at several levels. The first step is data sharing is mainly performed via enterprise resource planning (ERP) systems or electronic data interchange (EDI). Supply chain management systems provide tools for planning tasks. E-Commerce systems are used for the electronic support of business transactions and support all phases of a transaction (Alt & Fleisch, 2001).

GAME THEORIES

Game theoretic approaches were largely used to explain collaboration in supply chains. Their main goal is to develop models which compute or simulate the benefits and costs of collaboration. A key impact factor is information sharing. Therefore whereas IOIS themselves are often considered cost of information sharing, the benefits they accrue through enabling information sharing are well explained by game theoretic studies.

Generally speaking, game theory concerns the "analysis of situations involving conflict and cooperation" (Leng & Parlar, 2005, p. 187). In the context of interorganizational information sharing, game theoretic research analyzes the conditions under which cooperation yields more favorable results than isolated action. The research efforts in the game theory context can be distinguished into non-cooperative games where players act independently from each other and cooperative games in which players interact, exchange information, and execute action together. The latter are therefore of particular interest in the context of IOIS use. Cooperative games with two players usually use the Nash arbitration scheme for solution, whereas games that involve at least three players usually refer to the Shapley value and the nucleolus (Leng & Parlar, 2005).

Game theory-based analyses on information sharing have in common that the exchange of information, particularly the dissemination of demand by customer to the supplier yields considerable benefits to the whole supply chain. Trading partners can better optimize their own policies and reduce uncertainty which enhances the chance of correct decisions. Chu and Lee (2006) argue that a main problem to any supply chain is the fact that the stock level of the supply chain is determined by the suppliers which are upstream the supply chain and therefore less informed about market demand than downstream members (e.g. retailers). They conclude that it becomes necessary that the better informed downstream members share information with the less informed upstream members and thus call for information sharing to improve the efficiency of a supply chain. If a more differentiated look is made at the research findings, it becomes obvious that varying results exist concerning the benefits, profiting trading partners, and the conditions under which information sharing and therefore the use of IOIS yields benefits.

Another stream of research focuses on incentives to share information. For example, under the assumption that information sharing causes costs to the better informed part, the benefits must be fairly distributed in order to provide an incentive for information sharing (Chu and Lee, 2006). Costs of information sharing arise from necessary investments and maintenance of IOIS.

With a few exceptions game theoretic research concludes that information sharing between organizations can contribute to savings, cost decreases, and performance increases. The information flow can particularly result in a reduction of uncertainties which often induce supply chain members to behave in a suboptimal way. Simulations under different assumptions demonstrate that information sharing is useful in many cases. As IOIS are considered costs of the information flow it becomes obvious that these IOIS-related costs can be offset by increasingly efficient supply chains enabled by these systems.

COMPARISON OF THEORIES AND FRAMEWORK DEVELOPMENT

Although the theoretical approaches discussed above chiefly originate from different disciplinary backgrounds, they show numerous similarities in the context of IOIS use, information sharing, and interfirm coordination. Table 1 summarizes the main findings of analysis of the seven theories in respect of their suggested impact on IOIS use and the supposed impact of IOIS use.

Social exchange theory, embeddedness theory, and network theory provide explanations of factors that drive the use of IOIS and therefore consider IOIS use a dependent variable. In this context, especially trust plays a key role. All three theories imply that mutual trust between trading partners is a driver of an intensified information exchange and therefore of the use of IOIS. Besides that, social exchange theory also considers commitment and power important drivers of IOIS use, which is also demonstrated empirically. Whereas commitment is clearly positively related to IOIS use, power is a more complex mechanism related to IOIS use. Power is partly related to other factors that may be drivers of IOIS use themselves, such as firm size, sufficient funds or expertise which allows such firms to achieve high benefits. Thus such firms may exercise power to induce their trading partners to adopt and use IOIS. In addition to that, power is also interrelated with trust: if a company applies coercive power, it is likely to reduce its trading partner's trust. Under such circumstances, IOIS use may take place involuntarily and without trust.

Interestingly, the other discussed theories do not directly imply drivers of IOIS use. As they, however, point at considerable impacts resulting from IOIS use, all these approaches have in common that implicitly there are incentives to use IOIS. These incentives are based on the expectations of benefits achieved by IOIS. The factors that are part of the theories, however, do not contain perceived benefits as explicit variables.

The use of IOIS as an independent variable, i.e., a factor that impacts other variables, is explained by all analyzed theories. Based on the different assumptions, also the kinds of impacts differ from each other. The three theories that discuss trust (social exchange theory, embeddedness theory, and network theory) point at the double effect of IOIS use: if firms use IOIS they provide an infrastructure for intensifying information sharing. Mutual information sharing further increases trust as each trading partner gets more information about the other firm. Furthermore, IOIS can be regarded as a relationship-specific asset, which demonstrates commitment, as suggested by social exchange theory. Thus, in these theories, IOIS are part of a continuous and ever intensifying loop: trust facilitates the use of IOIS and the use of IOIS facilitates trust. If there are no external factors or substantial disadvantages of certain IOIS that distort this development, IOIS can be assumed to be a strong catalyst of intensive interorganizational relationships and collaboration. This development is further strengthened by the benefits achieved by information sharing and therefore IOIS use (see below).

The economics-oriented theories, i.e. transaction cost theory and agency theory, have in common that they put a strong focus on uncertainties, transaction costs, and information asymmetries.

Table 1. Main consequences of the discussed theories for IOIS use in interfirm relationships

Theory	Basic assumptions	Impact on IOIS use	Impact of IOIS usage	Missing issues
Social exchange Theory	Dyadic relationship is influenced by trust, commitment, and power.	Trust and commitment drive use of IOIS. Exercised power by influencer increases IOIS adoption by influencee (following or anticipating influencers' innovations).	IOIS as a proof of commitment. IOIS facilitate exchange of information and increase trust. IOIS can increase influencer's power. IOIS can increase influencee's power.	Interfirm networks (more than two firms) Transaction costs Competitive advantages Benefits and costs of IOIS
Embeddedness theory	Role of embedded relationship for formation and success of interfirm linkages, driven by information sharing, joint business processes, and trust.	Embeddedness positively impacts IOIS use.	IOIS facilitate information sharing and joint processes, thus increasing trust.	Transaction costs Opportunism Interfirm networks Benefits and costs
Transaction cost theory	Influence of asset specificity and uncertainty on coordination. Markets: loose relationship Hierarchies: highly integrated relationship	n/a	IOIS decrease transaction costs. Two possible impacts: electronic integration effect (toward hierarchy, more practiced) and electronic brokerage effect (toward market, less practiced).	Interfirm networks (hybrid forms between markets and hierarchies) Trust Power Benefits and costs
Agency theory	Information asymmetry: information advantage of agent over principal and potential opportunistic behavior by agent.	n/a	IOIS increase information transparency and control: reduce uncertainty for principle, increase information asymmetry if principal disseminates information, and reduces information asymmetry if agent disseminates information.	Transaction costs Interfirm networks Benefits and costs Power Trust
Resource-based view of the firm	Resources as a means of attaining and sustaining competitive advantages. IS as resource for single firm. IOIS as resource for interorganizational relationships.	n/a	IOIS increase competitiveness and thus achieve benefits.	Interpersonal relationships Trust Power Opportunism Governance mechanisms
Network theory	Interorganizational relationships between more than two partners. Hybrid forms between markets and hierarchies.	IOIS as objective of network. Trust increases IOIS use.	IOIS as enablers of network. IOIS use is increased by trust.	Transaction costs Benefits and costs Power Opportunism
Game theories	Uncertainties and information asymmetry among supply chain members which are reduced by information sharing.	n/a	Facilitate information sharing, thus allowing to achieve considerable benefits for all engaged trading partners (depending on external conditions).	Trust Power Interpersonal relationships Governance mechanisms

In respect of the impact of IOIS use, both theories have two different implications: in transaction cost theory IOIS might favor both market- and hierarchy-based coordination mechanisms. In agency theory IOIS use may decrease or increase the existing information asymmetries between principal and agent. In these two approaches the empirical evidence has to show which impacts are stronger. In transaction cost theory, practice demonstrates that IOIS rather increase higher integration, i.e., hierarchy-oriented coordination mechanisms. In agency theory, these impacts are not so obvious. However, power could serve as a possible explanation of how principal-agent relationships may be influenced by IOIS.

The resource-based view as well as game theory addresses benefits as factors impacted by IOIS. Both approaches conclude that IOIS increase benefits for both or all involved organizations. Interestingly, these two approaches make very different assumptions: While the resource-based view argues that the benefit of IOIS is related to its attributes as a valuable resource, game theories relate these benefits to the behavior and processes that are enabled by IOIS. Similarly, network theory argues that IOIS are enablers of interorganizational networks and certain processes within them.

The relations among the variables of the investigated seven theories discussed in Table 1 are summarized in the following framework (see Figure 1).

Based on the findings obtained by the analysis of the theories, one might wonder why the participation in IOIS use and interorganizational collaboration are not larger in practice (Madlberger, 2009). One possible reason lies in the characteristics of IOIS that are used in practice. Classical, wide-spread IOIS, such as electronic data interchange (EDI) systems, are often expensive to implement. Internet-based IOIS, e.g., b2b exchanges or XML/EDI are less expensive, but are often considered less attractive due to technology lock-in of established IOIS. Furthermore, like in many large IS implementations, firms are exposed to high risks of failure. If implementation costs are too high, the use of IOIS might lose its justification and the proposed tendency toward IOIS use and establishment of interfirm linkages diminishes. But if the cost-benefit relation of IOIS and interfirm collaboration is beneficial, there are no substantial arguments against the use of IOIS and interfirm collaboration.

Figure 1. A framework of seven theories investigating IOIS use and IOIS impacts

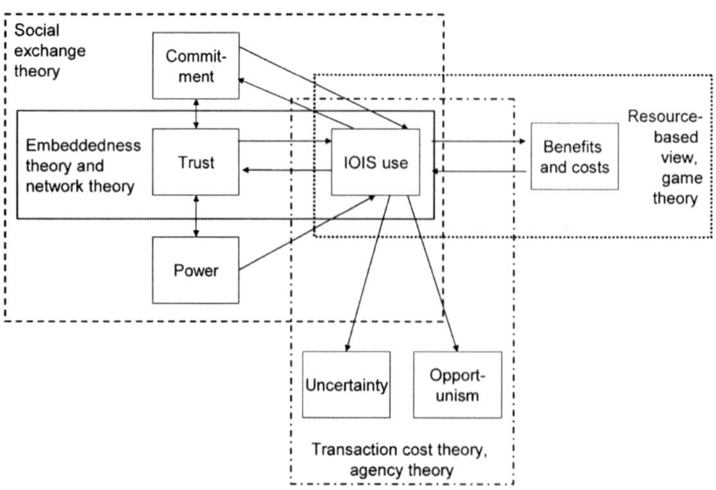

CONCLUSION

This chapter investigates the use and impacts of IOIS in companies to support their interorganizational relationships. Although the focus is put on the behavioral, business, and economic issues of IOIS, thus leaving out the technical perspective of IOIS, this research field is very interdisciplinary and can be subject of many, often very diverging theories. To the author's present knowledge a systematic analysis of theories in respect of their implications of IOIS is not available at present. The analysis presented in this chapter selects seven theories based on four main research areas, each of which has a different focus.

Despite the different backgrounds and even research disciplines (organization, sociology, economics, strategic management, and game theory) the congruence of findings is surprisingly high. All analyzed theories imply that information sharing and the use of IOIS is beneficial. The interesting issue in this result is that the same result is achieved in very different ways by the theories. The organization theories and network theory stress the key role of trust, social exchange theory in particular also commitment and power. The economics-related theories point at the positive, i.e., reducing effect on uncertainty and opportunism. Both phenomena negatively impact interorganizational relationships as well as the efficiency of interorganizational processes, such as supply chain management. The resource-based view of the firm suggests that IOIS are a resource that can contribute to obtain and sustain competitive advantages. This conclusion is based on the implication of the theory that IS are a resource. Therefore this finding has a different basis than the argumentations of the other theories. Finally, game theories use a mathematical approach to simulate and demonstrate formally the beneficial impacts of information sharing and thus IOIS. In addition, social exchange theory, embeddedness theory, and network theory also explain key antecedents of IOIS use.

The proposed framework can be considered a starting point for systematically investigating the complex drivers and implications of IOIS use and its benefits. Based on seven theories, the analysis should be further extended to more theoretical approaches to get a more complete understanding of the research field. To extend the analysis beyond the strict focus on the business administration and economics-related issue, several further research streams should be considered. First, theories grounded in IS research can contribute to a better understanding of the drivers of IOIS use and impacts from the technological perspective. Such an extension could provide insights whether the technological viewpoint strengthens or contradicts the findings based on the analysis made. Further valuable results could be achieved if social sciences as well as sociological theories were included in the analysis as they would bring further insights into the behavioral perspective that is not necessarily related to the economic dimension.

Additionally, there needs to be a clear conceptual differentiation between the use of IOIS and information sharing. In interesting research avenue is the identification of an optimum of information sharing and related IOIS. A limitation in this approach is that this distinction is not accounted for in the framework. To get more insights into the key dimensions of IOIS, a more structured approach of IOIS use and its benefits is needed. This implies a systematic review of different types of IOIS (e.g., EDI, Web portals, or electronic marketplaces), levels of usage intensity (e.g., with different trading partners or business areas), levels of frequency, and purpose (strategic and operational). Such an in-depth approach also calls for a thorough analysis of the costs and cost structures of IOIS and thus a strong integration of the economic perspective of IOIS.

REFERENCES

Alt, R., & Fleisch, E. (2001). Business networking systems: Characteristics and lessons learned. *International Journal of Electronic Commerce*, *5*(2), 7–27.

Amit, R., & Zott, C. (2001). Value creation in e-business. *Strategic Management Journal*, *22*(6/7), 493–520. doi:10.1002/smj.187

Bakos, Y., & Brynjolfsson, E. (1993). From vendors to partners: Information technology and incomplete contracts in buyer-supplier relationships. *Journal of Organizational Computing and Electronic Commerce*, *3*(3), 301–328. doi:10.1080/10919399309540206

Barney, J. (1991). Firm resources and sustained competitive advantage. *Journal of Management*, *17*(1), 99–120. doi:10.1177/014920639101700108

Chatfield, A. T., & Yetton, P. (2000). Strategic payoff from EDI as a function of EDI embeddedness. *Journal of Management Information Systems*, *16*(4), 195–224.

Chu, W. H. J., & Lee, C. C. (2006). Strategic information sharing in a supply chain. *European Journal of Operational Research*, *174*(3), 1567–1579. doi:10.1016/j.ejor.2005.02.053

Clark, T. H., Croson, D. C., & Schiano, W. T. (2001). A hierarchical model of supply-chain integration: Information sharing and operational interdependence in the US grocery channel. *Information Technology Management*, *2*(3), 261–288. doi:10.1023/A:1011497025090

Corsten, H., & Gössinger, R. (2008). *Einführung in das Supply Chain Management*. Munich, Germany: Oldenbourg.

Day, G. S. (1994). The capabilities of market-driven organizations. *Journal of Marketing*, *58*(4), 37–52. doi:10.2307/1251915

Doney, P. M., & Cannon, J. P. (1997). An examination of the nature of trust in buyer-seller relationships. *Journal of Marketing*, *61*(2), 35–51. doi:10.2307/1251829

Dovev, L. (2002). The competitive advantage of interconnected firms: An extension of the resource-based view. *Academy of Management Proceedings*, C1-7.

Dwyer, F. R., Schurr, P. H., & Oh, S. (1987). Developing buyer-seller relationships. *Journal of Marketing*, *51*(2), 11–27. doi:10.2307/1251126

Dyer, J. H., & Singh, H. (1998). The relational view: Cooperative strategy and sources of inter-organizational competitive advantage. *Academy of Management Review*, *23*(4), 660–679.

Eisenhardt, K. M. (1989). Agency theory: An assessment and review. *Academy of Management Review*, *14*(1), 57–74.

French, J. R., & Raven, B. (1959). The bases of social power. In Cartwright, D. (Ed.), *Studies in social power* (pp. 150–167). Ann Arbor, MI: Institute for Social Research.

Gaski, J. F., & Nevin, J. R. (1985). The differential effects of exercised and unexercised power sources in a marketing channel. *JMR, Journal of Marketing Research*, *22*(2), 130–142. doi:10.2307/3151359

Granovetter, M. (1985). Economic action and social structure: The problem of embeddedness. *American Journal of Sociology*, *91*(3), 481–510. doi:10.1086/228311

Grover, V., & Malhotra, M. K. (2003). Transaction cost framework in operations and supply chain management research: Theory and measurement. *Journal of Operations Management*, *21*(4), 457–473. doi:10.1016/S0272-6963(03)00040-8

Gulati, R., Nohria, N., & Zaheer, A. (2000). Strategic networks. *Strategic Management Journal*, *21*(3), 203–215. doi:10.1002/(SICI)1097-0266(200003)21:3<203::AID-SMJ102>3.0.CO;2-K

Gulati, R., & Singh, H. (1998). The Architecture of cooperation: Managing coordination costs and appropriation concerns in strategic alliances. *Administrative Science Quarterly*, *43*(4), 781–814. doi:10.2307/2393616

Hart, P. J., & Saunders, C. S. (1997). Power and trust: Critical factors in the adoption and use of electronic data interchange. *Organization Science*, *8*(1), 23–42. doi:10.1287/orsc.8.1.23

Holland, C. P. (1997). The evolution of electronic hierarchies in business markets. *Wirtschaftsinformatik*, *39*(3), 245–253.

Jarvenpaa, S. L., & Leidner, D. E. (1998). An information company in Mexico: Extending the resource-based view of the firm to a developing country context. *Information Systems Research*, *9*(4), 342–361. doi:10.1287/isre.9.4.342

Kankanhalli, A., Tan, B. C. Y., & Wei, K.-K. (2005). Contributing knowledge to electronic knowledge repositories: An empirical investigation. *Management Information Systems Quarterly*, *29*(1), 113–143.

Kanter, R. M. (1994). Collaborative advantage: The art of alliances. *Harvard Business Review*, *4*(July-August), 96–108.

Kingshott, R. P. J. (2006). The impact of psychological contracts upon trust and commitment within supplier-buyer relationships: A social exchange view. *Industrial Marketing Management*, *35*(6), 724–739. doi:10.1016/j.indmarman.2005.06.006

Kleinaltenkamp, M., & Jacob, F. (2002). German approaches to business-to-business marketing theory origins and structure. *Journal of Business Research*, *55*(2), 149–155. doi:10.1016/S0148-2963(00)00150-8

Konsynski, B. R., & McFarlan, F. W. (1990). Information partnerships – Shared data, shared scale. *Harvard Business Review*, *68*(5), 114–120.

Kwon, I. W. G., & Suh, T. (2004). Factors affecting the level of trust and commitment in supply chain relationship. *Journal of Supply Chain Management*, *40*(2), 4–14. doi:10.1111/j.1745-493X.2004.tb00165.x

Leng, M., & Parlar, M. (2005). Game theoretic applications in supply chain management: A review. *Infor*, *43*(3), 187–220.

Leuthesser, L., & Kohli, A. K. (1995). Relational behavior in business markets: Implications for relationship management. *Journal of Business Research*, *34*(3), 221–233. doi:10.1016/0148-2963(95)00006-E

Lin, F.-R., Huang, S.-H., & Lin, S.-C. (2002). Effects of information sharing on supply chain performance in electronic commerce. *IEEE Transactions on Engineering Management*, *49*(3), 258–268. doi:10.1109/TEM.2002.803388

Lin, H.-M. (2006). Interorganizational collaboration, social embeddedness, and value creation: A theoretical analysis. *International Journal of Management*, *23*(3), 548–558.

Madlberger, M. (2009). What drives firms to engage in interorganizational information sharing in supply chain management? *International Journal of e-Collaboration*, *5*(2), 18–42. doi:10.4018/jec.2009040102

Madlberger, M., & Roztocki, N. (2008). Cross-organizational and cross-border IS/IT collaboration: A literature review. *Proceedings of the 14th Americas Conference on Information Systems*, Toronto.

Malone, T. W., Yates, J., & Benjamin, I. (1987). Electronic markets and electronic hierarchies. *Communications of the ACM*, *30*(6), 484–497. doi:10.1145/214762.214766

Massetti, B., & Zmud, R. W. (1996). Measuring the extent of EDI usage in complex organizations: Strategies and illustrative examples. *Management Information Systems Quarterly*, *20*(3), 331–345. doi:10.2307/249659

Mayer, R. C., Davis, J. H., & Schoorman, F. D. (1995). An integrative model of organizational trust. *Academy of Management Review, 29*(3), 709–734.

Morgan, R. M., & Hunt, S. D. (1994). The commitment-trust theory in relationship marketing. *Journal of Marketing, 58*(3), 20–38. doi:10.2307/1252308

Nguyen, H. M., & Harrison, N. J. (2004). Electronic supply-chain orientation and its competitive dimensions. *Production Planning and Control, 15*(6), 596–607. doi:10.1080/09537280412331283946

Osborn, R. N., & Hagedoorn, J. (1997). The institutionalization and evolutionary dynamics of interorganizational alliances and networks. *Academy of Management Journal, 40*(2), 261–278. doi:10.2307/256883

Österle, H., Fleisch, E., & Alt, R. (2001). *Business networking: Shaping collaboration between enterprises*. Berlin, Germany: Springer.

Poulymenakou, A., & Klein, S. (2006). Networks as orchestrations. In Klein, S., & Poulymenakou, A. (Eds.), *Managing dynamic networks* (pp. 3–15). Berlin, Germany: Springer. doi:10.1007/3-540-32884-X_1

Premkumar, G., & Ramamurthy, K. (1995). The role of interorganizational and organizational factors on the decision mode for adoption of interorganizational systems. *Decision Sciences, 26*(3), 303–336. doi:10.1111/j.1540-5915.1995.tb01431.x

Reimers, K., & Klein, S. (2006). Network management framework. In Klein, S., & Poulymenakou, A. (Eds.), *Managing dynamic networks* (pp. 17–66). Berlin, Germany: Springer.

Uzzi, B. (1997). Social structure and competition in interfirm networks: The paradox of embeddedness. *Administrative Science Quarterly, 42*(1), 35–67. doi:10.2307/2393808

Wade, M. R., & Hulland, J. (2004). The resource-based view and information systems research: Review, extension, and suggestions for future research. *Management Information Systems Quarterly, 28*(1), 107–142.

Williamson, O. E. (1975). *Markets and hierarchies: Analysis and antitrust implications. A study in the economics of internal organization*. New York, NY: The Free Press.

Yoshino, M., & Rangan, S. (1995). *Strategic alliances: An entrepreneurial approach to globalization*. Boston, MA: Harvard Business School Press.

Chapter 4
Transaction Costs in Inter-Organizational Systems:
Theory and Selected Examples in Supply Management

Michael Essig
Bundeswehr University Munich, Germany

Raphael Boerner
Bundeswehr University Munich, Germany

ABSTRACT

Transaction Cost Economics (TCE) describes the fact that markets are incomplete. This might go without saying—but nevertheless TCE delivers rigorous instruments for microeconomic analysis combined with their application for managerial recommendations. As a result, TCE became quite popular in academia in the late 1990s and early 2000s. We show this by an analysis of scientific databases and journals.

Besides describing the core elements of TCE, this paper also shows the application of this concept for purchasing and supply decisions. Therefore, we do have a closer look on outsourcing problems, sourcing strategy decisions, and information technology/e-procurement adoption.

INTRODUCTION

Transaction Cost Economics (TCE) was once described as "revolutionary" in economic theory. Even though this seems to be a bit excessive, TCE is a major approach to combining the rigorous instruments of microeconomic analysis with the practical relevance of incomplete markets. Instead of comparing "relevance versus rigor," TCE offers the opportunity to combine both aspects through scientific research that combines a sound theoretical basis with concrete implications for management.

DOI: 10.4018/978-1-60960-768-5.ch004

Copyright © 2012, IGI Global. Copying or distributing in print or electronic forms without written permission of IGI Global is prohibited.

The fact that transaction costs occur both within companies and among companies in a market make TCE an ideal approach for inter-organizational (information) systems. Additionally, as a microeconomic-based approach, it can also be used for managerial purposes. In this chapter, we have determined an inter-organizational approach by using the perspective of a company using (and buying) outside resources, which means a concentration of supply management activities.

To develop these managerial and inter-organizational insights, we first start with the basics of transaction cost economics which ensures an understanding and comprehension of the context. This chapter illustrates the state of the art in TCE which implies a narrow description of the core elements of TCE, the problem of uncertainty and finally the current status in research.

In the second part of the present work, we are applying TCE to selected examples in/for procurement. The applications relate to outsourcing, procurement strategy formulation and e-procurement adaption.

BASICS OF TRANSACTION COST THEORY

Core Elements of Transaction Cost Economics

Aside from being a theory and agency of property rights, transaction cost economics is one of the core elements of new institutional economics. All three elements are closely linked, according to the theories developed by Coase (1937) and Williamson (1985), the main representatives of TCE.

There are a few basic behavioral assumptions of the new institutional economics that are important for a clear understanding of the heuristic TCE model formulated by Williamson (1985):

- Bounded rationality must be understood as a construct of decision-making behavior, which is located in between so-called absolute rationality and process rationality. Because of incomplete information and restricted human information processing, rationality never can be complete (Simon 1976).
- Opportunism is the main characteristic of the pursuit of individual interests (Williamson 1985).
- Methodological individualism means that multi-person organizations such as companies do not have their own personalities; they are just a conglomerate of individuals.
- Property rights are the main interest of the economic analysis in new institutional economics. They are handled in a purely physical or relative-legal manner. Because of this, Williamson (1989) considers the firm (and the cooperation) a "nexus of treaties."

Coase was the first to spread the idea that usage of markets to realize transactions normally incurs costs. The object of analysis is the transaction. Transactions in general are defined as "not the 'exchange of commodities,' but the alienation and acquisition, between individuals, of the rights of property and liberty created by society, which must therefore be negotiated between the parties concerned before labor can produce, or consumers can consume, or commodities be physically exchanged." (Commons, 1931, p. 652). Economic cooperation exists because there are transaction costs to using the market (or price mechanism). The costs of finding an exchange partner and agreeing to and controlling the transaction are defined as transaction costs. Aside from production costs, there are costs to finding a transaction partner, negotiating, contracting and managing contract fulfillment. Originally, Coase's idea "that there is a cost of using the price mechanism" (Coase, 1937, p. 390) limited transaction costs to the institution of markets. Based on the idea that the price mechanism is the most efficient way to handle economic transactions, Coase used transaction cost economics to explain the existence of the firm. Nowadays, transaction costs are used in a wider sense and exist (a) when using markets (transaction costs in a closer sense) and (b) when using organizations (hierarchy costs) for handling transactions. Hierarchy costs include costs for establishing a suitable organizational structure or an incentive system for employees. Transaction costs in this wider sense depend on:

- uncertainty as a result of opportunism (which will be analyzed in detail in chapter 2.2),
- strategic importance of the transaction,
- frequency of the transaction,
- asset specificity, which means, particularly, (1) site specificity, (2) physical asset specificity, (3) human capital specificity, (4) dedicated assets, and (5) brand name capital.

Williamson (1985) developed a heuristic model based on the ideas of Coase. In his opinion, "asset specificity is [the] most important and most distinctive" (Williamson 1989) characteristic of transactions. As Figure 1 shows, institutions provides the framework for transactions in general. Hence, the choice of institution determines and influences transaction costs. Concurrently,

Figure 1. Production cost and transaction cost

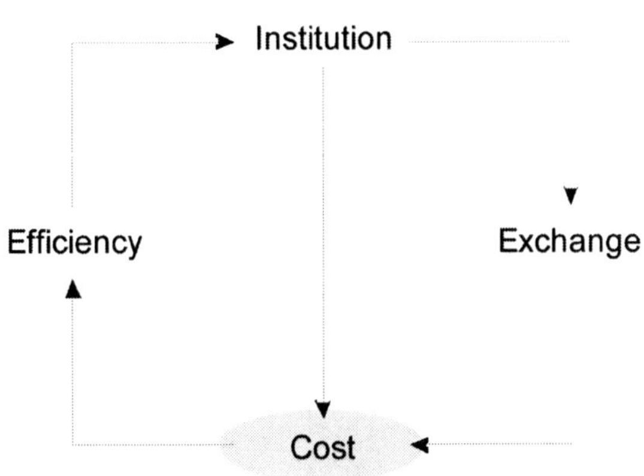

transaction costs constitute the choice of institution for processing.

Low specificity means a highly standardized good. It is easy to find transaction partners for standardized goods on markets; it is also easy to control their quality. As a result, unspecific transactions can be handled on markets with low transaction costs. On the other hand, it becomes more and more expensive to handle transactions with higher specificity in markets. The control problems are insoluble. It is impossible to give market partners detailed descriptions for manufacturing or R&D. There is a point of specificity where market advantages turn into disadvantages: where market transaction costs exceed hierarchical coordination costs. This is where hierarchically-steered companies start to exist.

It is not easy to define the "critical point" of specificity. Moreover, this dichotomy of market versus hierarchy has been criticized. One of the critical points is the "in-between" situation in the case of a middle degree of specificity, which causes interpretation problems. Neither market nor hierarchy can be preferred only on the basis of the marginal cost difference. Williamson himself argues that the institutional decisions are often based on "historical coincidence" (Williamson 1985).

As a consequence, a third *hybrid institution* with both market and hierarchical elements was introduced (Williamson 1990, Williamson 1991) and defined as a *cooperation* or *consortium*. The specificity-dependent cooperation costs X(s) have a pattern of cost behavior between the market and hierarchy (see Figure 2). The main reason for this was the empirical existence of a wide range of inter-organizational relationships, such as life-cycle supply contracts or joint ventures, which were neither market- nor hierarchically-steered. For example, the introduction of a just-in-time-based modular sourcing concept strongly integrates the supplier (Arnold, 1996, p. 1866). The supplier is held responsible for engineering activities and quality assurance for the specific module and handles the sub-suppliers. Therefore, he is linked strongly with his customer. Both parties, buyer and supplier, depend on each other, and nobody can end this business relationship easily. By installing a factory within a factory system (Arnold and Scheuing, 1997, p. 82), the supplier becomes more and more a kind of customer department. There exists neither a clear market relationship nor a clear hierarchical relationship.

The validity of the central hypothesis concerning cooperation mostly refers to vertical cooperation, especially make-or-buy decisions and vertical integration. Also, production costs are perceived to be negligible—markets are always seen as advantageous in terms of production cost because suppliers can make use of economies of scale.

The Problem of Uncertainty

In general, transactions (in this case, supply transactions) simply must be uncertain because the buyer never knows all aspects of the performance of his suppliers and their future development. With respect to the problem of restricted information, even "contracts are unavoidably incomplete" (Williamson, 1985, p. 190) because they can never cover all possibilities of future developments. We distinguish between three main types of uncertainty (see Figure 3): risk, uncertainty in a closer sense, and bounded rationality (Backhaus, Aufderheide and Spath, 1994, pp. 19 f.). Within risk and uncertain situations, the buyer knows all possible actions of the supplier in the future. For example, he knows that the supplier might end up with financial problems. In a risk situation, supply management has an idea about the probability of appearance and can decide whether or not such a risk is too high. Uncertainty in a closer sense means that the buying organization has no idea about this probability. Bounded rationality goes one step further: possible future actions of the supplier are unknown to the buyer. This is the most realistic situation—most buyers in fact do *not* know that the supplier might have financial

Figure 2. Cooperation and consortium as a hybrid institution (Williamson 1991)

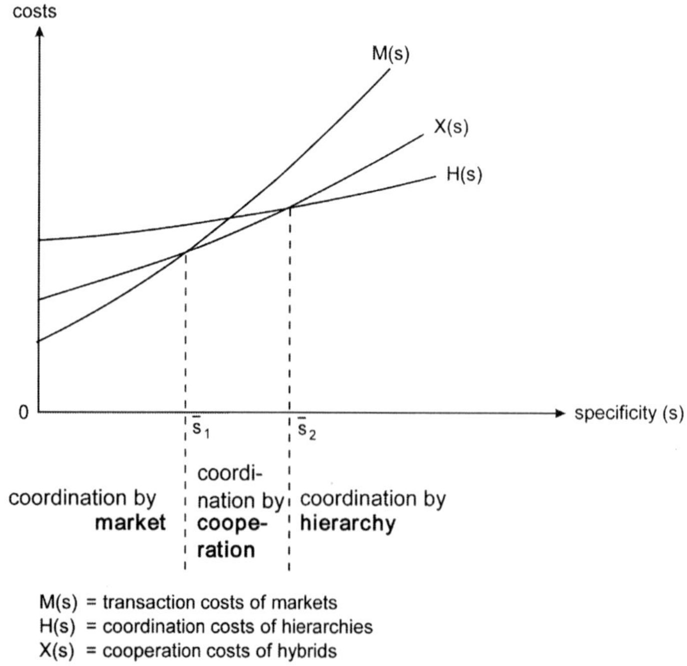

problems; if they did, they would not contract with the supplier.

Only in perfect markets is information complete (nirvana). In all other—realistic—market situations, we distinguish between two kinds of information deficit: ex ante and ex post information deficits. Information-seeking activities might be able to close or narrow ex ante deficits, but information-seeking is of course costly. For example, a buyer spends time on auditing a supplier (staff costs); he sends faxes (communication costs) and incurs traveling expenses, among other things. Transaction costs increase because information is not a free good in imperfect markets.

Ex post uncertainty seems to be a great problem. It means that suppliers react in a self-interested, opportunistic way after being awarded a contract. The buyer knows *that* suppliers will behave opportunistically, but the buyer does not know *how*. Therefore, agreements must be made before signing a contract to reduce ex post information risks.

Nelson (1970) and Darby/Karni (1973) developed three information-based exchange situations, based on the existence of transaction costs. Mainly, they analyze purchasing situations of consumers, but the results can be transferred to business-to-business transactions as well. The three situations (Darby/Karni call them "qualities") are: "Search qualities which are known before purchase, experience qualities which are known costlessly only after purchase, and credence qualities which are expensive to judge even after purchase." (Darby/Karni, 1973, p. 69).

Figure 3. Information problems for transactions (Backhaus, Aufderheide, and Spath, 1994, p. 20)

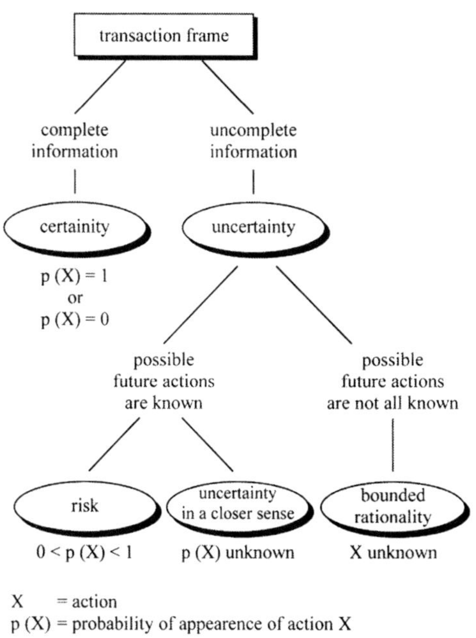

Complex industrial procurement situations are often a combination of these three qualities. Therefore, an information economics triangle helps to position combined supply situations (see Figure 4). For example, purchasing a new computer system solution for all business departments shows parts of all qualities: personal computers have experience qualities, which are known as ex ante (like the amount of RAM), and parts of the software functionality can be assessed after the customer-specific installation, but even after purchase the buying organization cannot be sure about the full adaptability of the system for all future releases.

State of the Art in Research

If we analyze the popularity of TCE both in business administration in general and in supply management, we can make use of some meta-data analyses. For this reason, we analyzed business administration-related databases, as well as specific journals. In all cases, we used the search term "transaction cost" and counted the number of articles in which this term occurs.

Searching the Science Direct and EBSCO databases, we find that the number of articles quadruples, from below 100 per year in the 1980s to 2009. From 1989 to 2009, the results from the EBSCO search increase from below 100 to more than 400; the results from Science Direct increase from below 200 to more than 800 (see Figure 5).

The picture is slightly different if we look into top-ranked management and business administra-

Figure 4. The information economics triangle (Weiber and Adler, 1995, p. 61)

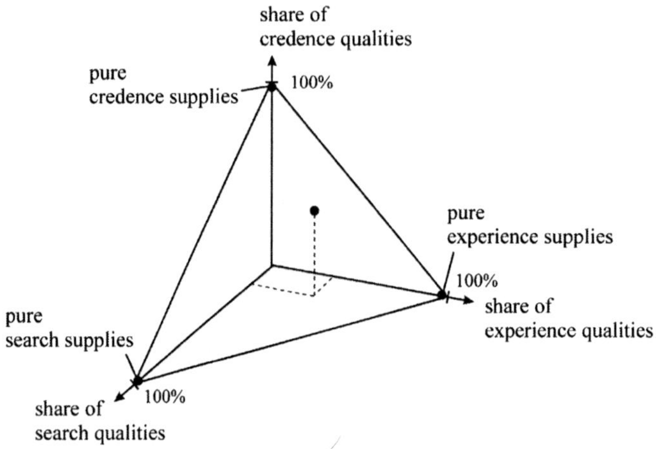

tion journals. As Figure 6 shows, we had a closer look at Academy of Management Journal, Academy of Management Review, Administrative Science Quarterly, and Management Science. Although the trend shows an increasing number, it is not as linear as we had previously observed from the EBSCO and Science direct databases. Instead, one can assume that the peaks have risen in the first half of the 2000 decade.

This declining trend since 2005/2006 can also be found if we analyze the Journal of Purchasing and Supply Management and its predecessor.

Figure 5. "Transaction cost" search results from Science Direct and EBSCO databases

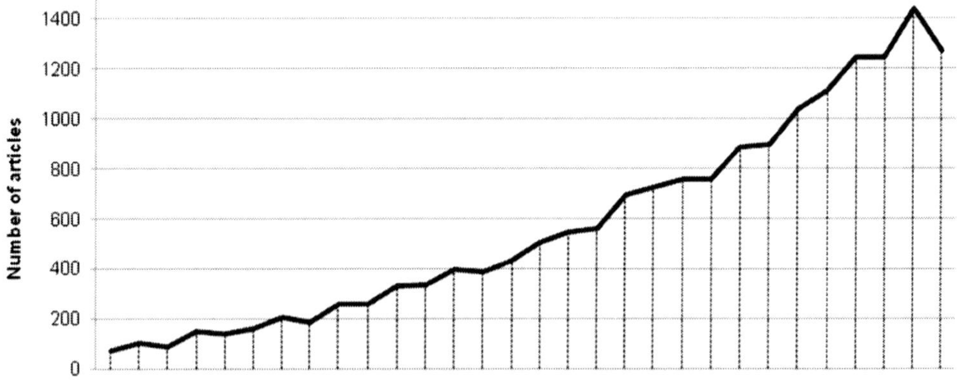

	1980	1981	1982	1983	1984	1985	1986	1987	1988	1989	1990	1991	1992	1993	1994	1995	1996	1997	1998	1999	2000	2001	2002	2003	2004	2005	2006	2007	2008	2009
Science direct	60	82	74	116	101	142	147	119	163	176	202	199	249	229	251	323	303	298	341	327	358	417	462	468	518	539	598	614	777	843
EBSCO	13	20	15	33	40	20	58	68	93	84	129	138	148	155	184	183	244	262	352	398	400	339	423	426	523	575	647	631	662	426

Figure 6. "Transaction cost" search results in top business journals

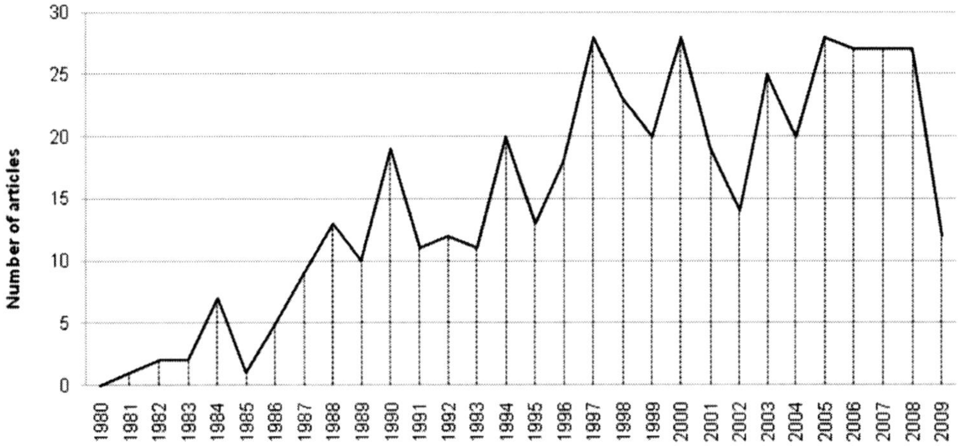

	1980	1981	1982	1983	1984	1985	1986	1987	1988	1989	1990	1991	1992	1993	1994
A. Of Mgmt. Journal	0	0	0	0	0	0	0	2	2	0	2	2	6	4	6
A. Of Mgmt. Review	0	1	0	1	2	0	1	1	5	5	14	2	1	3	5
Admin. Science Quarterly	0	0	0	0	4	1	2	2	4	2	2	4	3	1	4
Mgmt. Science	0	0	2	1	1	0	2	4	2	3	1	3	2	3	5

	1995	1996	1997	1998	1999	2000	2001	2002	2003	2004	2005	2006	2007	2008	2009
A. Of Mgmt. Journal	2	6	11	3	4	14	8	4	7	7	6	9	9	11	7
A. Of Mgmt. Review	4	6	11	12	9	11	4	4	9	3	9	8	9	8	5
Admin. Science Quarterly	5	5	5	2	3	2	4	2	3	2	2	1	2	4	0
Mgmt. Science	2	1	1	6	4	1	3	4	6	8	11	9	7	4	0

Figure 7 shows the numbers in detail. All together, the theory is of great popularity and did not really lose attractiveness for researchers, although the numbers were weaker in the last five years.

APPLICATION OF TRANSACTION COST: SELECTED EXAMPLES

The strategic perspective of supply management, which is an integrative approach combining purchasing, logistics, and materials management (Arnold 1989, p. 51 f., Arnold 1997, p. 2-9, Leenders/Fearon 1997, p. 3ff.), can be justified by the enormous profit impact of purchasing; materials costs are often more than 50% of sales income for industrial businesses (Dobler/Burt 1996, p. 27). It is "common sense" to understand purchasing as a relevant strategic activity in modern business theory. Since the 1980s, academics have published research on this topic (e.g., Arnold 1982, Grochla/Schonbohm 1980). As an important result of this research agenda, procurement has since been seen as a value chain activity that contributes significantly to competitive advantage, and is the basis for the fundamental mainstream research concept: "Purchasing is indeed strategic" (Carter/Narasimhan 1996, p. 20). Nevertheless, supply strategy *formulation* and the formulation process itself has not been a focused topic in purchasing research (Carr/Smeltzer 1997, p. 200).

Subsequent to the principles and relevance of TCE the applications will now be described in more detail based on selected examples from the perspective of strategic supply management. A

Figure 7. "Transaction cost" search results in the Journal of Purchasing and Supply Management

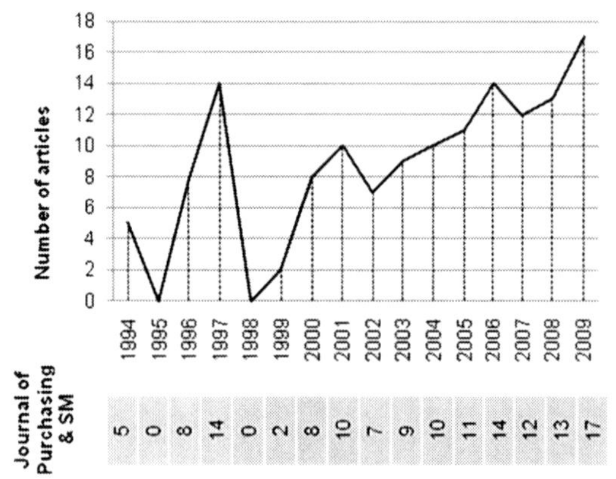

fundamental field of TCE affects the make-or-buy decision. It is the question whether or not purchasing is necessary (chapter 3.1). If necessary, an appropriate purchasing strategy is essential (chapter 3.2). After selection of the right strategy the question arises whether and how e-procurement could enhance purchasing (chapter 3.3).

Transaction Cost and Outsourcing

One of the major fields where TCE is used in business administration, supply management, and inter-organizational systems, is in the outsourcing (or make-or-buy) decision. In terms of its original meaning, the term *outsourcing* is an abbreviation for "outside resource using" (Quinn and Hilmer, 1994). To understand what this means, we have to analyze all three parts of this construct:

- *Outside* means creating value outside of the own company. With this exterior perspective, a company's border becomes increasingly interesting. The idea of a borderless organization means the integration of external partners for creating and adding value to end customers (Picot et al, 1996). Strategic networks arise. Early supplier involvement becomes a central element of the company's research & development strategy.
- This outside focus is not an end in itself. It means a strategic perspective on external *resources*. Following the resource-based view, the company can be understood as a unique complex of resources and knowledge (Penrose, 1959). Without these external resources, it would not be able to survive competition. It is supply management's job to analyze sourcing markets for obtaining competitive advantages. Therefore, purchasing must develop suitable instruments to perform a supplier-oriented strategy (Arnold, 1997).
- It is not enough to know about these external resources. They must be *used* by and for a company in order to reinforce its position in competition. Supply chain management is an approach that enable companies to exploit such resources for their individual purposes.

The outsourcing model consists of four major elements (see Figure 8): outsourcing subject, outsourcing object, outsourcing partner, and outsourcing design.

Outsourcing *subject* is the economic institution that plans to outsource (or not). The subject has to make the strategic outsourcing decision. Outsourcing *objects* are processes or process results that might be outsourced (Reichmann and Palloks, 1995). With regard to the activities of a company, we distinguish between (1) the company core (all activities that are necessarily connected with a company's existence), (2) core-close activities (directly linked with core activities), (3) core-distinct activities (supporting activities), and (4) disposable activities (activities with general availability). From an industrial perspective, the outsourcing object is closely linked with the degree of manufacturing penetration. Outsourcing *partners* are all possible suppliers for the activities considered for outsourcing. In this case, supplier

Figure 8. Outsourcing model

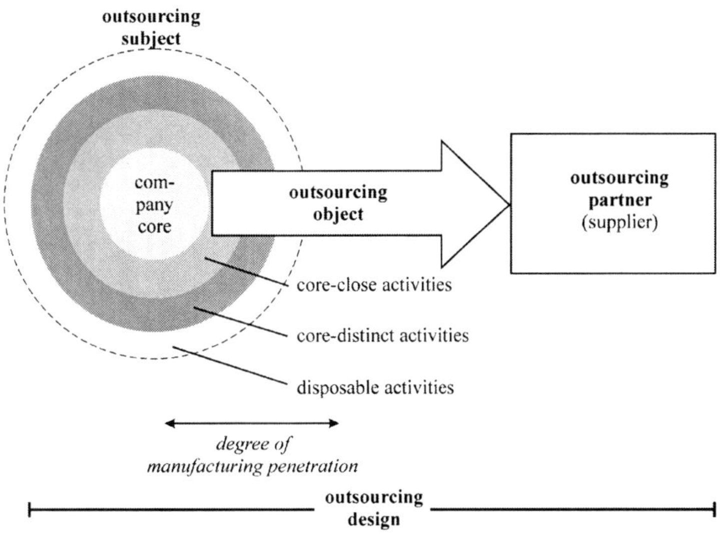

is a term in a wider sense. This supplier could also be an in-house supplier, e.g., an independent business unit within a group of firms. Outsourcing *design* is discussed below, basic design alternatives for the outsourcing decision can be based on the TCE institutions (see chapter 2.1 above).

The three major "governance structures" for economic activities (Williamson, 1985; Arnold, 1998) are linked as follows: As *Markets* steer transactions by the price mechanism, they are directly linked with outsourcing; *Hierarchies* are based on the centralization of property rights by management and therefore stand for insourcing. Administrative control mechanisms within a company facilitate the orientation on *one* target (e.g., the production of automobiles). *Hybrids* are a form of outsourcing because they all have market elements in their structures. We distinguish between internal and external outsourcing (see Figure 9). *External outsourcing* means spot transactions or long-term relationships with suppliers. *Internal outsourcing* refers to a higher degree of hierarchical steering (Zahn et al., 1998): by forming independent profit centers instead of hierarchical departments, the market element becomes relevant within a company (Krüger and Homp, 1997). If, for example, procurement operates as a profit center, all sourcing activities can be outsourced internally to an independent business unit. Internal outsourcing can also be organized as a horizontal cooperation of independent companies, sometimes by a general service company (joint venture) and even with capital investment.

The above described concept of specificity by Williamson of can be used as follows for the outsourcing decision. Goods and services with high specificity cannot be used in other transactions without huge additional costs. For example, paint shop equipment designed for the Volkswagen Golf can be used for a Mercedes only if it is redesigned and relocated. In such cases, quite often a total loss must be accepted if the original use is not a perfect fit.

Objects with *low specificity* can be governed with an external outsourcing design. Low specificity means that little information has to be exchanged with the transaction partner. External outsourcing partners are able to bundle demand and exploit economies of scale. Much information has to be exchanged before, during and after the exchange of goods and services with *high specificity*. The results are extremely high market transac-

Figure 9. Structural alternatives of outsourcing

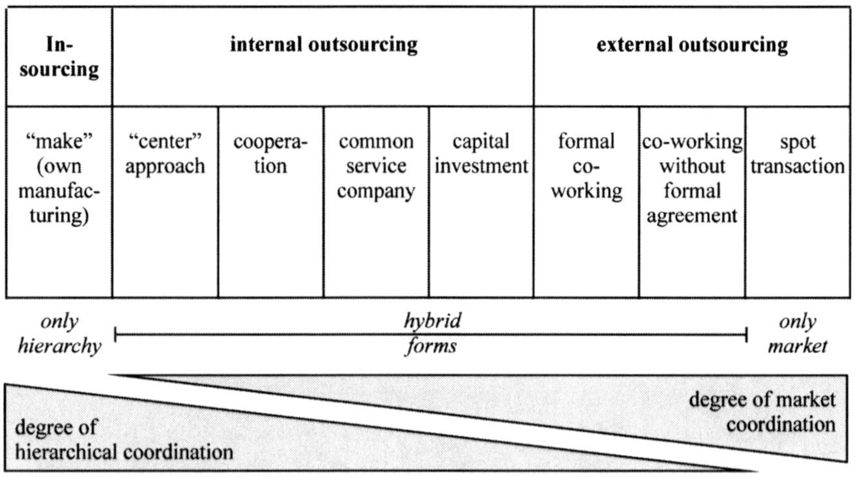

tion costs. It is not possible to realize large-scale effects because only a few customers exist (or perhaps only one). It makes sense to establish an internal outsourcing design for these transactions. Goods and services with the highest specificity are based on the company's core competencies. They should be kept under the full responsibility and control of a company (insourcing).

Therefore, management has to answer three questions about the outsourcing object:

- **Is the activity highly specific?** If so, normally, very high market transaction costs for communication and agreement exist. Economically, it makes no sense to outsource such an activity.
- **Is the activity strategically important?** Sometimes it is not helpful to outsource activities with low specificity because they are extremely important for a company's ability to survive. To get a concrete idea of this "strategic importance," we have to answer the following question.
- **Is the activity a core competence, a central part of competitive advantage?** Does it improve competitiveness in a general way, or does it not contribute to competitiveness in any way? Activities with no competitive contribution at all are typical outsourcing candidates. As activities increase their competitive contribution, they move step-by-step from external outsourcing to internal outsourcing to insourcing.

Together, the answers to these three questions help the firm arrive at an optimal outsourcing design. The recommendations of transaction cost economics often seem to be very short-term and only cost-based. With the implementation of "strategic importance" as a quality of transactions, we can add a long-term perspective. Williamson himself added "brand name capital" as one element of specificity. According to this, marketing and branding are a core competence. It is important to define outsourcing beyond just a "yes" or "no"-decision – according to TCE, it is a decision with a multitude of "hybrid" alternatives.

Transaction Cost, Information Economics, and Procurement Strategy

Because of the institutional approach, TCE seems to be a valid tool for funding the outsourcing decision. By including the problem of uncertainty (see chapter 2.2), it seems to also be an appropriate tool for strategic decision-making. As stated in the title and introduction, we do concentrate on supply management and therefore focus on strategic supply decisions from a TCE perspective. The question is how TCE can support the strategic supply decision-making process.

Therefore, we must focus on supply strategies themselves. We understand supply strategies as a mix of different sub-strategies (Arnold, 1996, p. 1872, Arnold, 1997, p. 124). Supply managers must define a supplier sub-strategy, an object sub-strategy, an area sub-strategy, a time sub-strategy, a subject sub-strategy, and a site sub-strategy. Every one of these sub-strategies has at least two attributes. These attributes are described as sourcing concepts. To find the appropriate strategy, one sourcing concept must be chosen for each sub-strategy. Together, the selected sourcing concepts characterize the supply strategy.

There are four alternative supplier sub-strategies, which refer to the number of suppliers: sole sourcing, single sourcing, dual sourcing, and multiple sourcing. Single sourcing means that only one supplier is responsible for delivering a specific part. In general, single sourcing will be chosen for e.g., complex parts, modules or systems that require closer supplier-customer relationships. Such an intensive vertical cooperation can be established only with one supplier because of the high amount of the specific investment that is necessary to increase the efficiency of such a close network relationship. If a buyer is forced to purchase from one supplier (monopolistic situation) the supplier concept is called sole sourcing (Owens Swift and Coe, 1994, p. 173).

To avoid supply risks, purchasing managers use the multiple sourcing concept. It is necessary to establish a wide supplier base. To intensify competition between suppliers is the central objective. Dual sourcing helps to combine the advantages of single sourcing and multiple sourcing. On the one hand, stronger relationships to suppliers can be built up. On the other hand, two suppliers are compensating for the risks of delivery and shipments.

Unit sourcing and modular sourcing are alternative object sub-strategies. Typically, a lot of different items with low complexity will be purchased. The buying company assembles these units into the end product. This means high manufacturing penetration. Today, modern management concepts promote the idea of a "lean" company. Instead of running their own manufacturing activities, a so-called first-tier supplier has to integrate a number of sub-suppliers and deliver a complete module or system (Eicke and Femerling, 1991). Modular sourcing means both supplying highly integrated modules and reducing the number of direct suppliers, to cut transaction costs.

The area sub-strategy defines the geographic area for sourcing activities. Local sourcing means a concentration on suppliers in the neighborhood or region. This might be useful to avoid logistical problems. It is not easy to define domestic sourcing. Filling the gap between local and global sourcing, it describes purchasing in the home country. With the emergence of the European Common Market and the Euro currency, the domestic market is no longer a single country; it is Europe in general. Global sourcing is a strategic approach to use worldwide supply markets (Arnold, 1989, Leenders and Fearon, 1993, pp. 491 ff.).

Time sub-strategies are closely linked with optimization of inventory. Stock sourcing helps to avoid supply risks by building up stocks. It is useful only for low-valued goods because of capital lockup (Arnold, 1996, p. 1868). Demand-tailored sourcing means both buying to current requirements and so-called "hand-to-mouth buying" (Scheuing, 1989, p. 147). Only the buyer tries to avoid own stocks. A stockless supply through all levels of the supply chain (buyer *and* supplier) is called just-in-time (Arnold and Bernard, 1989, Ansari and Modaress, 1990, p. 29). This creates a significant cost reduction and requires a close relationship between buyer and supplier (e.g., single sourcing).

Within the subject sub-strategy, we distinguish between individual sourcing and consortium sourcing. Consortium sourcing refers to a purchasing consortium (a horizontal supply alliance between buyers; Arnold and Essig, 1997, p. 10). Individual sourcing is a strategic decision which builds up a strong individual demand position in supply markets. It ignores the advantages of a consortium model.

Two alternative site sub-strategies (external sourcing and internal sourcing) differ with respect to the place of suppliers' value-added activities. External sourcing is the traditional site concept. Suppliers produce their modules or units in a plant more or less far away from the buyer's premises. With establishment of a modular sourcing model and/or just-in-time, a closer connection between buyer and supplier arises. To avoid supply risks, the supplier installs its own manufacturing equipment and employees on customer premises. This is called a "factory within a factory" (Arnold and Scheuing, 1997, p. 82).

It is the job of supply management to select the optimal sourcing model for every sub-strategy. Together, the chosen sourcing models are the supply strategy. Table 1 illustrates the idea of such a "sourcing toolbox": each line shows sourcing alternatives. Horizontally, there is an exclusion of concepts. The vertical columns represent the different concepts that have to be combined.

Although this might help to structure decisions, most important questions cannot be answered without the help of a sound theory: Which of the sourcing concepts fits best with a buying organization? Which combination contributes in an optimal way to a specific buying decision? What general recommendations for sourcing decisions can be given?

To answer these questions, we make use of TCE and use its elements to develop a sourcing portfolio. The dimensions of the portfolio refer to the concept of "specificity" in TCE. For giving recommendations concerning the optimal supply strategy in the portfolio, we take the approach of TCE to analyze (supply) transactions in detail. The definitions both of transactions and specificity have been given above.

In this case, specificity is used in two ways: First, it is the specificity of the transaction object (meaning the input needed by the company). In general, we distinguish between highly specific modules (individually produced by the supplier for the purchasing company) and commodities. Secondly, specificity refers to the site where suppliers add value. In some cases, supplier and buyer must be connected locally to realize the best results of the purchasing transaction (supplying process). Together, the two dimensions object specificity and site specificity are the basis for a sourcing portfolio. For a general understanding of the relationship between sourcing concepts and transaction types, we fix the position sourcing concepts in the specificity-based sourcing portfolio.

Table 1. Supply strategy as a combination of sourcing concepts

<table>
<tr><th>sub-strategy</th><th colspan="6">sourcing concepts</th></tr>
<tr><td>supplier sub-strategy</td><td>sole sourcing</td><td colspan="2">single sourcing</td><td colspan="2">dual sourcing</td><td>multiple sourcing</td></tr>
<tr><td>object sub-strategy</td><td colspan="3">unit sourcing</td><td colspan="3">modular sourcing</td></tr>
<tr><td>area sub-strategy</td><td colspan="2">local sourcing</td><td colspan="2">domestic sourcing</td><td colspan="2">global sourcing</td></tr>
<tr><td>time sub-strategy</td><td colspan="2">stock sourcing</td><td colspan="2">demand tailored sourcing</td><td colspan="2">just-in-time</td></tr>
<tr><td>subject sub-strategy</td><td colspan="3">individual sourcing</td><td colspan="3">consortium sourcing</td></tr>
<tr><td>site sub-strategy</td><td colspan="3">external sourcing</td><td colspan="3">internal sourcing
(factory within a factory-approach)</td></tr>
</table>

As mentioned above, high object specificity is connected with system supply respectively modular sourcing. Suppliers develop and produce modules exclusively for *one* customer. For example, the cockpit module for a Volkswagen Golf differs completely from the cockpit module for a Mercedes-Benz E-Class. This is mainly a design specificity because the basic technology (e.g., speedometer or climate control) might be the same. In contrast to modular sourcing, low object specificity means unit sourcing of more or less standardized items.

Site specificity is very high if the supplier is located on the buyer's site to produce exclusively his goods and to guarantee a continuous material flow. Typically, factory-within-a-factory systems make sense only for very valuable goods like modules and direct services connected with the final product. Within a just-in-time concept, object specificity and site specificity are slightly lower: a stockless supply means reduced capital costs for all types of goods, but the supplier must be able to deliver within a fixed time period. Therefore, he must not be geographically far away from his customer. As a result, the area sub-strategy is connected strongly with site specificity. For a factory within a factory, local sourcing must be established. Domestic sourcing makes it easier to realize a continuous material flow (just-in-time). Global sourcing is possible in the case of low site specificity.

Figure 10 shows the position of all sourcing concepts mentioned above in detail. These positions provide an overview of transaction attributes in the sense of specificity and their connection with sourcing concepts. It is necessary to consider different situations of uncertainty if purchasing managers are seeking an optimal strategy combination under the assumption of different attributes of specificity of a purchasing transaction.

Ex ante and ex post information deficits, as well as the three information economics-based supply situations (see chapter 2.2), are the bases to identify the three main supply strategy patterns within the sourcing portfolio (see Figure 11):

1. In the case of low object specificity and low site specificity, uncertainty can be reduced

Figure 10. The specificity-based sourcing portfolio

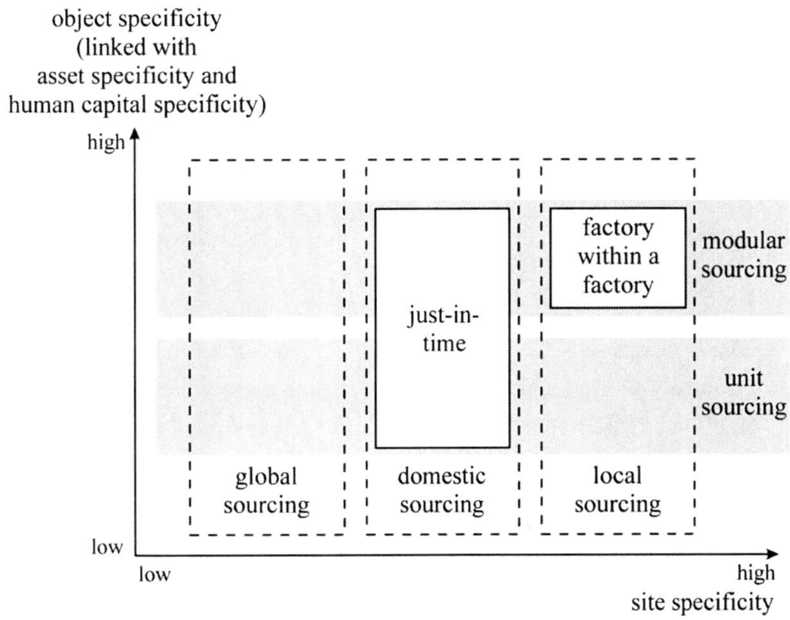

Figure 11. Information-oriented supply strategy formulation

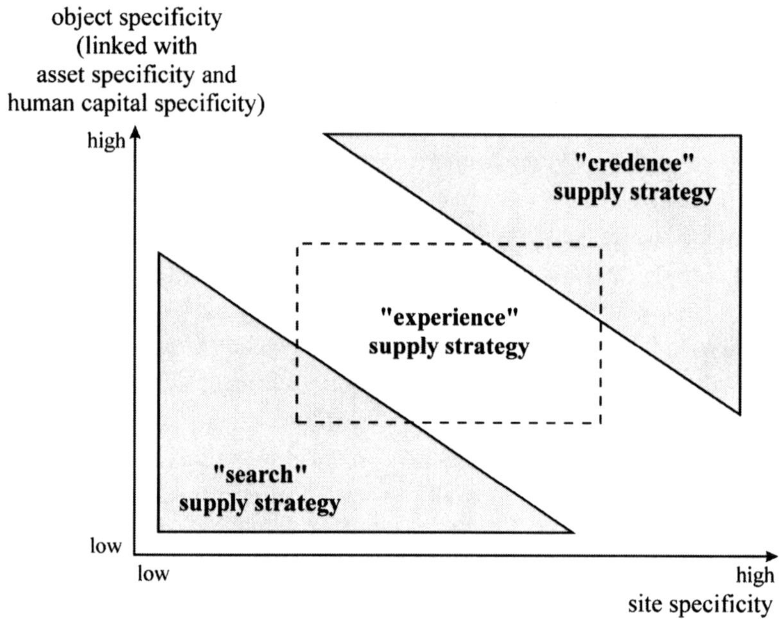

by ex ante information-seeking. Unit sourcing means a wider market transparency because of lower technical problems. On the other hand, global sourcing offers the opportunity to get information from a wider area, from suppliers all over the world. To reinforce competition among suppliers, multiple sourcing seems to be an appropriate supplier sub-strategy. Because in this case information-seeking is the main tool for reducing uncertainty, we call this strategy pattern—with reference to the contribution of Nelson (1970)—search supply strategy. As mentioned above, it combines global sourcing, unit sourcing and multiple sourcing.

2. The other extreme is a combination of high object specificity and high site specificity. To realize modular sourcing means to shift a lot of engineering and manufacturing responsibility to suppliers. In the long run, the buyer depends greatly on the supplier's future performance. Combined with a factory-within-a-factory design, this problem is aggravated because normally only one supplier is responsible for one module on a highly specific site. This combination with single sourcing can be very dangerous from the buyer's point of view. After signing a contract, it is difficult, and perhaps, in the short run, impossible, to substitute the supplier. On the other hand, the buyer has to deal with high ex post uncertainty because he will never have full information about the supplier's performance after awarding the contract. To minimize the information gap, information surrogates are used. Such surrogates are brand names or references, or reputation in general. From an information economics point of view, the key trait necessary on both sides to arrange such a buyer-supplier-relationship is trust. Referring to the work of Darby/Karni (1973), we call this pattern credence supply strategy. As mentioned above, it combines local sourcing, modular sourcing and single sourcing in a factory-within-a-factory design.

3. Between these extremes there is a medium strategy pattern. It is called experience supply strategy and combines elements of both patterns mentioned above, depending on a medium degree of object and site specificity.

Transaction Cost, Information Economics, and Information Technology

Observing inter-organizational (information) systems from a supply management perspective leads automatically to electronic procurement (e-procurement). For this paper, it gives us the chance to make concrete TCE-based recommendations at the next level. It would be the third step of an increasingly concrete application of TCE in the supply area, following outsourcing and strategic sourcing recommendations.

The so-called "revolution through electronic purchasing" (Telgen 1998) has to be discussed on an analytical basis. Therefore, TCE provides valuable input. The main advantage of web-based procurement is the high quantity and quality of information processing. The mixture of search, experience, and credence qualities requires different kinds of information that may not be available through either e- or non-e-procurement (classical procurement). By applying the TCE concept of making the transaction the "basic unit of analysis" (Williamson 1989), we are able to divide the transaction into a pre-decision phase (phase of information seeking), the decision itself and a post-decision phase (phase of information validation). Figure 12 provides an overview of information requirements for the purchasing transaction, concerning search, experience, and credence qualities.

By nature, search qualities can be inspected prior to the purchasing decision. E-procurement enables purchasers to extend speed, quantity, and quality of information processing. The internet makes suppliers all over the world easily accessible. Instead of finding data in actual sources like printed catalogs, buyers can now virtually find information with a mouse click. Reverse auctions allow purchasers to make real-time bidding comparisons. Pre-requisition is the kind of information exchanged in such supply transaction marketplaces; only search qualities can be expected by electronic exchange completely.

After the supplier has fulfilled the transaction, his quality can be measured. Computer-based programs help to confirm all aspects of the transaction, e.g., whether or not the delivery was on time, whether or not the number of parts supplied was as ordered, and so on. These data mostly come out of internal systems like ERP systems. We can describe this information as ex post validation information that helps to evaluate search qualities as well as experience qualities.

Experience and credence qualities cannot be examined before purchase. As a consequence of uncertainty and incomplete markets, buyers must use information substitutes. Such a substitute is the ex post validation information from a former purchase successfully fulfilled with the supplier. Additionally, references from other customers can be easily accessed through the web. Nowadays, in the B2C field, consumer reports on product satisfaction are available through websites like dooyoo.com.

The major element with credence qualities is trust. Without having the chance to totally evaluate a supplier's performance, even after the purchase, buyers have to build up trust-oriented relationships with their suppliers (Doney and Cannon 1997, Smeltzer 1997). Trust can be divided into inter-personal and inter-organizational parts. Interpersonal trust is directly connected with personal relationships of people within the company, e.g., between a buyer and a salesperson (Doney and Cannon 1997). Here, e-procurement has no direct influence. Electronic procurement might help to build organizational trust. An example is the branding of e-commerce activities, as Amazon does, for example.

Figure 12. Information qualities, procurement process, and e-procurement

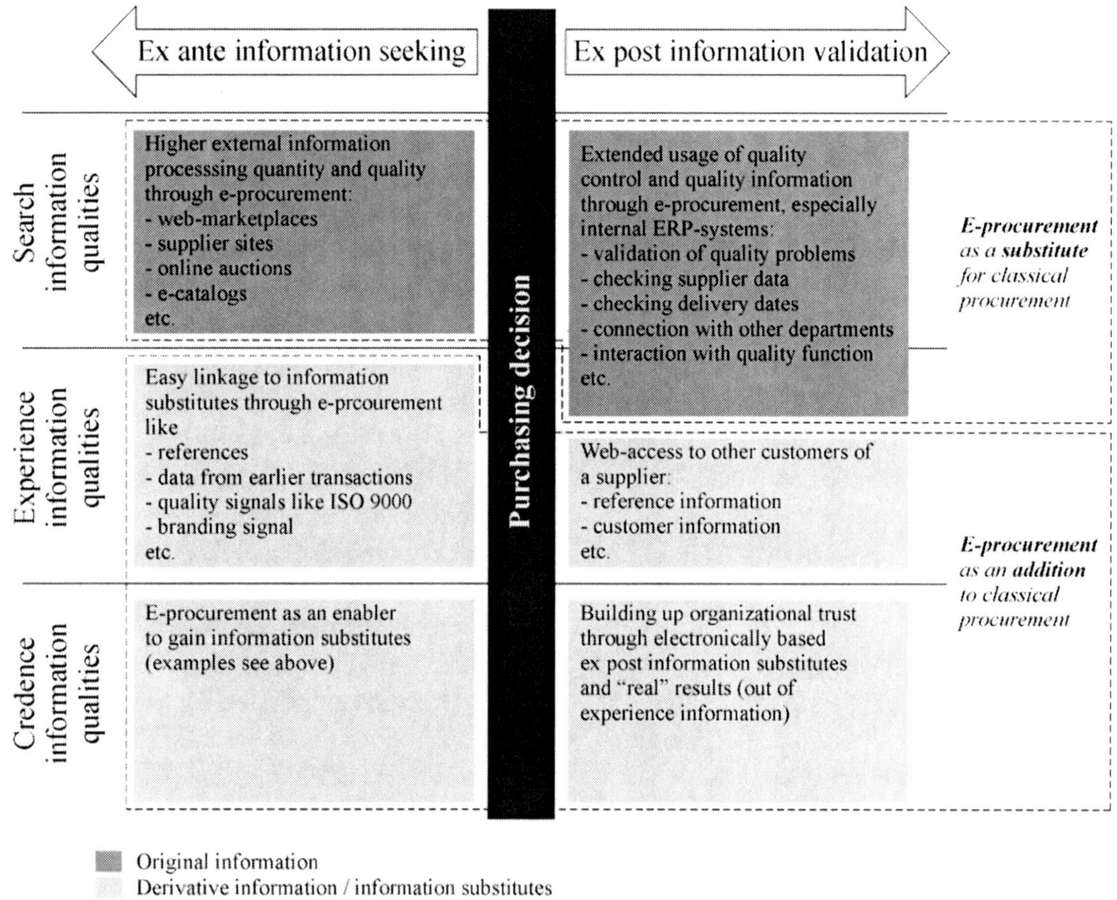

From a purchasing point of view, experience and credence qualities are the major challenge. As we show in the supply pyramid in Figure 13, these qualities improve with the installation of system suppliers because companies heavily rely on their performance and are not able to control this performance, due to their own knowledge deficits.

We maintain that e-procurement is useful for examining search qualities but fulfills only a support function in the case of experience and credence qualities. As a result, we see e-procurement as a potential complement to classical sourcing activities (see Figure 12). Depending on the information situation, e-activities can even replace non-e-activities, but there will always be a kind of information in supplier-buyer relationships for which personal contact is necessary.

Boer, Harink and Heijboer (2001) define five main forms of e-procurement: web-based enterprise resource planning (ERP), e-sourcing, e-tendering, e-reverse auctioning, and e-informing. ERP is based on a web-integrated enterprise resource planning system. In essence, a software system that is used internally as a materials planning and controlling system. E-sourcing is the process of identifying new suppliers over the web. E-tendering uses the internet to send RFQs to suppliers, and for suppliers to return them. E-reverse auctioning supports buyers in running a reverse auction. During a defined period of time, suppliers can bid for a defined purchasing good

Figure 13. Supply pyramid and information qualities

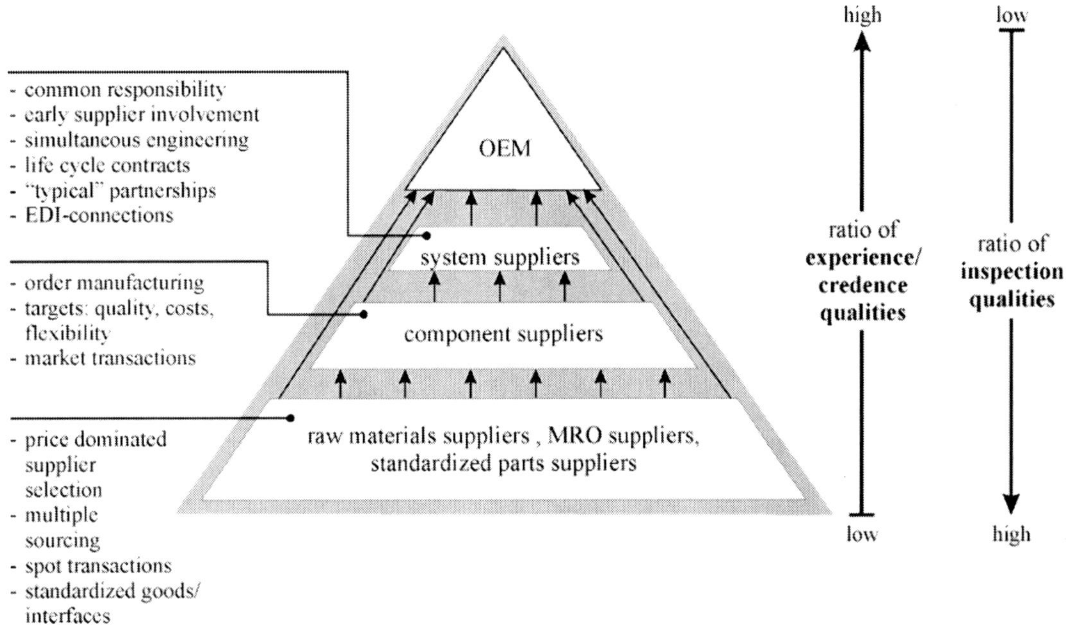

or service, winning only with the lowest price. E-informing represents all activities related to additional information through the web not directly connected with a contract.

The e-procurement matrix brings together information economics and transaction analysis (see Figure 14). By nature, original ex ante information-seeking is only possible for search qualities; ex post information validation is only possible for search and experience qualities. All information related to credence qualities can only be of a derived nature. The major source of controlling information is the ERP system, as mentioned above. By checking the on-time-delivery, quality and other supply factors of a supplier through ERP software, buyers are able to judge the supplier's performance precisely. The only other instrument that might be usable is general information available from other customers of a specific supplier (e-informing). Of course, e-informing can be an ex ante information-seeking instrument for all kinds of supplies as well.

There are major differences for the usage of all other e-procurement instruments in the ex ante phase of a purchasing transaction. E-sourcing and e-tendering might help obtain results for all supply situations, but e-reverse auctioning is only possible if supplies are "auctionable. As mentioned above, e-reverse auctioning concentrates on the price only. Without having the ability to check the quality of delivery after purchasing, e-reverse auctioning is useless. For example, choosing system suppliers is a very complex purchasing decision that affects the company's success dramatically. Undoubtedly, this decision is based on many factors, such as quality, engineering capabilities and trust.

The e-procurement matrix is a very simplified way to show the possibilities of e-procurement and its instruments, but it gives at least basic recommendations of the usage of different tools in that area.

RESULTS AND IMPLICATIONS

This paper had the aim not only to describe some basic elements of TCE, but also to show its usage

Figure 14. The e-procurement matrix

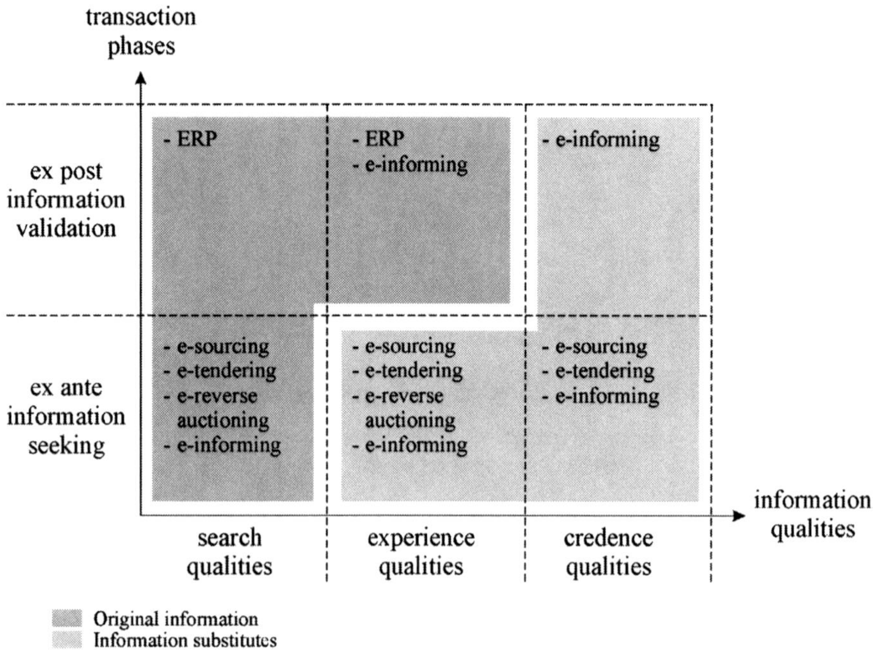

for inter-organizational management systems, in this case, from a supply management perspective. Of course, both the discussion of TCE and its applications in business administration is limited for such a popular theory. If we wrap up the concretization for e-procurement, we see interesting implications, from application to theory. Electronic (web-based) marketplaces are approaching – maybe, in reality, for the first time ever – the old economic idea of a "perfect market world." The field of economics has declared a kind of renaissance of neoclassical economic theory without (or with very low) transaction costs because of high reaction times for all market partners and almost full market transparency. In recent years, economics has taken a closer look at the value of information, beginning with marketing research, where considerations for levels of investment in market research activities have to be made. This has continued, on a more theoretical-analytical basis, with transaction cost economics. There are still problems with this kind of information analysis; Zajac and Olsen (1993) request a shift from transaction *cost* to information *value*. For example, strategic supply management does not only lower transaction costs, but it expands the possibilities of purchasing as well. This helps to create real added value by the purchasing function.

Instead of just "buying," e-procurement allows for completely new forms of exchange relationships with external partners/suppliers. The trend towards outsourcing will continue. As a consequence, virtual electronic networks between buying and selling companies, and between suppliers and customers, will arise (so-called "hybrids"). Therefore, supply management will have to redefine its roles of supplier relationship manager and cultural exchange partner. Within virtual exchange, cultural identity becomes more and more a problem because suppliers are members of a multitude of networks and might lose their own respective identities. TCE might support the idea of deciding whether or not hybrids are a cost-efficient institution, but without the value dimension, the answers will always be limited.

REFERENCES

Ansari, A., & Modarress, B. (1990). *Just-in-time purchasing*. New York, NY: Free Press.

Arnold, U. (1982). *Strategische Beschaffungspolitik: Steuerung und Kontrolle strategischer Beschaffungssubsysteme von Unternehmen*. Frankfurt, Germany: Lang.

Arnold, U. (1989). Ziele, Aufgaben und Instrumente des Materialmanagements. In *Beschaffung Aktuell, 9,* 47-54.

Arnold, U. (1996). Sourcing-Konzepte. In Kern, W., Schroeder, H.-H., & Weber, J. (Eds.), *Handwoerterbuch der Produktionswirtschaft* (2nd ed.). Stuttgart, Germany: Schaeffer-Poeschel.

Arnold, U. (1997). *Beschaffungsmanagement* (2nd ed.). Stuttgart, Germany: Schaeffer-Poeschel.

Arnold, U. (1998). Marktlich integrierte Kooperationen: Netzwerke und Allianzen in Beschaffung und Absatz. In Gassert, H., Prechtl, M., & Zahn, E. (Eds.), *Innovative Dienstleistungspartnerschaften: Neue Formen der Zusammenarbeit zwischen Industrie und Dienstleistern*. Stuttgart, Germany: Schaeffer-Poeschel.

Arnold, U., Bernard, K. N. (1989). Just-in-time. *Technovation*, 401-430.

Arnold, U., & Essig, M. (1997). *Einkaufskooperationen in der Industrie*. Stuttgart, Germany: Schaeffer-Poeschel.

Arnold, U., & Scheuing, E. E. (1997). Creating a factory within a factory. *Conference Proceedings of the 1997 NAPM Annual Conference*, Washington DC, May 4-7.

Backhaus, K., Aufderheide, D., & Spaeth, G. M. (1994). *Marketing fuer Systemtechnologien: Entwicklung eines theoretisch-oekonomisch begruendeten Geschaeftstypenansatzes*. Stuttgart, Germany: Schaeffer-Poeschel.

Boer, L. d., Harink, J., & Heijboer, G. (2001). A model for assessing the impact of electronic procurement forms. In *10th International Annual IPSERA Conference Proceedings*, Jönköping, (pp. 119-130).

Carr, A. S., & Smeltzer, L. R. (1997). An empirically based operational definition of strategic purchasing. *European Journal of Purchasing and Supply Management, 3*(4), 199–207. doi:10.1016/S0969-7012(97)00014-2

Carter, J. R., & Narasimhan, R. (1996). A comparison of North American and European future purchasing trends. *International Journal of Purchasing and Materials Management, 32*(2), 12–22.

Coase, R. H. (1937). The nature of the firm. *Economica, 4*, 386–405. doi:10.1111/j.1468-0335.1937.tb00002.x

Commons, J. R. (1931). Institutional economics. *The American Economic Review, 21*, 648–657.

Darby, M. R., & Karni, E. (1973). Free competition and the optimal amount of fraud. *The Journal of Law & Economics, 16*(4), 67–88. doi:10.1086/466756

Dobler, D. W., & Burt, D. N. (1996). *Purchasing and supply management: Text and cases* (6th ed.). New York, NY: McGraw-Hill.

Doney, P. M., & Cannon, J. P. (1997). An examination of the nature of trust in buyer-seller-relationships. *Journal of Marketing, 61*(4), 35–51. doi:10.2307/1251829

Eicke, H. v., & Femerling, C. (1991). *Modular sourcing: Ein Konzept zur Neugestaltung der Beschaffungspolitik*. München, Germany: Huss-Verlag.

Grochla, E., & Schonbohm, P. (1980). *Beschaffung in der Unternehmung: Einführung in eine umfassende Beschaffungslehre*. Stuttgart, Germany: Schaeffer-Poeschel.

Krüger, W., & Homp, C. (1997). *Kernkompetenz-Management: Steigerung von Flexibilität und Schlagkraft im Wettbewerb*. Wiesbaden, Germany: Gabler.

Leenders, M. R., & Fearon, H. E. (1993). *Purchasing and materials management*. Burr Ridge, IL: Irwin.

Leenders, M. R., & Fearon, H. E. (1997). *Purchasing and supply management* (11th ed.). Chicago, IL: McGraw-Hill/Irwin.

Nelson, P. (1970). Information and consumer behavior. *The Journal of Political Economy, 2*, 311–329. doi:10.1086/259630

Owens Swift, C., & Coe, B. J. (1994). Sourcing preference scale: Measuring preferences of purchasing managers for single sourcing or multiple sourcing of products. *Industrial Marketing Management, 23*(2), 171–180. doi:10.1016/0019-8501(94)90019-1

Penrose, E. (1959). *The theory of the growth of the firm*. New York, NY: Wiley.

Picot, A., Reichwald, R., & Wigand, R. T. (1996). *Die grenzenlose Unternehmung: Information, Organisation und Management* (2nd ed.). Wiesbaden, Germany: Gabler.

Quinn, J. B., & Hilmer, F. G. (1994). Strategic outsourcing. *Sloan Management Review, 35*, 43–55.

Scheuing, E. E. (1989). *Purchasing management*. Englewood Cliffs, NJ: Prentice Hall.

Simon, H. A. (1976). *Administrative behavior. A study of decision-making processes in administrative organization* (3rd ed.). New York, NY: Free Press.

Smeltzer, L. R. (1997). The meaning and origin of trust in buyer-supplier relationships. *International Journal of Purchasing and Materials Management, 33*(1), 40–48.

Telgen, J. (1998). Revolution through electronic purchasing. *7th International Annual IPSERA Conference Proceedings*, London, (pp. 499-504).

Weiber, R., & Adler, J. (1995). Informationsökonomisch begründete Typologisierung von Kaufprozessen. *Zeitschrift fuer betriebswirtschaftliche. Forschung, 47*(1), 43–65.

Williamson, O. E. (1985). *The economic institutions of capitalism*. New York, NY: Free Press.

Williamson, O. E. (1989). *Operationalizing the new institutional economics: The transaction cost economics perspective*. Working Paper, Berkeley.

Williamson, O. E. (1990). *Comparative economic organization: The analysis of discrete structural alternatives*. Walter A. Haas School of Business Working Paper, Berkeley.

Williamson, O. E. (1991). Comparative economic organization: Vergleichende ökonomische Organisationstheorie: Die Analyse diskreter Strukturalternativen. In Ordelheide, D., Rudolph, B., & Büsselmann, E. (Eds.), *Betriebswirtschaftslehre und ökonomische Theorie* (pp. 13–49). Stuttgart, Germany: Schaeffer-Poeschel.

Zahn, E., Barth, T., & Hertweck, A. (1998). Outsourcing unternehmensnaher Dienstleistungen in der Region Stuttgart: Ergebnisse einer empirischen Untersuchung. In Gassert, H., Prechtl, M., & Zahn, E. (Eds.), *Innovative Dienstleistungspartnerschaften: Neue Formen der Zusammenarbeit zwischen Industrie und Dienstleistern* (pp. 109–137). Stuttgart, Germany: Schaeffer-Poeschel.

Zajac, E. J., & Olsen, C. P. (1993). From transaction cost to transaction value analysis: Implications for the study of interorganizational strategies. *Journal of Management Studies, 30*(1), 131–145. doi:10.1111/j.1467-6486.1993.tb00298.x

Chapter 5
Trust and Transaction Cost in Supply Chain Cost Optimization:
An Exploratory Study

Ik-Whan G. Kwon
St. Louis University, USA

John H. Hamilton
St. Louis University, USA

Seock-Jin Hong
Bordeaux School of Management, France

ABSTRACT

The foundation of efficient and effective supply chain management rests on collaborative efforts by all parties involved in executing the supply chain optimization process. Every partner in the chain has to exercise its best effort to achieve the most efficient and effective results.

Research indicates that transaction cost can be reduced if partners practice trust-based collaborative supply chain operations. Studies also show that cooperation among and between potential supply chain partners sometimes can lead to collaboration if partners see an opportunity for mutual value creation. Collaboration may foster an environment conducive to building trust and form the basis for the first step toward making a tangible business commitment. As the level of trust within and outside an organization increases, speed of decision making increases, and subsequently, transaction costs decrease. The inverse is also true. Accordingly, trust and information sharing are central tenets of supply chains in reducing the transaction cost. As transaction cost decreases, total supply chain cost may also decrease making operations more competitive in the global market.

DOI: 10.4018/978-1-60960-768-5.ch005

Copyright © 2012, IGI Global. Copying or distributing in print or electronic forms without written permission of IGI Global is prohibited.

This chapter describes the relationship between trust and transaction cost in supply chain operations. Empirical findings from several research studies on trust and transaction cost in supply chain operations will be presented in support of the argument for managing transaction cost in supply chain management. A suggested future research agenda on this topic is also provided.

CONCEPT OF TRANSACTION COST THEORY

The tenet of transaction cost theory originally advanced by Coase (1937) is how the final price of goods and services is determined in the market. The theory argues that the final (optimum) price is determined in the market by "total cost." Labor, materials and other related costs such as administrative cost, search for better information, etc. constitute "total cost." In some cases, the transaction cost is sizeable. Indeed, North (1990) estimates that transaction costs may represent as much as 35-40% of the costs associated with economic activity. One recent study (Woolhandler, Campbell and Himmelstein, 2003) estimates that the average U.S. hospital devoted 23.4% of spending to administration.

Transaction costs, therefore, involve all of the costs associated with conducting exchanges between firms and can be decomposed into ex ante transaction costs (search and contracting costs), and ex post contracting costs (monitoring and enforcement costs) (Cheung, 1987; Williamson, 1981 and 2008; Hennart, 1993; North, 1990; Tadelis, 2007). Search costs include the costs of locating a desirable trading partner and then negotiating and writing a mutually acceptable contract. Monitoring and enforcement costs refer to the costs associated with monitoring the contract implementation and the procedures necessary to ensure that each party fulfills the predetermined set of obligations in the contracts. It is argued that if partners spend more time up front negotiating a mutually acceptable agreement, it is possible that this may reduce monitoring and enforcement costs because all of the expectations and obligations will have been clearly specified during the contracting phase (Dyer and Chu, 2003). Accordingly, they argue that any investigation into transaction cost should separate these types of transaction costs.

Many authors spend a considerable amount of time developing the transaction cost theory using external factors (e.g., Dyer and Chu, 2003, Williamson, 1981). Porter (1996), however, makes a significant contribution to internal transaction cost determination through his work on value chain analysis. Value chain analysis enables a firm to determine their core competencies and those that provide the lowest cost. Value chain analysis provides valuable insight for the firm to determine how it can lower internal transaction costs and thereby reduce the total transaction cost of goods and services.

A key absence in transaction cost theory related to supply chain management is a unified concept that integrates transaction cost theory into supply chain principles (information sharing and sharing rewards and risks) This paper will add to the body of knowledge of transaction cost theory by closing the gap by linking the transaction cost theory to supply chain management.

ATTRIBUTES FOR LOWERING TRANSACTION COST

Above studies seem to recognize the roles of transaction cost in determining the optimum prices of goods and services in the market. Tasks to locate and develop appropriate tools to achieve such goal (reducing transaction cost) are challenging and complex. Two approaches will be highlighted in this paper; information technology (IT) and the collaborative working relationship among and between business partners.

Information Technology (IT) and Transaction Cost

IT has enhanced our ability to search for information to reduce the transaction cost. Searching for reliable information and monitoring for the negotiation processes using information technology such as the internet, website, EDI and other means of communications has considerably reduced the total transaction cost more than Coase (1937) never envisioned at the time he developed transaction cost theory.

When information technology is used to enhance the quality of communication between and among firms and with the speed of connecting relevant trading partners, transaction costs can be minimized (Young-Ybarra and Wiersema, 1999). For example, electronic market places (EMPs) would have a dramatic impact on transaction costs as it (EMP) enables buyers and sellers to collaborate in the search for information, bargain and negotiate a contract and monitor contract performance electronically. Search for valuable information electronically will not only speed the search process so timely decision can be made, but more importantly enhances interactive opportunity between trading partners perhaps to resolve any differences in a timely fashion as well. The overall transaction cost will be lowered as a result.

Trust and Transaction Cost

Trust in exchange relationships has been hypothesized to be a valuable economic asset because it is believed to: (1) lower transaction costs and allow for greater flexibility to respond to changing market conditions (Gulati, 1995; Barney and Hansen, 1994; Uzzi, 1997; Dyer, 1997) and (2) lead to superior information sharing that improves coordination and joint efforts to minimize inefficiencies in business transactions (Aoki, 1988; Clark and Fujimoto, 1991; Nishiguchi, 1994). Trust promotes negotiating efficiency by enabling each party to be more flexible in granting concessions because of the expectation that the exchange partner will reciprocate in the future (Dore, 1983). This allows partners to achieve "serial equity" (equity over a longer period of time) rather than requiring immediate or "spot equity" (Ouchi, 1984; Dyer, 1997). Consequently, it reduces the need for partners to invest heavily prior bargaining. In addition, negotiations will likely be more efficient because partners will have greater confidence that information provided by the other organization is reliable. As observed by Zaheer, McEvily and Perrone (1998, p. 144), "Trust reduces the inclination to guard against opportunistic behavior (i.e., deliberate misrepresentation on the part of the exchange partner)." In a study of supplier-buyer relationships in the electrical equipment industry, Zaheer et al. (1998) found support for a negative relationship between inter-organizational trust and negotiation costs. Reduced transaction costs in exchange relationships could be a source of competitive advantage. Dyer and Chu's empirical study (2003) convincingly shows a statistically significant relationship between the level of trust and the amount of transaction cost. Duffy (2009) argues that end-to-end collaboration reduces administrative cost by 30% from the base line in consumer goods industry, 20% in automotive and electronics industries respectively.

The purpose of this chapter is to exam the roles of transaction cost theory in supply chain operations. More specifically, supply chain cost optimization will be reviewed from a hypothesis that collaborative relationships among supply chain participant lead to a lower transaction cost which reduces the total supply chain cost. Transaction cost theory is used as a guiding principle of this paper.

This paper consists of introduction, transaction cost theory in supply chain management, conceptual model, empirical evidence in literature, and future research arena in transaction cost theory in supply chain management. Summary and conclusion will be the last section of this paper.

TRANSACTION COST AND SUPPLY CHAIN COST OPTIMIZATION

Supply chain management is the systemic, strategic coordination of the traditional business functions and tactics across these business functions within a particular company and across businesses in the supply chain, for the purpose of improving the long-term performance of the individual companies and the supply chain as a whole (Mentzer, 2001). The main purpose of supply chain is to minimize the total supply chain cost thereby increasing the total supply chain profit for *all* participants (suppliers, manufacturers, distributors and others who participate in this process).

Supply chain management is built on three parts; foundation, engines, and goals. A structural snapshot is shown in Figure 1.

The ultimate goal for the supply chain management is to improve total profitability for all partners within the supply chain. However, such goal may not be achieved or even feasible if the supply chain foundation is not firmly established. Research indicates that business transactions become efficient and effective once commitment is established (Barney and Hansen, 1994; Dyer, 1997). Commitment, however, is seldom realized unless a certain level of trust between and among supply chain partners is formed. Collaboration between and among supply chain partners is the first step to establish such trust. A collaborative relationship is a long-term, win-win partnership between organizations based on joint value creation for the supply chain network focused on the end-customer needs. This type of supply chain is based on trust which in turn creates value for partners.

Figure 1. Supply chain process

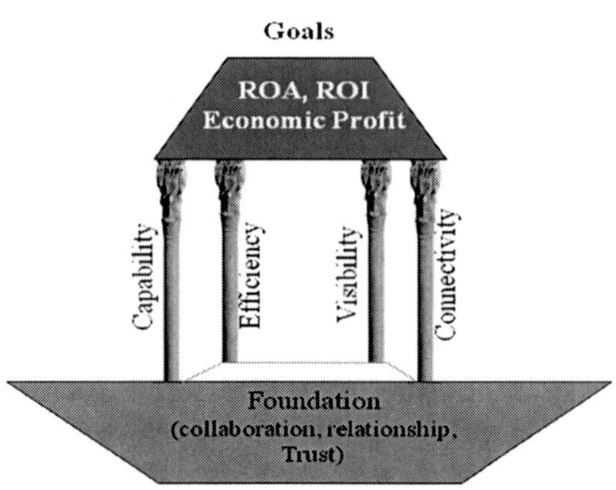

Accordingly, it is reasonable to argue that trust and information sharing are central tenets of supply chains. When not fully integrated because of lack of trust, or information sharing, the transaction costs of doing business increase and the ability to respond to potential risk/disruption diminishes (Eshkenazi, 2009). Some research reveals that one of the reasons for limiting collaboration among supply chain partners is the lack of trust among supply chain partners (Fawcett, 2009).

The premise of collaboration in supply chain performance improvement is that supply chain collaboration should look at developing close working relationships with customers and suppliers. Should these collaborative efforts succeed, then it is a reasonable expectation that performance improvements will be the result. For example, Simatupang and Sridharan (2005) argue that there is a strong correlation ($R^2 = 0.74$, $p < 0.01$) between a collaboration index (measured by degree of information sharing, degree of decision synchronization, and degree of incentive alignment) and the performance index (measured by fulfillment rate, inventory turnover, and responsiveness). Another research study further indicates that firms in supply chains with high levels of collaboration have a greater competitive advantage than those in less collaborative supply chains (Themistcloeous et al, 2004; Myhe and Speckman, 2005).

The supply chain operation in a typical case starts with cooperation (to capture extra benefits) which may lead to collaboration (to create future value) which in turn creates an environment conducive to building trust in future commitments where business transactions actually are consummated (Kwon and Suh, 2004). Morgan and Hunt (1994, p.23) in their seminal piece of work on relationship marketing, define commitment as "an exchange partner believing that an ongoing relationship with another is so important as to warrant maximum efforts at maintaining it; that is, the committed party believes that the relationship endures indefinitely."

When commitment is honored under such a positive environment, the transaction cost is set to decrease noticeably because trust allows each party to act in good faith, thereby skipping such tedious transactional activities as checking the accuracy of invoices, quality of products, endless communications to resolve differences, discrepancies etc., (Dyer and Chu, 2003). As trust within and outside an organization improves, the speed of decision making also increases and costs of making timely decision, therefore, decrease. For example, end-to-end collaboration in supply chain activities provided a 30% saving in administrative cost (Duffy, 2009; Dyer and Chu, 2003). Xie, Suh and Kwon (2010) concluded in their study that transaction cost and financial investment constructs have a strong relationship with continuance and behavioral commitment. A close collaboration with a selected partner is cited as one of the 10 most critical strategies for leading supply chain organizations (Poirier, Quinn and Swink, 2010). A strong positive correlation ($R^2 = 0.69$, $p < 0.05$) was reported between the degree of collaboration with suppliers and profitability in the automobile industry (Poirier, Quinn and Swink, 2010). On the other hand, a lack of trust among and between trading partners is cited as one of the four most important barriers for supply chain excellence (Fawcett et al., 2009).

CONCEPTUAL MODEL

Literature seems to suggest that the level of trust among and between the business partners indeed tends to lower the transaction cost (Dyer and Chu, 2003). If the amount of transaction cost is reduced due to information sharing (reduce search cost) and the level of trust (reduce ex post cost), it is a reasonable assumption to argue that the total supply chain cost will also be reduced.

Figure 2 presents a theoretical roadmap under supply chain operations that operationalises the link between the level of trust and total supply chain cost reduction.

Information Sharing

Information sharing has been singled out as the most important factor for a successful supply chain alliance (Handfield, 2002; Kwon and Suh, 2005). Information sharing and sharing the rewards and risks are considered as two major supply chain principles that enahnces the supply chain optimi-

Figure 2. Conceptual model

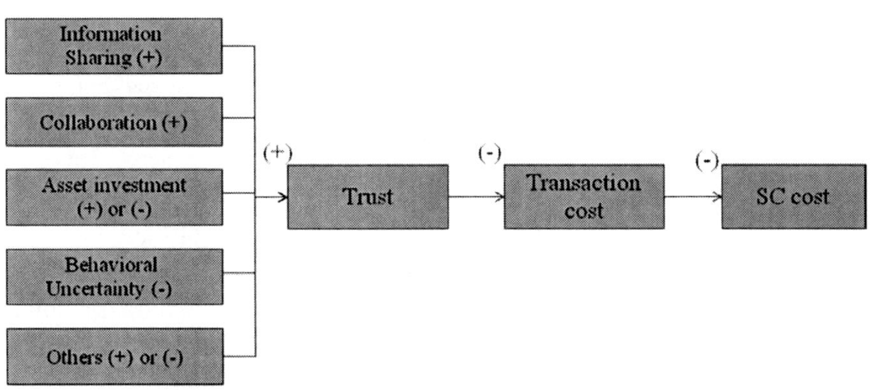

zation process. It has been suggested recently that supply chain partners not only share information on simple operational and tactical financial data, but also they exchange even critical strategic information such as forecasting, strategic goals, new product designs., etc to maximize the potentials from the supply chain alliance (Henderson, 2002). If partners share vital information, transaction becomes easier, efficient and effective. Accordingly, it is a reasonable to hypothesize that information sharing improves the opportunity to build trust which in turn reduces transaction cost.

Collaboration

North (1990) and Williamson (1981) argue that a sizeable part of the cost of goods and services contains transaction cost. North (1990) even suggested that the transaction cost amounts as much as 35 to 40% of total transaction cost. Dyer and Chu (2003) convincingly argued that there is a negative relationship between the trustworthiness and transaction cost. Kwon and Suh (2004 and 2005) provided empirical research results indicating the positive relationship between the degree of trust and the level of commitment. Therefore, it can be argued that collaboration creates an environment conducive to building trust which lowers the transaction cost. In other words, there is a positive relationship between the degree of collaboration and trust, and a negative relationship between the degree of collaboration and the amount of transaction cost.

Type of Asset Investment

When all the partners mutually commit specific asset investment, the interdependence between them is subsequently boosted, resulting in a more solid and interdependent relationship. Williamson (2008) was more specific of this argument; "because transaction-specific assets can be redeployed to alternative uses and users only at a loss of productive value, continuity preserving governance for such transactions is important." (p. 8). On the other hand, the asymmetrical specific asset investment among partners was found to be positively related to conflict among the partners (Suh, Xie and Kwon, 2005). Therefore, the direction of relationship between asset investment and the level of trust depends on whether partners engage in symmetrical (positive relationship) or asymmetrical asset investment (inverse relationship).

Partner's Behavioral Uncertainty

Behavioral uncertainty is defined as "the inability to predict partner behavior or changes in the external environment (Joshi and Stump, 1999, p.293). Behavioral uncertainty arises from the difficulties associated with monitoring the performance of transaction partners (Williamson, 1981). Therefore, behavioral uncertainty increases transactional costs even when contractual compliance is in place.

Other Attributes

There are many other attributes and factors that may be linked to variation of the level of trust which in turn may change the transaction cost.

EMPIRICAL EVIDENCE IN THE LITERATURE

Dyer and Chu (2003) studies the relationship between trust and transaction cost for the United States, Japan and Korea using the automobile industry as sample space. Samples in their study consist of three U.S. (General Motors, Ford, Chrysler), two Japanese (Toyota, Nissan), and three Korean (Hyundai, Daewoo, Kia) automakers and a sample of their Tier I suppliers. They investigated the relationship between the level of trust and ex ante total transaction cost, trust and ex post transaction cost and trust and the level of supplier information sharing.

Although there is no statistically significant relationship between the level of trust and ex ante transaction cost, there is a statistically significant relationship between the level of trust and ex post transaction cost ($p < 0.01$) with an inverse relationship, e.g. the higher the trust level the lower the total transaction cost. Such relationship is stronger for the United States sample than the other two countries. In addition, there is a strong positive relationship between the level of trust and the degree of information sharing as one partner would release more and pertinent information in a timely manner if a high level of trust is in place among trading partners. Their research result appears to confirm such hypothesis ($p < 0.01$).

Kwon and Suh (2004) attempts to measure the degree of relationship between cost (transaction cost variables—information sharing, behavioral uncertainty and asset specificity, and social exchange variables—perceived conflict, partner's reputation and perceived satisfaction), and the level of trust which leads to the degree of commitment. Samples came from supply chain professional organizations such as the American Inventory and Production Control Society (APICS), Council of Logistics Management (current Council for Supply Chain Management Professionals—CSCMP), and the Institute of Supply Management (ISM) in the St. Louis region.

Statistically reliable relationships were reported between the degree of information sharing and behavioral uncertainty ($p < 0.01$) and between behavioral uncertainty and the level of trust ($p < 0.01$). As to the individual variable, all variables listed above are related to the level of trust with p-values at least 0.05 except asset specificity where $p < 0.1$. Finally, their research reveals a positive and statistically significant relationship between the level of trust and the degree of commitment ($p < 0.01$).

The same authors re-analyzed the same data using path analysis in response to criticism that their 2004 study employed a least squared method to establish a casual relationship between independent variables and the level of trust, and between the level of trust and the degree of commitment. Kwon and Suh (2005) employed path analysis to establish the link between independent variables (asset investment, behavioral uncertainty, opportunistic behavior, degree of information sharing) and the level of trust and the degree of commitment in that sequence as shown in Figure 3 (Kwon and Suh, 2005).

The results confirm their previous study in that statistically significant relationships were established in the path model between trust and asset investment ($p < 0.01$), behavioral uncertainty ($p < 0.01$), opportunistic behavior ($p < 0.01$), and degree of information sharing ($p < 0.01$), and the level of trust and commitment ($p < 0.01$).

In a similar study conducted for a Korean industry as a sample space, Hong and Kwon (2009) hypothesized that business relationship will be sustained if there is a strong and reliable presence of information sharing based on the level of trust. The results are shown in Figure 4 (Hong and Kwon, 2009).

Based on a one-on-one interview with manufacturers and service providers in Incheon, Korea from May 9 to June 8, 2006 using 75 senior ex-

Figure 3. Conceptual path model (Kwon & Suh, 2005)

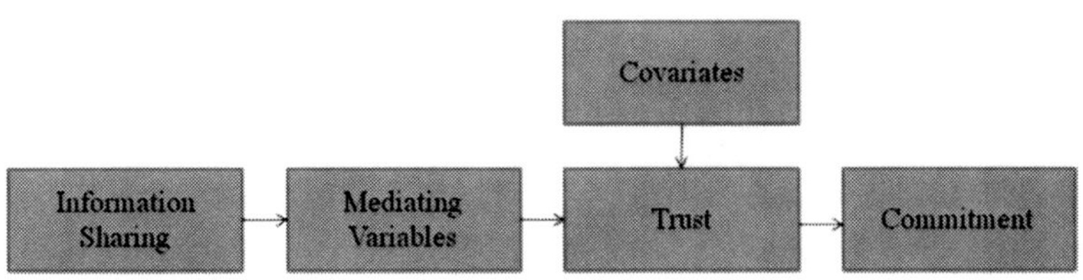

Figure 4. Conceptual model

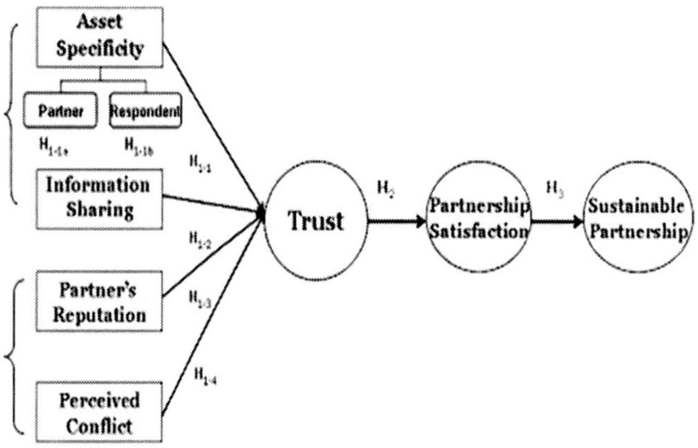

ecutives of the sample space, the authors found that there are strong and statistically significant relationships between sustainability of a business and the level of trust ($p < 0.003$), level of satisfaction ($P < 0.000$), and the level of information sharing ($p < 0.001$). If the inverse relationship between the degree of trustworthiness and transaction cost advanced by Dyer and Chu (2003) is correct, then it can be argued that Hong and Kwon's findings support hypothesis that the transaction cost would be lower if the partners have sustainable business relationship based on trust.

FUTURE RESEARCH

Empirical studies shown above appear to have established a reasonably clear link between collaboration and transaction cost in general and trust based commitment and supply chain cost in particular. However, empirical studies linking trust based collaboration to transaction cost at the micro/functional levels are not well defined and established. Recalling the Duffy's study (2009) argueing that a 30% of administrative cost saving is possible from collaborative supply chain in health care area, and

the 2010 Council for Supply Chain Management Professional's report on total administrative cost of $43 billion, and if we assume a minimum 30% of this cost (North, 1990) related to transaction cost, there is a significant room for improvement via collaborative logistics management.

Using the same conceptual model as Figure 2 especially on Covariate box, it is possible that cost savings through collaborative supply chain operations can be realized in several functional areas such as; maintaining and improving supply chain strategic plans, developing an effective supplier relationship management (SRM) program, establishing transparent sourcing strategies, lean based production processes, collaborative third party logistics management, inventory management using collaborative planning forecasting and replenishment (CPFR), and upgrading and maintaining customer relationship management (CRM). A roadmap to such process is shown in Figure 5.

Researchers in the supply chain management area, however, are facing a daunting challenge to operationalize the transaction cost theory into micro functional areas of the supply chain domain. As seen above, study after study points out the expected aggregated saving from transaction cost by using collaborative supply chain operations. But supply chain players are more interested in cost savings in their functional areas as shonw in Figure 5 (Covariates). Yet, the sources of such

Figure 5. Agenda for future research model

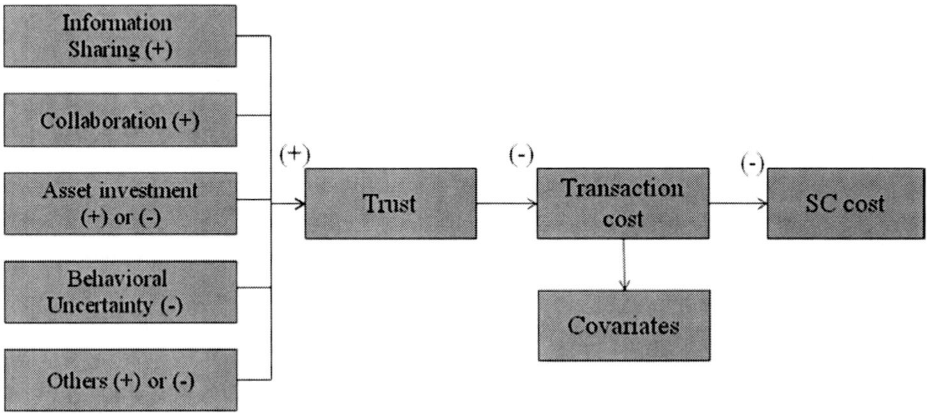

functional information in terms of transaction cost (ex ante as well as ex post) are not readily available from public and open sources. In spite of a common claim that each supply chain partner is willingly share critical information (cost), in reality such practice is rare than norm due perhaps to silo mentality that information is source of power maintaining unequal relationship in negotiation processes. Such challenge was echoed by Williamson (2008, p. 15) who raised a similar question: "transaction cost economic gives prominence to empirical testing of predictions with microanalytic data. How does supply chain management come out in these respects?" Scholars and researchers in the supply chain management field have not found an appropriate response to the above question at this time.

Since access to open sources of such "microanalytic data" is almost impossible, researchers have no choice but relying on proxy variables (yet to be developed) and/or private sources leaving objective verification of sources of information/data open to being challenged. However, like many other pioneer research breakthroughs, it is a matter of time that researchers in supply chain management fields will develop objective and measureable microanalytic data which allow us to be able to test a hypothesis that trust based collaborative partnership will decrease transaction cost and subsequent supply chain cost.

CONCLUSION

Transaction cost is a significant portion of total cost of goods and services. Managing and reducing the transaction cost may lead to a competitive cost advantage in the global marketplace. Search for ways to manage the transaction cost, therefore, should be an important research agenda.

Literature in this field appears to suggest two tools to reduce transaction cost; use of information technology which has been advanced much faster than other areas in supply chain optimization processes and building a strong collaborative relationship with trading partners. Literature is abundant linking information technology to transaction cost especially in the area of using RFID technology (Niederman, et al., 2007; Visich, et al., 2010)

A collaborative relationship may create an environment conducive to building trust. The literature supports a strong and positive relationship between the level of trust and the degree of information sharing which in turn improves the business environment for sustainable commitments where ultimate business is consummated.

However, testable microanalytic data is yet to be developed for empirical testing such a relationship in the functional areas in supply chain operations. We should not, nevertheless, be discouraged since "despite what almost 30 years ago may have appeared to be insurmountable obstacle to acquiring the relevant data[which are often primary data of a microanalytic kind], today transaction cost economies stands on a remarkably broad empirical foundation" (Geyskens, Steenkamp and Kumar, 2006).

The managerial implication appears to be rather straightforward. Improvement of information technologies will continue to enhance collaborative relationships through information sharing. Use of information technologies has been primarily in the areas of efficiency of transaction processing rather than enhancing collaboration via information sharing. One of the most difficult barriers in forming a successful supply chain partnership is the reluctance to information sharing-among and between trading partners. When and if such barriers are removed, then supply chain efficiency can be moved to the next level.

The other method, improving the level of trust and information sharing as a tool for reducing the transaction cost, is even more challenging because trust is abstract (hard to measure although many scholars have attempted to overcome such challenges) (Covey, 2006), complex (no single measurable tool available) and a long-term journey (it took us more than 20 years to understand the Japanese business culture). (Geyskens, Steenkamp and Kumar, 2006). However, research seems to indicate the reward from such a journey is substantial one that should not be ignored in this global market.

ACKNOWLEDGMENT

This chapter is partially funded by the Center for Supply Chain Management Studies at St. Louis University under Goals No. 3 in its Mission Statement

REFERENCES

Aoki, M. (1988). *Information, incentives, and bargaining in the Japanese economy*. New York, NY: Cambridge University Press. doi:10.1017/CBO9780511571701

Bakos, Y. J., & Kremerer, C. F. (1992). Recent applications of economic theory in information technology research. *Decisions Support Systems*, 365-386.

Barney, J. B., & Hansen, M. H. (1994). Trustworthiness as a source of competitive advantage. *Strategic Management Journal*, *15*, 175–190. doi:10.1002/smj.4250150912

Cheung, S. N. S. (1987). Economics organization and transactions costs. *The New Palgrave: A Dictionary of Economics*, *2*, 55-58.

Christiaanse, E., & Mrkus, N. L. (2003). Participation in collaboration electronic marketplaces. *Proceedings of the 36th Hawaii International Conference on Systems Science*, (pp. 1-44).

Clark, K. B., & Fujimoto, T. (1991). *Product development performance*. Boston, MA: Harvard Business School Press.

Clemons, E. K., Sashisdhar, P. R., & Row, M. C. (1993). The impact of Information Technology on the organization of economic activity: The move to the middle hypothesis. *Journal of Management Information Systems*, *10*(2), 9–33.

Coase, R. (1937). The nature of the firm. *Economica*, *4*(16), 386–405. doi:10.1111/j.1468-0335.1937.tb00002.x

Coase, R. (1960). The problem of social cost. *The Journal of Law & Economics*, *3*, 1–44. doi:10.1086/466560

Council for Supply Chain Management Professionals. (2010). *The status of logistics: Annual report*. Illinois: Lombard.

Covey, S. M. Jr. (2006). *The speed of trust*. New York, NY: Free Press.

Dore, R. (1983). Goodwill and the spirit of market capitalism. *The British Journal of Sociology*, *34*(4), 459–482. doi:10.2307/590932

Duffy, M. (2009). Is supply chain the cure for rising health care cost? *Supply Chain Management Review*, September, 28–35.

Dyer, J. (1997). Effective interfirm collaboration: How firms minimize transaction costs and maximize transaction value. *Strategic Management Journal*, *18*(7), 535–556. doi:10.1002/(SICI)1097-0266(199708)18:7<535::AID-SMJ885>3.0.CO;2-Z

Dyer, J., & Chu, W. (2003). The role of trustworthiness in reducing transaction costs and improving performance: Empirical evidence from the United States, Japan and Korea. *Organization Science*, *14*(1), 57–68. doi:10.1287/orsc.14.1.57.12806

Eshkenazi, A. (2009, May 29). APICS operations management now. *APICS Homepage*, 5-6.

Fawcett, S. S, Andrawski, J. C., Fawcett, A. M., & Magnan, G. M. (2009). The art of supply chain management. *Supply Chain Management Review*, November, 19-25.

Gefen, D. (2004). What makes an ERP implementation relationship worthwhile: Linking trust mechanisms and ERP usefulness? *Journal of Management Information Systems*, *21*(1), 263–288.

Geyskens, I., Steenkamp, J. E. M., & Kumar, N. (2006). Make, buy, or ally: A meta analysis of transaction cost theory. *Academy of Management Journal*, *49*(3), 519–543. doi:10.5465/AMJ.2006.21794670

Gulati, R. (1995). Familiarity breeds trust? The implications of repeated ties for contractual choice in alliances. *Academy of Management Journal*, *38*, 85–112. doi:10.2307/256729

Handfield, R. B. (2002, January). The new supply chain model. *APICS*, p. 24.

Henderson, R. (2002). *Going beyond the tactical*. White Paper. Lowell, MA: J.B. Hunt.

Hennart, J. F., & Anderson, A. E. (1993). Countertrade and the minimization of transaction costs: An empirical examination. *Journal of Law Economics and Organization*, *9*(2), 290–313.

Hong, S.-J., & Kwon, I.-W. (2009). *Study on impact of trust in supply chain partnership: A Korean case*. Paper presented at the 3rd International Conference on Operations and Supply Chain Management, at the Asian Institute of Medicine, Science and Technology in Malaysia, December 9-12.

Islamoglu, M., & Liebenau, J. (2007). Information Technology, transaction costs and governance structure: Integrating an institutional approach. *Journal of Information Technology*, *22*(3), 275–283. doi:10.1057/palgrave.jit.2000107

Joshi, A. W., & Stump, R. L. (1999). The contingent effect specific asset investment on joint action in manufacturer-supplier relationships: An empirical test of the moderating role of reciprocal asset investments, uncertainty, and trust. *Journal of the Academy of Marketing Science*, *27*(3), 291–305. doi:10.1177/0092070399273001

Kwon, I.-W., & Suh, T. (2004). Factors affecting the level of trust and commitment in supply chain relationships. *Journal of Supply Chain Management*, *40*(2), 4–14. doi:10.1111/j.1745-493X.2004.tb00165.x

Kwon, I.-W., & Suh, T. (2005). Trust, commitment and relationships in supply chain management: A path analysis. *Supply Chain Management: An International Journal*, *10*(1), 26–33. doi:10.1108/13598540510578351

Mentzer, J. T., DeWitt, W., Keebler, J. S., Min, S. H., Nix, N. W., Carlo, C. D., & Zacharia, Z. G. (2001). Defining the supply chain management. *Journal of Business Logistics*, *22*(2), 1–25. doi:10.1002/j.2158-1592.2001.tb00001.x

Morgan, R., & Hunt, S. (1994). The commitment-trust theory of relationship marketing. *Journal of Marketing*, *58*, 20–38. doi:10.2307/1252308

Myhe, N., & Speckman, R. R. (2005). Collaborative supply chain partnerships built upon trust and electronically mediated exchange. *Journal of Business and Industrial Marketing*, *20*(4-5), 179–186.

Niderman, F., Mathieu, R., Morley, R., & Kwon, I.-W. (2007). Examining RFID applications in supply chain management using a data lifecycle framework. *Communications of the ACM*, *50*(7), 92–101.

Nishiguchi, T. (1994). *Strategic industrial sourcing*. New York, NY: Oxford University Press.

North, D. C. (1990). *Institutions, institutional change and economic performance*. Cambridge, UK: Cambridge University Press.

Ouchi, W. (1980). Markets, bureaucracies, and class. *Administrative Science Quarterly*, *25*, 125–141. doi:10.2307/2392231

Ouchi, W. (1984). *The M-form society*. New York, NY: Avon Books.

Perrow, C. (1986). *Complex organizations: A critical essay*. New York, NY: McGraw-Hill, Inc.

Poirier, C. C., Quinn, F. J., & Swink, M. L. (2010). *Diagnosing greatness*, Ross publication.

Porter, M. E. (1996). What is strategy? *Harvard Business Review*, (November-December): 61–78.

Sampson, G. (2003). The myth of the diminishing firm. *Communications of the ACM*, *46*(11), 25–28. doi:10.1145/948383.948404

Simatupang, T. M., & Sridharan, R. (2005). The collaboration index: A measure for supply chain collaboration. *International Journal of Physical Distribution & Logistics Management*, *35*(1), 44–62. doi:10.1108/09600030510577421

Suh, T., Xie, H., & Kwon, I.-W. (2005). The effect of total and asymemetric specific asset investment on supplier-buyer relationship: A structural model. *Proceeding of the 2005 Winter American Marketing Association Conference*, San Antonio, Texas, February, (pp. 298-299).

Tadelis, S. (2007). The innovative organization: Creating value through outsourcing. *California Management Review*, *50*(1), 261–277.

Themistcloeous, M., Irani, Z., & Love, P. E. D. (2004). Evaluating the integration of supply chain Information Systems: A case study. *European Journal of Operational Research*, *159*(2), 393–405. doi:10.1016/j.ejor.2003.08.023

Uzzi, B. (1997). Social structure and competition in interfirm networks: The paradox of embeddedness. *Administrative Science Quarterly*, *42*, 35–67. doi:10.2307/2393808

Visich, J. K., Li, S., Khumawala, B. M., & Reyes, P. M. (2010). Empirical evidence of RFID impacts on supply chain performance. *International Journal of Operations & Production Management*, *29*(12).

Williamson, O. (1981). The economics of organizations: The transaction cost approach. *American Journal of Sociology*, *87*(3), 548–577. doi:10.1086/227496

Williamson, O. (2008). Outsourcing: Transaction cost economics and supply chain management. *Journal of Supply Chain Management*, *44*(2), 5–16. doi:10.1111/j.1745-493X.2008.00051.x

Woolhandler, S., Campbell, T., & Himmelstein, D. (2003). Costs of health care administration in the United States and Canada. *The New England Journal of Medicine*, 349.

Xie, Y. H., Suh, T., & Kwon, I.-W. (2010). Do magnitude and asymmetry of specific asset investment matter in supplier-buyer relationship? *Journal of Marketing Management*, *26*(9).

Young-Ybarra, C., & Wiersema, M. (1999). Strategic flexibility in Information Technology alliances: The influence of transaction cost economics and social exchange theory. *Organization Science*, *10*(4), 439–459. doi:10.1287/orsc.10.4.439

Zaheer, A., McEvily, B., & Perrone, V. (1998). Does trust matter? Exploring the effects of interorganizational and interpersonal trust on performance. *Organization Science*, *9*(2), 141–159. doi:10.1287/orsc.9.2.141

Chapter 6
Using Actor-Network Theory to Research the Adoption of Inter-Organizational Information Systems

Jim Underwood
University of Technology Sydney, Australia

Bruce McCabe
KPMG, Australia

ABSTRACT

Inter-organizational information systems depend at least as much on collaboration across organizational cultures as on the development of technical infrastructure for their success. Actor-network theory (ANT) is a useful approach for bringing together social and technical considerations. In this chapter we discuss key features of ANT and show how it might be applied to a particular case of IOIS adoption; this ANT approach is compared to co-evolutionary theory which was originally applied to this case. Some possible extensions to ANT are contemplated, and we offer advice to those attempting ANT-based research. We also give advice, based on ANT, to those undertaking IOIS development.

STUDYING TECHNOLOGY AND ORGANIZATIONAL CULTURE

In this chapter we discuss the adoption of inter-organizational information systems (IOIS). We define IOIS as systems that allow operational information to be sent across organizational boundaries (Johnston & Vitale, 1988). By 'operational information' we mean information that is directly used by business processes that support commercial relationships among the organizations; information that is structured to provide this support, as opposed to unstructured information included in emails or web pages. This implies that the collaborating organizations

DOI: 10.4018/978-1-60960-768-5.ch006

Copyright © 2012, IGI Global. Copying or distributing in print or electronic forms without written permission of IGI Global is prohibited.

will most likely need to adjust their internal systems and processes to the requirements of the interorganizational system, and this is one of the main impediments to IOIS adoption. Our discussion of adoption is not at the strategic level; we do not consider economic motivations, overall business strategies or top management attitudes that might impact the original decision to move to IOIS. Instead we consider how, as the IOIS are developed, the various intra-organisational actors (such as operational management) do or do not alter their objectives and procedures, and how the behaviour of these actors might affect success or otherwise of IOIS projects.

In their study of e-procurement systems in the Hong Kong textile industry Yen and Ng (2002) found that process reengineering represented a far greater challenge to IOIS adoption than did technology implementation. Thus in understanding the success or failure of IOIS we need theories and research methods that can help us to understand technical aspects of IOIS, the cultures of the collaborating organizations, and the interactions of technology and culture. This raises the problem of finding suitable frameworks, theories or approaches for researching interdisciplinary issues, such as the design and use of computer-based information systems. To understand the technical aspects of these systems we can draw upon computer science, network theories, relational database theory and the more traditional aspects of information science. For cultural aspects we have psychology, sociology and anthropology (all often referenced through organization studies, itself an interdisciplinary 'discipline'), as well as recent work on information behavior in information science (Wilson, 1997). But as well as the difficulty of becoming familiar with all these 'reference' disciplines, the information systems (IS) researcher needs theories for linking the technological and the cultural.

One approach is to look for a single theory that applies to both the social and the technical. Popular candidates in IS research have been information science (Shannon & Weaver, 1964), control theory (Beer, 1985) and general systems theory (Weinberg, 1975), most recently re-emerging as complexity theory (Goldspink & Kay, 2003). These theories have been effective in alerting IS researchers to important features of socio-technical systems, but have been unable to provide specific guidelines for conducting IS research projects. This is partly because the theories are in fact too general, describing results which apply in every circumstance, and partly because researchers have attempted to use mathematical versions of the theories, only to discover insurmountable problems of measurement when studying cultural aspects of systems.

Actor-network theory (ANT) deals with the relationship between the technical and the social in the most radical way—by defining it away. A major feature of ANT as a method is to emphasize a number of 'symmetries,' in particular a symmetry in how we think about 'humans' and 'non-humans.' ANT has been used in a considerable amount of IS research, although not extensively in IOIS. In the next section of this chapter we discuss the development of ANT, its main features, and some of its applications in IS research. We then introduce a case study of the introduction of IOIS by some large Australian organizations, and discuss the re-analysis of this case using ANT. The ANT analysis is compared with the original analysis of the case which used co-evolutionary theory. The final section summarises some advantages and benefits of ANT, suggests some possible improvements, and provides some guidelines for those contemplating using ANT for IOIS research.

VARIETIES OF ACTOR-NETWORK RESEARCH

ANT arose as a framework for interpreting research in science and technology studies. In attempting a sociological study of scientists in their laboratories, it became apparent that equipment, chemicals and scientific theories played more than passive or contextual roles in the trajectory of laboratory culture (Latour & Woolgar, 1979). To make sense of the work of the scientists, the sociologists had to understand the interactions of humans, institutions, technical artifacts and concepts. This eventually led to an emphasis on symmetry or, as Latour later recast it, not imposing 'a priori some spurious asymmetry among human intentional action and a material world of causal relations' (Latour, 2005 p. 76). Adding an intentional framework to our views of non-humans allows us to trace the success or otherwise of particular objects/concepts such as oxygen (Latour, 1987) or particular socio-technical projects such as an innovative urban transit system (Latour, 1996). The participants, human or otherwise, in the project, the evolution of a theory or the work of a laboratory, are called the *actors*. It is important that they be thought of as mediators that transmit effects on their own terms, that may or may not co-operate, rather than intermediaries, passive links in causal chains (Latour, 2005). In later work Latour also discusses a number of other symmetries: between success and failure, between adoption and resistance, and between macro and micro explanations. We will explain these symmetries as we describe a variety of ANT approaches.

It is worth noting here that actor-network theory is not usually considered a 'theory' (Latour, 1999) but a set of research approaches or attitudes (for example, about symmetry) to socio-technical systems. This means that ANT researchers differ in their ontologies (e.g. realist or constructionist), their objectives (to understand or to promote change), and their choice of conceptual tools. And ANT does not claim to provide complete explanations or predictions so much as tools for critiquing and sometimes reconciling other theoretical explanations of particular situations.

ANT and the Politics of Projects

The aspect of ANT that is most commonly used in IS research is the *translation* view of project development. As with many terms in ANT, 'translation' is used somewhat ambiguously; in this case we have an example of the interaction or symmetry of macro and micro explanations. At the macro level we speak of the translation (or transformation) of a chaotic collection of potential actors into a coherent assembly of allies working for the project. On the micro level we are concerned with conscripting individual actors as allies to the project, with translating the project's needs into the actor's personal goals. Clearly these are just two ways of theorising about the same phenomenon; the principle of symmetry suggests that neither way is primary, that neither a top-down nor a bottom-up approach is sufficient.

For a project to exist, for a theory to develop, the actors must assemble into a network, a loose, dynamic, always tentative collaboration. From the point of view of a particular actor (perhaps a project manager) who is trying to promote some idea, action or value, the objective is to assemble this network of allies. This of course has been 'known' since the beginning of time; the contribution of ANT is to analyse the formation of these alliances in terms of the intentions of actors, including non-human actors. This is most clearly explained in Callon's (1986) study of the development of a farmed scallop fishery, where actors included scallops, tides, wooden frames, fishermen, fishermen's co-operatives, markets and scientists (an example of symmetry with respect to different types of actor). Callon proposed four stages of translation in the development of networks—problematisation, intéressement, enrolment and mobilization—which move from getting the issue onto the agenda to having the final product accepted as a 'matter of fact' or a black box, something which is no longer questioned.

Problematisation involves constructing the problem. Some question or issue comes up and the sponsor identifies other actors who could be interested in the project. These actors are also constructed, in the sense that they are understood by the sponsor, but not yet by themselves, in terms of how they need the project. The project needs to be conceived as an *obligatory passage point*: the actors must learn not only that they have needs which the project will satisfy but also that the project is the only way these needs can be achieved.

For *intéressement* the sponsor must make the actors aware of their needs and have them acknowledge that the project may indeed provide the means of meeting those needs. This may mean, among other things, detaching some of the actors from interests in competing projects or perhaps including secondary actors who will help convince an original actor of their interest in the project. All sorts of technical devices, concepts, procedures and personal performances may be used in this process. As well as their own needs and the project, the actors should also be made aware of the other actors who are 'supporting' the project.

The actors must now be *enrolled* into a solid alliance and each start delivering on their part of the deal (which is not yet in writing). In many cases committees will form, documents will be produced, goals set and plans made. Many actors and performances need to be represented, by delegates, diagrams, mathematical models or test specifications. This is all achieved through the usual mixture of consent, negotiation, coercion, seduction, tricks and trials of strength.

Mobilisation is the last stage of translation. The original idea now needs to become commonplace and material (in the senses of both solid and relevant) for a multitude of as yet absent actors (Callon, 1986). If successful the project loses its identity and becomes part of everyday life; the network is said to have become a *black box*. The success or otherwise of the project at this stage is a test of the representations made during the translation process. There was no way of telling, until now, whether these representatives (be they diagrams or elected delegates) had the support of the masses. The proof of the project is in its acceptance.

The contributions of ANT are in its insistence on symmetry and on operationalising the assembly of allies. Thus, in the case of Aramis, the system of loosely coupled urban trains (Latour, 1996), the system itself was seen as an actor that was trying to come into being (a very useful way of conceptualising something that is in the process of being designed). The system failed because, although various parts such as couplings, motors and carriage bodies were able to enroll allies, the system as a whole could not. This example illustrates three instances of symmetry: the intentionality of non-humans (even those that do not yet exist), actors that act independently, even though they are parts of other actors, and narratives that take the same form, irrespective of whether the outcome is success or failure.

The ANT view of project translation was applied to a number of large IT projects in Norway. The case of the diffusion of Lotus Notes throughout Statoil (the Norwegian oil company) clearly illustrates the serendipitous emergence of infrastructure as an actor-network alliance. Notes entered Statoil as 'an amusing little side dish' packaged with Lotus Office Suite (Monteiro and Hepsø, 1998 p. 260). As a contribution to an organizational restructuring initiative a new IT research group attempted to use Notes to support discussion groups on best practice, buying credibility through an alliance with the MIT Center for Coordination Science. The less glamorous IT department, on the other hand, distributed Notes as an email system in a package with Lotus Office on the internal PC-based wide-area network. The take-up of Notes was slow—at one time in 1994, 85% of email messages still used the previous mainframe based system. By 1996 several thousand local Notes databases had evolved in Statoil and, with the introduction of a new version of the software, the IT department took the opportunity to rationalise the management of these databases. Switching to Notes as the preferred email tool was packaged with the transition to Windows '95, thus forming an alliance with Microsoft 'inevitability' (and the Rolling Stones). A further opportunistic alliance was formed with ISO 9001, as quality accreditation required the archiving of many documents, and this facility was provided by 'one button' in the Notes implementation. By 1997 there were 18,000 Notes users in Statoil. The Statoil example shows infrastructure developing as an alliance through hard work, seizing of opportunities and building on existing networks, without conforming to a predetermined plan.

A feature of the large complex alliances which are infrastructure is that they are 'slow and almost impossible to implement, but if successful irreversible and irresistible' (Hanseth and Monteiro, 1997 p. 207). This raises the question of how infrastructure can be changed. Hanseth and Monteiro use standards as a general example of infrastructure; standards are not static documents, but stable alliances of committees, researchers, technology providers and users. In a study of the internet protocol (IP) standard, Monteiro (1998) traces attempts to introduce a new IP standard. The need for this change is brought on by 'external' actors, the huge number of people (or machines) requiring unique internet addresses. The difficulty is that this same mass is inextricably aligned to the current standard, so that for any change to be acceptable it must be minimal (and hence ineffective?). The components of the actor-network become locked into one another in a deadly dance where none succeeds in breaking out.

So far we have looked at networks and alliances from the point of view of an 'outsider' or of a project sponsor. How do the actors see the alignment process? McMaster, Vidgen and Wastell (1998) propose a number of stages of induction through which an actor will pass before being aligned with a network. McMaster phrases the question as 'what and who should be included in the collective?' (1998 p. 346) which implies a one-sided judgement on the part of the existing network (in as much as it aligns on this question) but the stages described can as easily be seen as two-sided negotiation. The stages proposed are perplexity (what is this other?), consultation (establishing congruous values), hierarchy (finding, through translation, a possibly suitable place in the network) and institution (normalisation, acceptance). Clearly this sequence is the dual of Callon's phases of project development. While the network is gaining mass support and eventual black box status through the stages of problematisation, intéressement, enrolment and mobilisation the individual actors 'come on board' through the four stages of induction. The time scales of the two sequences do not coincide; the individual actor's induction time is usually short compared to the project history. We suspect that individual actors have the greatest chance of influencing the direction of the network during the enrolment phase, but this remains to be investigated. In any case, McMaster proposes that if actors join a network without passing through all stages of induction the probability of instability will increase. Ensuring that the stages of induction are followed properly is a question of due process and two models (both British) of due process are proposed: the courtroom and the parliament (where opposing parties represent the social and the technical). For IS development these might correspond to steering committee meetings (McMaster's example) and a JAD session (our example). In both cases a crucial issue is who is represented in what respect by whom.

The due process model was expanded by Tabak (2010) and applied to the attempt to introduce a corporate intranet into a major Australian entertainment distribution organization, where the researcher was employed as the internet content manager. Since employees often discovered things from the company's external facing internet site that were difficult to discover otherwise, a plan evolved to use the techniques learned from developing the internet as the basis for a company knowledge support system. At this stage problematisation had not even begun, and top management was not convinced that a company wide intranet was necessary. Nevertheless, the project promoters developed a number of web-based systems to support some processes in individual departments of the company. Some of these became obligatory points of passage for some employees (already allied to the project promoters) and so reached the intéressement stage; others fell by the wayside. The project only managed to enroll a significant proportion of employees when a technical innovation allowed it to connect successfully to a new ally, a spreadsheet application that was already widely used within the company. This shows the importance of choosing some allies that have already been 'black-boxed,' whose use is accepted as given.

Getting the Allies on Side: Scripting and Intentionality

To operationalise alliances, Latour's early work relied on the idea of inscription (Latour, 1992). An actor may have a script they wish to implement, such as 'be aware of intruders.' We might implement this script alone (by staying awake and alert), or we might conscript a network of allies, each of which might need to implement a related script ('increase the output voltage when motion is detected,' 'SMS this number when voltage increase is detected,' 'make sound when SMS is received'). Here we have the second, lower level, more operational meaning of translation. Making an alliance involves the translation of one actor's script into something that another actor will understand and be willing and able to implement. An obvious example is programming a computer to perform some task. Despite what computing texts may say, those of us who have attempted this are only too aware that the computer is a true mediator, that it may or may not do what we tell it.

This suggests one way of studying the development and maintenance of actor-networks is to 'follow the scripts,' looking in detail at how they are translated (or betrayed, another example of symmetry—Underwood, 2001b). This might involve looking in detail at conversations, emails, manuals and other types of text. Latour (2005), instead, suggests we 'follow the actors,' but the effect is similar (and scripts could be seen as actors as well). In any case, the important thing is to follow where the situation leads us, across boundaries, across levels, engaging with any type of actor we encounter, and drawing insights from whatever disciplines seem appropriate. We must resist trying to fit the data to some pre-conceived framework. This suggests a similarity with the grounded theory approach (Glasser, 1998), but ANT concentrates on the narrative and delays the construction of any theoretical model; there is an obstinate insistence on the details of the particular (Bakhtin, 1993).

From the point of view of a project promoter macro and micro translation are brought together by the *program* (Latour, 1992). This is a plan for inscribing a variety of actors with a variety of scripts in the hope that the actions of the conscripted actors will align and bring the project to mobilisation. Hanseth and Monteiro (1997) explore the necessity and mechanism of this alignment in the case of a project to facilitate the exchange among Norwegian health providers and agencies of information on lab tests and prescriptions. For a designer wishing to induce stable alignment important issues are the anticipation of use scenarios for various actors, the translation and inscription of desired behaviour (what they should do in order to maintain alignment), who is responsible for inscription and how strong (resistant to opposition) the inscriptions will be. For example, it became desirable (to the designers) to have general practitioners order drugs from pharmacies using a standard drug code. For the general practitioners this could be translated as 'have access to drug list' which had other useful data such as prices, but the central drug depot resisted, for commercial reasons, an inscription 'make drug list available.' In this case events in other networks changed the behaviour of the drug depot; an agreement with the European Community to allow other drug suppliers access to the Norwegian market encouraged the drug depot to be more cooperative, but also complicated the designers' task, since drug codes were not standard across companies. Other potential actors were difficult to align because they wished to appropriate the developing infrastructure to their own wider discourse. An attempt to align with the international EDIFACT standard for electronic record exchange meant moving from the single page data specification used by one local laboratory to a 500 page standard specification (Hanseth and Monteiro, 1997 p. 196), presumably because EDIFACT needs to align with a far greater mass of actors than will ever participate in the Norwegian lab network. Another attempt at standardisation was made by the Norwegian telecommunications network, who turned to the relevant IEEE committee known as Medix. 'The Medix effort adopted a standardization approach—perfectly in line with text books on information systems development—that the development should be based on an information model being a 'true' description of the relevant part of reality, that is, the health care sector, independent of existing as well as future technology. Individual messages would be derived from the model; more or less automatically. … for those involved in Medix the task of developing a Norwegian standardized lab report message had around 1990 been translated into the development of a proper object-oriented data model of the world-wide health care sector' (1997 p. 193).

In the above example we see many non-human actors who needed to be enrolled, actors such as standards, drug lists and the central drug depot, while human actors such as general practitioners were probably in fact represented by their non-human professional organizations. We can see the advantage of ascribing intentions to non-humans such as the drug depot—for the purposes of this project it is far simpler to accept the depot as a black box that 'resists' and use the simplistic explanation of 'commercial reasons' than to break the box open and attempt an explanation in terms of the intentions of the various managers, committee members, accountants and external lobbyists who have mobilised this resistance. We can also see in this description the symmetry between success and failure; the project did in fact fail, the network did not align, but this was neither necessary nor caused by the failure of particular actors. If external events had been timed differently, a very similar story may have ended in success. In particular, the advent of the agreement with the European Community could have provided a key ally, but the necessary standards had not yet been black-boxed, so that they attempted to conscript the Norwegian project to their own program of mobilisation.

APPLYING ANT TO AN IOIS PROJECT

In this section we discuss a study of IOIS adoption by a number of large Australian organizations (McCabe & Underwood, 2008). An iterative research approach was used. In the first phase, extensive interviews were conducted with systems initiators (executives identified as having overall responsibility for the e-commerce system within the initiator organization) and their trading partners from ten Australian e-commerce inter-organizational systems, covering a range of industries (including building and construction, manufacturing, finance, and agriculture) and business processes (including quoting, purchasing, invoicing, and project co-ordination). While the systems studied were all operational (thus excluding systems that had already failed), the emphasis was on understanding the enablers of engagement, and the sample appeared to be more than adequate for this purpose: it included systems where some trading partners had been engaged successfully while others had not, and systems that had struggled through difficult periods in their history.

Transcriptions of the interviews were interpreted through hermeneutic analysis and common themes were identified (Boyatzis, 1998). Based on the themes that emerged and the issues identified from the literature, it was decided to apply a co-evolutionary model (McCabe 2006) to the process of partner engagement. This was used as a framework for a detailed case study of one of the IOIS, with further interviews designed to capture all the decisions, events and changes that were important in the history of the system and engagement of trading partners.

Themes for Engagement in IOIS

Important themes affecting motivation to adopt IOIS that emerged from the initial interviews were:

1. Distributing benefits and costs fairly between initiators and trading partners was critical; differences significant enough to be perceived as unfair slowed engagement.
2. Adjusting to the value propositions that are important to different trading partners; even within one IOIS different trading partners often engaged for very different reasons depending on their circumstances and organizational priorities.
3. Identifying and selecting the right personnel to 'sell' the system to trading partners was an important enabler; better results were achieved when people were used with the same professional background as the personnel targeted.
4. Targeting the right people / job roles within trading partners was strongly linked to successful engagement; references were made to job roles such as logistics managers, billing managers, project directors, purchasing officers, content managers and designers.
5. Using other organizations to assist in the engagement process; positive and negative assessments of systems, received from trusted peers in the trading partner community, had considerable impact on engagement.
6. Providing trading partners with assistance and technical support.
7. Identifying competing priorities in partner organizations; when other priorities dominated management thinking, any new e-commerce project, even if recognised as valuable and viable, could not gain traction.
8. Minimising the organizational change required of trading partners.
9. Trading partner respondents described duplication of existing processes as reducing their motivation to adopt or make further use of a system; a common example of duplicated business processes was the requirement to re-enter data into an e-commerce IOS that had already been entered into an internal system.
10. Pre-packaging and removing complexity from the system, its implementation and the engagement process.
11. Addressing trading partner concerns over independence and lock-in; concerns about e-commerce systems increasing dependence on the initiator, increase the initiator's market power and/or make it more difficult to dismantle a trading relationship in future were sometimes a critical factor in engagement.
12. The need to solicit feedback from trading partners and to act upon it by adjusting the system and/or the way engagement was undertaken.

The study also identified a number of major turning points in each implementation project. These often related to changes in market conditions, availability of new technology, and changes in organizational structure or personnel. Interestingly, in only one case was a turning point related to one of the major themes above.

The Evolution of One IOIS

After themes and turning points had been identified in the ten organizations, one was selected for in depth study. This was the Australian subsidiary of an international supplier of industrial cleaning equipment, with around 200 employees (including an internal IT department of 3) and a turnover of about 90 million AUD. Most sales were made through 900 distributors, while 15% of sales were direct to a small number of very large (mostly government) customers. Of the 900 distributors, 180 were regarded as significant and just 3 accounted for 30% of sales. The distributors were not tied to the company; they offered products at different prices and also sold competing products.

The move to IOIS started in 1998, with the establishment of an online shopping mall on the company's server, where distributors were given pages where they could accept orders that were then transferred to the company's ordering system. This was technically the most feasible approach at the time and streamlined ordering for the system initiators, but did not integrate with the IT systems of the trading partners. The immediate reason for rejection of the system by the trading partners was, however, the exposure of an ambiguity in the agreed level of business collaboration—the company was unwilling to let the trading partners advertise competitors' products on their web pages.

By 2002 it was possible to contemplate installing systems at trading partners' sites, which would accept orders and transmit them to the company. The largest trading partner was chosen as the first participant, and considerable effort was put into tailoring the system to their needs. When it became clear that the same effort would be required for the second and subsequent participants, implementation was indefinitely postponed as uneconomical. Within a few months a new customer service manager had been appointed and simpler and cheaper technology became available; perhaps because of an assumed difference in power relationships, it was decided to offer a new system to smaller distributors. Initially only three distributors took up the offer, and it became apparent that there were problems with process integration that necessitated re-keying of orders. Over the next year this and a number of other process problems had been solved and twelve distributors had been enrolled. At this stage the CEO became actively involved and the improvements were consolidated in a new system release. Within six months the number of participating distributors had tripled.

IOIS Adoption as Co-Evolution

The above narrative was originally interpreted by McCabe (2006) in terms co-evolution. The first scholarly use of the term 'co-evolution' is ascribed to Erlich and Raven (1964) in their study of the evolutionary interaction between butterflies and plants. It refers to cases where there is two-way feedback between the evolutionary pathways of two species, with each applying selection pressure to variations in the other, in such a way as to encourage mutually beneficial behaviour. In the study of organizations and technology co-evolutionary theory has been applied to the selection of technology, and to changes in roles, routines and strategies. Kay and Cecez-Kecmanovic (2001) examined the effect of an information system implementation on a company, and the company on the information system in order to provide a deeper understanding of processes that underpin the resulting competitive advantages; Peters, Heng and Vet (2002) studied the evolution of an IS strategy within a leasing company and found the IS and organizational change co-evolved, without the adoption of formal strategies or planning methods.

While they did not explicitly use such a co-evolutionary model, Chatterjee, Grewal and Sambamurthy (2002 p. 66) noted that:

The effective assimilation of web technologies requires their integration into existing organizational work processes and this might necessitate changes to current technologies and work processes…however not many firms succeed in orchestrating the co-evolutionary changes to their technologies-in-use, organizational structures, processes, and incentive and reward systems to successfully assimilate Web technologies into their e-commerce initiatives.

This extract applies to the co-evolution of different aspects of information systems and their environment in on organization; with IOIS the co-evolution must occur across several organizations. Issues in different organizations, at different levels of detail, and from different discourses (IT, marketing, finance etc.) are intimately intertwined, and resistance or change in one area may affect progress in apparently unrelated areas. As one manager from the cleaning equipment supplier stated:

A lot of ideas started coming out of different places. So the idea for credit notes, the idea for adding service capabilities, came out of the customer service area, other ideas came from the warehouse, and from storemen. So one of the interesting observations from this project is that it is developing, and it keeps developing and growing because now there is input from all over the organization that has taken on a life of its own.

McCabe (2006) analysed co-evolution of the IOIS technology and business processes in the participating organisations using Rosenkopf and Nerkar's (1999) model of technology innovation. The IOIS evolves through feature selection at three levels, the trading system, trading operations and components. Within each level there are various communities (such as purchasing departments) which are the main agents of selection, but selection pressures also work across communities and across levels. Components are not only technical but social, including business processes, routines and informal networks based on trust. Evolution occurs erratically, sometimes speeding or slowing, sometimes changing direction, despite the best plans of the system's initiators.

Applying ANT to the Evolution of an IOIS

There are clear parallels between evolutionary theory and ANT. We can easily trace the IOIS described above through the stages problematisation, intéressement, enrolment and mobilisation. When, however, we look more closely at the history of the system we see that different functional components of the system moved through these stages at different paces, and that we need to consider also the evolution of subsystems at the level of trading operations and components. Web-based ordering, for instance, mobilised earlier than online order tracking, although this could have been otherwise, especially considering the problems with data re-entry. A significant number of partners were only enrolled when improved software components became available, presumably mobilised by an unknown network in a software company. This example emphasises the importance of finding allies that are already black-boxed. We could also find many examples of due process being followed or bypassed. The failure of the online shopping mall, for instance, resulted from incomplete consultation, so that trading partners were enrolled without clarifying the issue of advertising competitor's products.

The co-evolutionary analysis of the IOIS suggests some points where ANT might be clarified or expanded. Taken at face value, it appears that Callon's four stages of development assume that the project is well-defined before or during the problematisation phase while with co-evolution the final outcome is always contingent on ongoing interactions of components. This is not a real point of difference—if we use the full power of ANT and consider how translation at the macro level is enacted through micro translation of numerous scripts then it is apparent that a project is always undefined until it is completed. In a project to develop support flexible learning in an Australian university, all human actors assumed that the outcome would be a software system. When the network was black-boxed (on time and within budget of course) it turned out to be a paper-based handbook. Almost all the human actors (except the programmer) were happy. (Underwood, 2001a). The other point of interest is the 'co' in co-evolution. ANT normally considers only one program in a network; other interests that may lure away potential allies are thought of as part of the *anti-program.* In co-evolution there are always at least two complementary programs. This does not require any theoretical changes of ANT but does make the analysis more complex. Whether it is helpful to think of the co-evolving systems as constituting a 'super system' is an open question.

The mechanism of evolutionary theory has two key components—the selection of 'fittest' characteristics by the environment (macro or population level) and the usually faithful transmission of characteristics to the next generation (micro or individual level). The selection mechanism is fairly obvious; in modern evolutionary theory the transmission mechanism is explained via genes; the rare failures of transmission are ascribed to random mutations. With co-evolution the selection processes are more complex, but there is no question of transmission across species. When co-evolution is applied to IOIS selection is still fairly easy to conceptualise although not so visible, but it is not so clear what takes the place of genes. Richard Dawkins (1976) might say 'memes,' ANT would probably say 'scripts.'

What ANT adds to the co-evolutionary analysis is elucidation of the detail of 'how' selection, transmission and mutation work. This is where the symmetry between macro and micro becomes critical. As we have seen from the case study of the cleaning equipment supplier reciprocal selection occurs at all levels and across levels. It is not simply the initiating organization and its trading partners that are analogous to species in biological co-evolution; there are also various trading processes across organizations that are co-evolving, entangled in a web of selection, inscription and resistance. As ANT dissolves the demarcation between micro and macro, it also conflates selection and transmission. The mechanism of macro translation is micro translation, inscription. The IOIS initiator might wish to promote a script such as 'place your orders through my website.' A trading partner may accept or reject this script. Transmission succeeds or fails; selection occurs. The only distinction we might make is to regard selection as somewhat longer term, depending on a number of inscriptions, with the possibility of taking alternative paths if some inscriptions are rejected.

ANT also recognises that transmission is not exact, but is subject (almost always) to mutation. Different actors have different abilities, use different languages, and are connected to different other actors. The script must be translated rather than simply transmitted, and in translation it may be changed. Depending on the degree of change we may label the process as 'translation' or 'betrayal.' The trading partner (or their representative) may accept the script 'place my orders through your website' (already a slight translation) but may now need to transmit it to the ordering process which might translate it in part as 'connect our computer to your computer' or 're-key the order data'—which translation is made depends in part on what scripts my computer and your computer are prepared to accept.

The above description will be familiar to anyone who has designed and built a computer-based information system. Where ANT differs is in emphasising intentionality, in treating all actors as mediators, as having their own programs which may or may not be compatible with 'the' program. The purchasing department may be committed to the script 'don't change order processing—again!'; the finance department be promoting 'don't spend any more on IT upgrades'; the server may be saying 'don't ask for more memory.' These stories too are familiar, but most models used in IS research and practice are unable to deal with them. Intentionality also separates ANT from co-evolution—in evolution transmission, mutation and selection are all 'blind.'

It is interesting to review the themes derived in the original study in the light of ANT. Themes 1 and 2 refer to an actor deciding whether enrolment in the project represents good value for them—the need to make this judgement implies that the actor has competing programs or values that may or may not be compatible with the project. Themes 3 and 4 are about facilitating the translation process—this is often helped if both actors share a common discourse. Themes 5 and 6 involve calling upon extra allies—for theme 6 the project initiators may need to construct an additional actor, 'technical support.' Theme 7 refers to anti-programs—these are not just programs of resistance, but may be other projects making claims on the resources of the actor. Themes 8 and 9 deal with the difficulty of opening existing black boxes—the trading partners do not wish to change their established business processes. In theme 10 we see that the trading partners will feel more comfortable in alliances with systems that are already black-boxed. Theme 11, on the other hand, indicates that some actors resist enrolment for fear of being trapped in a black box with no hope of escape. Theme 12 recognises that the project is never fully defined—the purpose of change management is to allow the network to develop, not to control it.

By re-interpreting the themes is this way we can better see how they interact, and may be able to translate them into specific advice for supporting a project.

USING ANT IN RESEARCH AND PRACTICE

The most important advice for those contemplating using ANT in IS research is 'take ANT seriously, but not too seriously.' There are many aspects to ANT and many arguments have been canvassed about its philosophical position with regard to constructivism, humanism, postmodernism, instrumentalism and a host of other 'ism's. It is possible to make productive use of some aspects of ANT, such as Callon's stages of project translation or Latour's advice to 'follow the actors,' within a quite different research paradigm. But this is not 'doing ANT' and the researcher who does not embrace the spirit of the theory will be blind to the insights which are offered. The attitude that makes ANT both distinctive and powerful is the embracing of symmetry, the refusal to make a priori distinctions. Some ANT researchers (Hanseth, 2005) prefer not to mention symmetry, because they don't wish to deny common sense, because they wish to avoid provoking irrelevant philosophical arguments, or because they believe that insistence on symmetry masks some basic issues; it might, for instance, be difficult to discuss dehumanisation in an ANT context. McMaster and Wastell (2005), however, mount a spirited defense of symmetry. Still, ANT is not a theory about the nature of humans or technology, it is an approach to studying 'assemblies of hybrids.' The doctrine of symmetry advises us to treat the common dichotomies 'as if' they are meaningless. ANT does not usually take itself so seriously as to make claims about the essential nature of reality.

The most controversial symmetry is that which refuses to distinguish between humans and non-humans. This refusal brings a number of advantages. When modeling information systems we can fit particular activities into a network without knowing whether they will in the future be performed by people or machines. We can make the influence of IT on systems design and use explicit by thinking of it as an actor (e.g. 'SAP wants us to route all orders through a common process'). As well as drawing attention to the technology, this also helps us set boundaries for our investigations. With enough effort we might be able to explain SAP's intention as the result of particular lines of code within the software, or by a long history of the package's development, but this may be unnecessary for our purposes—that's just the way SAP is. Similarly, a particular (human) user may not want to lose control of manually checking order documents. If this is inconvenient to the project sponsor they may try to recruit allies or to trade off this desire for others less inconvenient; what is usually not helpful is to attempt to analyse too deeply the reason for the user's intention and to label it 'irrational.' Successful design depends on leaving many actors black-boxed. In IOIS the previous example may be extended from the user (human) to the trading partner (non-human).

In some cases it may be necessary to invent actors to perform missing actions (such as 'technical support' in the previous section). Whether these are human or non-human can be decided in later design.

We may need to consider organisations, business processes, individual users and software packages in the same analysis. Most theories and modeling tools would preclude systems and their subsystems (such as trading partners and business processes) from being modeled at the same level. Through viewing macro and micro levels symmetrically ANT allows us to follow actors and scripts wherever they lead, irrespective of the type or level of actor.

Symmetries between adoption and rejection, between success and failure, are similar. They should be unavoidable in the case of action research (where we cannot know the outcome until the research is almost complete) and desirable in other cases; we would like our theories to explain as many outcomes as possible. In both research and practice, however, we have a tendency to 'take sides,' to believe that outcomes which we favour are a result of 'good' actions, others the result of 'bad.' When considering adoption of technology we often claim that success comes from features of the technology, 'resistance' comes from cultural and psychological factors. IT project success is often attributed to the use of appropriate methodologies, failure to the unwillingness of obstinate humans to conform to the methodology. The principle of symmetry warns us against deciding what might explain success or failure before we have actually done the research.

Scripting and micro-translation are important aspects of ANT that are often neglected by IS researchers. When we conscript allies we hope that they will promote the scripts assigned to them in our program. These potential allies may, however, be of a different type or be operating in a different discourse (language, conceptual framework) from ourselves, and may need to re-interpret the script before enacting it. The most obvious example is when we expect software to implement a script such as 'allow only employees and invited visitors to enter the building.' The software might initially translate this as 'open the door for 40 seconds when a valid PIN number is entered.' Problems caused by this translation (e.g. tailgating, slow moving employees being trapped by the door) lead to extra scripts, adding to the complexity of the system until it either collapses or gives up. In many cases we can see that difficulties with IOIS occur when scripts apparently accepted are (possibly deliberately) misunderstood. Interestingly (and in accord with the principle of symmetry) a system can also succeed because of misunderstanding (Underwood 2001a).

Perhaps the most difficult aspect of ANT for researchers to accept is the possibility of unearthing contradictions (Underwood, 1992). As we follow actors and scripts we will be led through a world of hybrids where different actors have different interpretations for the same script, each attempting to make sense and form a basis for decisions in a chaotic world. Each actor initially rationalises the situation in terms of their 'home' discourse (IT, economics, office politics), but for mobilisation to occur these actors must eventually collude (perhaps unconsciously) in creating a shared local language and (il)logic. The researcher must try to tap into these local meanings, freeing themselves from the tunnel vision based on their own disciplinary lens. Only then can they understand the world of hybrids.

For practitioners, particularly project managers, the advice is similar to that for researchers, particularly with respect to embracing contradictions. Most project managers either take a Machiavellian view and promote superficial agreement and high sounding concepts while secretly working to their own goals, or insist on all players subscribing to detailed design specifications expressed in the language of some dominant discourse. They attempt to exert either covert or overt control. It might be thought that to deal with both paths a participant needs to strive for both types of control, but our experience with the case study suggests that successful project management is a matter of facilitation rather than control. In Latour's version of ANT we can't place ourselves outside the network. The project manager is just one more actor, who can promote programs through inscription of other actors but cannot expect to control the entire network. Further, openly with prototyping and unnoticed in life-cycle methodologies, the requirements for the system are constructed gradually along with the system, so there are no fixed goals against which to measure control. To help the project manager in such a situation we suggest a number of scripts which they might follow.

- **Don't be afraid of politics:** If political scripts are routinely included in our network they can, as with any other scripts, be more or less successfully translated to support our program.
- **Keep project boundaries broader and less technical:** The actor-network will evolve, sometimes becoming more focussed, sometimes growing, as the project progresses.
- **Avoid hierarchies of project definition:** The apparently least significant factor may rise to the highest importance at any moment.
- **Explicitly discuss the interests of possible technical actors:** They may be involved in facilitating or blocking alliances at any stage of IS development.
- **Keep track of important scripts:** We recommend what could be called a 'script audit,' where significant scripts are recorded and followed.
- **Continue de-scribing:** Keeping open decisions about what scripts the project supports and which have become 'losers,' likely to promote anti-programs.
- **Avoid linguistic dominance:** Through language dominance actors hope (consciously or otherwise) to pre-empt decisions which might otherwise be made during the development or even the operation of the information system.
- **Patch up (but don't cover up) differences:** 'A process of continuous and dynamic evaluation and debate between knowledgeable stakeholders recognising the need for shared values, individual autonomy and ambiguity, provides the best chance for information systems optimisation.' (Remenyi, 1999 p.18).

This advice could be summarised as 'let go of control' and 'don't be dominated by rigid objectives.' This, of course, is almost impossible in the culture of a modern organization, but in the world of hybrids celebrated by ANT it is the only approach possible. And when undertaking the development of IOIS, where some actors are large organisations and process-focussed practitioner communities jealous of their independence, it is the only approach with a chance of working.

REFERENCES

Bakhtin, M. M. (1993). *Toward a philosophy of the act* (Liapunov, V., Trans.). Austin, TX: University of Texas.

Beer, S. (1985). *Diagnosing the system*. Wiley.

Boyatzis, R. (1998). *Transforming qualitative information: Thematic analysis and code development*. Thousand Oaks, CA: SAGE.

Callon, M. (1986). Some elements of a sociology of translation: domestication of the scallops and the fishermen of Saint Brieuc Bay. In Law, J. (Ed.), *Power, action and belief: A new sociology of knowledge?* (pp. 196–233). London, UK: Routledge & Kegan Paul.

Chatterjee, D. R. G., & Sambamurthy, V. (2002). Shaping up for e-commerce: Institutional enablers of the organizational assimilation of web technologies. *Management Information Systems Quarterly*, *26*(2), 65–89. doi:10.2307/4132321

Dawkins, R. (1976). *The selfish gene*. Oxford, UK: Oxford UP.

Ehrlich, P., & Raven, P. (1964). Butterflies and plants: A study in co-evolution. *Evolution; International Journal of Organic Evolution*, *18*, 586–608. doi:10.2307/2406212

Emery, F. (1978). *The emergence of a new paradigm of work*. Canberra, Australia: Australian National University.

Glasser, B. (1998). *Doing grounded theory: Issues & discussions*. Mill Valley, CA: Sociology Press.

Goldspink, C., & Kay, R. (2003). Organizations as self-organizing and sustaining systems. *General Systems*, *32*(5), 459–474. doi:10.1080/0308107031000135017

Hanseth, Ø. (2005). Beyond metaphysics and theory consumerism. *Scandinavian Journal of Information Systems*, *17*(1), 159–166.

Hanseth, Ø., & Monteiro, E. (1997). Inscribing behaviour in information infrastructure standards. *Accounting. Management and Information Technology*, *7*(4), 183–211. doi:10.1016/S0959-8022(97)00008-8

Johnston, H., & Vitale, M. (1988). Creating competitive advantage with interorganizational systems. *Management Information Systems Quarterly*, *12*(2), 2. doi:10.2307/248839

Kay, R., & Cecez-Kecmanovic, D. (2001). *IS-organisation co-evolution: The future of IS*. Paper presented at the International Conference on Information Systems, New Orleans.

Latour, B. (1987). *Science in action*. Cambridge, MA: Harvard UP.

Latour, B. (1992). Where are the missing masses? The sociology of a few mundane artifacts. In Bjiker, W., & Law, J. (Eds.), *Shaping technology / building society*. Cambridge, MA: MIT Press.

Latour, B. (1996). *ARAMIS, or the love of technology*. Cambridge, MA: Harvard UP.

Latour, B. (1999). On recalling ANT. In Law, J., & Hassard, J. (Eds.), *Actor network theory and after*. Oxford, UK: Blackwell.

Latour, B. (2005). *Reassembling the social*. London, UK: Oxford UP.

Latour, B., & Woolgar, S. (1979). *Laboratory life*. Beverly Hills, CA: SAGE.

McCabe, B. (2006). *A coevolutionary framework for engaging trading partners in interorganisational e-commerce*. Unpublished PhD thesis, University of Technology, Sydney.

McCabe, B., & Underwood, J. (2008). *Enrolling actors in the co-evolution of inter-organisational information systems*. Paper presented at the 12th Pacific Asia Conference on Information Systems, Suzhou.

McMaster, T., Vidgen, R., & Wastell, D. (1998). *Networks of association in due process of IS development.* Paper presented at the Information Systems: current issues and future changes, Helsinki.

McMaster, T., & Wastell, D. (2005). The agency of hybrids: Overcoming the symmetophobic block. *Scandinavian Journal of Information Systems*, *17*(1), 175–182.

Monteiro, E. (1998). Scaling information infrastructure: the case of next-generation IP on the internet. *The Information Society*, *14*, 229–245. doi:10.1080/019722498128845

Montiero, E., & Hespø, V. (1998). Diffusion of infrastructure: mobilization and improvization. In Larsen, T. J., Levine, L., & de Gross, J. I. (Eds.), *Information Systems: Current issues and future changes*. Dordrecht, The Netherlands: Kluwer.

Peters, S., Heng, M., & Vet, R. (2002). Formation of the information systems strategy in a global financial services company. *Information and Organization*, *12*(1), 19–38. doi:10.1016/S1471-7727(01)00011-2

Remyeni, D. (1999). Language and a post-modern approach to information systems. *International Journal of Information Management*, *19*(1), 17–32. doi:10.1016/S0268-4012(98)00044-9

Rosenkopf, L., & Nerkar, A. (1999). On the complexity of technological evolution: Exploring co-evolution within and across hierarchical levels in optical disc Technology. In Baum, J., & McKelvey, B. (Eds.), *Variations in organization science, in honour of Donald T. Campbell*. Thousand Oaks, CA: SAGE.

Shannon, C. E., & Weaver, W. (1964). The mathematical theory of communication. [University of Illinois.]. *Urbana (Caracas, Venezuela)*, IL.

Tabak, E. (2010). Opportunistic translation in development and managment of an organisational intranet. In A. M. Rawani, H. Kettani & L. Zhang (Eds.), *International Conference on Innovation, Management and Service (ICIMS 2010)* (pp. 47-52). Singapore: World Academic Press.

Underwood, J. (1992). *Information systems work: Contradictions in practice and theory.* Paper presented at the Third Australian Conference on Information Systems, Wollongong.

Underwood, J. (2001a). *Meaning in IS development.* Unpublished PhD thesis, University of Wollongong.

Underwood, J. (2001b). Translation, betrayal and ambiguity in IS development. In Liu, K., Clark, R. J., Andersen, P. B., & Stamper, R. (Eds.), *Organizational semiotics: Evolving a science of information systems* (pp. 91–108). Boston, MA: Kluwer.

Weinberg, G. (1975). *An introduction to general systems thinking*. New York, NY: Wiley.

Wilson, T. (1997). Information behaviour: An interdisciplinary approach. *Information Processing & Management*, *33*, 551–572. doi:10.1016/S0306-4573(97)00028-9

Yen, G., & Ng, E. (2002). Migrating procurement onto the internet. *Electronic Commerce Research*, *2*(1-2), 113–134. doi:10.1023/A:1013348303943

Chapter 7
Organisational Change and Acceptance:
Perspectives of the Technology Acceptance Model

Marilyn Wells
CQ University, Australia

ABSTRACT

This chapter reports on the development of the technology acceptance model from 1986 when Davis investigated technology acceptance from an individual's view as to the ease of use and perceived usefulness of a system. Since then, many variations have been presented in attempts to explain how and what influences a computer system user's uptake of new technology within an organisation. Whilst all variations were developed explicitly to predict users' acceptance or rejection of new technology, these variations are in essence predictors of acceptance or rejection of change. Factors such as the organisational change environment and informal communication (rumours), together with social influence as exercised by colleagues should be considered major contributors to the perceptions of new technology and therefore acceptance. This chapter extends the original model to include the variations and proposes that rather than look at technology acceptance in isolation, acceptance of new technology should be viewed as acceptance of change. The author proposes the model Social Influence and Change Acceptance (SICAM) to reflect the inclusion of TAM's variations in an organizational change context.

INTRODUCTION

Change is an ongoing process in any organisation and changes due to the introduction of new technology or processes, and the ensuing relationships formed from those changes, provide a breeding ground for innovation and further avenues for change (Wells, 2009). Change literature tends to concentrate on organisational change as led from the top, and involves discussion of changing the organisation as a whole through changing or enhancing an organisation's core competencies (see for example, Prahalad, 2008). Whiteley (1995) suggests that changing core values of both

DOI: 10.4018/978-1-60960-768-5.ch007

Copyright © 2012, IGI Global. Copying or distributing in print or electronic forms without written permission of IGI Global is prohibited.

management and staff will produce a change in the organisation, whereas, Pettigrew (1987, 1979) suggests organisational change is brought about through changing culture *or* processes. Organisational change initiatives often cause staff affected by the change to resist the change. Therefore, there is a need to develop strategies that predict change acceptance and the subsequent acceptance by staff of that change.

The "Technology Acceptance Model" (TAM) was developed in 1986 by Davis to assist in predicting acceptance of new information systems (IS). The opposite of acceptance (non-acceptance) can be viewed as resistance to the new technology and by extension resistance to change acceptance. Since the initial TAM was proposed many researchers have extended TAM to include independent variables such as experience, relevance, gender, age, and social influence. This chapter reviews various extensions to TAM and proposes a conceptual model that incorporates some TAM variations and other factors in a framework that is useful to explain organisational change itself and not just change engendered by the introduction of new IS. When TAM and all its variations are viewed through the lens of organisational change, it can be seen as a model of change acceptance, not exclusively a model of technology acceptance. As change and the subsequent flow-on affect often causes staff uncertainty, it is relevant to look at the overall issues rather than focusing on technology alone as a means to explain staff behaviour.

This chapter will address the major variations to TAM since its proposal by Davis (1986) and offers some views and suggestions that will assist system implementers with introducing new technology into an organisation, and the consequent organisational change. Unlike previous meta-analyses of TAM (for example, Lee, Kozar and Larsen, 2003); this chapter does not offer a chronological study of TAM but rather introduces TAM to the reader through the major themes or concepts that have evolved since 1986.

RESEARCH METHODOLOGY

The research methodology for this chapter follows two paths. The first entails a qualitative review of literature since 1986 to 2009 involving significant stages of the evolution of TAM. A perceived bias in making this selection is that published research is assumed to have some significance. A second bias is evident in that by limiting the search and selection of papers based on the number of citations since publication, it is assumed that all papers will earn a similar number over time. A third bias is introduced as the number of citations depends on the type of study (qualitative or quantitative) and which evolution the researcher is using or proposing.

A search for studies related to TAM was undertaken across the publications types: referred journals, conference papers and proceedings, and theses. The keyword search criteria for indentifying the papers were "technology acceptance model" or "TAM." Irrelevant papers (such as those with the acronym TAM meaning test access mechanism) were removed from the list. Once the core set of articles was determined, the articles were sorted into categories based on the main concepts contained therein.

The second path for the research methodology from which Social Influence and Change Acceptance Model (SICAM) derives involved a qualitative study using a series of in-depth one-on-one conversational interviews as defined by Van Manen (1990). An interview guideline was compiled before the first round of interviews and this guide formed the basis of each interview (Patton, 1990). Each interview lasted an average of 45 minutes and, based on the participant's responses, a general conversation ensued around the original question. An amended set of questions were used for each subsequent session, based on the findings in the previous set of interviews. The data was collected from 21 interviews over a period of three years and totalled 17 hours of interview time. The conversational interviews were recorded to enable accurate transcriptions and to access easily the data for analysis (Creswell, 2007,).As with any conversation; all participants in an interview create a reality from the information gathered in the interview situation which is influenced by the interviewer's characteristics (Denzin and Lincoln, 2000).

This chapter does not seek to measure the differences between the constructs used in the TAM studies but rather seeks discuss the differing contexts where TAM has been applied and how organisations can use the information gathered here to facilitate information systems acceptance and organisational change.

PERSPECTIVES OF THE TECHNOLOGY ACCEPTANCE MODEL

As mentioned in the introduction to this chapter, TAM (Davis, 1986) (*Figure 1*) can be seen as an instance of change acceptance. This model has become widely used and modified by other researchers to represent their findings for research on reactions to new technology (Benbasat and Barki, 2007), and is one of the most influential models used to predict user acceptance of IS as it incorporates elements that address behavioural and attitudinal change.

Davis' model was based on the work carried out by Fishbein and Ajzen (1975) to develop the Theory of Reasoned Action (TRA). TRA proposes that behavioural intentions are at the base of individual behaviour and are a function of attitude or subjective norms that frame the behaviour. Whereas Davis's TAM looked at technology acceptance from an individual's view as to the ease of use and perceived usefulness of a system, TRA incorporates the element of subjective norm, which is an individual's perception of how referents feel about the required behaviour and the appropriateness of the individual's behaviour when compared to the referent. The more important the referent, the more important the referent's opinion will be perceived and therefore the more the influence it will be on subsequent behaviour (Wells, 2009). As will be shown later in this chapter, subject norm has been incorporated in TAM variations by many researchers.

Figure 1. Original technology acceptance model as developed by Davis, 1986 (p24)

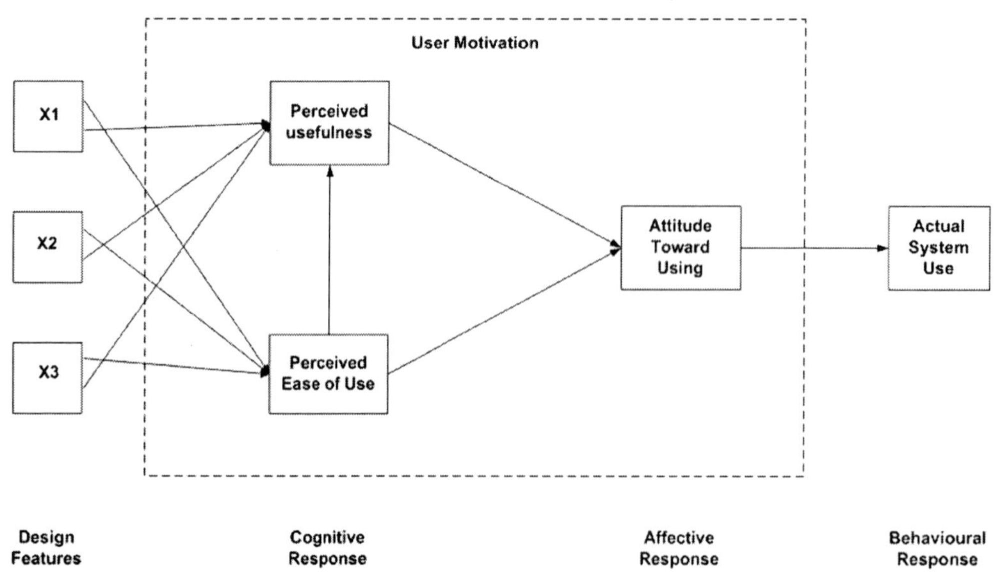

TAM as developed by (Davis, 1986) suggests that an individual's intention to use a system flows from the perceived usefulness and perceived ease of use of that system and that this intention is associated with actual system usage. Both TRA and TAM have behavioural elements which assume that once the intention to act has formed there will not be any constraints placed on those actions.

Technology Acceptance Model and User Perspective

Davis, Bagozzi and Warshaw (1989) developed the first variation to the original TAM model, and directly links perceived usefulness to behavioural intentions (refer to *Figure 2*).

This study claims that computer usage could be reasonably well predicted based on intentions and that the major factor in influencing intention to use a system was the perceived usefulness of the system. Ease of use was only secondary in determining intent, and after the initial learning period of using a new system had passed, and the user had assimilated the system processes, the overall usefulness of the system was the major determinant for intention to use. This indicates that experience is a factor when predicting usage of new information systems.

Davis (1989) found that there is a more significant relationship between usefulness and usage than between ease of use and usage and claims that users are prepared to cope with a system that they initially find difficult to use if they perceive that there are benefits to them such as functional usefulness, and suggests that while difficulty in using the system can discourage use, it is the provision of critically needed functions that win the day. Presumably, the difficulty with using the system will reduce over time as people become familiar with it, or just give up. This may have been so in 1989 when computer usage was far less than today when users have a higher level of expectation of a systems overall benefits and functionality. Davis further suggests perceived ease of use may be an influencing factor on usefulness, rather than being parallel, and therefore the chain of causality flows: ease of use > usefulness > usage. This flow may change with time and experience as the users' perception of what is an acceptably easy to use system changes, especially with advances in how systems are developed (Venkatesh and Davis, 1996).

Similar to Davis's study in 1989, Adams, Nelson and Todd (1992) undertook two studies where they compared perceptions about two different types of systems: one voicemail and email and the other software applications (WordPerfect, Lotus 1-2-3 and Harvard Graphics). The authors found that factors such as usefulness and ease of use may not be indicators of overall predictors of technology acceptance if usage of the new system is a job requirement. Adams, Nelson and Todd

Figure 2. Technology acceptance model (Davis, Bagozzi and Warshaw, 1989, p985)

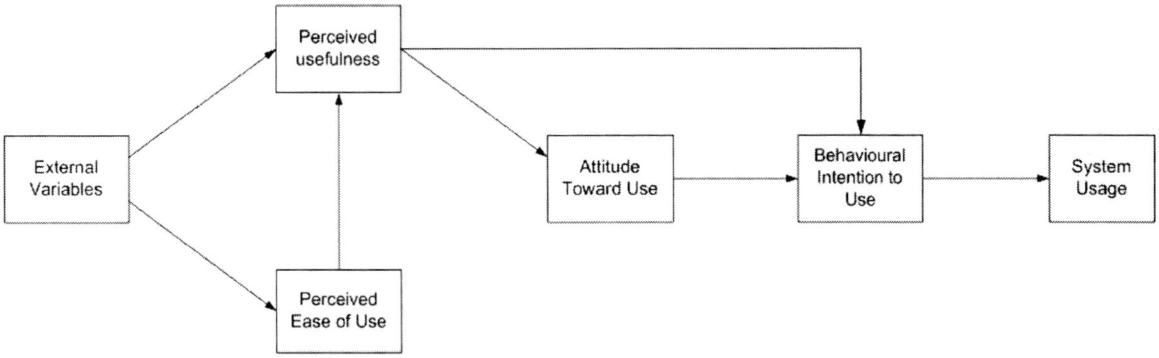

propose that the two factors of usefulness and ease of use may only influence technology acceptance usage of the system is voluntary. They also raise the possibility that new technology may be accepted and used if there is no alternative, even if usage is not mandated by job requirements, therefore these two factors can only be considered if there is a via alternative to the new system.

Wells (2009) and Klopping and McKinney (2004) propose that evidence for relating *perceived ease of use* to *perceived usefulness* is inconsistent. Wells (2009) suggests that the perceived ease of use will only relate to perceived usefulness if the user is inexperienced with IS and therefore may be unable to differentiate between the two. Once a user has the knowledge to evaluate the new system based on experience, he or she will be able to understand the difference, and therefore initial perceptions may change. Experience with IS determines whether a user will perceive a system as easy to use, as they can call on their knowledge or experience of prior systems usage, and place it in the context of the new system.

In a study of user expectation and user perceptions of an information system, Szajna and Scamell (1993) found that expectation influenced perceptions but not system usage Thus, knowledge gained from experience may frame user intentions towards the new system (Fishbein and Ajzen, 1975). A further study conducted in 1996 by Szajana using TAM from two different perspectives (pre-implementation and post-implementation) supports claims that experience determines both an individual's intention to use and usage behaviour. From a pre-implementation perspective the findings show that the more a system is perceived to be easy to use, the more likely a person is to use the system. This implies that once a person has experience of the new system, the person starts looking for other measures of usefulness, rather than how easy it is to use. The findings from Chau's (1996) study, using a simplified version of TAM without the attitude construct, correlate with Szajna's study (1996). Chau found that at the beginning "ease of use" influenced the user's perception of usefulness, and that the user's intention to use the system is only influenced by "near-term usefulness." Near-term usefulness is defined as how the system could improve job performance or job satisfaction, not necessarily, how the system could improve long-term career prospects (long-term usefulness).

Another element to consider under the experience variable is suggested by Venkatesh and Davis (1996). According to them, computer self-efficacy (knowledge and experience) influences technology acceptance and therefore the rejection of a new system may tie in with the lack of understanding of how to use the system rather than the lack of system functionality. This correlates with Fisher's findings (2006) where training (or lack thereof) was a factor for rejecting a new information system. Taylor and Todd (1995) discuss the relationship of experience to the technology acceptance and usage and the relevance to TAM. This again implies that a user's experience is a major factor when determining how the user perceives an information system, and that the longer a system is used, the more accepting of that system the users become. They also suggest that communication plays a significant part in technology acceptance, especially for inexperienced system users. Wells and Fisher (2007) support this view that experience and communication are major factors in gaining technology acceptance within an organisation.

Jackson, Chow and Leitch's (1997) study incorporated situational and intrinsic user involvement into TAM and suggest that user involvement be separated into psychological and participative components to enable system developers to understand the impact those factors have on systems development and subsequent usage. Swanson (1974) indicated that there is a positive link between involvement and appreciation of the new system, and Jackson, Chow, and Leitch's support this claim regarding their findings relating to intrinsic involvement and TAM. Intrinsic involvement also plays a significant part in shaping perceptions of the new information system, as those that participate tend to believe that the system is useful for their daily work (Jackson, Chow, and Leitch, 1997; Barki and Hartwick, 1989) (refer to *Figure 3*).

A possibility raised by Jackson, Chow, and Leitch (1997) is that of either resolved or unresolved conflict as a factor affecting user acceptance of a new system, especially the issue of whether the system features meet the needs of the user. The authors assume that if user conflict is absent then the user regards the system easy to use.

Technology Acceptance Model and Social Influence

Malhotra and Galletta (1999) introduced the importance that social influence of peers has on the adoption and usage of IS as a means of explaining what they saw as missing elements of TAM. They based their investigation upon the processes of social influence as determined by Kelman (1961, 1958), rather than use subjective norm from the TRA. Kelman's findings of the three processes of compliance, identification, and internalisation moves social influence into the area of power and states that acceptance of influence will occur as a combination of three functions:

- the relative importance of the anticipated effect;
- the relative power of the influencing agent; and
- the prepotency of the induced response.

Figure 3. Technology acceptance model extension (TAME) (Wells, 2009 [based on Jackson, Chow and Leitch, 1997, p363])

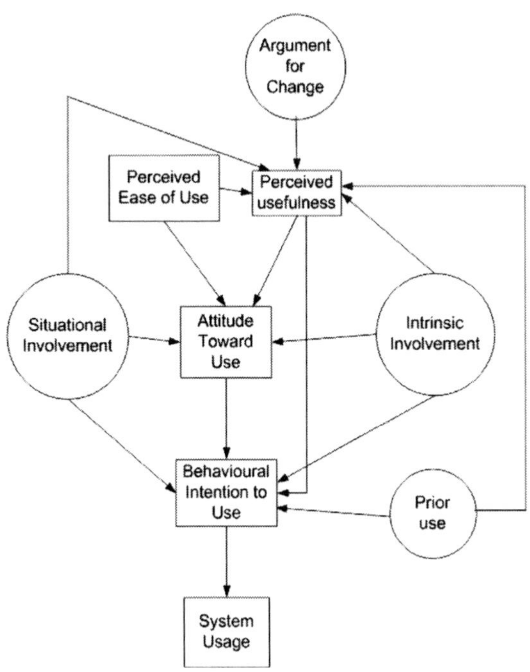

Malhotra and Galletta (1999) claim that when social influence induces compliance the effect is a negative attitude towards the new system, and when identification and internalisation are present the feeling towards the new system is positive.

There is further support for the premise of experience and social influence (subjective norm) as factors of technology acceptance in the extension of TAM developed by Venkatesh and Davis (2000). This version of the technology acceptance model, identified as TAM2 specifically introduces (amongst others) two new factors in addition to experience: subjective norm (social influence) and voluntariness. Venkatesh and Davis also incorporated into their model internalisation, identification and compliance from Kelman's (1958) work. They found that subjective norm affected perceived usefulness via internalisation and identification (image) as people used the system to gain status and influence within their work group. They also established that organisations who introduce new IS through mandatory use (compliance) are likely to have less success than those who use social influence to achieve their aims.

The purpose of TAM2 is to develop the constructs pertaining to perceived usefulness and to understand the addition's effects on users' perceptions over time as they gain more experience with an information system. A significant difference between TAM (1989) and TAM2 (2000) is that

TAM2 no longer has external variables that effect the "perceived ease of use." This is, in my opinion, a serious flaw as experience and subjective norm (social influence) must have bearing on a user's perception of how easy a new system is to use (refer to *Figure 4*).

Venkatesh (2000) carried out further investigation of the TAM constructs and extended the determinant of the perceived ease of use construct. This is a significant step forward in the flexibility of TAM and highlights behavioural experience as a major factor in understanding perceived ease of use and its relationship to behavioural intention to system usage.

In 2003, Venkatesh et al. transformed TAM and other IS theories into another model entirely "Unified Theory of Acceptance and Use of Technology" (UTAUT) (refer to *Figure 5*). In the new model, the authors have incorporated performance expectancy, effort expectancy and social influence as directly related to behavioural intention. The authors suggest that age and gender affect performance expectancy, and a previous study supports this claim (Venkatesh and Morris, 2000). Another important point to note with UTAUT and the later studies using TAM is that the research participants are from the business world and therefore fellow researchers can place some confidence that the results will have meaning for them in the *real world*, whereas participants in earlier studies were students, who may or may not have had significant business and/or computing experience.

Bhattacherjee and Premkumar (2004) developed a two-stage theoretical model of cognition change titled Extended Technology Acceptance Model (ETAM). They found that attitude perceptions fluctuated with time across the contexts of technology and usage, with the change dominant during early IT usage, rather than the later stages. Presumably this is because as the users become

Figure 4. Extension of Technology Acceptance Model (TAM2) (Venkatesh & Davis, 2000, p188)

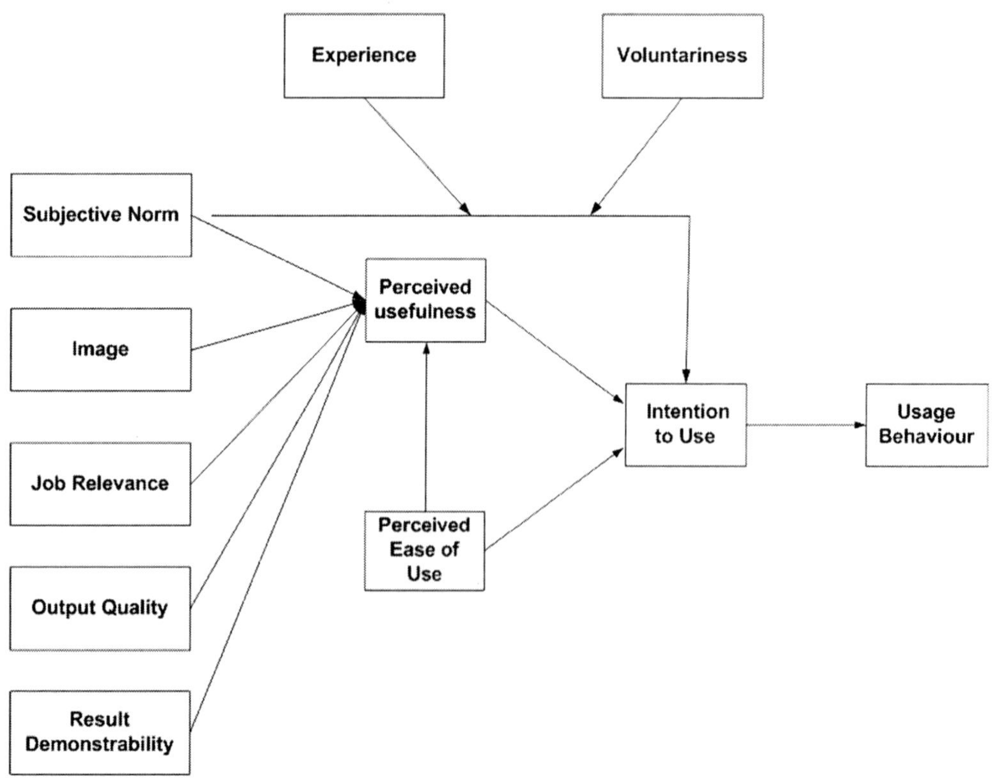

Figure 5. Unified theory of acceptance and use of technology (Wells, 2009 [based on Venkatesh, et al. 2003, p447])

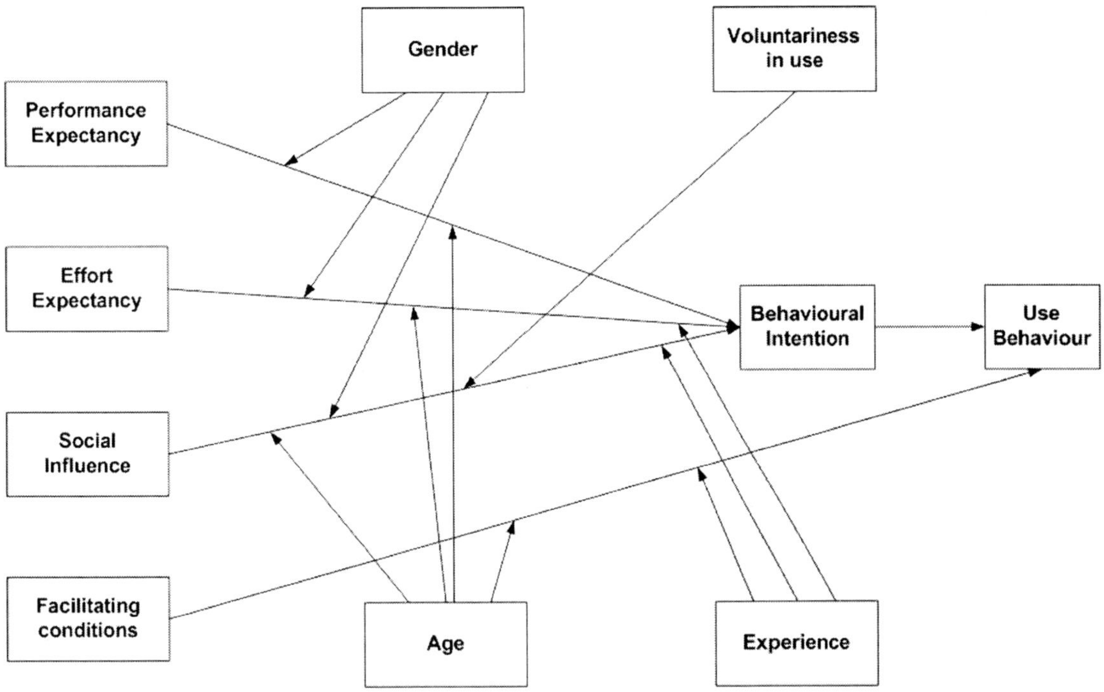

more experienced with the technology, user attitudes towards using it become settled.

Wixom and Todd (2005) propose that the research streams of user satisfaction and technology acceptance should integrate, as this would assist in better understanding the issues that surround the design and implementation stages of IS. The authors found user satisfaction is related directly to intention to use the system, and that other factors such as completeness, accuracy and currency of the data contributed to user satisfaction via the perception of information quality.

Technology Acceptance Model and Communication

Amoako-Gyampah and Salam (2004) discussed the effect of the influence of both training and communication on the shared beliefs users formed about the benefits of the new system, which in turn affects the perceived benefits of the system and the resulting adoption and use.

Building on Amoako-Gyampah and Salam's (2004) model Fisher (2006) found supporting evidence that communication was a variable that influenced users' perceptions of a new system. Fisher also found that users' reacted favourably to a new system if the rationale for implementing a new system was communicated clearly to all concerned. In an extension of Fisher's study, Wells and Fisher (2007) found that a method of communication during change is that of rumours circulated by those affected by the change. In a discussion on informal communication in the form of rumour and the effect, they found rumours had an effect on the perceived usefulness of a new system and that rumours heightened staff perceptions and attitude towards use, or the lack thereof, of a new information system.

The rumour activity discussed in Wells and Fisher's study centred on staff shared beliefs about the new system which were affected by perceived usefulness and perceived ease of use of the system. This focus on shared beliefs links back to a groupthink environment, as discussed earlier in this chapter, and exacerbated by the rumours (refer to *Figure 6*).

In a discussion of rumours and interpersonal communications, Allport and Postman (1947) propose "...a rumour public exists wherever there is a community of interest" (cited by Katz and Lazarfeld, 1955 p94).

During the implementation of a new information system the "community of interest" would be all stakeholders who are affected by the change of systems and disseminated by the informal networks within the organisation. Katz and Lazarfeld (citing Festinger, Schachter and Back, 1950) on rumour networks discuss how friendship acts as a link in a communication network and explore the existence of active communication channels between friends.

Festinger et al. (1948) describe the effect and spread of a rumour and its affect on group structure and group functions. The authors found that three principles emerged when looking at the outcome of the rumour: the principle of external control, the principle of cognitive unclarity and the principle of integrative explanation. The first principle asserts that rumours will germinate in situations where people have no control over developments affecting them; the second that rumours will evolve in situations that are unstructured; and, thirdly, issues surrounding the central theme of the rumour will be distorted so that they are consistent with the rumour. In conjunction with the effect of the rumour, they found that resistance emerged in response to a change in activities in a neighbourhood community. Wells (2009) found that negative perceptions fuelled staff resistance and a form of that resistance became rumours or other forms of informal communications. Burke and Wise (2003) suggest that rumours and gossip bring about a sense of social cohesion and give staff a forum to voice their uncertainty concerning organisational events.

Bordia and DiFonza (2004) have also reported the phenomena of *dread* rumours as a form of unofficial communication between staff members, which promotes active resistance to new systems and any phenomena that causes radical change to a workplace environment. As a new information system is an agent for change in the workplace, these rumours may be about any aspect of the new system such as the usefulness of the system or the lack of support or training on how the new system is going to replace or support daily work activities. These dread rumours can surface in the form of hidden agendas, political power plays, and lack of cooperation with those implementing the new system.

Bordia and DiFonza suggest that level of anxiety by those participating in spreading rumours fuels the momentum of the rumour. Randolph and Main (2005) reported that in such situations, employees often fear the loss of the ability to control their immediate workplace environment. Dread rumours play a significant part in highlighting the fear of staff to changes in the work environment (Wells and Fisher, 2007), particularly when the rumours are propagating amongst reference groups, groups by which an individual (or other groups) will frame their response to events and from which shared perspectives derive (Shibutani, 1955). By exchanging information, referent groups attempt to provide explanations to change events where the communication about those events is seen as lacking. Supporting the stance that referent groups are a source of influence when predicting attitudes to new technology, Rice and Aydin (1991) found that when predicting staff attitudes to new system, social information exchanges can account for a degree of influence. They suggest that, due to organisational complexity, other issues beside social information play a role in influencing attitudes to a new information system.

Staff who are feeling anxiety about a situation that they have no control over, tend to exchange

Figure 6. Extended techmology acceptance model with rumour activity (Wells and Fisher, 2007, p4)

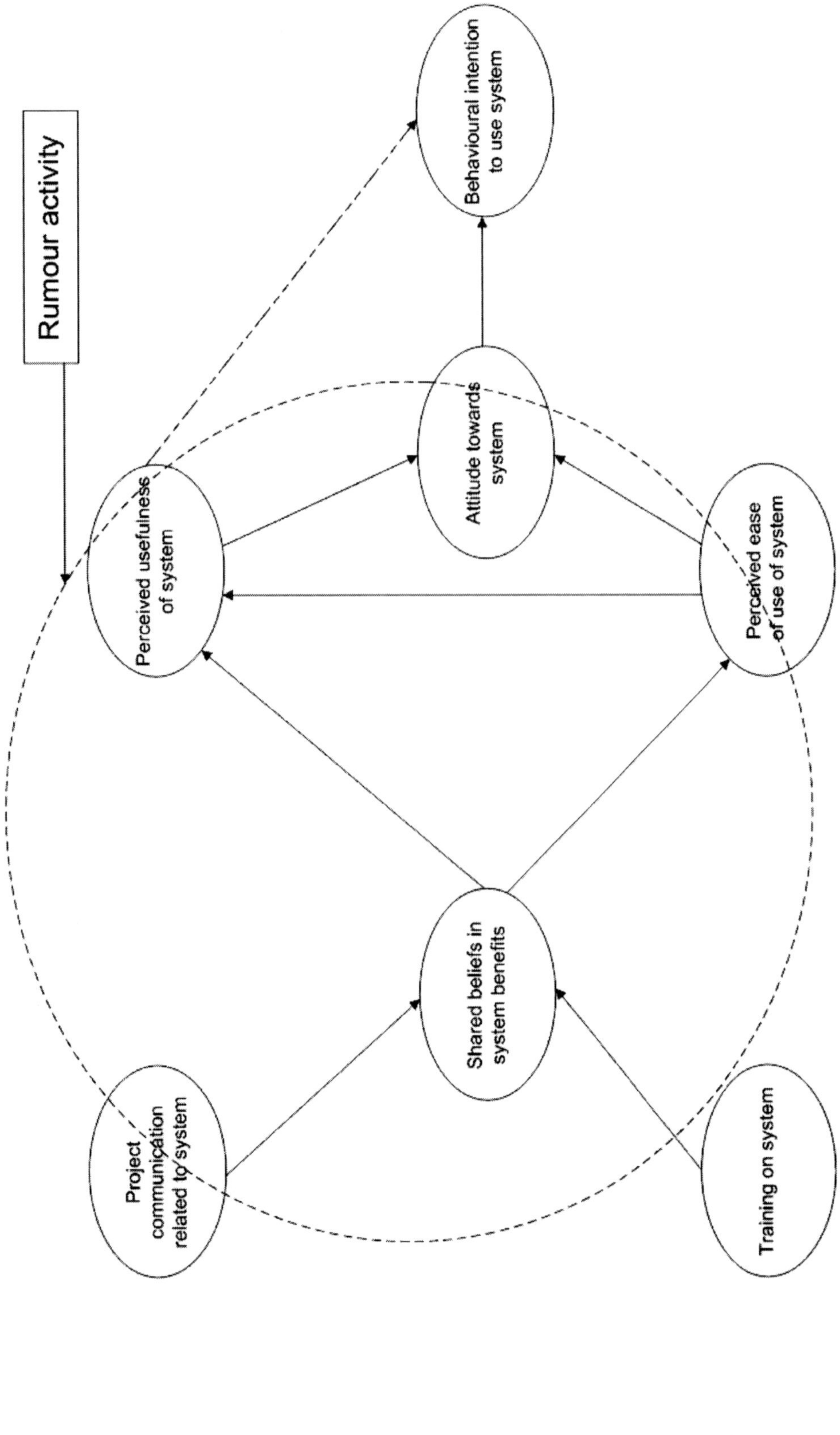

information and compare their perspective of the situation with other groups or individuals (Shibutani, 1955), and these discussions could start other rumours circulating (Michelson and Mouly, 2002). It is extremely difficult to halt a rumour, especially if it is a *dread* one, once the discussion starts (Wells and Fisher, 2007). Dread rumours are not the only outcome of discussions between groups or individuals during organisational change, though they are certainly the ones that seem to spread more rapidly and have longevity, compared to those that have more of a basis in fact. This observation is especially applicable if the communication for the rationale for change is perceived as being untrustworthy. Rumours can circulate throughout an organisation as an attempt to provide an explanation to the change event, and therefore can have the effect of drawing staff together to face what they see as adversity. Crampton, Hodge and Mishra (1998) discuss one of the benefits of rumour as fulfilling a social function and how they can act as an accelerator to combine the groups into a unified resistant front to the change. Conversely, it is possible that management may also leak information in an effort to test staff reaction to a proposed change. The extent to which this information circulates as rumour indicates the depth of feeling staff have of the proposed event.

Tension between the users of the old system and the implementers of the new is also reported in the literature, particularly when there is a perceived gap in the role each are playing in the project (Yang and Wu, 2003). Tension is often associated with a perceived lack of communication, with differing views held by the staff affected by the change (Wells and Fisher, 2007). Therefore, it is important that the rationale for change needs to be conveyed to all levels of the organisation—clearly and accurately in language easily understood by those at all levels of the organisation (Frantz, 2001). As Butler and Fitzgerald (2001) indicated, the level of communication between the user and technical staff is a factor for success during change surrounding a new information system. Therefore, appropriate communication can positively affect the perceptions of users and minimize the level of staff resistance and impact of rumours in an organisation.

Technology Acceptance Model and Change Acceptance

This section discusses the Social Influence and Change Management Model (SICAM) and places this model in the context of organisational change acceptance. Unlike many previous studies that use TAM (or a variant thereof), where the data has been self-reported via surveys and questionnaires, SICAM contributes to the ongoing discussion by using in-depth qualitative data which was collected via extensive unstructured interviews. The discussion in this section make the concept of SICAM relevant for explaining the issues that surround organisational change effected by the implementation of a new information system

To be able to gain the most from TAM and any variation the analysis needs to be at the individual level, rather than group or organisational. Using groups (i.e. departments or teams) would not accomplish the best outcome as different members of the group will have different levels of experiences, therefore different perceptions of the new system. The same reasoning can be applied to the organisational level due to the diversity of experience amongst the employees within the organisation. System implementers can draw on this diversity of experience by using volunteers to champion the new system and mentor colleagues through the early stages of system usage. This then brings the variables of organisational context and change management into consideration.

Organisations often fail to understand that technology itself will not necessarily bring about a desired change to people's daily work environment (Volkow, 2003). Similarly, Orlikowski (1996) proposes that organisational influences affect IS development rather than planned organisational change, and that situated change is further affected by organisational influences. Situated change is that which users make to the immediate work environment to improve daily tasks. Ciborra (1996) suggests that improvised organisational change has the potential danger of selecting daily processes that staff have devised to improve their own work environment, embedding knowledge from a novice, rather than some acting in the role of a knowledge gatekeeper (KG). A knowledge gatekeeper is a person who can facilitate (or not) the dissemination of information and an understanding organisational context to individuals, a group or the wider organisational community.

If change facilitators or agents and management impose an improvised solution upon staff that disregards improvements staff have made to their work environment, those staff members can become disenchanted with the replacement system, creating some resistance towards the new system (Qureshi and Davis, 2007). The KG can take on the role of interpreting technical requirements for the benefit of the users and, in turn, interpret the user requirements into technical language for the systems technicians.

As a contribution to the use of TAM, the author presents in *Figure 7* the Social Influence and Change Acceptance Model (SICAM) (Wells, 2009). Drawing on earlier work of Wells and Fisher (2007), which indicates that groupthink as communication emerges as a factor of resistance during change, the addition of a groupthink environment to explain the resistant behaviours based around the perceived usefulness and perceived ease of use of a new information system is valid. Social influence (indirect power) has been added to the mix as discussed previously, and the KG has been added as the conduit (or filter) of information that flows to the groupthink environment.

Experience was added previously to TAM and is retained in SICAM as the mediating factor between the groupthink environment and subse-

Figure 7. Social influence and change acceptance model (SICAM) (Wells, 2009)

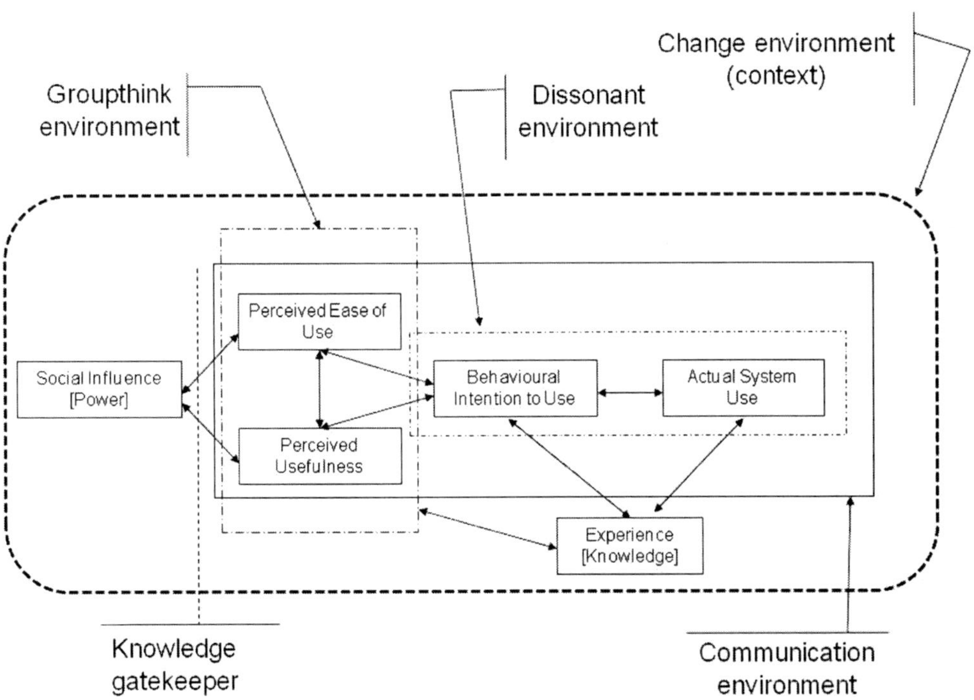

quent system usage as staff relate past experience to the current situation. Context is added as an additional influence as each organisation will have different requirements that cause a change.

As mentioned previously in the chapter, Bhattacherjee and Prekumar (2004) discussed cognitive change and Wells (2009) confirmed that cognitive dissonance is present as staff come to terms with a changing organisational environment. A cognitive dissonant environment has been added to extend TAM and explain resistant behaviours that surface as staff members rationalise the benefits of the new system and their consequent usage and acceptance of the new system.

Groupthink is a reaction whereby a group maintains its boundaries and rejects outside influence, thereby maintaining the status quo (Janis, 1972). Cognitive dissonance is the behaviour displayed by a person as they rationalise two opposing beliefs (Festinger, 1957). Groupthink and cognitive dissonance are potentially symptoms of resistance to change; therefore it is important to understand the dynamics of IS implementation. Festinger (1957, p13) defines dissonance as two elements that do not fit together, or to be more precise, "these two elements are in a dissonant relation if, considering these two elements alone, the obverse of one element would follow from the other." In a situation where a person considers alternatives to reach a decision, dissonance often arises where a person regards both alternatives meaningful and viable, and dissonance remains until the decision is rationalised. However, if a person considers the context of a situation, information or knowledge irrelevant, then they would disregard it and there would not be any instance of cognitive dissonance. Refer to *Figure 8*.

This potentially leads to conflict within the group and "the open expression of disagreement in a group leads to the existence of cognitive dissonance in the member," (Festinger, 1957, p261). If the cognition is irrelevant, then there is no dis-

Figure 8. A model of cognitive dissonance theory (Wells, 2009 based on Festinger, 1957)

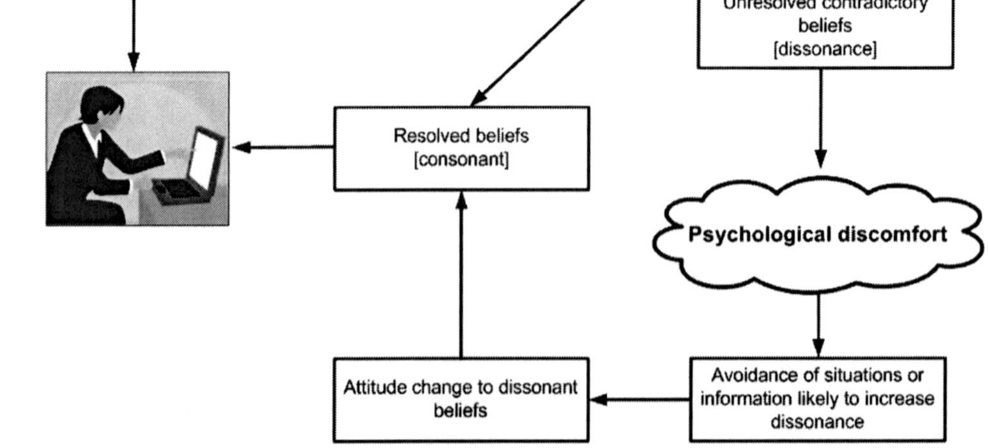

sonance, but if the cognition is relevant to the situation, then the group member changes attitude to resolve the dissonance.

It appears that there is still some lack of recognition of the impact on the social interaction among members of groups during and after an IS implementation. Nor are the implications of the changes necessarily well understood by those organisations that recognise the impact (Ishman, Pegels and Sanders, 2001). If an individual or group perceives the impact to be adverse, and that particular individual or group has overt or covert influence within the organisation, then there is a real risk of that project failing (Harley et al., 2006). The failure to recognise the effect of the perceptions of staff during this transition period has serious implications when trying to manage the various subcultures within an organisation.

The initiative to implement a new information system often causes considerable disruption, leads to substantial organisational change, and causes employees to feel displaced (Hartwick and Barki, 2001). This is especially the case if there is a lack of communication from senior management informing employees of the need for, and benefits of, the new system (McNish, 2002). When a major change to a personal workplace environment is the factor causing the change, "*pockets of user resistance*" may develop. These resistors of change can have influence over the behaviour of others within the workplace, either individually or collectively (Wells and Fisher, 2007). Those implementing the new systems do not necessarily consider the flow-on effect of these changes to other organisational groups and this again will cause anxiety within given staff groups if they find their daily work processes changing. There are many voices raised during a period of organisational change: acquiescent, dissident and neutral and for user expectations to be met. All voices should be heard.

The difference between organisational and user expectations and the final version of the product delivered as ready for use has been recognised as the cause of many conflicts and exacerbated what may already be a volatile situation between end-user expectation and designer/developer interpretation. Social influence, as perceived to be held by certain individuals within an organisation, plays a large part in communicating resistant behaviours within an organisation during a change event because of the potential that those individuals have of inducing behaviour and attitudes in those around them. Randolph and Main (2005) and Davenport (2000) suggest that announcement regarding the need for change should be clearly communicated to all levels of the organisation in an attempt to engage the systems users and therefore promote acceptance of the new system. When considering social and political aspects of an organisation, emphasis on the relevance of relations of referent power in the interaction between organisational subculture members and the role of KG during that process is almost mandatory.

The discussion presented in this section reinforces the importance of the roles that social information, social proximity, and social influence play in how people perceive new information system, and therefore a changing environment.

It appears that the very flexibility of TAM enables researchers to readily modify the model and it is perhaps because of this that TAM has been called one of the most powerful and influential computer usage models (McFarland and Hamilton, 2006; Chau, 1996; Igbaria, Guimaraes, and Davis, 1995). Bagozzi (2007), who considers that TAM and UTAUT in their current states (basic and evolved) is a "hotchpotch" of elements:

TAM is a remarkable model and has had an incredible effect on empirical research for a long time. On the one hand, it is too simple and leaves out important variables and processes. On the other hand, recent extensions of TAM (e.g. the UTAUT) have been a patchwork of many largely un-integrated and uncoordinated abridgements.

Wells's (2009) development of SICAM supports Benbasat and Barki (2007) on the need for an integrated model. In their paper discussing the various directions TAM has taken over the years, they theorise that TAM has become almost a "one size fits all" researcher model due to the constructs that have been added over the years. They note that with TAM evolving into UTAUT the model has almost devolved to Theory of Planned Behaviour (TPB), which in itself is an extension of Theory of Reasoned Action (TRA) and thus completing a circle of evolution/devolution. For example, whilst Davis, Bagozzi and Warshaw (1989) acknowledge that there are external factors that affect the perceived usefulness and perceived ease of use, they do not link external factors to other elements as does SICAM with the addition of the organisational environmental context affecting behavioural intention to use and actual system usage.

SICAM acknowledges the influence of referent groups on forming individual perceptions and attitudes with the inclusion of the groupthink environment and social influence and the Knowledge Gatekeeper (KG), which is linked to cognitive dissonance as a mediating factor on actual system usage as the user rationalises behavioural intention to use the system. SICAM includes experience (knowledge) as a moderating factor affecting perceptions within the groupthink environment and the eventual actual system use. SICAM acknowledges the role played by cognitive dissonance as the affective variable. In effect SICAM moves the usefulness of TAM from being focused on technology acceptance to that of the wider context of acceptance of organisational change.

Two contributions that SICAM offer the research community is the amalgamation of previous TAM variants into one model built around the organisational change context and the second is the proposal that TAM is essentially a model of change acceptance.

FUTURE RESEARCH DIRECTIONS

Technology Acceptance Model at the Cross-Roads

The creation of SICAM as derived from the interview data indicates the interrelationship of the issues and the need to take into account all environments and behaviours when planning organisational change. A limitation of this study is that it was undertaken at a single organisation and investigating the reaction to one change amongst many. This approach however provided the opportunity to explore in-depth the multiple issues involved in change acceptance. Future research should seek the perceptions of staff in many levels of the organisation, not only those from the most affected areas. Any chance to lessen resistance would increase the potential for a smoother change effort to be accomplished and therefore increase the viability of that change.

It would be beneficial in the context of organisational change to investigate further this focus of perception, within the framework of SICAM, to ascertain whether there is any difference in results. Another point raised by this study is the misunderstanding of what constitutes staff training and how training tailored to the needs of the staff member and the context of learning should be considered. It is recommended that change leaders should consider enacting change initiatives through organisational learning in the broader organisational view and in a more focused view, adequate individual staff training to increase staff ability to cope in uncertain situations and therefore decrease the potential negative effects that may arise through the use/abuse of power that emerged in this case, in some situations or circumstances.

CONCLUSION

This chapter has explored many variations of TAM and discussed various aspects that arise within an organisation during a time of change, and the social influence and power that clings to those aspects. The literature presented in this chapter includes discussion of various technology acceptance models explored for issues that will explain the reaction of staff to a new information system and subsequent organisational change.

TAM was originally developed as a model of prediction of user behaviour across differing types of end-users. With the subsequent additions to TAM by other researchers, the original model has become a list of user issues surrounding a new information system and most models have become quite specific as to the determinants required to explain the authors' stance. A new model, UTAUT, also slants heavily to explicit components of social influence.

SICAM borrows these other theories to provide a clearer explanation of the issues observed in any organisation, rather than using a current variation of TAM. Prior research has proven that the two constructs of perceived usefulness and perceived ease of use are antecedents to behavioural intention to use, and that intention is an antecedent to actual system use. The relationship between these two constructs exists as has been discussed in this chapter, and there is an assumption that these constructs will be part of any variation of TAM and applicable for any organisation. What will be different for each organisation is the breakdown of stressors, which most likely would be different for each organisational context. Therefore, using a TAM that has been broken down into the individual components is not appropriate, as each organisation will have different forces/stressors that arise during an IS implementation. Whilst there will be the usual suspects of resistance to change in its variations, there may be other issues that fuel the resistance and these issues need to be considered when implementing changes.

SICAM provides an organisation with an overview of the issues that will arise during organisational change and the effect of new technology on the organisational. These issues cannot be considered in isolation from each other as each issue has a holistic impact on the staff and organisation.

"All that is old is new again," only this time with a deeper appreciation of the issues that surround TAM and its interconnectedness to the particular organisational environment undergoing change.

REFERENCES

Adams, D., Nelson, R., & Todd, P. (1992). Perceived usefulness, perceived ease of use and user acceptance of information technology: A replication. *Management Information Systems Quarterly*, *16*(2). doi:10.2307/249577

Amoako-Gyampah, K., & Salam, A. F. (2004). An extension of the technology acceptance model in an ERP implementation environment. *Information & Management*, *41*(6), 731–745. doi:10.1016/j.im.2003.08.010

Bagozzi, R. P. (2007). The legacy of the technology acceptance model and a proposal for a paradigm shift. *Journal of the Association for Information Systems*, *8*(4), 224–254.

Barki, H., & Hartwick, J. (1989). Rethinking the concept of user involvement. *Management Information Systems Quarterly*, *13*(1), 53–63. doi:10.2307/248700

Benbasat, I., & Barki, H. (2007). Quo vadis, TAM? *Journal of the Association for Information Systems*, *8*(4), 211–218.

Bhattacherjee, A., & Premkumar, G. (2004). Understanding changes in belief and attitude toward information technology usage: A theoretical model and longitudinal test. *Management Information Systems Quarterly*, *28*(2), 229–254.

Bordia, P., & DiFonzo, N. (2004). Problem solving in social interactions on the Internet: Rumor as social cognition. *Social Psychology Quarterly*, *67*(1), 33–49. doi:10.1177/019027250406700105

Burke, L. A., & Wise, J. M. (2003). The effective care, handling and pruning of the office grapevine. *Business Horizons*, *46*(3), 71–76. doi:10.1016/S0007-6813(03)00031-4

Butler, T., & Fitzgerald, B. (2001). The relationship between user participation and the management of change surrounding the development of information systems: A European perspective. *Journal of End User Computing*, *13*(1), 12–24. doi:10.4018/joeuc.2001010102

Chau, P. K. (1996). An empirical assessment of a modified technology acceptance model. *Journal of Management Information Systems*, *13*(2), 185–204.

Ciborra, C. (1996). *Improvisation and Information Technology in organisations*. Paper presented at the International Conference on Information Systems (ICIS), Cleveland, Ohio, USA.

Crampton, S. M., Hodge, J. W., & Mishra, J. M. (1998). The informal communication network: Factors influencing grapevine activity. *Public Personnel Management*, *27*(4), 569–584.

Creswell, J. W. (2007). *Qualitative research design and inquiry: Choosing among five approaches* (2nd ed.). Thousand Oaks, CA: Sage Publications Inc.

Davenport, T. H. (2000). *Mission critical: Realizing the promise of enterprise systems*. Boston, MA: Harvard Business School Press.

Davis, F. D. (1986). *A technology acceptance model for empirically testing new end-user Information Systems: Theory and results*. Cambridge, MA: MIT.

Davis, F. D. (1989). Perceived usefulness, perceived ease of use, and user acceptance of Information Technology. *Management Information Systems Quarterly*, *13*(3), 319–340. doi:10.2307/249008

Davis, F. D., Bagozzi, R. P., & Warshaw, P. R. (1989). User acceptance of computer technology: A comparison of two theoretical models. *Management Science*, *35*(8), 982–1003. doi:10.1287/mnsc.35.8.982

Denzin, N. K., & Lincoln, Y. S. (2000). Methods of collecting and analyzing empirical materials. In Denzin, N. K., & Lincoln, Y. S. (Eds.), *Handbook of qualitative research* (2nd ed.). Thousand Oaks, CA: Sage Publications Inc.

Festinger, L. (1957). *A theory of cognitive dissonance*. London, UK: Tavistock Publications.

Festinger, L., Cartwright, D., Barber, K., Fleischl, J., Gottsdanker, J., & Keysen, A. (1948). A study of a rumour: Its origin and spread. *Human Relations*, *1*(4), 464–486. doi:10.1177/001872674800100405

Fishbein, M., & Ajzen, I. (1975). *Belief, attitude, intention, and behavior: An introduction to theory and research*. Reading, MA: Addison-Wesley Pub. Co.

Fisher, M. D. (2006). *Staff perceptions of an ERP systems implementation: A case study of three Australian universities*. Central Queensland University, Rockhampton.

Frantz, P. S. (2001). *Perceptions of selected administrators regarding enterprise planning software implementation best practices, and the relationship between these perceptions and selected variables*. University of Southern Mississippi.

Harley, B., Wright, C., Hall, R., & Dery, K. (2006). Management reactions to technological change: The example of enterprise resource planning. *The Journal of Applied Behavioral Science*, *42*(1), 58–75. doi:10.1177/0021886305284857

Hartwick, J., & Barki, H. (2001). Communication as a dimension of user participation. *Professional Communication*, *44*(1), 21–36. doi:10.1109/47.911130

Igbaria, M., Guimaraes, T., & Davis, G. B. (1995). Testing the determinants of microcomputer usage via a structural equation model. *Journal of Management Information Systems, 11*(4), 87–114.

Ishman, M., Pegels, C. C., & Sanders, G. L. (2001). Managerial information system success factors within the cultural context of North America and a former Soviet Republic. *The Journal of Strategic Information Systems, 10*(4), 291–312. doi:10.1016/S0963-8687(01)00055-5

Jackson, C. M., Chow, S., & Leitch, R. A. (1997). Toward an understanding of the behavioral intention to use an Information System. *Decision Sciences, 28*(2), 357–389. doi:10.1111/j.1540-5915.1997.tb01315.x

Katz, E., & Lazarfeld, P. F. (1955). *Personal influence* (*Vol. 2*). New York, NY: The Free Press.

Kelman, H. C. (1958). Compliance, identification, and internalisation: Three process of attitude change. *The Journal of Conflict Resolution, 2*(1), 51–60. doi:10.1177/002200275800200106

Kelman, H. C. (1961). Process of opinion change. *Public Opinion Quarterly, 25*(1), 57–78. doi:10.1086/266996

Klopping, I. M., & McKinney, E. (2004). Extending the technology acceptance model and the task-technology fit model to consumer e-commerce. *Information Technology, Learning and Performance Journal, 22*(1).

Lee, Y., Kozar, K., & Larsen, K. (2003). The technology acceptance model: Past, present, and future. *Communications of the Association for Information Systems, 12*(752), 780.

Malhotra, Y., & Galletta, D. F. (1999, January 5-8). *Extending the technology acceptance model to account for social influence: Theoretical bases and empirical validation.* Paper presented at the Proceedings of the 32nd Hawaii International Conference on System Sciences, Maui, Hawaii.

McFarland, D. J., & Hamilton, D. (2006). Adding contextual specificity to the technology acceptance model. *Computers in Human Behavior, 22*, 427–447. doi:10.1016/j.chb.2004.09.009

McNish, M. (2002). Guidelines for managing change: A study of their effects on the implementation of new information technology projects in organisations. *Journal of Change Management, 2*(3), 201–211. doi:10.1080/738552754

Michelson, G., & Mouly, V. S. (2002). You didn't hear this from us but...: Towards an understanding of rumour and gossip in organisations. *Australian Journal of Management, 27*, 1–10. doi:10.1177/031289620202701S07

Orlikowski, W. (1996). Improving organisational transformation over time: A situated change perspective. *Information Systems Research, 7*(1), 63–92. doi:10.1287/isre.7.1.63

Patton, M. Q. (1990). *Qualitative evaluation and research methods* (2nd ed.). Newbury Park, CA: Sage Publications, Inc.

Pettigrew, A. M. (1979). On studying organizational cultures. *Administrative Science Quarterly, 24*, 570–581. doi:10.2307/2392363

Pettigrew, A. M. (1987). Context and action in the transformation of the firm. *Journal of Management Studies, 24*(6), 649–670. doi:10.1111/j.1467-6486.1987.tb00467.x

Prahalad, C. K. (2008). The role of core competencies in the corporation. In Millson, M. R., & Wilemon, D. (Eds.), *The strategy of managing innovation and technology* (2nd ed., pp. 58–69). Upper Saddle River, NJ: Pearson Prentice Hall.

Qureshi, S., & Davis, A. (2007). *Managing resistance to organizational change: How GSS can reveal role related resistance behaviors.* Paper presented at the 40th Annual Hawaii International Conference on System Sciences (HICSS'07), Big island, HI.

Randolph, C., & Main, R. (2005). Exploring the power and politics of a PeoplesSoft implementation. In von Hellens, L., Nielsen, S., & Beekhuyzen, J. (Eds.), *Qualitative case studies on implementation of enterprise wide systems* (pp. 140–159). Hershey, PA: Idea Group, Inc.

Rice, R. E., & Aydin, C. (1991). Attitudes toward new organisational technology: Network proximity as a mechanism for social information processing. *Administrative Science Quarterly*, *36*(2), 219–244. doi:10.2307/2393354

Shibutani, T. (1955). Reference groups as perspectives. *American Journal of Sociology*, *60*(6), 562–569. doi:10.1086/221630

Swanson, E. B. (1974). Management Information Systems: Appreciation and involvement. *Management Science*, *21*(2), 178–188. doi:10.1287/mnsc.21.2.178

Szajna, B. (1996). Empirical Evaluation of the revised technology acceptance model. *Management Science*, *42*(1), 85–92. doi:10.1287/mnsc.42.1.85

Szajna, B., & Scamell, R. W. (1993). The effects of Information System user expectations on their performance and perceptions. *Management Information Systems Quarterly*, *17*(4), 493–516. doi:10.2307/249589

Taylor, S., & Todd, P. (1995). Assessing IT usage: The role of prior experience. *Management Information Systems Quarterly*, *19*(4), 561–570. doi:10.2307/249633

Van Manen, M. (1990). *Researching lived experience: Human science for an action sensitive pedagogy*. Albany, NY: State University of New York.

Venkatesh, V. (2000). Determinants of perceived ease of use: Integrating control, intrinsic motivation, and emotion into the technology acceptance model. *Information Systems Research*, *11*(4), 342–365. doi:10.1287/isre.11.4.342.11872

Venkatesh, V., & Davis, F. D. (1996). A model of the antecedents of perceived ease of use: Development and test. *Decision Sciences*, *27*(3), 451–481. doi:10.1111/j.1540-5915.1996.tb01822.x

Venkatesh, V., & Davis, F. D. (2000). A theoretical extension of the technology acceptance model: Four longitudinal field studies. *Management Science*, *46*(2), 186–204. doi:10.1287/mnsc.46.2.186.11926

Venkatesh, V., & Morris, M. G. (2000). Why don't men ever stop to ask for directions? Gender, social influence, and their role in technology acceptance and usage behaviour. *Management Information Systems Quarterly*, *24*(1), 115–139. doi:10.2307/3250981

Venkatesh, V., Morris, M. G., Davis, G. B., & Davis, F. D. (2003). User acceptance of Information Technology: Toward a unified view. *Management Information Systems Quarterly*, *27*(3), 425–478.

Volkow, N. (2003). *Interaction between Information Systems and organizational change: Case study of Petroleos Mexicanos*. London: Unpublished PhD, University of London.

Wells, M. A. (2009). *Perceptions of knowledge gatekeepers: Social aspects of information exchange in an organisation undergoing change*. Sydney: University of Western Sydney.

Wells, M. A., & Fisher, M. D. (2007). *The phenomena of uncontrolled communication as resistance during the implementation of an enterprise resource planning system*. Paper presented at the ANZAM 2007, Sydney, NSW, Australia.

Whiteley, A. (1995). *Managing change: A core values approach*. South Melbourne, Australia: Macmillan Education Australia Pty Ltd.

Wixom, B. H., & Todd, P. A. (2005). A theoretical integration of user satisfaction and technology acceptance. *Information Systems Research*, *16*(1), 85–102. doi:10.1287/isre.1050.0042

Yang, C., & Wu, C.-Y. (2003, October). *Perception difference between users and information professionals: A case study of TaiPower*. Paper presented at the ASIST Annual Meeting, Washington, DC.

Chapter 8
Business Case Development Risks in On and Offshore IT Outsourcing:
Unpacking the Theories

Anne C. Rouse
Deakin University, Australia

ABSTRACT

Outsourcing of IT-supported business processes (systems development; customer relationship management; helpdesk, etc.) has become increasingly common in Western economies since the late 1990s. Such outsourcing is totally dependent on the provision of inter-organizational information systems (IOSs), which act as the "glue" to link vendor(s) and client(s). Hence understanding the importance of IOSs, and conversely, the downsides or risks they embody, is a critical part of ensuring that outsourcing arrangements are successful. In this chapter the theory behind outsourcing is unpacked, and readers are alerted to sometimes-overlooked aspects of the IOSs on which outsourcing depends. These raise the risks, and reduce the benefits, of outsourcing if they are not well thought through. Decision makers are advised to explicitly include the notion of risk in their outsourcing business cases, including those risks associated with the IOSs that support outsourcing arrangements.

INTRODUCTION

An important business phenomenon of the last two decades has been the rapid growth of outsourcing. This is particularly so for complex, IT-supported business processes like systems development; IT service delivery; customer relationship management; helpdesk, etc. Such outsourcing has become increasingly common in western economies since the late 1990s. This outsourcing is also proving to be an important source of income for developing countries such as India, China, the Philippines and the former Soviet Republic, which are able to provide services from "offshore."

DOI: 10.4018/978-1-60960-768-5.ch008

Copyright © 2012, IGI Global. Copying or distributing in print or electronic forms without written permission of IGI Global is prohibited.

This chapter will illustrate that inter-organizational systems (IOSs) are the glue which holds together these types of outsourcing arrangements. It will then argue that, given this, understanding the importance, and conversely, the downsides or risks that IOSs embody, is a critical part of ensuring that outsourcing arrangements are successful.

The chapter also identifies deficiencies in the business cases typically developed by purchasing firms when deciding to outsource. These deficiencies are even more critical if this involves offshore delivery. The chapter outlines several key IOS-related issues firms need to take into account when investigating the business case for offshore outsourcing. These include a realistic assessment of the risks associated with sending customer data to countries with limited sanctions against release of such data. This risk is inherent in all cross-national IOSs, but is heightened when data is sent to countries where high levels of corruption exist. They also include risks associated with replacing face to face organizational controls with those mediated by IOSs.

The chapter is essentially a literature review, but is informed by a series of ten focus groups conducted by the author with purchaser and vendor staff involved in outsourcing arrangements (n = 46). Services supplied within these outsourcing arrangements included back-end operations; delivery of mainframe IT services; software development; help desk operations and desktop support. Details are reported in Rouse (2002). The organization of the chapter is as follows: after providing a background to the growth of outsourcing, particularly business process outsourcing (BPO), the chapter then explores inter-organizational systems (IOSs). It then canvasses the importance of taking into account risks as well as costs and benefits when developing the business case on which the sourcing decision is made. The chapter then explores in more detail the risks associated with outsourcing, especially when it is provided offshore. It also focuses on those risks that are associated with replacing internal, face to face direction and coordination with electronically mediated coordination. Finally the chapter provides examples of typical risks associated with this IOS mediation and suggests some implications.

BACKGROUND

The Rise of Complex, IT-Supported Outsourcing

In this section the focus is not on all types of outsourcing, but rather on complex IT-supported outsourcing. Willcocks and Lacity (1998, p 3) defined such outsourcing as the

> *...handing over to a third party [of the] management of IS/IT assets, resources and/or activities for required results.*

This definition excludes outsourcing of simple services, such as cleaning, catering, or garbage collection, but would include delivery of IT services of all kinds, as well as what has come to be known as "business process outsourcing" or BPO. BPO involves delivery of complex IT-supported business services rather than simply IT services.

Outsourcing is essentially the business-to-business delivery of services, where the vendor, rather than the client, is responsible for determining how the service is to be performed. This differentiates it, for example, from supply of contract labor where such labor is controlled by client managers. A key defining aspect of outsourcing is that it involves delegating responsibility for "how" to produce the required results to the vendor. The client retains responsibility for defining "what" services are to be produced, and how the quality of these services is to be judged.

When services are outsourced, instead of controlling the behavior of service staff directly as happens in a "hierarchical" organization, the purchaser controls performance through a mix of formal and informal controls (see Choudhury and Sabherwal, 2003, for a discussion).

The formal controls typically revolve around a legal contract, which includes a "service level agreement" or SLA. While this will differ according to the type of outsourcing, the SLA specifies the services to be delivered, the performance criteria, the consequences of service failure, and the roles to be performed by various players within the vendor and client organizations. Hence another way of viewing outsourcing is to see it as the replacement of largely *informal within-firm controls* (O'Reilly, 1989) by largely *formal, contractual, control* mechanisms. Informal controls are seen in the day to day supervision of internally-employed staff, relying largely on their cultural knowledge, norms and understanding.

In real life, the contractual controls associated with outsourcing are usually still supplemented by informal controls. However, these are largely exercised via IOSs. This difference demands a realistic assessment of the changes that take place when face-to-face coordination and control of known internal staff (within a hierarchy) are replaced by arms-length control, managed by legal contracts and supported and coordinated only through the use of IOSs. The chapter will return to this issue later.

In discussing outsourcing, it is worth noting that there are two quite different types of outsourcing – with different quality characteristics, and importantly, different control processes. These are illustrated in Table 1. The first type is "project based" outsourcing, where the vendor is responsible for delivering a set of specified requirements by a certain date (and at a certain price). In most cases such projects are extremely complex, and information systems play a crucial role in budgeting for, and then coordinating and controlling the complex set of project activities. The second type involves continuous delivery of specified services, which might include the performance of discrete business processes (such as the preparation of tax returns or the handing of all simple customer transactions). These have much in common with other continuous delivery systems, such as the provision of manufactured products making up a supply chain.

Outsourcing Depends on Effective IOSs

It is no coincidence that the rise of outsourcing occurred after the development of a range of new technologies for linking firms through IT and IOSs.

Although firms had used external bureaus to carry out batch processing of data in the sixties and seventies, this was generally cumbersome and rarely matched a client's individual needs. Once the price of internal computer systems dropped in the 1980s, and the price of mini-computers became affordable, many bureau-users brought their data processing in-house. However, by the late 1980s the possibilities of "outsourcing" IT

Table 1. Project-based and process-based outsourcing

	Project-based outsourcing	Process-based outsourcing (including business process and IT outsourcing)
Service	Creation of a complex artifact of some kind	Continuous delivery of specified services or performance of specified business processes over a defined period
Examples	Development of an information system; building design and/or construction; new product design, etc.	Customer service; help desk; data centre hosting; provision of network services
Control-mechanism	Planned against actual (deliverables, budget, timeline)	Delivery of services as specified in the service level agreement

services began to be promoted by vendors. At that time the improvements in telecommunications, databases, and workstations (by then, almost all PC-based) meant that it had become feasible for vendors to host applications for clients within their own data centers – at some distance from clients' sites. As well, the client and vendor could use the Internet, email and phone to coordinate activities remotely. As far as clients were concerned, they could access systems via their PCs, and support staff via email (or telephone), and it mattered little to their own employees whether services were provided in-house or via an external party. In essence, the emergence of inter-organizational systems *enabled* the growth of an outsourcing vendor market.

These IOSs also reduced the transaction costs (discussed below) of engaging an external provider (Clemons and Row, 1992). Cost-reductions were probably the most important motivations for the adoption of outsourcing (Lacity and Willcocks, 2001) and the message that outsourcing would reduce the costs of firms' IT services was spread widely. However, this claim was based on assumptions that do not necessarily hold up under investigation. During the late 1990s, newer vendor markets grew up, when vendors began to offer not only outsourced IT-services but the whole IT-supported "process." The business literature soon became replete with examples from human resources, customer service, back end processing, etc (Rouse and Corbitt, 2004; Halvey and Melby, 2007). Again, such outsourcing was dependent on the availability of effective IOSs.

More recently still, vendor firms began to exploit salary differentials between first and third world countries to provide outsourced services from countries such as India, the Philippines, China, and the former Soviet Republic. This is described as "offshore" outsourcing (Lacity and Rottman, 2008). As with other forms of outsourcing, delivery of services offshore was only possible because of the underlying IOS technology, which in turn depended on IT/communications infrastructure in both host and purchaser locations.

These changes have had profound effects in western economies, transferring a range of IT and service jobs to developing nations. But they have introduced additional risks that are not always perceived by decision-makers.

THE NATURE OF INTERORGANIZATIONAL SYSTEMS

Without the development of IOSs, there would not have been the growth in outsourcing, as outsourcing would have had to remain a local endeavor. Indeed, it is a moot point whether even simple outsourcing (such as catering, cleaning, or garbage collection) could be performed efficiently without the use of some kinds of IOSs. However, the IOSs that support outsourcing are of different types.

Types of IOSs

Eom (2005, p 4) define an inter-organizational System (IOS) as

> *an information and management system that transcends organizational boundaries via electronic linkages.*

Originally, an IOS was conceived of as a cross-organizational system that allowed a more-or-less automated flow of *structured information* between organizations (e.g. Barrett, 1987, p 6). IOSs were an important topic of research in the fields of logistics and supplier-purchaser coordination. Such systems were critical in enabling forecasting of needs and the coordinated supply of products via delivery systems that embraced networks of multiple firms. By reducing the need for large inventories, such IOSs streamlined supply chains and reduced their costs (Eom, 2005). Many of the original challenges in this field centred on the development of agreed standards (such as EDI – electronic data interchange, and more recently, XML – extensible markup language). Such standards would allow data to move between firm databases with limited human intervention. Although such structured IOSs had major impact on the efficiencies of supply chains and networks, they are not necessarily related to outsourcing. Outsourcing is in essence about service-delivery rather than physical product-delivery, and so less dependent on exchange of structured data.

However, it was soon realized that IT could also enhance *communication* between organizations at multiple levels, even though much of this communication was (and remains) informal rather than structured. Hence the concept of IOS came to embrace IT tools such as electronic mail, and search engines (for finding information held in unstructured formats) that supported the coordination of inter-organizational activities, and the delivery of services using non-structured data. This more modern view of an IOS is reflected in Eom's definition above. As vendor and purchaser are physically separated, IOSs of this kind are necessary to ensure the level of integration needed for effective vendor-client cooperation.

Given this, IOSs can be divided into three categories:

- **Type 1:** those that simply provide access to systems hosted or managed by other firms (normally, in modern systems, enabled by the Internet and local browsers);
- **Type 2:** those that enable the automated exchange of structured data between different firms (such as EDI or XML-based systems);
- **Type 3:** those that enable exchange of unstructured data (such as email and related technologies like wikis, bulletin boards, and shared data repositories, like Youtube etc).

Several characteristics of these three types of systems are shown in Table 2. Outsourcing tends to rely heavily on IOSs of the first and third type, rather than on the automated exchange of structured data associated with manufacturing and supply chain systems.

Since the turn of the century, a new variation of Type 1 IOSs can be seen in developments such as "applications service providers" (ASPs) (Currie and Seltsikas, 2001); "software as a service" (SaaS) (Kaplan, 2007) and hosting of data on remote computers, sometimes on the other side of the world, in "the cloud" (Hayes, 2008, p 9). Users of such systems are often members of the public or non-IT staff within purchaser firms, so their expectations of simplicity and ease-of-use are high. Users can now access such systems over the Internet via browsers, but in that case, instead of accessing the vendor's systems — as happens, with, for example, airline bookings — the client user accesses the client's own data, which is stored on the vendor's servers, and used in applications hosted by the vendor.

The role of IOSs of the first type are discussed at length in typical Information Systems textbooks, beginning with the importance of American Hospital Supplies' use of terminals within client sites (Johnston and Vitale, 1988; Clemons and Row, 1988), and Sabre's impact on the airline reservations industry (Clemons and Row, 1988; Hopper, 1990). Such IOSs have been greatly simplified by the emergence of common Internet protocols, and, in particular, by the development of modern browsers, which provide a common user interface to many disparate systems. No longer do users of such systems need to undertake long and detailed training to be able to access information held in other firms' databases.

Much of the literature on IOSs is concerned with those of the second type, which automate the exchange of data between databases held in different firms. It is these types that have revolutionized the management of product supply chains in industry such as the car industry and other manufacturing chains and enabled just-in-time manufacturing and reduced inventories.

Table 2. Three types of inter-organizational system

IOS Type	Description	Key benefits	Key challenges
Type 1	Enable access to systems hosted or managed by other firms (e.g. McKessons', Sabre, etc)	Can interact with suppliers'/purchasers' systems directly without the need of a human intermediary	Prior to development of browsers, users required substantial training in use of the 'foreign' system – failure to master the alternative system in depth made effective use impossible. Heavily dependent on inter-organizational negotiation.
Type 2	Automatic exchange of structured data (e.g. EDI, or XML-based)	Automation of exchange of structured information from one database to another - enabled range of new applications and revolutionizing of supply chains	Development of complex applications required – at substantial expense. Intermediaries often required prior to the Internet to handle authentication, security, and other aspects of the information exchange. Heavily dependent on common standards, as well as inter-organizational negotiation in relation to long-term planning.
Type 3	Exchange of unstructured information (e.g. email, shared document repositories, bulletin boards, etc)	Support for the informal activities of workgroups	Attenuation of information richness. Cultural and language-based misunderstanding. Need for good search and presentation tools. Involve many of the challenges of other types of IOSs, but these are not necessarily recognized.

Less research seems to have been conducted into the inter-organizational social systems that are based on unstructured data and inter-employee communications, that is, the third type of IOS. Where these types of IOS have been studied, the research often uses terms such as "knowledge management" or "e-collaboration" rather than "IOS."

Table 2 indicates that the different types of IOSs present a range of challenges to management. So, for example, while interface issues are of paramount importance when IOSs of the first type are developed, these are less salient to IOSs of the third type. With these, issues of culture, language, and tacit knowledge are paramount. Some issues overlap the groups, so all three types of IOSs present availability and security challenges, as the data exchanged between network members needs to be authenticated, and to be protected against denial of service, privacy breaches, system contamination, or data corruption. This is particularly difficult for IOSs of the third kind, where the human element can often be the major source of insecurity (Greinstein and Vasarhelyi, 2000).

COSTS AND RISKS OF OUTSOURCING (LOCAL AND OFFSHORE)

This chapter examines the IOS-related risks for complex outsourcing, so this section details some of the salient characteristics of outsourcing. While almost all outsourcing arrangements rely on a legal contract, this tends only to set the scene for day to day management of the outsourcing arrangement. It is IOSs, particularly of Types 1 and 3, which enable the crucial collaboration that leads to successful outsourcing arrangements, particularly when these involve offshore service delivery or data hosting. As vendor and client are almost always physically separated, without the level of integration provided by IOSs, the coordination needed would be impossible.

A range of factors determine the success, or otherwise, of outsourcing arrangements. While these affect all types of outsourcing to some extent, their importance grows as the processes that are outsourced move from simple to complex, and from local to offshore.

The focus group informants studied by Rouse (2002) observed that the search for reduced long-term costs is behind most outsourcing decisions. This is also confirmed in the academic literature (Lacity and 2001)–there are few firms that knowingly choose the more expensive option for service delivery. In some cases this may mean paying more in the short term to a vendor, because a firm has chosen not to establish a particular function in-house. Even then, this is usually because in the long term, this is a more efficient strategy. Given the salience of cost savings to the sourcing decision, it is critical that the business case accurately determines costs of the outsourced option and of the alternative "counterfactual."

Yet Rouse's focus group informants revealed that determining whether outsourcing will be cheaper or not is a particularly difficult endeavor. Decisions depend on a long chain of different assumptions about services that will be needed over the contract period, how unequivocally these can be specified; the capacity of the vendor to deliver these at the quality required and price quoted; and the relative costs that alternative scenarios will involve. If any one of these assumptions is not met, a potential cost-saving can quickly become a very expensive additional expense. This generally, in turn, leads to high levels of dissatisfaction amongst purchasers, and can quickly erode the relationship between client and vendor (Rouse, 2002).

Despite the growth of outsourcing, evidence of widespread cost savings from local, onshore IT and business process outsourcing has been mixed, at best (Rouse and Corbitt, 2003a; Domberger et al, 2002). This may be why so many firms in the US, Europe and the Pacific Basin are now considering offshore outsourcing, instead. However, there is as yet virtually no systematic independent evidence about the success (or otherwise) of offshore outsourcing, even though anecdotal and case study evidence is published widely. Unfortunately, reports of cost savings by informants at a particular time do not mean that verified costs will be saved over the life of these cases, and certainly tell us nothing about whether the general population of those firms that outsource experience net cost savings. To complicate matters, some case studies of "offshore outsourcing" relate to what are described as "captive centres" (in, for example, Lacity and Rottman, 2008). Captive centres are not "outsourcing" at all, but rather firm subsidiaries that have been located offshore to take advantage of lower salaries.

There certainly appears to be a significant gap between portrayal in the trade literature of the benefits of offshore outsourcing and the reality experienced by many firms (Overby, 2003). Substantial benefits from offshore outsourcing are promised by vendors (and often by sourcing consultants), based largely on the salary differentials between developed and developing nations but salaries, increasingly, are only part of the costs associated with offshore outsourcing. According to Lacity et al (2009, p 142).

Achieving total cost savings has been difficult in the context of offshore outsourcing because of all the additional challenges and practices needed to ensure success.

Moreover, once a firm enters into an offshore arrangement, it has few options if expected benefits do not eventuate, and any change of vendor (or worse, re-insourcing or "backsourcing") will be time-consuming and expensive (Overby, 2003; Hirschheim, 1998). Yet it is difficult to establish the realistic likelihood of promised benefits due to the lack of systematic probabilistic academic research into outsourcing – that is, research where large random samples are gathered so that confidence intervals can be calculated (Rouse and Corbitt, 2003a). The case studies making up the bulk of academic research into offshore outsourcing are necessarily non-random, and they may be poor exemplars of the average firms' likely offshore outsourcing experiences. Given the complexities of establishing "success," or otherwise, we may never know, other than anecdotally, how common, nor how destructive, are the risks associated with outsourcing.

We can, however, encourage firms that are engaged in outsourcing (particularly offshore outsourcing) to develop better "business cases" to support their decision whether or not to outsource offshore. This will have benefits beyond the individual firm, because poorly-developed business cases have two negative consequences. Firstly, they encourage firms to adopt sourcing choices that should have been flagged as inappropriate. Secondly, unless they are countered by public reviews (which are extremely rare), the unachievable "expected" benefits that are often promoted to the press (and sometimes reported in academic case studies) add to an unrealistic community portrayal of the benefits and risks associated with outsourcing (and offshore) arrangements.

Drawing on transaction and risk theory, Rouse (2009) coined a basic outsourcing equation that she argued should be investigated as part of the development of the business case for a sourcing choice.

Savings(or negative savings) = Production cost savings – (Transactions costs + Risk exposure costs)

Drawing on her focus group studies, Rouse also pointed out that while production cost savings are highly visible, transaction costs and risk exposure are quite difficult to discern.

Rouse's "outsourcing equation" is drawn from transaction cost theory (Williamson, 1989) which argues that there are two key costs that need to be accounted for: the *production* costs (the costs of actually delivering the specified services) and the *transaction* costs (the costs of coordination and control of the vendor-client arrangement. These latter do not include just the day to day costs of coordination, but all costs associated with finding and contracting with the other player, as well as the costs of monitoring performance, and acting where this does not match the original contract.

Rouse's focus group informants revealed that transaction costs are particularly difficult to establish, and the high proportion of them reporting no savings suggests that with outsourcing, transaction costs are often as high as, if not higher, than the production cost savings associated with the vendor's bid. Rouse and Corbitt's survey of purchasers (Rouse and Corbitt, 2003a) reveals that a majority of firms fail to obtain cost savings, and a sizeable minority report that outsourcing IT leads to even greater costs than before services were outsourced.

Transaction costs are also substantially higher in situations where the service is highly tailored to the needs of the particular vendor ("asset specific") and where there is a high level of uncertainty (Williamson, 1981).

Risks can be seen as a particular kind of cost, as they can be converted to a notional cost by multiplying their likelihood by the cost of the negative consequences that might arrive – often labeled the "risk exposure" (Bahli & Rivard, 2005; Vaughan, 1997). So for example, if there is a 40 per cent chance that the $1million savings projected for the outsourcing arrangement will be completely eaten up by unexpected variations (a common occurrence) then the risk exposure for this particular risk would be $400,000. The risk exposure costs for commonly-occurring risks should be included in the development and comparison of different sourcing scenarios, however, Rouse's focus group informants suggested this is rarely done. Perhaps this is because, given the low success rates reported by Rouse and Corbitt

(2003a), few outsourcing arrangements would be entered into if risks were costed in this way.

Dozens of different types of outsourcing risks have been reported in the literature – Lacity et al (2009) identified at least 43 different risks in their overview of the academic literature; a similar long list was classified into twenty-three groups by Martens and Teuteberg (2009). However, some of those cited by Lacity et al and Martens and Tueteberg are management failures (like poor project management, or "inflexible contract"), rather than risks.

Three important risks are:

1. the risk that vendors will deliberately (or unwittingly) under quote (Willcocks et al., 2002);
2. the risk of post-contracting variations – generally charged for at a premium (Cullen and Willcocks, 2003); and
3. risks associated with the nature of the IOSs that link vendor and client. It is these latter that are the focus of this chapter.

Unfortunately, many of the risks associated with outsourcing seem to go unrecognized, and this can lead to problems during the life of the outsourcing arrangement (Lacity et al, 2009). According to Rouse's focus group informants, outsourcing risks tend to eventuate more frequently than is typically expected; and this inevitably lead to additional purchaser costs, often substantial ones. These costs reduce, and in many cases, reverse, the cost savings that were the primary reason most firms entered into their outsourcing arrangement. In other words, instead of saving money by outsourcing, firms can end up paying more to outsource their services. This explanation helps to make sense of the survey research that Rouse and Corbitt (2003a) reported.

Since the time line and costs to revert an outsourcing decision are long and expensive, firms that encounter risks that should have been foreseen may need to absorb substantial cost increases for many years before anything can be done to counter them. This uses up resources (both financial and management attention) that should be redirected elsewhere in the firm.

It is easy to see how this might happen when the process by which sourcing decisions are made is examined. The outsourcing decision always depends on the comparison of two hypothesized scenarios, that is, projections of what "might" happen under different circumstances. The first scenario involves the purchaser retaining service-provision in-house (the "counterfactual" if outsourcing is chosen). The second involves the services being delivered by an external party. Both scenarios depend heavily upon a range of assumptions and projections about likely service demands, costs of delivery, how much intervention will need to take place (if there are problems, etc) (Hodge and Rouse, 2006).

It is only after a sourcing arrangement has finished that it is possible to determine whether the actual experience (the "factual") of the selected option actually matched that projection. Even then, it is not at all clear what the theoretical "counterfactual" would have really cost. So after-the-event comparisons are themselves difficult to undertake (as illustrated in Rouse and Corbitt, 2003b).

OUTSOURCING RISKS INHERENT TO INTER-ORGANIZATIONAL SYSTEMS

This chapter concentrates on outsourcing risks related particularly to the use of IOSs to support outsourcing. The focus groups conducted by Rouse (2002) suggest there are two major categories of risks associated particularly with IOSs. The first is related to the handing over of sensitive data to the vendor; the second to the move from largely informal within-organizational controls to formal controls that are supplemented by informal controls exercised largely remotely and mediated by technology.

Data-Related Risks

Complex IT-supported outsourcing almost always involves handing over the client firm's data to the vendor, given that almost all business processes carried out in firms are now information-intensive (Rouse and Watson, 2005). Even supposedly simple services such as Help Desk support normally require that sensitive customer information be made available to vendor staff. This transfer of data takes place within the IOS, and introduces a range of new risks that are not always thought through by those who are making the decision whether to outsource or not. Moving data beyond the confines of the purchaser organization, particularly if this involves offshore hosting, can introduce security, cultural, language, and political risks as well as risks associated with different legal jurisdictions (O'Donnell & Glassberg, 2005, p 41; Rouse and Watson, 2005). A further risk for accessing data held offshore is the quality of telecommunications infrastructure in the country where the system is hosted, which has important reliability implications. Many firms have been surprised to find that the infrastructure in developing nations is not necessarily as reliable as that in the US or Europe (Rao, 2004).

The more distant the vendor site, the higher the data risks – with offshore outsourcing to developing nations (sometimes labeled "farshoring") the most risky (Rao, 2004; Rouse and Watson, 2005). Such outsourcing involves substantially different cultural attitudes (to, for example, privacy of data); and different legal jurisdictions, with often very different penalty treatments for breaches of privacy and confidentiality (Rouse and Watson, 2005). Furthermore, many of the popular offshore sites are in countries with very high levels of corruption (Transparencies International, 2009), meaning that legal remedies have limited power to protect data from theft. There have been a number of highly-publicized failures where outsourcing vendors did not safeguard the data supplied to them by vendors, though not all of these were in developing nations (Rouse and Watson, 2005). Unfortunately once a data breach occurs, there is little firms can do to regain the trust of their customers.

Risks Related to IOS-Supported Control Processes

Complex IT-supported outsourcing substitutes the use of IT-mediated controls for the informal interpersonal controls associated with a hierarchical employment-based service, in which managers direct the activities of their subordinates. This too introduces new outsourcing risks that are not always well thought through.

The quality of the outsourced service supplied to the purchaser depends on the coordinated actions of a range of staff working for both client and vendor. Yet outsourcing involves replacing the face-to-face supervision that is associated with a hierarchy. Staff who perform outsourced tasks are no longer the known individuals, selected and vetted by the client firm, and able to be quickly redirected if circumstances change. Instead tasks are performed by anonymous vendor staff controlled by an arms-length outcomes-based contract, supplemented by the day to day controls provided by Type 3 IOSs such as email. These technologies involved attenuation of information richness (Daft and Lengel, 1986), something that is not necessarily easily observed. The focus group informants studied by Rouse (2002) gave several instances of confusion and misunderstanding as a result of this attenuation.

For a service process to work, all players need to share a common language, based on common cultural understandings. They also need to know what behavior is required and how and when to act (Shostack, 1993). This is particularly difficult to ensure when coordination and control is exercised remotely, without the benefit of face-to-face meetings, so it is not surprising that many misunderstandings and problems occur with outsourcing (Willcocks and Kern, 2001). Replacing controls based largely on tacit understandings and social mores with explicit text-based controls (codified into documents and transmitted via IOSs) will only work when there is substantial "cultural compatibility" (Hancox and Hackney, 2000) but this is less likely when vendor and client come from dramatically different national and cultural settings.

These IOS-related risks of outsourcing are associated with the fact that informal controls are essentially only possible because both managers and employees operate within, and understand a range of taken-for-granted assumptions that are often described as the internal "culture" (Rouse, 2008; O'Reilly, 1989). Firm and national culture act as a form of shortcut to allow individuals to act without having to formally check what is and is not acceptable behavior, but because norms, and the meanings inherent in language, are taken for granted, this process can lead to major confusion across different organizational and national cultures.

The focus group informants studied by Rouse (2002) reported that (corporate) cultural misunderstandings can be a source of continual difficulty in outsourcing arrangements. This is because employees of both vendor and client do not realize that the other player will not necessarily behave, nor understand language, in the expected way. Again, these risks are magnified when outsourcing involves vendors in developing countries where not only different firms are involved, but the national ways of doing business, and of behaving in relation to issues of legality, can differ markedly (Winkler, et al., 2008).

Problems of confusion are most likely to occur with Type 3 IOSs, in the use of technologies like email or wikis to carry out coordination and day to day controls, where information richness is reduced compared to face to face discussion. Cultural problems are also likely to be magnified in "crisis" situations, where the substitution of semi-formal IT-mediated controls, and misunderstandings that cause delays, can lead to substantially reduced responsiveness. However, the design of Type 1 and 2 IOSs, too, needs to consider issues associated with offshore service delivery (such as currency, technology and data standards, and technology infrastructure etc).

In Tables 3 and 4, these IOS-related risks are summarized, and categorized depending on whether they are likely to be seen in all outsourcing-related IOSs, or whether they are more likely to be found in offshore outsourcing arrangements. Examples are taken from those raised by Rouse's (2002) focus group members. Table 3 focuses on risks related to the sending of data outside the firm via an IOS, while Table 4 focuses on risk associated with the substitution of formalized organizational controls, mediated by an IOS, for informal, largely face-to-face, organizational controls.

The way both classes of IOS risks operate will differ to some extent according to whether the outsourcing is project or process-based (as discussed earlier). For example, project-based outsourcing may not always involve sending sensitive live corporate data to the vendor (though it frequently does). Furthermore, with project-based outsourcing, many of the risks associated with outsourcing are common to most project-based activities. Whether the development of an IOS is carried out by outsourced or internal staff, for example, there are likely to be communication problems, and differences in cultural understandings between users and system developers. However, these are likely to be magnified in an outsourced situation because there are fewer opportunities for face to face meetings where such issues can be identified and addressed.

Table 3. Data related outsourcing risks introduced when inter organizational systems are involved

Risk	Inherent to an IOS	Magnified for offshore outsourcing	Example
Data interception	X		Sensitive information is hacked while being transmitted between vendor and client
Access becomes unreliable	X		Client cannot access own records due to telecommunications failure
Data theft	X	X	Provider staff steal data (especially in jurisdictions where this is neither illegal nor frowned upon)
Privacy breach	X	X	Vendor staff fail to safeguard data, or (as happened in the US) threaten to publish sensitive records. (This is less likely in Australia, NZ or Europe because of stringent privacy protection).
Data destroyed due to failure of poor infrastructure		X	Records destroyed by floods, electricity failures, etc.
Data destroyed due to political unrest		X	Records damaged by terrorists, war

Table 4. Organizational control-related outsourcing risks introduced when inter organizational systems are involved

Risk	Inherent to an IOS	Magnified For offshore outsourcing	Example
Cultural confusions due to different language/terms	X	X	Staff in both organizations use the same term, but it has different meanings in the different organizational or national culture
Cultural confusions due to different firm, or national culture	X	X	Staff in one organization do not recognize that they are expected to do a range of unstated work that is seen by the other party as being inherent to a given request.
Misunderstandings due to information attenuation	X		Staff misinterpret instructions or information because of the lack of information richness in the electronic communication
Misunderstandings due to incorrect cultural expectations		X	Firm staff expect that few vendor staff would be willing to risk jail and opprobrium by stealing data (as happens in Australia) when those sanctions and values are not in places in the vendor's location
Crucial information overlooked	X		Staff miss critical information that is in a written document – a face to face meeting would have highlighted the importance
Delayed processes because of asynchronous communication	X		Messages are sent but not acted on because they are not seen till later
Cultural confusion due to different norms	X		Purchaser and provider staff have very different expectations about what the other will do, which are not surfaced in face to face meetings
Reduced responsiveness	X		Delays introduced by time differences, or by the need to set up video/audio conferencing.

SOLUTIONS AND RECOMMENDATIONS

IOSs have been enormously important in allowing firms to interact and coordinate value chain activities, including vendor-client outsourcing arrangements which rely largely on Type 3 IOSs. They have enabled substantial efficiencies, and improved operational and financial performance. However, IOSs are not merely technology systems – they are social systems in which vendor and client staff behavior, and cultural expectations, are a core aspect of the system's success.

While vendors would encourage firms to believe that outsourcing normally leads to cost savings, Transaction cost economics argues that this will only occur when there is intense competition between a sizeable number of vendors (often missing in BPO and IT markets) and when production cost savings are not outweighed by increased transaction costs. Risk management theory (Vaughan, 1997) adds in the importance of risk exposure. It is critical, then, that the business case on which outsourcing decisions are made does, in fact, accurately incorporate all transaction and risk exposure costs. This requires a more thoughtful analysis of assumptions and risks.

This chapter has highlighted that IOSs introduce additional risks that may not easily be recognized, and that these risks are increased when outsourcing involves vendors located outside the cultural and legal environments of the decision-makers. In that case, few decision-makers seem to recognize that their own taken-for-granted assumptions about infrastructure, language, behaviors, national attitudes, and legal sanctions may not operate in developing countries, and that such incorrect assumptions can be a continual source of unforeseen costs, or service failures.

Furthermore, such failures themselves can be sources of substantial unforeseen second-order costs, as executives may need to fly quickly to offshore sites to address crises; staff may need to be relocated for longer periods; and legal consequences (such as being sued by customers whose data is stolen) may be high.

Managing these IOS-related risks requires recognition of the richness and complexity of the control processes that take place within hierarchies, and the extent to which these rely on cultural expectations. This in turn requires careful investigation and analysis. Vendor and client alike must devote the required attention, skill, and resources to surfacing and articulating what needs to be done by each player in the service-delivery process. This is more easily achieved when formal systems are designed (for Type 1 and Type IOSs, for example) but is probably most crucial for Type 3 IOSs where the human element plays such an important role.

Firms have been exhorted for decades to "do their homework" when making significant sourcing decisions (Lacity and Hirschheim, 1993) and in the end, this is the message of this chapter. However the chapter argues that "doing your homework" involves exploring in depth all of the assumptions underlying the decision, capturing all costs (not just production costs) associated with service delivery under each scenario considered; and realistically considering the gamut of risks that might be encountered, including the magnitude of the consequences of these risks, and their likelihood.

In this chapter several IOS-specific risks have been discussed that may be overlooked when the outsourcing decision is investigated. The author argues that this overlooking usually occurs because success relies on taken-for-granted assumptions. Unless alerted to potential difficulties, it seems that managers often assume that common terms used by vendor and client staff will mean the same thing; that the culture of both will be similar; and that the legal/ security/infrastructure environments in which both operate will be similar. None of these assumptions are necessarily valid, and so challenging these is an important part of the "sensitivity analysis" that should take place when the business-case for sourcing is developed.

FUTURE RESEARCH DIRECTIONS

As more and more firms move to outsource their complex IT-based processes, particularly when this involves vendors located overseas, the challenges confronting IOS researchers will multiply. While in future the topics of cooperative systems development and common standards, which were identified in the 1980s and 1990s, will still have currency, the growing move to Type 3 IOSs will require additional research focused on these less structured technologies for supporting inter-firm cooperation.

Such research will need to recognize the complex social nature of the inter-organizational system, and the importance of informal IOS-based control processes alongside the formal, legalistic control processes. There has to date been little comprehensive multi-dimensional research on IOS risk (Hughes et al, 2004), and what research has been done has not tended to consider this risk in the context of outsourcing (i.e. of business-to-business service-delivery). Within the outsourcing literature, on the other hand, very little systematic investigation of risks and their likelihoods has been undertaken, as evidenced by the piecemeal approach adopted in the articles identified by Martens and Teuteberg (2009). In particular, little research to date has considered IOS-related risks when a service is provided by sites located in very different legal/cultural/infrastructure/ethical environments to that found in western countries.

New organizational forms, supported by Type 3 IOSs have great potential. So more investigations into the risks associated with cross-national IOSs should be undertaken, as should investigations into how the notion of risks is incorporated into considerations of costs and benefits of such systems.

CONCLUSION

IOS-supported offshore outsourcing clearly can be successful in certain circumstances, and such outsourcing has the potential to lead to substantial benefits for both vendor and clients. But success is by no means guaranteed.

Thoughtful planning is the cornerstone of good outsourcing arrangements, including planning for how the IOS-based social systems are to work. Since outsourcing now frequently involves dealing with vendors from other cultures, it is important to take a social-technical-cultural view of arrangements, and to recognize the risks associated with substituting IOS-based working arrangements for face-to-face interpersonal relationships. Firms must carefully consider the types of risks that IOSs bring to these forms of inter-organizational cooperation.

REFERENCES

Baeker, R. M. (1993). *Readings in groupware and computer supported cooperative work* (p. 399). San Francisco, CA: Morgan Kauffman.

Bahli, B., & Rivard, S. (2003). The information technology outsourcing risk: A transaction cost and agency theory-based perspective. *Journal of Information Technology, 18*(3), 211–221. doi:10.1080/0268396032000130214

Barrett, S. S. (1987). Strategic alternatives and inter-organizational system implementation: An overview. *Journal of Management Information Systems, 3*(3), 5–16.

Choudhury, V., & Sabherwal, R. (2003). Portfolios of control in outsourced software development projects. *Information Systems Research, 14*(4), 291–314. doi:10.1287/isre.14.3.291.16563

Clemons, E., & Row, M. (1992). Informational technology and industrial cooperation: The changing economics of coordination and ownership. *Journal of Management Information Systems*, *9*(2), 9–28.

Cullen, S., & Willcocks, L. P. (2003). *Intelligent outsourcing: Eight building blocks to IT success*. Oxford, UK: Buttterworth-Heineman.

Currie, W., & Seltsikas, P. (2001). Exploring the supply-side of IT outsourcing: evaluating the emerging role of application service providers. *European Journal of Information Systems*, *10*(3), 123–134. doi:10.1057/palgrave.ejis.3000393

Daft, R. L., & Lengel, R. H. (1986). Organizational information requirements, media richness and structural design. *Management Science*, *32*(5), 554–571. doi:10.1287/mnsc.32.5.554

Domberger, S., Jensen, P. H., & Stonecash, R. E. (2002). Examining the magnitude and sources of cost savings associated with outsourcing. *Public Performance and Management Review*, *26*(2), 148–168. doi:10.1177/1530957602238260

Eom, S. B. (2005). *Inter-organizational information systems in the Internet age*. Hershey, PA: Idea Group.

Greinstein, M., & Vaserhelyi, M. (2000). *Electronic commerce: Security, risk management and control*. McGraw-Hill/Irwin.

Halvey, J. K., & Melby, B. M. (2007). *Business process outsourcing. Processes strategies and contracts*. Wiley.

Hancox, M., & Hackney, R. (2000). IT outsourcing: Frameworks for conceptualizing practice and perception. *Information Systems Journal*, *10*, 217–237. doi:10.1046/j.1365-2575.2000.00082.x

Hayes, B. (2008). Cloud computing. *Communications of the ACM*, *51*(7), 9–10. doi:10.1145/1364782.1364786

Hirschheim, R. A. (1998). *Backsourcing: An emerging trend?* Infoserver. Retrieved from http://www.infoserver.com/sep1998/html/academic.html

Hodge, G. A., & Rouse, A. C. (2006). Outsourcing government IT services: An Australian case study. In Boyne, G. A. (Eds.), *Public service performance: Perspectives on performance and management* (pp. 212–232). Cambridge, UK: Cambridge University Press.

Hopper, D. (1990). Rattling SABRE – New ways to compete on information. *Business Review (Federal Reserve Bank of Philadelphia)*, *4*(July), 118–125.

Hughes, M., Powell, P., Panteli, N., & Golden, W. (2004). Risk mitigation and risk absorption in IOS: A proposed investigative study. *Proceedings of the 13th European Conference on Information Systems (ECIS 2004)*. June Turku, Finland.

Johnston, H. R., & Vitale, M. R. (1988). Creating competitive advantage with inter-organizational information systems. *Management Information Systems Quarterly*, *12*(2), 153–165. doi:10.2307/248839

Kaplan, J. M. (2007). SaaS: Friend or foe. *Business Communications Review*, 48-53.

Lacity, M., Khan, S. A., & Willcocks, L. (2009). A review of the IT outsourcing literature: Insights for practice. *The Journal of Strategic Information Systems*, *18*(3), 130–146. doi:10.1016/j.jsis.2009.06.002

Lacity, M., & Rottman, J. (2008). *Offshore outsourcing of information technology work*. New York, NY: Palgrave-McMillan. doi:10.1057/9780230582965

Lacity, M., & Willcocks, L. (2001). *Global information technology outsourcing*. UK: Wiley.

Martens, B., & Teuteberg, F. (2009). Why risk management matters in IT outsourcing: A systematic literature review and elements of a research agenda. *Proceedings of the 17th European Conference on Information Systems (ECIS 2009).* June. Verona, Italy.

O'Donnell, J. B., & Glassberg, B. C. (2005). A typology of inter-organizational systems. In Eom, S. (Ed.), *Inter-organizational information systems in the Internet age*. Hershey, PA: Idea Group.

O'Reilly, C. (1989). Corporations, culture, and commitment: Motivation and social control in organizations. *California Management Review, 31*, 9–25.

Overby, S. (2003, September 1). The hidden costs of offshore outsourcing. *CIO Magazine*. Retrieved March 19, 2010, from http://www.cio.com/archive/090103/

Rao, M. T. (2004). Key issues for global outsourcing: Country and individual factors. *Information Systems Management*, 16–24. doi:10.1201/1078/44432.21.3.20040601/82472.3

Rouse, A. C. (2002). *Information technology outsourcing revisited: Success factors and risks.* Unpublished doctoral thesis. Melbourne, Australia: University of Melbourne.

Rouse, A. C. (2008). *Managing e-collaboration risks in business process outsourcing, Encyclopedia of e-Collaboration* (pp. 424–429). Hershey, PA: Information Science Reference.

Rouse, A. C. (2009). *The governance implications when it is outsourced. Information Technology governance and service management: Frameworks and adaptations* (pp. 285–295). Hershey, PA: Information Science Reference.

Rouse, A. C., & Corbitt, B. J. (2003a). Revisiting IT outsourcing risks: Analysis of a survey of Australia's top 1000 organizations. *14th Australasian Conference on Information Systems 2003, Perth, Western Australia, 26-28 November, 2003: Delivering IT and e-business value in networked environments.* Edith Cowan University, Joondalup, WA (pp. 1-11).

Rouse, A. C., & Corbitt, B. J. (2003b).Minimising risks in IT outsourcing: Choosing target services, *PACIS 2003: Proceedings of the Seventh Pacific Asia Conference on Information Systems*, University of South Australia, Adelaide, S. Aust. (pp. 927-940).

Rouse, A. C., & Corbitt, B. J. (2004). IT-supported business process outsourcing (BPO): The good, the bad and the ugly. In C.-P. Wei (Ed.), *Information Systems Adoption and Business Productivity, PACIS 2004: Proceedings of the Seventh Pacific Asia Conference on Information Systems.* Shanghai, China (pp. 1-14).

Rouse, A. C., & Watson, D. J. (2005). Cyberfraud and identity theft: The hidden costs of business process outsourcing. *Monash Business Review, 1*(2), 30–39. doi:10.2104/mbr05018

Shostack, G. L. (1993). How to design a service. *European Journal of Marketing, 16*(1), 49–63. doi:10.1108/EUM0000000004799

Transparencies International. (2009). *Corruption perception index 2009.* Retrieved from http://www.transparency.org/policy_research/surveys_indices/cpi/2009

Vaughan, E. J. (1997). *Risk management.* UK: Wiley.

Willcocks, L. P., & Kern, T. (2001). *The relationship advantage: Information technologies, sourcing and management.* Oxford, UK: Oxford University Press.

Willcocks, L. P., Kern, T., & Van Heck, E. (2002). The winner's curse in IT outsourcing: Strategies for avoiding relational trauma. *California Management Review*, *44*(2), 47–69.

Williamson, O. E. (1981). The economics of organization: The transaction cost approach. *American Journal of Sociology*, *87*, 548–577. doi:10.1086/227496

Williamson, O. E. (1989). *Operationalizing the new institutional economics: The transaction cost economics perspective.* Walter A. Haas School of Business Working Paper. University of California, Berkeley.

Winkler, J., Dibbern, J., & Heinzl, A. (2008). The impact of cultural differences in offshore outsourcing: Case study results from German-Indian application development projects. *Information Systems Frontiers*, *10*(2), 243–258. doi:10.1007/s10796-008-9068-5

KEY TERMS AND DEFINITIONS

BPO: Business process outsourcing. Outsourcing of relatively complex business processes or activities that are supported by information technologies.

Business Process: A set of interrelated organizational activities performed by a number of individuals with the goal of generating customer value. This process can be intra-organizational or inter-organizational.

Captive Centre: A wholly-owned or partly-owned business unit that performs services overseas (usually in a developing nation) so as to take advantage of lower salary costs. While occasionally described as "outsourcing" this does not necessarily involve an external party.

Inter-Organizational System (IOS): An information and management system that links separate organizations via electronic linkages, so transcending organizational boundaries.

Offshoring: Offshore outsourcing or cross-national outsourcing, where the vendor and client operate in different countries. Sometimes this term is used to describe the allocation of work to a wholly-owned or partly-owned subsidiary, sometimes termed a "captive centre"; however this does not necessarily involve outsourcing.

Outsourcing: Assigning, to required results, responsibility for all or a portion of the activity and tasks involved in a business process to an external provider. The provider is responsible for management of organizational assets, resources and/or activities.

Risk: The likelihood or probability of some consequence seen as undesirable, although the term is often used synonymously with "downside." Risk exposure is calculated as the probability of an undesirable consequence multiplied by its (negative) magnitude.

Risk Management: The process of evaluating and selecting alternative responses to risk.

Chapter 9
The Theory of Constraints: A Management Philosophy

Shams Rahman
RMIT University, Australia

ABSTRACT

In the late 1970s, a new approach to the management of operations was developed by Goldratt. Now known as the theory of constraints (TOC), it provides a coherent management theory for running an organisation. It has two major components: a philosophy which underpins the working principle of on-going improvement and a generic approach for investigating, analyzing, and creating solutions to problems, called the "thinking process" (TP). Several books, numerous articles, and a few journal special issues have been published on TOC. This chapter provides a comprehensive review of TOC concepts, philosophy, and working principles.

INTRODUCTION

Businesses are competing increasingly on responsiveness and service. Companies cannot survive if they fail to obtain competitive advantages by providing a high level of service and distributing in shorter delivery times with quicker inventory turnover. Since the early 1970s, three important approaches have evolved for companies to achieve competitive advantages, each challenges old assumptions and ways of doing things. These are just-in-time (JIT) (Moden, 1993), or lean manufacturing (Womack and Jones, 1996), total quality management (TQM) (Deming, 1986) and theory of constraints (TOC) (Goldratt, 1988).

Developed by Eli Goldratt in the mid-1980s (Goldratt, 1988) TOC evolved from the Optimized Production Timetables (OPT) system (Goldratt, 1980), later known by the commercial name of Optimized Production Technology (OPT®). As a marketing tool for the OPT system, Goldratt illustrated OPT concepts in a novel (Goldratt

DOI: 10.4018/978-1-60960-768-5.ch009

Copyright © 2012, IGI Global. Copying or distributing in print or electronic forms without written permission of IGI Global is prohibited.

and Cox, 1984) in which the theory is gradually unravelled through the context of an everyday production situation. The concepts identified in this book (*The Goal)* were more fully developed as results from actual OPT implementation became known. A second book, *The Race* (Goldratt and Fox, 1986), was written to illustrate overcoming difficulties encountered in implementation. It introduced a logistical system for material flow, called drum-buffer-rope (DBR), and gradually, the focus of OPT has moved from the production floor to encompass all aspects of business. By 1987, the overall concept became known as the theory of constraints (TOC), which Goldratt viewed as "an overall theory for running an organisation" (Goldratt, 1988, p.453). This refinement to OPT recognised that the main constraint in most organisations may not be physical but rather managerial and policy related. To address the policy constraints and effectively implement the process of ongoing improvement, Goldratt (1990, 1994) developed a generic approach, 'Thinking Process' (TP).

In the following section provides a review of existing literature, highlighting the areas of TOC application and its impact on organisational performance.

BACKGROUND

The theory of constraints (TOC) is a system-based management philosophy which seeks to understand and identify the core causes that limit a system from achieving higher performance versus its goal (Goldratt, 1988). Although a relatively new approach, applications of TOC concepts and tools have been published widely in academic literature and the popular press. This body of literature has been written to:

- demonstrate the basic concepts of TOC;
- review TOC literature;
- review the historical development of OPT as well as TOC and TP applications;
- define and categorise concepts and terms;
- demonstrate the impact of OPT software on organisational performance;
- compare aspects of TOC with other operations management tools such as material requirement planning (MRP) and Kanban, linear programming, and total quality management;
- compare the TOC performance measures with traditional cost accounting and activity-based cost accounting management;
- develop a TOC-based framework for operations management.

Much of the earlier TOC studies focused on manufacturing companies (Rahman, 1998). The application to service organisations is relatively new. The TOC tools have been implemented across a variety of service organisations, including: livestock production; education institutions; the health sector; military health services and the banking sector. These studies used either the five-focusing steps or the TP mapping tools of TOC.

The TOC tools have been applied in conjunction with other management techniques. For example, Ehie and Sheu (2005) implemented a combined six-sigma and TOC approach in an automobile components production facility and made substantial cost-savings for the company. Recently, Lacerda et al. (2010) applied TP in conjunction with process engineering in an academic institution to redesign processes related to the delivery of various academic programs. The improvement through integration of TOC and other tools doesn't come as a surprise. A study by Pirasteh and Farah (2006) concluded that when lean management, six sigma and TOC principles are implemented together, it is possible to realise cost savings up to nine times higher than the independent application of either lean or six sigma.

A number of Fortune 500 companies including Boeing, Ford Motor Company, General Motors,

General Electric and Lucent Technologies have deployed TOC solutions and achieved significant improvements (Watson et al., 2007). In a comprehensive study of a wide variety of companies, Mabin and Balderstone (2000) reported that the deployment of TOC tools has produced higher levels of throughput while reducing inventory, order-to-delivery lead time and manufacturing cycle time.

The purpose of this chapter is to present a comprehensive review of developments to the concept, philosophy and working principles of TOC.

THE CONCEPT

The concept of TOC can be summarised as:

1. **Every system must have at least one constraint.** If it were not true, then a real system, such as a profit making organisation would make unlimited profit. A constraint therefore, "is anything that limits a system from achieving higher performance versus its goal" (Goldratt, 1988, p.453).
2. **The existence of constraints represents opportunities for improvement.** Contrary to conventional thinking, TOC views constraints as positive, not negative. Because constraints determine the performance of a system, a gradual elevation of the system's constraints will improve its performance.

There are two major components of TOC. First, a philosophy which underpins its working principle. It consists of the five focusing steps and two prerequisites of ongoing improvement, (the drum-buffer-rope [DBR] scheduling methodology and the buffer management information system), and is usually referred to as TOC's 'logistics' paradigm. The second component of TOC is a generic approach for investigating, analysing and solving complex problems, the 'Thinking Process' (TP). In addition, TOC prescribes new performance measurements which are quite different from the traditional cost-accounting system. Integrating these components a comprehensive framework of TOC is presented in Figure 1.

Within the TOC paradigm the goal of a profit making organisation is to make money now and in the future, without violating two necessary conditions: providing satisfaction to internal customers (employees) and providing satisfaction to external customers (Dettmer, 1997). The relationship between the goal and two other necessary conditions is shown in Figure 1a. This sequence of relationship is similar to the balanced scorecard model (Kaplan and Norton, 1996), in the sense that they represent an interactive link between financial (goal) and non-financial (two necessary conditions: satisfying employee and customer) parameters. However, unlike the scorecard model, the internal business process (five-focusing steps in the case of the TOC paradigm) is independent of the two necessary conditions.

The goal of the system is measured by three traditional financial measures; net profit, return on investment and cash flow (see Figure 1b); which are direct results of three operational level measures: throughput, inventory and operating expenses. The implementation of the five-focusing steps of TOC is governed by the drum-buffer-rope (DBR) methodology and managed through the use of time-buffers (T-B) when the constraint is physical. However, when the constraint is market or policy related TOC's continuous improvement process is managed by the five mapping tools of the thinking process (TP) (Figure 1c). These components are discussed in the following sections.

PHILOSOPHY

The working principle of TOC provides a focus for a continuous improvement process. The principle consists of five focusing steps (Goldratt, 1990, p.5), summarised in Figure 2.

The steps are:

Figure 1. A comprehensive TOC framework (Source: Adapted from Gupta et al., 2002)

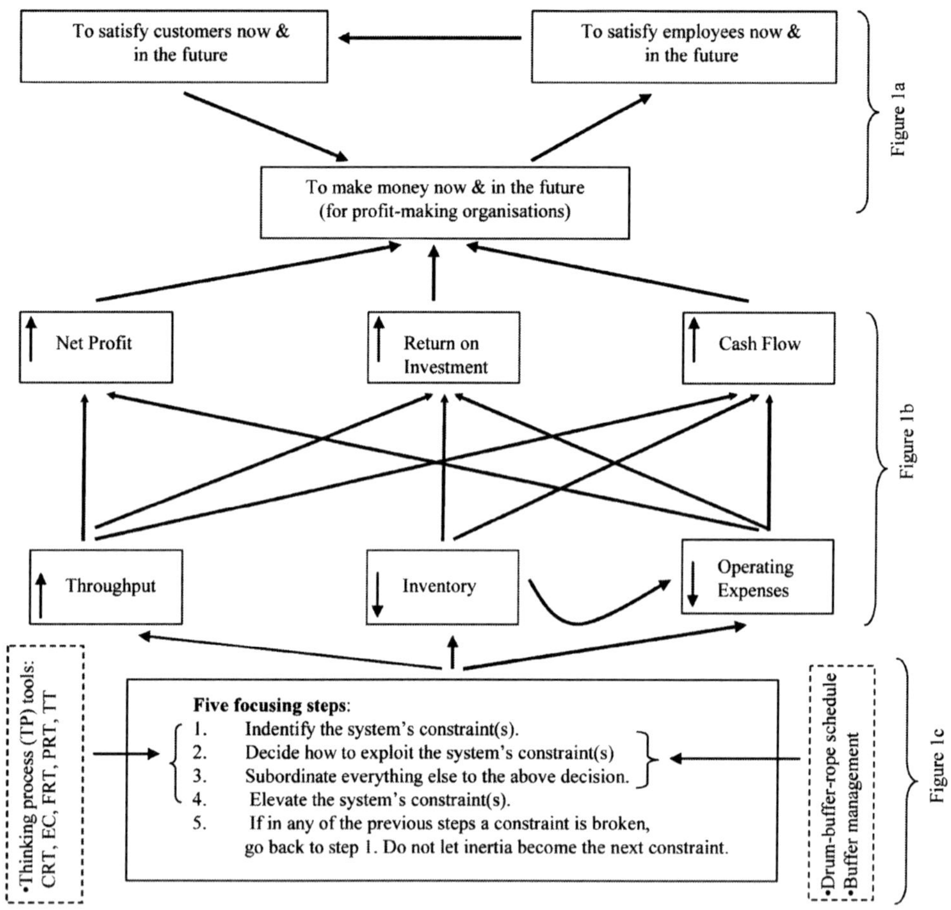

1. **Identify the system's constraint(s).** The TOC assertion is that any organisation has only a handful of real constraints, these can be physical, market related or policy constraints.
   - **Physical constraints:** can be such things as material supplies, machine capacity, workforce capacity, space availability and so on. Generally, organisations have very few physical constraints and they are the easiest to identify. For instance, if a process is shut down by the unavailability of raw materials, this is a materials constraint.
   - **Market constraints:** also known as an external constraint, a market constraint exists if an organisation possesses excess capacity to market demand. Market constraints are relatively harder to identify, when compared with physical constraints.
   - **Policy constraints:** In principle, there should be no policy constraints. However, in reality, most constraints to organisational performance are around policy, in the form of procedures, rules and methods (Goldratt, 1990). Goldratt (1994) developed a technique called a Current Reality Tree to identify policy constraints.

Figure 2. The five-focusing steps of TOC (source: Reid, 2007)

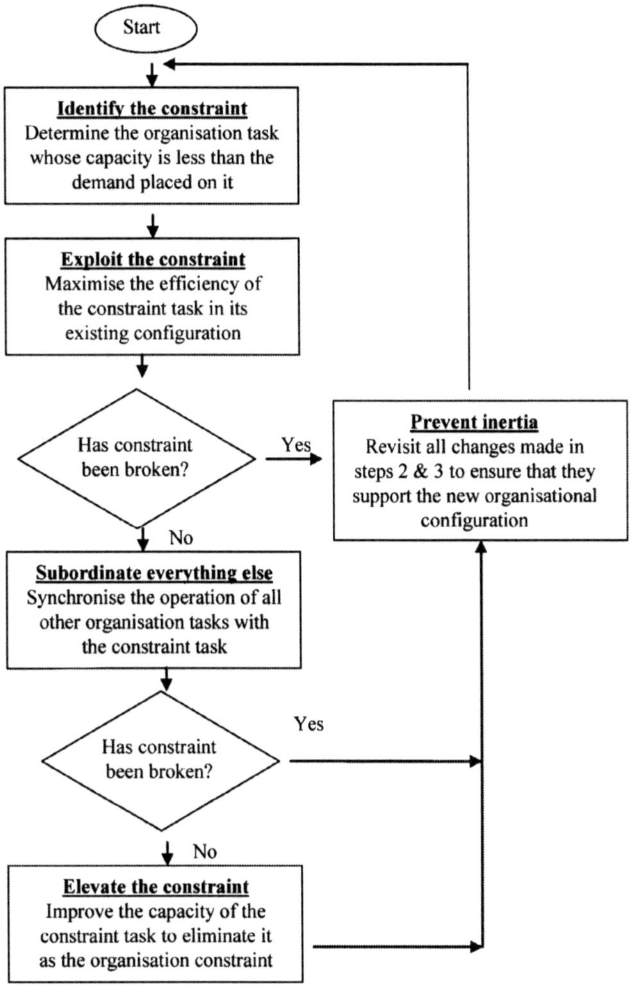

Irrespective of the forms of constraint, it is important to identify and prioritise them according to their impact on the goal(s) of an organisation.

2. **Decide how to exploit the system's constraint(s).** The aim of this step is to exploit any constraint as profitably as possible. If the constraint is physical, the objective is to make it as effective as possible. This means that all non-value adding tasks and time at the constraint must be eliminated. This is likely to uncover unused capacity and help achieve higher throughput, without additional costs. On the other hand, a market or policy constraint should not be exploited but eliminated and replaced with a policy which will support an increase to throughput.
3. **Subordinate everything else to the above decision.** The third step focuses on the management of non-constraints elements of the system. Subordinating everything else means that every other component of the

system (non-constraints) must be adjusted to support the maximum effectiveness of the constraint. Because constraints dictate a firm's throughput, resource synchronisation with the constraint provides the most effective manner of resource utilisation. Non-constraint resources contain productive capacity (capacity to support the constraint throughput) and idle capacity (capacity to protect against system disruptions and capacity not currently needed). If non-constraint resources are used beyond their productive capacity to support the constraint, they do not improve throughput but increase unnecessary inventory. On the other hand, if the non-constraints are ignored, they may turn into constraint resources. Although it sounds simple, this is the most difficult step to accomplish (Smith, 2000), since, "it often requires a paradigm shift in managerial thinking" (Reid, 2007, p. 215).

4. **Elevate the system's constraint(s).** If existing constraints are still the most critical in the system, rigorous improvement efforts on these constraints will improve their performance. As the performance of the constraints improves, the potential of non-constraint resources can be better realised, leading to improvements in overall system performance. Eventually the system will encounter a new constraint.
5. **If, in any of the previous steps, a constraint is broken, go back to step 1.** Do not let inertia become the next constraint. The first part of this step makes TOC a continuous process. The second part is a reminder that no policy (or solution) is appropriate (or correct) for all time or in every situation. It is critical for an organisation to recognise that as its business environment changes, business policy needs to be refined to take account of those changes. Failure to implement step 5 may lead an organisation to disaster.

The sequence of five-focusing steps of TOC is similar to the Shewhart Cycle (Plan-Do-Study-Act) (Deming, 1986) in the sense that the steps represent an iterative approach to implementing a continuous improvement process. However, compared to TQM, Lean thinking, and six-sigma approaches, which tend to improve every aspect of a process, the five-focusing steps of TOC concentrate on the constraint task. For instance, the main thrust of Lean and TQM is to increase productivity and improve quality by eliminating waste and reducing variation in every task of a process. In contrast, TOC concentrates its improvement efforts only on the task/activity that limits the performance of the system as a whole.

The five-focusing steps of TOC have evolved into what is now called the process of ongoing improvement (POOGI). POOGI is an integration of five-focusing steps and two prerequisites for TOC implementation. The first prerequisite is to define the purpose of the system and the second is to define measurements that align the system to the purpose. In the following subsection a hypothetical case demonstrates the application of the five-focusing steps of TOC.

A Case Study of the Five-Step Focusing Process

Adapted from Srinivasan (2004), this hypothetical case study demonstrates the application of the five-focusing steps of TOC in a manufacturing environment, where the constraints are considered to be physical.

A company produces two products, X and Y. There are four operations required to produce X and Y using three raw materials and one purchased part (component). The objective of this hypothetical manufacturing system is to maximise profit. The raw material requirements, costs, demand (production level) and other details associated with the manufacturing system are given in Table 1. For example, the weekly demand for product X is 100 per week. The production of X involves three manufacturing operations (A, B, C) and one assembly operation (D). It requires two raw materials (RM1 and RM2) and a component part. The per unit cost of RM1, RM2, RM3 and Part are $10, $10, $15 and $5 respectively. The sequence of these operations and the time required in each operation are shown in Figure 3. The total operations time available at each operation is 1600 minutes per week and the total operating expenses per week is $3000. The selling price for X and Y are $50 and $60 per unit respectively. Thus, the profit contribution of a unit X is $25 ($50 - $5-$10-$10) and the profit contribution of a unit Y is $35 ($60 - $10 - $15).

Considering the above information and process details we implement the five-focusing steps.

Step 1: Identify the System's Constraint(s)

A capacity analysis was conducted on all four operations. The results are shown in Table 2. A comparison between total available time and total operations time required for each operation indicates that operation B (total operations time = 2050 min > total time available = 1600 min) is the constraint of the current system.

Step 2: Decide How to Exploit the System's Constraint(s)

Due to the capacity constraint at operation B, the current manufacturing system is unable to produce to meet the demand for units of X and Y. The question therefore is: given the situation, what would be the best product mix that would generate maximum profit? This can be investigated from two perspectives: one, traditional measurement (cost world); or two, TOC measurement (throughput world).

Cost World Perspective

Since product Y has a higher profit margin ($35 per unit) than product X ($25 per unit), management of the system may produce as many units of Y as possible through the constraint operation B first and then produce product X using the remaining capacity of B. Based on this approach, management can produce all 50 units of Y that are demanded, utilising 1350 minutes (50 x 27 min) of operation B per week. The remaining 250 minutes (1600 - 1350 min) can be utilised to produce 35 units (250/7) of product X. Thus, the system is capable of producing 35 units of X and 50 units of Y. This product mix will generate a net profit of - $375 ($25 x (35) + $35 x (50) - $3000).

Table 1. Production requirements for product X and Y

Product	Production/week	Raw Materian	Cost / unit ($)	Sale / unit ($)	Required Operations	Total operations time available for each operation (min / week)
X	100	Part	5	50	A,B,C,D	1600
		RM1	10			
		RM2	10			
Y	50	RM2	10	60	A,B,C,D	
		RM3	15			

Figure 3. A hypothetical production system (Source: Adapted from Srinivasan, 2004)

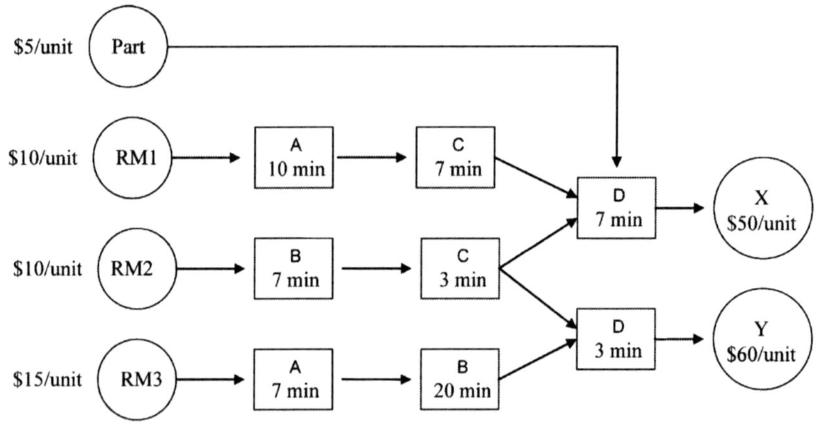

Throughput World Perspective

From this perspective, the aim of the system is to extract maximum throughput ($ per unit time) from the constraint operation B. Data analysis indicates that it requires 27 minutes at operation B to produce one unit of Y, and it contributes $35 per unit. Therefore, the rate at which Y generates profit is $1.30 per minute ($35/27). On the other hand, it requires 7 minutes at operation B to produce one unit of X, and it contributes $25 per unit. Hence, the rate at which X generates profit is $3.57 per minute ($25/7). The management will prefer to produce X first and then produce Y with the remaining capacity of operation B. Using the throughput world concept management can produce all 100 units of X that are demanded using 700 minutes (100 x 7 min) of operation B per week. The remaining 900 minutes (160 - 700 min) can be utilised to produce 33 units (900/27) of product Y. The system is therefore capable of producing 100 units of X and 33 units of Y. This product mix will generate a net profit of $655 ($25 x (100) + $35 x (33) - $3000). The analysis shows that management using the cost world concept will incur a loss of $375, whereas, adopting throughput world concept management will make a profit of $655.

Table 2. Capacity analysis of the manufacturing system

Operation	Load of produce 100 units of X	Load of produce 50 units of Y	Total operation time required	Total time available
A	1000	350	1350	1600
B	700	1350	2050	1600
C	1000	150	1150	1600
D	700	150	850	1600

Step 3: Subordinate Everything Else to the Above Decision

This means that the utilisation of operations A, C, and D (non-constraints) must be adjusted to support the maximum effectiveness of operation B (constraint operation). The management of the production system must ensure that operation B is fully utilised and operation A processes only 33 units of RM3 each week to produce product Y. Any more units A produces, beyond these 33 units, will remain as inventory in front of Operation B.

Step 4: Elevate the System's Constraint(s)

Since management has exploited the constraint operation B, the next step to take is to elevate the constraint. Now, in addition to the physical constraint B, management may find demand mix as a (market) constraint. Since, the rate at which X generates profit ($3.57 per min) at the constraint operation is higher than Y ($1.30 per min), ideally, the management would prefer to have more demand for product X. So, the management has two choices: one, to acquire another resource B; two, to generate more demand for product X. Either of these choices would elevate the constraint, however, the elevation of the constraint through demand increase would pose greater challenges to management than elevating constraint through resource acquisition. An adoption of the latter option (resource B acquisition), will shift constraint from operation B to another operation.

Step 5: If, in any of the Previous Steps, a Constraint is Broken, Go Back to Step 1

Since the current constraint is broken, management's aim now is to take step 1 to step 5 again. This process is known as the process of ongoing improvement (POOGI).

Many studies have successfully applied the five-focusing steps of TOC to real world situations in both the manufacturing and service sectors (Gupta et al., 2002; Pegels and Watrous, 2005; Reid, 2007).

DRUM-BUFFER-ROPE MANAGEMENT

The logistics paradigm of the TOC has evolved from the scheduling software, Optimised Production Technology (OPT®) which, in turn, is based on the following eight rules (Goldratt and Fox, 1986, p.179):

- **Rule 1:** Balance flow, not capacity.
- **Rule 2:** The level of utilisation of a non-bottleneck is not determined by its own potential but by some other constraint in the system.
- **Rule 3:** Utilisation and activation of a resource are not synonymous.
- **Rule 4:** An hour lost at a bottleneck is an hour lost for the total system.
- **Rule 5:** An hour saved at a non-bottleneck is just a mirage.
- **Rule 6:** Bottlenecks govern both throughput and inventories.
- **Rule 7:** The transfer batch may not, and for many times should not, be equal to the process batch. The process batch should be variable, not fixed.
- **Rule 8:** Schedules should be established by looking at all the constraints simultaneously. Lead times are the result of a schedule and cannot be predetermined.

Rule 1 suggests that the aim of a system should be to synchronise the flow for smoother and quicker movement of the products through manufacturing or supply chain systems. The aim should never be to balance the capacities of subsystems or improve the utilisation of all equipment and human resources. Variability due to common causes is inherent to any system (Deming, 1986). Therefore, if more than one operation within a set of dependent operations in a system operates close to 100 per cent of capacity, there is a high likelihood that the system will experience interference in the movement of products, especially if processing times are variable.

Rule 2 through to Rule 6 are related to step 2 and step 3 of the five-focusing steps of TOC which deal with the management of constraint. Rule 7 is that the transfer batch need not be the same as the process batch. The process batch size is the level of production each time a job is run. Often, the size of the process batch is determined by trading off various costs such as economic order quantity (EOQ)/economic batch quantity (EBQ) models. On the other hand, the size of the transfer batch is the size of the batch of products/components moved from one operation-station to another. Research suggests that considerable reductions in batch flow times can be obtained by using a transfer batch that is smaller than the process batch (Meredith and Shafer, 1999). Also, since the economics of different operations within a manufacturing system can vary, the process batch does not have to be the same size for all operations.

Often, schedules are determined sequentially without taking into account all constraints in a system. Rule 8 says that schedules should be established by investigating all the constraints simultaneously. Also, in contrast to the MRP approach to the estimation of lead times, Rule 8 maintains that lead times are the result of a schedule and cannot be predetermined.

When OPT® became available initially it was presented as a competitor for MRP (I and II) and JIT. Many companies successfully implemented OPT®-based software. It also attracted considerable criticism, and continues to be criticised, because of the claim that it offers an optimal schedule, and because the algorithm on which it is based has never been revealed in the literature.

The implementation of the TOC logistical system is governed by the drum-buffer-rope (DBR) methodology and managed through the use of time-buffers (T-B). The name of the method is based on metaphors developed in *The Goal* (Goldratt and Cox, 1984). The *drum* is the system schedule or the pace at which the constraint works. *Rope* provides communication between critical control points to ensure their synchronisation. *Buffer* is strategically placed inventory, to protect the system's output from the variations that occur in the system.

The DBR methodology synchronises resources and material utilisation in an organisation. Resources and materials are used only at a level that contributes to the organisation's ability to achieve throughput. Because random disruptions are inevitable in any organisation, DBR methodology provides a mechanism for protecting total throughput of the system by the use of time-buffers (T-B). Time-buffers contain inventory and protect constraint schedules from the effects of disruptions at non-constraint resources. The use of time-buffers (T-B) as an information system to effectively manage and improve throughput (T) is referred to as buffer management. It provides information based on planned and actual performance and is used for monitoring the inventory (I) in front of a protected resource to compare its actual and planned performance (Schragenheim and Ronen, 1990). Three types of time-buffer (T-B) are used in buffer management (Lockamy and Cox, 1991):

1. **Constraint buffers:** contain parts which are expected to wait a certain amount of time in front of a capacity constraint resource (CCR), thus protecting the constraint's planned schedule. A capacity constraint resource (CCR) is a resource that is not a bottleneck at present, but, if not managed properly, can become a constraint.
2. **Assembly buffers:** contain parts/subassemblies which are not processed by a capacity constraint resource (CCR), but need to be assembled with capacity constraint resource (CCR) parts.
3. **Shipping buffers:** contain products which are expected to be finished and ready to ship at a certain time before the due date, thus protecting delivery date performance.

Figure 4 shows the locations of these three types of T-Bs. Note that an assembly buffer is not required before every assembly operation. It is required only before an assembly operation that is fed by both capacity constraint resource (CCR) and non-CCR parts. The constraint buffer is lo-

Figure 4. A hypothetical drum-buffer-rope configuration (Source: Adapted from Rahman, 1998)

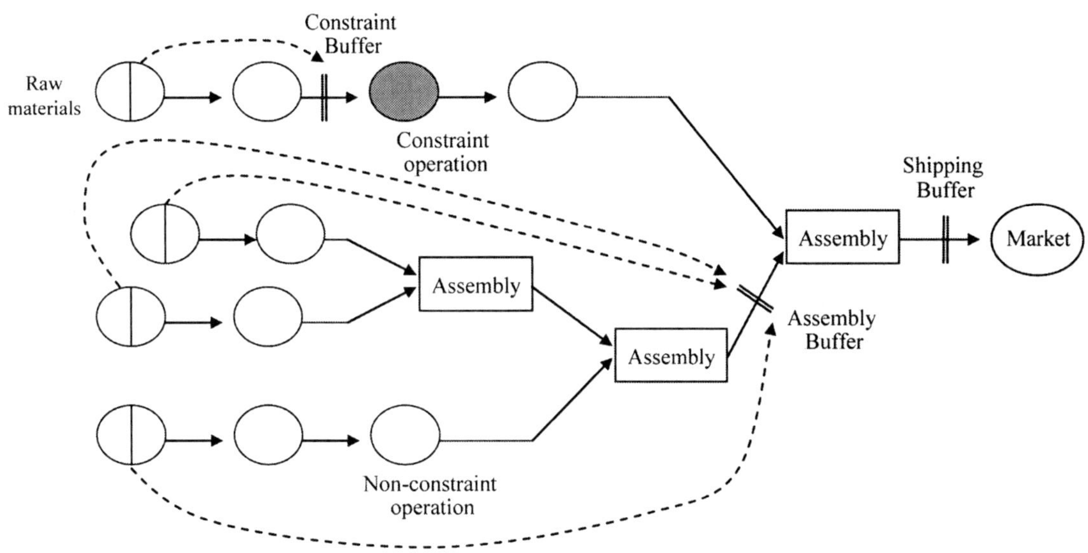

cated in front of the capacity constraint resource (CCR) and the shipping buffer is located at the end of the process. The use of time-buffers (T-B) in buffer management can help spot the causes of disruptions, without upsetting throughput. Moreover, by continually reducing buffer sizes, production cycle time can be reduced, which in turn may reduce lead time. For a detailed discussion of Drum-Buffer-Rope (DBR) methodology and buffer management, readers are referred to Goldratt and Fox (1986).

PERFORMANCE MEASUREMENT OF TOC

TOC assumes that the goal of an organisation is to make money both now and in the future. To measure an organisation's performance in achieving this goal, two sets of measurements have been prescribed by Goldratt and Fox (1986, p.31): global (financial) measurements and operational measurements (see Figure 1b). Since global measurements can be expressed through operational measurements, these are defined first.

Operational Measurements

1. **Throughput (T):** the rate at which the system generates money through sales (output which is not sold is inventory, Not throughput). Throughput defined within the TOC paradigm differs from its traditional definition. In traditional usage, throughput (T) is the rate at which the system produces products. At the conceptual level, it can be argued that the TOC definition of throughput (T) is similar to the traditional definition of marginal revenue. Throughput (T) is represented as sales minus 'totally variable' cost, and the general definition of contribution margin is revenue minus variable costs.
2. **Inventory (I):** All the money invested in things the system intends to sell. Inventory (I) includes any physical inventories such as raw material, work in process, unsold finished products, and includes tools, building,

capital equipment and furnishings. Thus any investment in fixed assets (e.g. equipment, building etc) or variables assets (e.g. raw materials) is considered as inventory (I). The direct labour or resource time used to make products is not taken into account while calculating the finished products inventory (I) value. Similarly, TOC does not use the value-adding concept (conversion from raw material to work-in-process, and finished product) of a cost-accounting system.

3. **Operating Expense (OE):** All the money the system spends in turning inventory into throughput. Operating expense includes expenditures such as direct and indirect labour, supplies, outside contractors and interest payments. A detailed explanation of these definitions can be found in Goldratt and Fox (1986). Figure 5 shows the constituents of throughput, inventory, and operating expense and the relationships between them.

Building on this, there are three global measurements.

Global Measurements

1. **Net profit (NP):** An absolute measurement in dollars, expressed as total Throughput (T) minus Operating Expense (OE).
2. **Return on Investment (ROI):** A relative measurement which equals Net Profit (NP) divided by the inventory (I).
3. **Cash Flow (CF):** A 'red line' of survival which is an 'on-off' type measurement, *i.e* when a company has enough cash, it is not so important, but when there is not enough

Figure 5. Relationships between inventory, throughput, and operating expenses (Source: Adapted from Srinivasan, 2004)

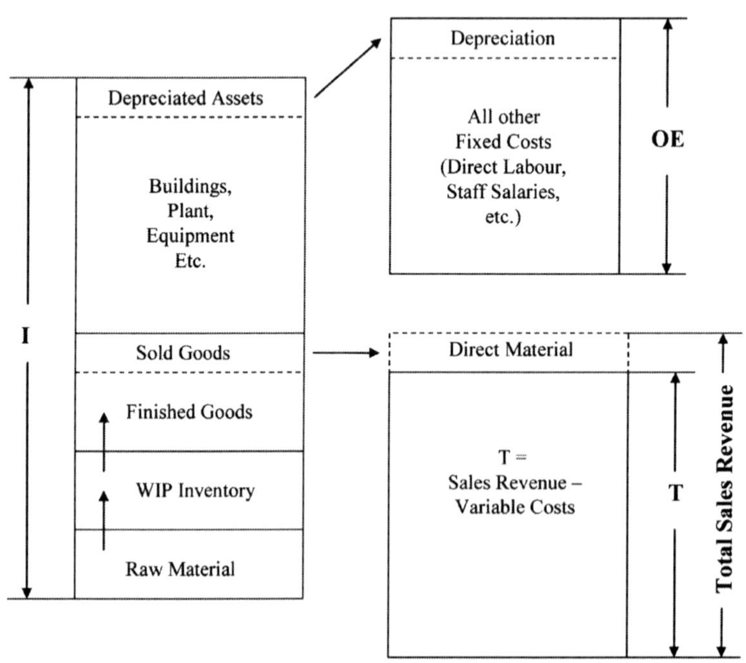

cash, nothing is more important than cash for its survival.

Since the two sets of performance measurements are related, it is possible to assess the impact of each of the operational measurements on the global measurements (Figure 1b). When throughput (T) is increased without adversely affecting inventory (I) and operating expense (OE), then all three global measurements are simultaneously improved. The same result is obtained when operating expense (OE) is decreased without harming throughput (T) and inventory (I). However, the impact of inventory (I) is not so simple. When inventory (I) is decreased, only ROI and cash flow (CF) are improved, but net profit (NP) remains unchanged. The impact of reduced inventory, however, can be realised indirectly through the reduction of carrying costs which is a component of the operating expense (OE). Although, the operational measurements of TOC are quite different from traditional cost accounting measurements, they can be used to describe traditional measurements such as inventory turns (T divided by I), productivity (T divided by OE), and return on investment ((T - OE) divided by I).

Management traditionally emphasises reduction of operating expense (OE) first, followed by increasing throughput (T) and, finally, reducing inventory (I). Goldratt suggests that the biggest gains can be realised by first increasing throughput (T), then by reducing inventory (I). The reduction of operating expense (OE) should be the last priority. The rationale for this order of priority is based on the fact that the reward from decreasing costs (OE costs and I costs) is finite (a theoretical lower limit is zero, a realistic limit is of course considerably higher), but theoretically, increased profit from improved sales is unrestricted.

Clearly, the performance measurements of TOC are very different from traditional cost accounting systems. Maskell (1991, p.45-7) identified five problem areas associated with traditional accounting systems: lack of relevance; cost distortion; inflexibility; subjection to the needs of financial accounting and impediment to progress in world class manufacturing. World class companies increasingly compete on competitive edges that are nonfinancial in nature: throughput time, inventory turnover, process flexibility, on-time delivery, product introduction responsiveness etc. As a result, there exists a mismatch between the goal of the company and traditional accounting practices. Among others, Umble and Srikanth (1990) recommended the use of the performance measurements of TOC, suggesting that traditional accounting systems be replaced by the system that can adequately evaluate the effect of managerial actions on the productivity and profitability of the entire firm.

THINKING PROCESS OF TOC

Implementing the five focusing steps to a typical production environment can yield rapid and substantial improvements in operations as well as profits (Noreen *et. al*, 1995). However, this process of continuous improvement takes the production operations to a point where the constraint shifts from factory floor to market. In such a case, constraint could be market demand (insufficient demand) which is a managerial/policy constraint rather than a physical constraint. Policy constraints are generally difficult to identify and evaluate, and frequently require involvement and cooperation across functional areas.

Goldratt (1994) developed a generic approach to address policy constraints and create breakthrough solutions for them using common sense, intuitive knowledge and logic. This procedure is referred to as the Thinking Process (TP).

According to Goldratt (1990), while dealing with constraints managers are required to make three generic decisions:

1. Decide what to change.
2. Decide what to change to.
3. Decide how to cause the change.

To address these decisions, the TP prescribes a set of five tools, in the form of cause and effect diagrams. The decision questions, associated tools and their purposes are summarised in Table 3. The TP process starts with the first decision question, 'What to change?' *i.e* to identify core problems. Current Reality Tree (CRT) is used for this purpose. A Current Reality Tree (CRT) is a logical structure that depicts the state of reality as it currently exists in a given system.

Once a core problem has been identified, the next question becomes, 'What to change to.' The second step in the process is therefore to search for a plausible solution to the core problem. This requires other tools such as Evaporating Cloud (EC) and Future Reality Tree (FRT). A Future reality Tree (FRT) is a strategic tool used to plan major changes. The implementation of these changes is likely to improve a system.

With the 'What to change to' question decided, the organisation is left with the question, 'How to do it' or 'How to change.' The Prerequisite Tree (PRT) and Transition Tree (TT) diagrams are used to identify obstacles to implementation and devise detailed plans for overcoming these obstacles.

Gupta et al. (2004) suggested that, compared to the Thinking Process (TP) tools, traditional

Table 3. Thinking process tools and their roles

Generic questions	Purpose	TP tools
What to change?	Identify core problems	Current Reality Tree (CRT)
What to change to?	Develop simple, practical solutions	Evaporative Cloud (EC) Future Reality Tree (FRT)
How to cause the change?	Implement solutions	Prerequisite Tree (PRT) Transition Tree (TT)

strategic management tools can only address two issues of the planning process: analysis (what to change) and implementation (how to cause the change). However, the most critical aspect in strategic planning is the formulation of the strategy by asking the question, 'What to change to?' It seems that traditional approaches to strategic planning lack the necessary tools to address this question.

Clearly, there is a need to investigate the potential synergy between Thinking Process (TP) and strategic management tools. Many have already identified synergies, for example, TP tools and the tools associated with quality management, value chain management and process reengineering are mutually supportive. The Deming-cycle can be used in conjunction with Current Reality Tree (CRT) to identify the core problem, and process mapping and Current Reality Tree (CRT)/Future Reality Tree (FRT) can be used to augment each other (Watson et al., 2007).

The thinking process (TP) tools have been successfully applied in a variety of settings. Scoggin et al. (2003) demonstrated how a team of employees used TP tools to document reality, identify a core conflict, develop proposed changes to address the core problem and create several detailed action plans to implement changes. Rahman (2002) described an application of TP tools not only to identify critical success factors in supply chain management, but also to understand causal relationships between these factors. Klein and Debruine (1995) utilised TP tools to identify deficiencies in industry-level and corporate-level strategies. Dettmer (2003) and Boyd et al. (2001) provided insight into strategy formulation using these tools.

The TP tools are interrelated, in the sense that output of one tool is used as the input from another (see Figure 6). The TP analysis generally starts with the identification of core problems, using CRT, which then become the inputs for the EC tool. The output of EC becomes the input for the FRT and so on. It is not the purpose of this chapter to discuss these tools in great detail. For a detailed discussion readers are referred to Goldratt (1994), Noreen *et. al* (1995), Kendall (1998), Scoggin et al. (2003) and Chaudhari and Mukhopadhyay (2003). However, using an example from supply chains, an application of CRT is demonstrated in the following section.

A Case Study of CRT Application

A Current Reality Tree (CRT) is used to identify the core problem or constraint of a system. The CRT is particularly effective when the constraint is policy or market related, as opposed to a physical constraint. In this example CRT is applied to identify core problems which reduce the effectiveness and efficiency of supply chains. This case is taken from Rahman (2002).

Guidelines for Constructing a Current Reality Tree

The Current Reality Tree (CRT) identifies cause-and-effect relationships in a system. It is constructed from the top down by identifying undesirable effects (UDEs), and depicting probable causes for those effects (effect-cause). It is, however, read from the bottom up (cause-effect), when the construction is complete. The following steps should be considered to develop a CRT (Noreen, et al., 1995, p.156):

Figure 6. Relationships between the TOC thinking process tools (Source: adapted from Watson et al., 2007)

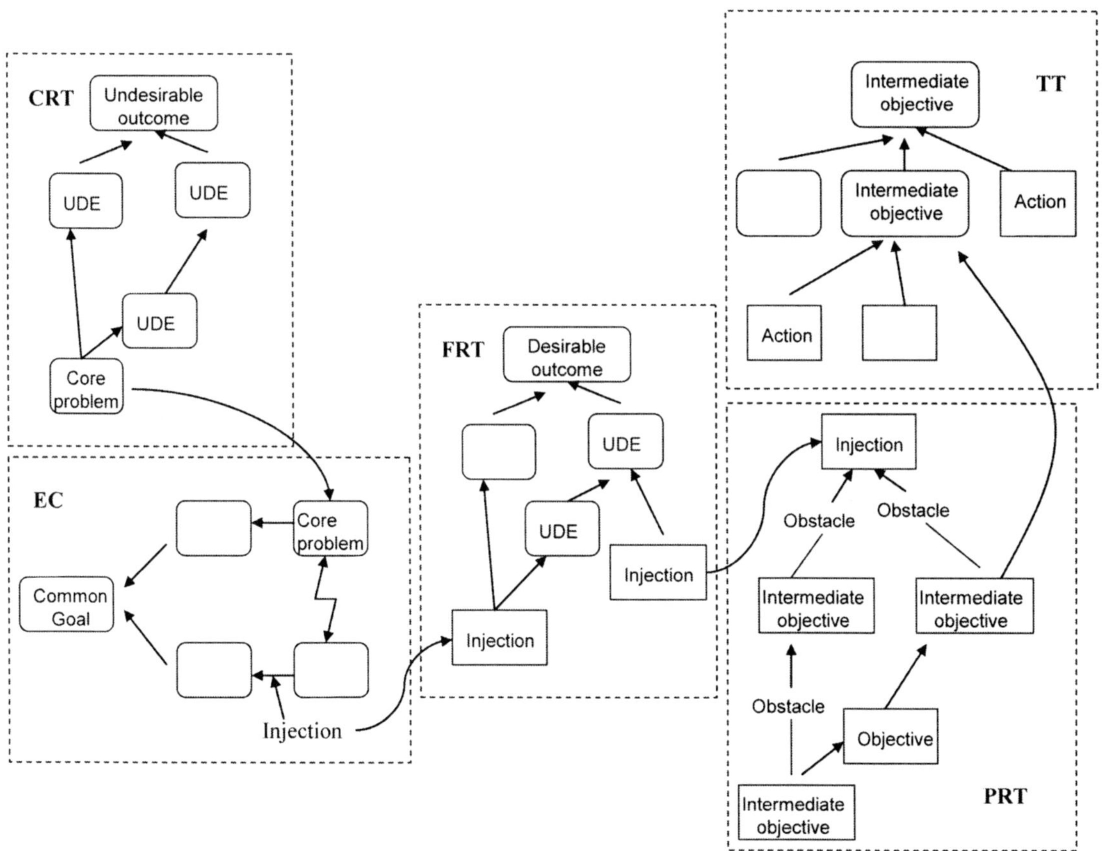

- **Step 1:** Identify a list of Undesirable Effects (UDEs) that describe the area being analysed. It is recommended to begin with a list of five to ten UDEs.
- **Step 2:** Connect one or more UDEs to other UDEs if they are causally related. Depict cause-and-effect relationships with an arrow.
- **Step 3:** Connect all other UDEs to the result of Step 2. Scrutinise each entry and arrow along the way. Stop when all the UDEs have been connected.
- **Step 4:** Read the tree from the bottom up, scrutinising again each arrow and entry along the way. Make any necessary corrections.
- **Step 5:** Ask yourself if the tree as a whole reflects your intuition about the area being analysed. If not, check for each arrow and revise.
- **Step 6:** Don't hesitate to expand the tree to connect other UDEs that exist but were not included in the original UDE list.
- **Step 7:** Present the tree to someone (or a group) who will help you surface and challenge the assumptions captured.
- **Step 8:** Decide that the CRT is complete. Identify the core problem or problems.

Constructing a CRT Diagram for an Aspect of a Supply Chain

In our case study, forty-four people participated in a group-based model building exercise in supply chains. The purposes of this exercise were to:

- Identify the consequences (effects) of failing to organise and run efficient supply chains.
- Determine possible causes of these consequences.
- Develop causal relationships between causes and effects.

Participants were split into six groups, each of which used nominal group technique (NGT) to brainstorm and identify five to ten undesirable effects (UDEs) of failing to organise and run an efficient supply chain. Groups then identified factors most likely to cause such UDEs. The number of UDEs identified by these groups ranged between four and eight. After a detailed discussion, groups agreed to consider the following UDEs for the model building process.

- Long cycle time
- High cost of managing inventory
- Low customer service
- High distribution cost
- High cost of supply chain.

Using the Guidelines discussed above they developed a CRT diagram for the first UDE: long cycle time (Figure 7).

Long Cycle Time

The criticality of cycle time or delay in a supply chain (including both product flow time and information flow time) was highlighted by Forrester (1958) some fifty years ago. Stalk and Hout (1990) and Mason-Jones and Towill (1999) had emphasised the importance of reduction of total cycle time. In order to avoid what was called the 'bullwhip effect' (Lee, et al., 1997) or 'Forrester effect' (Hines, 1997), total cycle time is reduced by improved coordination and communication among supply chain partners and by aligning product-process design with appropriate supply chain structure (Figure 7).

This example not only identifies elements of successful supply chain management (SCM), but also develops the causal relationships between these elements. Understanding the dynamic nature of the supply chain (SC) through cause and effect relationships is critical to the formulation of supply chain growth strategies. For instance,

Figure 7. Causal relationships based on cycle time (Source: Rahman, 2002)

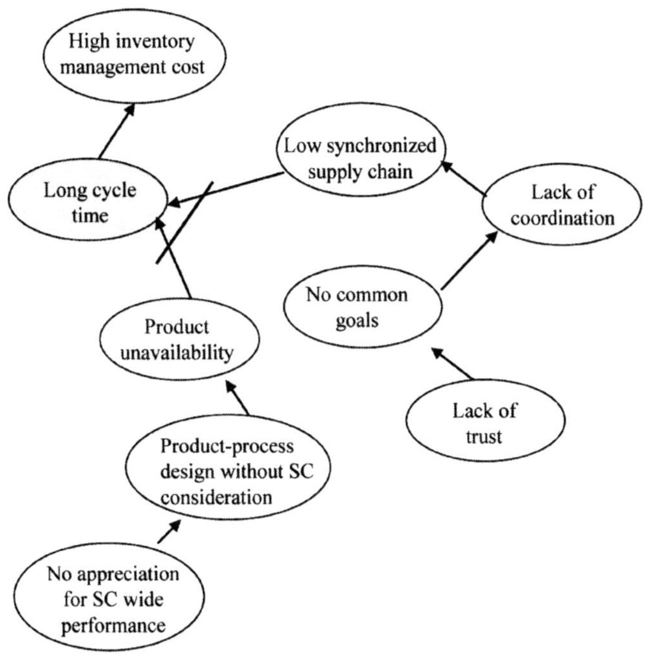

consider the case of 'long cycle times' shown in Figure 7. The cause and effect diagram in Figure 7 identifies cycle time as an element of successful SCM, as well as the following two factors or 'paths' to show the main causes of the problem:

- **Path 1:** No appreciation for supply chain (SC) wide performance → Product-process design without SC consideration → Product unavailability → Long cycle time.
- **Path 2:** Lack of trust → No common goals → Lack of coordination → Low synchronised supply chain → Long cycle time.

Problems such as long cycle times are influenced by complex interrelationships between many factors. With a better understanding of these relationships, managers are able to devise strategies for further improvement and growth in supply chains.

ISSUES AND FUTURE RESEARCH

The TOC tools provide a systematic way to analyse a situation as part of its planning process and to find a feasible and implementable strategy. However, these tools are not beyond criticism. There are number of issues or deficiencies associated with TOC solutions and the TOC thinking process.

Issues Associated with TOC Solutions

Issue 1: TOC Solutions Are Not Always Optimal

A common criticism is that the TOC tools produce solutions that are feasible, but not always optimal. Many authors compared the linear programming (LP) and TOC approaches to the product mix problem and found that TOC solutions are marginally inferior to LP solutions (Lee and Plenert, 1993). Although algorithms have been suggested to overcome such deficiency (Fredendall and Lea, 1997), much more research is required to minimise the confusion about the application of the TOC tools.

Issue 2: Ill-Defined Procedure for Applying TOC

When ill-defined procedures are adopted for applying TOC, and the results are compared with the results of the JIT solution, the strengths and weaknesses of the two systems were found to be inconclusive (Lea and Min, 2003). The inclusion of two necessary conditions, such as providing satisfaction to employees and customers to the goal of the system (see Figure 1a), has helped to define the characteristics of TOC systems (Gupta and Boyd, 2008).

Issues Associated with TP Implementation

Issue 1: Lack of TP Tool Validity and Reliability

Many authors argue that because TP mapping tools rely on subjective and qualitative assessment and interpretation of the subject matter they are unreliable. For wider applicability of the TP tools, the issue of validity and reliability must be resolved.

Issue 2: TP Tools are Less User-Friendly

Although the TP tools have undergone improvement in the past, they are still considered to be less user-friendly. Since the proponents of TOC have failed to educate top management in how to use these tools, which was the original intent, Goldratt has introduced a new tool called Viable Vision (Watson, et al. 2007).

The issues related to the TOC solution and TP implementation need to be addressed and resolved. As Watson et al. (2007, p. 398) highlighted, "If TOC is to gain the elusive mainstream acceptance … researchers and practitioners will need to address (these) deficiencies."

CONCLUSION

The theory of constraints (TOC) is a relatively new approach to the management of operations. Over the last three decades, it has evolved from a production scheduling software package to a coherent management theory for running an organisation. This chapter provides a comprehensive review of TOC concepts, philosophy and working principles. The TOC philosophy and tools have been successfully implemented in various organisational settings, including both production and service operations. Many Fortune 500 companies have implemented TOC solutions and achieved substantial improvements in the management of inventory, throughput and manufacturing and delivery lead time. The researchers and practitioners of TOC have identified synergies between the TOC and other management tools such as TQM, Six Sigma, Linear Programming, Lean management and strategic management. There is evidence that when a process improvement is undertaken by combining TOC and other management tools, a step function improvement can be realised. However, the application of TOC tools is not beyond criticism. There are a number of deficiencies associated with TOC implementation, these include generation of sub-optimal solutions, lack of TP tool validity and reliability, ill-defined procedure for applying TOC and user-unfriendliness. In order to get wider use and to gain mainstream acceptance, of TOC its proponents need to resolve these deficiencies.

REFERENCES

Boyd, L., & Gupta, M. C. (2004). Constraint management: What is the theory? *International Journal of Operations & Production Management*, *24*(4), 350–371. doi:10.1108/01443570410524631

Chaudhari, C. V., & Mukhopadhyay, S. K. (2003). Application of theory of constraints in an integrated poultry industry. *International Journal of Production Research*, *41*(4), 799–817. doi:10.1080/0020754031000065548

Deming, E. (1986). *Out of the crisis*. Cambridge, MA: MIT Press.

Dettmer, H. W. (1997). *Goldratt's theory of constraints: A system approach to continuous improvement*. Milwaukee, WI: ASQ Quality Press.

Dettmer, H. W. (2003). *Strategic navigation: A system approach to business strategy*. Milwaukee, WI: ASQ Quality Press.

Ehie, I., & Sheu, C. (2005). Integrating six sigma and theory of constraints for continuous improvement: a case study. *Journal of Manufacturing Technology Management*, *16*(5), 542–553. doi:10.1108/17410380510600518

Forrester, J. (1958). Industrial dynamics: A major breakthrough for decision makers. *Harvard Business Review*, (July-August): 37–66.

Forrester, J. (1961). *Industrial dynamics*. Cambridge, MA: MIT Press.

Fredendall, L., & Lea, B. (1997). Improving product mixed heuristic in the theory of constraints. *International Journal of Production Research*, *35*, 1535–1544. doi:10.1080/002075497195100

Goldratt, E. M. (1988). Computerized shop floor scheduling. *International Journal of Production Research*, *26*(3), 443–455. doi:10.1080/00207548808947875

Goldratt, E. M. (1990). *What is this thing called theory of constraints and how should it be implemented?*New York, NY: North River Press.

Goldratt, E. M. (1994). *It's not luck*. England: Gower.

Goldratt, E. M., & Cox, J. (1984). *The goal: An ongoing improvement process*. England: Gower.

Goldratt, E. M., & Fox, R. E. (1986). *The race*. New York, NY: North River Press.

Gupta, M., Ko, H.-J., & Min, H. (2002). TOC-based performance measures and five focusing steps in a job-shop manufacturing environment. *International Journal of Production Research*, *40*(4), 907–930. doi:10.1080/00207540110097185

Gupta, M. C., & Boyd, L. (2008). Theory of constraints management: A theory for operations management. *International Journal of Operations & Production Management*, *28*(10), 991–1012. doi:10.1108/01443570810903122

Gupta, M. C., Boyd, L., & Sussman, L. (2004). To better maps: A TOC primer for strategic planning. *Business Horizons*, *47*(2), 15–26. doi:10.1016/j.bushor.2003.10.001

Hines, P., Lamming, R., Jones, D., Cousins, P., & Rich, N. (2000). *Value stream management: Strategy and excellence in the supply chain*. London, UK: Prentice Hall.

Kaplan, R. S., & Norton, D. P. (1996). *The Balanced Scorecard: Translating strategy into action*. US: Harvard Business Press.

Kendall, G. I. (1998). *Securing the future: Strategies for exponential growth using the theory of constraints*. Boca Raton, FL: Lucie Press/APICS Series on Constraints Management.

Klein, D. J., & Debruine, M. (1995). A thinking process for establishing management policies. *Review of Business*, *16*(3), 37.

Lacerda, D. P., Cassel, R. A., & Rodrigues, L. H. (2010). Service process analysis using process engineering and the theory of constraints thinking process. *Business Process Management Journal*, *16*(2), 264–281. doi:10.1108/14637151011035598

Lea, B.-R., & Min, H. (2003). Selection of management accounting systems in just-in-time and theory of constraints-based manufacturing. *International Journal of Production Research*, *41*(13), 2879. doi:10.1080/0020754031000109134

Lee, H. L., Padmannabhan, V., & Whang, S. (1997). The bullwhip effect in supply chains. *Sloan Management Review*, *38*(3), 93–102.

Lee, T., & Plenert, G. (1993). Optimising theory of constraints when new product alternatives exist. *Production and Inventory Management Journal*, *3*, 51–57.

Mabin, V. J., & Balderstone, S. J. (2000). *The world of the theory of constraints: A review of the international literature*. Boca Raton, FL: St Lucie Press.

Maskell, B. H. (1991). *Performance measurement for world class manufacturing – A model for American companies*. Connecticut: Productivity Press.

Mason-Jones, R., & Towill, D. R. (1999). Total cycle time compression and the agile supply chain. *International Journal of Production Economics*, *62*, 61–73. doi:10.1016/S0925-5273(98)00221-7

Meredith, J. K., & Shafer, S. M. (1999). *Operations management for MBAs*. Danvers, MA: John Wiley & Sons.

Moden, Y. (1993). *Toyota manufacturing system: Linking the seven functional areas*. Portland, OR: Productivity Press.

Noreen, E., Smith, D., & Mackey, J. (1995). *The theory of constraints and its implications for management accounting*. MA: North River Press.

Pegels, C. C., & Watrous, C. (2005). Application of the theory of constraints to a bottleneck operation in a manufacturing plant. *Journal of Manufacturing Technology Management*, *16*(3), 302–311. doi:10.1108/17410380510583617

Pirasteh, R., & Farah, K. S. (2006). Continuous improvement trio. *APICS Magazine*, *16*(5), 31–33.

Rahman, S. (1998). Theory of constraints: A review of the philosophy and its applications. *International Journal of Operations & Production Management*, *18*(4), 336–355. doi:10.1108/01443579810199720

Rahman, S. (2002). The theory of constraints' thinking process approach to developing strategies in supply chains. *International Journal of Physical Distribution and Logistics Management*, *32*(10), 809–828. doi:10.1108/09600030210455429

Reid, R. A. (2007). Applying the TOC five-step focusing process in the service sector: A banking sub-system. *Managing Service Quality*, *17*(2), 209–234. doi:10.1108/09604520710735209

Schragenheim, E., & Ronen, B. (1990). Drum-Buffer shop floor control. *Production and Inventory Management*, Third Quarter, 18-22.

Scoggin, J. M., Segelhorst, R. J., & Reid, R. A. (2003). Applying the TOC thinking process in manufacturing: A case study. *International Journal of Production Research*, *41*(4), 767–797. doi:10.1080/0020754031000065557

Smith, D. (2000). *The measure nightmare: How the theory of constraints can resolve conflicting strategies, policies and measures*. Boca Raton, FL: St. Lucie Press.

Srinivasan, M. M. (2004). *Streamlined – 14 principles for building and managing the lean supply chain*. Cincinnati, OH: Thomson.

Stalk, G., & Hout, T. (1990). *Competing against time*. London, UK: Free Press.

Umble, M., & Srikanth, M. L. (1990). *Synchronous manufacturing: Principles for world class excellence*. Cincinnati, OH: South-Western Publishing.

Watson, K. J., Blackstone, J. H., & Gardiner, S. C. (2007). The evolution of a management philosophy: The theory of constraints. *Journal of Management, 25*, 387–402.

ADDITIONAL READING

Choe, K., & Herman, S. (2004). Using theory of constraints tools to manage organizational change: a case study of Euripa Labs. *International Journal of Management and Organisational Behaviour, 8*(6), 540–558.

Coad, P. (2004). *Agile Manufacturing for Software Engineering: Applying the Theory of Constraints for Business Results*. Upper Saddle River, NJ: Prentice-Hall.

Cooper, M. J., & Loe, T. W. (2000). Using theory of constraints' thinking processes to improve problem-solving skills in marketing. *Journal of Marketing Education, 22*(2), 137–146. doi:10.1177/0273475300222008

Cox, J. F., & Spencer, M. (1998). *The Constraints Management Handbook*. Boca Raton: St Lucie Press.

Kendall, G. I. (2004). *Viable Vision: Transforming Total Sales into Net Profits*. Boca Raton: J. Ross Publishing.

Klapholz, R., & Klarman, A. (2004). *The Cash Machine: using Theory of Constraints for Sales Management*. Great Barrington, MA: North River Press.

Lang, L. (2006). *Maximising Profitability: The Theory of Constraints Approach to Maximising Profitability (Workbook plus CD)*. Denver, CO: Throughput Publishing.

Rohen, B., & Pass, S. (2007). *Focused Operations Management: Achieving More with Existing Resources*. San Francisco, CA: Wiley.

Sabbaghi, A., & Vaidyanathan, G. (2004). SWOT analysis and theory of constraint in information technology projects. *Information Systems Education Journal, 23*(2), 1–19.

Tripp, J. (2005). *TOC Executive Challenge: A Goal Game*. Great Barrington, MA: North River Press.

KEY TERMS AND DEFINITIONS

Constraint: A constraint is anything that limits an organisation from achieving higher performance versus its goal. The constraints may be physical, market-related and/or policy-oriented.

Drum-Buffer-Rope (DBR): DBR is the scheduling methodology which synchronises resources and material utilisation in an organisation. The drum is the pace at which the constraint should work. Rope is the communication link between critical control points in a system. Buffer is strategically positioned inventory to protect a system's output.

Inventory (I): Inventory is all the money invested in things an organisation intends to sell.

Optimised Production technology (OPT®) – OPT® is a theory of constraints-based software package for production scheduling.

Theory of Constraints (TOC): TOC is a system-based management philosophy developed by Eliyahu Goldratt. It seeks to investigate and understand complex human-based systems and provide solutions using a systematic approach.

Throughput (T): Throughput is the rate at which an organisation generates money through sales. The output which is not sold is not throughput, but inventory.

Chapter 10
The Effect of Merger and Acquisitions on the IS Function:
An Overview and a Potential Agent-Based Approach

Andrea Genovese
University of Naples "Federico II", Italy

Khole Gwebu
University of New Hampshire, USA

Barry Shore
University of New Hampshire, USA

Sebastian Titz
University of Naples "Federico II", Italy

Venky Venkatachalam
University of New Hampshire, USA

Jing Wang
University of New Hampshire, USA

ABSTRACT

Merger and acquisition (M&A) activity has many strategic and operational objectives. One operational objective is to develop common and efficient information systems that can be the source of creating significant cost savings for the joined companies. In combining the IS divisions of the acquiring firm with that of the acquired firm there are many hurdles when the technical and social system are to be integrated. Exactly how this process will evolve and exactly what results can be achieved is hard to determine. This chapter identifies some of the major factors associated with the integration process and proposes Agent Based Simulation as a possible methodology to study this phenomenon.

INTRODUCTION

Merger and acquisition (M&A) activity has increased in the last decade and a half (Gupta et al. 2002). It promises increased efficiency, increased market share, operating synergy, diversification, strategic realignment, and acquisition of new products, technologies, patents, and talents (Gupta et al. 2002; Stylianou and Jeffries 1996). Bringing together different organizations does present its own special challenges. Cartwright and Cooper (1993) contend that two-thirds of these M&A fail to meet their goals.

DOI: 10.4018/978-1-60960-768-5.ch010

Copyright © 2012, IGI Global. Copying or distributing in print or electronic forms without written permission of IGI Global is prohibited.

One area in which cost savings and great efficiency gains can be achieved is Information Systems (IS). The impact of an M&A process on IS is considerable. In most cases the IS division from the acquired company is absorbed into the IS division of the acquiring company (Wijnhoven et al. 2006). In this process the surviving IS division may include new staff, hardware, software, and procedures. It is during the post-merger process that value is created (Jemison and Haspeslagh 1991) and synergies achieved (Birkinshaw et al. 2000).

While IS synergy is often expressed as one of the justifications of an M&A, studies have shown that IS professionals are often excluded from the M&A planning process (Stylianou and Jeffries 1996; Johnson 1989). In some cases, IS professionals are not even aware of the merger activities until the official announcement is made (Stylianou and Jeffries 1996). Corresponding to this apparent lack of involvement of IS professionals in the planning stages, there has been very little conceptual or empirical work in the area of IS integration resulting from M&A activities (Robbins and Stylianou 1999).

The purpose of this chapter is to identify and study the factors that affect the successful integration of IS divisions during M&As using and Agent-based Modeling approach. Additionally, this study also proposes agent based simulation as a way for M&A decision makers to better understand the impact of these factors on IS divisions after an M&A. Agent-based Modeling (ABM) has been successfully employed to study various complex socio-technical systems (Axelrod 1997).

The rest of the chapter is organized as follows. In the next section we review extant literature on the factors that influence the success or failure of M&As. Thereafter, we discuss the relationship between the factors identified in the literature review, the merged IS division and the merged organization. We illustrate potential applications of modeling for IS division integration in an M&A scenario and identifiy the relevant variables. We conclude the chapter by pointing out the usefulness of the study and the proposed Agend-based simulation approach and suggesting directions for future research.

Theoretical Background

The factors that influence the success or failure of M&A have been studied in a number of fields such as Finance (Champagne and Kryzanowski 2008), Strategic Management (Homburg and Bucerius 2006), Organizational Behavior (Larsson and Finkelstein 1999), and Accounting (Black et al. 2007) just to name a few. However, little is known about the factors that influence the successful integration of IS in M&As. Extant studies have suggested that successful integration of the acquiring and acquired IS divisions may be dependent upon IS (Evgeniou 2002), organizational (Mehta and Hirschheim 2007) and human (Legare 1998) factors.

IS Factors

The difficulty in merging IS in organizations is related to the compatibility of the IS architectures and the skills possessed by IS employees in the acquired and acquiring companies (Harvey and Lusch 1998). Studies have found that a large number of firms have encountered significant IS incompatibility problems after mergers (Evgeniou 2002). Integration of non-compatible systems may be extremely difficult and time-consuming, which may in turn result in the ultimate failure of the IS integration endeavor (Stylianou and Jeffries 1996; Robbins and Stylianou 1999; McKiernan and Merali 1995). Extant literature has demonstrated that having incongruent IS platforms and infrastructure presents serious challenges that can potentially jeopardize organizational objectives (McKiernan and Merali 1995). Large variations in IT platforms and infrastructure between merging organizations can make an M&A more difficult or more costly or both. Although information technology may be an asset to one of the organization pre-merger, it may turn into a liability post-merger if it cannot be successfully integrated with other information technologies in the merged organization. By contrast, standardized architecture and infrastructure is conducive for integration and synergy.

It is also essential for the merged organization to ensure that it has personnel with adequate knowledge and skills. With respect to IS, skills can be considered to be the aggregate technical knowledge of the personnel on the IS division (Rahul and Kwanghui 2007). The higher the skill levels the better since employees can respond quickly and effectively to IS issues that are likely to arise post-merger such as system incompatibilities, and they can exploit related opportunities arising from the M&A. Skill obsolescence is another issue that needs to be considered because of the changing environment and the fast development of new applications and systems. Employees need to be constantly trained to ensure that they have adequate skills to respond to various technology related challenges post merger (Choi et al. 2008).

The way information technologies are coordinated and controlled within each of the merging organizations pre-merger also influences the integration approach. In some organizations the coordination and control of information systems is centralized while in others it is decentralized or distributed (Main et al. 1989). When systems are centralized they are coordinated and controlled by a single organizational unit, whereas decentralized systems are coordinated and controlled by individual organizational business units (Gordon and Gordon 2000). Such subtle differences can pose challenges when attempting to merge the systems of two different organizations (Main et al. 1989). If the coordination and control of the systems of one company is centralized while that of the other company is decentralized or distributed, the time, effort and money required to merge the managerial aspects of the two IS divisions is likely to be high.

Fiedler et al. (1996) define three categories to measure Information Systems Architecture: Processing Decentralization, Network Connectivity, Shared Applications. For each of these measures two degrees are introduced: low and high. On the basis of the different possible combinations of the categories, several kinds of IS architectures are defined: centralized, decentralized, centralized cooperative, distributed cooperative. Their values are shown in Table 1.

Wijnhoven et al. (2006) describes four methods of post-merger IT integration. Figure 1 depicts these different methods. First, *renewal* describes abandoning both legacy IT- Systems and replacing them with a new system for the merged organization. In the *takeover* method the IT system of one organization will be used for the combined organization and the other system is shut down. These two approaches allow for total systems integration. *Standardization* keeps parts of both prior IT systems and combines these to a new one resulting in complete or partial integration. The

Table 1. Information Systems typologies (Fiedler et al. 1996)

	Processing Decentralization (PD)	Network Connectivity (NC)	Shared Applications (SA)
Centralized	Low	Low	Low
Decentralized	High	Low	Low
Centralized Cooperative	Low	High	High
Distributed Cooperative	High	High	High

Figure 1. IT integration methods, A and B are IT-systems before the merger, C after (Wijnhoven et al., 2006)

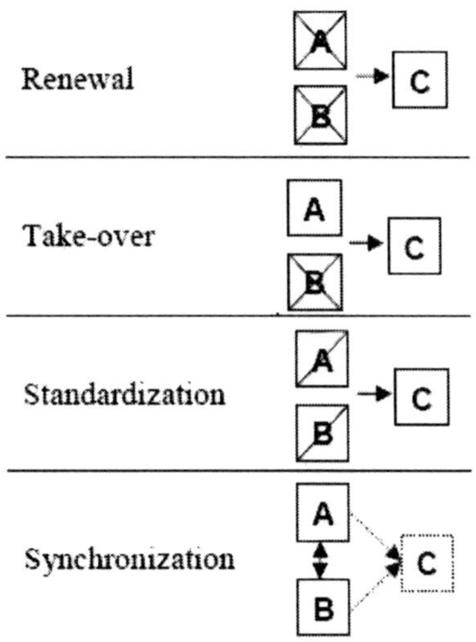

fourth way, *synchronization*, aims for the co-existence of both systems by linking them together (Wijnhoven et al. 2006).

Organizational Factors

Organizational factors such as corporate culture, firm size, top management's support of IS integration, organizational structure, firms' prior experience with M&A activities all influence the ability of the firms to bring IS systems together (Robbins and Stylianou 1999; Schweiger and Goulet 2005; Weber and Pliskin 1996).

Corporate culture represents beliefs, norms, ideologies, values, and assumptions shared by employees of a company (Schein 1992; Sathe 1985). Corporate cultures differ across organizations (Hofstede et al. 1990). While some organizations have individualistic competitive cultures others have more collaborative/collective cultures (Baron 2004). For firms with competitive corporate cultures, employee performance is judged on an individual basis then a reward or punishment is administered on an individual basis. A collaborative/collective culture on the other hand does not discriminate performance on an individual basis but considers employees as groups and therefore rewards and punishes team work and group effort. This has been shown to influence organizational interaction between the acquiring and acquired firms (Schweiger and Goulet 2005; Lubatkin et al. 1999). Differences between the acquiring and acquired firms' corporate culture can lead to challenges during integration, and limit the achievement of IS synergies (Schweiger and Goulet 2005). Studies have found that differences in corporate culture are related to polarization, negative evaluations of counterparts, anxiety, ethnocentrism in M&A top management teams, and top management team turnover in the acquired firms (Lubatkin et al. 1999; Sales and Mirvis 1984). Corporate cultural differences have also been found to be negatively related to IS integration and effectiveness (Weber and Pliskin 1996). One of the major objectives of M&A is for knowledge and skills to transfer across workers post-merger. Prior literature suggests that corporate culture will play a critical role in the transfer of knowledge and skills (Salleh and Goh 2002). If an acquiring firm has a competitive culture and the acquired firm has a collaborative culture, conflicts are likely to emerge when employees in the merged organization attempt to work with each other.

Prior research has hypothesized that size differences between merging organizations may impact the outcome of the M&A (Kusewitt 1985). Kusewitt (1985) detected a significant negative relationship between the relative size of merging firms and post-merger performance. This implies that the larger the merger, the more complicated and difficult it is to manage the merged firm. For merging IS divisions, knowledge and skill transfer between employees of the two organizations is likely to become more complex as the relative size of the firms increases.

Human Factors

The integration of two IS divisions involves not only the consolidation of technologies and systems, but also the integration of personnel (Legare 1998). Together with systems integration, the acquiring and acquired companies' IS professionals must overcome the conflict that often occurs when two organizations merge. Conflict may occur when employees' jobs are threatened, technical skills are very different, work load uneven, morale is not good, and retention is a problem (Stylianou and Jeffries 1996). For example, Brahma and Srivastava, have found that while executive retention positively impacts M&A performance, employee stress has a negative impact (Brahma and Srivastava 2007). When these issues are neither recognized nor addressed, they can jeopardize the success of the synergy realization sought, and even disrupt existing business processes.

A major problem that the integration of two bodies of employees presents is that knowledge and skill may not transfer across the two organizations. While the employees who are at a skill/knowledge disadvantage may want to share their limited skills/knowledge, employees with a skill/knowledge advantage are more likely to be reluctant to spend time on skill/knowledge-sharing because they will perceive few or no benefits from such endeavors (Husted and Michailova 2002). This can be derived from Thomas (1992) theoretical framework that classifies the behavior of an individual on the basis of two dimensions: assertiveness and cooperativeness. Thomas defines:

- assertiveness as the attempt to satisfy one's own concerns;
- cooperativeness as the attempt to satisfy other's concerns.

Five possible behaviors related to different degrees of cooperativeness and assertiveness can be defined, as depicted in Figure 2.

The Relationship Between IS Divisions and Post-Merger Performance

Each of the abovementioned factors contributes to the performance of the IS division in the merged organization. Since the IS divisions' actions post-merger are likely to impact organizational performance it is imperative for senior management involved in pre-merger activities to recognize and understand the potential impact of the factors on the merged firm. Figure 3 summarizes the relationship between the abovementioned factors, the merged IS division and the merged organization.

Typically the role of newly formed IS division will be to employ various IS assets such as hardware, software and people to facilitate the execution of various tactical and strategic organizational objectives including:

- the ability to exploit opportunities arising from the merger;
- the ability to avoid problems stemming from the merger;

Figure 2. Behaviors depending on different degrees of cooperativeness and assertiveness (Thomas 1992)

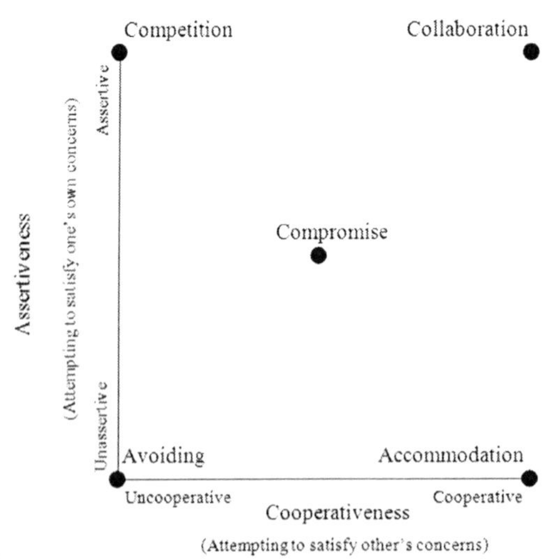

Figure 3. Factors influencing IS division merger success and post-merger organizational performance

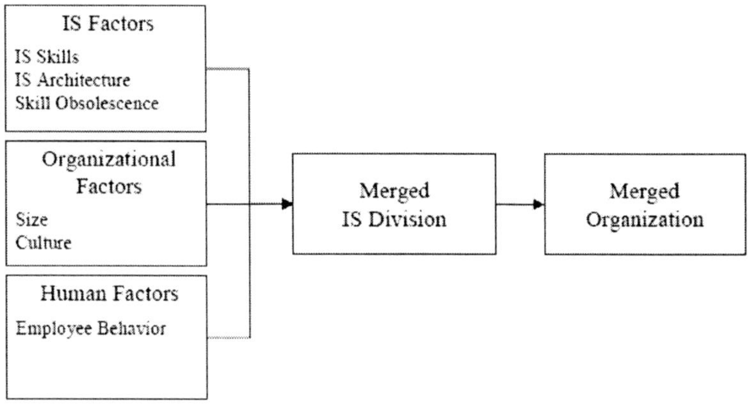

- end user satisfaction with the integration process and integrated systems;
- IS assessment of the success of the integration process and integrated systems (Stylianou and Jeffries 1996).

Thus it is essential for the IS division to be aligned with the needs of the newly merged organization. Effective alignment of the IS division can only be achieved if the impacts of the abovementioned factors are well understood by senior management.

The above discussion suggests that factors at multiple levels (e.g. individual employee, organizational, national) all play a role in the success of IS integration in M&As. These factors may also interact with each other to affect the outcome of the merger. To reflect the true underlying complexity and dynamism of M&A IS integration phenomena, an approach is needed that is inherently multiple-level and can also handle the interplay among the factors that are at different levels. It turns out to be very difficult to study the interaction among two different firms and their sets of employees in order to assess the compatibility of the two organizations through traditional mathematical, deterministic and even linguistic modeling techniques. For this reason, in the following section a novel innovative methodology is proposed for M&A research - agent-based simulation.

Agent Based Simulation

Agent Based simulation is a technique in which the behavior of "agents" is observed through a series of interactions over a specified number of iterations. In this way it is possible to reproduce an environment with all its real features and variables, forecast and explore future scenarios related to it, experiment with possible alternative decisions by setting different values for the variables in the model, and analyze the effects of these changes. Franklin and Graesser (1996), define an agent as: "*... a system which is part of an environment, capable of perceiving what surrounds it and of acting consequently, to achieve objectives and to pursue what it plans for the future*". Wooldridge (2002), defines an agent as a computational system, interacting with an environment and endowed with the following features:

- **Independence:** the capability of acting without the control of humans or devices
- **Social ability:** the capability of interacting with entities through a language;
- **Reactiveness:** the possibility of answering in a precise way to environmental signals;

- **Proactiveness:** the capability of acting to achieve an objective.

Agent based models can be comprised of a single agent (Single-Agent-Models or Centralized Models) or a set of agents (Multi-Agent-System, *MAS*). A *MAS* represents situations in which many agents act in the same environment, activating interactions among themselves. The main feature of MAS is that it can depict aggregated level behavioral properties not belonging to a specific agent.

As stated by Billari *et al.* (2006) and Weiss (1999), the development of a MAS needs a complete description for a set of basic *building blocks*, as follows.

- **The object of the simulation.** It has to be specified what is the phenomenon/problem to be reproduced, defining the space where the simulation takes place.
- **The agents' population.** Agents can be grouped in different classes with common characteristics reproducing the various components of the system; characteristics agents are endowed with should be specified.
- **The adaptive capability of each agent category.** Agents of each category present a specific adaptive capability, i.e. the degree of re-activeness and pro-activeness.
- **The interaction paradigm among agents.** Each agent can interact with agents of the same or of other categories. In the literature, several interaction paradigms have been defined, such as cooperation, competition, negotiation (see for instance Weiss (1999)). On the base of the selected paradigm, the agents evolve in the simulation space in a different way.

The desirable properties of the ABM methodology have spurred its use by researchers to reproduce and study many different complex social systems. For instance it has been used to study consumer behavior (Schenk et al. 2007), knowledge sharing (Wang et al. 2009), urban evacuation strategies (Chen & Zhan 2008) and financial markets (Boer et al. 2007) just to name a few. There are also prior applications of ABM in the area of collaboration (Dekker 2007) and on the economic effects of mergers (Kerber, 2001), both central parts of our model.

A possible way of reproducing a M&A context within an agent-based simulation would be provided by representing two populations from different firms (an Acquiring firm and a Targeted firm) in order to assess their integration dynamics. The model should implement the factors identified in the literature review.

An agent-based simulation approach has several advantages over traditional approaches in modeling IS division integration in M&A. Traditional conceptual and empirical models use a set of independent variables at one level to explain one or more dependent variables at the same level of analysis. They do not relate a global parameter to local ones (Anderson 1999; Drogoul and Ferber 1994).

In the case of IS integration in M&A, these traditional models do not ask questions of how organizational level outcomes such as IS integration success are influenced by the behavior of technical staff of the acquiring and acquired organizations. An agent-based approach, by contrast, asks how changes in employees' decision rules, the interconnections among them, or the objective division employees adopt produce different outcomes in IS integration. It models complex behaviors by examining the emergence of higher level orders from lower level interactions among heterogeneous, autonomous individuals (Anderson 1999; Lewin et al. 1998). Such an approach is inherently multilevel because order is considered an emergent property. Accordingly, it is appropriate in addressing issues related to IS integration in M&A.

Further, interactions and interdependency are central to the case of M&A IS integration. Adopting traditional analytical techniques is problematic because these approaches have to abstract away interactions for the sake of deducibility and tractability. Simple boxes-and-arrow causal models are also inadequate for modeling systems with complex interconnections and feedback loops, even when nonlinear relationships between dependent and independent variables are introduced by means of exponents, logarithms, or interaction terms (Anderson 1999).

In contrast, the agent-based approach demonstrates an appreciation for modeling interactions instead of simplifying them away (Anderson 1999). Rather than making nonlinear systems tractable by reducing them to a set of independent and dependent variables and error terms, an agent-based approach allow investigators to focus on agents, their interactions and interdependencies with each other and their environments, and their effort to achieve higher fitness. By capturing interactions and tracing their impact, we can reveal the complexity of relationships in business processes and phenomena.

On the basis of the surveyed literature and of the proposed theoretical framework, several variables and dynamics are identified as fundamental building blocks for a potential agent-based model aimed to evaluate IS integration in post-merger scenarios. In the following section, the characteristics of this model will be introduced and the relevant variables defined.

The Framework of an Agent-Based Model for IS Integration in M&A Scenarios

According to the ABM building blocks classification previously, some descriptions will be provided about the object of the simulation, the classes of agents, the adaptive capability of each agent category and the interaction paradigm among agents.

Object of the Simulation

The object of the simulation is the reproduction of the interaction among employees of an IT department in a post-merger scenario. The environment of the simulation will reproduce the merged IT department.

Agent Population

In the simulation environment, two sets of agents are created, representing the employees' populations from the two merging organizations. These agent sets are endowed with the following variables, coming from the previous literature analysis:

- **Number of Employees:** Number of employees in each organization: both the acquiring and acquired firms' IT departments are characterized by an initial population of employees; in the model, this is translated into the number of agents belonging to each agent set. The value of the initial population can vary in a given range.
- **IS Architecture:** For every organization, the architecture of the IT infrastructure is described as centralized, decentralized, or distributed. When two organizations having a different organizational architecture are merging, communication and knowledge exchange will be more difficult.
- **Skill Level:** Every individual within the organization (agent) is characterized by a given skill level. The skill level is composed of a basic value (related to the organization the individual belongs to) plus a random value varying in a given range. Skill levels are set at initiation for each agent.
- **Power Distance:** Power Distance is the "degree of inequality among people" (Hofstede 1993). The power distance remains the same during the simulation. The

power distance is also a measure of willingness of the members of the two organizations to cooperate. It expresses also the influence of national culture on corporate behaviors.

- **Skill Obsolescence Level:** Captures the fact that skills can lose their importance overtime. The value of this variable is related to the speed of technological change in the environment. Skill obsolescence level is set for the whole simulation and is a global parameter.

The Adaptive Capability of Each Agent's Category

Agents in both agent sets are endowed with high pro-activeness, as agents are representing employees who try to maximize their utility.

The Interaction Paradigm Among Agents

To clarify the interaction paradigm among agents, let's consider the interaction between two employees:

- an employee *i*, coming from the acquiring firm;
- an employee *j*, coming from the acquired firm.

Given that from the previous literature review it emerges that the two employees have at their disposal 5 different kind of behaviors each, based on the different degrees of assertiveness cooperativeness, and 5x5=25 different kinds of outcomes are possible. Therefore, the paradigm should be able to reflect this and the effect of the interaction on the skill level of the employees.

CONCLUSION

One of the primary reasons for engaging in a merger and acquisition is to benefit from the integration of the two Information Systems departments. If this process is carried out successfully then the resulting Information Systems division will likely be smaller than the sum of the two original divisions and in addition there will be considerable organization learning that occurs as a result of the merger.

The purpose of this chapter has been to identify the major factors influencing the outcomes of the Merger and Acquisition activity on the IS division, through a careful scrutiny of the literature, that reveals the critical variables which can influence the outcome of an IS integration. Such variables include IS, Organizational and Human factors.

The large number of identified variables and the complexity of their interaction suggest that agent-based simulation could be a viable tool for studying the way in which these variables interacted. Therefore, agent-based simulation characteristics have been introduced and discussed; the framework of a potential ABM for studying M&A effects in IS departments has been also provided.

Future researches should focus on the development, calibration and application of this tool on famous IS integration cases.

REFERENCES

Anderson, P. (1999). Complexity theory and organization science. *Organization Science: A Journal of the Institute of Management Sciences, 10*(3), 216.

Axelrod, R. (1997). *The complexity of cooperation: Agent-based models of competition and collaboration*. Princeton, NJ: Princeton University Press.

Baron, J. N. (2004). Employing identities in organizational ecology. *Industrial and Corporate Change, 13*(1), 3–32. doi:10.1093/icc/13.1.3

Billari, F. G., Fent, T., Prskawetz, A., & Scheffran, J. (Eds.). (2006). *Agent-based computational modelling: Applications in demography, social, economic and environmental sciences (contributions to economics)*. Heidelberg, Germany: Physica-Verlag.

Birkinshaw, J., Bresman, H., & Hakanson, L. (2000). Managing the post-acquisition integration process: How the human integration and task integration processes interact to foster value creation. *Journal of Management Studies, 37*(3), 395–425. doi:10.1111/1467-6486.00186

Black, E. L., Carnes, T. A., Jandik, T., & Henderson, B. C. (2007). The relevance of target accounting quality to the long-term success of cross-border mergers. *Journal of Business Finance & Accounting, 34*(1/2), 139–168. doi:10.1111/j.1468-5957.2006.01269.x

Boer, K., Kaymak, U., & Spiering, J. (2007). From discrete-time models to continuous-time, asynchronous modeling of financial markets. *Computational Intelligence, 23*(2), 142–161. doi:10.1111/j.1467-8640.2007.00302.x

Brahma, S. S., & Srivastava, K. B. L. (2007). Communication, executive retention, and employee stress as predictors of acquisition performance: An empirical evidence. *ICFAI Journal of Mergers & Acquisitions, 4*(4), 7–26.

Cartwright, S., & Cary, L. C. (1993). The role of culture compatibility in successful organizational marriage. *The Academy of Management Executive, 7*(2), 57–70. doi:10.5465/AME.1993.9411302324

Champagne, C., & Kryzanowski, L. (2008). The impact of past syndicate alliances on the consolidation of financial institutions. *Financial Management, 37*(3), 535–569. doi:10.1111/j.1755-053X.2008.00024.x

Chen, X., & Zhan, F. B. (2008). Agent-based modelling and simulation of urban evacuation: Relative effectiveness of simultaneous and staged evacuation strategies. *The Journal of the Operational Research Society, 59*(1), 25–33. doi:10.1057/palgrave.jors.2602321

Choi, J., Derek, L. N., & Hemant, K. J. (2008). Information Technology skill management: A Systems dynamics approach. In *Proceedings of the 41st Hawaii International Conference on System Sciences*.

Dekker, A. (2007). Studying organisational topology with simple computational models. *Journal of Artificial Societies and Social Simulation, 10*(4), 6. Retrieved from http://jasss.soc.surrey.ac.uk/10/4/6.html.

Drogoul, A., & Ferber, J. (1994). Multi-agent simulation as a tool for studying emergent processes in societies. In Gilbert, N., & Doran, J. (Eds.), *Simulating societies: The computer simulation of social phenomena*. London, UK: UCL Press Limited.

Evgeniou, T. (2002). Information integration and information strategies for adaptive enterprises. *European Management Journal, 20*(5), 486. doi:10.1016/S0263-2373(02)00092-0

Fiedler, K. D., Grover, V., & Teng, J. T. C. (1996). An empirically derived taxonomy of information technology structure and its relationship to organizational structure. *Journal of Management Information Systems, 13*(1), 9–34.

Franklin, S., & Graesser, A. (1996). Is it an agent, or just a program? A taxonomy for autonomous agents. In *Proceedings of the Third International Workshop on Agent Theories, Architectures and Languages*, (pp. 21-35).

Gordon, J., & Gordon, S. (2000). Structuring the interaction between IT and business units: Prototypes for service delivery. *Information Systems Management, 17*(1). doi:10.1201/1078/43190.17.1.20000101/31209.2

Gupta, D., & Gerchak, Y. (2002). Quantifying operational synergies in a merger/acquisition. *Management Science*, *48*(4), 517–533. doi:10.1287/mnsc.48.4.517.209

Harvey, M., & Lusch, R. F. (1998). Beyond traditional due diligence for mergers and acquisitions in the 21st century. *Review of Business*, *19*(3), 17.

Hofstede, G., Neuijen, B., Ohayv, D. D., & Sanders, G. (1990). Measuring organizational cultures: A qualitative and quantitative study across twenty cases. *Administrative Science Quarterly*, *35*(2). doi:10.2307/2393392

Homburg, C., & Bucerius, M. (2006). Is speed of integration really a success factor of mergers and acquisitions? An analysis of the role of internal and external relatedness. *Strategic Management Journal*, *27*(4), 347–367. doi:10.1002/smj.520

Husted, K., & Michailova, S. (2002). Diagnosing and fighting knowledge-sharing hostility. *Organizational Dynamics*, *31*(1), 60–73. doi:10.1016/S0090-2616(02)00072-4

Jemison, D. B., & Haspeslagh, P. C. (1991). *Managing acquisitions: Creating value through corporate renewal* (1st ed.). Free Press.

Johnson, M. (1989). Compatible information systems a key to merger success. Healthcare financial management. *Journal of the Healthcare Financial Management Association*, *43*(6), 56–61.

Kerber, W., & Saam, N. J. (2001). Competition as a test of hypotheses: Simulation of knowledge-generating market processes. *Journal of Artificial Societies and Social Simulation*, *4*(3), 2.

Kusewitt, J. B. (1985). An exploratory study of strategic acquisition factors relating to performance. *Strategic Management Journal*, *6*, 151–169. doi:10.1002/smj.4250060205

Larsson, R., & Finkelstein, S. (1999). Integrating strategic, organizational, and human resource perspectives on mergers and acquisitions: A case survey of synergy realization. *Organization Science*, *10*(1), 1–26. doi:10.1287/orsc.10.1.1

Legare, T. L. (1998). The human side of mergers and acquisitions. *Human Resource Planning*, *21*(1), 32–41.

Lewin, R., Parker, T., & Regine, B. (1998). Complexity theory and the organization: Beyond the metaphor. *Complexity*, *3*(4), 36–40. doi:10.1002/(SICI)1099-0526(199803/04)3:4<36::AID-CPLX7>3.0.CO;2-I

Lubatkin, M., Schweiger, D., & Weber, Y. (1999). Top management turnover in related M&A's: An additional test of the theory of relative standing. *Journal of Management*, *25*(1), 55–73.

Main, T. J., & Short, J. E. (1989). Managing the merger: Building partnership through IT planning at the new Baxter. *Management Information Systems Quarterly*, *13*(4), 469–484. doi:10.2307/248735

Mckiernan, P., & Merali, Y. (1995). Integrating Information Systems after a merger. *Long Range Planning*, *28*(4), 54–62. doi:10.1016/0024-6301(95)00027-G

Mehta, M., & Hirschheim, R. (2007). Strategic alignment in mergers and acquisitions: Theorizing IS integration decision making. *Journal of the Association for Information Systems*, *8*(3), 143–174.

Rahul, K., & Kwanghui, L. (2007). The impact of acquisitions on the productivity of inventors at semiconductor firms: A synthesis of knowledge-based and incentive-based perspectives. *Academy of Management Journal*, *50*(5), 113–115.

Robbins, S., & Stylianou, A. C. (1999). Post-merger systems integration: The impact on IS capabilities. *Information & Management*, *36*(4), 205. doi:10.1016/S0378-7206(99)00018-X

Sales, A. L., & Mirvis, P. H. (1984). When cultures collide: Issues in acquisition. In Kimberly, J. R., & Quinn, R. E. (Eds.), *Managing organizational transitions* (pp. 107–133). Homewood, IL: Irwin.

Salleh, Y., & Goh, W. K. (2002). Managing human resources towards achieving knowledge management. *Journal of Knowledge Management, 6*(5), 457–468. doi:10.1108/13673270210450414

Sathe, V. (1985). *Culture and related corporate realities: Text, cases, and readings on organizational entry, establishment, and change*. Homewood, IL: R.D. Irwin.

Schein, E. H. (1992). *Organizational culture and leadership*. San Francisco, CA: Jossey-Bass.

Schenk, T., Löffler, G., & Rauh, J. (2007). Agent-based simulation of consumer behavior in grocery shopping on a regional level. *Journal of Business Research, 60*(8), 894–903. doi:10.1016/j.jbusres.2007.02.005

Schweiger, D. M., & Goulet, P. K. (2005). Facilitating acquisition integration through deep-level cultural learning interventions: A longitudinal field experiment. *Organization Studies, 26*, 1477–1499. doi:10.1177/0170840605057070

Stylianou, A. C., & Jeffries, C. J. (1996). Corporate mergers and the problems of IS integration. *Information & Management, 31*(4), 203. doi:10.1016/S0378-7206(96)01082-8

Thomas, K. (1992). Overview of conflict and conflict management. *Journal of Organizational Behavior, 13*(3), 263–264. doi:10.1002/job.4030130306

Wang, J., Gwebu, K., Shanker, M., & Troutt, M. D. (2009). An application of agent-based simulation to knowledge sharing. *Decision Support Systems, 46*(2), 532–541. doi:10.1016/j.dss.2008.09.006

Weber, Y., & Pliskin, N. (1996). The effects of information systems integration and organizational culture on a firm's effectiveness. *Information & Management, 30*(2), 81–90. doi:10.1016/0378-7206(95)00046-1

Weiss, G. (1999). *Multiagent systems, a modern approach to distributed artificial intelligence*. Cambridge, MA: MIT Press.

Wijnhoven, F., Spil, T., Stegwee, R., & Fa, R. T. (2006). Post-merger IT integration strategies: An IT alignment perspective. *The Journal of Strategic Information Systems, 15*(1), 5–28. doi:10.1016/j.jsis.2005.07.002

Wooldridge, M. (2002). *An introduction to multiagent systems*. New York, NY: John Wiley and Sons.

Chapter 11
Information Management for Public Budget Decision Making:
Insights from Organization and Budget Theories

Yaotai Lu
Florida Atlantic University, USA

Khi V. Thai
Florida Atlantic University, USA

ABSTRACT

Information is very important throughout the government budgetary process which consists of budget preparation, budget appropriations, budget execution, and auditing and evaluation. When their budgets are prepared, agencies need various sources of data including those related to all types of government revenues and expenditures, economic conditions, agency needs, and services to provide. In each phase of the budgetary process, data are needed for decision making concerning the amount of money to allocate, the programs to establish, outputs to measure, performance to evaluate, and goals and objectives to accomplish. In the United States, these data have been provided via various types of budgetary techniques, including line-item budgeting, program budgeting, planning-program budgeting systems, performance budgeting and zero-based budgeting.

INTRODUCTION

After a budget is adopted or approved, it is implemented or executed and different types of information are needed, including monthly financial information. Then, in the final phase of the budgetary process, financial data are audited, and other data are used for program evaluation and auditing and evaluation data or information are fed into the first three phases of the process. Figure 1 shows information that flows to each phase of the budgetary process.

As the budget preparation and budget appropriations phases require critical decisions, for the purpose of this chapter, we merge these two

DOI: 10.4018/978-1-60960-768-5.ch011

Copyright © 2012, IGI Global. Copying or distributing in print or electronic forms without written permission of IGI Global is prohibited.

Figure 1. Information Used in the Budgetary Process

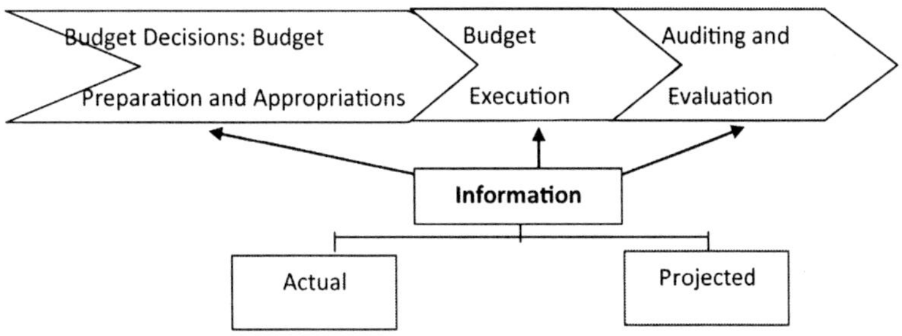

phases into one, that is called the budget decision phase. In the budget decision process, the executive branch "proposes" a budget, but the legislative "disposes" it. In other words, the executive branch submits a budget request after carefully preparing it; and the legislative branch has the power of the purse, and makes final budget allocations for the entire government. Historical developments of budgetary theories, have proved that

1. When preparing budgets, the executive branch tends to provide necessary information supporting its budget requests. Indeed, as explained later in this chapter, various budgetary approaches, from line-item budgeting to the current new performance budgeting, have provided various types of information supporting its budget requests.
2. When reviewing budget requests submitted by the executive branch, and making final budget decisions, legislators examine information provided in budget requests but also weigh factors other than information. Legislative budget decisions are driven by legislators' and voters' preferences, which may not be based on a rational basis as justified in budget requests. This has led to the existing perception of fiscal bias.

From the perspective of sound budget decisions, all relevant information needs to be collected and used for rational decisions. In reality, however, it is mostly a myth that a rational individual or an organization can make decisions completely in a logical manner. As shown in Figure 1, there are two types of information: actual information such as actual expenditures, actual revenues, and actual number of retirees who receive annual social security benefits; and projected information such as estimated revenues, estimated expenditures, and projected number of retirees who will receive social security benefits in future years, projected costs and projected benefits of a new program. Information based on a projected future faces future uncertainties. Moreover, it is very difficult to project or measure, in monetary terms, public program benefits and costs due to many reasons, including external costs and benefits. Consequently, those policy makers who favor a public program or policy tend to project lower costs and higher benefits; and those who oppose it tend to project higher costs and lower benefits. Finally, the information for budget decisions is complex and relates to a great number of factors, such as the chief executive's main goals, current programs, new services to provide, new goods to produce, groups of people who have various demands and interests, personal and non-personal costs, prices and inflation, increase or decrease of intergovernmental grants, goods and services to be purchased, increase or decrease of tax resources and other revenue, tax expenditures, debt, and indicators of performance. In addition, budget decision makers who represent different groups of people and political parties, have distinct interests in budget decisions.

Considering these elements, budget decision making is a rational as well as political process. There are multiple purposes in this long process in a narrow sense. One is to determine goals and objectives and allocating limited financial resources to reach these goals and objectives. Another purpose is to reduce risks and increase executive performance in terms of efficiency, effectiveness, and equity. Still another purpose is to improve government accountability. To attain these purposes in budgetary decision making, information management is of supreme importance for agency administrators, budget officials, chief executive, and legislators.

The purpose of this chapter is to explore information management for the budget decision phase of the budgetary process (Figure 1), to examine limited use of information for budget decisions, and finally to explain usefulness of information.

INFORMATION-DRIVEN BUDGETARY TECHNIQUES OR APPROACHES

Budget Functions

For different actors, budget serves different functions. For actors who fight for limited resources, budget is a political instrument by which government allocates public resources among a variety of needs. This is also the viewpoint of the political model of budgeting previously discussed in this chapter. For government management, budget is a tool of strategic planning which decides on objectives of the budget entity and on resources to attain these objectives (Schick, 1966; Mikesell, 2007); an instrument of financial management to ensure that resources are obtained and expended efficiently and effectively in attaining governmental objectives and goals (Schick, 1966; Hyde, 2002; Willoughby, 2002; Axelrod, 1988); a leverage to pressure government agencies to manage their specific tasks and programs effectively and efficiently (Schick, 1966; Axelrod, 1988). From the perspective of economists and top government officials, a budget may serve as an economic instrument that directs a budget entity's economic growth, investment, and development (Hyde, 2002; Axelrod, 1998).

The Budget Cycle and Decision Making

A budget is formulated and executed throughout the budget cycle which consists of four phases. In the first phase, execution preparation, the chief executive instructs government departments and agencies to prepare their budget requests. The instruction is based on the preferences of the chief executive and information the chief executive and his/her budget specialists collect from various sources. It may specify an agency ceiling, or a percentage of increase or decrease, and overall priority directions. Government departments build up their budget estimate based on services provided in the last budget period, services to be provided in the upcoming year, and an agency forecast of conditions in the upcoming year (Mikesell, 2007). When a budget office consolidates budget requests made by operating departments, it keeps budget requests consistent with the policies of the chief executive and holds administrative hearings for reconciliation of agency requests or budget office adjustments.

Information collected by the executive and operating agencies is bounded. The bounds or constraints include, but are not limited to, inaccurate forecast of revenues, preferences of political parties and interest groups, potential risks of planned programs, environmental changes, and changes of laws and policies. The extent of boundedness varies at different levels of budget entities, either federal, or state, or local.

In the second phase of a budget cycle, legislators review the budget document the chief executive transmits to the legislature. The legislators may take into account the interest of their constituents, or interest groups that support them in the election campaign, or the values of their political parties. Budget serves as a political instrument in this phase of budget cycle. In the U.S. federal government, Congress has its own budget office (CBO) and budget committees. Both CBO and budget committees and subcommittees in both chambers collect their own information from sources different from those of the executive branch. Thus, they build up their own budget and review the executive budget based on their preferences and information they collect. Chances are that there are great differences in budget between Congress and the executive branch. Conversely, in many local governments, legislature may not have access to information resources, thus approving executive budget without making a large percentage of adjustments. However, in recent years at higher levels of government, especially federal government, with Social Security, Medicare, Medicaid and other entitlement taking an increasingly larger section of the federal budget, discretionary spending has become much smaller. Thus, legislators have limited political power to control over incremental budget without changing the substantive law that creates the payment rules. But on the other hand, there will be more conflicts in the fight for more limited discretionary spending. When a political system is volatile, politics of budgetary decision making that underlie the budget process have changed fundamentally and made formal rules both "more necessary and more vulnerable" (Posner, 2009), thus producing more bounds and constraints.

In the third phase of a budget cycle, operating agencies carry out their approved budget. In this process, apportionments or allotments are requested and approved; thus appropriations are spent and programs are implemented. Laws forbid operating agencies from spending more money than appropriations. Therefore, a budget entity has two equally important tasks during budget execution. One is to monitor and control spending in both amount and purpose. The other is to improve performance of budgeted programs to improve efficiency and effectiveness of spending appropriations. A government needs information to implement various budget controls, like preventive controls to block actions that would violate control standards, feed-forward controls that implement diagnostic actions in the spending process, feedback controls that provide correction measure in the future budget cycle, and internal controls within operating agencies (Mikesell, 2007; Thompson & Zumeta, 1981). These controls may prevent and eliminate politics of manipulating budgeted resources (Hale & Douglass, 1977). Concurrently, government, especially operating agencies, needs information about services and products to be provided by the government itself or to be purchased through contracting-out, outsourcing, and public-private partnership. In addition, legislature demands information for supervising execution of the approved budget.

In the fourth phase of the budget cycle, budget is audited and evaluated based on the information generated in the first three phases and the performance of public program implementation. The audit and evaluation is performed by both internal and external auditors. An audit of the executed budget is categorized into financial audits and performance audits (Mikesell, 2007). The former focuses on financial statement audits and financial-related audits while the latter targets economy and efficiency audits and program audits. The purpose of financial audits is to assure that the audited agency has presented appropriate financial statements in accordance with generally accepted accounting principles and has complied with laws in the process of carrying out transactions permitted by the adopted budget. Performance audits purport to secure that the audited agency has acquired and used its resources economically and efficiently, that the budgeted programs have achieved their intended objectives and goals effectively and efficiently with compliance of laws and regulations.

Audit and evaluation is an indispensible check to ensure that the adopted budget achieves its policy and management outcomes. Meanwhile, it provides information for decision making in the next budget cycle.

Table 1 summarizes information management and decision making in different phases of the budget cycle.

Budgetary Techniques and Decision Making

Generally speaking, budgetary decision-making requires a large amount of information. However, when budgetary technique is concerned, different types of information are required for different budgetary techniques. This suggests that different formats of budget have different orientations. On the other hand, even with the same financial input, different formats of budget are likely to produce distinct outputs and outcomes. According to Government Finance Officials Association (GFOA), budget is a governmental operation guide for activities and services a budget organization intends to carry out; it is also a policy document that should include organization-wide nonfinancial goals and objectives, long-term financial policies, short-term initiatives of the financial development, and budget priorities in the upcoming budget year. These principles support the flow of public service provision through budget as shown in Figure 2 (Mikesell, 2007).

Budget technique focuses on different factors in the system of government expenditures and public service delivery. Line-item budgeting focuses on the resources to be purchased; traditional performance budgeting on outputs (like tasks and activities) to be achieved; program

Table 1. Information Management and Budget Decision-Making

Budget cycle	Supporting Theories	Major Actors	Information Needed	Strategy	Orientation
Executive Preparation	Rational model, incremental model, punctuated equilibrium	Executive administrators, interest group, political parties	Needs, problems, time, personal and nonpersonal cost, revenue, economy, executive policies, financial status, outcomes	Top-down and/or bottom-up	Policies of the executive chief
Legislative Consideration	Rational model, political model, incremental model, agency theory, punctuated equilibrium	Legislators, executive administrators, interest groups, politicians, media	Needs and problems of constituents and interest groups, problems, revenue, financial status, economy, legal constraints, social outcomes	Bargaining and compromise	Preferences of constituents
Budget Execution	Rational model, agency model, transaction-cost model	Executive administrators, legislators, interest groups	Spending limit, ways of organization, market factor, environmental changes, cash flow, private partners	Organizing and managing	Efficiency, effectiveness, accountability
Audit and Evaluation	Rational model, agency model, transaction-cost model	Executive administrators, legislators, and auditors	Legal information, budget policies and standards, financial statements, input and output, performance	Data analysis	Trouble shooting

Figure 2. The Flow of Public Service

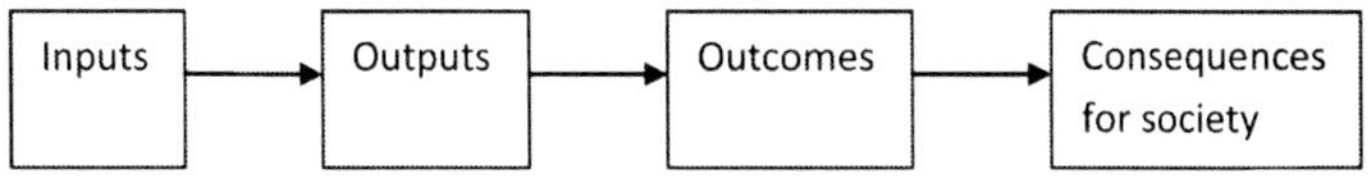

budgeting on benefits and costs of a program to be delivered; planning, programming, budgeting system on goals and objectives; new performance budgeting on the societal goal, or the outcome; and zero-base budgeting on final results. In addition, different budget techniques provide different information for budgetary decisions and different organization forms to implement the adopted budget. Consequently, each budgetary technique results in its own budget format. For example, line-item budgeting leads to a budget format, which shows how much money allocated to each item of expenditures such as salary and wages, office supplies, travel etc. The following section analyzes decision making with six major budget formats.

Line-Item Budgeting

As a basic format of budget, line-item budget is used by government organizations to present their expenditure against commodities, labor, services, and other resources to be purchased in the upcoming budget period. The resources to be purchased are broken down and grouped by cost centers and objects. The budget item groups are usually displayed incrementally in comparison with previous budget periods.

To create a line-item budget, a budgeteer collects information regarding the resources to be purchased in the new budget period. The information related to budget estimate involves not only the categories of resources, but also their amount, function, quality, cost, and specifications, among many other factors (Tyer & Willand, 1997; Borgia & Coyner, 1996). The budgeteer faces a variety of bounds in predicting nonpersonal cost for the budget and a large number of contingencies and uncertainties in the estimate of personal costs, market growth, and internal and external environmental changes. Even with a budget limit, the budgeteer still has a great number of options to make.

Line-item budget provides a place for everything, and everything is in its place. Under a specific expenditure category within the budget, there may be many relevant sub-categories. In this way, line-item budget provides a clear picture of what is exactly needed for various levels of operation of a budget cost center. Concurrently, line-item budget exerts control over expenditure within budget limit and the accountability for the expenditure within the budget cost center (Schick, 1971).

Obviously, line-item budgeting focuses on scrutiny of inputs rather than considers outputs, thus controlling costs and ignoring outputs and outcomes (Kelly & Rivenbark, 2003; Mikesell, 2007). Since line-item budget does not include performance requirements, a budgeteer does not need to collect relevant information regarding the activities and functions of a budget program. In this sense, line-item budget seldom collects information for considering a different alternative of service provision or goods production. From this perspective, the budgeteer may have fewer bounds and certainties than when he/she creates budget of other formats.

In addition, with line-item budget, cost estimate and appropriations are made on an administrative-department basis, not on the basis of services to be provided and objectives to be achieved. Under this broad categorization, line-item budget does not need any information for comparing consequences of spending because it does not include social outcomes. This means that in some cases, the programs that produce greater social results may be ignored by the budget agency (Mikesell, 2007). Moreover, with a focus only on cost of resources to be purchased, line-item budget excludes social costs, transaction cost, and incremental cost of actions. Budgeteers do not have to collect information regarding these excluded costs. As a result, a program's social value is not determined; and impediments occur in the process of carrying out the budget.

Line-item budget is the simplest, but the most fundamental budget format. It applies to small organizations. With line-item budget, information management is less bound than in other budget formats. Considering its characteristics, line-item budget is usually combined with other budget formats.

Program Budgeting

Program budgeting is a response to the requirement of economic analysis and financial pressure in the U.S. federal government. Different from a line-item budgeting that focuses on what the organization purchases, program budgeting focuses on public services or programs the organization provides. It allocates resources on the basis of programs that are linked to fundamental missions of the budget organization. Programs are constructed according to what products or services the budget entity intends to provide and what objectives the budget organization intends to achieve (Smithies, 1955; Lehan, 1981; Gianakis & McCue, 1999; Mikesell, 2007). In this sense, expenditure is proposed on the basis of the objectives the budget organization intends to attain; the final expenditure decision should be based on all budget claims (Smithies, 1955). Program budgeting takes into account the definition of the budget organization's objectives and determination of programs based on the major issues to be resolved (Novick, 2002). Since programs are created regardless of administrative organizations, program budgeting breaks down administrative boundaries between agencies within the government. This means that a budgeted program may be implemented by more than one government departments or agencies.

In addition, program budgeting is mostly based on cost-benefit analysis. The main goal of program budgeting is to rationalize budgetary decision-making by two means. One is cost-benefit analysis regarding alternative ways of achieving proposed goals; the other is determination of output evaluation measurement that is used to effectively attain chosen objectives (Schick, 1966). Cost-benefit analysis is a key tool an organization uses to adjust stated programs and originally established objectives. In the program budgeting process, budget organization keeps on examining program benefits through comparing costs with anticipated outcomes.

Moreover, program budgeting has an important time element. It requires that a multi-year program and financial plan be developed each year with projection of resource demands for ten or more years into the future (Novick, 2002; Bourdeaux, 2008). Budget time lasts more than one year while appropriation is made annually. This means that program budgeting helps determine the total cost of the multi-year program, but the appropriation remains annual.

Information management for program budget is a complex process. First of all, the budget agency collects information to determine a policy objective. The information comes from a variety of sources. Owing to bounded rationality, the objective is likely to be imperfect. Secondly, it is not an easy job to construct a program and determine the final program in the budget. Budgeteers facilitate numerous comparisons of alternative methods of pursuing the selected objective. For each alternative method, cost-benefit analysis is conducted. The most cost-effective program might be chosen to attain the budget agency's objective. However, administrative bounds may not lead agency administrators and the chief executive to the program that requires the least cost to achieve the expected result because "administrators traditionally have incentives toward larger budgets for prestige or advancement" (Mikesell, 2007, p. 208). In addition, expected outputs or contribution to the selected objective may not actually arise due to contingencies or environmental changes. The implemented program may prove problematic. Once the program gets started, it is hard to change or adjust it when it is found faulty.

Information management also involves data regarding deployment of resources, structures of program organization, recognition of long-term activities and the unallocable service programs (Mikesell, 2007). Deployment of resources includes not only core components but also complementary components. Without complementary resources, a program will not work effectively. Considering characteristics of program budget, a program may need overlapping organization structure to achieve its desired objectives. In addition, some activities, like scientific research and long-term investment, may not be completed within one year. They may be considered subprograms because of their long time and expenditure cycle. Some service programs may not be separated lest they should not permit operating economies when functioning separately.

Program budgeting is bounded because it has a number of problems that arise due to the technique itself. When the executive branch prepares program budget, it may not consider political factors because it depends on cost-benefit analysis and rational analysis. However, when the legislature reviews the program budget that the executive branch transmits, it may propose new programs aimed to attain political or social results. Besides, many public services have more than one objective; program budgeting emphasizes one set of policy choices at the cost of another (Mikesell, 2007; Gianakis & McCue, 1999).

With respect to information provision, program budgeting creates information and analytical burden in the budgetary process (Schick, 1966). The burden costs time and money on the part of budget organization. When a program is organized across departments, it cannot completely displace an organizational unit to satisfy expectations of all parties in the budget process. This is especially true when responsibility and accountability are concerned because responsibility and accountability are assigned to an organizational unit rather than to a program (Mikesell, 2007).

Planning, Programming, and Budgeting System

As previously discussed, program budgeting focuses on cost-benefit analysis and evaluation of output (Schick, 1966). On this basis, programming is intended to efficiently accomplish expected goals (Tyler & Willand, 1997). In the practice of public budgeting, planning is implemented to determine goals and objectives, program authorization, and approaches to achieve expected goals and objectives (Schick, 1966). Actually, budgeting is a strategic planning process in which public resources are allocated (Meyers, 1994; Axelrod, 1988; Hyde, 2002) and public programs are financed for select governmental goals (Cleveland, 1915; Robin, 1990b). When planning is combined with budgeting, specific approaches are identified to expend public financial resources for predetermined purposes. As a result, planned public services are delivered and public goods produced in an administration process.

Budgeting has an interdisciplinary dimension that embraces emerging economic and scientific theories in its operation and evolution (Kelly, 2003). When systems theory was developed in the 1960s, it was quickly adopted as a tool to integrate various components that are interrelated and interdependent in the budgetary process. This integration has resulted in a new budgetary technique — the planning, programming, budgeting system (PPBS). In this system, planning processes, programming approaches, and budgeting principles and tools are incorporated (Miller, 1996; Borgia & Coyner, 1996). PPBS is intended to establish appropriately selected programs through cost-benefit analysis to efficiently and effectively accomplish predetermined goals and objectives with financially estimated resources needed by service deliverers. It aims to produce high quality budgetary decisions that focus more on results rather than on financial input (Borgia & Coyner, 1996). In addition, PPBS emphasizes long-range planning when allocating financial resources (Axelrod, 1995; Borgia & Coyner, 1996; Ahmad, Grizzle, & Pettijohn, 2003). It evaluates costs on the basis of multi-year impacts.

Considering its characteristics, PPBS is a complicated mechanism that involves a large variety of components. This implies that PPBS needs enormous amounts of information in its operation to accomplish budgeting purposes (Schick, 1966). Actually, PPBS has changed the information system of budgeting (Ahmad et al., 2003). In its programming process, information pertaining to substitutable alternatives is collected for benefit-cost analysis and determination of course of action for program operation (Schick, 1966; Kelly, 2003). In the planning process, long-term goals and objectives are determined on the basis of cost-effectiveness analysis. With sophisticated analytical techniques, quantitative data are analyzed to measure output and performance of budgetary cost in proposed programs. Based on program requirements and proposed goals and objectives, financial resources are projected over a long term. PPBS requires a comprehensive improvement of the accounting and information system (Axelrod, 1995). When agencies do not have clear objectives, or when they do not have expertise to perform programming, planning, and budgeting, PPBS does not function properly to yield appropriate budgetary decisions (Kelly, 2003).

Performance Budgeting

Performance budgeting organizes expenditure around work programs and activities. It does not focus only on resources to be purchased as line-item budgeting does, or on the public services provided by the budget agency as program budget does. Rather, performance budgeting combines performance information and allocated resources (Mikesell, 2007). It classifies expenditure based on the volume of workload (or activity) and the cost of resources. This means that performance budgeting emphasizes outputs, the ratio of workload, and the cost to finish the workload, that is, unit cost of a budgeted activity (McNab & Melese, 2003). Unit cost is the key measurement of performance of implementing planned activities. Performance budgeting leads to a budget format that presents unit cost by activity and evaluates efficiency in performance of the activities (Seckler-Hudson, 2002; Lehan, 1981; Kelly & Rivenbark, 2003).

Unit cost is a key, but not the only measure to evaluate performance. Low cost in most cases suggests reduced quality. Therefore, to ensure that intended objectives are accomplished both quantitatively and qualitatively, performance budgeting requires the application of performance standards for tasks, activities, and direct outputs. This means that besides unit cost, performance is also evaluated against particular standards regarding accomplishment of the planned activities and intended objectives.

It is important to note that performance measures are not the end product of the budget organization. Rather, they are adopted as the means to the end, that is, the accomplishment of budget objectives. Performance measures may be misleading or irrelative in some cases. A police department may intentionally reduce the reporting of crimes so as to lower the local crime rate and thus fulfill the performance requirement of low crime rate although the actual crime rate is not as low as reported. Therefore, establishing appropriate performance measures and reaching an executive-legislative consensus are key premises to performance budgeting.

Since performance budget mainly considers whether an activity is being performed at low cost, decision making for performance budget has a focus on information management that is different from that of other budget formats. First, information is sought for performance structure. Budgeteers and decision makers should know the needs of the people within the budget jurisdiction; They must find the appropriate needs from among the many options as the planned activities and budget objectives according to particular values and policies. They should collect information for determining fiscal policy to carry out the budget, and locate responsibility for administration of the budget and accountability for results with the right departments and/or particular persons (Seckler-Hudson, 2002). Based on the activities, costs, and performance measures, budgeteers and decision makers determine demand, work load, productivity, and effectiveness for the budget (Mikesell, 2007). Second, information is needed for resource requirement. It should be determined how much money and other resources shall be allocated to each budget program and at what rate of expenditure (Seckler-Hudson, 2002). Third, because detailed information about input, output, and measurement is needed to evaluate performance of planned activities, decision power is decentralized from top officials to department administrators and experts. Top officials may focus their time and energy on guiding policies while department administrators collect detailed information for evaluating performance and improving management and efficiency.

Performance budget focuses on the management process. In the process of carrying out budgetary decisions, information is needed to determine whether the actual cost and performance are consistent with the prediction in the adopted budget, thus justifying the value of budget program. Hence, information is collected continuously throughout budget execution.

New Performance Budgeting

New performance budgeting (NPB), also called results budgeting, focuses on results or outcomes of budget programs. It was created on the basis of the Government Performance and Results Act of 1993 (GPRA) and the National Performance Review conducted under the leadership of Vice President Al Gore in 1993. The creation of NPB was also affected by expenditure control budgeting proposed by Osborne and Gaebler in their book *Reinventing Government* (1992). Expenditure control budgeting is a results-oriented budget system that takes into account some budget advantages in the private sector. It intends to hold government accountable for the result of budgetary inputs and reward agencies for cost-saving and high performance in serving citizens as private businesses serve their clients.

The essential idea of NPB is that "the societal goal, the outcome or result, is what matters for government performance, not the direct output or activity of the agency" (Mikesell, 2007, p. 214). To make NPB, a budget agency should include objectives or a strategic plan in the budget and link annual performance plans and annual budgets to the strategic plan. The major purpose is to justify what results the agency intends to achieve and how to achieve them. Besides, the agency should provide performance measures in the budget to connect the strategic plan with the performance results. It is important to note that performance measures do not transform inputs into outputs. The outputs are actually activities the budget agency intends to perform by using budgeted resources. They are accomplished through applying output measures. Meanwhile, performance measures ensure that the outputs accomplished achieve the agency's expected results—broader societal consequences. According to Mikesell (2007, p. 217), "if the purpose of measuring performance is evaluating the results achieved by a program, outcome measures are superior to output measures."

Unlike other budget formats, NPB permits flexible execution. A budget agency is not constrained by strict rules regarding how to spend the appropriation during budget execution. It is also permitted to retain some portion of the unspent funds in the next budget period rather than returning them to the general treasury. Moreover, NPB requires that the budget agency focus on service outcomes with their annual financial report. Budget audit and evaluation emphasize outcomes rather than how money is spent. This principle conforms to the requirement of the Federal Chief Financial Officers Act of 1990 about developing and reporting systematic measures of performance for the budget agencies, and on the state level, to the requirement of the Governmental Accounting Standard Board (GASB) about including service efforts and accomplishment in annual financial statements (Mikesell, 2007; Joyce, 1993).

NPB combines certain features of both program budget and traditional performance budget. It focuses on results or outcomes as program budget does; and it emphasizes performance measurement as traditional performance budget does, but for different purposes from those of traditional performance budget. Traditional performance budget's performance measurement focuses on the budget agency's productivity whereas new performance budget's performance measurement concentrates on outcomes or the agency's societal consequences (Mikesell, 2007).

Considering the characteristics of NPB, information collection for decision making related to NPB has its own features while sharing some features with other budget formats. Like other budget formats, NPB needs information for determining budget objectives or strategic plan. This is a process in which there are numerous uncertainties and bounds. Unlike other budget formats, NPB requires a close connection between objectives and outcomes (broad social consequences). This means that objective determination is a key point for NPB. Administrators and legislators may collect different information and thus determine different objectives. This is one of key constraints for NPB because it is different for legislators and administrators to reach consensus. Another key point of decision making related to NPB is selecting output performance measures. Information is needed to determine the measure related to the people to be served, measurability of the measure, measure based on outcome, significance of the measure, and manageability of the measure. This is a rational process and may finally cause performance measurement to be an information burden. In reality, developing performance measures is problematic for the ultimate results because there is no standard performance measure that works well for all agencies (Joyce, 1993).

Zero-Base Budgeting

Zero-based budgeting (ZBB) has three basic elements, including identification of decision units, analysis of decision units and the formulation of decision packages, and priority ranking (Taylor, 1977; Tyer & Willand, 1997). A decision unit is a basic entity for which a budget is prepared. The decision unit manager formulates decision packages based on different levels, such as minimum level (or survival level), a current or maintenance level, intermediate level, and an enhancement or improvement level (Axelrod, 1988). Decision packages are aggregated to form the total of a budget request for the decision unit. Then, the decision-unit manager ranks the decision packages on the basis of objectives and the effects of different funding levels. The ranked decision packages are reviewed, revised, or supplemented at higher levels of management (Kelly, 2003). As budget cut is one of the major objectives of ZBB, in the ranking process, the packages whose budget expenditure lie within a reasonable range around the estimated budget cut line are finally selected (Taylor, 1977).

ZBB requires justifying all budget requests, including requests of programs that are being currently implemented. It requires submission of different levels of budget requests rather than focuses on the existing budget base and/or the marginal changes from year to year in incremental budgeting. Therefore, compared with other budgetary techniques, ZBB is "first and foremost a rejection of the incremental decision-making model of budgeting" (Hyde, 2002, p. 456). In addition, compared with incremental budgeting, ZBB is more effective in cutting budgets, in providing better information regarding the use of public resources, and in attaining organizational objectives.

ZBB adopts a mechanism similar to rational model for decision making. Budgeteers at different levels of budget organization and decision makers need a huge amount of information for formulating and selecting budget requests. Decision unit managers formulate possible decision packages they are able to think of, each at different levels. They need data to justify the goal of each decision package, its funding levels, principal customers to be served, outputs, performance effects, implementation strategies, and organization form, among other factors. They collect detailed information for priority analysis, especially spending information and performance information because ZBB takes budget cut as a major objective. For programs that are implemented, decision unit managers seek possibilities to reduce their funding level, analyze their cons and pros in the budget process, and prioritize them appropriately.

The chief executive needs information for determining how to identify decision units according to the flow of responsibility for budgetary decision making in the budget organization. He/she studies current policies and proposes his/her own policies, thus generating information to determine objectives for the proposed budget. The chief executive also predicts revenue status and obtains financial information to determine degrees of funding to attain selected objectives. Decision makers seek and analyze information for determining the budget organization's objectives. Each possible objective is analyzed on the basis of different levels of funding, different levels of output, and various degrees of social consequences. All objectives are prioritized according to these analyses.

To take the format of ZBB, the budget organization must analyze the advantages and disadvantages of the existing budget process and determine the extent by which ZBB format is linked to the current budgeting and information system (Taylor, 1977). Moreover, the budget organization should determine whether or not current technical and procedural structures apply to ZBB requirement. Overall, what information is collected and produced depends on who are information users in the budget process, what budget format is currently adopted, and what objectives the budget organization intends to attain.

Given its characteristics, ZBB had a number of constraints. Ranking decision packages has little impact on decision making because decision units use different criteria when determining priority order, and because top management cannot rank decision packages rationally in case of ambiguous objectives and inadequate performance data (Schick, 1978). Taking into account political impacts for priority ranking hardly works well in selecting objectives and budget programs (Hyde, 2002). Finally, ZBB is time-consuming. It increases cost and produces confusion and frustration among budget analysts, but it provides few budgetary benefits (Schick, 1978).

Table 2 summarizes the major characteristics of budgetary decision making with various budgetary techniques.

Analyses demonstrate that each budgetary technique has particular strengths as well as weaknesses. No budgetary technique is perfect in every aspect. Practice and research shows that a hybrid of various budgetary techniques is an appropriate mechanism for government budget decisions. Information management depends on budgetary techniques to be adopted and organization structure of the budget entity.

Table 2. Major Characteristics of Budget Decision Making under Various Budgetary Techniques

Budget Format	Major Theories	Situation / Environments	Information	Strategy	Orientation
Line-item	Rational model, incrementalism	Relatively structured environment	Less bounded information management	Expenditure control	Control
Program	Political model, rational model, incremenatalism	Multi-dimensional environmental factors as inputs	Multi-structured information management	Cost-benefit analysis	Planning
PPBS	Political model, transaction model	Multi-dimensional environment	Multi-structured, clear information needed	Cost-benefit, cost-effectiveness analysis	Planning and performance management
Performance	Rational model, transaction-cost model, agency model	Relatively transparent, but subtle environment	Relatively clear information request and management	Performance measurement by unit cost	Management (productivity oriented)
New Performance	Rational model, political model, agency model	Not well-structured environment	Flexible, subtle information management	Measuring performance by result criteria	Management (societal consequence oriented)
Zero-base	Rational model, political model	Mixture of rational and multi-standard inputs	Multi-level and multi-purpose information management	Ranking by funding level and objectives	Control and management

Bounded Rationality and Incrementalism

In budget decisions, the rational comprehensive model is a theory based on the reasoning of economists, mathematicians, and psychologists. The rational model is based on the following assumptions:

- Policy makers are capable of identifying a social problem; have clear goals or and objectives; and are able to rank them in accord with their importance;
- Policy makers have a full range of alternatives to achieve a selected goal or objective, and full information to predict the consequences – benefits and costs – of each alternative with certainty;
- Policy makers are able to choose the best alternative to achieve that selected goal, or objective (Lasswell, 1963; Edwards, 1967; Forester, 1984; Zey, 1992).

However, these assumptions can only work in abstract, ideal conditions. In real-life situations, the rational comprehensive model has no applications and is impossible to follow. For one thing, not all decision makers are able to identify and clearly define a problem. As a matter of fact, decision makers are frequently faced with ambiguous, poorly defined problems. For another, decision makers may not be able to obtain complete and uncertain information about alternatives and consequences of each alternative. Actually, owing to incomplete information regarding the range and content of values and preferences, and to lack of consistent criteria, it is almost impossible to rank supposed alternatives and choose the most rational one. In addition, more often than not, decision makers have inadequate time, limited skill, and scarce resources for solving problems (Forester, 1984; Morçöl, 2007).

The uncertainties actual decision-making individuals face in a decision-making process imply that pure rationality in real life does not exist and that decision makers are "intendedly and boundedly rational," thus "bounded rationality"

(Simon, 1947). According to Simon (1957, 1986), compared with the size of problems whose solution should approximate objective rationality in the real world, the capacity of the human mind for solving complex problems is very small. Under bounded conditions it is not reasonable to talk about seeking all alternatives. Simon (1997, p. 292) claimed that "the generation of alternatives is a lengthy and costly process and one where, in real-world situations, even minimal completeness can seldom be guaranteed." Lindblom (1959) endorsed this argument. He contended that it is never possible to sort out and rank all the values of objectives pertaining to a particular problem. Perrow (1986) also conceded that when a decision maker gets engaged in problem solving, he/she conducts a limited search for alternatives and selects the first satisfactory one rather than keeps searching for the optimal one.

According to Simon (1957), in the decision-making process, "economic man" seeks to maximize utility through obtaining all information about the problem and analyzing all possible alternatives while "administrative man" recognizes his constraints and seeks a satisfactory alternative without examining all possible behavior alternatives and without ascertaining he has obtained all the alternatives. Thus, when making decisions to solve problems, "administrative man" chooses to satisfice and does the best he can with the capacity he has.

Decision making occurs in social, political, cultural, and organizational contexts that encompass various categories of bounds. Forester (1984) assumed four categories of bounded rationality where bounds occur due to different factors. With bounded rationality I, bounds come into existence due to cognitive limits; the problem is ambiguous, information imperfect, time limited; the decision maker seeks to satisfice with lower expectations. With bounded rationality II, bounds occur due to social differentiation. Because of the division of labor, the decision maker is faced with a complicated network that consists of other decision makers, staff, and clients. In this kind of setting, information collected by decision makers is "not only imperfect, but it is of highly varying quality, in equally varying locations, with less than simpler and direct accessibility" (Forester, 1984, p. 26). With bounded rationality III, bounds are produced due to pluralist conflict. Different actors may have distinct interests. As a result, decision makers are confronted with various responses, like opposition, intransigence, suspicion, and support. In a more complex practical environment of decision making, the problem is defined in plural and multiple fashions; the information that decision makers collect can be politically manipulated and thus distorted. Considering conflicting interests, bargaining and incremental compromise become major practical strategies to make decisions. With bounded rationality IV, bounds upon rationality are distortions that arise in historical, social, and political-economic structures. These structures encompass inequalities of resources and power; and distortion thus formed is one obvious characteristic of a decision-making setting; it constitutes the context in which decision makers and other actors work and affects rationality in decision making. Owing to structural distortions, information for decision making may blur into misinformation or reflect the interests of the relevant participants in the process of decision making. Strategies taken to make decisions in the environment of severe structural distortion and inequality are those that endorse "effective equality, substantive democratic participation and voice," and that reject "the continuation and perpetuation of systematic racial, sexual, and economic domination" (Forester, 1984, p. 28).

In reality, the concept of "bounded rationality" does not imply that decision makers give up rational or efficient organizational efforts; rather, they seek to maximize utilities to whatever extent possible based on what they have (Denhardt, 2004). In order to curtail the negative effects of individual rationality, organizations take measures to impose their rationality standards on individual decision makers in the decision-making process.

Following the direction of "bounded rationality," Lindblom (1959) outlined the approach of "successive limited comparatives," also called incremental method. Different from rational methods, incremental method of decision making does not require comprehensive information. Nor does it attempt to identify all possible consequences of each alternative. Considering the constraints on time and information, decision makers circumvent a comprehensive examination of all alternative solutions and restrict their focus to a limited number of options (Braybrooke & Lindblom, 1963). According to Lindblom (1959), the most effective policies or decisions are those that are implemented and agreed upon by competing parties. Therefore, in a policy (decision) making process, policy (decision) makers can simplify the process by making comparisons among incremental or marginal changes. This saves time and guards against errors.

Generally speaking, the incremental method permits action where the comprehensive rational model is paralyzed (Hayes, 2007). It describes how decisions are made under circumstances in which preconditions for rational decision making are not satisfied. However, in certain cases of decision making, unstable environments or policy shifts contribute to large nonincremental changes (True, 2000; True, Jones, & Baumgartner, 1999). Therefore, Baumgartner and Jones (1993) contended that there is a state of equilibrium in policy (decision) making followed by a punctuated change which is followed again by equilibrium. Besides, great changes in policy may occur over a long period.

Political Theory of Budget Decisions

While rational, a comprehensive approach emphasizes net value, and seeks efficiency, it usually ignores who receives benefits and how much (Wildavsky, 1961). Proponents of the bounded rationality model argue that uncertainties and bounds are an important factor that affects rational decision making (Simon, 1947). Part of bounds or constraints includes political elements and bargaining between groups. With incremental model, consensual bargaining between budgetary participants is a means to reach final budget decisions. These models suggest that budgetary decision making is not only economically oriented but also politically oriented (Wildavsky, 1961, 1992; Fenno, 1966).

Rubin (1990b) observed that the public budgeting process has four characteristics including multiple actors with different goals, vulnerability to the environment, separation of taxpayer and decision maker, and constraints. Together, these characteristics determine that budgetary decision making is a process that is replete of politics. The political nature relates to interest groups as participants in budgeting process, preferences of each group and the degree to which preferences prevail, political resources of various groups, and coalition of groups and/or other actors in case of interest conflicts. According to Wildavsky (1961, p. 184), "the most crucial aspect of budgeting is whose preferences are to prevail in disputes about which activities are to be carried on and to what degree, in the light of limited resources."

On the one hand, budgetary decision making is a process of resource allocation politics by which limited public resources are allocated among distinct interest groups (Rubin, 1990b; Wildavsky, 1961). These different groups of people compete against each other by means of political forces for the limited public resources because, as multiple actors, they have different preferences. Concurrently, conflicts exist between different branches of government, between the chief executive and subordinate agencies, between agencies of the same level of government, and between different political parties. The competition and conflicts are resolved by transforming distinct preferences into voting power or veto power through the political system (Wildavsky, 1961).

On the other hand, budgetary decision making is a process of revenue politics (Rubin, 1990b). In this process, government determines revenue resources, tax burden for different groups of people and other social entities, and the mechanism by which revenue is raised, and the economic and social effects of revenue-raising policies. Relevant groups of people and other social entities bargain for a reduced tax burden by employing political power and the political system. In the American political system, every significant interest has representation in the budgetary decision-making process. When bargaining occurs among groups, no single coalition of interest and its representatives is so powerful as to determine what is going to be in the budget (Wildavsky, 1961). Therefore, the result of bargaining is usually a compromise.

Generally, in modern democracies a political model of budgeting provides a mechanism through which actors from different groups communicate preferences and bargain for greater benefits through the political system. Policy makers seek information from various groups for budget decisions that aim to satisfy most relevant groups. In addition, conflicts are mitigated or resolved through bargaining and political mediation.

The Application of Rational Model and Incremental Model in Budget Decisions

In the realm of budget decisions, the rational approach and incremental approaches are frequently applied in practice. Rational model emphasizes net value achievement and efficiency (Haveman, 1970). To rationally select a program, policy makers must consider all the society's value preferences and their relative weights, all the available alternatives to achieve this program, and all the consequences of each alternative. They must calculate the ratio of the achieved social value to the sacrificed societal value of each alternative, and then select the most efficient alternative (Dror, 1968). Budgeted or funded programs are thus determined based on rational analysis to maximize benefits. Therefore, through rational choice, policy makers attempt to achieve maximum benefits in relation to costs. It does not consider who gets the maximum benefits. This aspect will be discussed later in the part of political theory of public budgeting.

The fundamental principle of incrementalism is usually applied in public budgeting. In the process of budget preparation, budgeters limit their activity to a small number of items and seek small increase from the base budget, which is provided by actual spending of the previous budget period. To prepare budget, an agency appraises the current situation based on actual results of previous periods and estimates incremental changes. Incremental budget is derived by transforming incremental changes into incremental inputs; incremental outputs are denoted in terms of revenue and expenses (Wu, 1981). When uncertain conditions arise because of knowledge limitations, budget complexity, and different purposes of budget participants, incremental budgeting involves bargaining among policy makers (Wildavsky, 1964). For the most part, incremental budgeting focuses on sorting out increments to the base budget, pays special attention to these increments, and concentrates on marginal adjustments of the base budget.

Incremental budgeting is more suitable to stable environments. When budget environment has changed, incremental budgeting may fail to work well in the new environment (Rubin, 1990a). In addition, incremental budgeting tends to rely on three points: simple decision in case of complexity, stable and specific budgetary roles, and stable and consensual budgetary bargaining (Meyers, 2002). But in budgeting practices, budget calculations are often complex and nonincremental (Domke, 1984; Schulman, 1975; Rubin, 1990a). In an agency, budget may have numerous unstable roles due to institutional changes (Meyers, 2002). Moreover, competition usually arises for budgetary resources (Natchez & Bupp, 1973). These factors determine that budget equilibrium with small increments is punctuated by great changes in budgetary reality.

To sum up, in the budgeting process, rational model and incremental model are frequently implemented through different budgetary formats. Disadvantageous as they are in some aspects, they demonstrate a number of features and represent general principles in public budgeting. Rational model is a vital tool for seeking efficiency. Incremental model is elastic and elusive. It is not necessarily important to determine how much change is considered as an incremental adjustment. In reality, incremental model can be modified to fit almost every budgetary circumstance (Schick, 1983).

Information Management and Decision Making

As stated above, information management is an indispensible part of making budgetary decisions because various types of rational information provide a backup about maximum benefits to be achieved in a certain context. Bounded rationality, uncertainty, and political impact suggest that information be managed systematically to serve various purposes of budget during a budget process. Under various theoretical models, decision makers take measures to manage information in distinct manners to satisfice with what they have.

Information management and decision making under the models discussed in the previous sections are specified in Table 3.

Organizational environments have great impact on decision-making processes and choices. Table 3 demonstrates that decision-making conditions or environments are different under the different models discussed, thus leading to differences in problem definition, quality of information required, strategy for decision making, and budgeting goals. To make appropriate decisions, decision makers must examine the environments their organization is confronted with, and establish their own decision support system that consists of information sources and decision aids. The decision support system thus established may provide timely, accurate information for high-quality analysis, save costs, and produce better understanding of problems (Stemp, Minkin, Thomopoulos, & Stemp, 1985). It assists decision makers to find appropriate strategies to address the problems they face.

The theoretical models of budgetary decision-making provide vital components for the decision support system by which decision makers clearly define problems and create problem strategies. Under the rational model, decision makers combine the available alternatives of values with the resources they have to attain satisfying objectives. They seek and use information in a rational manner to make decision choices. Accumulated information and decision aids in the organizational decision support system contribute to improved decisions from generation to generation. Incremental model, with a stable environment, assists decision makers to concentrate analysis costs on incremental adjustments. Information requirements are based on previous performance and incremental objectives. Decision makers under the environments of incremental model benefit both from sorting limited objective increments and from utilizing the performance information of implemented policies (decisions). Particular analysis tools can serve as vital decision aids in the decision support system.

Political model of budget provides decision makers with a mechanism to analyze values, interests, and impacts of all parties involved in the decision process. Decision makers under the political model compare political power of each of the parties involved, thus determining what strategies to use in negotiations with other parties. Political model of budget contributes featured elements in the decision support system, such as political influence, representatives, competition, and compromise.

Table 3. Theoretical Framework of Budgetary Decision-Making

Models	Elements of Information Management and Problem Strategies						
	Actors	**Situation**	**Problem**	**Designing**	**Information**	**Strategy for decision making**	**Budgeting goals**
Rational Comprehensive Model	Rational actors	Unbounded conditions	Clearly defined	Alternatives with biggest payoff	Perfect information	Optimize Maximize	Maximum economic efficiency
Bounded rationality Model	Fallible actors	Constraints and uncertainties in the environment	Ambiguous scope	Objectives determined by cognitive limits	Information with varying quality	Satisficing,, lower expectation	Satisficing goals for revenue and expenditure
Incremental Model	Agencies, decision makers, groups of competing interest	Constraints on time and information, competing parties	Varying interpretation of increments	Limited alternatives, incremental adjustments	Limited, accessible information	Successive comparison, sorting increments	Budgetary stability, simplicity, accuracy
Political Model	Actors in competing groups and political systems	Political system, values, beliefs, conflicts	Multiple problem definitions (value, interest, impacts)	Objectives determined by political power	Manipulated, contested information	Political competition, bargaining, compromise	Political outcomes of resource allocation
Transaction-cost Model	Administers, private service and product providers	Inscrutable market bargaining,, opportunism	Vaguely defined, multifaceted prediction	Contract oriented for high efficiency	Imperfect information	Governance structure	Improvement of budget execution efficiency
Agency Model	Principals and agents	Preference of self-interest	Economic/business and political definitions	Reducing cost, improving quality	Information withheld	Contractual agreements	Reducing spending and improving service quality

Transaction-cost model (Coase, 1937; Williamson, 1975, 1981, 1985, 1999; Ferris & Graddy, 1998) encourages decision makers to analyze inscrutable market and the nature of transaction, and determine an efficient and effective governance structure of the transaction. This requires that decision makers identify uncertainties and try to reduce transaction costs, thus improving transaction efficiency. Similarly, agency model (Ferris & Graddy, 1998; Jensen, 1983; Perrow, 1986) calls for decision makers to seek and analyze both the nature of goods and/or services to be purchased and interests of the principal and the agent. The purpose is to enter into a contract that specifies rights and obligations of both sides. From perspectives of the decision support system, both transaction-cost model and agency model link specific need of information for business operation and problem strategy orientation.

Overall, each model discussed above provides particular components of an organization's decision support system. Each model assists decision makers in understanding a portion of decision environments. A combination of various models creates a decision support system that helps public administrators make more effective decisions to solve the organization's problem.

CONCLUSION

Budgeting is a usual mechanism for a budget entity to attain its goals and objectives. In both the public and private sector, budgeting serves the same or similar functions. For example, budgeting plays a role in strategic planning, as a financial management instrument, and an economic instrument. However, due to the fact that government is the authorized power to levy taxes, that government is responsible for social and economic aspects within its jurisdiction, and that government does not consider making profits as its major role, public budgeting has particular functions that private budgeting does not share. For example, in the public sector, budgeting may function as a political instrument for government to allocate public resources among a variety of needs, as an instrument to stabilize the economy and as an instrument of democracy to provide benefits for a particular social group. Public budget, once passed by legislature, is a legal document, which allows government to collect revenue from individuals and private institutions. A private entity is driven by profit-making, and its business budget is based on revenues it generates.

The public and private sectors have distinct budgetary processes. Transparency and public accountability are very important. Government at any level must experience a transparent and legal budget cycle to have a budget passed by the legislature, carried out by the executive branch, and audited by internal or external entities. For business entities, budget does not have to be passed through a transparent and legal process. In the public sector, there are a variety of types of budget making participants. Interest groups play an increasingly important role in affecting budget decision making. Political parties exert great influence and impact on determining what is finally in a budget. These phenomena do not exist in the private sector.

Compared with the private sector, budgeting in the public sector is susceptible to legal constraints. Since public budget is concerned with many domains throughout society, and each domain has legal controls, public budgeting is subject to various legal constraints and certainties. Once a government budget is passed, it is transparent internally and externally, thus people and media may oversee its execution process. Consequently, a government budget is fixed while a private sector budget is flexible. Indeed, in a fiscal year, when sales increase, which requires increased production, business executives do not have to go through a lengthy process for additional budget allocation. In the public sector, overspending an approved budget is prohibited. Depending on the size of government, a budget is prepared months (18 months for the U.S. Federal government) before the fiscal year starts. Budget amendments normally occur to cope with unpredicted social and economic changes. However, in order to get additional budget allocations, the chief executive has to go through a legislative process for budget supplemental appropriations.

Government budget decisions are complicated. They involve a great variety of factors. Some factors are under control of budgeteers and decision makers, but some are not. Because of bounded rationality and uncontrollable factors in the environment, budget agencies are faced with a great number of uncertainties and constraints. Information management intends to reduce these uncertainties and risks in the budgetary process so that budget decision making will be more rational; thus public resources are expended efficiently, effectively, and equitably. Organization theories and budget theories as well produce considerable impacts on the practice of public budgetary decision making and relevant information management. Importance is attached to the appropriate combination of theoretic function and budget formats and goals in the budget process.

REFERENCES

Ahmad, A. A., Grizzle, G. A., & Pettijohn, C. D. (2003). Patterns of change: Information change and congressional budget deliberations revisited. *Journal of Public Budgeting, Accounting & Financial Management, 15*(1), 1–22.

Axelrod, D. (1988). *Budgeting for modern government.* New York, NY: St. Martin's Press.

Axelrod, D. (1995). *Budgeting for modern government* (2nd ed.). New York, NY: St. Martin's Press.

Baumgartner, F. R., & Jones, B. D. (1993). *Agendas and instability in American politics*. Chicago, IL: University of Chicago Press.

Borgia, C. R., & Coyner, R. S. (1996). The Evolution and success of budgeting systems at institutions of higher education. *Public Budgeting and Financial Management, 7*(4), 467–492.

Bourdeaux, C. (2008). The problem with programs: Multiple perspectives on program structures in program-based performance-oriented budgets. *Public Budgeting & Finance, 28*(2), 20–47. doi:10.1111/j.1540-5850.2008.00904.x

Braybrooke, D., & Lindblom, C. (1963). *A strategy of decision*. New York, NY: Free Press.

Cleveland, F. A. (2002). Evolution of the budget idea in the United States. In Hyde, A. C. (Ed.), *Government Budgeting: Theory, Process, Politics* (3rd ed., pp. 7–19). Thompson Learning. (Original work published 1915)

Coase, R. (1937). The nature of the firm. *Economica, 4*, 385–405. doi:10.1111/j.1468-0335.1937.tb00002.x

Denhardt, R. B. (2004). *Theories of public organization* (4th ed.). Belmont, CA: Wadsworth/Thomson Learning.

Domke, W. K. (1984). Waste, weapons, and resolve: Defense posture and politics in the defense budget. *Policy Sciences, 16*, 371–390. doi:10.1007/BF00135955

Dror, Y. (1968). *Public policy-making re-examined.* San Francisco, CA: Chandler.

Edwards, W. (1967). The theory of decision making. In Edwards, W., & Tversky, A. (Eds.), *Decision making: Selected readings* (pp. 13–64). Middlesex, UK: Penguin Books.

Fenno, R. F. Jr. (1966). *The power of the purse: Appropriation politics in congress*. Boston, MA: Little Brown.

Ferris, J., & Graddy, E. (1998). A contractual framework for new public management theory. *International Public Management Journal, 1*(2), 225–240. doi:10.1016/S1096-7494(99)80092-0

Forester, J. (1984). Bounded rationality and the politics of muddling through. *Public Administration Review*, (January/February): 23–31. doi:10.2307/975658

Gianakis, G. A., & McCue, C. P. (1999). *Local government budgeting: A managerial approach.* Westport, CT: Praeger.

Goldberg, V. P. (1985). Productions functions, transaction costs and new institutionalism. In Fiewel, G. R. (Ed.), *Issues in contemporary microeconomics and welfare* (pp. 395–402). Albany, NY: State University of New York Press.

Hale, G. E., & Douglass, S. R. (1977). Politics of budget execution. *Administration & Society, 9*(3), 367–378. doi:10.1177/009539977700900305

Haveman, R. H. (1970). *The economics of the public sector*. New York, NY: John Wiley.

Hayes, M. (2007). Policy making through disjointed incrementalism. In Morçöl, G. (Ed.), *Handbook of decision making* (pp. 39–59). Boca Raton, FL: Taylor & Francis Group.

Hyde, A. C. (Ed.). (2002). *Government budget: Theory, process, and politics* (3rd ed.). Thompson Learning.

Jensen, M. C. (1983). Organization theory and methodology. *Accounting Review*, *8*(2), 319–337.

Joyce, P. G. (1993). Using performance measures for federal budgeting: Proposals and prospects. *Public Budgeting & Finance*, *13*(4), 3–17. doi:10.1111/1540-5850.00987

Kelly, J. A., & Rivenbark, W. C. (2003). *Performance budgeting for state and local government*. Armonk, NY: M.E. Sharpe.

Kelly, J. M. (2003). The long view: Lasting (and fleeting) reforms in public budgeting in the twentieth century. *Journal of Public Budgeting, Accounting, & Financial Management*, *15*(2), 309–326.

Lehan, E. A. (1981). *Simplified governmental budget*. Chicago, IL: Municipal Finance Officers Association.

Lesswell, H. D. (1963). *The Future of Political Science*. New York, NY: Atherton.

Lindblom, C. E. (1959). The science of muddling through. *Public Administration Review*, *19*(1), 79–88. doi:10.2307/973677

McNab, R. M., & Melese, F. (2003). Implementing the GPRA: Examining the prospects for performance budgeting in the federal government. *Public Budgeting & Finance*, *23*(2), 73–95. doi:10.1111/1540-5850.2302006

Meyers, R. T. (1994). *Strategic Budgeting*. Ann Arbor, MI: University of Michigan Press.

Mikesell, J. L. (2007). *Fiscal administration: Analysis and applications for the public sector* (7th ed.). Belmont, CA: Thomas Wadsworth.

Miller, G. J. (1996). Productivity and the budget process. In Rabin, J. W., Hildrith, W. B., & Miller, G. J. (Eds.), *Budgeting: Formulation and Execution*. Athens, GA: Carl Vinson Institute of Government, University of Georgia.

Morçöl (Ed.), *Handbook of decision making* (pp. 3–18). Boca Raton, FL: Taylor & Francis Group.

Morçöl, G. (2007). Decision making: An overview of theories, contexts, and methods. In G.

Natchez, P. B., & Bupp, I. C. (1973). Policy and priority in the budgetary process. *The American Political Science Review*, *67*, 951–963. doi:10.2307/1958637

Novick, D. (2002). What program budgeting is and is not? In Hyde, A. C. (Ed.), *Government budgeting: Theory, process, and politics* (pp. 475–482). Pacific Grove, CA: Thompson Learning.

Osborn, D., & Gaebler, T. (1992). *Reinventing government: How the entrepreneurial spirit is transforming in public sector*. Reading, MA: Addison-Wesley.

Perrow, C. (1986). *Complex organizations: A critical essay* (3rd ed.). New York, NY: McGraw-Hill, Inc.

Posner, P. L. (2009). Budget process reform: Waiting for Godot. *Public Administration Review*, *69*(2), 233–244. doi:10.1111/j.1540-6210.2008.01969.x

Rubin, I. S. (1990a). Budget theory and budget practice: How good the fit? *Public Administration Review*, *50*(2), 179–189. doi:10.2307/976865

Rubin, I. S. (1990b). *The politics of public budgeting: Getting and spending, borrowing and balancing*. Chatham, NJ: Chatham House of Publishers, Inc.

Schick, A. (1966). The road to PPB: The stages of budget reform. *Public Administration Review*, *26*(December), 243–258. doi:10.2307/973296

Schick, A. (1971). *Budget Innovation in the States*. Washington, D.C.: The Brookings Institute.

Schick, A. (1978). The road from ZBB. *Public Administration Review*, *39*(2), 177–180. doi:10.2307/976294

Schick, A. (1983). Incremental budgeting in a decremental age. *Policy Sciences*, *16*(1), 1–25. doi:10.1007/BF00138465

Schulman, P. R. (1975). Nonincremental policy making: Notes Toward an alternative paradigm. *The American Political Science Review*, *69*, 1354–1370. doi:10.2307/1955293

Seckler-Hudson, C. (2002). Performance budgeting in government. In Hyde, A. C. (Ed.), *Government budgeting: Theory, process, and politics* (pp. 462–474). Pacific Grove, CA: Thompson Learning.

Simon, H. A. (1947). *Administrative behavior: A study of decision making process in administrative organization*. New York, NY: McMillan Co.

Simon, H. A. (1957). *Models of man*. New York, NY: Wiley & Sons.

Simon, H. A. (1986). Rationality in psychology and economics. In Hogarth, R. M., & Reder, M. W. (Eds.), *Rational choice: The contrast between economics and psychology* (pp. 25–40). Chicago, IL: The University of Chicago Press.

Simon, H. A. (1997). *Models of bounded rationality* (*Vol. 3*). Cambridge, MA: The MIT Press.

Smithies, A. (1955). *The budgetary process in the United States*. New York, NY: McGraw-Hill.

Stemp, S. D., Minkin, J. E., Thomopoulos, J., & Stemp, M. W. (1985). *Decision support system*. Montvale, NJ: National Association of Accountants.

Taylor, G. M. (1977). Introduction to zero-based budgeting. *The Bureaucrat*, *6*(1), 33–55.

Thompson, F., & Sumeta, W. (1981). Control and controls: A reexamination of control patterns in budget execution. *Policy Sciences*, *13*(1), 25–50. doi:10.1007/BF00155931

True, J. L. (2000). Avalanches and incrementalism: Making policy and budgets in the United States. *American Review of Public Administration*, *30*(1), 3–18. doi:10.1177/02750740022064524

True, J. L., Jones, B. D., & Baumgartner, F. R. (1999). Punctuated equilibrium theory: Explaining stability and changes in American policymaking. In Sabatier, P. (Ed.), *Theories of the policy process*. Boulder, CO: Westview.

Tyler, C., & Willand, J. (1997). Public budgeting in America: A twentieth century retrospective. *Journal of Public Budgeting, Accounting, & Financial Management*, *9*(2), 189–219.

Wildavsky, A. (1961). Political implications of budgetary reform. *Public Administration Review*, *21*(3), 183–190. doi:10.2307/973628

Wildavsky, A. (1964). *The politics of the budget process*. Boston, MA: Little Brown.

Wildavsky, A. (1992). Political implications of budget reform: A retrospective. *Public Administration Review*, *52*(3), 594–599. doi:10.2307/977170

Williamson, O. E. (1975). *Markets and hierarchies: Analysis and antitrust implications*. New York, NY: Free Press.

Williamson, O. E. (1981). The economics of organizatioins: The transactin cost approach. *American Journal of Sociology*, *87*, 548–577. doi:10.1086/227496

Williamson, O. E. (1985). *The economic institutions of capitalism*. New York, NY: The Free Press.

Williamson, O. E. (1999). Public and Private Bureaucracies: A transaction cost economics perspective. *Journal of Law Economics and Organization*, *15*, 306–342. doi:10.1093/jleo/15.1.306

Willoughby, W. F. (2002). The movement for budgetary reform in the states. In A. C. Hyde (Ed.), *Government budgeting: Theory, process, and politics* (pp. 20-23). Thomson Learning. Wu, F. H. (1981). Incrementalism in financial strategic planning. *Academy of Management Review, 6*(1), 133-143.

Zey, M. (Ed.). (1992). *Decision making: Alternatives to rational choice models*. Newbury Park, CA: Sage.

Chapter 12
The Value of Sociotechnical Theories for Implementation of Clinical Information Systems

Joanne Callen
The University of Sydney, Australia

Andrew Georgiou
The University of Sydney, Australia

Julie Li
The University of Sydney, Australia

Johanna Westbrook
The University of Sydney, Australia

ABSTRACT

The following chapter provides an overview of sociotechnical theories that can be used to understand, design, implement, and evaluate clinical information systems in health care settings. The sociotechnical approach is one that seeks to identify the dynamics between technology and the social, professional, and cultural environment in which it is used. Theories and models covered include: the technology and information technology acceptance models; a multi-level integration framework approach; social cognition theory; theories that propose a fit between individuals, tasks and the technology; diffusion of innovation theory, and a contextual implementation model. The frameworks presented in this chapter are not exhaustive but are most relevant to the complexity of information and communication technology use in health care settings.

INTRODUCTION

Socio-technical theories of organizational life were first derived from studies conducted in the 1950s (Trist & Bamforth, 1951). In essence these theories espoused the view that to improve organisational performance consideration needs to be given to optimizing both technical work processes and the social systems within the work environment.

This chapter presents an overview of sociotechnical theories which are applicable to understanding, designing and evaluating the implementation processes of clinical information systems in health care settings. Contemporary health organisations

DOI: 10.4018/978-1-60960-768-5.ch012

Copyright © 2012, IGI Global. Copying or distributing in print or electronic forms without written permission of IGI Global is prohibited.

are complex, composed of deeply interdependent and interrelated social and technical elements where changes to one aspect will affect the other (Wears & Berg, 2005). The introduction of any new technology into a complex organisational setting will entail innovation in clinical roles, work processes, and culture change (Ash, et al., 2003; Ash, Sittig, Campbell, Guappone, & Dykstra, 2006; Ash, Sittig, Dykstra, Campbell, & Guappone, 2009; Berg, 1998; Callen, Braithwaite, & Westbrook, 2007; Callen, Braithwaite, Westbrook, Callen, & Westbrook, 2009; Coiera, 2004; Gosling, Westbrook, & Coiera, 2003; Kaplan, 1997; Massaro, 1993) whilst the attitudes and utility of technology is simultaneously socially shaped (Coiera, 2004). Implementation of information systems in any environment must take account of the users of the system and the organizational context to ensure the technology fits and works within this framework

The sociotechnical approach to clinical information systems implementation is one which seeks to identify the dynamics between technology and the social, professional, and cultural environment in which it is used (Berg, 1999). The limitations of a purely technocentric approach to implementation became apparent when early projects were less than successful and purported benefits of Information and Communication Technology (ICT) rarely realised (Berg, 2004; Littlejohns, Wyatt, & Garvican, 2003; Whetton, 2005). Causes of implementation failure extend beyond poor system design to the erroneous perceptions and theories about how medical work is conducted (Aarts, Ash, & Berg, 2007; Aarts & Gorman, 2007; Wears & Berg, 2005). Clashes between the model of health care work inscribed in these tools with the actual nature of work has resulted in staff resistance and decreased organisational uptake of ICT, as well as the facilitation of some unexpected and negative effects in efficiency and patient safety (Ash, et al., 2009; Berg, 2004; Han, et al., 2005; Koppel, et al., 2005). It has been advanced that ICT in health care is being used to address the 'wicked problem', of how to deliver sustainable health delivery systems facilitated by information technologies (Westbrook, et al., 2007). Wicked problems are dynamic with multiple sets of complex, interacting issues that evolve in an emergent social context and solutions applied will often contain within them other wicked problems, and will generate new wicked problems (Ritchey, 2005; Rittel & Webber, 1973). Sociotechnical theories provide a useful paradigm within which to appreciate and explain the magnitude and complexity of the task of implementing clinical information systems.

The theories and models presented in this chapter are not exhaustive. Some frameworks are presented as models which represent an abstract view of a complex reality whereas some are described as theories which attempt to explain a group of facts or phenomenon. There are many valuable theories and models which can inform IT implementation. However those presented in this chapter are most relevant for the implementation of clinical information systems.

MODELS

Technology Acceptance Model (TAM) and Information Technology Acceptance Model (ITAM)

Two early information system evaluation models which have utilized attitude theory from psychology are the technology acceptance model (TAM) (Davis, 1989, 1993) and the information technology adoption model (ITAM) (Dixon, 1999). Davis (Davis, 1989) developed a validated measure which can be used to predict perceived usefulness and perceived ease of use of the technology, which he theorized were fundamental determinants of whether the system would be used. The TAM (Figure 1) proposes that a users' attitude to the system will have a major impact on how the system is viewed. The attitude towards using the system is dependent upon the perceived usefulness or value of the system and the perceived ease of use. The design features of a system indirectly affect an individual's attitude towards using the system through their direct impact on the users' perceived usefulness of the system and perceived ease of use (Davis, 1993). Therefore, computer systems which appear difficult to use and are difficult for individuals to navigate affect how they view the technology. Davis tested his model on 112 users who rated two different software systems (an electronic mail system and a text editor) via a questionnaire for perceived ease of use, perceived usefulness, attitudes towards using the system and actual use of the system. Results showed that the motivational variables in the model: attitudes toward using, perceived usefulness and perceived ease of use, completely mediated the effect of system design features on usage (Davis, 1993). Interestingly the usefulness of the system was found to be the most important variable in predicting use. Thus this model suggests that users might accept a difficult to use system as long as it was perceived to be of value in their jobs (Davis, 1993).

The ITAM (Davis, 1993; Dixon, 1999) builds on the work of Davis and also incorporates Rogers' Diffusion of Innovation Theory (Rogers, 1995) to provide a framework for information technology adoption with a focus on individual users (Figure 2). Individuals have capabilities such as knowledge, skills, and resources (Dixon, 1999). The technology also has a number of software and hardware requirements and the interface between these and the capabilities of the user determine the fit of the individual to the technology (Dixon, 1999). The IT user fit impacts on an individual users' perception of both the usefulness and ease of use of the technology. Roger's constructs of relative advantage, compatibility etc are included in the ITAM definition of perceived ease of use variable (Rogers, 1995). The ITAM is valuable as a predictor of whether an individual user will adopt a technology and it also highlights a number of areas where implementation strategies might be targeted in order to increase system acceptance and use (Dixon, 1999). However, both the TAM and the ITAM do not acknowledge the influence of organizational and clinical context, which have been shown to impact on the successful implementation of clinical information systems (Ash, et al., 2003; Callen, et al., 2007; Massaro, 1993; Southon, Sauer, & Dampney, 1997).

Multi-Level Integration Framework for Information Technology Implementation

Another approach with a behavioural science perspective to guide technology implementations

Figure 1. Technology Acceptance Model (TAM) (© 1993, Elsevier. Used with permission)

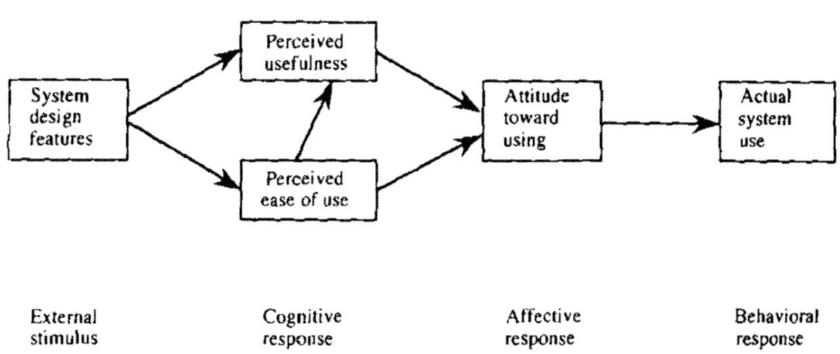

Figure 2. Information Technology Acceptance Model (ITAM) (© 1999, Elsevier. Used with permission)

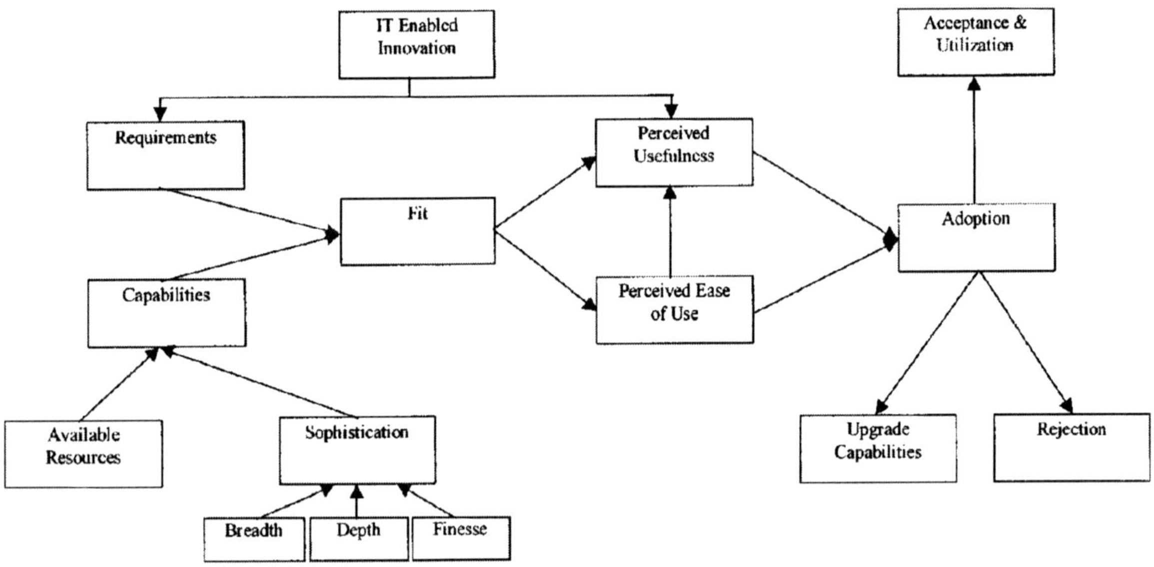

integrates a number of theories and models which are seen as complementary rather than competitive (Kukafka, Johnson, Linfante, & Allegrante, 2003). This integrative framework for IT implementation is based on a model used for planning health promotion programs where the primary aim is to modify how people behave. The multi-level integration framework consists of five phases with each phase identifying variables of interest (for example, organizational needs, support and education) and evaluation components. The first phase of the proposed framework consists of assessing the goals and needs of the organization with each subsequent phase building on this assessment. The focus of this first stage is to ensure that the technology matches the needs of the organization and that end-users are engaged from the outset. The focus of the second phase is on the system specifications and matching the needs of the end users. Phase three emphasizes the behaviours and organizational factors (such as computer access) associated with the use of the system. Phase four identifies those factors which influence behaviours linked to IT use, such as: perceived usefulness and ease of use; enabling factors such as the skills needed to use the system; and reinforcing factors including rewards and incentives. The final phase focuses on strategies to induce IT system use. The IT implementation framework proposed by Kukafka et al. is derived from an assessment of the literature utilizing a number of theories of human behaviour (Kukafka, et al., 2003). The value of the multi-level integration framework lies in the integration of a number of theories of human behaviour and its acknowledgement that there is no 'single bullet' solution for difficult IT implementations in healthcare settings.

Social Cognitive Theory

Social Cognitive Theory (Bandura, 1986) is a model of human behaviour which has been used to explain individual's reactions to computer technology (Bolt, Killough, & Koh, 2000; Compeau & Higgins, 1995; Compeau, Higgins, & Huff, 1999). The model is based on triadic reciprocality which asserts that the personal and cognitive factors of an individual, their behaviour in a given situation, and an individual's environment, impact on each other in a reciprocal fashion. An important aspect of the theory is that self efficacy or an individual's beliefs in his/her ability to perform a particular behaviour, for example use of a computer, influences what an individual chooses to do and subsequently their effort and persistence in undertaking that behaviour (Compeau & Higgins, 1995). This is particularly relevant to an individual's perceptions of their ability to use technology and hence can assist in our understanding of usage of clinical information systems in the workplace. Training programs aimed at making individuals more competent and comfortable with computer use need to take into account the concept of self efficacy.

Fit Between Individual, Task and Technology

It has been recognized that the implementation of clinical information systems needs to take account of the clinical environment as well as the human-computer interaction process. Several researchers (Aarts & Peel, 1999; J Aarts, Peel, & Wright, 1998) have proposed models which place emphasis on the fit between the clinical environment, the task and the technology. Aarts et al. present a model which describes the stages in the implementation of health information systems with associated personal requirements necessary to achieve each stage (Aarts, et al., 1998). The underlying premise of the model is the necessity of achieving an effective fit between the domains of clinical work, the technology and the organization. This model does not claim to be explanatory but rather attempts to place the implementation process within an organisational change framework (Aarts, et al., 1998). An interesting model developed specifically for the clinical environment which also takes account of fit has been proposed by Ammenwerth et al.(Ammenwerth, et al., 2006) The FITT model (Fit between Individuals, Task and Technology) arose from a review of the literature and considers the interaction or fit of the individual or users (taking into account for example, computer anxiety, motivation), the technology (hardware, software, network and usability, functionality, performance) and the clinical tasks and processes (for example, documentation, test orders) (Ammenwerth, et al., 2006) (Figure 3). Underlying this theory is the assertion that the aim of an IT implementation is to reach an ideal fit between attributes of the individual, task and technology. To improve this fit the hospital or clinical unit management can influence these attributes with interventions to facilitate the uptake of the technology. Examples of interventions include: user involvement in system selection; user training sessions, reorganization of tasks and clarification of responsibilities, and hardware and software upgrades (Ammenwerth, et al., 2006). Ammenwerth et al presents a case study applying the model to a computer based nursing documentation system and this provides a useful application of the theory in a naturalistic setting (Ammenwerth, et al., 2006).

Diffusion of Innovation Theory (DOI)

The implementation of new information systems in health care settings is seen by a number of researchers as a study in organizational change (Ash, et al., 2000; Benjamin & Levinson, 1993; Lorenzi & Riley, 2000; Metz, 1986; Southon, et al., 1997). Models of change management can guide information system implementers to assist in their understanding of why people resist new technology and what strategies could be employed to overcome this resistance. Roger's diffusion of innovation (DOI) theory, based on extensive empirical work, is a key change management theory applicable to technology implementations in health care settings (Rogers, 1995). This theory proposes an explanation of how individuals and groups adopt new ideas or practices over time. Roger's theory proposes five attributes of an innovation each of which is directly applicable to clinical information system: relative advantage; compatibility; complexity; trialability and observability. Implementation teams need to consider these attributes. For example, the attribute of

Figure 3. FITT (Fit between Individuals, Task and Technology) framework (© 2006, Ammenwerth et. al. Used with permission)

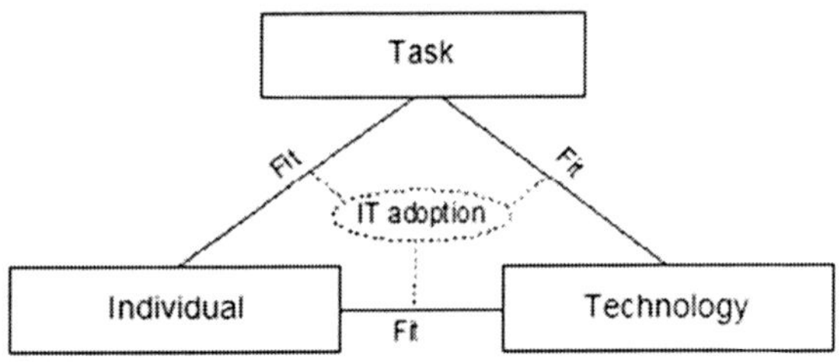

relative advantage underscores the need to present to the users the advantage of the new system over the old method of doing things. If users don't perceive a relative advantage by using the new technology they will be less likely to embrace it. In relation to an organization's response to a new idea or system, the DOI theory defines five factors (complexity, centralization, formalization, connectedness and slackness) which need to be taken into account to facilitate the uptake of the innovation. For example, Rogers proposes that organizations with a higher degree of centralization and formalization will be less likely to favour innovations. Roger's theory provides a framework for explaining how an innovation, which results in large-scale change, permeates throughout an organisation, industry or social environment. The DOI theory has been harnessed as the key theoretical paradigm in a number of studies of technology uptake in health care settings (Ash, 1997; Ash, et al., 2004; Ash, Lyman, Carpenter, & Fournier, 2001; Ash, et al., 2007).

Contextual Implementation Model (CIM)

The Contextual implementation model (CIM) is a multiple perspectives model of clinical information system implementation which arose from qualitative data collected from four clinical units in two large hospitals. The model focused attention on diversity at three levels or contexts: the organisational level; the clinical or departmental level, and the individual level (Callen, Braithwaite, & Westbrook, 2008) (Figure 4). Within each of these three contextual levels are dimensions for consideration which affect physicians' attitudes to, and use of, a clinical information system. The clinical information system in this study was a computerised provider order entry system used to order and view all diagnostic and radiological tests. The dimensions for consideration relating to these levels such as 'culture', 'clinical profile' and 'ways of working', and the levels themselves are interrelated and all impact on clinicians' use and acceptance of computerised order management systems. The CIM provides a contextual differences perspective which can be used to facilitate the implementation of clinical information systems. The value of this model is that it views clinical information system implementations from a sociotechnical perspective, acknowledging the complexity and diversity of clinical and organisational environments, and differences between users which need to be taken into account if implementations are to be successful and benefits to patients realised. The sociotechnical approach to patient care information systems emphasizes a user-oriented, work practice perspective (Berg, 1999).

CONCLUSION

The sociotechnical implementation models and theories outlined in this chapter provide useful

Figure 4. Contextual Implementation Model (CIM) (© 2007, BMJ Publishing Group Ltd. Used with permission)

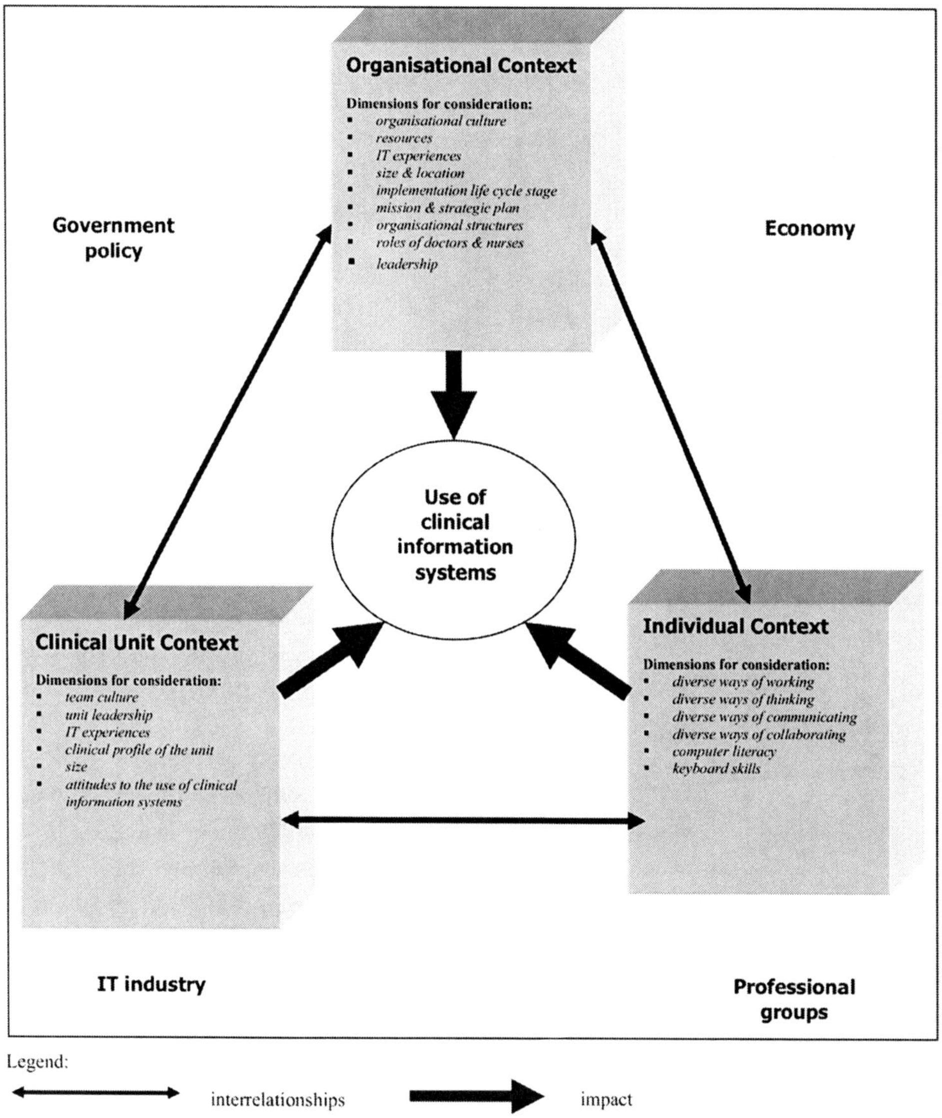

frameworks for understanding the relationship between social and technical systems within a clinical work practice and organizational context. There value lies in their ability to inform and facilitate the implementation process. Clinical information systems are dynamic and continue to evolve over the multiple phases of the implementation process (Callen, et al., 2008; Kaplan, 2001). They represent technical artefacts which embody implicit theories about how work is conducted and the clinical context within which they operate; successful implementation of the artefact in real clinical environments relies upon the accuracy and applicability of these theories (Woods, 1998). These models serve as a framework to guide implementations to ensure their safe and efficient use and improve the likelihood of uptake by clinicians.

REFERENCES

Aarts, J., Ash, J., & Berg, M. (2007). Extending the understanding of computerized physician order entry: Implications for professional collaboration, workflow and quality of care. *International Journal of Medical Informatics*, *76*, 4–13. doi:10.1016/j.ijmedinf.2006.05.009

Aarts, J., & Gorman, P. (2007). IT in health care: Sociotechnical approaches "to err is system". *International Journal of Medical Informatics*, *76*(Supplement 1), S1–S3. doi:10.1016/S1386-5056(07)00078-0

Aarts, J., & Peel, V. (1999). Using a descriptive model of change when implementing large scale clinical information systems to identify priorities for further research. *International Journal of Medical Informatics*, *56*(1-3), 43–50. doi:10.1016/S1386-5056(99)00045-3

Aarts, J., Peel, V., & Wright, G. (1998). Organizational issues in health informatics: A model approach. *International Journal of Medical Informatics*, *52*(1-3), 235–242. doi:10.1016/S1386-5056(98)00142-7

Ammenwerth, E., Iller, C., Mahler, C., Ammenwerth, E., Iller, C., & Mahler, C. (2006). IT-adoption and the interaction of task, technology and individuals: A fit framework and a case study. *BMC Medical Informatics and Decision Making*, *6*, 3. doi:10.1186/1472-6947-6-3

Ash, J. (1997). Organizational factors that influence information technology diffusion in academic health sciences centers. *Journal of the American Medical Informatics Association*, *4*(2), 102. doi:10.1136/jamia.1997.0040102

Ash, J., Anderson, J., Gorman, P., Zielstorff, R., Norcross, N., & Pettit, J. (2000). Managing change: Analysis of a hypothetical case. *Journal of the American Medical Informatics Association*, *7*(2), 125. doi:10.1136/jamia.2000.0070125

Ash, J., Gorman, P., Lavelle, M., Stavri, P., Lyman, J., & Fournier, L. (2003). Perceptions of physician order entry: Results of a cross-site qualitative study. *Methods of Information in Medicine*, *42*(4), 313–323.

Ash, J., Lyman, J., Carpenter, J., & Fournier, L. (2001). *A diffusion of innovations model of physician order entry*.

Ash, J., Sittig, D. F., Dykstra, R. H., Guappone, K., Carpenter, J., & Seshadri, V. (2004). *The unintended consequences of computerized physician order entry*. Presentation at the IT in Health Care Sociotechnical Approaches 2nd International Conference, Portland, Oregon, USA. Sept 12-14.

Ash, J. S., Sittig, D. F., Campbell, E., Guappone, K., & Dykstra, R. H. (2006). An unintended consequence of CPOE implementation: Shifts in power, control, and autonomy. *AMIA ... Annual Symposium Proceedings / AMIA Symposium. AMIA Symposium*, 11–15.

Ash, J. S., Sittig, D. F., Dykstra, R., Campbell, E., & Guappone, K. (2009). The unintended consequences of computerized provider order entry: Findings from a mixed methods exploration. *International Journal of Medical Informatics*, *78*(Suppl 1), S69–S76. doi:10.1016/j.ijmedinf.2008.07.015

Ash, J. S., Sittig, D. F., Dykstra, R. H., Guappone, K., Carpenter, J. D., & Seshadri, V. (2007). Categorizing the unintended sociotechnical consequences of computerized provider order entry. *International Journal of Medical Informatics*, *76*(Suppl 1), S21–S27. doi:10.1016/j.ijmedinf.2006.05.017

Bandura, A. (1986). *Social foundations of thought and action*. Englewood Cliffs, NJ.

Benjamin, R., & Levinson, E. (1993). A framework for managing IT-enabled change. *Sloan Management Review*, *34*(4), 23–33.

Berg, M. (1998). Medical work and the computer-based patient record: A sociological perspective. *Methods of Information in Medicine*, *37*, 294–301.

Berg, M. (1999). Patient care information systems and health care work: A sociotechnical approach. *International Journal of Medical Informatics*, *55*(2), 87–101. doi:10.1016/S1386-5056(99)00011-8

Berg, M. (2004). *Health information management: Integrating information technology in health care work*. Routledge.

Bolt, M., Killough, L., & Koh, H. (2000). Testing the interaction effects of task complexity in computer training using the social cognitive model. *Decision Sciences*, *32*(1), 1–20. doi:10.1111/j.1540-5915.2001.tb00951.x

Callen, J., Braithwaite, J., & Westbrook, J. (2007). Cultures in hospitals and their influence on attitudes to, and satisfaction with, the use of clinical information systems. *Social Science & Medicine*, *65*(3), 635–639. doi:10.1016/j.socscimed.2007.03.053

Callen, J., Braithwaite, J., & Westbrook, J. (2008). Contextual implementation model: a framework for assisting clinical information system implementations. *Journal of the American Medical Informatics Association*, *15*(2), 255–262. doi:10.1197/jamia.M2468

Callen, J., Braithwaite, J., Westbrook, J. I., Callen, J., & Westbrook, J. I. (2009). The importance of medical and nursing sub-cultures in the implementation of clinical information systems. *Methods of Information in Medicine*, *48*(2), 196–202.

Coiera, E. (2004). Four rules for the reinvention of health care. *BMJ (Clinical Research Ed.)*, *328*(7449), 1197–1199. doi:10.1136/bmj.328.7449.1197

Compeau, D., & Higgins, C. (1995). Application of social cognitive theory to training for computer skills. *Information Systems Research*, *6*(2), 118. doi:10.1287/isre.6.2.118

Compeau, D., Higgins, C., & Huff, S. (1999). Social cognitive theory and individual reactions to computing technology: A longitudinal study. *Management Information Systems Quarterly*, *23*(2), 145–158. doi:10.2307/249749

Davis, F. (1989). Perceived usefulness, perceived ease of use, and user acceptance of information technology. *Management Information Systems Quarterly*, *13*(3), 319–340. doi:10.2307/249008

Davis, F. (1993). User acceptance of information technology: System characteristics, user perceptions and behavioral impacts. *International Journal of Man-Machine Studies*, *38*(3), 475–487. doi:10.1006/imms.1993.1022

Dixon, D. (1999). The behavioral side of information technology. *International Journal of Medical Informatics*, *56*(1-3), 117–123. doi:10.1016/S1386-5056(99)00037-4

Gosling, A., Westbrook, J., & Coiera, E. (2003). Variation in the use of online clinical evidence: A qualitative analysis. *International Journal of Medical Informatics*, *69*(1), 1–16. doi:10.1016/S1386-5056(02)00046-1

Han, Y., Carcillo, J., Venkataraman, S., Clark, R., Watson, R., & Nguyen, T. (2005). Unexpected increased mortality after implementation of a commercially sold computerized physician order entry system. *Pediatrics*, *116*(6), 1506–1512. doi:10.1542/peds.2005-1287

Kaplan, B. (1997). Addressing organizational issues into the evaluation of medical systems. *Journal of the American Medical Informatics Association*, *4*(2), 94. doi:10.1136/jamia.1997.0040094

Kaplan, B. (2001). Evaluating informatics applications—Some alternative approaches: theory, social interactionism, and call for methodological pluralism. *International Journal of Medical Informatics*, *64*(1), 39–56. doi:10.1016/S1386-5056(01)00184-8

Koppel, R., Metlay, J., Cohen, A., Abaluck, B., Localio, A., & Kimmel, S. (2005). Role of computerized physician order entry systems in facilitating medication errors. *Journal of the American Medical Association, 293*, 1197–1203. doi:10.1001/jama.293.10.1197

Kukafka, R., Johnson, S., Linfante, A., & Allegrante, J. (2003). Grounding a new information technology implementation framework in behavioral science: A systematic analysis of the literature on IT use. *Journal of Biomedical Informatics, 36*(3), 218–227. doi:10.1016/j.jbi.2003.09.002

Littlejohns, P., Wyatt, J. C., & Garvican, L. (2003). Evaluating computerised health information systems: Hard lessons still to be learnt. *BMJ (Clinical Research Ed.), 326*(7394), 860–863. doi:10.1136/bmj.326.7394.860

Lorenzi, N., & Riley, R. (2000). Managing change: An overview. *Journal of the American Medical Informatics Association, 7*(2), 116. doi:10.1136/jamia.2000.0070116

Massaro, T. (1993). Introducing physician order entry at a major academic medical center: I. Impact on organizational culture and behavior. *Academic Medicine, 68*, 20–25. doi:10.1097/00001888-199301000-00003

Metz, E. (1986). Managing change toward a leading-edge information culture. *Organizational Dynamics, 15*(2), 28–40. doi:10.1016/0090-2616(86)90035-5

Ritchey, T. (2005). *Wicked problems: Structuring social messes with morphological analysis*. Swedish Morphological Society.

Rittel, H., & Webber, M. (1973). Dilemmas in a general theory of planning. *Policy Sciences, 4*(2), 155–169. doi:10.1007/BF01405730

Rogers, E. (1995). *Diffusion of innovations*. Free press.

Southon, F., Sauer, C., & Dampney, C. (1997). Information technology in complex health services: organizational impediments to successful technology transfer and diffusion. *Journal of the American Medical Informatics Association, 4*(2), 112. doi:10.1136/jamia.1997.0040112

Trist, E., & Bamforth, K. (1951). Some social and psychological consequences of the longwall method of coal-getting: An examination of the psychological situation and defences of a work group in relation to the social structure and technological content of the work system. *Human Relations, 4*(1), 3–38. doi:10.1177/001872675100400101

Wears, R. L., & Berg, M. (2005). Computer technology and clinical work: Still waiting for Godot. *Journal of the American Medical Association, 293*(10), 1261–1263. doi:10.1001/jama.293.10.1261

Westbrook, J. I., Braithwaite, J., Georgiou, A., Ampt, A., Creswick, N., & Coiera, E. (2007). Multimethod evaluation of information and communication technologies in health in the context of wicked problems and sociotechnical theory. *Journal of the American Medical Informatics Association, 14*(6), 746–755. doi:10.1197/jamia.M2462

Whetton, S. (2005). *Health informatics: A socio-technical perspective*. Oxford University Press.

Woods, D. (1998). Designs are hypotheses about how artifacts shape cognition and collaboration. *Ergonomics, 41*(2), 168–173. doi:10.1080/001401398187215

ADDITIONAL READING

Aarts, J., & Berg, M. (2006). Same systems, different outcomes--comparing the implementation of computerized physician order entry in two Dutch hospitals. *Methods of Information in Medicine, 45*(1), 53–61.

Ammenwerth, E., Gräber, S., Herrmann, G., Bürkle, T., & König, J. (2003). Evaluation of health information systems—problems and challenges. *International Journal of Medical Informatics*, *71*(2-3), 125–135. doi:10.1016/S1386-5056(03)00131-X

Anderson, J., & Aydin, C. (2005). *Evaluating the organizational impact of healthcare information systems*. Springer Verlag. doi:10.1007/0-387-30329-4

Berg, M. (2001). Implementing information systems in health care organizations: myths and challenges. *International Journal of Medical Informatics*, *64*(2-3), 143–156. doi:10.1016/S1386-5056(01)00200-3

Berg, M., Aarts, J., & Van Der Lei, J. (2003). ICT in health care: sociotechnical approaches. *Methods of Information in Medicine*, *42*(4), 297–301.

Beuscart-Zephir, M. C., Anceaux, F., Menu, H., Guerlinger, S., Watbled, L., & Evrard, F. (2005). User-centred, multidimensional assessment method of Clinical Information Systems: a case-study in anaesthesiology. *International Journal of Medical Informatics*, *74*(2-4), 179–189. doi:10.1016/j.ijmedinf.2004.07.005

Beuscart-Zephir, M. C., Elkin, P., Pelayo, S., & Beuscart, R. (2007). The human factors engineering approach to biomedical informatics projects: state of the art, results, benefits and challenges. *Yearbook of Medical Informatics*, 109–127.

Beuscart-Zephir, M. C., Pelayo, S., Anceaux, F., Meaux, J. J., Degroisse, M., & Degoulet, P. (2005). Impact of CPOE on doctor-nurse cooperation for the medication ordering and administration process. *International Journal of Medical Informatics*, *74*(7-8), 629–641. doi:10.1016/j.ijmedinf.2005.01.004

Braithwaite, J., Westbrook, M., Iedema, R., Mallock, N., Forsyth, R., & Zhang, K. (2005). A tale of two hospitals: assessing cultural landscapes and compositions. *Social Science & Medicine*, *60*(5), 1149–1162. doi:10.1016/j.socscimed.2004.06.046

Callen, J., Westbrook, J., & Braithwaite, J. (2006). The effect of physicians' long-term use of CPOE on their test management work practices. *Journal of the American Medical Informatics Association*, *13*(6), 64. doi:10.1197/jamia.M2152

Coiera, E. (2007). Putting the technical back into socio-technical systems research. *International Journal of Medical Informatics*, *76*(Suppl 1), S98–S103. doi:10.1016/j.ijmedinf.2006.05.026

England, I., Stewart, D., & Walker, S. (2000). Information technology adoption in health care: when organisations and technology collide. *Australian health review: a publication of the Australian Hospital Association, 23*(3), 176.

Fox, W. (1995). Sociotechnical system principles and guidelines: past and present. *The Journal of Applied Behavioral Science*, *31*(1), 91–105. doi:10.1177/0021886395311009

Georgiou, A., Ampt, A., Creswick, N., Westbrook, J., & Braithwaite, J. (2009). Computerized Provider Order Entry--what are health professionals concerned about? A qualitative study in an Australian hospital. *International Journal of Medical Informatics*, *78*(1), 60–70. doi:10.1016/j.ijmedinf.2008.09.007

Goodhue, D., & Thompson, R. (1995). Task-technology fit and individual performance. *Management Information Systems Quarterly*, 213–236. doi:10.2307/249689

Greenhalgh, T., Potts, H. W., Wong, G., Bark, P., & Swinglehurst, D. (2009). Tensions and paradoxes in electronic patient record research: a systematic literature review using the meta-narrative method. *The Milbank Quarterly*, *87*(4), 729–788. doi:10.1111/j.1468-0009.2009.00578.x

Greenhalgh, T., Robert, G., Macfarlane, F., Bate, P., & Kyriakidou, O. (2004). Diffusion of innovations in service organizations: systematic review and recommendations. *The Milbank Quarterly*, *82*(4), 581–629. doi:10.1111/j.0887-378X.2004.00325.x

Greenhalgh, T., Stramer, K., Bratan, T., Byrne, E., Mohammad, Y., & Russell, J. (2008). Introduction of shared electronic records: multi-site case study using diffusion of innovation theory. *BMJ*, *337*, a1786.

Kaplan, B. (2001). Evaluating informatics applications—clinical decision support systems literature review. *International Journal of Medical Informatics*, *64*(1), 15–37. doi:10.1016/S1386-5056(01)00183-6

Kaplan, B., Brennan, P., Dowling, A., Friedman, C., & Peel, V. (2001). Toward an Informatics Research Agenda Key People and Organizational Issues. *Am Med Inform Assoc*, *8*(3), 235–241. doi:10.1136/jamia.2001.0080235

Kaplan, B., & Shaw, N. (2004). Future directions in evaluation research: people, organizational, and social issues. *Methods of Information in Medicine*, *43*(3), 215–231.

Niazkhani, Z., van der Sijs, H., Pirnejad, H., Redekop, W. K., Aarts, J., & Niazkhani, Z. (2009). Same system, different outcomes: comparing the transitions from two paper-based systems to the same computerized physician order entry system. *International Journal of Medical Informatics*, *78*(3), 170–181. doi:10.1016/j.ijmedinf.2008.06.012

Norman, D. (2004). *Emotional Design: Why we love (or hate) everyday things*. New York: Basic Books.

Pasmore, W. (1995). Social science transformed: the socio-technical perspective. *Human relations (New York, NY)*, *48*(1), 1–21.

Peute, L., Aarts, J., Bakker, P., & Jaspers, M. (2009). Anatomy of a failure: A sociotechnical evaluation of a laboratory physician order entry system implementation. *International Journal of Medical Informatics*.

Stoop, A. P., & Berg, M. (2003). Integrating quantitative and qualitative methods in patient care information system evaluation: guidance for the organizational decision maker. *Methods of Information in Medicine*, *42*(4), 458–462.

Tsiknakis, M., & Kouroubali, A. (2009). Organizational factors affecting successful adoption of innovative eHealth services: A case study employing the FITT framework. *International Journal of Medical Informatics*, *78*(1), 39–52. doi:10.1016/j.ijmedinf.2008.07.001

Westbrook, J., Braithwaite, J., Gibson, K., Paoloni, R., Callen, J., & Georgiou, A. (2009). Use of information and communication technologies to support effective work practice innovation in the health sector: a multi-site study. *BMC Health Services Research*, *9*(1), 201. doi:10.1186/1472-6963-9-201

KEY TERMS AND DEFINITIONS

Contextual Implementation Model (CIM): A multiple perspectives model of clinical systems implementation focused on diversity at three levels or contexts: the organisational, clinical/departmental, and individual. Each contextual level contain unique dimensions for consideration during implemenation phases which influence clinicians' attitudes to, and use of, a clinical information system.

Diffusion of Innovation (DOI) Theory: A change management theory which aims to explain how, why, and at what rate individuals and groups adopt new ideas and practices over time.

Fit between Individual, Task, and Technology (FITT) Framework: A systems implementation model advocating the recognition of the clinical environment and the human-computer interaction process. Specifically, it highlights the necessity of achieving a fit between clinical work, technology, and the organisation into which the system is introduced.

Information Technology Acceptance Model (ITAM): An incorporation of the TAM and DOI frameworks, the ITAM predicts user adoption of technology through measurement of the fit between individual capabilities such as knowledge, skills, and resources, and the software and hardware requirements of the technology.

Social Cognitive Theory: A human behaviour model used to explain individual reactions to computer technology. It asserts that an individual's perceptions of their ability to use technology determine their persistence and effort to undertake that behaviour.

Sociotechnical Theory: A framework emphasising the relationship and interdependence between the social and technical aspects of a system.

Technology Acceptance Model (TAM): A system evaluation theory which predicts user acceptance and use of technology. The model proposes that user decisions about how and when they will use the technology are influenced by the degree to which a person believes that using a particular system would enhance his or her job performance, and the degree to which a person believes that using a particular system would be free from effort.

Wicked Problem: A complex issue composed of multiple dynamic, interdependent components which change with the evolving social context. Solutions to wicked problems often create other wicked problems.

APPENDIX

Table 1. Comparison of sociotechnical approaches to clinical information system implementation

Model/Framework	Key elements	Advantages	Limitations
Technology Acceptance Model (TAM) (Davis, 1989; 1993)	Aim was to develop valid measurement scales for predicting user acceptance of computers. 2 determinants which cause people to accept or reject IT are: *Perceived usefulness* (the degree to which a person believes that using the system would enhance job performance) *Perceived ease of use* (the degree to which a person believes that using the system would be free of effort). Model developed from a review of previous literature.	The 2 new scales exhibited high convergent, discriminant and factorial validity. These measures for predicting and explaining system use have value for vendors (in early user acceptance testing) and information system managers (in emphasising the value of the system for users work). Perceived usefulness was significantly more strongly linked to usage than ease of use. Therefore users may tolerate a difficult interface to access functionalities in the system that helps them do their job. The TAM provided a foundation for further research on why users accept or reject information technology.	The TAM has been applied to studies on clinical information system implementations however the major limitation is that it does not take into account the impact of the organisational or clinical context. Davis asserts that his model is only of use for IT systems which are used voluntarily. Usage measures employed were self reported.
Information Technology Adoption Model (ITAM) (Dixon 1999)	The ITAM model was designed to provide a structure for designing and evaluating strategies for IT implementation. The end user has *sophistication* derived from their knowledge and skills which may be defined in terms of breadth, depth and finesse (ability to transfer knowledge and skills from one area to another). The end user also has available *resources* (information technology (IT), time, money). Resources combined with sophistication will give *capabilities* available for the IT. The technology itself has *requirements* (money, time, knowledge, skills). From the *requirements* of the IT and the *capabilities* of the user, one can determine a *fit of an individual to the technology*. The *IT user fit* will affect *usefulness and ease of use*. Rogers (1995) constructs are included in the ease of use and usefulness items. All these perceptions lead to the individual forming an intent to change and making a decision to adopt the IT. If adopted (used once) the person may continue using the IT, reject the IT or upgrade their capabilities.	Builds on the TAM In the *perceived usefulness* takes into account Rogers (1995) constructs of relative advantage, subjective norms, compatibility and feedback. In *perceived ease of use* includes usability, perceived behavioural control and support.	Does not take into account organisational or clinical context in relation to use of the system.

Continued on following page

Table 1. Continued

Model/Framework	Key elements	Advantages	Limitations
Multi-level integration framework (Kukafka et al. 2003)	Aim was to present a framework intended to guide synthesis of more than one theoretical perspective for the purpose of planning IT implementations. Used the PRECEDE/PROCEDE conceptual framework used for planning health promotion programs to account for multiple determinants of behaviour. Developed from a systematic review of the literature (24 articles) and measured the extent to which the studies reported in the articles addressed various phases of the proposed IT implementation framework. The framework is based on 2 propositions: IT use is complex, multi-dimensional and influenced by a variety of individual and organisational level factors, Success in achieving change is enhanced by active participation from the user group The framework is structured around 5 phases of implementation with each phase building on the previous and with each phase including a suggested evaluation. Based on literature using a number of behavioural theories.	Includes an evaluation component in each phase. Reported that none of the studies in the sample included a sufficiently broad set of empirically investigated influencing factors. Promotes the use of multiple models to assist in IT implementations. Acknowledges human and organisational factors as important in IT implementations.	Literature review included different and short time frames for inclusion of studies from the search (1997-2002; 1998-2002; 1999-2002). Generalisability of findings needs to be tested with further studies.
Social Cognitive theory (Bandura, 1986)	A behavioural model based on triadic reciprocality. Triadic reciprocality refers to the relationship between the environment, the person (including personality) and their behaviour and each influence each other. Social Cognitive theory includes two important constructs relevant for explanation of IT usage: Individuals are more likely to undertake behaviours they believe will result in valued outcomes and, Self efficacy which is defined as one's beliefs about their ability to perform a specific behaviour. The concept of self efficacy acknowledges that the user requires the requisite skills and confidence to use IT.	Widely accepted and empirically validated model of individual behaviour. Social Cognitive theory suggests that both self efficacy and outcomes expectations are important components of whether individuals will use computers. Training programs need to include strategies for improving self efficacy of users.	Self efficacy and outcomes expectations need to be tested with users involved in IT implementations in a variety of health care settings.

Continued on following page

Table 1. Continued

Model/Framework	Key elements	Advantages	Limitations
Eight stage implementation model (Aarts et al. 1998)	Aim was to describe a model which accounts for the stages of implementation of an information system. The model had eight stages of information system changes and the personal requirements necessary to realise these. Within these stages there need to be an 'effective' fit between *clinical work, the organisation of medicine and the health care system* and the *information and communication technology (ICT).* 'Effective' fit means that the three domains will mould each other. The three levels of clinical work which should fit with the ICT are: interaction with the patient in relation to diagnosis and treatment learning from patients – clinicians improve their practice through accumulated experience organising and managing clinical practice (scheduling, reporting, billing etc). The model was derived from the literature and authors thoughts and experiences using a sociotechnical perspective.	The model presents a practical guide for implementation of ICT and acknowledges the complexity of implementations, the notion of a dynamic process of organisational change with interactions (briefly noted but not fully described) at each stage. The model describes three levels of clinical work which is important when considering how clinicians (and others) use ICT. The model acknowledges the process of continuous alignment between work practices and ICT. The model serves as a conceptual basis for a unit of study in health informatics with students working through the eight stages as modules of their higher degree program.	The model is not explanatory but does identify domains that are relevant for implementing ICT in health. The authors acknowledge that they do not explain the exact nature of the interactions at each stage which they state requires further research. The model needs to be tested with other clinical information system implementations in a range of health care settings.
FITT theory (Ammenwerth et al. 2006)	The aim was to present a framework (the FITT theory) to better analyse the socio-organisational-technical factors which influence IT adoption. The FITT theory (Fit between Individuals, Task and Technology) is based on the premise that clinical IT adoption depends on the fit between the attributes of the users, the technology and the clinical tasks. The user must be sufficiently motivated and knowledgeable and the technology must offer sufficient functionality and performance to support clinical tasks. There are also external influencing factors on fit such as staff changes, staff workload, rising complexity of the task and new software standards. The FITT theory was based on a literature review of IT adoption frameworks.	A case study of the FITT theory is presented based on the implementation of a computer based nursing process documentation system. The case study provides specific examples of the importance of the interaction between task and user which underlies the importance of examining the impact of technology on clinicians' work practices. There is also emphasis on differences between clinical areas in terms of users and tasks.	The theory needs to be tested with other clinical information system implementations in a range of health care settings.

Continued on following page

Table 1. Continued

Model/Framework	Key elements	Advantages	Limitations
Diffusion of Innovation Theory (Rogers, 1995)	This theory proposes how individuals and groups adopt new ideas or practices over time. Rogers described *characteristics of adopters* (innovators; early adopters; early majority; late majority and laggards) and of the innovation or technology if applied to ICT implementations. *Innovation characteristics* which impact on adoption rates include: *relative advantage* (degree to which the innovation is perceived as better than the way something is currently undertaken); *compatibility* (degree to which the innovation is consistent with existing values); *complexity* (the degree to which the innovation is difficult); *trialability* (degree to which one can experiment with or trial the innovation); and *observability* (degree to which the results of the innovation are visible). *Organisational factors* which impact positively on diffusion include: high complexity; low centralisation, low formalisation, high connectedness and organisational slackness. Based on extensive empirical work of agricultural innovations and subsequently applied to information technology diffusion.	Focus is on the speed of diffusion of the innovation in terms of organisational and technological readiness. Innovation characteristics described in the DOI model are applicable to clinical information system implementations in particular relative advantage, complexity and trialability.	The DOI theory proposes organisational readiness features, for example, low formalisation, as important for diffusion. These features manifest differently in different health care organisations. If the DOI model is proposing an 'ideal' organisational structure then this does not acknowledge structural differences which are present in health care facilities such as hospitals.
Contextual implementation model (CIM) (Callen et al. 2008)	The CIM is a multiple perspectives model of clinical information system implementation. Its core underlying theme focuses on *contextual differences* or diversity at three levels: *the organisational level;* *the clinical or department level, and* *the individual level.* Within each of these three contextual levels are *dimensions for consideration* such as organisational and/or team culture, IT experiences, diverse ways of ways of working, communicating and thinking, diverse keyboard skills etc. The three levels of contextual differences and their dimensions for consideration are situated with the complex external environment of the organisation which includes: influences from professional bodies; government policy; the economic environment and the information technology industry. The model was derived from empirical data collected from observations and interviews in four clinical units in two hospitals in relation to the use of a computerised provider order entry system.	The model arose from data collected in the field. The value of this model is that it views clinical information system implementations from a sociotechnical perspective acknowledging the complexity and diversity of clinical and organisational environments and differences between users.	The model needs to be tested with a range of clinical information system implementations in diverse clinical units, hospitals and countries. The model does not take into account the phases of implementation.

Chapter 13
Diffusion of Innovation Theory and the Problem of Context for Inter-Organizational Information Systems:
The Example of Feral Information Systems

Luke Houghton
Griffith University, Australia

Don Kerr
University of the Sunshine Coast, Australia

ABSTRACT

This chapter argues that diffusion theory models like the technology acceptance model (TAM) need to be rethought of in light of contextual factors that are becoming increasingly important in modern inter-organisational settings. This is due to the growing complexity of organizations with respect to different organisational types, contexts, and political structures that have been shown in research literature to hinder information systems acceptance. The chapter looks at possible contextual factors that are ignored by TAM by critiquing its parent diffusion theory (diffusion of innovations). This approach was considered best as there are many variations of TAM, but the diffusion of innovations (DOI) theory underlies all these variations. The chapter also recommends a way forward for research into inter-organisational information systems by examining an example situation of Feral Information Systems (FIS) to illustrate the problem. The chapter concludes with a discussion about future research directions.

DOI: 10.4018/978-1-60960-768-5.ch013

Copyright © 2012, IGI Global. Copying or distributing in print or electronic forms without written permission of IGI Global is prohibited.

INTRODUCTION

In the short history of the information systems discipline, there has been a healthy debate about the role technology has and how we have come to understand the problem of accepting technological innovations (Davis 1989, Bagozzi 2007). The TAM was built on the backbones of the theory of reasoned action (Hale, Householder and Green 2003) and diffusion of innovations (DOI) (Rogers 1995). The theory of reasoned action assumes a great deal of well thought out straight-forwardness in structured management decision making and ultimately presents the notion that organizational life is linear and actions well planned, as does DOI. Management scholars like Johns (2006) have questioned the straightforward view of research in organizations because it lacks a reasonable explanation of the problem of context. Johns in particular describes context as a form of constraint that, 'can serve as a main effect or interact with personal variables such as disposition to affect organizational behavior,' or what he later calls a 'bundle of stimuli'. Such a grouping is unique to each setting and therefore changes in each organization. Johns also argues that findings in organizational behaviour research point towards the idea that many studies owe their findings to contextual variables that aren't described or clearly articulated. Very few scholars in the information systems field have attempted to map or even discuss these problems in relation to inter-organizational information systems.

This concern about how context affects the acceptance of inter-organizational information systems has manifested itself in information systems research through an emerging view of the problem of feral information Systems (Kerr, Houghton and Burgess 2007). Feral information systems (FIS) are defined as:

"An information system [computerised] that is developed by individuals or groups of employees to help them with their work, but is not condoned by management nor is part of the corporation's accepted information technology infrastructure. Its development is [or may be] designed to circumvent existing organisational information systems" (Houghton and Kerr, 2006, p 137, Kerr Houghton and Burgess 2007)).

The original concern for Feral Information Systems comes from a research project (cited above) conducted in 2004-2008 in which key actors were found to be building deliberately working around systems. After two different data collection phases, the authors found significant evidence of systems that existed without official consent, support or IT architecture. The term 'feral' was applied to these kinds of information systems because much like 'feral' children or people who wander outside the boundaries of society, they continue to exist and grow independent to the mainstream. The systems found by the authors were created with the express purpose of augmenting; working around and bypassing existing 'sanctioned' information systems architecture. A key point here is that the purpose of the system's creation suits the social network that drives it. For example, an FIS belongs to a culture that believes it's necessary to work around established information systems architecture. FIS can also be thought of as a reaction to rejecting technology because of its cumbersome nature, the fact that it doesn't match workflow (see Alter 2004) and a host of other factors discussed by authors like Orlikowski (1992).

Orlikowski highlights a constructivist approach, arguing that technology is a byproduct and facilitator of human accomplishment and a part of the social order, our norms and ideas. Technology becomes an extension of the stratification and intentionality of its users, part of the constitutional properties of the organization and most importantly the tools for significance, power and legitimizing of practices. FIS can be seen as part of a constitutional context of an organization and part of the social network that makes practice. The technology is merely the *byproduct* of the social interactions around the system.

Table 1. The influence of technology on actions - from Orlikowski (1992)

Theory	Practice
Technology as a Product of Human Action	The design, modification and appropriation of technology
Technology as a Medium of Human Action	Technology facilitates and constrains human action through the provision of interpretive schemes, facilities, and norms
Institutional Conditions of Interaction with Technology	Institutional Properties influence humans in their interaction with technology, for example, intentions, professional norms, state of the art in materials and knowledge, design standards, and available resources (time, money, skills)
Institutional Consequences of Interaction with Technology	Interaction with technology influences the institutional properties of an organization, through reinforcing or transforming structures of signification, domination, and legitimation

An example related to one of the authors was of a line manager from a major Australian mining company who when faced with a system he/she didn't understand, developed a workaround in the form of a complex spreadsheet for determining requirements for material planning. This has major ramifications for this manager who had to account for his/her actions to strategic elements of the business and in addition was blacklisted by the IT department.

A key problem here is that effective use of technology depends on context and interactions with it, including the way individuals use the technology according to their own view of the world (Orlikowski 1992). FIS are usually developed as an effort to improve an individual's or work group's way of handling the job because those systems in use need to be navigated around in order to complete assigned work. The phenomena is increasingly being facilitated by new and improved user development tools, however they in turn can present a real problem for organizations as they represent a version of what Orlikowski (1992) refers to as "technology in use". In many cases this attempt to circumvent existing organizational systems can have detrimental effects as many organizational systems have been implemented as a result of careful upper management planning that usually involves higher-level functions of the implemented software such as accurate forecasting. FIS arise out of a context and a place where an interaction with technology and culture has occurred. More importantly we argue that FIS are an example of a technology in use that results when major technological innovations are not accepted or well understood.

TAM and DOI models assume that innovations diffuse overtime, in a straightforward, well-structured manner. This means the model is well equipped to handle straightforward and well-structured innovations, (i.e. Malcolm Gladwell's example of the Hush Puppies in *The Tipping Point*) and acts as a mediator for explaining innovations. However, as a model when innovations are complex and diffused differently or prove difficult as in FIS, the model fails to give adequate explanations of acceptance. What if, in the case of FIS, the innovation that's accepted is not the one that was planned?

The case of FIS shows that some adoptions are fraught with disaster (Houghton and Kerr [2006]) because organizational goals and social system goals differ. For example, Archer-Lean, Clark and Kerr (2006, page 26) state that "Language and the communication forms that people use are not simply a means to help convey a pre-existing reality; rather, they affect perception of reality". This statement is an example of the problems organisation face with, apparently well structured innovations being subject to differing "perceptions of reality". The context of social interactions and the strategic IS plan don't match (Archer-Lean,

Clark and Kerr [2006]). Quattrone and Hooper (2001) suggest that from this conflict of interests, different social groups invent their own technology and adopt it according to their own ad-hoc innovation cycle.

This is no more evident that in the realm of inter-organizational information systems, where there may be two or three clashing cultures, different structures of decision making hierarchy, different agendas and most importantly different business processes and norms in both organisations. A problem with context, as noted by research such as Johns (2006), points towards the idea that a generalized model of innovation such as DOI, would have problems with radically different contexts.

Compare this with organisational and management literature noting the problem of context in research studies on organisations and a problem emerges. How does diffusion theory and the models like TAM account for context?

The seemingly endless development of TAM models as a 'one-size-fits-all' model for information systems uptake and acceptance do not have a strong case for the growing non-linearity of the modern organisations and such models do not help explain the FIS phenomenon. They also have a weaker case when faced with inter-organisational information systems. Problems like: council mergers, acquisitions and takeovers are cases in point. The problem isn't necessarily with TAM, but the assumptions derived from its parent diffusion theory (See Tornatzky and Klein 1982) as the following section suggests.

This chapter looks at possible contextual factors that are ignored by diffusion theory models and recommends a way forward for research in inter-organisational information systems.

BACKGROUND

Inter-organisational Information Systems (henceforth IOS) are those which tie together different from different organizations (see Markus and Wigland [2005]). They have the unique problem in that they bring data and business processes of one organization as well as bringing together the workflow of the different organizations into a singular space.

A dominant focus of the research so far into IOS has been the reliance on the use of TAM to explore adoption and uptake issues. In a study done on literature in the IOS field, Robey, Im and Wareham (2008) highlighted some future research directions needed to extend the field of IOS. In particular they were concerned with the straightforwardness of adoption studies and called for new theoretical perspectives. They noted:

The influence of social context on IOS adoption can thus be studied using new theoretical perspectives that incorporate IOS characteristics as explanatory variables (p.510).

More specifically:

Jasperson et al. express concerns that IS innovations may fail to fulfill their promise because, over time, post-adoptive behaviors become habitualized through non- reflective mental scripts that engage only "a selected subset of the technology's features… many of the perceived potential benefits of an innovation, so important in predicting the adoption decision, may actually never be realized because the innovation is used in unanticipated ways (p.511).

The authors argue that problems such as FIS are one of those 'non-reflective mental scripts' discussed by Robey et al (2008) above. This is specifically aimed at the overuse of adoption studies in IOS and how the field itself lacks more social critique and advanced analysis of complex issues. In citing Fichman (2004) the authors argue that a great majority of adoptions are bias because of the positive framing of adoption studies. As the quote above notes, this can create an imbalanced view of adoption. In the case of FIS, it fails to adequately explain some of the contextual and organizational problems mentioned earlier.

Robey et. al (2008) also discuss the over reliance on adoption models, is the problem of fashionable organizations and management fads. This leads to information systems that are implemented for reasons that are not necessarily in the best interest of the organization. In some cases, it means information systems that slow down business processes, create expensive failures and raise questions as to the motives of implementing large scale information systems packages (see Quattrone and Hooper [2001] for example). Robey et al (2008) in citing Fichmann (2004) make the following point:

To counteract the pro-innovation bias of innovation theory, Fichman draws attention to alternative theories of social contagion and management fashion, which suggest that adoption of innovation often hinges on the behavior of adopters other than the focal adopter. Research on managerial fads and fashions shows that even inefficient technologies may be adopted when powerful, fashion-setting organizations lead the way. Likewise, efficient technologies can be rejected when fashion-setting organizations reject them.

And:

As a consequence of social pressure, firms may adopt innovations that are not right for them and, thus, experience outcomes that fail to meet expectations (p. 509).

While the authors fail to cite case studies, the recent lawsuits on companies such as HP[1] and SAP[2] point towards growing problems in the field. Very few scholars are investigating the problems associated with technical innovations and there is a clear need to investigate the reasons for problems and adopting IOS systems is at the heart of such matters. The following section outlines some problems with diffusion theory and points towards the need for more research.

CONTEXTUAL PROBLEMS THAT CHALLENGE ADOPTION MODELS: THE EXAMPLE OF FIS

Problems with Diffusion Theory Based Models

Diffusion means the communication about new ideas, technologies or processes (Rogers, 1995). Diffusion theory explains and predicts the influence of a wide range of factors on the innovation adoption and implementation decision. The predicators include the factors from the focal system (individuals such as targeted adopters, managers and champions as well as the organization's structure and culture), the perceived nature of the innovation itself (its advantages, compatibility and complexity), communication channels (e.g. formal and informal, resource intensive or inexpensive) and time.(e.g. the rate of diffusion over time). This theoretical framework is over fifty years old and has its roots in rural sociology where it was used to explain and predict how agricultural innovations were diffused. It has been applied in over 4000 studies of innovation adoption across a wide range of areas (see Burgess [2007] for a comprehensive account), including scholarly disciplines, primarily communications, sociology, marketing and organization science (see Bradford and Florin 2003 and Rogers 1995 for examples).

While undeniably popular and useful, this traditional approach to innovation adoption and diffusion has well-understood limitations that have been identified by innovation researchers themselves (Rogers, 1995, Wolfe 1994, Drazin and Schoonhoven 1996).

Much of the DOI research has focused on the process of technological innovation. This literature is developing arguments about the technological innovation process that challenges traditional adoption and diffusion theory. While it would be naïve to suggest that one set of assumptions about innovation is 'right' or 'wrong' for all possible research projects, enough work has been done to suggest that the traditional approach to innovation research should not automatically be seen as the source of correct assumptions. IS research is a case in point of technological innovation where the following four claims do not neatly align with diffusion theory:

1. *Technological innovation is fundamentally competitive and conflicting.* For technological innovation to happen, networks of interest groups must be attracted into a new technological system, and their commitment to it preserved.
2. *Technological innovation is underdetermined – there is no single "best solution"*
3. While the economists of innovation believe that technological "trajectories" make some innovation paths more likely than others the complex interplay between technological supply and market demand cannot be captured strictly with reference to the characteristics of the technology. An example of this is the VHS/Beta video player format wars of the late 1970's and early 1980's. Beta was a superior technology developed by Sony but was locked out of the market by the other competitors, namely Toshiba and Sanyo and in Europe, Phillips (Sartorius and Zundel (2005)
4. *Technological innovation cycles between periods of stability and change.* There is considerable technological literature to support the view that there are periods of incremental innovation in which technology appears to develop along well understood paths, which are then followed abruptly by periods of radical innovation in which the certainties of the past era are abandoned. Culture also plays a significant role here and is more complex than standard management definitions such as: "the way things are done around here" indicate. Culture is a complex organization of social history, norms and partnerships based on a network of human arrangements (Kilduff and Tsai, 2003). Culture is established through an on-going process whereas the forced implementation of an innovation may pose problems for adoption such as a lack of user acceptance (see principle 8 of Mumford 2006), resistance to training or "feral information systems" (Kerr, Houghton and Burgess 2007). An example of this would be the photographic industry where high speed film technology was replaced almost overnight with digital photography.

Other methodological limitations of diffusion theory include:

1. Defining technology characteristics that allow cross-study comparisons (Wolfe, 1994);
2. Pro innovation bias of adoption and diffusion research (Rogers, 1995) i.e. assuming that technological innovation is positive and will be adopted by a target population over time. *"This bias tends to lay the 'blame' of poor adoption on adopting individuals and organisations, rather than on systems or situations, and does little to help IS research understand the crucial problem of trying to learn which innovations will be of benefit, and which will not".* (Allen, 2000, p.213);
3. The difficulties of recalling past adoption decisions accurately (Rogers, 1995);
4. Inconsistency of previous research findings (Wolfe, 1994);
5. Lack of attention to community and population-level dynamics Drazin and Schoonhoven 1996);
6. A prime interest in existing literature to investigate innovation activities and their

associations, where adoption of one or more innovations is examined as the dependent variable and linked to attributes of the organization, the individual respondent and the innovation itself (Gallivan, Spitler, & Koufaris 2004). In "diffusion studies, adoption is often conceived as the dependent variable" (Russell and Hoag, 2004, p106);
7. Other restrictions that have been identified include the relative lack of attention to the adoption and diffusion stemming from the conceptualization of fixed, and unchanging innovations being diffused from producers to adopters (Allen, 2000).

While most of these concerns cycle around different issues, the higher order concept that links these issues together is context.

When we take these ideas as a framework and apply them to technological innovations an interesting pattern emerges (Table 2).

Johns (2006) notes that organisational behaviour research has a high sensitivity to context. In particular he argues that any research undertaken has to pay attention to context because the slightest change in a setting can actually change the relationships between the variables in a research program. So sensitive are these shifts that the uptake or rejection technical innovations could in reality be sensitive to context and therefore the reasons for acceptance, adoption and proliferation all depend on context.

A key assumption of DOI (and derivatives like TAM) is that it is applicable to all innovation-based contexts. The key argument being made here is: DOI does not pay attention to context. However, in order to demonstrate the key problems with DOI and context, the authors present a short framework that challenges some of the key assumptions of the innovation literature as it relates to technical contexts.

SOME KEY CONTEXTUAL FACTORS IGNORED BY DIFFUSION THEORY

Factor 1: Organizational Types

The literature surrounding innovations is replete with exemplars of technical innovations in a certain types of organisations. Most of these studies are focused on the ideas surrounding innovations and changes to organisational structure that were already planned, linear and part of an overarching change management process (Lowe and Locke [2007] discuss this in light of ERP's and the history of change that occurs over the lifetine of a package). Certain organisational types such as Government Owned Corporations (GOCs) (sometimes called QUANGOS in Britain for example) have a unique historical context, in that they were

Table 2. Problems with DOI Ideology

Problem with Diffusion Models	Technology Problem	Outcome of conflict
Technological innovation is fundamentally competitive and conflicting.	Technology acceptance may be partial and incomplete	Feral Information Systems (Kerr, Houghton and Burgess 2007),
Technological innovation is underdetermined – there is no single "best solution	Technical systems is designed for a best fit	A technical innovation may result in long lead times, a failure to understand context (Johns 2006) and other organizational issues (Orlikowski 2000, Miller, Fern and Cardinal (2007)
Technological innovation cycles between periods of stability and change.	Technological Innovation on a broad scale often focuses on major process improvements	Processes are often complex (see Stacey 2003) and legal, political issues are involved.

once state institutions that are now seeking profit. Campbell, McDonald and Sethibe (2010) have discussed this and brought to light some interesting factors for discussion including the idea that budgets and other factors present challenges that are unique in each case. As such these organisations tend to have fragmented partnerships across a broad array of departments and connections that are at time underhanded or ambiguously defined which means ambiguity challenges the 'one size fits all' systems model.

Other organisations have proved difficult to define in terms of structure like: not for profit, heavily unionised industries and volunteer organisations (see Sok, Sia, Boh and Tang (2003)). Such places are not necessarily streamlined like profit motivation ventures and a technical innovation in this sense may be haphazardly implemented. DOI assumes a linearity of context in organisational structure, particularly in it's derivative forms (TAM for example) and fails to recognise the social structures and arrangements that underpin the contexts in such settings.

Factor 2: Political Realities: The Ideal of a Best Solution

Whilst it could be argued that political contexts set the boundary for most innovations, the reality of this is not represented by the literature. Perhaps, this is because the mapping of political structures and the role they play in innovation is underdetermined by researchers or that politics being endemic in human affairs disappears from the line of sight (Quattrone and Hooper 2001). Most large scale technical innovations are political because they involve complex processes of negotiation and reconstruction of organisational realities (Orlikowski 2000).

As our leaders shape the decision making process, they also shape the tools through which we will engage and do so through complex processes of negotiation and debate with key stakeholders (Mitroff and Linstone 1993). Systems that are mandated have little political opposition, but ones that emerge from a process of complex political debate, surely do not represent a context of smooth acceptance present in DOI derivatives. Acceptance is a matter of incentives, negotiation and as researchers have discovered, workarounds and FIS (Kerr, Houghton and Burgess 2007). Post implementation these issues do not simply evaporate, they continue on and grow into complex problems despite promises from the literature pointing towards the contrary. Barker and Frolick (2003) highlight how ignoring key user problems, or the context of work, can destroy ERP implementations in complex settings. On the other side of the argument, Gargeya and Brady (2005) make the same point saying that if a cultural context isn't ready, the system will not succeed. Despite these challenges there has been very little change in researching how we adopt complex information systems.

Factor 3: Complexity, Social Networks, and Workplace Arrangements

The other important ignored contextual factor in evaluating innovations for DOI and derivative models is organisational complexity, social networks and workplace arrangements. A workplace can have any number of possible groups that form complex social networks in any given moment (Kilduff and Tsai 2003). Social networks often revolve around identities (Russell and Hoag 2004, Wenger 2004) and these are pursued by people who have built established arrangements in their social networks over a period of time.

Workplace arrangements may be easily mapped onto an organisational chart or put into a business process document, but it doesn't actually mean that work is negotiated this way or that the workplace actually operates in this fashion. Arrangements exist for bypassing organisation processes and in some cases reward systems (culturally acceptable benefits) are in place for organisational sub-systems to resist management strategy. As well as this, strategy often focuses on abstract terminology (see Mintzberg 2007) and pays little attention to what is actually done and how it is undertaken.

As some argue (Stacey [2003], Shankun [2001]) rationality for decision-making may not actually be based on the way in which complex adaptive organisational processes actually work. We may find ourselves changing and learning in the traditional organisational sense (Argyris [2003]), by questioning and challenging the assumptions we hold about technical innovations; however such learning may be emergent (Miller [1996]) and the by-product of complex interactions between people processes and systems. That is, our learning and hence technical innovations may be what we find useful because of our inability to forecast, because of complexity, rather than what we have diligently planned.

Factor 4: Mandated Systems

A final contextual factor argued to challenge the idea of linear innovations is the idea of mandated systems. Some organisations make unilateral strategic decisions to implement technical innovations and include a lack of operational input when they do so. This presents a different context altogether, a coercive context that is so often argued against in organisational change literatures (Bovey and Hede 2001*, McGuire and Hutchings 2006). Technical innovations present a unique context are ideally suited for molding organisational change processes (McAdam and Galloway 2005) and data generated by that process, into a seamless hybrid where the two in theory are perfectly integrated.

In reality, a mandated system is akin to a mandated change, likely to be accepted for a time (time enough to measure an innovation) but probably reluctantly accepted or worked around (see below) over the long haul. Mandated systems may produce a culture of conflict (as shown above) and in reality may produce the opposite ideal over an extended period of time. This makes what once appears to be accepted, not *actually* accepted over a longer time span. These kinds of systems also fall into the category of what Robey et. al (2008) call 'fashionable' systems.

Recent research conducted by the authors has provided a useful example of how systems can sometimes falter to be accepted and instead

THE EXAMPLE OF FIS

As mentioned earlier, FIS are those designed to work around established processes for the purpose of developing more effective working arrangements. The design of new work is at the heart of systems development (Gargeya and Brady [2005]) and indeed the broader promise of strategic alignment. FIS that are developed in response to adoption present a contextual challenge for diffusion theory. When looking at the contextual factors above four reasons are important for discussion.

The type of organization, as Barker and Frolick (2002) highlight, has a lot to do with the success of any systems development. In IOS the separate organisational cultures don't merge as such but interrelate between businesses. This presents yet another case for making FIS' and could explain how they are developed. Secondly, the political arrangements can produce a problem for adoption that diffusion theory may not realise as noted in Kilduff and Tsai (2003). They use the example of unionism in a factory to highlight how the slightest change in a social system can bring about completely new arrangements and partnerships between social systems. The politics of an engineering culture for example and the effects of implementing a mandated system in such an environment is something that challenges the contextual issues with diffusion theory. From this short example the amount of context that is ignored by diffusion models and ideas like TAM, present a problem that needs further research. What role would these contextual factors play in hindering or facilitating technical innovations in IOS for example?

DISCUSSION

The concept of a generalized holistic view of innovation seems reasonable; however there is no place in either TAM or DOI that is able to handle arguably the most significant factor associated with adoption, namely contextual stimuli. Contextual problems such as: organisational size and structure, government owned versus non-government owned, demographics and those mentioned above, are well documented problems in the information systems development literature. Orlikowski 1992 touched on these contextual factors when describing the different conditions of use of software where "the way software was used varied significantly depending on the group or even the individual. The inflexibility of these systems means that the use of the software cannot "vary significantly" so the only option left to individuals is to develop their own versions to either circumvent the system or adapt to its use through easy to use, contextually relevant FIS. This aspect of adoption is not a component of any version of TAM.

Moreover, TAM highlights an acceptance where issues of politics and change are considered in equilibrium. Orlikowski argues that technological issues, for example, bring out consequences that may be unpredictable. The way in which these inflexible systems are used will differ from context to context because of the nature of the power relationships, technical infrastructure and other institutional or operational pressures. Although the intention to improve the system and business operations is clear from IS literatures, it goes beyond 'critical success factors' and depends deeply on the problem areas Orlikowski discusses. For example, the 1990's saw a link forged between change planning and ERP system development literatures showing a common assumption that a new system can be shaped around an organisational change process. The IS literature has neither acknowledged the problems Orlikowski highlighted, neither has much work been done to clarify or understand such problems despite them gaining a great deal of attention in organisational and management literatures.

IOS comes with the assumption that business process integration and strategic alignment are a given, yet this chapter raises the interesting problem of contextual factors that has not really received much attention in the literature. Are these just myths of the information systems literature or are they proven through the rigours of research and practice? The growing law suits against technology vendors suggests that the promises are still in the wind. As Robey et. al (2008) point out, a majority of the IOS literature assumes that diffusion theory is an acceptable model. In this chapter however some questions have been asked of it, and the example of the growing trend of FIS was provided to highlight some of these concerns.

FUTURE RESEARCH DIRECTIONS

While these contextual factors really only begin to scratch the surface of the usefulness of TAM and the contextual factors surrounding the implementation of IOS, it has raised a few interesting points for further research. Firstly, when we begin to understand technical innovations we have to understand the context that produced it. For IOS, we cannot allow ourselves to use linear models to evaluate that change because in doing so, we may miss out on the interacting complexity that lies under the surface between two organisations. Issues such as politics, power, culture, negotiation and workplace arrangements need to be carefully investigated to see how and if they relate to innovation and most importantly the implementation of IOS. In particular for this chapter, if we are to assume that TAM and subsequent models do not provide a close a fit to the problem domain as previously suggested, then how can we assess context? Secondly, in what way will these problems impact on future IOS developments if they are ignored.

Future research needs to understand different patterns of context in technical innovations and as Johns (2006) notes, understand how sensitive the variables are. More to the point, in order to understand the concerns raised by the socio-technical aims (Mumford 2006) and the ideal of social informatics (Lamb and Kling [2003]) more attention needs to be paid to how context impacts large-scale technical IOS implementations. For example, if a system is mandated, what is the likelihood of resistance? What contextual problems: social, technical and community wise, stem from actions like these? Another example could be, in mergers and acquisitions when technological systems innovate and collide, how do two complex social interactions force changes in context… and how does that hinder innovation? Does it establish power groups?

Future research needs to look more closely at how DOI constructs would impact FIS and vice versa. A major limitation of this paper is that it fails to address the constructs of DOI and instead focuses on systemic issues with context. Before the claims of this paper can be substantiated, future research needs to be conducted on how the resistance of users impacts on DOI constructs and so forth. This would help clarify empirically exactly how well this problems are explained by DOI and user resistance. Future research should begin to model contextual factors related to DOI and understand the differing and various impacts it has on organisations, perhaps case by case or qualitatively as Johns (2006) suggests.

CONCLUSION

This chapter discussed the problem of relying on linear models of acceptance for IOS acceptance and ultimately implementation. It provided the contemporary example of FIS to support the idea that TAM was a problem and suggested future research into the deepening contextual factors that impact both IS and IOS implementation across different cultures and organizations. The chapter also raised the challenge to other researchers to follow suit and begin to find more contextual factors in future research.

REFERENCES

Alter, S. A. (2004). A work system view of DSS in its fourth decade. *Decision Support Systems*, *38*(3), 319–327. doi:10.1016/j.dss.2003.04.001

Archer-Lean, C., Clark, J., & Kerr, D. (2006). Evading technological determinism in ERP implementations: Towards a consultative social approach. *Australasian Journal of Information Systems*, *13*(2), 19–30.

Argyris, C. (2003). A life full of learning. *Organization Science*, *24*(7), 1178–1192. doi:10.1177/01708406030247009

Bagozzi, R. P. (2007). The legacy of the technology acceptance model and a proposal for a paradigm shift. *Journal of the Association for Information Systems*, *8*(4), 244–254.

Barker, T., & Frolick, M. N. (2003). ERP implementation failure: A case study. *Information Systems Management*, *20*(4), 43–47. doi:10.1201/1078/43647.20.4.20030901/77292.7

Bradford, M., & Florin, J. (2003). Examining the role of innovation diffusion factors on the implementation success of enterprise resource planning systems. *International Journal of Accounting Information Systems*, *4*(3), 205–225. doi:10.1016/S1467-0895(03)00026-5

Burgess, K. (2007). *The role of social factors in generating innovation in mature industry supply chains*. Unpublished Doctoral Thesis, RMIT.

Campbell, J., McDonald, C., & Sethibe, T. (2010). Public and private sector IT governance: Identifying contextual differences. *Australasian Journal of Information Systems, 16*(2).

Drazin, R., & Schoonhoven, C. B. (1996). Community, population, and organization effects on innovation: A multilevel perspective. *Academy of Management Journal, 39*(5), 1065–1083. doi:10.2307/256992

Fichman, R. G. (2004). Going beyond the dominant paradigm for Information Technology innovation research: Emerging concepts and methods. *Journal of the Association for Information Systems, 5*(8), 314–355.

Gallivan, M. J., Spitler, V. K., & Koufaris, M. (2004). Does Information Technology training really matter? A social information processing analysis of coworkers' influence on IT usage in the workplace. *Journal of Management Information Systems, 22*(1), 153–192.

Gargeya, V., & Brady, C. (2005). Success and failure factors of adopting SAP in ERP system implementation. *Business Process Management Journal, 11*(5), 511–516. doi:10.1108/14637150510619858

Hale, J. L., Householder, B. J., & Greene, K. L. (2003). The theory of reasoned action. In Dillard, J. P., & Pfau, M. (Eds.), *The persuasion handbook: Developments in theory and practice* (pp. 259–286). Thousand Oaks, CA: Sage.

Houghton, L., & Kerr, D. V. (2006). A study into the creation of feral information systems as a response to an ERP implementation within the supply chain of a large government-owned corporation. *International Journal of Internet and Enterprise Management, 4*(1), 135–147.

Johns, G. (2006). The essential impact of context on organisational behaviour. *Academy of Management Review, 31*(2), 386–408. doi:10.5465/AMR.2006.20208687

Kerr, D. V., Houghton, L., & Burgess, K. (2007). Power relationships that lead to the development of Feral Systems. *Australasian Journal of Information Systems, 14*(2), 141–152.

Kilduff, M., & Tsai, W. (2003). *Social networks and organizations*. USA: Sage.

Lamb, R., & Kling, R. (2003). Reconceptualizing users as social actors in Information Systems research. *Management Information Systems Quarterly, 27*(2), 197–236.

Lowe, A., & Locke, J. (2007). *Biography of an ERP: Tracing the fabrication of a virtual object*. (Department of Accounting Working Paper Series, Number 93). Hamilton, New Zealand: University of Waikato.

Markus, L., Steinfield, C. W., Wigand, R. T., & Minton, G. (2006). Industry-wide Information Systems standardization as collective action: The case of the US residential mortgage industry. *Management Information Systems Quarterly, 30*, 439–465.

McGuire, D., & Hutchings, K. (2006). A Machiavellian analysis of organisational change. *Journal of Organizational Change Management, 19*(2), 192–209. doi:10.1108/09534810610648906

Miller, D. (1996). A preliminary topology of organisational learning: Synthesising the literature. *Journal of Management, 22*(3), 485–505. doi:10.1177/014920639602200305

Miller, D. J., Fern, M. J., & Cardinal, L. B. (2007). The use of knowledge for technological innovation within diversified firms. *Academy of Management Journal, 50*(2), 308–326. doi:10.5465/AMJ.2007.24634437

Mintzberg, H. (2007). *Tracking strategies*. USA: Oxford University Press.

Mitroff, I. I., & Linstone, H. A. (1994). *The unbounded mind*. USA: Oxford University Press.

Mumford, E. (2006). The story of socio-technical design: Reflections on its successes, failures and potential. *Information Systems Journal, 16*, 317–342. doi:10.1111/j.1365-2575.2006.00221.x

Orlikowski, W. (1992). The duality of technology: Rethinking the concept of technology in organizations. *Organization Science, 3*(3), 398–427. doi:10.1287/orsc.3.3.398

Orlikowski, W. J. (2000). Using technology and constituting structures: A practice lens for studying technology in organizations. *Organization Science, 11*(4), 404–420. doi:10.1287/orsc.11.4.404.14600

Quattrone, P., & Hopper, T. (2001). What does organisational change mean? Speculations of a taken for granted category. *Management Accounting Research, 12*(4), 403–435. doi:10.1006/mare.2001.0176

Robey, D., Im, G., & Wareham, J. D. (2008). Theoretical foundations of empirical research on interorganizational systems: Assessing past contributions and guiding future directions. *Journal of the Association for Information Systems, 9*(9), 497–518.

Rogers, E. M. (1995). *Diffusion of innovations*. New York, NY: Free Press.

Russell, D. M., & Hoag, A. M. (2004). People and information technology in the supply chain: Social and organizational influences on adoption. *International Journal of Physical Distribution & Logistics Management, 34*(1/2), 102–122. doi:10.1108/09600030410526914

Sartorius, C., & Zundel, S. (2005). *Time strategies, innovation and environmental policy*. Cheltenham, UK: Edward Elgar.

Shakun, M. F. (2001). Unbounded rationality. *Group Decision and Negotiation, 10*(2), 97–118. doi:10.1023/A:1008708222157

Sok, C., Sia, S. K., Boh, W. F., & Tang, M. (2003). Misalignments in ERP implementation: A dialectic perspective. *International Journal of Human-Computer Interaction, 16*(3), 81–100.

Stacey, R. (2003). Learning as an activity of interdependent people. *The Learning Organization, 10*(6), 323–331. doi:10.1108/09696470310497159

Tornatzky, L. G., & Klein, R. J. (1982). Innovation characteristics and innovation adoption-implementation: A meta-analysis of findings. *IEEE Transactions on Engineering Management, 29*, 28–45.

Venkatesh, V., & Bala, H. (2008). Technology acceptance model 3 and a research agenda on interventions. *Decision Sciences, 39*(2), 273–315. doi:10.1111/j.1540-5915.2008.00192.x

Wenger, E. (2004). Knowledge management as a doughnut: Shaping your knowledge strategy through communities of practice. *Ivey Business Journal Online*, January/February 2004.

Wolfe, R. A. (1994). Organizational innovation: Review, critique and suggested research directions. *Organizational Dynamics, 31*(3), 403.

ENDNOTES

1. http://www.computerworlduk.com/management/it-business/supplier-relations/news/index.cfm?newsid=18517
2. http://www.informationweek.com/news/global-cio/trends/showArticle.jhtml?articleID=207000149

Chapter 14
Public E-Procurement Implementation:
Insights from the Structuration Theory

José Rodrigues Filho
Universidade Federal da Paraíba, Brazil

Flavio Perazzo Barbosa Mota
Universidade Federal da Paraíba, Brazil

ABSTRACT

Today most e-government and e-procurement research and discussion are done in a quite utilitarian and technical way. This follows the worldwide positivist and utilitarian approach to research that neglects the social, organizational, cultural, and political aspects of social life. Therefore, most research initiatives are based on a market-driven and utilitarian approach in which technology is treated as a mere tool. So, under the use of a traditional top-down model or the "tool-approach," information and communication technologies (ICTs) have been implemented in developing countries detached from their social and political context, as an instrumental, static, elitist, and uncritical utilitarian approach, neglecting a deep investigation of how social, economic, and political factors are embedded in technology. In addition, most of the literature on e-procurement has been studied primarily from a business-to-business (B2B) perspective, and the field of public sector procurement has been neglected. Although public e-procurement has similarities with the private sector, it also has some special characteristics that make it different. Therefore, it is not clear to what extent recent decisions on public e-procurement have been optimal. In the broad competing views of information technology (IT), interpretative or constructivist approaches see the use of IT as the result of conflicts, negotiations, and interpretations of various interests that make it socially constructed. These competing views of technology help the formulation of an appropriate debate on e-procurement that holds enormous potential for cost savings, efficiency and

DOI: 10.4018/978-1-60960-768-5.ch014

Copyright © 2012, IGI Global. Copying or distributing in print or electronic forms without written permission of IGI Global is prohibited.

benefit gains, and transparency. In this work, an attempt was made to show how qualitative research traditions like structuration theory (specifically the perspective of "dialectic of control") and qualitative research analysis can be used in the analysis of e-procurement in Brazil, leading to results that differ substantially from the mainstream positivist research that does not always touch the barriers and challenges that can constrain the adoption and implementation of public e-procurement projects.

INTRODUCTION

In recent years, developing countries have increasingly adopted ICT to enhance government services and business transactions. In Brazil, for instance, e-procurement is a very basic e-government tool that is said to have the potential to improve efficiency in government administration and achieve better governance.

However, despite the enthusiastic discourse of public administration modernization through the adoption and development of ICT, literature has shown that successful implementation of e-procurement technology remains a challenge in both developed and developing countries. It is stated that e-procurement requires a fundamental transformation of traditional government organization and development infrastructure, in addition to financial and human resources. In that case, a "successful transparent e-procurement system requires policies, legislation, and a legal framework conducive to reorganizing the Government and its services to the citizens, businesses and institutions" (United Nations, 2006, p. iii).

It is stated that the benefits of e-procurement are numerous in terms of enhancing transparency of transactions, saving time and lowering costs, increasing productivity, and standardizing and integrating processes. However, there are a multitude of barriers and challenges, especially in developing countries, where infrastructures are underdeveloped and human resources in both private and public sector are not trained. It is mentioned that before "an e-procurement system can achieve maximum potential, a strong infrastructure must be developed, ICT services expanded, innovative policies administered to establish a secure online environment, standard developed" (United Nations, 2006, p.3), and leadership and government reorganization are required.

Today most e-government and e-procurement research and discussion are done in a quite utilitarian and technical way. This follows the worldwide positivist and utilitarian approach to research that neglects the social, organizational, cultural and political aspects of social life. Therefore, most research initiatives are based on a market-driven and utilitarian approach in which technology is treated as a mere tool. So, under the use of a traditional top-down model or the "tool-approach", ICTs have been implemented in developing countries detached from their social and political context, as an instrumental, static, elitist, and uncritical utilitarian approach, neglecting a deep investigation of how social, economic, and political factors are embedded in technology.

Although public e-procurement has similarities with the private sector, it also has some special characteristics that make it different. Therefore, it is not clear to which extent recent decisions on public e-procurement have been optimal. Further to this, IT is not value neutral, because it is developed and designed by hegemonic interests to manipulate, control, and dominate public consciousness (Feenberg, 1996).

As the implementation of e-procurement is extremely challenging and its impacts are unclear, a number of e-procurement initiatives have been abandoned in recent times (Cuganesan & Lee, 2006). This has increased the preoccupation with the use of e-procurement technology (Davila, Guppa & Palmer, 2003), especially when its expected growth rate has been moving downwards: "Recent market observations indicate that the adoption and integration of e-procurement technologies into the business mainstream is occurring at a much slower than expected pace" (Davila et al, 2003, p. 12).

In this work we propose to move from the dominant positivist research paradigm used to fit most e-procurement studies to other paradigms of organizational study as proposed by Burrell and Morgan (1979), contemplating e-procurement with interpretivism, radical humanism, and radical structuralism, in an attempt to provide answers to the many questions related to social and organizational changes.

In the broad competing views of IT, interpretative or constructivist approaches see the use of IT as the result of conflicts, negotiations, and interpretations of various interests that make it socially constructed. These competing views of technology help the formulation of an appropriate debate on e-procurement that holds enormous potential for cost savings, efficiency and benefit gains, transparency, in addition to the expansion of democratic practice. However, if we continue to follow the current path, e-procurement will perpetuate a system of muted democracy and exclusion.

In this work, an attempt was made to show how qualitative research traditions like structuration theory (specifically the perspective of "dialectic of control") and qualitative research analysis can be used in the analysis of e-procurement in Brazil, leading to results that differ substantially from the mainstream positivist research that does not always touch the barriers and challenges that can constrain the adoption and implementation of public e-procurement projects.

FROM DOMINANT POSITIVISM TO A QUALITATIVE APPROACH TO E-PROCUREMENT

Under the use of a traditional top-down model or the "tool-approach", ICTs have been implemented in developing countries detached from their social and political context, as an instrumental, static, elitist, and uncritical utilitarian approach, neglecting a deep investigation of how social, economic, and political factors are embedded in technology.

What is more, it is stated that there is a lack of training in qualitative research methods such as action research, critical research and interpretative research, especially in the American business schools that usually adopt a functionalist and positivist perspective (Trauth, 2001, Orlikowski, 1991). In addition, it is recognized that information systems (IS) research is guided in most parts of the world: "by a dominant, positivist worldview that sanctioned methodologies consistent with a positivist research perspective" (Trauth, 2001, p. 11).

Trauth has mentioned all the pressure that researchers have to face to remain in the methodological mainstream, when the academic politics of publishing (publish or perish) can dissuade them from ever choosing qualitative research: "He argues that a solely rational view of the publication process that doesn't incorporate the social and political views impedes publication of qualitative research" (Trauth, 2001, p. 285). If the interpretative perspective is suffering such pressure, what about the critical theory perspective that tries to expose inherent conflicts and contradictions, and all sorts of exploitation, manipulated interests, power relations and (mis)use of IS, especially due to the greater number of IS failures all over the world.

It has been stated that in the United States alone, only 62% of software projects were considered successful (Verner et al, 2006). Due to the worldwide spending in IT that is estimated to reach 1.48 trillion US dollars by 2010 (Urbach,

Smolnik & Riempp, 2009), it is urgent to develop more critical research work not only to measure IS success but to identify the interested groups involved in such transactions that, in many instances, result in negative consequences for the population as a whole.

In the developing world the pressure not to develop interpretative and critical theory research work in the field of IT goes beyond that of the developed world, because to embark on this kind of academic work means a complete isolation of the researcher. This is unfortunate, when it becomes so clear that these two perspectives can be useful to annul the violent isolation of men and women from one another.

Despite the enthusiastic view all over the world about the launching of e-procurement systems and the benefits already mentioned in the literature, there seem to be some contradictions that, with few exceptions, are explored in most academic studies. While it is mentioned that e-procurement in Brazil is intended to provide an instrument for social control of public expenditure through its public transparency, in the benefit of citizens and society, there are claims that the use of IT results in reinforcing and increasing power control only over lower bureaucracy (Sanchez, 2003). Consequently, ICTs may not have brought more transparency in the areas where the political elite, legislators and the high bureaucracy deal with high public resources transactions. In this case, e-government can reinforce dominant institutions at the expense of reducing citizenship (Rodrigues Filho, 2010).

Structuration Theory: The Study of IT in Organizations

Structuration theory has been widely used to explore IT use in organizations, in addition to its uses in other areas of management qualitative research. Therefore, Giddens' structuration theory is a very rich paradigm to be used in interpretative and critical studies. He is considered to be a critical theorist especially because he takes power seriously, and is: "concerned with questions of structure, its reproduction and social transformation – all of which are central to the broader critical tradition" (Prasad, 2005, p. 184). It is argued that this: "represents a serious attempt to blend the central assumptions of the interpretive traditions with those of structuralism within a wider framework of power and domination that is more the hallmark of the critical tradition" (Prasad, 2005, p. 185).

Due to the complexity of structuration theory, it is claimed that translating Giddens' ideas in the application of empirical work is open to question, especially in the field of IS: "where structuration theory enjoys considerable popularity". It is argued that there is a tendency to emphasize human action (agency), neglecting social structure that mediates (by facilitation or constraint) the human action (Prasad, 2005, p.184).

In his structuration theory, Giddens (1984) does not explicitly address the issue of technology. It was in the influential work of Orlikowski (1992) that the attempt was made to use structuration theory to study technology within organizational settings. Based on Orlikowski's (1992) framework, that tries to analyze the interaction between human action and social structures, some research work has been done in Brazil involving the implementation of e-government initiatives, including e-procurement.

As mentioned, structuration theory is concerned with the interplay of agents' actions and social structures, and can be used in the study of e-procurement as a system of management control. Although power is centrally implicated in the concept of control, both power and domination still remain unexplored in the management control literature. Giddens (1984) maintains that in power struggles the dialectic of control is always in operation. Therefore, power relations and its contradictions and conflicts in organizations involve reproduced relations of autonomy and dependence. They involve a two-way process, even where the power of one individual is minimal in comparison to that of another (Giddens, 1979).

Consequently, if e-procurement, as a control system, is designed and implemented to constrain the behavior of subordinates, yet those subordinates also have the potential to manipulate any control mechanism to their advantage: "Even new control mechanisms will provide skilled and knowledgeable subordinates in organisations with new opportunities to exploit the control potentials for their own benefits" (Nandan, 1998, p. 135). In that case, management control systems cannot be seen as foolproof systems to bring about coordination and control in organizations.

For the analysis of power in social systems, the dialectic of control as proposed by Giddens (1979, 1984) can be seen as a rich concept to integrate the top-down and bottom-up positions. In this work it is argued: "that the two-way character of power makes it a form of control in which the less powerful are usually able to exert some control over the more powerful" (Nandan, 1998, p.139), as it is implicit in the agency oriented conception of power in Giddens' structuration theory. In short, the dialectic of control means that those in a subordinate position can influence the activities of their superiors, because they have some resources at their disposal. The duality of structure means that social structures (signification, domination, and legitimation) are constituted by human actions and, at the same time, are the medium of this constitution.

There are few studies on qualitative research in Brazil that try to take a more critical stance on e-government when compared to studies that use a quantitative or qualitative positivist approach (Rodrigues Filho & Mota, 2010). However, while structuration theory has been used in the study of implementation of some IT applications in both public and private institutions in Brazil, emphasizing the duality of technology, qualitative content analysis, as proposed by (Glaser & Laudel, 2009) has been used in local e-government implementations, demonstrating citizens' frustration with the lack of improvement in interaction and political participation (Rodrigues Filho & Santos Junior, 2009). Other critical studies on e-government in Brazil have stated that it is an isolated sector for technical professionals, because the wider society is absent in its politico-organizational architecture (Marcondes & Jardim, 2003).

In the next sections an attempt is made to describe one of the most important e-government initiatives (e-procurement) in Brazil and to apply the structurational model in order to show that the mainstream quantitative and qualitative positivist research approaches do not always touch the barriers and challenges that can constrain the adoption and implementation of e-procurement projects, especially in terms of power and context.

PUBLIC E-PROCUREMENT INITIATIVE IN BRAZIL

The public administration in Brazil has been undergoing technological, political, social and economic changes, seeking a management model based on the principles of New Public Management (NPM), with the support of ICTs. The movement to rethink the role of the public administration began with the preparation and publication of a government official document in 1995, which resulted in, among other measures, the inclusion of the principle of efficiency in the country's federal constitution, stating the government adaptation to new concepts and tasks assigned to the state. Thus, over the last decade, the Brazilian government has searched for solutions to modernize and computerize all the spheres of the administrative public sector. Therefore, the use of electronic tools in the federal government increased substantially, either through the Internet or other applications to automate administrative processes.

The new public administration reform in Brazil is similar to many other reforms that have taken place all over the world in the transition of the bureaucratic model to a managerial model, using techniques of the private sector in the public administration (Fadul & Silva, 2008). Thus, it is stated that the Brazilian public reform is intended to offer better and more qualified information to support public managers' decisions, aiming to increase transparency, and democratic initiatives with citizen orientation (Bresser-Pereira, 1998).

It was natural, therefore, that this reform movement in Brazil was to reach one of the most controversial areas of the public administration: procurement. Public procurement in Brazil is very much regulated with a law that contemplates all procedures necessary for public administration purchasing and contracting. In 2002, the initiative was to use the potential of ICTs in this area, when a new law was passed bringing about the possibility to have the procurement processes working electronically, through the Internet portal named "Comprasnet". This portal operates a reverse auction system called "pregão". In the electronic space of pregão, the reverse public auctions occur without the real presence of the public official or reverse auctioneer in charge of the e-procurement process. The bids are made electronically by suppliers, previously registered on Comprasnet. Specifically, the operation of pregão happens in a division/sector of each public institution in Brazil responsible for the purchasing process. This implies that each institution individually is responsible for the buying process.

Therefore, Comprasnet is the Brazilian government's e-procurement system of the direct administration, including many public foundations and autonomous agencies. It was set up, firstly, by the Secretariat of Logistics and IT in the Brazilian Ministry of Planning, Budget and Management. This is a Web-based online procurement system used by more than 2,000 federal government procurement units, that enables online price quoting and reverse auction commodity purchases: "Comprasnet is a system where Brazil Federal Government organizations register their procurement needs (i.e. goods and services they need to buy). The system automatically informs registered suppliers by e-mail and the supplier may download the bidding documents"(Almeida, 2006, p. 497).

It is estimated that more than 200,000 registered suppliers of goods and services to the federal government are affected by this system. Comprasnet "was introduced to automate the procurement process. The aim of automation is to render the procurement process uniform without centralizing the buying process of the Federal organizations. It was also intended to reduce procurement costs and give more transparency to the process" (Almeida, 2006, p. 498). In addition, it is stated that: "the system aimed to increase the number of government suppliers; to reduce participation costs for these suppliers; and to increase competition among suppliers, which should also bring about cost reductions and better quality of goods and services acquired" (Almeida, 2006, p.498).

The official discourse praised Comprasnet as a world pioneer. It is mentioned that it is the only system in Brazil acknowledged by the World Bank (BIRD) and by the Inter-American Development Bank (IDB) as a secure system: "According to a 2006 World Bank study in electronic procurement, Comprasnet achieved the maximum efficiency standards in indicators for evaluating transparency, in divulging the auctions as well as their results, and in using competitive bidding methods" (Santana, 2007, p. 5).

There is considerable evidence of e-procurement annual cost savings and efficiency and effectiveness gains in the private sector that can potentially reach the same level in the public sector where perceived benefits are not substantiated by consistent quantitative and/or qualitative evidence, due to the lack of standardized measurement procedures and criteria. However, other studies on e-procurement, especially on e-auctions, have raised some concerns (Davila et al, 2003; Emiliani & Stec, 2004; Smeltzer & Carr 2003). While it is stated that "E-auctions can reduce purchase prices, save time, streamline the bidding process" enhancing competition, the "risks of e-auctions include damaging supplier relationships, switching to suppliers who are not capable, underestimating the total costs associated with using suppliers with lower purchase prices, and negatively impacting the supply market in the long run by driving out qualified suppliers" (Hartley, Lane & Duplaga, 2006).

Some researchers have mentioned that in private firms there were varying return on investments (ROI) on their e-auction programs (Handfield, Straight & Stirling, 2002), and "e-auction use has not reached the initial optimistic projections made in the late 1990s" (Hur, Mabert & Hartley, 2007). In addition, concerns with ethics and supplier relationships may be the barriers to e-auction adoption in many firms, besides limited economic benefits (Hur et al, 2007). It is stated: "that while many supply managers are not philosophically opposed to e-auctions, they cannot economically justify e-auction costs" (Hur et al, 2007). While, it has been demonstrated (Jap, 2003): "that e-auctions may increase suppliers' mistrust of buying firms, since the open-bid process was considered exploitative and unfair" (Hur et al, 2007).

Methodology

The case study was conducted over a time period of four months in five Brazilian public institutions, between July and October of 2009. Semi-structured interviews were conducted in the workplaces to gather information on the project of e-procurement implementation in each institution. The interviewees were selected from auction executives and auctioneers, and 12 of them were interviewed during this period, with each interview lasting about two hours, on average. The second author took notes on all significant conversations, and tape-recorded the in-depth personal interviews. After each interview he listened to it repeatedly and transcribed its important sections. Our present analysis draws on notes taken by the interviewer, revised literature information, and transcriptions of in-depth personal interviews.

In addition, secondary data was collected from various sources in public institutions in Brazil responsible for e-procurement activities. An extensive literature review was done on e-government in both Brazil and other countries. As e-procurement in Brazil is mediated through the Web portal named Comprasnet, which aims to provide information to the public administration, some information was also obtained from Comprasnet. Due to space limitations it is not possible to discuss all the issues covered in the e-procurement study that can be found in the recent work developed by Mota (2010).

FROM EFFICIENCY AND BENEFIT GAINS TO RISKS AND CONTRADICTIONS

All interviewees stressed that the implementation of e-procurement in the public administration resulted in cost savings, which seems to be the main factor for many government agencies to adopt it. There is no doubt that high volumes of purchases will help in getting better prices and higher savings from suppliers. Other vital benefits mentioned by the interviewees were process efficiency, transparency in the process, and better information flow between government agencies and suppliers.

It is stated that cost and time are the two most important measures for the success of procurement processes (Eadie et al, 2007). In a United States survey in 2001, 75% of the respondents cited reduction in costs (Eadie et al, 2007), while in Australia this figure was between 75 and 80% (Hawking et al 2004). Cost reduction has also been highlighted in the United Kingdom (Erridge, Fee & McIlroy, 2001) and in China (Kong, Li & Love, 2001). It is also mentioned that time savings through e-procurement has been achieved. In Sweden, for instance, it was found that reduction in time has been proved to be a relevant e-procurement driver: "E-procurement is a rapid efficient method of finding and connecting new sources, being a lean channel for communication" (Knudsen, 2003, 723).

However, some interviewees have expressed some risks associated with e-procurement: lack of integration between the government system and the system used by the suppliers, and connectivity; system failures and out of date technological infrastructure; resistance to change; in addition to poor product acquisition that resulted from the poor system codification system. This shows that the implementation of e-procurement is extremely challenging.

Literature has shown that the above factors remain as barriers to implementation of a system of e-procurement. Resistance to change is pointed out as: "one of the biggest barriers to the introduction of e-procurement within the public sector" (Eadie et al, 2007, p. 111). For Davila et al (2003), resistance to change and leadership are seen as cultural barriers that are highlighted as barriers in the United States. It is stated that these: "produce a slowdown in adoption of e-procurement and result in a failure to reap many of the perceived benefits. Therefore a cultural change needs to take place prior to adoption of an e-procurement system" (Eadie et al, 2007, p. 111). In addition, some interviewees mentioned that the government does not have the appropriate technology to carry out e-procurement. The lack of IT infrastructure and training were also mentioned as vital barriers to e-procurement.

Security of transactions and confidentiality were not mentioned by the interviewees, but these seem to be significant barriers to e-procurement in other countries. Legal issues were not raised as a barrier to e-procurement in Brazil, but it is known that Web-based systems will need to be tested in court in some cases in order to overcome this barrier. To talk about the drivers or benefits of IT in general and e-procurement in particular without touching on power relations is to have a limited view of the whole problem.

It is argued that e-procurement is an instrument of control and domination that: "imposes a mode of organizing and changing social relationships" (Dillard et al, 2005, p. 115). There are different types of control: personal, social, and dialectic control described by Giddens (1984), as all forms of dependence in which subordinates can influence the activities of their superiors. Therefore, Giddens' (1984, p. 16) notion of agency, known as dialectic of control, recognizes that: "all forms of dependence offer some resource whereby those who are subordinate can influence the activities of their superiors". In this case, structuration theory holds the view that people are empowered within organizations as they have the action (agency) to draw upon existing rules and resources in the social system to face or resist the dominant actors.

It was found in this research that some people choose to refuse to use e-procurement, thereby constraining the public administration because the e-procurement technology is not truly accepted and appropriated. It is an instrument of management control, thus re-enforcing the structure of domination where the human agents (users and managers) actively use and appropriate it, because unintentionally they reinforce the institutionalized control imposed on them through the technology. However, it became clear that some sectors do not rely on the e-procurement system, and resist using it.

Public e-procurement is not just a quick fix that can speed up the buying process in the public administration. In some institutions, it became clear that not all users involved in the bidding process fully understand it, constraining the specifications of products and services, a key factor to achieve quality. In other words, it was argued that the lack of concern of some sectors at the time of description causes the acquisition of products and services to be of poor quality. It was mentioned that another issue that influences the quality of goods and services occurs when the bid requires a prior sample for standardization of specifications.

It is evident that particular attention is needed, because suppliers do not always deliver the ordered product as it should be. Most interviewees confirmed that users of products in the institutions studied always complained about the poor quality of some products that in the traditional procurement process would never have been acquired. This demonstrates the dual character of this technology, because while it enables human action, it also limits the e-procurement itself. By resisting using the system, users exercise their human action to face the most powerful that always are mentioning the positive aspects of e-procurement, but neglect to mention the lack of transparency in the system adoption and implementation.Unfortunately, neither the users of products acquired by the e-procurement system nor people responsible for its distribution within each organization were interviewed.

While it was found in this work that e-procurement is an extremely rich tool for managerial control in the public administration, it was neglected that power relations involve a two-way process, even where the power of one individual is minimal in comparison to that of another (Giddens, 1984). Through the dialectic of control it is possible to understand how actors exercise human action (agency) to counteract powerful agents that dominate social systems.

Therefore, following the theoretical understanding of Giddens (1979), it was noted that the introduction of e-procurement is supported through human actions, including legal measures adopted, the commitment of top management, users' involvement, and the recognition of suppliers. This is an example of an effective way to control the understanding and the actions of users, who are taking the rules, knowledge and assumptions incorporated in the system and implemented to perform tasks. This was perceived to be a reaffirmation of the status quo, with reinforcement of legitimation, signification and domination structures in the Brazilian public administration (Giddens, 1979), indicating that there are many unsolved and inherent questions embedded in e-procurement, that can be broadened with the use of research approaches outside the standard positivist dominance.

In short, we have found that there are some contradictions in the implementation and use of e-procurement in public institutions in Brazil, at both the federal and state levels, that need to be investigated as part of a deep auditing of the e-procurement system in terms of costs, transparency, and appropriation.

CONCLUSION

Public e-procurement in Brazil is one of the most important applications of e-government that is shared across multiple public foundations and agencies, realizing economies of scale. It has been mentioned that the benefits of e-procurement will enhance transparency, save time and lower costs, streamline and integrate processes, and increase productivity.

The lack of transparency and accountability are prevalent in public procurement, but it is mentioned that e-procurement encourages full computerization of procurement procedures and is a deterrent to lack of compliance and corruption, facilitating transparent public decision making. However, it is worth mentioning that technology alone will not solve these problems, especially in the public sector, that involves governance, and organizational and behavioral changes. If the benefits are so great, why are the information and statistics needed to analyze the procurement process not available or so incomplete? There is a need for a deep audit of e-procurement activities in developing countries, especially in Brazil.

E-procurement is an extremely rich tool for managerial control in the public administration, but it is neglected that power relations involve a two-way process, even where the power of one individual is minimal in comparison to that of another (Giddens, 1984). Structuration theory facilitates understanding through the dialectic of control of how actors exercise human action (agency) to counteract powerful agents that dominate social systems. Giddens' idea of the dialectic of control in the contextual study of public e-procurement as a management control tool was emphasized, highlighting the public interest role of management controls in the context of public sector reforms.

In this empirical work done in Brazil it was found that some people choose to refuse to use public e-procurement, thereby constraining the public administration because the e-procurement technology is not truly accepted and appropriated. It is an instrument of management control, thus re-enforcing the structure of domination where the human agents (users and managers) actively use and appropriate it, because unintentionally they reinforce the institutionalized control imposed on them through the technology. However, it became clear that some sectors do not rely on the e-procurement system, and resist using it.

The research findings show that there are many unsolved and inherent questions embedded in public e-procurement, that can be broadened with the use of research approaches outside the standard positivist dominance that do not always touch the challenges that constrain the adoption and implementation of e-government projects, especially in developing countries.

REFERENCES

Almeida, M. O. (2006). Role of ICT in diminishing collusion in procurement. *International Public Procurement Conference Proceedings,* 21-23 September. Rome, Italy.

Bresser-Pereira, L. C. (1998). *Reforma de Estado para a cidadania: A reforma gerencial brasileira na perspectiva internacional.* Brasília: ENAP.

Burrell, G., & Morgan, G. (1979). *Sociological paradigms and organizational analysis.* London, UK: Heinemann Press.

Cuganesan, S., & Lee, R. (2006). Intra-organisational influences in procurement networks controls: The impacts of information technology. *Management Accounting Research, 17*, 141–170. doi:10.1016/j.mar.2005.12.005

Davila, A., Guppa, M., & Palmer, R. (2003). Moving procurement systems to the Internet: The adoption and use of e-procurement technology models. *European Management Journal, 21*(1), 11–23. doi:10.1016/S0263-2373(02)00155-X

Dillard, J. F., Ruchala, L., & Yuthas, K. (2005). Enterprise resource planning systems: A physical manifestation of administrative evil. *International Journal of Accounting Information Systems, 6*, 107–127. doi:10.1016/j.accinf.2005.02.001

Eadie, R., Perera, S., Heaney, G., & Carlysle, J. (2007). Drivers and barriers to public sector e-procurement within Northern Ireland's Construction Industry. *Itcon, 12*, 103–120.

Emiliani, M., & Stec, D. (2004). Aerospace parts supplier's reaction to online reverse auctions. *Supply Chain Management, 9*(2), 139–153. doi:10.1108/13598540410527042

Erridge, A., Fee, R., & McIlroy, J. (2001). *Best practice procurement: Public and private sector perspectives.* Burlington, MA: Gover.

Fadul, E. M. C., & Silva, L. P. (2008). *Retomando o debate sobre a reforma do Estado e a nova administração pública. XXXII EnANPAD.* Rio de Janeiro, Brazil: ANPAD.

Feenberg, A. (1996). Marcuse or Habermas: Two critiques of technology. *Inquiry, 39*, 45–70. doi:10.1080/00201749608602407

Giddens, A. (1979). *Central problems in social theory.* Berkeley, CA: University of California Press.

Giddens, A. (1984). *The constitution of society.* Cambridge, MA: Polity Press.

Gläser, J., & Laudel, G. (2009). *Expertinterviews und qualitative Inhaltsanalyse*. Wiesbaden, Germany: VS Verlag.

Handfield R. B., Straight S. L. & Stirling WA. (2002). Reverse auctions: How do supply managers really feel about them. *Inside Supply Management, 13*(11), 56–61.

Hartley, J. L., Lane, M. D., & Duplaga, E. A. (2006). Exploring the barriers to the adoption of e-auctions for sourcing. *International Journal of Operations & Production Management, 26*(2), 202–221. doi:10.1108/01443570610641675

Hawking, P., Stein, A., Wyld, D., & Forster, S. (2004). E-procurement: Is the ugly duckling actually a swan down under? *Asia Pacific Journal of Marketing and Logistics, 16*(1), 1–26. doi:10.1108/13555850410765140

Hur, D., Mabert, V. A., & Hartley, J. L. (2007). Getting the most out of reverse e-auction investment. *Omega, 35*, 403–416. doi:10.1016/j.omega.2005.08.003

Jap, S. D. (2003). An exploratory study of the introduction of online reverse auctions. *Journal of Marketing, 67*, 96–107. doi:10.1509/jmkg.67.3.96.18651

Knudsen, D. (2003). Aligning corporate strategy, procurement strategy and e-procurement tools. *International Journal of Physical Distribution & Logistics Management, 33*(8), 720–734. doi:10.1108/09600030310502894

Kong, C., Li, H., & Love, P. (2001). An e-commerce system for construction material procurement. *Construction Innovation, 1*(1), 43–54.

Marcondes, C. H., & Jardim, J. M. (2003). Políticas de informação governamental: A construção do governo eletrônico na administração federal do Brasil. *Revista de Ciência da Informação, 4*(2).

Mota, F. P. B. (2010). *Processo eletrônico de compras públicas na perspectiva da DUALIDADE da tecnologia: Um estudo comparado no contexto brasileiro e paraibano. Dissertação (Mestrado em Administração)*. João Pessoa: Universidade Federal da Paraíba.

Nandan, R. K. (1998). The dialectic of power – Implications for management accounting and control research. *Journal of Pacific Studies, 22*, 133–158.

Orlikowski, W. J. (1991). *Relevance versus rigor in Information Systems research: An issue of quality – The role of institutions in creating research norms*. Panel Presentation at the IFIP TC8/WG 8.2 Working Conference on the Information Systems Research Challenges, Perception and Alternative Approaches, Copenhagen, Denmark.

Orlikowski, W. J. (1992). The duality of technology: Rethinking the concept of technology in organizations. *Organization Science, 3*(3), 398–427. doi:10.1287/orsc.3.3.398

Prasad, P. (2005). *Crafting qualitative research*. Armonk, NY: M.E. Sharpe.

Rodrigues, F. J., & Santos, J. R. Jr. (2009). Local e-government in Brazil – Poor interaction and local politics as usual. In Reddick, C. G. (Ed.), *Handbook of research on strategies for local e-government adoption and implementation – Comparative studies* (*Vol. 2*, pp. 863–878). Hershey, PA: IGI Global.

Rodrigues Filho, J. (2010). E-government in Brazil – Reinforcing institutions or reducing citizenship? In Reddick, C. (Ed.), *Politics, democracy and e-government – Participation and service delivery* (pp. 347–362). Hershey, PA: IGI Global. doi:10.4018/978-1-61520-933-0.ch021

Rodrigues Filho, J., & Mota, F. P. B. (2010). *E-government research – From a utilitarian quantitative and qualitative positivist approach to an in-depth critical and reflexive engagement with theoretical issues*. Qualitative Research on Administration and Organization Conference, New Mexico, 2010.

Sanchez, O. A. (2003). O poder burocrático e o controle da informação. *Lua nova Revista de Cultura e Política, 58*, 89-119.

Santana, R. (2007). *Electronic procurement allow for inspection by society. Global forum on governance: Modernising government: strategies & tools for change*. Retrieved from http://www.oecd.org/dataoecd/0/51/39612372.pdf

Smeltzer, L., & Carr, A. (2003). Electronic reverse auctions: Promises, risks, and conditions for success. *Industrial Marketing Management, 32*(6), 481–488. doi:10.1016/S0019-8501(02)00257-2

Trauth, E. M. (2001). The choice of qualitative methods in IS research. In Trauth, E. M. (Ed.), *Qualitative research in IS: Issues and trends* (pp. 1–19). Hershey, PA: Idea Group Publishing.

United Nations. (2006). *E-procurement. Economic and social commission for Asia and the Pacific Asian*. Thailand: Development Bank Institute.

Urbach, N., Smolnik, S., & Riempp, G. (2009). The state of research on information systems success – A review of existing multidimensional approaches. *Business & Information Systems Engineering, 1*(4), 315–325. doi:10.1007/s12599-009-0059-y

Uzal, R., Debnath, N. C., Montejano, G., & Riesco, D. (2005). *Software engineer first duty: The preliminary financial feasibility analysis of real world software projects*. IEEE International Symposium on Signal Processing and Information Technology. Retrieved from http://www.computer.org/portal/web/csdl/doi/10.1109/ISSPIT.2005.1577185

Verner, J. C.ox, K., & Bleistein, S. J. (2006). Predicting good requirements for in-house development projects. In *Proceedings of the 2006 ACM/IEEE International Symposium on Empirical Software Engineering*, Rio de Janeiro, (pp. 154–163).

Chapter 15
The Technology Acceptance Model: A "Localized" Version to Predict Purchasing Behavior in Internet Shopping

Kanokwan Atchariyachanvanich
Matsuyama University, Japan

Hitoshi Okada
National Institute of Informatics, Japan

Shiro Uesugi
Matsuyama University, Japan

ABSTRACT

This chapter examines the factors affecting consumer purchasing behavior in Internet shopping. Multiple group analysis and structural equation modeling were applied to investigate whether the existing model of Consumer Acceptance of Virtual Stores is able to identify those factors in Japan and South Korea. The results of online questionnaires completed by 1,111 Japanese online customers and by 998 Korean online customers revealed that the model failed. Therefore, localized models for Japan and South Korea were developed. According to the localized models, perceived trust is the most important factor affecting purchasing behavior of Japanese customers. In South Korea, purchasing behavior is highly related to perceived usefulness and perceived service quality. These differences in the ways that online customers of different nationalities perceive purchasing through the Internet will yield insights that can help e-commerce vendors increase the number of customers in different world market segments.

INTRODUCTION

Since Electronic Commerce (EC) emerged in cyberspace, Business-to-Customer (B2C) EC has become a way for consumers to purchase products or services through the Internet. B2C is commonly perceived as Internet shopping and was introduced as an EC application in the early 1990s (Turban et al., 2002). It is rapidly extending its coverage to most business sectors among countries around the world. The United States (US) is the world's earliest and largest adopter of EC, but Japan and South Korea are the dominant markets for EC in Asia. Despite the wide accep-

DOI: 10.4018/978-1-60960-768-5.ch015

Copyright © 2012, IGI Global. Copying or distributing in print or electronic forms without written permission of IGI Global is prohibited.

tance and development of advanced technology in Japan, the EC market in Japan is still lagging behind that of the US. According to a survey on B2C EC markets in Japan and the US (Ministry of Economy, Trade, and Industry, 2006), customer support services in the US EC market is slow and its EC system is unsafe. The EC market in Japan needs improvement of connections between the EC system and other systems in a company, and the Japanese EC system lacks customer relationship management. In 2006, the B2C EC market size of Japan was smaller than that of the US, and the B2C EC growth rate of Japan was two times slower than that of the US (Ministry of Economy, Trade, and Industry, 2007). On the other hand, South Korea has played an important role in the global EC market. As South Korea's high-speed infrastructure continues to grow, along with the new government's initiatives to promote digital convergence, demand for EC transactions is increasing. According to statistics, Korean EC transactions in 2008 totaled USD 524 billion, an increase of 17 percent from USD 423 billion in 2007 (Ahn, 2009). Although the government of South Korea is actively promoting EC industries, the total volume of B2C EC increased from 11,359 billion Korean won in 2008 to 12,043 billion Korean won in 2009, an increase of 6 percent (Statistics Korea, 2010).

Because a better understanding of the factors affecting purchase decisions can provide a crucial grasp of consumer behavior in cyberspace (Limayem et al., 2000), the government and/or business sectors should consider an appropriate model for identifying the these factors in order to increase the growth rate of the B2C EC market. However, the existing EC model, based on the Technology Acceptance Model (TAM), might not be able to identify perfectly the factors influencing the purchasing behavior of online customers. It is vital to demonstrate whether the existing EC model is applicable to investigate online customers in any country. If not, a localized model will be further developed.

The objectives of this chapter are to investigate whether the existing EC model is able to identify the factors affecting consumer purchasing behavior in Internet shopping in Japan and South Korea by conducting a comparative study and to develop localized models of purchasing behavior for Internet shopping in Japan and South Korea if the existing EC model turns out to be inapplicable. The next section provides background information on the theoretical model of consumer behavior and discusses the literature in the domain of EC consumer behavior. The third section describes the methodologies applied in this chapter. The fourth section presents the findings of a comparative study and demonstrates the localized models. The last section contains conclusions and future research directions.

Theoretical Models OF EC Markets

To study and analyze consumer behavior in the use of EC, most researchers have applied several theories used in information system research. In this section, background information and a review of the state-of-the-art related theories will be discussed. Recently, predictors of consumer behavior in purchasing through the Internet have been investigated. In studies of consumer behavior, several theories have been applied. These include the theory of planned behavior (TPB), the theory of reasoned action (TRA), and TAM.

The model frequently employed to conduct such investigations is the TAM (Kwong et al., 2002). TAM was designed to explain the determinants of user acceptance of a wide range of end-user computing technologies (Davis, 1986). TAM is an adaptation of TRA to the field of information systems. TAM posits that perceived usefulness (PU) and perceived ease of use (PEOU) are the primary determinants of an individual's intention to use a system. The usage intention serves as a mediator of actual system use. PU is defined as "the prospective user's subjective probability that using a specific application system will increase his or her job performance within an organizational context" and PEOU refers to "the degree to which the prospective user expects the target system to be free of effort" (Davis, 1986; Davis et al., 1989).

Using the constructs of TAM as a basis, Monsuve et al. (2004) proposed adding exogenous factors to the framework of consumers' intentions to shop online. Their review indicates that attitude toward online shopping and intention to shop online are not only affected by ease of use, usefulness, and enjoyment, but also by exogenous factors like consumer traits, situational factors, product characteristics, previous online shopping experiences, and trust in online shopping. Ahn et al. (2004) extended TAM to examine the quality factors of Internet shopping malls. They hypothesized that five perceived quality factors would positively affect perceived ease of use and usefulness. By using structural equation modeling (SEM), found that customers evaluate the quality of Internet shopping malls in terms of online features and offline features. Online quality of information, service, and systems positively affect the perceived ease of use and usefulness, while offline quality of product and delivery positively affect usefulness. Both online and offline features have greater effects on usefulness, attitude, and intention to use than either online or offline features separately. Liu and Wei (2003) developed a theoretical model of consumers' EC adoption intention by adding perceived risk to the two constructs of TAM. They also investigated the moderating effect of product type on the relationships between consumers' perceptions about EC and consumers' intention to adopt EC. The results indicate that consumers' EC adoption decisions are more strongly influenced by their perceptions of risk when they consider purchasing goods, as compared to services. Conversely, consumers' EC adoption decisions are more strongly influenced by their perceptions of ease of use when they consider purchasing services over the Internet.

Limayem et al. (2000) developed a model based on the TPB in order to explain the relationship between individuals' intentions to purchase through the Internet and their actual behavior of purchasing online. A longitudinal study to empirically test the validity of the proposed model was also conducted. The results provided strong support for positive effects of personal innovativeness on attitude and intentions to purchase online. By applying TPB, George (2004) investigated the relationships between Internet purchasing and beliefs about the privacy and trustworthiness of the Internet. The results indicate that beliefs about trustworthiness positively affect attitudes toward buying online, which in turn positively affect purchasing behavior. Beliefs about self-efficacy in purchasing positively affect perceived behavioral control, which in turn affects Internet purchasing behavior. Hence, respondents who believed in the trustworthiness of the Internet and in their own abilities to purchase online were more likely to purchase through the Internet than were those without such beliefs.

A model of consumers' intention to adopt electronic grocery shopping was developed by Verhoef and Langerak (2001). They applied the TRA to examine the relationship between the (dis)advantages of electronic grocery shopping, in comparison to traditional in-store shopping, and consumers' perception of the innovation characteristics (i.e., relative advantage, compatibility, and complexity) of electronic grocery shopping, as well as the relationship between consumers' perception of these characteristics and their intention to adopt electronic grocery shopping. The results showed that the advantages and disadvantages of physical effort and time pressure that are related to traditional in-store shopping positively influenced consumers' perception of the characteristics of electronic grocery shopping, and consumers' perception of the relative advantage and compatibility of electronic grocery shopping positively influenced their intention to adopt it. In addition, consumers' perception of the complexity of electronic grocery shopping negatively influenced their intention to adopt it.

Ding et al. (2003) used TRA to analyze factors that influence customers to make online purchases. The factors consist of three concepts of marketing strategy, content, context, and infrastructure, as well as consumer service. They found that content, context, and consumer service-related factors are significant in determining customers' attitude to purchase online. Consumer service-related factors are the essential determinants. A comparative study among online customers in China, South Korea, and Japan revealed that the effect of infrastructure on consumers' attitude to purchase online is not so significant in China.

Prior research has adopted many theories to explain the determinants of online purchasing behavior. This study selected TAM as a base model for four reasons. First, TAM was originally meant to explain computer usage behavior (Davis, 1986) but has been widely applied to a diversity in technologies and users such as Internet shopping malls (Ahn et al., 2004), and mobile commerce (Yang, 2005). Second, in the past 20 years, TAM and its extensions have been established as the core models of much research and have been significantly developed in the literature. Third, according to a meta-analysis (King & He, 2006), TAM is considered to be a robust model in predicting determinants of, as well as effects on, consumer adoption and use of new technologies. Fourth, in numerous empirical studies, TAM has been found to explain more than 40% of the variance in usage intentions and behavior (Davis et al., 1989; Venkatesh, 1999). Thus, TAM provides a concrete theoretical background for constructing our research model.

Research Methodology

The studies in the previous section mainly focused on the development of models of online purchasing behavior based on several theories about personal behavior and attitude. TAM was selected as the base model for several reasons. We first tested the consumers' acceptance of virtual stores model, developed by Chen et al. (2004), to evaluate whether or not it could be localized for adoption in Japan and South Korea. Of the existing models of customer behavior and attitude, Chen's model includes the largest numbers of factors affecting purchasing behavior. Its respondents were requested to consider virtual stores which mainly operated and shipped products within the US; therefore, it is highly likely that most were online customers in the US. However, most EC studies, if possible, are compared with those conducted in the US because the US is regarded as the world's earliest and largest EC adopter and represents the largest share of all EC in the world (Ahn, 2009).

As Japan is regarded as one of the largest EC markets, EC vendors who want to invest in the EC industry in Japan should take the following observation into consideration. Japanese market characteristics are a mystery to most foreign observers and the consumption behavior of Japanese customers is notably different from other societies (Synodinos, 2001). On the other hand, South Korea is a rival of Japan in Information and Communication Technology (ICT), and its EC market was reported as a national Internet business in a national survey (Ministry of Information and Communication, 2006). In addition, the number of Internet users in South Korea is dramatically increasing. Thus, EC in South Korea was selected to be compared with that in Japan and the US.

To investigate whether the existing EC model is applicable to any country and to compare purchasing behavior of online consumers in the US with those of Japan and South Korea, the model of consumer acceptance of virtual stores (Chen et al., 2004) was used as a test bed. This model (Figure 1) is regarded as the model of purchasing behavior for the US because its online customer survey was conducted in the US. The outcomes of this section will be further developed as part of a localized model of purchasing behavior in Japan and South Korea.

Structural Equation Modeling

The research models were tested using a structural equation modeling (SEM) technique suitable for higher complex predictive models. SEM is the only multivariate technique that allows the simultaneous estimation of multiple equations. Thus, SEM techniques are used to test a structural theory; SEM is the equivalent of performing factor analysis and regression analysis (multiple regression) in one step. Its characteristics include:

1. Estimation of multiple and interrelated dependence relationships;
2. Representing unobserved concepts in these relationships and correcting for measurement error in the estimation process;
3. Defining a model to explain the entire set of relationships;
4. Using a maximum likelihood function to obtain the estimated values in the models; and
5. Allowing the simultaneous estimation of multiple equations.

Confirmatory Factor Analysis

Confirmatory factor analysis (CFA) is used to provide a confirmatory test of measurement theory. Structural equation models often involve both a measurement theory and a structural theory. A measurement theory specifies how measured variables logically and systematically represent constructs involved in a theoretical model. In other words, a measurement theory specifies a series of relationships that suggest how measured variables represent a latent construct that is not measured directly. One of the biggest advantages of CFA is its ability to assess the construct validity of a proposed measurement theory. Construct validity is the extent to which a set of measured items actually reflects the theoretical latent construct those items are designed to measure. Therefore, it deals with the accuracy of measurement. Evidence of construct validity provides confidence that item measures taken from a sample represent the actual true score that exists in the population. There are four requirements for construct validity:

Figure 1. Theoretical model for consumers' acceptance of virtual stores (adapted from Chen et al. (2004))

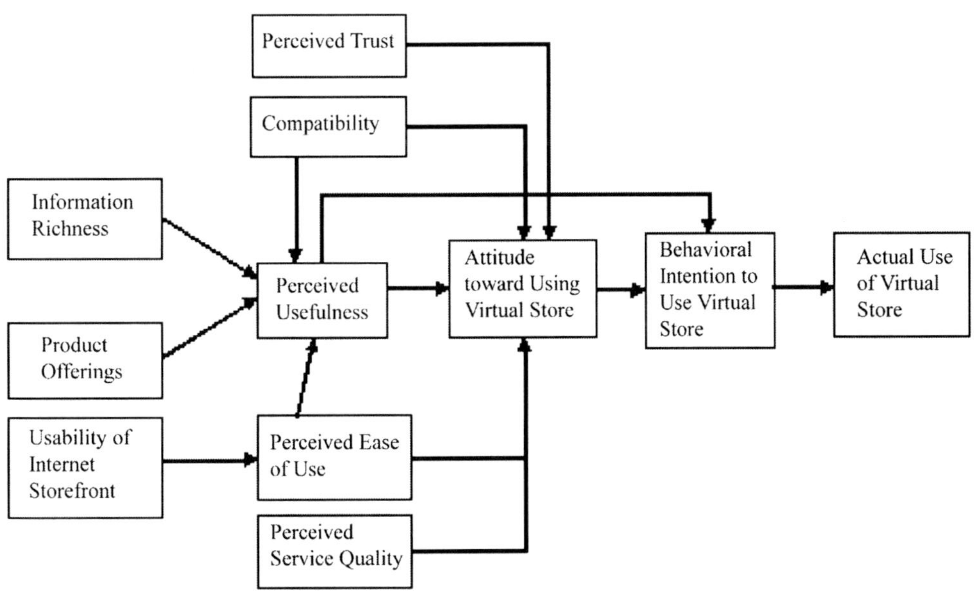

1. Standardized loading estimates should be 0.5 or higher, and ideally 0.7 or higher;
2. Variance extracted (VE) should be 0.5 or greater to suggest adequate convergent validity;
3. Variance estimates for two factors also should be greater than the square of the correlation between the two factors to provide evidence of discriminant validity; and
4. Construct reliability should be 0.7 or higher to indicate adequate convergence or internal consistency.

Multiple Group Analysis

Multigroup analysis provides a mechanism for imposing severe restrictions on the model and for considering the evaluation of the identification criterion across groups because the two groups under study are tested simultaneously (Byrne, 2001). A selected moderator variable is put into the model by using a multigroup analysis technique, after the analysis of the main effects is done. Each moderator variable is split using its median to form two groups. Multigroup analyses are calculated by comparing the two subgroups, the one with high values versus the one with low values of the moderator variables.

Initially, an overall chi-square (χ^2) difference test is performed to determine whether or not the factor loadings of the proposed model are invariant across the two subgroups of each moderator variable. Specifically, the restricted model imposing equality constraints on all parameters across subgroups is compared with the unrestricted model allowing all of these parameters to vary freely across subgroups. If the χ^2 of the restricted model is significantly larger than the χ^2 of the unrestricted model, the assumption of invariance is not tenable. In other words, this test assesses the null hypothesis that the moderator variables did not have any effect on the parameters.

Measurement Development

A web-based survey with an online questionnaire attached was chosen to investigate the factors and consumer internet purchasing behavior. Advantages of web-based surveys over e-mail surveys include better display, greater interactivity, greater ease of completion, and better data quality (Ilieva et al., 2002). The online questionnaire contained two sections. The first section was designed to gather demographic data including age, gender, education level, marital status, and annual income. The second section had multi-item scales to measure various constructs of the research model. Each question asked respondents to rate their perception regarding Internet shopping according to a 5-point Likert scale ranging from 1 ("strongly disagree") to 5 ("strongly agree").

The measures were developed from the literature. The scales for all constructs in this study were adapted from Chen et al. (2004), except the construct of attitude towards purchasing over the Internet, which was adapted from Limayem et al. (2000).

Data Collection in Japan

Because the web-based survey was conducted in Japan, a Japanese version of the questionnaire was administered. The questionnaire, originally written in English, was translated into Japanese by bilingual speakers whose native language was Japanese and whose background was IT-oriented. The questionnaire was then translated back into English by another bilingual speaker whose native language was English and whose background was also IT-oriented. The English versions were then compared, and no item was found to pertain to a specific cultural context in terms of language or to a specific IT-related context.

This study applied cluster sampling to select Internet shoppers from Japanese Internet users. The survey process consisted of three steps:

1. To draw potential Internet shoppers who have purchased a product or service through Internet shopping from among Internet users, an invitation to fill out an Internet questionnaire was electronically mailed to 6,000 registered opt-in-mail members of "goo Research" of NTT Resonant Inc., Japan, (www.goo.ne.jp) on March 15, 2007. From March 16 to 19, 2007, the respondents answered a pre-test questionnaire posted on the goo website, which counted 2,926 samples recorded in the database as potential Internet shoppers.
2. The potential Internet shoppers were clustered based on the percentages of age groups and gender of Internet users reported by the Ministry of Internal Affairs and Communications (2006). This prevents an excess of responses from highly educated respondents or young respondents and ensures that the respondents will be selected randomly. If the percentages of respondents in each age group and gender were higher than the aforementioned clusters, the system would randomly select respondents from each cluster. In this way, 2,000 respondents were randomly selected as potential respondents, and each received an opt-in mail with an invitation for the post-test questionnaire attached.
3. The post-test questionnaire was administered during the period of March 20-25, 2007. The percentages of target Internet shoppers were recorded until they reached the clusters based on the percentages of age groups and gender of Internet shoppers reported by the Ministry of Internal Affairs and Communications (2005). The system automatically stopped gathering the online questionnaire data when the clusters were completed.

After all three steps were completed, 1,111 target responses were collected, successfully reaching the clusters of target respondents set in the second and third steps. The respondents received a point as a reward from the goo website if they completed the online questionnaire. To replicate the distribution of online customers of Internet shopping in Japan, sample weighting[1] was applied to assign a weighted variable to each response. The weighted variable was created based on the percentages of gender and age group (Ministry of Internal Affairs and Communications, 2005). Then each response in the dataset was weighted by its weighted variables. As a result, the distribution of the dataset was then applicable to the distribution of online customers of Internet shopping in Japan. The percentages of gender (52.2% male and 47.8% female) and age group (7.4% (15-19), 19.7% (20-29), 21.8% (30-39), 18.9% (40-49), 18.5% (50-59), and 13.8% (over 60)) for the 1,111 respondents are presented in Table 1.

Data Collection in South Korea

All the questions were posted for registered opt-in-mail users of an Internet service operated by a Korean research company, which is a partner of "goo Research" of NTT Resonant Inc. in Japan. Because the survey was conducted in South Korea, a Korean version of the questionnaire was administered. The questionnaire, originally written in English, was translated into Korean by bilingual speakers whose native language was Korean and whose background was IT-oriented. The questionnaire was then translated back into English by other bilingual speakers whose native language was English and whose background was also IT-oriented. The English versions were then compared, and no item was found to pertain to a specific cultural context in terms of language or to a specific IT-related context. Cluster sampling was also applied to select the Internet shoppers from Korean Internet users. The survey process was the same as that of Japanese Internet users' sampling. The post-test questionnaire period ran from March 22 to 26, 2007.

Table 1. Demographic data of respondents in Japan

Category	Percentage (%)	Category	Percentage (%)
Gender:		Marital Status:	
Male	52.2	Single	39.8
Female	47.8	Married	60.2
Age:		Annual Income: (1 USD = 122.61 JPY)	
15-19	7.4	Less than 24,468 USD	13.2
20-29	19.7	24,469-48,936 USD	33.8
30-39	21.8	48,937-73,403 USD	19.4
40-49	18.9	Greater than 73,404 USD	18.2
50-59	18.4	Missing values	15.4
>=60	13.8		
Education level:		No. of Purchases within 6 months:	
Secondary School	3.0	1-5	30.0
High School	30.3	6-10	42.7
Vocational School	10.4	11-15	9.2
College	10.1	16-20	9.5
Bachelor Degree	39.6	20-25	1.3
Master Degree	4.1	26-30	4.5
Doctoral Degree	1.9	Over 30	2.8
Others	0.6		

After completing the post-test questionnaires, 998 responses were found to be complete and usable. For the 998 respondents, percentages for gender (54.1% male and 45.9% female) and age group (27.3% (under 19), 22.3% (20-29), 23.9% (30-39), 11.1% (40-49), 8.6% (50-59), and 6.7% (over 60)) were the same as those from the computer and Internet usage survey conducted in 2006 by the Ministry of Information and Communication (Ministry of Information and Communication, 2006). Therefore, our results predicted the same trend as the ministry's study of online customers in South Korea. Table 2 presents the demographic data of respondents.

DATA ANALYSIS

The data were analyzed using a two-step approach (Anderson & Gerbing, 1988) using the statistical program SPSS and a covariance-based program AMOS. In the first step, the measurement model was examined for instrument validity and refinement by using confirmatory factor analysis (CFA). The second step involved confirming the relationships and testing the hypotheses of the research model by using the SEM technique.

Measurement Model

The validity of each construct was assessed by examining the standardized factor loadings of its hypothesized items obtained from the measurement model. The construct validity is acceptable if each item has a minimum factor loading of 0.50 on its hypothesized construct (Hair et al., 2006). In addition, the internal consistency of the measurement model was assessed by computing the construct reliability (CR). After the validation of the measurement model for Japan was performed, all constructs were found to have construct reliability higher than 0.70. The coefficients of VE indicate the percentage of the variance in the construct that is explained by an individual item. Most VEs of the constructs were found to be lower than the acceptance level of 0.50 (Hair et al., 2006); therefore, the items cannot adequately explain the variance in the constructs.

Table 2. Demographic data of respondents in South Korea

Category	Percentage (%)	Category	Percentage (%)
Gender: Male Female	 54.1 45.9	Marital Status: Single Married	 56.7 43.3
Age: <= 19 20-29 30-39 40-49 50-59 >=60	 27.3 22.3 23.9 11.1 8.6 6.7	(1,078 USD = 1M. KRW) Less than 2,156 USD 2,157-5,390 5,391-8,624 Greater than 8,625 Missing value	 18.2 42.3 14.3 3.3 21.9
Education level: Secondary School High School Vocational School College Bachelor Degree Master Degree Doctoral Degree	 16.2 30.8 0.3 10.0 37.3 4.3 1.1	No. of Purchases within 6 months: 1-5 6-10 11-15 16-20 20-25 26-30 Over 30	 45.0 30.8 7.5 9.0 1.4 3.5 2.8

Figure 2. Comparison of purchasing behavior among the US, Japan and South Korea

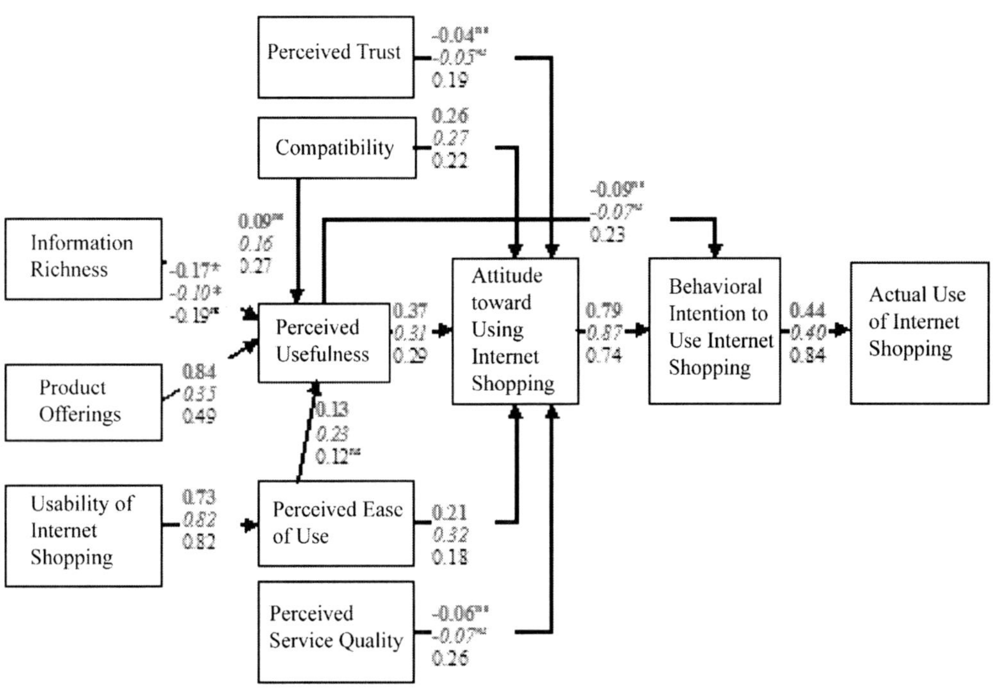

All paths are significat at p<0.001, except *significant at the 0.05 level
TM in significant at the 0.05 level

Bold letter presents Japan
Italic letter presents South Korea
Normal letter presents US (Chen et al., 2002)

For the validation of the measurement model of South Korea, the coefficients of VE, the reliability coefficients and factor loadings of its constructs were analyzed. Almost all of the VEs of the constructs were lower than the acceptance level of 0.50 (Hair et al., 2006); therefore, the items cannot adequately explain the variance in the constructs.

Structural Model

Figure 2 shows the results of the structural model of purchasing behavior of Japanese and South Korean samples and the structural model of the US sample from Chen et al. (2004)'s study. The estimated path effects (standardized) are presented. All standardized path coefficients are significant at the .01 significance level, except those paths marked with one asterisk and "ns", which indicate the .05 significance level and insignificance, respectively. The normal-style coefficients that are reported in Figure 2 for each of these paths belong to the US samples (Chen et al., 2004), whereas the bold and italic coefficients belong to the Japanese and South Korean samples, respectively.

The structural model of the Japanese samples shows that attitude towards using Internet shopping was predicted by perceived ease of use (β = 0.21, p < .01), perceived usefulness (β = 0.37, p < .01), and compatibility (β = 0.26, p < .01), but not by perceived service quality (β = -0.06, p > .05) or perceived trust (β = -0.04, p > .05). Actual use of Internet shopping was positively influenced by behavioral intention to use Internet shopping (β = 0.44, p < .01), which was positively related to attitude toward using Internet shopping (β = 0.79, p < .01) but not significantly related to perceived usefulness (β = -0.07, p > .05).

The analysis of the South Korea model shows that attitude towards using Internet shopping was significantly predicted by perceived ease of use (β = 0.32, p < .01), perceived usefulness (β = 0.31, p < .01), and compatibility (β = 0.27, p < .01), but not by perceived service quality (β = -0.07, p > .05) or perceived trust (β = -0.05, p > .05). Actual use of Internet shopping was positively influenced by behavioral intention to use Internet shopping (β = 0.40, p < .01), which was positively related to attitude toward using Internet shopping (β = 0.87, p < .01) but not significantly related to perceived usefulness (β = -0.07, p > .05).

The results of both models indicate that perceived usefulness is not significantly related to behavioral intention to use Internet shopping. This is in contrast to the significance of perceived usefulness indicated in Chen et al. (2004)'s study. In addition, perceived trust and perceived service quality are not significantly related to attitude toward using Internet shopping.

To assess if the US model is applicable to Internet shopping in Japan and South Korea, fit indices for the models of factors affecting purchasing behavior between t Japan, and South Korea were calculated. The $\chi^2(835, N = 1,111)$ of the Japan model is 4081.202, $p < .001$ and the $\chi^2(835, N = 998)$ of the South Korea model is 3090.475, $p < .001$. Their root mean square errors of approximation (RMSEA) were 0.056, 0.059 and 0.052, respectively. These indices indicate good fit and reasonable errors of approximation in the population and were lower than the recommended limit of 0.07 (Hair et al., 2006). The comparative fit index (CFI) of the US model is 0.91. However, the CFIs of the Japan and South Korea models are 0.88 and 0.87, which did not meet the recommended levels of 0.90 (Byrne, 2001). This implies that the US model cannot be well fit to the Japan and South Korea samples. This poor fit of the US model implies that the EC model for the US is not applicable as the EC model for Japan and South Korea. Therefore, revised models of purchasing behavior for Japan and South Korea are proposed.

Revised Model of Purchasing Behavior in Internet Shopping

In this section, a localized model of purchasing behavior in Internet shopping for Japan and South Korea is developed based on the result of the comparative study in the previous section. First, the country variable is assessed to determine if it has an effect on the model of purchasing behavior in Internet shopping. The samples of Japanese and South Korean respondents are combined and analyzed by applying a multiple-group analysis technique. The country variable or moderator variable is Japan and South Korea. Next, it is determined if the factors of purchasing behavior are different. Finally, the localized model is developed.

The multiple-group analysis was begun by testing an overall chi-square difference in order to determine whether or not the factor loadings of the proposed model were invariant across the two country subgroups Specifically, the restricted model, which imposed equality constraints on all five parameters across subgroups, was compared with the unrestricted model, which allowed all of these parameters to vary freely across subgroups. If the χ^2 of the restricted model were significantly larger than the χ^2 of the unrestricted model, the assumption of invariance would not be tenable. In other words, this test assessed the null hypothesis that the moderator variables did not have any effect on the five parameters. As can be seen from Table 3, this null hypothesis was rejected ($\Delta\chi^2 \geq 15.09$, $p < .05$, $\Delta DF = 5$). This finding implies that the US model cannot explain the purchasing behavior of Internet shopping in Japan and South Korea. Therefore, the model of purchasing behavior should be localized for Japan and South Korea.

Localized Model of Purchasing Behavior for Japan

After the model assessment was performed, the reliability coefficients and the coefficients of VE were obtained; these are presented in Table 4. The validity of each construct was assessed by examining the standardized factor loadings of its hypothesized items obtained from the measurement model. The internal consistency of the measurement model was assessed by computing the composite reliability (CR). All constructs had composite reliability higher than the acceptance level of 0.60 (Bagozzi & Yi, 1988). This suggests that the data have high internal reliability. The coefficients of VE indicate the percentage of the variance of the construct that is explained by an individual item. All constructs had VEs higher than the acceptance level of 0.50 (Bagozzi & Yi, 1988); therefore, it is concluded that the items can adequately explain the variance in the constructs.

Figure 3 shows the results of the structural paths of the model of purchasing behavior in Internet shopping for Japan. The estimated path

Table 3. Results of multiple-group analysis of purchasing behavior

Path	Country		Chi-Square Difference($\Delta DF=1$)
	Japan	South Korea	
U → PEOU	0.704 (11.380)	0.706 (11.206)	$\Delta\chi^2 = 2.050$
T → A	0.963 (14.000)	0.959 (12.931)	$\Delta\chi^2 = 0.050$
CP → A	0.792 (18.377)	0.778 (16.944)	$\Delta\chi^2 = 0.491$
PEOU → A	0.194 (3.518)	0.241 (4.378)	$\Delta\chi^2 = 0.394$
SQ → A	0.255 (2.767)	0.298 (3.223)	$\Delta\chi^2 = 0.531$

$\Delta\chi^2$ for all gammas set equal across subgroups ($\Delta DF = 5$): 34.26
*Chi-square difference is significant at the 5% level.

Table 4. Factor loadings and reliability of measured constructs of purchasing behavior for the Japan model

Constructs	Items	Variance Extracted	Construct Reliability	Standardized Factor Loadings
Attitude toward Using Internet Shopping	USE1	0.70	0.97	0.752
	USE2			0.912
Perceived Ease of Use	PEOU1	0.66	0.99	0.722
	PEOU3			0.786
	PEOU4			0.910
	PEOU5			0.888
	PEOU6			0.746
Compatibility	CP1	0.77	0.99	0.862
	CP2			0.928
	CP3			0.845
Perceived Service Quality	SQ4	0.57	0.99	0.728
	SQ7			0.709
	SQ8			0.792
	SQ9			0.787
Perceived Trust	T2	0.74	0.99	0.798
	T3			0.927
	T4			0.943
	T6			0.805
	T7			0.806
Usability of Internet Shopping Website	U1	0.68	0.99	0.818
	U2			0.837

effects (standardized) are presented. All path coefficients, except the ones marked by asterisks, are significant at the .01 level, which indicates strong support for all the hypothesized relationships. The structural model test estimated the goodness-of-fit of the research models. The $\chi^2(221, N=1{,}111)$ of the Japan model was calculated to be 1245.542, $p < .001$. The root mean square residual (RMR) is 0.039, which is lower than the accepted limit of 0.05 (Byrne, 2001). The comparative fit index (CFI) of 0.94 is higher than the recommended level of 0.90. Overall, the revised model of purchasing behavior in Internet shopping for Japan appears to be statistically well fit.

Attitude towards using Internet shopping was predicted by perceived ease of use ($\beta = 0.09$, $p < .01$), perceived service quality ($\beta = 0.17$, $p < .001$), perceived trust ($\beta = 0.49$, $p < .001$), and compatibility ($\beta = 0.09$, $p < .05$) which accounted for 35% of the variance in the purchasing attitude.

Localized Model of Purchasing Behavior for South Korea

After the model assessment was performed, the reliability coefficients and the coefficients of VE were obtained; these are presented in Table 5. All constructs have composite reliability higher than the acceptance level of 0.60 (Bagozzi & Yi, 1988). This suggests that the data have high internal reliability. In addition, all constructs have VEs higher than the acceptance level of 0.50 (Bagozzi & Yi, 1988); therefore, it is concluded that the items can adequately explain the variance in the constructs.

Figure 3. Localized model of purchasing behavior in internet shopping for Japan

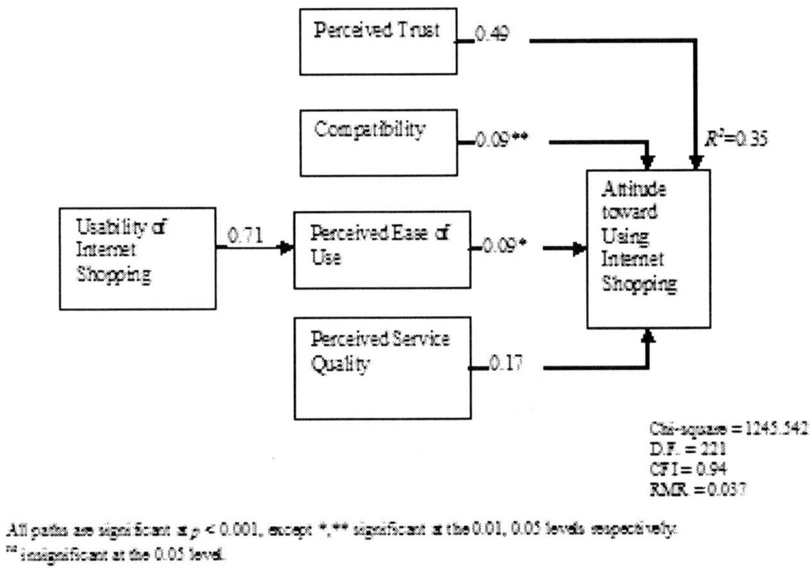

Table 5. Factor loadings and reliability of measured constructs of purchasing behavior for the South Korea model

Constructs	Items	Variance Extracted	Construct Reliability	Standardized Factor Loadings
Attitude toward Using Internet Shopping	USE1	0.52	0.96	0.622
	USE2			0.804
Perceived Ease of Use	PEOU1	0.55	0.99	0.704
	PEOU3			0.657
	PEOU4			0.645
	PEOU5			0.851
	PEOU6			0.815
Perceived Service Quality	SQ4	0.50	0.99	0.622
	SQ7			0.671
	SQ8			0.702
	SQ9			0.816
Perceived Trust	T2	0.70	0.99	0.807
	T3			0.933
	T4			0.922
	T6			0.760
	T7			0.757
Usability of Internet Shopping Website	U1	0.62	0.99	0.792
	U2			0.789

Figure 4 shows the results of the structural paths of the model of purchasing behavior in Internet shopping for South Korea. The estimated path effects (standardized) are presented. All path coefficients, except the ones marked by asterisks, are significant at the .01 level, which indicates strong support for all the hypothesized relationships. The structural model test estimated the goodness-of-fit of the research models. The $\chi^2(221, N=998)$ of the South Korea model was calculated to be 1292.584, $p < .001$. The root mean square residual (RMR) is 0.037, which is lower than the accepted limit of 0.05 (Byrne, 2001). The comparative fit index (CFI) of 0.91 is higher than the recommended level of 0.90. Overall, the revised model of purchasing behavior in Internet shopping for South Korea appears to be statistically well fit.

Attitude towards using Internet shopping was predicted by perceived ease of use ($\beta = 0.13$, $p < .05$), perceived service quality ($\beta = 0.22$, $p < .01$), and perceived trust ($\beta = 0.43$, $p < .01$), which accounted for 31% of the variance in purchasing attitude.

FUTURE RESEARCH DIRECTIONS

Despite several significant findings and implications, this chapter has two limitations. First, we have not considered information about specific products, services, and Internet shopping websites. Because various products and services can be purchased from several Internet shopping websites, the empirical results for the model of purchasing behavior might be biased. For example, the respondents may have focused only on some particular products or services or on products that are not sold on the Internet. Therefore, the factors influencing actual attitudes toward using Internet shopping for a particular product, service, or Internet shopping website may be different from those we assumed in this study. Second, the respondents were all Internet users who had shopped online at least once within six months of answering the questionnaire. We could not differentiate between the attitudes and intentions of Internet users who have shopped online and those who have not. Therefore the measurement of attitude toward purchasing should be further refined.

Figure 4. Localized model of purchasing behavior in Internet shopping for South Korea

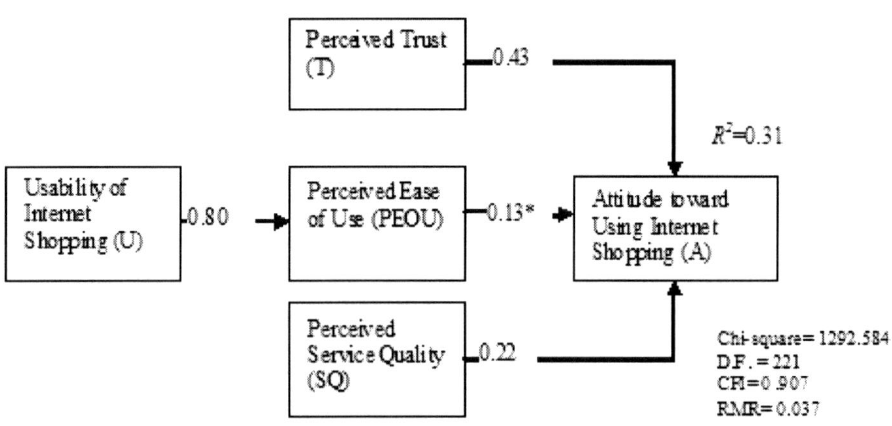

All paths are significant at 0.01 level, except * significant at the 0.05 level.
ns insignificant at the 0.05 level.

Further studies can be conducted by following these guidelines. First, a verification system should be developed for critical success factors of EC based on the localized model. The system would help in verifying these factors of the EC sites and in allocating resources for creating the factors. In addition, the localized model can be used and assessed by EC companies in the real EC market. For example, an EC company can assess if the factors in the localized model exist in its EC system. The assessment can be done by cross-checking the factors against those that are found in the EC system. Second, the localized model may be further analyzed to determine if it is affected by the characteristics of online customers: gender, marital status, age group, income level, education level, net-orientation, and innovativeness. Each of these seven potential moderators has been found to be relevant in the context of purchase and repurchase behaviors in previous studies (Bellman et al., 1999; Limayem et al., 2000; Yang, 2005). These differences will yield insights that can help managers to better serve different customer demographics.

CONCLUSION

The goals of this chapter were to investigate whether the EC model of the US is applicable to the EC models for other countries, to develop a model for exploring the factors influencing the success of Internet shopping, and to identify the factors related to the success of EC. In order to fulfill these objectives, consumer behavior modeling and online consumer behavior analysis were conducted by applying the structural equation modeling technique. In a comparative study, a country variable was introduced to assess its effects on the model of purchasing behavior in Internet shopping. Country variable was found to have a significant effect; the samples from Japan and South Korea could not be adequately fit in the EC model of the US. Therefore, the EC model of the US is unable to identify the significant factors affecting online purchasing behavior in Japan and South Korea. It was therefore necessary to develop the EC model for Japan and South Korea. The factors of the purchasing behavior models were also found to differ for Japan and South Korea.

Why the model of Chen et al. (2004) works for the US country but not for Japan and South Korea may be explained in two ways: by the maturity of their EC markets and by cultural differences among those three countries. The EC market in the US is more mature than those of Japan and South Korea. Online consumers in the US adopted Internet shopping many years ago. This is perhaps one of the many factors that influence their acceptance of shopping through the Internet. On the other hand, because the EC market in Japan and South Korea was developed later than that in the US, Japanese and Korean online consumers' attitude towards Internet shopping may be differently affected by the factors that are significant for online consumers in the US.

Empirical studies have found that the TAM model is unable to predict the use of technology equally well across cultures (Straub et al., 1997). Moreover, the consumption behavior of Japanese customers is notably different from other societies (Synodinos, 2001). The results of this study indicate that compatibility has no correlation in the localized model of purchasing behavior for South Korea. Perceived trust is the most important factor affecting purchasing behavior of online customers in both localized models of Japan and South Korea. Purchasing behavior in South Korea is significantly related to perceived usefulness and perceived service quality.

These results may not only help EC vendors increase the number of customers in different world market segments, guide managers in conducting EC business, supporting EC strategy planning, and promoting EC adoption, but may also provide the theoretical grounds for studying other factors influencing the success of EC.

REFERENCES

Ahn, C. (2009). *Korea: E-commerce industries.* Retrieved from http://www.mitc.com/PDFs/Korea-E-Commerce.pdf

Ahn, T., Ryu, S., & Han, I. (2004). The impact of the online and offline features on the user acceptance of Internet shopping malls. *Electronic Commerce Research and Applications, 3*, 405–420. doi:10.1016/j.elerap.2004.05.001

Anderson, J. C., & Gerbing, D. W. (1998). Structural equation modeling in practice: A review and recommended two-step approach. *Psychological Bulletin, 103*(3), 411–423. doi:10.1037/0033-2909.103.3.411

Bagozzi, R., & Yi, T. (1988). On the evaluation of structural equation models. *Journal of the Academy of Marketing Science, 16*(1), 74–94. doi:10.1007/BF02723327

Bellman, S., Lohse, G. L., & Johnson, E. J. (1999). Predictors of online buying behavior. *Communications of the ACM, 42*(12), 32–38. doi:10.1145/322796.322805

Byrne, B. M. (2001). *Structural equation modeling with AMOS: Basic concepts, applications, and programming.* New York, NY: Lawrence Erlbaum Associates Inc.

Chen, L., Gillenson, M. L., & Sherrell, D. L. (2004). Consumer acceptance of virtual stores: A theoretical model and critical success factors for virtual stores. *ACM SIGMIS Database, 35*(2), 8–31. doi:10.1145/1007965.1007968

Cocharan, W. G. (1977). *Sampling techniques.* John Wiley & Sons.

Davis, F. D. (1986). *A technology acceptance model for empirically testing new end-user information systems: Theory and results.* Doctoral dissertation, Sloan School of Management, Massachusetts Institute of Technology, 1986.

Davis, F. D., Bagozzi, R. P., & Warshaw, P. R. (1989). User acceptance of computer technology: A comparison of two theoretical models. *Management Science, 35*, 982–1003. doi:10.1287/mnsc.35.8.982

Ding, X., Iijima, J., & Ho, S. (2003). An exploratory study on influential factors of online consumer behavior. *Proceedings from The 3rd Asian eBusiness Workshop*, (pp. 3-44).

George, J. F. (2004). The theory of planned behavior and Internet purchasing. *Internet Research, 14*(3), 198–212. doi:10.1108/10662240410542634

Hair, J. F., Black, B., Babin, B., Anderson, R. E., & Tatham, R. L. (2006). *Multivariate data analysis* (6th ed.). New Jersey: Prentice-Hall.

Ilieva, J., Baron, S., & Healey, N. M. (2002). Online surveys in marketing research: Pros and cons. *International Journal of Market Research, 44*(3), 361–376.

King, W. R., & He, J. (2006). A meta-analysis of the technology acceptance model. *Information & Management, 43*, 740–755. doi:10.1016/j.im.2006.05.003

Kwong, T., Cheung, C., Zhu, L., Limayem, M., & Viehland, D. (2002). Online consumer behavior: An overview and analysis of the literature. *Proceedings from The Six Pacific Asia Conference on Information System,* (pp. 813-827).

Limayem, M., Khalifa, M., & Frini, A. (2000). What makes consumers buy from Internet? A longitudinal study of online shopping. *IEEE Transactions on Systems, Man, and Cybernetics. Part A, Systems and Humans, 30*(4), 421–432. doi:10.1109/3468.852436

Liu, X., & Wei, K. K. (2003). An empirical study of product differences in consumers' e-commerce adoption behavior. *Electronic Commerce Research and Applications, 2*, 229–239. doi:10.1016/S1567-4223(03)00027-9

Ministry of Economy. Trade and Industry. (2006). *Market research report on e-commerce for year 2005*. Ministry of Economy, Trade, and Industry, Japan. Retrieved from www.meti.go.jp/policy/it_policy/statistics/outlook/060901outlook.pdf

Ministry of Economy, Trade, and Industry. (2007). *Market research report on e-commerce for year 2006*. Ministry of Economy, Trade, and Industry, Japan. Retrieved from www.meti.go.jp/policy/it_policy/statistics/outlook/H18EC_070330.pdf

Ministry of Information and Communication. (2006). *Survey on the computer and Internet usage. Internet Statistic Reports*. National Internet Development Agency of Korea. Retrieved from http://isis.nida.or.kr/eng/

Ministry of Internal Affairs and Communications. (2005). *Communications usage trend survey in 2004. Telecommunications Bureau*. Tokyo, Japan: MIC.

Ministry of Internal Affairs and Communications. (2006). *Communications usage trend survey in 2005. Telecommunications Bureau*. Tokyo, Japan: MIC.

Monsuve, T. P., Dellaert, B. G. C., & Ruyter, K. (2004). What drives consumers to shop online? A literature review. *International Journal of Service Industry Management*, *15*(1), 102–121. doi:10.1108/09564230410523358

Shang, R.-A., Chen, Y.-C., & Shen, L. (2005). Extrinsic versus intrinsic motivations for consumers to shop on-line. *Information & Management*, *42*, 401–413. doi:10.1016/j.im.2004.01.009

Statistics Korea. (2010). *E-commerce and cyber shopping survey in 2009 and in the fourth quarter 2009*. Retrieved from http://kostat.go.kr

Straub, D., Keil, M., & Brenner, W. (1997). Testing the technology acceptance model across cultures: A three country study. *Information & Management*, *33*, 1–11. doi:10.1016/S0378-7206(97)00026-8

Synodinos, N. E. (2001). Understanding Japanese consumers: Some important underlying factors. *The Japanese Psychological Research*, *43*(4), 235–248. doi:10.1111/1468-5884.00181

Turban, E., King, D., Lee, J., Warkentin, M., & Chung, H. M. (2002). *Electronic commerce 2002: A managerial perspective*. New Jersey: Prentice-Hall.

Venkatesh, V. (1999). Creation of favorable user perceptions: Exploring the role of intrinsic motivation. *Management Information Systems Quarterly*, *23*, 239–260. doi:10.2307/249753

Verhoef, P. C., & Langerak, F. (2001). Possible determinants of consumers' adoption of electronic grocery shopping in the Netherlands. *Journal of Retailing and Consumer Services*, *8*, 275–285. doi:10.1016/S0969-6989(00)00033-3

Yang, K. C. C. (2005). Exploring factors affecting the adoption of mobile commerce in Singapore. *Telematics and Informatics*, *22*, 257–277. doi:10.1016/j.tele.2004.11.003

ENDNOTE

[1] Sample weighting is used to correct disproportional sample sizes and adjust the collected data to represent the population from which the sample was drawn (Cocharan, 1977). During the period of data collection, the 2005 estimate of population of online customers (Ministry of Internal Affairs and Communications, 2005) was the most recent one suitable for sample weighting.

Chapter 16
Perceived Benefits from a Local Government Public Procurement Initiative:
A Diffusion of Innovation Perspective

Md Mahbubur Rahim
Monash University, Australia

Adarsh P. Bantwal
Monash University, Australia

ABSTRACT

In recent years, government organisations are expressing a growing interest in the uptake of eProcurement systems in order to achieve many of the benefits that their counterparts in the private sector have reported. These systems represent a specific instance of internet-based inter-organisational initiatives that streamline organisational purchasing processes and facilitate electronic exchange of transactions and other procurement related documents between organisations and their suppliers. Although some literature exists on the adoption of e-procurement systems within the government sector, relatively little has been focused on the outcomes of these systems particularly within the Australian local government context. Furthermore, much of the attention of the existing eProcurement literature is on understanding adoption decisions of these systems from the perspective of senior management, and few research efforts have been made to examine how employees who actually use these systems perceive the benefits arising from these systems. In addition, although the role of demographic characteristics of users is recognised in the innovation adoption and broader IS/IT adoption literatures, it is not clearly known how the demographic characteristics of employees (who interact with such systems) may influence their perceptions about eProcurement benefits. To address this gap in the literature, we analyse the views captured from sixty employees working in three large city councils located in the state of Victoria, Australia. The findings indicate that the outcomes of eProcurement systems adoption were largely seen in a positive light as the employees reported favourably about the attainment of benefits from their use of these systems.

DOI: 10.4018/978-1-60960-768-5.ch016

Copyright © 2012, IGI Global. Copying or distributing in print or electronic forms without written permission of IGI Global is prohibited.

More specifically, efficiency improvement and establishing control were perceived as the two most important benefits. However, except user type, popular demographic characteristics of employees (e.g. gender, job role, working experience at councils) were not related to their perceptions of eProcurement benefits. These findings offer limited support for the views expressed in the existing innovations and IS/IT adoption literatures. The implications of these findings are discussed, and future directions of research are proposed.

INTRODUCTION

Inter-organsiational systems which connect two or more organisations electronically come in several forms. One important application of such systems is known as e-procurement which automates the labour-intensive procurement function of organisations and facilitates transactions and information exchange between organisations and their suppliers. In particular, eProcurement refers to the application of e-commerce technologies to an organisation's purchasing activities (Garrido-Samaniego et al, 2010). When properly employed, these technologies can deliver considerable benefits (Attaran, 2001). For example, General Electric (GE) - a multinational manufacturing electrical and electronic manufacturing company, benefited from the use of web-based procurement systems in terms of shorter bidding process, reduced purchasing price, and availability of worldwide suppliers (Watson et al, 2000). Likewise, Cathay Pacific Airways saved $38 million annually by adopting an Oracle Internet Procurement solution (Farhoomand, 2001). Motorola, another renowned telecommunication manufacturing giant, is reported to have made a savings of $2.5 billion dollars on its goods and services acquired through an Internet-based e-Procurement system (Schneider, 2006). The wide publicity about eProcurement benefit stories has generated a strong interest on the part of the government agencies to introduce these systems. Moreover, the need to introduce greater levels of transparency into the procurement practices (Ancarani, 2005; Singer et al., 2009) has further fueled the government sector's interest to consider adopting eProcurement systems. According to Wirtz et al (2010), local government agencies too regard it important to introduce eProcurement technologies largely due to considerable decline in their income and growing pressure to optimise costs. Likewise, Padhi and Mohapatra (2010) reported a rising trend of the application of eProcurement systems in industry and government departments alike.

In the recent years, several initiatives have been reported to promote the notion of eProcurement within the government sector. For example, in the European Union, eProcurement in the government sector came into public focus as it was recognised to have a potential to improve efficiency, transparency and the opening up of public procurement activities (European Union, 2005). In Hong Kong, the government has embarked on an eProcuremnt program to enable electronic transaction between suppliers and the participating departments in respect of departmental purchases of non-construction related goods and services up to $1.43 million (2009). The Mauritius government signed a MoU with the Andhra Pradesh (AP) government of India to use AP's e-procurement platform for its projects and in its administration (2009). According to Vaidya et al. (2006; 2008) many government agencies worldwide consider e-procurement as a priority and have either implemented or are in a process of implementing buy-side eProcurement initiatives as part of their e-government agendas. For example, in Malaysia, the government has undertaken eProcurement project within the broader e-government initiative of its multimedia super corridor applications (Kaliannan et al, 2010). Even United Nations (UN) affiliated organisations are undertaking a variety of eProcurement projects (Walker and Harland, 2008).

In the state of Victoria, Australia, the state government too had launched an eProcurement initiative (known as EC4P) to encourage state government agencies and local government bodies to develop eProcurement capabilities (Braue, 2004). In response, several large city councils in Victoria implemented web-enabled eProcurement systems beginning from 2005. It is not however known how the council employees who use eProcurement systems perceive the benefits received from their use of these systems because there is evidence (Elbanna, 2010) which suggests that eProcurement systems may not be put into significant use although such systems are initially accepted with enthusiasm. Hence, although there is a call by Attaran (2001) for senior management to believe in the benefits of e-procurement technologies, we argue that empirical evaluation of benefits from employees' perspective is needed. We further argue that it is important to examine employee views about eProcurement systems benefits because the impact of introducing these systems may be interpreted differently by the senior council management owing to their socio-political stake in the adoption decision making process. Hence, instead of measuring eProcurement benefits from the perspective of senior management, it is quite essential to develop understanding about how those employees who actually use these systems at councils perceive the benefits arising from their use of these systems.

Another motivation for this research was triggered by the existing innovation and IS/IT adoption literature in which several scholars (e.g. Igbaria and Parasuraman, 1989; Vallerand, 1997; Venkatesh and Morris, 2000, Branca, 2008) have argued that demographic characteristics of individuals in general may affect how they perceive IS/IT adoption. As the eProcurement systems are founded on new web-based technologies and a systematic analysis of the influence of the employees' demographic characteristics on their views about benefits perceived from their use of these systems has not yet been reported in the literature, it is necessary to initiate further studies to examine this relationship. Although a plethora of eProcurement literature is available, much attention of the literature is on the factors affecting adoption of eProcurement systems. There is a genuine lack in the literature about an evaluation of eProcurement benefits from the perspective of employee (user) characteristics. We thus address this deficiency in the literature by undertaking a research on the relationships between employees' (who use eProcurement systems) demographic variables and their perceptions of the benefits arising from their use of web-enabled eProcurement systems at the Australian local government context.

The primary objectives of our research are therefore two fold:

1. To find out the extent to which local council employees (who use eProcurement systems) report the perceived benefits from their use of these systems;
2. To explore whether the employees' perceptions of eProcurement benefits significantly vary based on their demographic characteristics.

The above mentioned research concerns were addressed by identifying four major categories of benefits drawn from the eBusiness literature, developing a survey instrument which operatiaonlised these benefits, and then administrating the survey questionnaires among two hundred employees at three Melbourne-based city councils which have introduced web-enabled eProcurement systems in recent years. The responses received from sixty participating employees indicate that the outcomes of eProcurement systems adoption was seen largely in a positive light by the employees as they reported favourably about the attainment of benefits from their use of these systems. More specifically, efficiency improvement and establishing control were perceived as the two most important benefits. In contrast, socio-political benefits involving the desire to advance council's image and improving its relationship with suppliers was considered less important.

Furthermore, the demographic characteristics of employees (e.g. gender, job role, working experience at councils) in broad sense were not found to be related to their perceptions of eProcurement benefits. An exception is however the type of eProcurement user which is clearly related to employees' perceptions of benefits. These findings are useful to government decision makers as they can help guide the prospective government agencies in planning for justifying investment in the introduction of eProcurement systems. For theory, the findings can assist the eBusiness researcher community in shaping future directions of eProcurement research within the local government sector.

The rest of this chapter has been organised as follows. The next section explains the significance of procurement process in organisations, describes the key activities involved in the procurement process, identifies its weaknesses, explains how automation and streamlining of the procurement process using eProcurement systems can generate benefits, and discusses the role of employees' demographic characteristics from the viewpoint of innovation adoption. This is followed by a set of research hypotheses which link employees' (who use eProcurement systems) demographic characteristics with their perceived benefits received from these systems. The research approach is then described. The survey data collected from sixty responding employees from three large Melbourne-based city councils are then analysed and discussed. Finally, the contributions and some limitations of this study are indicated, and future research directions are proposed.

BACKGROUND LITERATURE ANALYSIS

Procurement and its Significance

Procurement is generally described as the process of purchasing goods and/or services and managing its timely acquisition by an organisation (Gebauer and Segev, 2000). Goods and services may be either direct or indirect. Direct goods (e.g. parts for vehicle, components for computers, and ingredients for pharmaceuticals) are those that are exclusively required for a buying organisation's end-product. On the other hand, indirect goods (e.g. office supplies, software) are those which are consumed by an organisation but are not associated directly with the organisation's end-product (Gebauer and Segev, 2000). Government agencies are more concerned with purchase of indirect goods. However, public sector e-procurement is more than simple automation of indirect good for use by the government agencies. According to Vaidya and Hyde (2011), public procurement practices must take into account at least the following four elements: the Internet/e-commerce (enabler); process automation and integration (action); the practice of public procurement (process): and value for money principles (objective). As such, public electronic procurement has been defined as the use of any Internet-based Inter-organizational Information System, which automates and integrates any part of the procurement process in order to improve efficiency and quality in public procurement, and promote transparency and accountability in the wider public sector (Vaidya and Hyde, 2011).

Regardless of the sector (public or private), procurement function has assumed increasingly greater prominence in the last few years due to the following reasons. First, as more functional units of an organisation take part in purchasing activities, the ability to make correct purchasing decisions becomes more significant (Afsharipour et al, 2006). Second, a better understanding of procurement practices allows an organisation to improve its relationships with suppliers. In turn, better relationships with suppliers are characterised by informed negotiations about prices and delivery arrangements, assurance of procurement from preferred suppliers, and increased sharing of information which aids in developing improved purchasing strategies (Gebauer and Segev, 2000). Third, there is a greater concern in particular for the government bodies for establishing transparency into purchasing practices (Ancarani, 2005; Rahim and As-Saber, 2009; Singer et al., 2009)

The Procurement Process

Procurement processes at organisations vary depending on type of products procured (Narasimhan and Carter, 1998). As the public administration (including local councils) do not administer production function (Wirtz et al, 2010), we restrict our focus to describing those key activities which are involved in indirect procurement. According to Neef (2001), there are four major activities (shown in Figure 1) in a typical indirect procurement process. The selection of goods is the first task. This stage is often a convoluted process requiring searching through supplier catalogues. When catalogues cannot be found, direct contact with the supplier is necessary. The next stage is the requisition process. Here, the requisitions may be sent to a central department. This is a time consuming process. Each requisition then needs to be approved, in the third stage. Approval is based on the nature of the goods including its cost. In the fourth stage, once approval is received, a purchase order (PO) is created. The processing for the PO is a source of inefficiency because often PO processing takes several weeks and it is hard to identify its status once processing has commenced.

The traditional paper-based procurement process however has been criticised for a number of reasons. The procurement process is labour-intensive and expensive which often allows collusive bidding activities resulting in inefficiency and wastes (Liao, et al., 2002). The government sector in particular is known to suffer from weak enforcement mechanisms to manage corruption and wasteful purchase practices (Thai, 2005). In response to these weaknesses, a new class of web-based eProcurement systems is developed by several software vendors that facilitate the purchase of goods and services electronically by automating the key activities outlined in Figure 1 (Hawking and Stein, 2002).

E-Procurement Systems and Benefits of Adopting E-Procurement Systems

The term e-procurement is not free from a debate. Vaidya et al. (2006) acknowledges that confusion exists in defining the term e-procurement primarily because not all e-procurement solutions focus on all the stages of procurement process as shown in Figure 1. In this chapter, we focus on those e-procurement systems which automate and streamline all the four stages of the procurement process. Popular eProcurement solutions which satisfy this requirement include Enterprise Buyer professionals (EBP) from SAP and iProcurement from Oracle among others. As such, although general e-mail, internet-based fax, and buying from supplier web-sites can be used in support of procurement, we do not consider them as the complete end-to-end e-procurement solution. This view is consistent with the opinions of Vaidya et al. (2006).

We argue that successful implementation of eProcurement systems in organisations can offer

Figure 1. Procurement model proposed by Neef (2001)

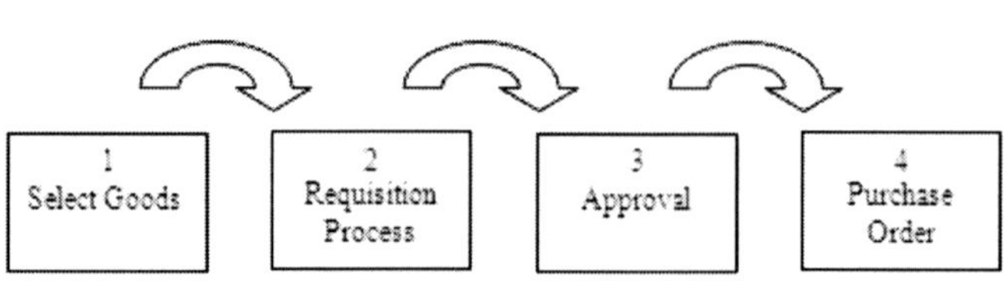

a range of benefits. Some scholars like Croom (2000), Attaran (2001), and Neef (2001) grouped eProcurement benefits into several categories. Croom identified two types of benefits: operative and strategic. Operative benefits are concerned with what eProcurement systems can help reduce (e.g. PO costs, ordering cycle, inventory costs, error rates). Strategic benefits on the other hand relate to what eProcurement systems can help increase (e.g. increased control over the procurement process, relationship with business partners). This classification was extended by Attaran (2001) who added 'opportunity' as another benefit of e-procurement systems. In contrast, in his book Neef (2001) identified three types of eProcurement benefits: process efficiency, compliance, and leverage.

In this chapter, we have grouped eProcurement benefits into four categorises depending on the level at which these benefits are more visible: organisational level benefits (e.g. efficiency improvement, control enhancement and image advancement), and supply-chain level benefits (e.g. improved relationships with suppliers), and argue that the perceptions of employees about these benefits may vary based their demographic characteristics. These benefits are discussed below.

Efficiency Improvement

Efficiency refers to meeting objectives at minimum costs (Garrido et al., 2008). eProcurement systems help improve manual purchasing process efficiency (Minahan, 2001; Wu et al, 2007) via reduced paperwork, lowered cost of preparing purchase orders, shortened order cycles and decentralisation of the procurement process. The digitisation of all documents pertaining to the entire procurement process means that there is very little involvement of physical papers. Croom and Johnston (2003) suggest that a reduction in paperwork and an increase in automation for creating purchase related documents in turn reduces the number of errors. In addition, documents can be prepared and dispatched quickly (Reddick, 2004). A recent case study report published in M2 Presswire (2009) indicated that by using COA eProcurement solutions the Gloucester city council reduced time taken to procure goods by 75%.

Furthermore, digitisation allows organisations for keeping a more accurate audit trail and the tracking of orders (Reddick, 2004). Reducing the cost of preparing purchase related documents is another benefit of e-Procurement systems. According to Parida et al (2005), organizations using eProcurement systems have reported savings of up to 42%, especially in larger firms. In another study, Bandiera et al. (2008) reported a 22% improvement in procurement related administrative costs.

Use of eProcurement systems further help organisations shorten their order cycles considerably. A long order cycle is normally caused by delays in transmitting documents between various groups. According to Rahim et al (2008), a requisition form often has to wait at several locations before it is picked up and sent to the next relevant department for processing. Waiting times may be experienced where someone has to pick up the requisition from the buyer, where someone has to verify it at an approval station and where the supplier has to manually sift through potentially hundreds of such orders originating from various locations (Kalakota and Robinson, 1999). Hence, a single remedy to the long waiting times may be introduced by eProcurement systems which send requisitions directly to all the concerned parties. This view is also supported by Osmonbekov et al (2002).

Control Enhancement

Control is defined as the regulation of an activity (Merriam-Webster, 2009). A lack of control in the procurement of goods and services may lead to such problems as maverick purchasing practices (Garrido et al, 2006), difficulty in maintaining audit trails and reduced visibility of overall spending (Attaran, 2001). It is often difficult to adequately address these issues in the manual procurement process. By automating the procurement process, eProcurement systems can improve control on purchasing practices. For example, through punch functionality supported by eProcurement systems employees can gain direct access to their suppliers' systems to visually confirm technical specifications and price descriptions (Teo et al, 2009) and this functionality thus allows purchasing from the catalogues of approved suppliers only thus reducing maverick buying practices (Puschmann and Alt, 2005). Likewise, these systems address the difficulty in maintaining audit trails by electronically linking purchase orders, invoices and receipts (Croom, 2001; Angeles, 2006). According to a report published in Long-Term Living (2009), use of eProcurement systems helps organisations maintain internal consistency in procurement procedures which in turn enhances control on purchasing function.

Image Advancement

Use of eProcurement systems can even help organisations create a positive image (Kaliannan, 2009; Leipold et al, 2004). Image is established in two ways. First, by demonstrating that organisations provide a fair opportunity for all stakeholder participation in their procurement process (Liao et al, 2002). This is particularly important to government bodies as they are expected to uphold the rights of all participants. For example, a recent report published in BERNAMA (2008) indicates that the state government of Penang, Malaysia launched eprocurement initiative to give more opportunities to the contractors and suppliers to work for the state government. Second, an enhanced image is also established when eProcurement systems help maintain compatibility between organisations. According to Daniel and White (2005), forming linkages with other organisations is quickly becoming both popular and necessary as the world markets become more volatile. Use of eProcurement systems enable organisations to foster links electronically which in turn helps them to appear more technology savvy.

Improved Relationships with Suppliers

The usage of eProcurement systems can provide organisations with an opportunity to extend and improve their existing relationships with suppliers (Puschman and Alt, 2005; Scriven, 2003; Aghesin, 2001). Through the use of these systems, a small number of dedicated suppliers can provide goods and services at lower cost because the organisation will be buying in greater volumes (Gebauer and Segev, 2000). This provides the suppliers with an incentive to maintain the relationship. The relationship is beneficial for both buying organisations and suppliers. The eProcurement systems further allow several aspects of the supplier relationship management to be automated. Once a supplier receives a "preferred" status, purchases are more likely to head its way than a supplier which is not deemed "preferred". This is because the eProcurement system makes it easy to look up preferred suppliers.

Another beneficial aspect is the increased communication and sharing of information between suppliers and buying organizations (Brun et al., 2004). Changes in the market may require adjustments to orders at very short notices. The speed of the eProcurement systems can help ensure that suppliers receive the correct instructions before an order is dispatched. This provides a competitive advantage to the supplier (Dai and Kauffman, 2006). With new eProcurement systems, the supplier can receive both strategic and operational information from the buying organisation. This increased sharing of information allows them to plan their production and hence is rewarding for both entities which in turn contributes to strengthening business relationship with suppliers.

In summary, we argue that the attainment of these benefits needs empirical confirmation from the perspective of employees who are the user of the eProcurement systems particularly at the government context. We further expect that these benefits, if experienced by employees, are expected to further accelerate the rate of adoption of eProcurement systems in government organisations.

E-Procurement as an Innovation in the Government Sector

Rogers (1995) defines an innovation as 'an idea or artifact perceived to be new by the relevant unit that may adopt the innovation'. Building on this definition, Vaidya et al (2008) argue that e-procurement systems can be regarded to be an innovation that helps transforms the traditional paper-based public procurement processes. An e-procurement system in the government sector when interconnected with an organisation's internal financial system has the potential to minimise transaction processes inefficiencies and can improve control on spending particularly low value and routine commodities.

Demographic Characteristics and Adoption of Innovation: An Overview

Adoption of innovation is often measured in terms of rate of adoption and innovativeness behaviour. Usually, the rate of adoption determines the success of the innovation, while innovativeness refers to the degree to which an individual is relatively earlier in adopting new ideas than other individuals (Rogers, 1995). According to Branca (2008), two major sets of constructs have been hypothesised to contribute to the prediction of innovativeness and innovation adoption decisions: attributes of the innovation itself and personal-social characteristics. A large number of innovation adoption studies have focused on the association between individuals' usage of innovations and their demographic characteristics (Steenkamp et al, 1999; Lee at al, 2003). The findings of these studies are mixed about the role of the demographic characteristics on the usage behaviour of innovations.

The influence of demographic characteristics of people using various types of ICT-based innovative systems is recgonised in both theoretical and empirical studies. Our observation is consistent with the views expressed by Branca (2008). Popular theoretical frameworks from social psychology literature such as Theory of Reasoned Action (Fishbein and Ajzen, 1975), and Theory of Planned Behaviour (Ajzen, 1991) which are widely used in the IS/IT adoption literature do not deny the possibility that external factors (e.g. demographic variables and personality characteristics) will have a relationship with the usage behaviour of individuals for IT applications. The IS/IT adoption literature further contains a number of other theoretical frameworks which acknowledge that the demographic characteristics of people (who use ICT applications) have an influence on their intention and/or extent of ICT use. For example, Technology Adoption Model (TAM) of Davis et al. (1989) is an adaptation of TRA and is specifically designed to suit the IS/IT adoption context. It incorporates several external variables (e.g. user characteristics) which may influence users' belief structure towards perceived ease of use and usefulness of IT/IS applications.

Another popular model known as the Interactional model (Nelson, 1990) seeks to explain the need for individual adjustment necessary to use information-driven technologies. The central tenet of the model is the notion that organisational context and differences in individuals affect their attitudes and usage behaviour. More specifically, individuals may vary in terms of their demographic characteristics and cognitive styles which in turn affect their attitudes for using innovative technologies. MIS success model (Zmud, 1979) represents another theoretical framework which portrays the manner in which individual differences influence MIS success. The model further reflects the impact of individual differences upon the attitudes held by potential MIS users and upon the tendencies for MIS users to involve themselves in the MIS development effort. Individual differences are grouped into three categories: cognitive style, personality, and demographic/situational variables.

The IS/IT literature also contains empirical evidence which suggests that demographic characteristics of individuals affect their perceptions and actual usage behaviour of various types of ICT applications (Mumford and Bank, 1967; Lucas, 1978; Keillor et al., 1997; Nachmias et al, 2000; Speier and Venkatesh, 2002). Thus, building on the notion of the role of demographic characteristics of individuals as recognised in the innovation adoption and broader IS/IT adoption theoretical and empirical literatures, we conjecture that the perceptions of employees (who use eProcurement systems) about benefits arising from their usage of eProcurement systems may also vary depending on their demographic characteristics. However, this assumption cannot be accepted without empirical confirmation. As such, there is a clear need to investigate the association between employees' perceptions of benefits and their demographic characteristics in relation to eProcurement systems contexts.

RESEARCH HYPOTHESES

Drawing on the innovation and broader IS/IT adoption literature, we have identified four demographic characteristics of employees (e.g. gender, job role, type of eProcurement user, and working experience in councils) that may potentially influence their perceptions of benefits from their use of eProcurement systems. Detailed explanations are offered below.

Gender

We argue that the perceptions of male employees about the benefits from their use of eProcurement systems are likely to be greater than those of their female counterparts. This is because unlike females, use of IT-based systems (including eProcurement systems) by male employees is generally driven by their expectations of the usefulness of the system (Venkatesh and Morris, 2000). Thus, it can be argued that male employees are expected to use eProcurement systems to seek more efficiency and productivity improvements and increased ability to exert control. On the other hand, female employees generally demonstrate greater anxiety towards the use of IT systems (Heinseen et al, 1987; Venkatesh and Morris, 2000) and exhibit a lack of confidence in the execution of their tasks using complex technologies like eProcurement systems. Moreover, female employees' use of IT systems is often influenced by their perceived ease of technology use (Vallerand, 1997). As the eProcurement systems are usually complex in nature, female employees are more likely to form low expectations of benefits from their use of these systems. These arguments lead to the following hypothesis:

H1: There is a significant difference in the perceptions of eProcurement systems benefits between male and female employees

Job Role

We argue that job roles held by employees may have an influence on their perceptions of benefits arising from their use of eProcurement systems. One reason for this assertion is the existence of differences in perceived information needs between managerial and operational employees (Hjelt, 2006). This means that the attitudinal beliefs of employees having managerial responsibilities towards perceived usefulness of eProcurement applications to address their information needs would be low. Their needs are so diverse that the eProcurement systems alone may not be adequate to satisfy all their information requirements. Hence, these employees are more likely to demonstrate low expectation of benefits from eProcurement systems than those of operational employees who are primarily concerned with improving their efficiency and productivity using eProcurement systems. Thus, the following hypothesis is developed:

H2: There is a significant difference in the perceptions of eProcurement systems benefits between managerial and operational employees

Type of eProcurement User

We argue that those employees who use eProcurement systems on a regular basis tend to become more familiar with the functionalities offered by these systems and are in a position to better appreciate how the systems could be used in support of performing their tasks. Regular users can also overcome anxiety which they may initially have towards the use of eProcurement systems. As these users grow confidence, they begin to experiment with a variety of functionalities offered by the eProcurement systems which may not ordinarily be explored by more casual users. Hence, employees using eProcurement systems regularly may demonstrate more positive expectation of benefits than those of casual users. This assertion thus leads to the following hypothesis:

H4: There is a significant difference in the perceptions of eProcurement systems benefits between casual and regular eProcurement systems users

Working Experience at Councils

We argue that experienced employees who have been working at councils for a long period of time tend to be more rigid in changing their work style because habits and norms which they have formed over the years are much stronger among them than for new employees. Thus, perceptions about compatibility of the eProcurement systems with employees' past experience and work practices at councils would play a vital role in determining their views towards benefits expected from their use of these systems. In addition, those new employees who have joined councils are more likely to have been trained in the use of latest variety of IT applications during their academic programmes at tertiary institutions. Hence, they may have better appreciation of the benefits that could potentially be delivered by eProcurement systems. As such, the following hypothesis is derived:

H3: There is a significant difference in the perceptions of eProcurement systems benefits between new and experienced employees

RESEARCH APPROACH

Our intention is to discover the existence of possible relationships between employees' demographic characteristics and their perceptions of benefits arising from their use of web-enabled eProcurement systems at councils. Hence, our research can be considered exploratory in nature for which according to Yin (2004) an exploratory survey is deemed appropriate. The Municipal Association of Victoria (MAV) was contacted for information regarding those local government councils which had implemented eProcurement systems. A subsequent response from the Association indicated that five councils in Victoria had implemented these systems. These councils were invited to participate in the research project, but only three expressed an interest. Given the exploratory nature of our research, a convenience sampling strategy was adopted and a total of two hundred questionnaires were distributed among those three participating councils. The intended participants of the survey were the employees whose job responsibilities involve interacting with the eProcurement systems as a part of their routine activities. A total of sixty usable questionnaires were returned resulting in a response rate of 30%. According to Hikmet and Chen (2003), there is a debate about the reasonable and acceptable response rate in social research. Many IT/IS researchers (e.g. Walstrom and Wilson, 1997) had faced a problem with low response rates (e.g.

10%). Moreover, other Australian IT scholars (e.g. Lin and Pervan, 2003) have also reported a low response rate (e.g. 7%). Considering these, the response rate (30%) for this research project was regarded satisfactory.

An initial survey instrument was developed that included 16 items which operationalised employees' perceptions about for broad categories of eProcurement benefits reported in Section 2. These items were identified from the relevant literature sources but were refined to suit the eProcurement systems context. Each item was measured on a scale of 1 to 5 where 1 means strongly agree, 2 means agree, 3 means neutral, 4 means disagree, and 5 means strongly disagree. A summary of these items is shown in Table 1. A total of 4 items were used to measure the perceptions of efficiency-related benefits. The focus of these items is to determine the degree to which the eProcurement systems return the benefits relating to reduced costs and faster procurement task processing. Another 6 items were used to measure the control enhancement benefits. Control benefits determine such aspects as compliance and transparency of purchasing practice. Two items were used to measure how well the e-Procurement systems help advance the progressive image of the councils. Finally, 3 more items were used to measure if the eProcurement systems help councils in improving relationships with their suppliers. Relationships with suppliers were expected to allow for greater amounts of information sharing and increased collaboration.

Employee demographic characteristics were measured on a dichotomous scale. Two types of job roles were identified: managerial and opera-

Table 1. E-procurement benefits and their operationalisations

Benefit categories	Item Measurement	Literature Sources
Efficiency related benefits	EF01: I think the use of the e-procurement system in my organisation helps reduce paperwork EF02: I think the use of the e-procurement system in my organisation helps reduce the cost of preparing purchase orders EF03: I think the use of the e-procurement system in my organisation facilitates quicker receipt of ordered items from our suppliers EF04: I think the use of the e-procurement system in my organisation helps delegate more authority to the employees	Panayiotou et al (2004), Parida et al (2005)
Control benefits	C1: I think the use of the e-procurement system in my organisation helps improve compliance with organisational procurement policies C2: I think the use of the e-procurement system in my organisation helps my organisation to exert greater control on procurement function C3: I think the use of the e-procurement system in my organisation helps reduce maverick buying practices C4: I think the use of the e-procurement system in my organisation helps improve transparency into our procurement practices C5: I think the use of the e-procurement system in my organisation helps establish management accountability for our procurement decisions C6: I think the use of the e-procurement system follows an organisation-wide procurement strategy	Garrido et al (2006), Scriven (2003)
Image	I1:I think the use of the e-procurement system in my organisation helps improve the image of our procurement function I2: I think the use of the e-procurement system in my organisation helps in advancing the progressive image of our organisation	Leipold et al (2004), Kaliannan (2009)
Relationship with suppliers	RS1:I think the use of the e-procurement system in my organisation helps improve relationship with suppliers RS2: I think the use of the e-procurement system in my organisation facilitates greater information sharing with our suppliers RS3: I think the use of the e-procurement system in my organisation facilitates greater collaboration with our suppliers	Puschmann and Alt (2005), Gebauer and Segev (2000)

tional. Working experience was measured using two categories: new staff (having less than 5 years experience at the council) and experienced staff (with over 5 years working experience at the councils). Two types of eProcurement users (i.e. regular and casual) were identified based on their frequency of eProcurement use. Use of these systems was measured on a scale of 1 to 5 where 1 means always, 2 means quite often, 3 means sometimes, 4 means seldom, and 5 means never. Employees are considered as regular users who selected a rating of 1 and 2 and casual users are those employees who chose a rating of 3 and over.

The initial survey instrument was reviewed by three domain experts who were selected following the guidelines of Kitchenham and Pfleeger (2002). Based on the suggestions given by the domain experts, several questionnaire items were rephrased to improve clarity and one item (Item C6) was removed from the control benefit. SPSS, a popular statistical software, was used to analyse employees' responses. More specifically, student t-tests were performed to find out whether a significant difference in employees' perceptions of eProcurement benefits can be observed based on their demographic characteristics.

EMPIRICAL FINDINGS

Characteristics of the Participating Employees

A profile of the surveyed employees is provided in Table 2. A number of observations can be made: (a) a dominance of female users (65%) of the eProcurement system is visible, (b) employees representing managerial roles (13.3%) is limited. This makes sense because not all employees are expected to have high level of managerial responsibilities, (c) in terms of job experience, about an equal proportion of the participating council employees are new staff and experienced staff, and d) a slight majority of the employees (58.3%) are regular users of the eProcurement system.

Inter-Correlation Matrix Between Employee Characteristics

The inter-correlation matrix for the employee characteristics is shown in Table 3. Gender is found to be negatively related to work experience (r = -.059), and user type (r = -.053). This means that female employees are likely to have less job experience with the councils and tend to be casual users of eProcurement systems. Job role is also negatively related to user type (r = -.133), implying that operational employees tend to be casual users of eProcurement systems.

Evaluating E-Procurement Benefit Categories

A factor analysis was conducted to ascertain the existence of the four broad categories of eProcurement systems benefits reported in Section 2. The results (shown in Table 4) provide partial support for the theoretically derived categories. Instead of four, only three broad categories of benefits

Table 2. A summary of employee profile

Characteristics of employees	Frequency	Percent
Gender		
Male	21	35
Female	39	65
Job Role		
Managerial	8	13.3
Non-managerial	52	86.7
Working years at the council 1 to 5 years Over 5 years	 31 29	 51.6 48.3
Type of eProcurement user		
Casual Regular	25 35	41.7 58.3

Table 3. Correlation matrix

Characteristics	Correlation and Significance	Gender	Job Role	Work Experience	User Type
Gender	Pearson Correlation	1	.123	-.059	-.053
	Sig. (2-tailed)		.348	.652	.687
Job Role	Pearson Correlation	.123	1	.085	-.133
	Sig. (2-tailed)	.348		.518	.313
Work experience	Pearson Correlation	-.059	.085	1	.141
	Sig. (2-tailed)	.652	.518		.283
User type	Pearson Correlation	-.053	-.133	.141	1
	Sig. (2-tailed)	.687	.313	.283	

* Correlation is significant at the 0.05 level (2-tailed).

Table 4. Results of factor analysis

Benefit item description	Benefit categories			Cronbach alpha
	Efficiency	Control	Socio-political	
ER01: I think the use of the e-procurement system in my organisation helps reduce paperwork	.737			.678
ER02: I think the use of the e-procurement system in my organisation helps reduce the cost of preparing purchase orders	.738			
ER04: I think the use of the e-procurement system in my organisation helps delegate more authority to the employees	.677			
C01: I think the use of the e-procurement system in my organisation helps improve compliance with organisational procurement policies		.808		.875
C02: I think the use of the e-procurement system in my organisation helps my organisation to exert greater control on procurement function		.714		
C03: I think the use of the e-procurement system in my organisation helps reduce maverick buying practices		.690		
C04: I think the use of the e-procurement system in my organisation helps improve transparency into our procurement practices		.868		
C05: I think the use of the e-procurement system in my organisation helps establish management accountability for our procurement decisions		.736		
I01: I think the use of the e-procurement system in my organisation helps improve the image of our procurement function			.768	.895
I02: I think the use of the e-procurement system in my organisation helps in advancing the progressive image of our organisation			.766	
RS01: I think the use of the e-procurement system in my organisation helps improve relationship with suppliers			.721	
RS02: I think the use of the e-procurement system in my organisation facilitates greater information sharing with our suppliers			.845	
RS03: I think the use of the e-procurement system in my organisation facilitates greater collaboration with our suppliers			.812	
Kaiser-Meyer-Olkin Measure of Sampling Adequacy: .796 Bartlett's Test of Sphericity: Approx. Chi-Square = 478.474, df = 78, Sig = .000 Total variance explained: 69%				

have emerged. Two of them include *efficiency-related* and *control* Benefits which are consistent with the literature analysis. However, *image* and *relationship with suppliers* were collapsed into a new single category which is named as *socio-political* benefits. The reliability of each of these three broad categories of benefits was calculated using Cronbach Alpha (Nunnaly, 1978) (shown in the 4th column of Table 4) and was found to be satisfactory.

An arithmetic mean for each of the three benefit categories is reflected in Figure 2. The participating employees had more favourable perceptions towards efficiency related benefits (mean: 2.36) as compared to those of control (mean: 2.43) and socio-political benefits (mean: 2.73). Furthermore, in broad sense, the mean perceptions of employees towards overall benefits are also quite favourable (mean: 2.53). Out of three categories of benefits, employees had least favourable views towards the attainment of socio-political benefits.

Testing Hypotheses

We have performed student t-tests (shown in Table 5, 6, 7, and 8) to find out whether a significant difference in employees' perceptions about eProcurement benefits can be observed based on their gender, job role, work experience at council, and user type. With the exception of efficiency related benefits, the female employees were found to have more favourable perceptions towards control, socio-political and overall benefits. However, the differences are not statistically significant. Hence, hypothesis H1 is not supported.

In terms of job role, managerial employees demonstrated more favourable perceptions towards overall eProcurement systems benefits. They also had more favourable views about control benefits. In contrast, operational employees displayed greater favourable perceptions towards efficiency related and socio-political benefits. These differences are not however statistically significant. Therefore, hypothesis H2 is rejected.

In terms of work experience of employees at councils, it was found that new employees dem-

Figure 2. Mean value of e-procurement benefits

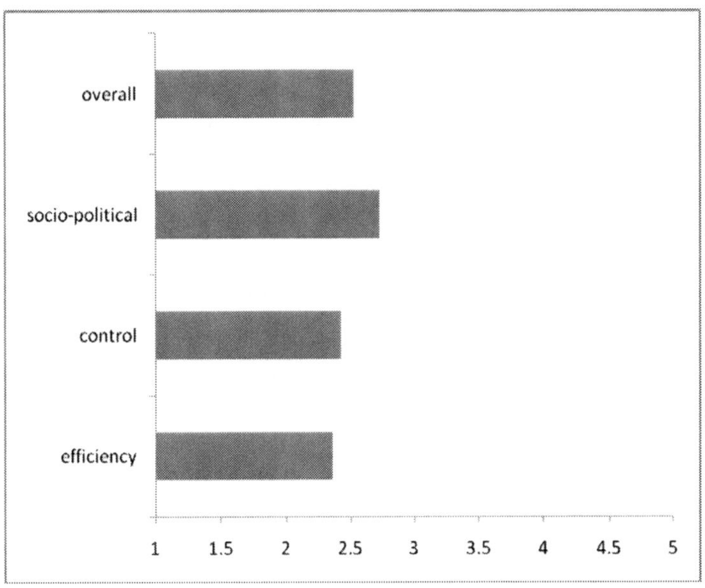

Table 5. Student t-test results based on gender

Type of benefits	Mean Rating		t-value	df	p-value
	Male	Female			
Overall benefits	2.64	2.47	1.109	58	2.72
Efficiency related benefits	2.33	2.38	-.284	58	.778
Control benefits	2.52	2.38	.726	58	.471
Socio-political benefits	2.95	2.61	1.865	58	.067

Table 6. Student t-test results based on job role

Type of benefits	Mean Rating		t-value	df	p-value
	Managerial	Non-managerial			
Overall benefits	2.51	2.53	-.074	58	.941
Efficiency related benefits	2.41	2.35	.227	58	.821
Control benefits	2.20	2.46	-1.005	58	.319
Socio-political benefits	2.90	2.70	.740	58	.462

onstrated more favourable perceptions towards all types of eProcurement benefits as opposed to more experienced employees at councils. However, such differences were not found to be statistically significant. As such, hypothesis H3 is rejected.

On the matter of the variations in the eProcurement perceptions towards overall benefits, user type appeared to be a significant differentiator. Student t-test results support the existence of a statistically significant difference in the perceptions of casual and regular users towards overall benefits ($p = .026$) and control benefits ($p= .000$). However, no such differences were noted with regard to efficiency related and socio-political benefits. Hence, the hypothesis H4 received partial support.

DISCUSSION

The empirical findings presented in the previous section are important for several reasons. First, the mean perceptions of employees towards all types of benefits (Figure 1) lean more towards favourable side. This implies that in broad sense the impact of eProcurement systems was seen largely in a positive light by the participating employees. This finding is consistent with the

Table 7. Student t-test results based on work experience

Type of benefits	Mean Rating		t-value	df	p-value
	New Employees	Old Employees			
Overall benefits	2.49	2.57	-.585	58	.561
Efficiency related benefits	2.31	2.42	-.659	58	.512
Control benefits	2.38	2.48	-.522	58	.604
Socio-political benefits	2.70	2.76	-.351	58	.727

Table 8. Student t-test results based on user types

Type of benefits	Mean Rating		t-value	df	p-value
	Casual User	Regular User			
Overall benefits	2.72	2.39	2.28	58	.026*
Efficiency related benefits	2.49	2.27	1.257	58	.214
Control benefits	2.80	2.16	3.865	58	.000*
Socio-political benefits	2.78	2.69	.483	58	.631

Note: * means statistically significant at 95% confidence level

views of many eBusiness scholars (Neef, 2001; Croom, 2001; Puschman and Alt, 2005). However, employees had most favourable perceptions about the attainment of efficiency improvement benefit. This reinforces previous research by Harringan et al. (2008) who conducted a survey on eProcurement systems use within the Irish ICT industry and reported that more respondents considered efficiency improvement and reduction of purchase transaction costs as the primary benefits of eProcurement systems.

This study found increased control over procurement process as another benefit which is consistent with the views of Puschmann and Alt (2005). However, control benefit was considered to be the second most important benefit. This finding too is consistent with the observations of Harrigan et al. (2008) who indicated a reduction in maverick purchasing was less frequently mentioned by the survey respondents in Ireland. Our study further found improved relationships with suppliers to be yet another benefit which supports the views of Scriven (2003) and Puschmann and Alt (2005). However, unlike efficiency and control benefits, improved relationships with suppliers was reported by the employees to be the least experienced benefit. Even this finding is consistent with the observations of Harringan et al. (2008). We thus suggest that the inter-organisational type of eProcurement systems benefit is perceived to a lesser extent than that of intra-organisational benefit. The implication is that the introduction of the eProcurement systems at the participating councils are inward focussed and aimed less at strategic level of enhancing collaboration and information sharing with suppliers.

Second, although such demographic characteristics as gender, job role, and work experience of employees were not found to be statistically significant factor to differentiate the perceptions of employees towards various types of eProcurement benefits, but still some insightful observations were made. For example, managerial employees considered exerting control via the eProcurement systems to be more important than operational employees. This makes sense because of management's intention to introduce eProcurement systems to control maverick buying practices. On the other hand, operational employees indicated more favourable perceptions about efficiency related benefits. This finding too makes sense because the primary concern of these employees may have is how to use the eProcurement systems in support of improving their productivity and efficiency.

Third, those new employees who are not working at the councils for a very long period of time demonstrated more positive perceptions about all types of benefits. It can be argued that the new employees perhaps have prior exposure and training in the use of latest generation of IT applications during their academic programs undertaken at their tertiary institutions, and hence they may have greater appreciation of the merits of IT systems (including eProcurement systems) used at work places. Moreover, they are likely to be less influenced by the existing inertia of the councils and may be more keen to apply their academically earned skills and knowledge into practice than those experienced employees who have been working at the councils for a longer period of time.

Fourth, a significant difference in views was observed between casual and regular users of eProcurement systems about control and overall benefits. The presence of more positive perceptions of employees who regularly use these systems about the overall benefits makes sense because more active users of information technologies may have more positive attitudes towards the use of eProcurement systems, are keen to use these systems more innovatively, and are more optimistic and appreciative of the impacts that IT-based e-procurement systems can create.

CONCLUSION

The research project reported in this chapter addressed the following two research questions:

1. What is the extent of perceived benefits arising from the use of eProcurement systems by employees working at the local government bodies?
2. Do the perceptions of employees working at the local government bodies about the benefits arising from their use of eProcurement systems significantly differ based on their demographic characteristics?

To answer these questions, a questionnaire was developed based on eBusiness literature analysis which was subsequently distributed among two hundred employees at three local councils situated in the state of Victoria, Australia which have introduced web-enabled eProcurement systems in recent years. A total of sixty completed responses were received which were then analysed. With regard to the first question, we find that efficiency improvement and establishing control were perceived to be the two most important benefits. In contrast, socio-political benefits involving the desire to advance councils' image and improve councils' relationship with suppliers was considered less important. These findings about e-procurement benefits provide some support to the current impression given in the eBusiness literature. However, there was no evidence to suggest that the degree of e-procurement systems benefits perceived by employees was spectacular.

On the matter of the second question, our findings indicate that the demographic characteristics of the participating councils' employees in broad sense are not related to their perceptions of eProcurement benefits. However, evidence was found which suggests the presence of a clear relationship between employees' usage behavior of their eProcurement systems (expressed in terms of casual and regular users) and their perceptions of benefits. In other words, those employees who perceived greater extent of eProcurement benefits indeed tend to be the more regular users of these systems. Likewise, employees who are casual eProcurement users are reported to have low appreciation of benefits arising from their use of these systems. Therefore, our study did not provide a strong support to the views expressed in the innovations adoption and broader IS/IT adoption literatures.

These findings make contributions to theory and practice. For theory, a major contribution to the eBusiness literature is the construction of an empirically validated survey instrument for the measurement of eProcurement benefits. Another contribution is the confirmation of a partial significant relationship between employees' demographic characteristics and their perceived benefits arising from their use of eProcurement systems. To practice, the survey instrument can be used by organisations (which have implemented eProcurement systems) as a tool to assess eProcurement success by evaluating the degree to which the eProcurement benefits cited in literature are being really reported by their employees. Senior management can focus their attention to those specific benefits areas that would further require improvement.

There are several ways this research can be further extended. The use of a small sample size (n = 60) may have restricted the outcomes of our analysis. For future research in this area, a much larger sample size is needed. Longitudinal studies could also be carried out to find out whether the perceptions of employees about eProcurement benefits change over time. Finally, in order to develop an improved understanding about the perceptions of eProcurement benefits among supply chain partners, further studies should be undertaken in which the views of both the councils and their suppliers (who participate in online procurement relationships with councils) are to be analysed.

REFERENCES

Advanced Business Solutions. (2009). *COA solutions: Gloucester city council cuts time taken to procure good by 75% using COA Solutions' e-Procurement.* M2 Presswire, Coventry, September 15.

Afsharipour, A., Afshari, A., & Sahaf, L. (2006). *E-procurement in automotive supply chain of Iran*. Master's thesis, Lulea University of Technology, Sweden. Retrieved from http://epubl.luth.se/1653-0187/2006/08/LTU-PB-EX-0608-SE.pdf

Ancarani, A. (2005). Towards quality e-services in the public sector: The evolution of web sites in the local public service sector. *Managing Service Quality, 15*(1), 6–23. doi:10.1108/09604520510575236

Angeles, R. (2006). Business-to-business e-procurement corporate initiative: A descriptive empirical study. *ICEC 2006 Conference, Fredericton, NB, Canada.*

Anonymous. (2008). *E-procurement to ensure fair tender for contractors*. Bernama, Kuala Lumpur, Jul 17.

Anonymous,. (2009). E-procurement. *Long-Term Living, 58*(7), 22–24.

Attaran, M. (2001). The coming age of e-procurement. *Industrial Management & Data Systems, 101*(4), 177–181. doi:10.1108/02635570110390080

Branca, A. S. (2008). Demographic influences on behavior: An update to the adoption of bank delivery channels. *International Journal of Bank Marketing, 26*(4), 237–259. doi:10.1108/02652320810884786

Braue, D. (2004, 5 October). Why government isn't buying e-Procurement. *CIO*, 1-6.

Brun, A., Corti, D., & Cozzini, S. (2004). Value assessment of e-procurement projects: A modular methodology. *Production Planning and Control, 15*(7), 742–760. doi:10.1080/09537280412331298184

Croom, S., & Johnston, R. (2003). E-service: Enhancing customer service through e-procurement. *International Journal of Service Industry Management, 14*(5), 539–555. doi:10.1108/09564230310500219

Elbanna, A. (2010). From intention to use to actual rejection: The journey of an e-procurement system. *Journal of Enterprise Information Management, 23*(1), 81–99. doi:10.1108/17410391011008914

Eprocurement.gov. (2009). *News clip*. Retrieved from http://www.eprocurement.gov.in/news/sign.jpg

European Union. (2005). *E-procurement action plan*. Retrieved from http://europa.eu.int/idabc/en/document/3824/194

Farhoomand, A. (2001). *E-procurement at Cathay Pacific Airways: E-business valuation*. Centre for Asian Business Cases. The University of Hong Kong.

Garrido, M. J., Gutierrez, A. M., & San Jose, R. (2006). The impact of e-procurement on the structure of the buying centre. *International Journal of Electronic Business*, *4*(6), 463–482. doi:10.1504/IJEB.2006.011696

Garrido, M. J., Gutierrez, A. M., & San Jose, R. (2008). Organizational and economic consequences of business e-procurement intensity. *Technovation*, *28*, 615–629. doi:10.1016/j.technovation.2007.12.004

Garrido-Samaniego, M. J., Gutierrez-Arranz, A. M., & Jose-Cabezudo, R. S. (2010). Assessing the impact of e-procurement on the structure of the buying centre. *International Journal of Information Management*, *30*, 135–143. doi:10.1016/j.ijinfomgt.2009.08.004

Gebauer, J., & Segev, A. (2000). Emerging technologies to support indirect procurement: Two case studies from the petroleum industry. *Information Technology Management*, *1*(1/2), 107–128. doi:10.1023/A:1019160605755

GovPro. (2009). An update about the e-procurement pilot programme. *GovProcurement Newsletter*, September, pp. 1-2.

Harrigan, P. O., Boyd, M. M., Ramsey, E., & Ibbotson, P. (2008). The development of e-procurement within the ICT manufacturing industry in Ireland. *Management Decision*, *46*(3), 481–500. doi:10.1108/00251740810863906

Hawking, P., & Stein, A. (2002). E-Procurement: Drivers, barriers and practices. *Conference Proceedings of the 2002 Australian Conference on Information Systems,* Melbourne, Australia.

Hikmet, N., & Chen, S. K. (2003). An investigation into low mail survey response rates of information technology users in health care organizations. *International Journal of Medical Informatics*, *72*(1-3), 29–34. doi:10.1016/j.ijmedinf.2003.09.002

Hjelt, M. (2006). *End-user attitudes towards EDM use in project work: A case study of the Kamppi Center project.* Master of Science Thesis. Sweden: Swedish School of Economics and Business Administration.

Igbaria, M., & Parasuraman, S. (1989). A path analytic study of individual characteristics, computer anxiety and attitudes toward microcomputers. *Journal of Management*, *15*(3), 373–383. doi:10.1177/014920638901500302

Kalakota, R., & Robinson, M. (1999). *e-Business: Roadmap for success.* Addison-Wesley Longman, USA.

Kaliannan, M., Awang, H., & Raman, M. (2009). Government purchasing: A review of e-procurement system in Malaysia. *The Journal of Knowledge Economy & Knowledge Management*, *4*(Spring), 27–37.

Kitchenham, B., & Pfleeger, S. L. (2002). Principles of survey research questionnaire evaluation. *Software Engineering Notes*, *27*(3), 20–23. doi:10.1145/638574.638580

Lee, E., Lee, J., & Eastwood, D. (2003). A two-step estimation of consumer adoption of technology-based service innovations. *The Journal of Consumer Affairs*, *37*(2), 256–282. doi:10.1111/j.1745-6606.2003.tb00453.x

Leipold, K., Klemow, J., Holloway, F., & Vaidya, K. (2004). The World Bank e-procurement for the selection of consultants: Challenges and lessons learned. *Journal of Public Procurement*, *4*(3), 319–339.

Lin, C., & Pervan, G. (2003). The practice of IS/IT benefits management in large Australian organisations. *Information & Management*, *41*(1), 13–24. doi:10.1016/S0378-7206(03)00002-8

Narasimhan, R., & Carter, J. R. (1998). Linking business unit and material sourcing strategies. *Journal of Business Logistics*, *19*(2), 155–170.

Neef, D. (2001). *E-Procurement: From strategy to implementation*. New Jersey: Prentice Hall.

Padhi, S. S., & Mohapatra, P. K. J. (2010). Adoption of e-procurement in the government departments. *Electronic Government: An International Journal*, *7*(1), 41–51. doi:10.1504/EG.2010.029890

Parida, V., Sophonthummapharn, K., & Parida, U. (2005). Understanding e-procurement: Qualitative case studies. Lulea University of Technology. Retrieved from http://www.ebrc.fi/kuvat/Parida_Sophonthummapharn_Parida_paper.pdf

Puschmann, T., & Alt, R. (2005). Successful use of e-procurement in supply chains. *Supply Chain Management*, *10*(2), 122–133. doi:10.1108/13598540510589197

Rahim, M. M., & As-Saber, S. (2009). Motivations and challenges of e-procurement systems adoption: The experience of an Australian City Council. In *Proceedings of the Conference on Administration, Society, and Education (e-CASE)*, January, Singapore.

Reddick, G. C. (2004). The growth of e-procurement in American state governments: A model & empirical evidence. *Journal of Public Procurement*, *4*(2), 151–176.

Rogers, E. M. (1995). *Diffusion of innovations*. New York, NY: The Free Press.

Schneider, G. P. (2006). *Electronic commerce*. Boston, MA: Thomson Course Technology.

Scriven, G. (2003). Interoperability in Australian government e-procurement – Strategy versus reality. *Conference Proceedings of the 7th Pacific Asia Conference on Information System*, Adelaide, South Australia, July 10-13, 2003.

Singer, M., Konstantinidis, G., Roubik, R., & Beffermann, E. (2009). Does e-procurement save the state money? *Journal of Public Procurement*, *9*(1), 58–78.

Steenkamp, J. B., Hofstede, F., & Wedel, M. (1999). A cross-national investigation into the individual and national cultural antecedents of consumer innovativeness. *Journal of Marketing*, *63*(2), 55–69. doi:10.2307/1251945

Teo, T. S. H., Lin, S., & Lai, K.-H. (2009). Adopters and non-adopters of e-procurement in Singapore: An empirical study. *Omega*, *37*, 972–987. doi:10.1016/j.omega.2008.11.001

Thai, K. V. (2001). Public procurement re-examined. *Journal of Public Procurement*, *1*(1), 9–50.

US Congress. (2001). *E-Government Bill of 2001*. Bill introduced into the US Senate by Joseph Lieberman, May 1.

Vaidya, K., & Hyde, M. (2011). Inter-organisational information systems assimilation: An empirical evaluation in light of the diffusion of innovation theory. *International Journal of Business Information Systems*, *7*(3), 247–258. doi:10.1504/IJBIS.2011.039330

Vaidya, K., Sajeev, A. S. M., & Callender, G. (2006). Critical factors that influence e-procurement implementation success in the public sector. *Journal of Public Procurement*, *6*(1&3), 70–99.

Vaidya, K., Sajeev, A. S. M., Johnston, J., & Cox, M. A. (2008). *Assimilation of public procurement innovation: an empirical; analysis in the light of transaction cost theory*. In Annual Conference of International Purchasing and Supply Education and Research Association, 9-12 March, Perth, Australia.

Vallerand, R. J. (1997). Toward a hierarchical model of intrinsic and extrinsic motivation. *Advances in Experimental Social Psychology*, 271–360. doi:10.1016/S0065-2601(08)60019-2

Venkatash, V., & Morris, M. (2000). Why don't men ever stop to ask for directions? Gender, social influence, and their role in technology acceptance and usage. *Management Information Systems Quarterly*, *24*, 115–139. doi:10.2307/3250981

Walker, H., & Harland, C. (2008). E-procurement in the United Nations: Influences, issues, and impact. *International Journal of Operations & Production Management*, *28*(9), 831–857. doi:10.1108/01443570810895276

Walstrom, K. A., & Wilson, R. L. (1997). An examination of executive information systems (EIS) users. *Information & Management*, *32*(2), 75–83. doi:10.1016/S0378-7206(97)00010-4

Wirtz, B. (2010). An empirical analysis of the acceptance of e-procurement in the German public sector. *International Journal of Public Administration*, *33*, 26–42. doi:10.1080/01900690903188768

World Bank. (2003). *Electronic government procurement (e-GP): World Bank draft strategy*. Washington, DC: World Bank.

Yin, R. K. (2003). *Case study research: Design and methods*. Newbury Park, CA: Sage Publications Inc.

Compilation of References

Aarts, J., Ash, J., & Berg, M. (2007). Extending the understanding of computerized physician order entry: Implications for professional collaboration, workflow and quality of care. *International Journal of Medical Informatics, 76*, 4–13. doi:10.1016/j.ijmedinf.2006.05.009

Aarts, J., & Gorman, P. (2007). IT in health care: Sociotechnical approaches "to err is system". *International Journal of Medical Informatics, 76*(Supplement 1), S1–S3. doi:10.1016/S1386-5056(07)00078-0

Aarts, J., & Peel, V. (1999). Using a descriptive model of change when implementing large scale clinical information systems to identify priorities for further research. *International Journal of Medical Informatics, 56*(1-3), 43–50. doi:10.1016/S1386-5056(99)00045-3

Aarts, J., Peel, V., & Wright, G. (1998). Organizational issues in health informatics: A model approach. *International Journal of Medical Informatics, 52*(1-3), 235–242. doi:10.1016/S1386-5056(98)00142-7

Adams, D., Nelson, R., & Todd, P. (1992). Perceived usefulness, perceived ease of use and user acceptance of information technology: A replication. *Management Information Systems Quarterly, 16*(2). doi:10.2307/249577

Advanced Business Solutions. (2009). *COA solutions: Gloucester city council cuts time taken to procure good by 75% using COA Solutions'e-Procurement.* M2 Presswire, Coventry, September 15.

Afsharipour, A., Afshari, A., & Sahaf, L. (2006). *E-procurement in automotive supply chain of Iran.* Master's thesis, Lulea University of Technology, Sweden. Retrieved from http://epubl.luth.se/1653-0187/2006/08/LTU-PB-EX-0608-SE.pdf

Ahmad, A. A., Grizzle, G. A., & Pettijohn, C. D. (2003). Patterns of change: Information change and congressional budget deliberations revisited. *Journal of Public Budgeting, Accounting &. Financial Management, 15*(1), 1–22.

Ahn, T., Ryu, S., & Han, I. (2004). The impact of the online and offline features on the user acceptance of Internet shopping malls. *Electronic Commerce Research and Applications, 3*, 405–420. doi:10.1016/j.elerap.2004.05.001

Ahn, C. (2009). *Korea: E-commerce industries.* Retrieved from http://www.mitc.com/PDFs/Korea-E-Commerce.pdf

Almeida, M. O. (2006). Role of ICT in diminishing collusion in procurement. *International Public Procurement Conference Proceedings,* 21-23 September. Rome, Italy.

Alt, R., & Fleisch, E. (2001). Business networking systems: Characteristics and lessons learned. *International Journal of Electronic Commerce, 5*(2), 7–27.

Alter, S. A. (2004). A work system view of DSS in its fourth decade. *Decision Support Systems, 38*(3), 319–327. doi:10.1016/j.dss.2003.04.001

Amit, R., & Zott, C. (2001). Value creation in e-business. *Strategic Management Journal, 22*(6/7), 493–520. doi:10.1002/smj.187

Ammenwerth, E., Iller, C., Mahler, C., Ammenwerth, E., Iller, C., & Mahler, C. (2006). IT-adoption and the interaction of task, technology and individuals: A fit framework and a case study. *BMC Medical Informatics and Decision Making, 6*, 3. doi:10.1186/1472-6947-6-3

Amoako-Gyampah, K., & Salam, A. F. (2004). An extension of the technology acceptance model in an ERP implementation environment. *Information & Management, 41*(6), 731–745. doi:10.1016/j.im.2003.08.010

Ancarani, A. (2005). Towards quality e-services in the public sector: The evolution of web sites in the local public service sector. *Managing Service Quality*, *15*(1), 6–23. doi:10.1108/09604520510575236

Anderson, J. C., & Gerbing, D. W. (1998). Structural equation modeling in practice: A review and recommended two-step approach. *Psychological Bulletin*, *103*(3), 411–423. doi:10.1037/0033-2909.103.3.411

Anderson, P. (1999). Complexity theory and organization science. *Organization Science: A Journal of the Institute of Management Sciences*, *10*(3), 216.

Angeles, R. (2006). Business-to-business e-procurement corporate initiative: A descriptive empirical study. *ICEC 2006 Conference, Fredericton, NB, Canada.*

Anonymous,. (2009). E-procurement. *Long-Term Living*, *58*(7), 22–24.

Anonymous. (2008). *E-procurement to ensure fair tender for contractors*. Bernama, Kuala Lumpur, Jul 17.

Ansari, A., & Modarress, B. (1990). *Just-in-time purchasing*. New York, NY: Free Press.

Aoki, M. (1988). *Information, incentives, and bargaining in the Japanese economy*. New York, NY: Cambridge University Press. doi:10.1017/CBO9780511571701

Archer-Lean, C., Clark, J., & Kerr, D. (2006). Evading technological determinism in ERP implementations: Towards a consultative social approach. *Australasian Journal of Information Systems*, *13*(2), 19–30.

Argyris, C. (2003). A life full of learning. *Organization Science*, *24*(7), 1178–1192. doi:10.1177/01708406030247009

Armstrong, C. P., & Sambamurthy, V. (1999). Information Technology assimilation in firms: The influence of senior leadership and IT infrastructures. *Information Systems Research*, *10*(4), 304–327. doi:10.1287/isre.10.4.304

Arnold, U. (1982). *Strategische Beschaffungspolitik: Steuerung und Kontrolle strategischer Beschaffungssubsysteme von Unternehmen*. Frankfurt, Germany: Lang.

Arnold, U. (1997). *Beschaffungsmanagement* (2nd ed.). Stuttgart, Germany: Schaeffer-Poeschel.

Arnold, U., & Essig, M. (1997). *Einkaufskooperationen in der Industrie*. Stuttgart, Germany: Schaeffer-Poeschel.

Arnold, U. (1998). Marktlich integrierte Kooperationen: Netzwerke und Allianzen in Beschaffung und Absatz. In Gassert, H., Prechtl, M., & Zahn, E. (Eds.), *Innovative Dienstleistungspartnerschaften: Neue Formen der Zusammenarbeit zwischen Industrie und Dienstleistern*. Stuttgart, Germany: Schaeffer-Poeschel.

Arnold, U. (1996). Sourcing-Konzepte. In Kern, W., Schroeder, H.-H., & Weber, J. (Eds.), *Handwoerterbuch der Produktionswirtschaft* (2nd ed.). Stuttgart, Germany: Schaeffer-Poeschel.

Arnold, U. (1989). Ziele, Aufgaben und Instrumente des Materialmanagements. In *Beschaffung Aktuell, 9,* 47-54.

Arnold, U., & Scheuing, E. E. (1997). Creating a factory within a factory. *Conference Proceedings of the 1997 NAPM Annual Conference*, Washington DC, May 4-7.

Arnold, U., Bernard, K. N. (1989). Just-in-time. *Technovation*, 401-430.

Ash, J. (1997). Organizational factors that influence information technology diffusion in academic health sciences centers. *Journal of the American Medical Informatics Association*, *4*(2), 102. doi:10.1136/jamia.1997.0040102

Ash, J., Anderson, J., Gorman, P., Zielstorff, R., Norcross, N., & Pettit, J. (2000). Managing change: Analysis of a hypothetical case. *Journal of the American Medical Informatics Association*, *7*(2), 125. doi:10.1136/jamia.2000.0070125

Ash, J., Gorman, P., Lavelle, M., Stavri, P., Lyman, J., & Fournier, L. (2003). Perceptions of physician order entry: Results of a cross-site qualitative study. *Methods of Information in Medicine*, *42*(4), 313–323.

Ash, J. S., Sittig, D. F., Campbell, E., Guappone, K., & Dykstra, R. H. (2006). An unintended consequence of CPOE implementation: Shifts in power, control, and autonomy. *AMIA ... Annual Symposium Proceedings / AMIA Symposium. AMIA Symposium*, 11–15.

Ash, J. S., Sittig, D. F., Dykstra, R., Campbell, E., & Guappone, K. (2009). The unintended consequences of computerized provider order entry: Findings from a mixed methods exploration. *International Journal of Medical Informatics*, *78*(Suppl 1), S69–S76. doi:10.1016/j.ijmedinf.2008.07.015

Ash, J. S., Sittig, D. F., Dykstra, R. H., Guappone, K., Carpenter, J. D., & Seshadri, V. (2007). Categorizing the unintended sociotechnical consequences of computerized provider order entry. *International Journal of Medical Informatics*, *76*(Suppl 1), S21–S27. doi:10.1016/j.ijmedinf.2006.05.017

Ash, J., Lyman, J., Carpenter, J., & Fournier, L. (2001). *A diffusion of innovations model of physician order entry.*

Ash, J., Sittig, D. F., Dykstra, R. H., Guappone, K., Carpenter, J., & Seshadri, V. (2004). *The unintended consequences of computerized physician order entry.* Presentation at the IT in Health Care Sociotechnical Approaches 2nd International Conference, Portland, Oregon, USA. Sept 12-14.

Attaran, M. (2001). The coming age of e-procurement. *Industrial Management & Data Systems*, *101*(4), 177–181. doi:10.1108/02635570110390080

Australian Government Information Management Office. (2006). *Strategic guide to e-procurement. Commonwealth of Australia*. AGIMO.

Axelrod, R. (1997). *The complexity of cooperation: Agent-based models of competition and collaboration.* Princeton, NJ: Princeton University Press.

Axelrod, D. (1988). *Budgeting for modern government.* New York, NY: St. Martin's Press.

Axelrod, D. (1995). *Budgeting for modern government* (2nd ed.). New York, NY: St. Martin's Press.

Backhaus, K., Aufderheide, D., & Spaeth, G. M. (1994). *Marketing fuer Systemtechnologien: Entwicklung eines theoretisch-oekonomisch begruendeten Geschaeftstypenansatzes.* Stuttgart, Germany: Schaeffer-Poeschel.

Baeker, R. M. (1993). *Readings in groupware and computer supported cooperative work* (p. 399). San Francisco, CA: Morgan Kauffman.

Bagozzi, R. P. (2007). The legacy of the technology acceptance model and a proposal for a paradigm shift. *Journal of the Association for Information Systems*, *8*(4), 224–254.

Bagozzi, R., & Yi, T. (1988). On the evaluation of structural equation models. *Journal of the Academy of Marketing Science*, *16*(1), 74–94. doi:10.1007/BF02723327

Bahli, B., & Rivard, S. (2003). The information technology outsourcing risk: A transaction cost and agency theory-based perspective. *Journal of Information Technology*, *18*(3), 211–221. doi:10.1080/0268396032000130214

Bakhtin, M. M. (1993). *Toward a philosophy of the act* (Liapunov, V., Trans.). Austin, TX: University of Texas.

Bakos, Y., & Brynjolfsson, E. (1993). From vendors to partners: Information technology and incomplete contracts in buyer-supplier relationships. *Journal of Organizational Computing and Electronic Commerce*, *3*(3), 301–328. doi:10.1080/10919399309540206

Bakos, Y. J., & Kremerer, C. F. (1992). Recent applications of economic theory in information technology research. *Decisions Support Systems*, 365-386.

Bandura, A. (1986). *Social foundations of thought and action.* Englewood Cliffs, NJ.

Barker, T., & Frolick, M. N. (2003). ERP implementation failure: A case study. *Information Systems Management*, *20*(4), 43–47. doi:10.1201/1078/43647.20.4.20030901/77292.7

Barki, H., & Hartwick, J. (1989). Rethinking the concept of user involvement. *Management Information Systems Quarterly*, *13*(1), 53–63. doi:10.2307/248700

Barney, J. (1991). Firm resources and sustained competitive advantage. *Journal of Management*, *17*(1), 99–120. doi:10.1177/014920639101700108

Barney, J. B., & Hansen, M. H. (1994). Trustworthiness as a source of competitive advantage. *Strategic Management Journal*, *15*, 175–190. doi:10.1002/smj.4250150912

Baron, J. N. (2004). Employing identities in organizational ecology. *Industrial and Corporate Change*, *13*(1), 3–32. doi:10.1093/icc/13.1.3

Barrett, S. S. (1987). Strategic alternatives and inter-organizational system implementation: An overview. *Journal of Management Information Systems*, *3*(3), 5–16.

Baumgartner, F. R., & Jones, B. D. (1993). *Agendas and instability in American politics*. Chicago, IL: University of Chicago Press.

Beer, S. (1985). *Diagnosing the system*. Wiley.

Bellman, S., Lohse, G. L., & Johnson, E. J. (1999). Predictors of online buying behavior. *Communications of the ACM*, *42*(12), 32–38. doi:10.1145/322796.322805

Benbasat, I., & Barki, H. (2007). Quo vadis, TAM? *Journal of the Association for Information Systems*, *8*(4), 211–218.

Benjamin, R., & Levinson, E. (1993). A framework for managing IT-enabled change. *Sloan Management Review*, *34*(4), 23–33.

Berg, M. (1998). Medical work and the computer-based patient record: A sociological perspective. *Methods of Information in Medicine*, *37*, 294–301.

Berg, M. (1999). Patient care information systems and health care work: A sociotechnical approach. *International Journal of Medical Informatics*, *55*(2), 87–101. doi:10.1016/S1386-5056(99)00011-8

Berg, M. (2004). *Health information management: Integrating information technology in health care work*. Routledge.

Bhattacherjee, A., & Premkumar, G. (2004). Understanding changes in belief and attitude toward information technology usage: A theoretical model and longitudinal test. *Management Information Systems Quarterly*, *28*(2), 229–254.

Billari, F. G., Fent, T., Prskawetz, A., & Scheffran, J. (Eds.). (2006). *Agent-based computational modelling: Applications in demography, social, economic and environmental sciences (contributions to economics)*. Heidelberg, Germany: Physica-Verlag.

Birkinshaw, J., Bresman, H., & Hakanson, L. (2000). Managing the post-acquisition integration process: How the human integration and task integration processes interact to foster value creation. *Journal of Management Studies*, *37*(3), 395–425. doi:10.1111/1467-6486.00186

Black, E. L., Carnes, T. A., Jandik, T., & Henderson, B. C. (2007). The relevance of target accounting quality to the long-term success of cross-border mergers. *Journal of Business Finance & Accounting*, *34*(1/2), 139–168. doi:10.1111/j.1468-5957.2006.01269.x

Boer, K., Kaymak, U., & Spiering, J. (2007). From discrete-time models to continuous-time, asynchronous modeling of financial markets. *Computational Intelligence*, *23*(2), 142–161. doi:10.1111/j.1467-8640.2007.00302.x

Boer, L. d., Harink, J., & Heijboer, G. (2001). A model for assessing the impact of electronic procurement forms. In *10th International Annual IPSERA Conference Proceedings*, Jönköping, (pp. 119-130).

Bolt, M., Killough, L., & Koh, H. (2000). Testing the interaction effects of task complexity in computer training using the social cognitive model. *Decision Sciences*, *32*(1), 1–20. doi:10.1111/j.1540-5915.2001.tb00951.x

Bordia, P., & DiFonzo, N. (2004). Problem solving in social interactions on the Internet: Rumor as social cognition. *Social Psychology Quarterly*, *67*(1), 33–49. doi:10.1177/019027250406700105

Borgia, C. R., & Coyner, R. S. (1996). The Evolution and success of budgeting systems at institutions of higher education. *Public Budgeting and Financial Management*, *7*(4), 467–492.

Bourdeaux, C. (2008). The problem with programs: Multiple perspectives on program structures in program-based performance-oriented budgets. *Public Budgeting & Finance*, *28*(2), 20–47. doi:10.1111/j.1540-5850.2008.00904.x

Bowker, G., & Star, S. L. (2000). *Sorting things out: Classification and its consequences*. Cambridge, MA: MIT Press.

Boyatzis, R. (1998). *Transforming qualitative information: Thematic analysis and code development*. Thousand Oaks, CA: SAGE.

Boyd, L., & Gupta, M. C. (2004). Constraint management: What is the theory? *International Journal of Operations & Production Management*, *24*(4), 350–371. doi:10.1108/01443570410524631

Bradford, M., & Florin, J. (2003). Examining the role of innovation diffusion factors on the implementation success of enterprise resource planning systems. *International Journal of Accounting Information Systems*, *4*(3), 205–225. doi:10.1016/S1467-0895(03)00026-5

Brahma, S. S., & Srivastava, K. B. L. (2007). Communication, executive retention, and employee stress as predictors of acquisition performance: An empirical evidence. *ICFAI Journal of Mergers & Acquisitions*, *4*(4), 7–26.

Branca, A. S. (2008). Demographic influences on behavior: An update to the adoption of bank delivery channels. *International Journal of Bank Marketing, 26*(4), 237–259. doi:10.1108/02652320810884786

Braue, D. (2004, 5 October). Why government isn't buying e-Procurement. *CIO*, 1-6.

Braybrooke, D., & Lindblom, C. (1963). *A strategy of decision*. New York, NY: Free Press.

Bresser-Pereira, L. C. (1998). *Reforma de Estado para a cidadania: A reforma gerencial brasileira na perspectiva internacional*. Brasília: ENAP.

Brun, A., Corti, D., & Cozzini, S. (2004). Value assessment of e-procurement projects: A modular methodology. *Production Planning and Control, 15*(7), 742–760. doi:10.1080/09537280412331298184

Burgess, K. (2007). *The role of social factors in generating innovation in mature industry supply chains*. Unpublished Doctoral Thesis, RMIT.

Burke, L. A., & Wise, J. M. (2003). The effective care, handling and pruning of the office grapevine. *Business Horizons, 46*(3), 71–76. doi:10.1016/S0007-6813(03)00031-4

Burn, J., & Robins, G. (2003). Moving towards e-government: A case study of organisational change processes. *Logistics Information Management, 16*(2), 25–36. doi:10.1108/09576050310453714

Burrell, G., & Morgan, G. (1979). *Sociological paradigms and organizational analysis*. London, UK: Heinemann Press.

Butler, T., & Fitzgerald, B. (2001). The relationship between user participation and the management of change surrounding the development of information systems: A European perspective. *Journal of End User Computing, 13*(1), 12–24. doi:10.4018/joeuc.2001010102

Byrne, B. M. (2001). *Structural equation modeling with AMOS: Basic concepts, applications, and programming*. New York, NY: Lawrence Erlbaum Associates Inc.

Callen, J., Braithwaite, J., & Westbrook, J. (2007). Cultures in hospitals and their influence on attitudes to, and satisfaction with, the use of clinical information systems. *Social Science & Medicine, 65*(3), 635–639. doi:10.1016/j.socscimed.2007.03.053

Callen, J., Braithwaite, J., & Westbrook, J. (2008). Contextual implementation model: a framework for assisting clinical information system implementations. *Journal of the American Medical Informatics Association, 15*(2), 255–262. doi:10.1197/jamia.M2468

Callen, J., Braithwaite, J., Westbrook, J. I., Callen, J., & Westbrook, J. I. (2009). The importance of medical and nursing sub-cultures in the implementation of clinical information systems. *Methods of Information in Medicine, 48*(2), 196–202.

Callon, M. (1986). Some elements of a sociology of translation: domestication of the scallops and the fishermen of Saint Brieuc Bay. In Law, J. (Ed.), *Power, action and belief: A new sociology of knowledge?* (pp. 196–233). London, UK: Routledge & Kegan Paul.

Campbell, J., McDonald, C., & Sethibe, T. (2010). Public and private sector IT governance: Identifying contextual differences. *Australasian Journal of Information Systems, 16*(2).

Carr, A. S., & Smeltzer, L. R. (1997). An empirically based operational definition of strategic purchasing. *European Journal of Purchasing and Supply Management, 3*(4), 199–207. doi:10.1016/S0969-7012(97)00014-2

Carter, J. R., & Narasimhan, R. (1996). A comparison of North American and European future purchasing trends. *International Journal of Purchasing and Materials Management, 32*(2), 12–22.

Cartwright, S., & Cary, L. C. (1993). The role of culture compatibility in successful organizational marriage. *The Academy of Management Executive, 7*(2), 57–70. doi:10.5465/AME.1993.9411302324

Cash, J. I. J., & Konsynski, B. R. (1985). IS redraws competitive boundaries. *Harvard Business Review, 63*(2), 134–142.

Champagne, C., & Kryzanowski, L. (2008). The impact of past syndicate alliances on the consolidation of financial institutions. *Financial Management, 37*(3), 535–569. doi:10.1111/j.1755-053X.2008.00024.x

Chandler, A. D. (1980). *The visible hand: The managerial revolution in American business*. Boston, MA: Harvard University Press.

Chatfield, A. T., & Yetton, P. (2000). Strategic payoff from EDI as a function of EDI embeddedness. *Journal of Management Information Systems*, *16*(4), 195–224.

Chatterjee, D., Grewal, R., & Sambamurthy, V. (2002). Shaping up for e-commerce: Institutional enablers of the organisational assimilation of web technologies. *Management Information Systems Quarterly*, *26*(2), 65–89. doi:10.2307/4132321

Chau, P. K. (1996). An empirical assessment of a modified technology acceptance model. *Journal of Management Information Systems*, *13*(2), 185–204.

Chaudhari, C. V., & Mukhopadhyay, S. K. (2003). Application of theory of constraints in an integrated poultry industry. *International Journal of Production Research*, *41*(4), 799–817. doi:10.1080/0020754031000065548

Chen, X., & Zhan, F. B. (2008). Agent-based modelling and simulation of urban evacuation: Relative effectiveness of simultaneous and staged evacuation strategies. *The Journal of the Operational Research Society*, *59*(1), 25–33. doi:10.1057/palgrave.jors.2602321

Chen, L., Gillenson, M. L., & Sherrell, D. L. (2004). Consumer acceptance of virtual stores: A theoretical model and critical success factors for virtual stores. *ACM SIGMIS Database*, *35*(2), 8–31. doi:10.1145/1007965.1007968

Cheung, S. N. S. (1987). Economics organization and transactions costs. *The New Palgrave: A Dictionary of Economics, 2*, 55-58.

Child, J. (2000). Theorizing about organization cross-nationality. In Chen, J. L. C., & Peterson, R. B. (Eds.), *Advances in International Comparative Management, 13* (pp. 27–75). Greenwich, CT: JAI Press.

Chircu, A. M., & Kauffman, R. J. (2000). Reintermediation strategies in business-to-business electronic commerce. *International Journal of Electronic Commerce*, *4*(4), 7–42.

Choi, J., Derek, L. N., & Hemant, K. J. (2008). Information Technology skill management: A Systems dynamics approach. In *Proceedings of the 41st Hawaii International Conference on System Sciences*.

Choudhury, V., & Sabherwal, R. (2003). Portfolios of control in outsourced software development projects. *Information Systems Research*, *14*(4), 291–314. doi:10.1287/isre.14.3.291.16563

Christiaanse, E., & Mrkus, N. L. (2003). Participation in collaboration electronic marketplaces. *Proceedings of the 36th Hawaii International Conference on Systems Science*, (pp. 1-44).

Chu, W. H. J., & Lee, C. C. (2006). Strategic information sharing in a supply chain. *European Journal of Operational Research*, *174*(3), 1567–1579. doi:10.1016/j.ejor.2005.02.053

Ciborra, C. U. (2000). *From control to drift: The dynamics of global information infrastructures*. Oxford, UK: Oxford University Press.

Ciborra, C. (1996). *Improvisation and Information Technology in organisations*. Paper presented at the International Conference on Information Systems (ICIS), Cleveland, Ohio, USA.

Clark, T. H., Croson, D. C., & Schiano, W. T. (2001). A hierarchical model of supply-chain integration: Information sharing and operational interdependence in the US grocery channel. *Information Technology Management*, *2*(3), 261–288. doi:10.1023/A:1011497025090

Clark, K. B., & Fujimoto, T. (1991). *Product development performance*. Boston, MA: Harvard Business School Press.

Clemons, E. K., Sashisdhar, P. R., & Row, M. C. (1993). The impact of Information Technology on the organization of economic activity: The move to the middle hypothesis. *Journal of Management Information Systems*, *10*(2), 9–33.

Clemons, E., & Row, M. (1992). Informational technology and industrial cooperation: The changing economics of coordination and ownership. *Journal of Management Information Systems*, *9*(2), 9–28.

Cleveland, F. A. (2002). Evolution of the budget idea in the United States. In Hyde, A. C. (Ed.), *Government Budgeting: Theory, Process, Politics* (3rd ed., pp. 7–19). Thompson Learning. (Original work published 1915)

Coase, R. H. (1937). The nature of the firm. *Economica*, *4*, 386–405. doi:10.1111/j.1468-0335.1937.tb00002.x

Coase, R. (1960). The problem of social cost. *The Journal of Law & Economics*, *3*, 1–44. doi:10.1086/466560

Cocharan, W. G. (1977). *Sampling techniques*. John Wiley & Sons.

Coiera, E. (2004). Four rules for the reinvention of health care. *BMJ (Clinical Research Ed.)*, *328*(7449), 1197–1199. doi:10.1136/bmj.328.7449.1197

Commons, J. R. (1931). Institutional economics. *The American Economic Review*, *21*, 648–657.

Compeau, D., & Higgins, C. (1995). Application of social cognitive theory to training for computer skills. *Information Systems Research*, *6*(2), 118. doi:10.1287/isre.6.2.118

Compeau, D., Higgins, C., & Huff, S. (1999). Social cognitive theory and individual reactions to computing technology: A longitudinal study. *Management Information Systems Quarterly*, *23*(2), 145–158. doi:10.2307/249749

Consortium for Global Electronic Commerce. (2002). *Measuring and improving value of e-procurement initiatives*. Madison, WI: University of Wisconsin-Madison, Consortium for Global Electronic Commerce (CGEC).

Cooper, R. B., & Zmud, R. W. (1990). Information Technology implementation research: A technological diffusion approach. *Management Science*, *36*(2), 123–139. doi:10.1287/mnsc.36.2.123

Copeland, D. G., & McKenney, J. L. (1988). Airline reservation systems - Lessons from history. *Management Information Systems Quarterly*, (September): 353–370. doi:10.2307/249202

Corsten, H., & Gössinger, R. (2008). *Einführung in das Supply Chain Management*. Munich, Germany: Oldenbourg.

Council for Supply Chain Management Professionals. (2010). *The status of logistics: Annual report*. Illinois: Lombard.

Covey, S. M. Jr. (2006). *The speed of trust*. New York, NY: Free Press.

Crampton, S. M., Hodge, J. W., & Mishra, J. M. (1998). The informal communication network: Factors influencing grapevine activity. *Public Personnel Management*, *27*(4), 569–584.

Creswell, J. W. (2007). *Qualitative research design and inquiry: Choosing among five approaches* (2nd ed.). Thousand Oaks, CA: Sage Publications Inc.

Croom, S., & Johnston, R. (2003). E-service: Enhancing customer service through e-procurement. *International Journal of Service Industry Management*, *14*(5), 539–555. doi:10.1108/09564230310500219

Cuganesan, S., & Lee, R. (2006). Intra-organisational influences in procurement networks controls: The impacts of information technology. *Management Accounting Research*, *17*, 141–170. doi:10.1016/j.mar.2005.12.005

Cullen, S., & Willcocks, L. P. (2003). *Intelligent outsourcing: Eight building blocks to IT success*. Oxford, UK: Buttterworth-Heineman.

Currie, W., & Seltsikas, P. (2001). Exploring the supply-side of IT outsourcing: evaluating the emerging role of application service providers. *European Journal of Information Systems*, *10*(3), 123–134. doi:10.1057/palgrave.ejis.3000393

Daft, R. L., & Lengel, R. H. (1986). Organizational information requirements, media richness and structural design. *Management Science*, *32*(5), 554–571. doi:10.1287/mnsc.32.5.554

Damsgaard, J., & Lyytinen, K. J. (2001). The role of intermediating institutions in the diffusion of Electronic Data Interchange (EDI). How industry associations in the grocery sector intervened in Hong Kong, Finland, and Denmark. *The Information Society*, *17*(3), 195–210. doi:10.1080/01972240152493056

Darby, M. R., & Karni, E. (1973). Free competition and the optimal amount of fraud. *The Journal of Law & Economics*, *16*(4), 67–88. doi:10.1086/466756

Davenport, T. H. (2000). *Mission critical: Realizing the promise of enterprise systems*. Boston, MA: Harvard Business School Press.

Davila, A., Guppa, M., & Palmer, R. (2003). Moving procurement systems to the Internet: The adoption and use of e-procurement technology models. *European Management Journal*, *21*(1), 11–23. doi:10.1016/S0263-2373(02)00155-X

Davis, F. D. (1986). *A technology acceptance model for empirically testing new end-user Information Systems: Theory and results*. Cambridge, MA: MIT.

Davis, F. D. (1989). Perceived usefulness, perceived ease of use, and user acceptance of Information Technology. *Management Information Systems Quarterly, 13*(3), 319–340. doi:10.2307/249008

Davis, F. D., Bagozzi, R. P., & Warshaw, P. R. (1989). User acceptance of computer technology: A comparison of two theoretical models. *Management Science, 35*(8), 982–1003. doi:10.1287/mnsc.35.8.982

Davis, F. (1993). User acceptance of information technology: System characteristics, user perceptions and behavioral impacts. *International Journal of Man-Machine Studies, 38*(3), 475–487. doi:10.1006/imms.1993.1022

Davis, F. D. (1986). *A technology acceptance model for empirically testing new end-user information systems: Theory and results.* Doctoral dissertation, Sloan School of Management, Massachusetts Institute of Technology, 1986.

Dawkins, R. (1976). *The selfish gene*. Oxford, UK: Oxford UP.

Day, G. S. (1994). The capabilities of market-driven organizations. *Journal of Marketing, 58*(4), 37–52. doi:10.2307/1251915

de Vaujany, F. (2008). Capturing reflexivity modes in IS: A critical realist approach. *Information and Organization, 18*(1), 51–72. doi:10.1016/j.infoandorg.2007.11.001

Dekker, A. (2007). Studying organisational topology with simple computational models. *Journal of Artificial Societies and Social Simulation, 10*(4), 6. Retrieved from http://jasss.soc.surrey.ac.uk/10/4/6.html.

Del Val, P., & Fuentes, C. M. (2003). Resistance to change: A literature review and empirical study. *Management Decision, 41*(2).

Deming, E. (1986). *Out of the crisis*. Cambridge, MA: MIT Press.

Denhardt, R. B. (2004). *Theories of public organization* (4th ed.). Belmont, CA: Wadsworth/ Thomson Learning.

Denzin, N. K., & Lincoln, Y. S. (2000). Methods of collecting and analyzing empirical materials. In Denzin, N. K., & Lincoln, Y. S. (Eds.), *Handbook of qualitative research* (2nd ed.). Thousand Oaks, CA: Sage Publications Inc.

Dettmer, H. W. (1997). *Goldratt's theory of constraints: A system approach to continuous improvement*. Milwaukee, WI: ASQ Quality Press.

Dettmer, H. W. (2003). *Strategic navigation: A system approach to business strategy*. Milwaukee, WI: ASQ Quality Press.

Dhillon, G. (2004). Dimensions of power and IS implementation. *Information & Management, 41*(5), 635–644. doi:10.1016/j.im.2003.02.001

Dillard, J. F., Ruchala, L., & Yuthas, K. (2005). Enterprise resource planning systems: A physical manifestation of administrative evil. *International Journal of Accounting Information Systems, 6*, 107–127. doi:10.1016/j.accinf.2005.02.001

Ding, X., Iijima, J., & Ho, S. (2003). An exploratory study on influential factors of online consumer behavior. *Proceedings from The 3rd Asian eBusiness Workshop*, (pp. 3-44).

Dixon, D. (1999). The behavioral side of information technology. *International Journal of Medical Informatics, 56*(1-3), 117–123. doi:10.1016/S1386-5056(99)00037-4

Dobler, D. W., & Burt, D. N. (1996). *Purchasing and supply management: Text and cases* (6th ed.). New York, NY: McGraw-Hill.

Dobson, P. J. (2001). The philosophy of critical realism-An opportunity for Information Systems research. *Information Systems Frontiers, 3*(2), 199–210. doi:10.1023/A:1011495424958

Domberger, S., Jensen, P. H., & Stonecash, R. E. (2002). Examining the magnitude and sources of cost savings associated with outsourcing. *Public Performance and Management Review, 26*(2), 148–168. doi:10.1177/1530957602238260

Domke, W. K. (1984). Waste, weapons, and resolve: Defense posture and politics in the defense budget. *Policy Sciences, 16*, 371–390. doi:10.1007/BF00135955

Doney, P. M., & Cannon, J. P. (1997). An examination of the nature of trust in buyer-seller relationships. *Journal of Marketing, 61*(2), 35–51. doi:10.2307/1251829

Doolin, B. (2004). Power and resistance in the implementation of a medical management Information System. *Information Systems Journal*, *14*(4), 343–362. doi:10.1111/j.1365-2575.2004.00176.x

Dore, R. (1983). Goodwill and the spirit of market capitalism. *The British Journal of Sociology*, *34*(4), 459–482. doi:10.2307/590932

Dovev, L. (2002). The competitive advantage of interconnected firms: An extension of the resource-based view. *Academy of Management Proceedings*, C1-7.

Drazin, R., & Schoonhoven, C. B. (1996). Community, population, and organization effects on innovation: A multilevel perspective. *Academy of Management Journal*, *39*(5), 1065–1083. doi:10.2307/256992

Drogoul, A., & Ferber, J. (1994). Multi-agent simulation as a tool for studying emergent processes in societies. In Gilbert, N., & Doran, J. (Eds.), *Simulating societies: The computer simulation of social phenomena*. London, UK: UCL Press Limited.

Dror, Y. (1968). *Public policy-making re-examined*. San Francisco, CA: Chandler.

Duffy, M. (2009). Is supply chain the cure for rising health care cost? *Supply Chain Management Review*, September, 28–35.

Dwyer, F. R., Schurr, P. H., & Oh, S. (1987). Developing buyer-seller relationships. *Journal of Marketing*, *51*(2), 11–27. doi:10.2307/1251126

Dyer, J. H., & Singh, H. (1998). The relational view: Cooperative strategy and sources of interorganizational competitive advantage. *Academy of Management Review*, *23*(4), 660–679.

Dyer, J. (1997). Effective interfirm collaboration: How firms minimize transaction costs and maximize transaction value. *Strategic Management Journal*, *18*(7), 535–556. doi:10.1002/(SICI)1097-0266(199708)18:7<535::AID-SMJ885>3.0.CO;2-Z

Dyer, J., & Chu, W. (2003). The role of trustworthiness in reducing transaction costs and improving performance: Empirical evidence from the United States, Japan and Korea. *Organization Science*, *14*(1), 57–68. doi:10.1287/orsc.14.1.57.12806

Eadie, R., Perera, S., Heaney, G., & Carlysle, J. (2007). Drivers and barriers to public sector e-procurement within Northern Ireland's Construction Industry. *Itcon*, *12*, 103–120.

Edwards, W. (1967). The theory of decision making. In Edwards, W., & Tversky, A. (Eds.), *Decision making: Selected readings* (pp. 13–64). Middlesex, UK: Penguin Books.

Ehie, I., & Sheu, C. (2005). Integrating six sigma and theory of constraints for continuous improvement: a case study. *Journal of Manufacturing Technology Management*, *16*(5), 542–553. doi:10.1108/17410380510600518

Ehrlich, P., & Raven, P. (1964). Butterflies and plants: A study in co-evolution. *Evolution; International Journal of Organic Evolution*, *18*, 586–608. doi:10.2307/2406212

Eicke, H. v., & Femerling, C. (1991). *Modular sourcing: Ein Konzept zur Neugestaltung der Beschaffungspolitik*. München, Germany: Huss-Verlag.

Eisenhardt, K. M. (1989). Agency theory: An assessment and review. *Academy of Management Review*, *14*(1), 57–74.

Elbanna, A. (2010). From intention to use to actual rejection: The journey of an e-procurement system. *Journal of Enterprise Information Management*, *23*(1), 81–99. doi:10.1108/17410391011008914

Elgarah, W., Falaleeva, N., Saunders, C. S., Ilie, V., Shim, J. T., & Courtney, J. F. (2005). Data exchange in interorganizational relationships: Review through multiple conceptual lenses. *The Data Base for Advances in Information Systems*, *36*(1), 8–29.

Emery, F. (1978). *The emergence of a new paradigm of work*. Canberra, Australia: Australian National University.

Emiliani, M., & Stec, D. (2004). Aerospace parts supplier's reaction to online reverse auctions. *Supply Chain Management*, *9*(2), 139–153. doi:10.1108/13598540410527042

Eom, S. B. (2005). *Inter-organizational information systems in the Internet age*. Hershey, PA: Idea Group.

Eprocurement.gov. (2009). *News clip*. Retrieved from http://www.eprocurement.gov.in/news/sign.jpg

Erridge, A., Fee, R., & McIlroy, J. (2001). *Best practice procurement: Public and private sector perspectives*. Burlington, MA: Gover.

Erwin, D. G., & Garman, A. N. (2010). Resistance to organizational change: Linking research to practice. *Leadership & Development Journal*, *31*(1), 39–56. doi:10.1108/01437731011010371

Eshkenazi, A. (2009, May 29). APICS operations management now. *APICS Homepage*, 5-6.

European Union. (2005). *E-procurement action plan*. Retrieved from http://europa.eu.int/idabc/en/document/3824/194

Evgeniou, T. (2002). Information integration and information strategies for adaptive enterprises. *European Management Journal*, *20*(5), 486. doi:10.1016/S0263-2373(02)00092-0

Fadul, E. M. C., & Silva, L. P. (2008). *Retomando o debate sobre a reforma do Estado e a nova administração pública. XXXII EnANPAD*. Rio de Janeiro, Brazil: ANPAD.

Farhoomand, A. (2001). *E-procurement at Cathay Pacific Airways: E-business valuation*. Centre for Asian Business Cases. The University of Hong Kong.

Fawcett, S. S, Andrawski, J. C., Fawcett, A. M., & Magnan, G. M. (2009). The art of supply chain management. *Supply Chain Management Review*, November, 19-25.

Feenberg, A. (1996). Marcuse or Habermas: Two critiques of technology. *Inquiry*, *39*, 45–70. doi:10.1080/00201749608602407

Fenno, R. F. Jr. (1966). *The power of the purse: Appropriation politics in congress*. Boston, MA: Little Brown.

Ferris, J., & Graddy, E. (1998). A contractual framework for new public management theory. *International Public Management Journal*, *1*(2), 225–240. doi:10.1016/S1096-7494(99)80092-0

Festinger, L. (1957). *A theory of cognitive dissonance*. London, UK: Tavistock Publications.

Festinger, L., Cartwright, D., Barber, K., Fleischl, J., Gottsdanker, J., & Keysen, A. (1948). A study of a rumour: Its origin and spread. *Human Relations*, *1*(4), 464–486. doi:10.1177/001872674800100405

Fichman, R. G., & Kemerer, C. F. (1997). The assimilation of software process innovations: An organizational learning perspective. *Management Science*, *43*(10), 1345–1363. doi:10.1287/mnsc.43.10.1345

Fichman, R. G., & Kemerer, C. F. (1999). The illusory diffusion of innovations: An examination of assimilation gaps. *Information Systems Research*, *10*(3), 255–275. doi:10.1287/isre.10.3.255

Fichman, R. G. (2004). Going beyond the dominant paradigm for Information Technology innovation research: Emerging concepts and methods. *Journal of the Association for Information Systems*, *5*(8), 314–355.

Fiedler, K. D., Grover, V., & Teng, J. T. C. (1996). An empirically derived taxonomy of information technology structure and its relationship to organizational structure. *Journal of Management Information Systems*, *13*(1), 9–34.

Fink, D. (2003). Case study analysis of the 3 Rs of informational technology benefit management. *Benchmarking an International Journal*, *10*(4).

Fishbein, M., & Ajzen, I. (1975). *Belief, attitude, intention, and behavior: An introduction to theory and research*. Reading, MA: Addison-Wesley Pub. Co.

Fisher, M. D. (2006). *Staff perceptions of an ERP systems implementation: A case study of three Australian universities*. Central Queensland University, Rockhampton.

Forester, J. (1984). Bounded rationality and the politics of muddling through. *Public Administration Review*, (January/February): 23–31. doi:10.2307/975658

Forrester, J. (1958). Industrial dynamics: A major breakthrough for decision makers. *Harvard Business Review*, (July-August): 37–66.

Forrester, J. (1961). *Industrial dynamics*. Cambridge, MA: MIT Press.

Franklin, S., & Graesser, A. (1996). Is it an agent, or just a program? A taxonomy for autonomous agents. In *Proceedings of the Third International Workshop on Agent Theories, Architectures and Languages*, (pp. 21-35).

Frantz, P. S. (2001). *Perceptions of selected administrators regarding enterprise planning software implementation best practices, and the relationship between these perceptions and selected variables*. University of Southern Mississippi.

Fredendall, L., & Lea, B. (1997). Improving product mixed heuristic in the theory of constraints. *International Journal of Production Research*, *35*, 1535–1544. doi:10.1080/002075497195100

French, J. R., & Raven, B. (1959). The bases of social power. In Cartwright, D. (Ed.), *Studies in social power* (pp. 150–167). Ann Arbor, MI: Institute for Social Research.

Gal, U., Lyytinen, K., & Yoo, Y. (2008). The dynamics of IT boundary objects, information infrastructures, and organisational identities: The introduction of 3D modelling technologies into the architecture, engineering, and construction industry. *European Journal of Information Systems*, *17*, 290–304. doi:10.1057/ejis.2008.13

Gallivan, M. J., Spitler, V. K., & Koufaris, M. (2004). Does Information Technology training really matter? A social information processing analysis of coworkers' influence on IT usage in the workplace. *Journal of Management Information Systems*, *22*(1), 153–192.

Gardner, R. S., & Ash, C. G. (2003). ICT enabled organisations: A model for change management. *Logistics Information Management*, *16*(2), 18–25. doi:10.1108/09576050310453705

Gargeya, V., & Brady, C. (2005). Success and failure factors of adopting SAP in ERP system implementation. *Business Process Management Journal*, *11*(5), 511–516. doi:10.1108/14637150510619858

Garrido, M. J., Gutierrez, A. M., & San Jose, R. (2006). The impact of e-procurement on the structure of the buying centre. *International Journal of Electronic Business*, *4*(6), 463–482. doi:10.1504/IJEB.2006.011696

Garrido, M. J., Gutierrez, A. M., & San Jose, R. (2008). Organizational and economic consequences of business e-procurement intensity. *Technovation*, *28*, 615–629. doi:10.1016/j.technovation.2007.12.004

Garrido-Samaniego, M. J., Gutierrez-Arranz, A. M., & Jose-Cabezudo, R. S. (2010). Assessing the impact of e-procurement on the structure of the buying centre. *International Journal of Information Management*, *30*, 135–143. doi:10.1016/j.ijinfomgt.2009.08.004

Gaski, J. F., & Nevin, J. R. (1985). The differential effects of exercised and unexercised power sources in a marketing channel. *JMR, Journal of Marketing Research*, *22*(2), 130–142. doi:10.2307/3151359

Gebauer, J., & Segev, A. (2000). Emerging technologies to support indirect procurement: Two case studies from the petroleum industry. *Information Technology Management*, *1*(1/2), 107–128. doi:10.1023/A:1019160605755

Gefen, D. (2004). What makes an ERP implementation relationship worthwhile: Linking trust mechanisms and ERP usefulness? *Journal of Management Information Systems*, *21*(1), 263–288.

George, J. F. (2004). The theory of planned behavior and Internet purchasing. *Internet Research*, *14*(3), 198–212. doi:10.1108/10662240410542634

Geyskens, I., Steenkamp, J. E. M., & Kumar, N. (2006). Make, buy, or ally: A meta analysis of transaction cost theory. *Academy of Management Journal*, *49*(3), 519–543. doi:10.5465/AMJ.2006.21794670

Gherardi, S. (2009). Introduction: The critical power of the practice lens. *Management Learning*, *40*(2), 115–128. doi:10.1177/1350507608101225

Gianakis, G. A., & McCue, C. P. (1999). *Local government budgeting: A managerial approach*. Westport, CT: Praeger.

Giddens, A. (1984). *The constitution of society-Outline of the theory of structuration*. Berkley, CA: University of California Press.

Giddens, A. (1979). *Central problems in social theory*. Berkeley, CA: University of California Press.

Gläser, J., & Laudel, G. (2009). *Expertinterviews und qualitative Inhaltsanalyse*. Wiesbaden, Germany: VS Verlag.

Glasser, B. (1998). *Doing grounded theory: Issues & discussions*. Mill Valley, CA: Sociology Press.

Goldberg, V. P. (1985). Productions functions, transaction costs and new institutionalism. In Fiewel, G. R. (Ed.), *Issues in contemporary microeconomics and welfare* (pp. 395–402). Albany, NY: State University of New York Press.

Goldratt, E. M. (1988). Computerized shop floor scheduling. *International Journal of Production Research*, *26*(3), 443–455. doi:10.1080/00207548808947875

Goldratt, E. M. (1990). *What is this thing called theory of constraints and how should it be implemented?*New York, NY: North River Press.

Goldratt, E. M. (1994). *It's not luck*. England: Gower.

Goldratt, E. M., & Cox, J. (1984). *The goal: An ongoing improvement process*. England: Gower.

Goldratt, E. M., & Fox, R. E. (1986). *The race*. New York, NY: North River Press.

Goldspink, C., & Kay, R. (2003). Organizations as self-organizing and sustaining systems. *General Systems*, *32*(5), 459–474. doi:10.1080/0308107031000135017

Gordon, J., & Gordon, S. (2000). Structuring the interaction between IT and business units: Prototypes for service delivery. *Information Systems Management*, *17*(1). doi:10.1201/1078/43190.17.1.20000101/31209.2

Gosling, A., Westbrook, J., & Coiera, E. (2003). Variation in the use of online clinical evidence: A qualitative analysis. *International Journal of Medical Informatics*, *69*(1), 1–16. doi:10.1016/S1386-5056(02)00046-1

GovPro. (2009). An update about the e-procurement pilot programme. *GovProcurement Newsletter*, September, pp. 1-2.

Granovetter, M. (1985). Economic action and social structure: The problem of embeddedness. *American Journal of Sociology*, *91*(3), 481–510. doi:10.1086/228311

Gregor, S. (2006). The nature of theory in Information Systems. *Management Information Systems Quarterly*, *30*(3), 611–642.

Greinstein, M., & Vaserhelyi, M. (2000). *Electronic commerce: Security, risk management and control*. McGraw-Hill/Irwin.

Grochla, E., & Schonbohm, P. (1980). *Beschaffung in der Unternehmung: Einführung in eine umfassende Beschaffungslehre*. Stuttgart, Germany: Schaeffer-Poeschel.

Grover, V., & Malhotra, M. K. (2003). Transaction cost framework in operations and supply chain management research: Theory and measurement. *Journal of Operations Management*, *21*(4), 457–473. doi:10.1016/S0272-6963(03)00040-8

Gulati, R., Nohria, N., & Zaheer, A. (2000). Strategic networks. *Strategic Management Journal*, *21*(3), 203–215. doi:10.1002/(SICI)1097-0266(200003)21:3<203::AID-SMJ102>3.0.CO;2-K

Gulati, R., & Singh, H. (1998). The Architecture of cooperation: Managing coordination costs and appropriation concerns in strategic alliances. *Administrative Science Quarterly*, *43*(4), 781–814. doi:10.2307/2393616

Gulati, R. (1995). Familiarity breeds trust? The implications of repeated ties for contractual choice in alliances. *Academy of Management Journal*, *38*, 85–112. doi:10.2307/256729

Gupta, M., Ko, H.-J., & Min, H. (2002). TOC-based performance measures and five focusing steps in a job-shop manufacturing environment. *International Journal of Production Research*, *40*(4), 907–930. doi:10.1080/00207540110097185

Gupta, M. C., & Boyd, L. (2008). Theory of constraints management: A theory for operations management. *International Journal of Operations & Production Management*, *28*(10), 991–1012. doi:10.1108/01443570810903122

Gupta, M. C., Boyd, L., & Sussman, L. (2004). To better maps: A TOC primer for strategic planning. *Business Horizons*, *47*(2), 15–26. doi:10.1016/j.bushor.2003.10.001

Gupta, D., & Gerchak, Y. (2002). Quantifying operational synergies in a merger/acquisition. *Management Science*, *48*(4), 517–533. doi:10.1287/mnsc.48.4.517.209

Hair, J. F., Black, B., Babin, B., Anderson, R. E., & Tatham, R. L. (2006). *Multivariate data analysis* (6th ed.). New Jersey: Prentice-Hall.

Hale, G. E., & Douglass, S. R. (1977). Politics of budget execution. *Administration & Society*, *9*(3), 367–378. doi:10.1177/009539977700900305

Hale, J. L., Householder, B. J., & Greene, K. L. (2003). The theory of reasoned action. In Dillard, J. P., & Pfau, M. (Eds.), *The persuasion handbook: Developments in theory and practice* (pp. 259–286). Thousand Oaks, CA: Sage.

Halvey, J. K., & Melby, B. M. (2007). *Business process outsourcing. Processes strategies and contracts*. Wiley.

Han, Y., Carcillo, J., Venkataraman, S., Clark, R., Watson, R., & Nguyen, T. (2005). Unexpected increased mortality after implementation of a commercially sold computerized physician order entry system. *Pediatrics*, *116*(6), 1506–1512. doi:10.1542/peds.2005-1287

Hancox, M., & Hackney, R. (2000). IT outsourcing: Frameworks for conceptualizing practice and perception. *Information Systems Journal, 10*, 217–237. doi:10.1046/j.1365-2575.2000.00082.x

Handfield R. B., Straight S. L. & Stirling WA. (2002). Reverse auctions: How do supply managers really feel about them. *Inside Supply Management, 13*(11), 56–61.

Handfield, R. B. (2002, January). The new supply chain model. *APICS*, p. 24.

Hanseth, Ø. (2005). Beyond metaphysics and theory consumerism. *Scandinavian Journal of Information Systems, 17*(1), 159–166.

Hanseth, Ø., & Monteiro, E. (1997). Inscribing behaviour in information infrastructure standards. *Accounting. Management and Information Technology, 7*(4), 183–211. doi:10.1016/S0959-8022(97)00008-8

Harley, B., Wright, C., Hall, R., & Dery, K. (2006). Management reactions to technological change: The example of enterprise resource planning. *The Journal of Applied Behavioral Science, 42*(1), 58–75. doi:10.1177/0021886305284857

Harrigan, P. O., Boyd, M. M., Ramsey, E., & Ibbotson, P. (2008). The development of e-procurement within the ICT manufacturing industry in Ireland. *Management Decision, 46*(3), 481–500. doi:10.1108/00251740810863906

Hart, P. J., & Saunders, C. S. (1997). Power and trust: Critical factors in the adoption and use of electronic data interchange. *Organization Science, 8*(1), 23–42. doi:10.1287/orsc.8.1.23

Hartley, J. L., Lane, M. D., & Duplaga, E. A. (2006). Exploring the barriers to the adoption of e-auctions for sourcing. *International Journal of Operations & Production Management, 26*(2), 202–221. doi:10.1108/01443570610641675

Hartwick, J., & Barki, H. (2001). Communication as a dimension of user participation. *Professional Communication, 44*(1), 21–36. doi:10.1109/47.911130

Harvey, M., & Lusch, R. F. (1998). Beyond traditional due diligence for mergers and acquisitions in the 21st century. *Review of Business, 19*(3), 17.

Haveman, R. H. (1970). *The economics of the public sector*. New York, NY: John Wiley.

Hawking, P., Stein, A., Wyld, D., & Forster, S. (2004). E-procurement: Is the ugly duckling actually a swan down under? *Asia Pacific Journal of Marketing and Logistics, 16*(1), 1–26. doi:10.1108/13555850410765140

Hawking, P., & Stein, A. (2002). E-Procurement: Drivers, barriers and practices. *Conference Proceedings of the 2002 Australian Conference on Information Systems*, Melbourne, Australia.

Hayes, B. (2008). Cloud computing. *Communications of the ACM, 51*(7), 9–10. doi:10.1145/1364782.1364786

Hayes, M. (2007). Policy making through disjointed incrementalism. In Morçöl, G. (Ed.), *Handbook of decision making* (pp. 39–59). Boca Raton, FL: Taylor & Francis Group.

Henderson, R. (2002). *Going beyond the tactical.* White Paper. Lowell, MA: J.B. Hunt.

Hennart, J. F., & Anderson, A. E. (1993). Countertrade and the minimization of transaction costs: An empirical examination. *Journal of Law Economics and Organization, 9*(2), 290–313.

Hikmet, N., & Chen, S. K. (2003). An investigation into low mail survey response rates of information technology users in health care organizations. *International Journal of Medical Informatics, 72*(1-3), 29–34. doi:10.1016/j.ijmedinf.2003.09.002

Hines, P., Lamming, R., Jones, D., Cousins, P., & Rich, N. (2000). *Value stream management: Strategy and excellence in the supply chain.* London, UK: Prentice Hall.

Hirschheim, R. A. (1998). *Backsourcing: An emerging trend?* Infoserver. Retrieved from http://www.infoserver.com/sep1998/html/academic.html

Hjelt, M. (2006). *End-user attitudes towards EDM use in project work: A case study of the Kamppi Center project.* Master of Science Thesis. Sweden: Swedish School of Economics and Business Administration.

Hodge, G. A., & Rouse, A. C. (2006). Outsourcing government IT services: An Australian case study. In Boyne, G. A. (Eds.), *Public service performance: Perspectives on performance and management* (pp. 212–232). Cambridge, UK: Cambridge University Press.

Hofstede, G., Neuijen, B., Ohayv, D. D., & Sanders, G. (1990). Measuring organizational cultures: A qualitative and quantitative study across twenty cases. *Administrative Science Quarterly*, *35*(2). doi:10.2307/2393392

Holland, C. P. (1997). The evolution of electronic hierarchies in business markets. *Wirtschaftsinformatik*, *39*(3), 245–253.

Homburg, C., & Bucerius, M. (2006). Is speed of integration really a success factor of mergers and acquisitions? An analysis of the role of internal and external relatedness. *Strategic Management Journal*, *27*(4), 347–367. doi:10.1002/smj.520

Hong, S.-J., & Kwon, I.-W. (2009). *Study on impact of trust in supply chain partnership: A Korean case*. Paper presented at the 3rd International Conference on Operations and Supply Chain Management, at the Asian Institute of Medicine, Science and Technology in Malaysia, December 9-12.

Hopper, D. (1990). Rattling SABRE – New ways to compete on information. *Business Review (Federal Reserve Bank of Philadelphia)*, *4*(July), 118–125.

Houghton, L., & Kerr, D. V. (2006). A study into the creation of feral information systems as a response to an ERP implementation within the supply chain of a large government-owned corporation. *International Journal of Internet and Enterprise Management*, *4*(1), 135–147.

Hughes, M., Powell, P., Panteli, N., & Golden, W. (2004). Risk mitigation and risk absorption in IOS: A proposed investigative study. *Proceedings of the 13th European Conference on Information Systems (ECIS 2004)*. June Turku, Finland.

Hur, D., Mabert, V. A., & Hartley, J. L. (2007). Getting the most out of reverse e-auction investment. *Omega*, *35*, 403–416. doi:10.1016/j.omega.2005.08.003

Husted, K., & Michailova, S. (2002). Diagnosing and fighting knowledge-sharing hostility. *Organizational Dynamics*, *31*(1), 60–73. doi:10.1016/S0090-2616(02)00072-4

Hyde, A. C. (Ed.). (2002). *Government budget: Theory, process, and politics* (3rd ed.). Thompson Learning.

Hyde, M. (2002). *An empirical examination of inhibitors affecting web-based interorganizational applications*. PhD Dissertation (Unpublished), Southern Illinois University at Carbondale, USA

Iacovou, C., Benbasat, I., & Dexter, A. (1995). EDI and small organizations: Adoption and impact of technology. *Management Information Systems Quarterly*, (December): 465–485. doi:10.2307/249629

Igbaria, M., Guimaraes, T., & Davis, G. B. (1995). Testing the determinants of microcomputer usage via a structural equation model. *Journal of Management Information Systems*, *11*(4), 87–114.

Igbaria, M., & Parasuraman, S. (1989). A path analytic study of individual characteristics, computer anxiety and attitudes toward microcomputers. *Journal of Management*, *15*(3), 373–383. doi:10.1177/014920638901500302

Ilieva, J., Baron, S., & Healey, N. M. (2002). Online surveys in marketing research: Pros and cons. *International Journal of Market Research*, *44*(3), 361–376.

Ishman, M., Pegels, C. C., & Sanders, G. L. (2001). Managerial information system success factors within the cultural context of North America and a former Soviet Republic. *The Journal of Strategic Information Systems*, *10*(4), 291–312. doi:10.1016/S0963-8687(01)00055-5

Islamoglu, M., & Liebenau, J. (2007). Information Technology, transaction costs and governance structure: Integrating an institutional approach. *Journal of Information Technology*, *22*(3), 275–283. doi:10.1057/palgrave.jit.2000107

Jackson, C. M., Chow, S., & Leitch, R. A. (1997). Toward an understanding of the behavioral intention to use an Information System. *Decision Sciences*, *28*(2), 357–389. doi:10.1111/j.1540-5915.1997.tb01315.x

Jap, S. D. (2003). An exploratory study of the introduction of online reverse auctions. *Journal of Marketing*, *67*, 96–107. doi:10.1509/jmkg.67.3.96.18651

Jarvenpaa, S. L., & Ives, B. (1990). Executive involvement and participation in the management of Information Technology. *Management Information Systems Quarterly*, *15*(2), 205–227. doi:10.2307/249382

Jarvenpaa, S. L., & Leidner, D. E. (1998). An information company in Mexico: Extending the resource-based view of the firm to a developing country context. *Information Systems Research*, *9*(4), 342–361. doi:10.1287/isre.9.4.342

Jehn, K. A. (1997). A qualitative analysis of conflict types and dimensions in organizational groups. *Administrative Science Quarterly*, *42*, 530–557. doi:10.2307/2393737

Jemison, D. B., & Haspeslagh, P. C. (1991). *Managing acquisitions: Creating value through corporate renewal* (1st ed.). Free Press.

Jensen, M. C. (1983). Organization theory and methodology. *Accounting Review*, *8*(2), 319–337.

Jiang, J. J., Muhanna, W. A., & Klein, G. (2000). User resistance and strategies for promoting acceptance across system types. *Information & Management*, *37*, 25–36. doi:10.1016/S0378-7206(99)00032-4

Johns, G. (2006). The essential impact of context on organisational behaviour. *Academy of Management Review*, *31*(2), 386–408. doi:10.5465/AMR.2006.20208687

Johnson, M. (1989). Compatible information systems a key to merger success. Healthcare financial management. *Journal of the Healthcare Financial Management Association*, *43*(6), 56–61.

Johnston, R. B., & Gregor, S. (2000). A theory of industry-level activity for understanding the adoption of interorganizational systems. *European Journal of Information Systems*, *9*(4), 243–251. doi:10.1057/palgrave/ejis/3000375

Johnston, H., & Vitale, M. (1988). Creating competitive advantage with interorganizational systems. *Management Information Systems Quarterly*, *12*(2), 2. doi:10.2307/248839

Joshi, A. W., & Stump, R. L. (1999). The contingent effect specific asset investment on joint action in manufacturer-supplier relationships: An empirical test of the moderating role of reciprocal asset investments, uncertainty, and trust. *Journal of the Academy of Marketing Science*, *27*(3), 291–305. doi:10.1177/0092070399273001

Joyce, P. G. (1993). Using performance measures for federal budgeting: Proposals and prospects. *Public Budgeting & Finance*, *13*(4), 3–17. doi:10.1111/1540-5850.00987

Kalakota, R., & Robinson, M. (1999). *e-Business: Roadmap for success.* Addison-Wesley Longman, USA.

Kaliannan, M., Awang, H., & Raman, M. (2009). Government purchasing: A review of e-procurement system in Malaysia. *The Journal of Knowledge Economy & Knowledge Management*, *4*(Spring), 27–37.

Kankanhalli, A., Tan, B. C. Y., & Wei, K.-K. (2005). Contributing knowledge to electronic knowledge repositories: An empirical investigation. *Management Information Systems Quarterly*, *29*(1), 113–143.

Kanter, R. M. (1994). Collaborative advantage: The art of alliances. *Harvard Business Review*, *4*(July-August), 96–108.

Kaplan, R. S., & Norton, D. P. (1996). *The Balanced Scorecard: Translating strategy into action.* US: Harvard Business Press.

Kaplan, B. (1997). Addressing organizational issues into the evaluation of medical systems. *Journal of the American Medical Informatics Association*, *4*(2), 94. doi:10.1136/jamia.1997.0040094

Kaplan, B. (2001). Evaluating informatics applications—Some alternative approaches: theory, social interactionism, and call for methodological pluralism. *International Journal of Medical Informatics*, *64*(1), 39–56. doi:10.1016/S1386-5056(01)00184-8

Kaplan, J. M. (2007). SaaS: Friend or foe. *Business Communications Review*, 48-53.

Katz, E., & Lazarfeld, P. F. (1955). *Personal influence* (*Vol. 2*). New York, NY: The Free Press.

Kay, R., & Cecez-Kecmanovic, D. (2001). *IS-organisation co-evolution: The future of IS.* Paper presented at the International Conference on Information Systems, New Orleans.

Kelly, J. A., & Rivenbark, W. C. (2003). *Performance budgeting for state and local government.* Armonk, NY: M.E. Sharpe.

Kelly, J. M. (2003). The long view: Lasting (and fleeting) reforms in public budgeting in the twentieth century. *Journal of Public Budgeting, Accounting, &. Financial Management*, *15*(2), 309–326.

Kelman, H. C. (1958). Compliance, identification, and internalisation: Three process of attitude change. *The Journal of Conflict Resolution*, *2*(1), 51–60. doi:10.1177/002200275800200106

Kelman, H. C. (1961). Process of opinion change. *Public Opinion Quarterly*, *25*(1), 57–78. doi:10.1086/266996

Kendall, G. I. (1998). *Securing the future: Strategies for exponential growth using the theory of constraints*. Boca Raton, FL: Lucie Press/APICS Series on Constraints Management.

Kerber, W., & Saam, N. J. (2001). Competition as a test of hypotheses: Simulation of knowledge-generating market processes. *Journal of Artificial Societies and Social Simulation*, *4*(3), 2.

Kerr, D. V., Houghton, L., & Burgess, K. (2007). Power relationships that lead to the development of Feral Systems. *Australasian Journal of Information Systems*, *14*(2), 141–152.

Kilduff, M., & Tsai, W. (2003). *Social networks and organizations*. USA: Sage.

King, W. R., & He, J. (2006). A meta-analysis of the technology acceptance model. *Information & Management*, *43*, 740–755. doi:10.1016/j.im.2006.05.003

Kingshott, R. P. J. (2006). The impact of psychological contracts upon trust and commitment within supplier-buyer relationships: A social exchange view. *Industrial Marketing Management*, *35*(6), 724–739. doi:10.1016/j.indmarman.2005.06.006

Kitchenham, B., & Pfleeger, S. L. (2002). Principles of survey research questionnaire evaluation. *Software Engineering Notes*, *27*(3), 20–23. doi:10.1145/638574.638580

Klein, D. J., & Debruine, M. (1995). A thinking process for establishing management policies. *Review of Business*, *16*(3), 37.

Klein, S., Schellhammer, S., Reimers, K., & Riemer, K. (2008). *Evolutionary paths of Inter-organizational Information Systems (IOIS)*. Paper presented at the 12th Annual Conference of the International Society for New Institutional Economics (ISNIE 2008), June 20-21 2008, Rotman School of Management, University of Toronto, Canada.

Kleinaltenkamp, M., & Jacob, F. (2002). German approaches to business-to-business marketing theory origins and structure. *Journal of Business Research*, *55*(2), 149–155. doi:10.1016/S0148-2963(00)00150-8

Klopping, I. M., & McKinney, E. (2004). Extending the technology acceptance model and the task-technology fit model to consumer e-commerce. *Information Technology, Learning and Performance Journal*, *22*(1).

Knudsen, D. (2003). Aligning corporate strategy, procurement strategy and e-procurement tools. *International Journal of Physical Distribution & Logistics Management*, *33*(8), 720–734. doi:10.1108/09600030310502894

Kong, C., Li, H., & Love, P. (2001). An e-commerce system for construction material procurement. *Construction Innovation*, *1*(1), 43–54.

Konsynski, B. R., & McFarlan, F. W. (1990). Information partnerships – Shared data, shared scale. *Harvard Business Review*, *68*(5), 114–120.

Koppel, R., Metlay, J., Cohen, A., Abaluck, B., Localio, A., & Kimmel, S. (2005). Role of computerized physician order entry systems in facilitating medication errors. *Journal of the American Medical Association*, *293*, 1197–1203. doi:10.1001/jama.293.10.1197

Kotter, J. A., & Schlesinger, L. A. (1979). Choosing strategies for change. *Harvard Business Review*, *57*(2), 106–114.

Krovi, R. (1993). Identifying the causes of resistance to IS implementation. *Information & Management*, *25*, 327–335. doi:10.1016/0378-7206(93)90082-5

Krüger, W., & Homp, C. (1997). *Kernkompetenz-Management: Steigerung von Flexibilität und Schlagkraft im Wettbewerb*. Wiesbaden, Germany: Gabler.

Kukafka, R., Johnson, S., Linfante, A., & Allegrante, J. (2003). Grounding a new information technology implementation framework in behavioral science: A systematic analysis of the literature on IT use. *Journal of Biomedical Informatics*, *36*(3), 218–227. doi:10.1016/j.jbi.2003.09.002

Kurnia, S., & Johnston, R. B. (2000). The need for a processual view of Interorganizational Systems. *The Journal of Strategic Information Systems*, *9*(4), 295–319. doi:10.1016/S0963-8687(00)00050-0

Kusewitt, J. B. (1985). An exploratory study of strategic acquisition factors relating to performance. *Strategic Management Journal, 6*, 151–169. doi:10.1002/smj.4250060205

Kwon, I. W. G., & Suh, T. (2004). Factors affecting the level of trust and commitment in supply chain relationship. *Journal of Supply Chain Management, 40*(2), 4–14. doi:10.1111/j.1745-493X.2004.tb00165.x

Kwon, I.-W., & Suh, T. (2004). Factors affecting the level of trust and commitment in supply chain relationships. *Journal of Supply Chain Management, 40*(2), 4–14. doi:10.1111/j.1745-493X.2004.tb00165.x

Kwon, I.-W., & Suh, T. (2005). Trust, commitment and relationships in supply chain management: A path analysis. *Supply Chain Management: An International Journal, 10*(1), 26–33. doi:10.1108/13598540510578351

Kwong, T., Cheung, C., Zhu, L., Limayem, M., & Viehland, D. (2002). Online consumer behavior: An overview and analysis of the literature. *Proceedings from The Six Pacific Asia Conference on Information System,* (pp. 813-827).

Lacerda, D. P., Cassel, R. A., & Rodrigues, L. H. (2010). Service process analysis using process engineering and the theory of constraints thinking process. *Business Process Management Journal, 16*(2), 264–281. doi:10.1108/14637151011035598

Lacity, M., Khan, S. A., & Willcocks, L. (2009). A review of the IT outsourcing literature: Insights for practice. *The Journal of Strategic Information Systems, 18*(3), 130–146. doi:10.1016/j.jsis.2009.06.002

Lacity, M., & Rottman, J. (2008). *Offshore outsourcing of information technology work.* New York, NY: Palgrave-McMillan. doi:10.1057/9780230582965

Lacity, M., & Willcocks, L. (2001). *Global information technology outsourcing.* UK: Wiley.

Lamb, R., & Kling, R. (2003). Reconceptualizing users as social actors in Information Systems research. *Management Information Systems Quarterly, 27*(2), 197–236.

Larsson, R., & Finkelstein, S. (1999). Integrating strategic, organizational, and human resource perspectives on mergers and acquisitions: A case survey of synergy realization. *Organization Science, 10*(1), 1–26. doi:10.1287/orsc.10.1.1

Latour, B. (1987). *Science in action.* Cambridge, MA: Harvard UP.

Latour, B. (1996). *ARAMIS, or the love of technology.* Cambridge, MA: Harvard UP.

Latour, B. (2005). *Reassembling the social.* London, UK: Oxford UP.

Latour, B., & Woolgar, S. (1979). *Laboratory life.* Beverly Hills, CA: SAGE.

Latour, B. (1992). Where are the missing masses? The sociology of a few mundane artifacts. In Bjiker, W., & Law, J. (Eds.), *Shaping technology / building society.* Cambridge, MA: MIT Press.

Latour, B. (1999). On recalling ANT. In Law, J., & Hassard, J. (Eds.), *Actor network theory and after.* Oxford, UK: Blackwell.

Lave, J., & Wenger, E. (1991). *Situated learning - Legitimate peripheral participation.* Cambridge, UK: Cambridge University Press.

Lea, B.-R., & Min, H. (2003). Selection of management accounting systems in just-in-time and theory of constraints-based manufacturing. *International Journal of Production Research, 41*(13), 2879. doi:10.1080/0020754031000109134

Lee, Y., Kozar, K., & Larsen, K. (2003). The technology acceptance model: Past, present, and future. *Communications of the Association for Information Systems, 12*(752), 780.

Lee, H. L., Padmannabhan, V., & Whang, S. (1997). The bullwhip effect in supply chains. *Sloan Management Review, 38*(3), 93–102.

Lee, T., & Plenert, G. (1993). Optimising theory of constraints when new product alternatives exist. *Production and Inventory Management Journal, 3*, 51–57.

Lee, E., Lee, J., & Eastwood, D. (2003). A two-step estimation of consumer adoption of technology-based service innovations. *The Journal of Consumer Affairs, 37*(2), 256–282. doi:10.1111/j.1745-6606.2003.tb00453.x

Leenders, M. R., & Fearon, H. E. (1993). *Purchasing and materials management.* Burr Ridge, IL: Irwin.

Leenders, M. R., & Fearon, H. E. (1997). *Purchasing and supply management* (11th ed.). Chicago, IL: McGraw-Hill/Irwin.

Legare, T. L. (1998). The human side of mergers and acquisitions. *Human Resource Planning*, *21*(1), 32–41.

Lehan, E. A. (1981). *Simplified governmental budget*. Chicago, IL: Municipal Finance Officers Association.

Leibenstein, H. (1976). *Beyond economic man: A new foundation for microeconomics*. Cambridge, MA: Harvard University Press.

Leipold, K., Klemow, J., Holloway, F., & Vaidya, K. (2004). The World Bank e-procurement for the selection of consultants: Challenges and lessons learned. *Journal of Public Procurement*, *4*(3), 319–339.

Leng, M., & Parlar, M. (2005). Game theoretic applications in supply chain management: A review. *Infor*, *43*(3), 187–220.

Leonardi, P. M., & Barley, S. R. (2008). Materiality and change: Challenges to building better theory about technology and organizing. *Information and Organization*, *18*(3), 159–176. doi:10.1016/j.infoandorg.2008.03.001

Lesswell, H. D. (1963). *The Future of Political Science*. New York, NY: Atherton.

Leuthesser, L., & Kohli, A. K. (1995). Relational behavior in business markets: Implications for relationship management. *Journal of Business Research*, *34*(3), 221–233. doi:10.1016/0148-2963(95)00006-E

Levina, N., & Vaast, E. (2005). The emergence of boundary spanning competence in practice: Implications for implementation and use of Information Systems. *Management Information Systems Quarterly*, *29*(2), 335–363.

Levine, H. G., & Rossmoore, D. (1995). Politics and the function of power in a case study of IT-implementation. *Journal of Management Information Systems*, *11*(3), 115–133.

Lewin, R., Parker, T., & Regine, B. (1998). Complexity theory and the organization: Beyond the metaphor. *Complexity*, *3*(4), 36–40. doi:10.1002/(SICI)1099-0526(199803/04)3:4<36::AID-CPLX7>3.0.CO;2-I

Limayem, M., Khalifa, M., & Frini, A. (2000). What makes consumers buy from Internet? A longitudinal study of online shopping. *IEEE Transactions on Systems, Man, and Cybernetics. Part A, Systems and Humans*, *30*(4), 421–432. doi:10.1109/3468.852436

Lin, F.-R., Huang, S.-H., & Lin, S.-C. (2002). Effects of information sharing on supply chain performance in electronic commerce. *IEEE Transactions on Engineering Management*, *49*(3), 258–268. doi:10.1109/TEM.2002.803388

Lin, H.-M. (2006). Interorganizational collaboration, social embeddedness, and value creation: A theoretical analysis. *International Journal of Management*, *23*(3), 548–558.

Lin, C., & Pervan, G. (2003). The practice of IS/IT benefits management in large Australian organisations. *Information & Management*, *41*(1), 13–24. doi:10.1016/S0378-7206(03)00002-8

Lindblom, C. E. (1959). The science of muddling through. *Public Administration Review*, *19*(1), 79–88. doi:10.2307/973677

Littlejohns, P., Wyatt, J. C., & Garvican, L. (2003). Evaluating computerised health information systems: Hard lessons still to be learnt. *BMJ (Clinical Research Ed.)*, *326*(7394), 860–863. doi:10.1136/bmj.326.7394.860

Liu, X., & Wei, K. K. (2003). An empirical study of product differences in consumers' e-commerce adoption behavior. *Electronic Commerce Research and Applications*, *2*, 229–239. doi:10.1016/S1567-4223(03)00027-9

Lorenzi, N., & Riley, R. (2000). Managing change: An overview. *Journal of the American Medical Informatics Association*, *7*(2), 116. doi:10.1136/jamia.2000.0070116

Lowe, A., & Locke, J. (2007). *Biography of an ERP: Tracing the fabrication of a virtual object*. (Department of Accounting Working Paper Series, Number 93). Hamilton, New Zealand: University of Waikato.

Lubatkin, M., Schweiger, D., & Weber, Y. (1999). Top management turnover in related M&A's: An additional test of the theory of relative standing. *Journal of Management*, *25*(1), 55–73.

Mabin, V. J., & Balderstone, S. J. (2000). *The world of the theory of constraints: A review of the international literature*. Boca Raton, FL: St Lucie Press.

Madlberger, M. (2009). What drives firms to engage in interorganizational information sharing in supply chain management? *International Journal of e-Collaboration*, *5*(2), 18–42. doi:10.4018/jec.2009040102

Madlberger, M., & Roztocki, N. (2008). Cross-organizational and cross-border IS/IT collaboration: A literature review. *Proceedings of the 14th Americas Conference on Information Systems,* Toronto.

Main, T. J., & Short, J. E. (1989). Managing the merger: Building partnership through IT planning at the new Baxter. *Management Information Systems Quarterly*, *13*(4), 469–484. doi:10.2307/248735

Malhotra, Y., & Galletta, D. F. (1999, January 5-8). *Extending the technology acceptance model to account for social influence: Theoretical bases and empirical validation.* Paper presented at the Proceedings of the 32nd Hawaii International Conference on System Sciences, Maui, Hawaii.

Malone, T. W., Yates, J., & Benjamin, I. (1987). Electronic markets and electronic hierarchies. *Communications of the ACM*, *30*(6), 484–497. doi:10.1145/214762.214766

Marcondes, C. H., & Jardim, J. M. (2003). Políticas de informação governamental: A construção do governo eletrônico na administração federal do Brasil. *Revista de Ciência da Informação, 4*(2).

Markus, M. L., & Robey, D. (1988). Information Technology and organizational change: Causal structure in theory and research. *Management Science*, *34*(5), 583–599. doi:10.1287/mnsc.34.5.583

Markus, M. L. (1983). Power, politics and MIS implementation. *Communications of the ACM*, *26*(6), 430–444. doi:10.1145/358141.358148

Markus, L., Steinfield, C. W., Wigand, R. T., & Minton, G. (2006). Industry-wide Information Systems standardization as collective action: The case of the US residential mortgage industry. *Management Information Systems Quarterly*, *30*, 439–465.

Martens, B., & Teuteberg, F. (2009). Why risk management matters in IT outsourcing: A systematic literature review and elements of a research agenda. *Proceedings of the 17th European Conference on Information Systems (ECIS 2009).* June. Verona, Italy.

Maskell, B. H. (1991). *Performance measurement for world class manufacturing – A model for American companies*. Connecticut: Productivity Press.

Mason-Jones, R., & Towill, D. R. (1999). Total cycle time compression and the agile supply chain. *International Journal of Production Economics*, *62*, 61–73. doi:10.1016/S0925-5273(98)00221-7

Massaro, T. (1993). Introducing physician order entry at a major academic medical center: I. Impact on organizational culture and behavior. *Academic Medicine*, *68*, 20–25. doi:10.1097/00001888-199301000-00003

Massetti, B., & Zmud, R. W. (1996). Measuring the extent of EDI usage in complex organizations: Strategies and illustrative examples. *Management Information Systems Quarterly*, *20*(3), 331–345. doi:10.2307/249659

Mayer, R. C., Davis, J. H., & Schoorman, F. D. (1995). An integrative model of organizational trust. *Academy of Management Review*, *29*(3), 709–734.

McCabe, B. (2006). *A coevolutionary framework for engaging trading partners in interorganisational e-commerce.* Unpublished PhD thesis, University of Technology, Sydney.

McCabe, B., & Underwood, J. (2008). *Enrolling actors in the co-evolution of inter-organisational information systems.* Paper presented at the 12th Pacific Asia Conference on Information Systems, Suzhou.

McFarland, D. J., & Hamilton, D. (2006). Adding contextual specificity to the technology acceptance model. *Computers in Human Behavior*, *22*, 427–447. doi:10.1016/j.chb.2004.09.009

McGhee, J. (2003). Strategy as orchestrating knowledge. In Cummings, S., & Wilson, D. C. (Eds.), *Images of strategy* (pp. 136–163). Blackwell, UK.

McGuire, D., & Hutchings, K. (2006). A Machiavellian analysis of organisational change. *Journal of Organizational Change Management*, *19*(2), 192–209. doi:10.1108/09534810610648906

Mckiernan, P., & Merali, Y. (1995). Integrating Information Systems after a merger. *Long Range Planning*, *28*(4), 54–62. doi:10.1016/0024-6301(95)00027-G

McMaster, T., & Wastell, D. (2005). The agency of hybrids: Overcoming the symmetophobic block. *Scandinavian Journal of Information Systems*, *17*(1), 175–182.

McMaster, T., Vidgen, R., & Wastell, D. (1998). *Networks of association in due process of IS development.* Paper presented at the Information Systems: current issues and future changes, Helsinki.

McNab, R. M., & Melese, F. (2003). Implementing the GPRA: Examining the prospects for performance budgeting in the federal government. *Public Budgeting & Finance*, *23*(2), 73–95. doi:10.1111/1540-5850.2302006

McNish, M. (2002). Guidelines for managing change: A study of their effects on the implementation of new information technology projects in organisations. *Journal of Change Management*, *2*(3), 201–211. doi:10.1080/738552754

Mehta, M., & Hirschheim, R. (2007). Strategic alignment in mergers and acquisitions: Theorizing IS integration decision making. *Journal of the Association for Information Systems*, *8*(3), 143–174.

Mentzer, J. T., DeWitt, W., Keebler, J. S., Min, S. H., Nix, N. W., Carlo, C. D., & Zacharia, Z. G. (2001). Defining the supply chain management. *Journal of Business Logistics*, *22*(2), 1–25. doi:10.1002/j.2158-1592.2001.tb00001.x

Meredith, J. K., & Shafer, S. M. (1999). *Operations management for MBAs*. Danvers, MA: John Wiley & Sons.

Metz, E. (1986). Managing change toward a leading-edge information culture. *Organizational Dynamics*, *15*(2), 28–40. doi:10.1016/0090-2616(86)90035-5

Meyer, A. D., & Goes, J. B. (1988). Organizational assimilation of innovations: A multilevel contextual analysis. *Academy of Management Journal*, *31*(4), 897–923. doi:10.2307/256344

Meyers, R. T. (1994). *Strategic Budgeting*. Ann Arbor, MI: University of Michigan Press.

Michaels, C. F., & Carello, C. (1981). *Direct perception*. Englewood Cliffs, NJ: Prentice-Hall.

Michelson, G., & Mouly, V. S. (2002). You didn't hear this from us but...: Towards an understanding of rumour and gossip in organisations. *Australian Journal of Management*, *27*, 1–10. doi:10.1177/031289620202701S07

Mikesell, J. L. (2007). *Fiscal administration: Analysis and applications for the public sector* (7th ed.). Belmont, CA: Thomas Wadsworth.

Miller, D. (1996). A preliminary topology of organisational learning: Synthesising the literature. *Journal of Management*, *22*(3), 485–505. doi:10.1177/014920639602200305

Miller, D. J., Fern, M. J., & Cardinal, L. B. (2007). The use of knowledge for technological innovation within diversified firms. *Academy of Management Journal*, *50*(2), 308–326. doi:10.5465/AMJ.2007.24634437

Miller, G. J. (1996). Productivity and the budget process. In Rabin, J. W., Hildrith, W. B., & Miller, G. J. (Eds.), *Budgeting: Formulation and Execution*. Athens, GA: Carl Vinson Institute of Government, University of Georgia.

Mingers, J. (2004). Realizing Information Systems: Critical realism as an underpinning philosophy for Information Systems. *Information and Organization*, *14*, 87–103. doi:10.1016/j.infoandorg.2003.06.001

Ministry of Economy, Trade, and Industry. (2007). *Market research report on e-commerce for year 2006.* Ministry of Economy, Trade, and Industry, Japan. Retrieved from www.meti.go.jp/policy/it_policy/statistics/outlook/H18EC_070330.pdf

Ministry of Economy. Trade and Industry. (2006). *Market research report on e-commerce for year 2005.* Ministry of Economy, Trade, and Industry, Japan. Retrieved from www.meti.go.jp/policy/it_policy/statistics/outlook/060901outlook.pdf

Ministry of Information and Communication. (2006). *Survey on the computer and Internet usage. Internet Statistic Reports*. National Internet Development Agency of Korea. Retrieved from http://isis.nida.or.kr/eng/

Ministry of Internal Affairs and Communications. (2005). *Communications usage trend survey in 2004. Telecommunications Bureau.* Tokyo, Japan: MIC.

Ministry of Internal Affairs and Communications. (2006). *Communications usage trend survey in 2005. Telecommunications Bureau.* Tokyo, Japan: MIC.

Mintzberg, H. (2007). *Tracking strategies*. USA: Oxford University Press.

Mitroff, I. I., & Linstone, H. A. (1994). *The unbounded mind*. USA: Oxford University Press.

Moden, Y. (1993). *Toyota manufacturing system: Linking the seven functional areas*. Portland, OR: Productivity Press.

Monsuve, T. P., Dellaert, B. G. C., & Ruyter, K. (2004). What drives consumers to shop online? A literature review. *International Journal of Service Industry Management*, *15*(1), 102–121. doi:10.1108/09564230410523358

Monteiro, E. (1998). Scaling information infrastructure: the case of next-generation IP on the internet. *The Information Society*, *14*, 229–245. doi:10.1080/019722498128845

Montiero, E., & Hespø, V. (1998). Diffusion of infrastructure: mobilization and improvization. In Larsen, T. J., Levine, L., & de Gross, J. I. (Eds.), *Information Systems: Current issues and future changes*. Dordrecht, The Netherlands: Kluwer.

Morçöl (Ed.), *Handbook of decision making* (pp. 3–18). Boca Raton, FL: Taylor & Francis Group.

Morçöl, G. (2007). Decision making: An overview of theories, contexts, and methods. In G.

Morgan, R. M., & Hunt, S. D. (1994). The commitment-trust theory in relationship marketing. *Journal of Marketing*, *58*(3), 20–38. doi:10.2307/1252308

Mota, F. P. B. (2010). *Processo eletrônico de compras públicas na perspectiva da DUALIDADE da tecnologia: Um estudo comparado no contexto brasileiro e paraibano. Dissertação (Mestrado em Administração)*. João Pessoa: Universidade Federal da Paraíba.

Mumford, E. (2006). The story of socio-technical design: Reflections on its successes, failures and potential. *Information Systems Journal*, *16*, 317–342. doi:10.1111/j.1365-2575.2006.00221.x

Myhe, N., & Speckman, R. R. (2005). Collaborative supply chain partnerships built upon trust and electronically mediated exchange. *Journal of Business and Industrial Marketing*, *20*(4-5), 179–186.

Nandan, R. K. (1998). The dialectic of power – Implications for management accounting and control research. *Journal of Pacific Studies*, *22*, 133–158.

Narasimhan, R., & Carter, J. R. (1998). Linking business unit and material sourcing strategies. *Journal of Business Logistics*, *19*(2), 155–170.

Natchez, P. B., & Bupp, I. C. (1973). Policy and priority in the budgetary process. *The American Political Science Review*, *67*, 951–963. doi:10.2307/1958637

Neef, D. (2001). *E-Procurement: From strategy to implementation*. New Jersey: Prentice Hall.

Nelson, P. (1970). Information and consumer behavior. *The Journal of Political Economy*, *2*, 311–329. doi:10.1086/259630

Nguyen, H. M., & Harrison, N. J. (2004). Electronic supply-chain orientation and its competitive dimensions. *Production Planning and Control*, *15*(6), 596–607. doi:10.1080/09537280412331283946

Niderman, F., Mathieu, R., Morley, R., & Kwon, I.-W. (2007). Examining RFID applications in supply chain management using a data lifecycle framework. *Communications of the ACM*, *50*(7), 92–101.

Nishiguchi, T. (1994). *Strategic industrial sourcing*. New York, NY: Oxford University Press.

Noreen, E., Smith, D., & Mackey, J. (1995). *The theory of constraints and its implications for management accounting*. MA: North River Press.

North, D. C. (1990). *Institutions, institutional change and economic performance*. Cambridge, UK: Cambridge University Press.

Novick, D. (2002). What program budgeting is and is not? In Hyde, A. C. (Ed.), *Government budgeting: Theory, process, and politics* (pp. 475–482). Pacific Grove, CA: Thompson Learning.

O'Donnell, J. B., & Glassberg, B. C. (2005). A typology of inter-organizational systems. In Eom, S. (Ed.), *Inter-organizational information systems in the Internet age*. Hershey, PA: Idea Group.

O'Reilly, C. (1989). Corporations, culture, and commitment: Motivation and social control in organizations. *California Management Review*, *31*, 9–25.

Orlikowski, W. J. (1992). The duality of technology: Rethinking the concept of technology in organizations. *Organization Science*, *3*(3), 398–427. doi:10.1287/orsc.3.3.398

Orlikowski, W. J. (2000). Using technology and constituting structures: A practice lens for studying technology in organizations. *Organization Science*, *11*(4), 404–428. doi:10.1287/orsc.11.4.404.14600

Orlikowski, W. J., & Barley, S. R. (2001). Technology and institutions: What can research on Information Technology and research on organizations learn from each other? *Management Information Systems Quarterly*, *25*(2). doi:10.2307/3250927

Orlikowski, W. J., & Iacono, C. S. (2001). Research commentary: Desperately seeking the "IT" in IT research - A call to theorizing the IT artifact. *Information Systems Research*, *12*(2), 121–134. doi:10.1287/isre.12.2.121.9700

Orlikowski, W. (1996). Improving organisational transformation over time: A situated change perspective. *Information Systems Research*, *7*(1), 63–92. doi:10.1287/isre.7.1.63

Orlikowski, W. J. (1991). *Relevance versus rigor in Information Systems research: An issue of quality – The role of institutions in creating research norms*. Panel Presentation at the IFIP TC8/WG 8.2 Working Conference on the Information Systems Research Challenges, Perception and Alternative Approaches, Copenhagen, Denmark.

Orlikowski, W. J., & Scott, S. V. (2008). *The entangling of technology and work in organizations*. Working Paper, Department of Management, Information Systems and Innovation Group, London School of Economics, February 2008.

Osborn, R. N., & Hagedoorn, J. (1997). The institutionalization and evolutionary dynamics of interorganizational alliances and networks. *Academy of Management Journal*, *40*(2), 261–278. doi:10.2307/256883

Osborn, D., & Gaebler, T. (1992). *Reinventing government: How the entrepreneurial spirit is transforming in public sector*. Reading, MA: Addison-Wesley.

Österle, H., Fleisch, E., & Alt, R. (2001). *Business networking: Shaping collaboration between enterprises*. Berlin, Germany: Springer.

Ouchi, W. (1980). Markets, bureaucracies, and class. *Administrative Science Quarterly*, *25*, 125–141. doi:10.2307/2392231

Ouchi, W. (1984). *The M-form society*. New York, NY: Avon Books.

Overby, S. (2003, September 1). The hidden costs of offshore outsourcing. *CIO Magazine*. Retrieved March 19, 2010, from http://www.cio.com/archive/090103/

Owens Swift, C., & Coe, B. J. (1994). Sourcing preference scale: Measuring preferences of purchasing managers for single sourcing or multiple sourcing of products. *Industrial Marketing Management*, *23*(2), 171–180. doi:10.1016/0019-8501(94)90019-1

Padhi, S. S., & Mohapatra, P. K. J. (2010). Adoption of e-procurement in the government departments. *Electronic Government: An International Journal*, *7*(1), 41–51. doi:10.1504/EG.2010.029890

Parida, V., Sophonthummapharn, K., & Parida, U. (2005). Understanding e-procurement: Qualitative case studies. Lulea University of Technology. Retrieved from http://www.ebrc.fi/kuvat/Parida_Sophonthummapharn_Parida_paper.pdf

Patton, M. Q. (1990). *Qualitative evaluation and research methods* (2nd ed.). Newbury Park, CA: Sage Publications, Inc.

Pegels, C. C., & Watrous, C. (2005). Application of the theory of constraints to a bottleneck operation in a manufacturing plant. *Journal of Manufacturing Technology Management*, *16*(3), 302–311. doi:10.1108/17410380510583617

Penrose, E. (1959). *The theory of the growth of the firm*. New York, NY: Wiley.

Perrow, C. (1986). *Complex organizations: A critical essay*. New York, NY: McGraw-Hill, Inc.

Peters, S., Heng, M., & Vet, R. (2002). Formation of the information systems strategy in a global financial services company. *Information and Organization*, *12*(1), 19–38. doi:10.1016/S1471-7727(01)00011-2

Pettigrew, A. M. (1979). On studying organizational cultures. *Administrative Science Quarterly*, *24*, 570–581. doi:10.2307/2392363

Pettigrew, A. M. (1987). Context and action in the transformation of the firm. *Journal of Management Studies*, *24*(6), 649–670. doi:10.1111/j.1467-6486.1987.tb00467.x

Picot, A., Reichwald, R., & Wigand, R. T. (1996). *Die grenzenlose Unternehmung: Information, Organisation und Management* (2nd ed.). Wiesbaden, Germany: Gabler.

Pirasteh, R., & Farah, K. S. (2006). Continuous improvement trio. *APICS Magazine*, *16*(5), 31–33.

Poirier, C. C., Quinn, F. J., & Swink, M. L. (2010). *Diagnosing greatness*, Ross publication.

Porter, M. E. (1996). What is strategy? *Harvard Business Review*, (November-December): 61–78.

Posner, P. L. (2009). Budget process reform: Waiting for Godot. *Public Administration Review*, *69*(2), 233–244. doi:10.1111/j.1540-6210.2008.01969.x

Poulymenakou, A., & Klein, S. (2006). Networks as orchestrations. In Klein, S., & Poulymenakou, A. (Eds.), *Managing dynamic networks* (pp. 3–15). Berlin, Germany: Springer. doi:10.1007/3-540-32884-X_1

Prahalad, C. K. (2008). The role of core competencies in the corporation. In Millson, M. R., & Wilemon, D. (Eds.), *The strategy of managing innovation and technology* (2nd ed., pp. 58–69). Upper Saddle River, NJ: Pearson Prentice Hall.

Prasad, P. (2005). *Crafting qualitative research*. Armonk, NY: M.E. Sharpe.

Premkumar, G., & Ramamurthy, K. (1995). The role of interorganizational and organizational factors on the decision mode for adoption on interorganizational systems. *Decision Sciences*, *26*, 303–336. doi:10.1111/j.1540-5915.1995.tb01431.x

Purvis, R. L., Sambamurthy, V., & Zmud, R. W. (2001). The assimilation of knowledge platforms in organizations: An empirical investigation. *Organization Science*, *12*(2), 117–135. doi:10.1287/orsc.12.2.117.10115

Puschmann, T., & Alt, R. (2005). Successful use of e-procurement in supply chains. *Supply Chain Management*, *10*(2), 122–133. doi:10.1108/13598540510589197

Quattrone, P., & Hopper, T. (2001). What does organisational change mean? Speculations of a taken for granted category. *Management Accounting Research*, *12*(4), 403–435. doi:10.1006/mare.2001.0176

Quinn, J. B., & Hilmer, F. G. (1994). Strategic outsourcing. *Sloan Management Review*, *35*, 43–55.

Qureshi, S., & Davis, A. (2007). *Managing resistance to organizational change: How GSS can reveal role related resistance behaviors*. Paper presented at the 40th Annual Hawaii International Conference on System Sciences (HICSS'07), Big island, HI.

Rahim, M. M., & As-Saber, S. (2009). Motivations and challenges of e-procurement systems adoption: The experience of an Australian City Council. In *Proceedings of the Conference on Administration, Society, and Education (e-CASE),* January, Singapore.

Rahman, S. (1998). Theory of constraints: A review of the philosophy and its applications. *International Journal of Operations & Production Management*, *18*(4), 336–355. doi:10.1108/01443579810199720

Rahman, S. (2002). The theory of constraints' thinking process approach to developing strategies in supply chains. *International Journal of Physical Distribution and Logistics Management*, *32*(10), 809–828. doi:10.1108/09600030210455429

Rahul, K., & Kwanghui, L. (2007). The impact of acquisitions on the productivity of inventors at semiconductor firms: A synthesis of knowledge-based and incentive-based perspectives. *Academy of Management Journal*, *50*(5), 113–115.

Ramiller, N. C., & Swanson, E. B. (2003). *Whether, when, and how to innovate with Information Technology: What do empirical studies tell us?* Information Systems Working Paper 2-03, The Anderson School at UCLA, March.

Randolph, C., & Main, R. (2005). Exploring the power and politics of a PeoplesSoft implementation. In von Hellens, L., Nielsen, S., & Beekhuyzen, J. (Eds.), *Qualitative case studies on implementation of enterprise wide systems* (pp. 140–159). Hershey, PA: Idea Group, Inc.

Ranganathan, C., Teo, T. S. H., Dhaliwal, J., Ang, J. S. K., & Hyde, M. (2001). Facilitators and inhibitors for deploying business-to-business e-Commerce applications: A multi-method, cross-cultural study. *Proceedings of the 22nd Annual International Conference on Information Systems.* New Orleans, LA, (pp. 593-600).

Rao, M. T. (2004). Key issues for global outsourcing: Country and individual factors. *Information Systems Management*, 16–24. doi:10.1201/1078/44432.21.3.20040601/82472.3

Reckwitz, A. (2002). Toward a theory of social practice - A development in culturalist theorizing. *European Journal of Social Theory*, *5*(2), 243–263. doi:10.1177/13684310222225432

Reddick, G. C. (2004). The growth of e-procurement in American state governments: A model & empirical evidence. *Journal of Public Procurement*, *4*(2), 151–176.

Reid, R. A. (2007). Applying the TOC five-step focusing process in the service sector: A banking subsystem. *Managing Service Quality*, *17*(2), 209–234. doi:10.1108/09604520710735209

Reimers, K., & Klein, S. (2006). Network management framework. In Klein, S., & Poulymenakou, A. (Eds.), *Managing dynamic networks* (pp. 17–66). Berlin, Germany: Springer.

Reimers, K., & Li, M. (2008). Interaction of technological and institutional change in the development of an electronic commerce system in China's pharmaceutical distribution chain - A transaction cost perspective. In *Proceedings of the International Conference on Health Informatics (HEALTHINF)*, January 28-31 2008, Funchal, Portugal.

Reimers, K., Johnston, R. B., & Klein, S. (2004). The shaping of inter-organisational Information Systems: Main design considerations of an international comparative research project. In *Proceedings of the 17th Bled eCommerce Conference "eGlobal"*, June 21-23 2004, Bled, Slovenia.

Reimers, K., Johnston, R. B., & Klein, S. (2009). Understanding resilience and evolution of IOIS in the Australian pharmaceutical distribution industry. In *Proceedings of the Thirtieth International Conference on Information Systems*, December 16-18 2009, Phoenix.

Reimers, K., Johnston, R. B., Klein, S., Wagner, T., & Schellhammer, S. (2008). *Beyond mutual shaping - Rethinking symmetry and causality in the treatment of socio-material systems.* Paper presented at the Joint Conference of the Society for Social Studies of Science (4S) and the European Association for the Study of Science and Technology (EASST), August 20-23 2008, Rotterdam, The Netherlands.

Remyeni, D. (1999). Language and a post-modern approach to information systems. *International Journal of Information Management*, *19*(1), 17–32. doi:10.1016/S0268-4012(98)00044-9

Rice, R. E., & Aydin, C. (1991). Attitudes toward new organisational technology: Network proximity as a mechanism for social information processing. *Administrative Science Quarterly*, *36*(2), 219–244. doi:10.2307/2393354

Ritchey, T. (2005). *Wicked problems: Structuring social messes with morphological analysis*. Swedish Morphological Society.

Rittel, H., & Webber, M. (1973). Dilemmas in a general theory of planning. *Policy Sciences*, *4*(2), 155–169. doi:10.1007/BF01405730

Robbins, S., & Stylianou, A. C. (1999). Post-merger systems integration: The impact on IS capabilities. *Information & Management*, *36*(4), 205. doi:10.1016/S0378-7206(99)00018-X

Robey, D., Im, G., & Wareham, J. D. (2008). Theoretical foundations of empirical research on Interorganizational Systems: Assessing past contributions and guiding future directions. *Journal of the Association for Information Systems*, *9*(9), 497–518.

Robey, D., & Boudreau, S. (1999). Accounting for the contradictory organizational consequences of Information Technology: Theoretical direction and methodological implications. *Information Systems Research*, *10*(2), 167–185. doi:10.1287/isre.10.2.167

Robey, D., Im, G., & Wareham, J. D. (2008). Theoretical foundations of empirical research on interorganizational systems: Assessing past contributions and guiding future directions. *Journal of the Association for Information Systems*, *9*(9), 497–518.

Rodon, J., Pastor, J. A., Sesé, F., & Christiaanse, E. (2008). Unraveling the dynamics of IOIS implementation: An actor-network study of an IOIS in the Seaport of Barcelona. *Journal of Information Technology*, *23*, 97–108. doi:10.1057/palgrave.jit.2000131

Rodrigues Filho, J. (2010). E-government in Brazil – Reinforcing institutions or reducing citizenship? In Reddick, C. (Ed.), *Politics, democracy and e-government – Participation and service delivery* (pp. 347–362). Hershey, PA: IGI Global. doi:10.4018/978-1-61520-933-0.ch021

Rodrigues Filho, J., & Mota, F. P. B. (2010). *E-government research – From a utilitarian quantitative and qualitative positivist approach to an in-depth critical and reflexive engagement with theoretical issues*. Qualitative Research on Administration and Organization Conference, New Mexico, 2010.

Rodrigues, F. J., & Santos, J. R. Jr. (2009). Local e-government in Brazil – Poor interaction and local politics as usual. In Reddick, C. G. (Ed.), *Handbook of research on strategies for local e-government adoption and implementation – Comparative studies* (*Vol. 2*, pp. 863–878). Hershey, PA: IGI Global.

Rogers, E. M. (1995). *Diffusion of innovations*. New York, NY: Free Press.

Rosenkopf, L., & Nerkar, A. (1999). On the complexity of technological evolution: Exploring co-evolution within and across hierarchical levels in optical disc Technology. In Baum, J., & McKelvey, B. (Eds.), *Variations in organization science, in honour of Donald T. Campbell*. Thousand Oaks, CA: SAGE.

Rouse, A. C. (2008). *Managing e-collaboration risks in business process outsourcing, Encyclopedia of e-Collaboration* (pp. 424–429). Hershey, PA: Information Science Reference.

Rouse, A. C. (2009). *The governance implications when it is outsourced. Information Technology governance and service management: Frameworks and adaptations* (pp. 285–295). Hershey, PA: Information Science Reference.

Rouse, A. C., & Watson, D. J. (2005). Cyberfraud and identity theft: The hidden costs of business process outsourcing. *Monash Business Review*, *1*(2), 30–39. doi:10.2104/mbr05018

Rouse, A. C. (2002). *Information technology outsourcing revisited: Success factors and risks*. Unpublished doctoral thesis. Melbourne, Australia: University of Melbourne.

Rouse, A. C., & Corbitt, B. J. (2003a). Revisiting IT outsourcing risks: Analysis of a survey of Australia's top 1000 organizations. *14th Australasian Conference on Information Systems 2003, Perth, Western Australia, 26-28 November, 2003: Delivering IT and e-business value in networked environments*. Edith Cowan University, Joondalup, WA (pp. 1-11).

Rouse, A. C., & Corbitt, B. J. (2003b).Minimising risks in IT outsourcing: Choosing target services, *PACIS 2003: Proceedings of the Seventh Pacific Asia Conference on Information Systems*, University of South Australia, Adelaide, S. Aust. (pp. 927-940).

Rouse, A. C., & Corbitt, B. J. (2004). IT-supported business process outsourcing (BPO): The good, the bad and the ugly. In C.-P. Wei (Ed.), *Information Systems Adoption and Business Productivity, PACIS 2004: Proceedings of the Seventh Pacific Asia Conference on Information Systems*. Shanghai, China (pp. 1-14).

Rubin, I. S. (1990a). Budget theory and budget practice: How good the fit? *Public Administration Review*, *50*(2), 179–189. doi:10.2307/976865

Rubin, I. S. (1990b). *The politics of public budgeting: Getting and spending, borrowing and balancing*. Chatham, NJ: Chatham House of Publishers, Inc.

Russell, D. M., & Hoag, A. M. (2004). People and information technology in the supply chain: Social and organizational influences on adoption. *International Journal of Physical Distribution & Logistics Management*, *34*(1/2), 102–122. doi:10.1108/09600030410526914

Sales, A. L., & Mirvis, P. H. (1984). When cultures collide: Issues in acquisition. In Kimberly, J. R., & Quinn, R. E. (Eds.), *Managing organizational transitions* (pp. 107–133). Homewood, IL: Irwin.

Salleh, Y., & Goh, W. K. (2002). Managing human resources towards achieving knowledge management. *Journal of Knowledge Management*, *6*(5), 457–468. doi:10.1108/13673270210450414

Sampson, G. (2003). The myth of the diminishing firm. *Communications of the ACM*, *46*(11), 25–28. doi:10.1145/948383.948404

Sanchez, O. A. (2003). O poder burocrático e o controle da informação. *Lua nova Revista de Cultura e Política, 58*, 89-119.

Santana, R. (2007). *Electronic procurement allow for inspection by society. Global forum on governance: Modernising government: strategies & tools for change*. Retrieved from http://www.oecd.org/dataoecd/0/51/39612372.pdf

Sartorius, C., & Zundel, S. (2005). *Time strategies, innovation and environmental policy*. Cheltenham, UK: Edward Elgar.

Sathe, V. (1985). *Culture and related corporate realities: Text, cases, and readings on organizational entry, establishment, and change*. Homewood, IL: R.D. Irwin.

Schein, E. H. (1992). *Organizational culture and leadership*. San Francisco, CA: Jossey-Bass.

Schenk, T., Löffler, G., & Rauh, J. (2007). Agent-based simulation of consumer behavior in grocery shopping on a regional level. *Journal of Business Research*, *60*(8), 894–903. doi:10.1016/j.jbusres.2007.02.005

Scheuing, E. E. (1989). *Purchasing management*. Englewood Cliffs, NJ: Prentice Hall.

Schick, A. (1966). The road to PPB: The stages of budget reform. *Public Administration Review*, *26*(December), 243–258. doi:10.2307/973296

Schick, A. (1971). *Budget Innovation in the States*. Washington, D.C.: The Brookings Institute.

Schick, A. (1978). The road from ZBB. *Public Administration Review*, *39*(2), 177–180. doi:10.2307/976294

Schick, A. (1983). Incremental budgeting in a decremental age. *Policy Sciences*, *16*(1), 1–25. doi:10.1007/BF00138465

Schneider, G. P. (2006). *Electronic commerce*. Boston, MA: Thomson Course Technology.

Schragenheim, E., & Ronen, B. (1990). Drum-Buffer shop floor control. *Production and Inventory Management*, Third Quarter, 18-22.

Schulman, P. R. (1975). Nonincremental policy making: Notes Toward an alternative paradigm. *The American Political Science Review*, *69*, 1354–1370. doi:10.2307/1955293

Schweiger, D. M., & Goulet, P. K. (2005). Facilitating acquisition integration through deep-level cultural learning interventions: A longitudinal field experiment. *Organization Studies*, *26*, 1477–1499. doi:10.1177/0170840605057070

Scoggin, J. M., Segelhorst, R. J., & Reid, R. A. (2003). Applying the TOC thinking process in manufacturing: A case study. *International Journal of Production Research*, *41*(4), 767–797. doi:10.1080/0020754031000065557

Scriven, G. (2003). Interoperability in Australian government e-procurement – Strategy versus reality. *Conference Proceedings of the 7th Pacific Asia Conference on Information System*, Adelaide, South Australia, July 10-13, 2003.

Seckler-Hudson, C. (2002). Performance budgeting in government. In Hyde, A. C. (Ed.), *Government budgeting: Theory, process, and politics* (pp. 462–474). Pacific Grove, CA: Thompson Learning.

Sewell, W. H. (2005). *Logics of history – Social theory and social transformation*. Chicago, IL: The University of Chicago Press.

Shakun, M. F. (2001). Unbounded rationality. *Group Decision and Negotiation*, *10*(2), 97–118. doi:10.1023/A:1008708222157

Shang, R.-A., Chen, Y.-C., & Shen, L. (2005). Extrinsic versus intrinsic motivations for consumers to shop on-line. *Information & Management*, *42*, 401–413. doi:10.1016/j.im.2004.01.009

Shannon, C. E., & Weaver, W. (1964). The mathematical theory of communication. [University of Illinois.]. *Urbana (Caracas, Venezuela)*, IL.

Shibutani, T. (1955). Reference groups as perspectives. *American Journal of Sociology*, *60*(6), 562–569. doi:10.1086/221630

Short, J. E., & Venkatraman, N. (1992). Beyond business process redesign: Redefining Baxter's business network. *Sloan Management Review*, *34*(1), 7–21.

Shostack, G. L. (1993). How to design a service. *European Journal of Marketing, 16*(1), 49–63. doi:10.1108/EUM0000000004799

Silva, L., & Backhouse, J. (2003). The Circuits-of-power framework for studying power in institutionalization of Information Systems. *Journal of the AIS, 4*(6), 294–336.

Simatupang, T. M., & Sridharan, R. (2005). The collaboration index: A measure for supply chain collaboration. *International Journal of Physical Distribution & Logistics Management, 35*(1), 44–62. doi:10.1108/09600030510577421

Simon, H. A. (1976). *Administrative behavior. A study of decision-making processes in administrative organization* (3rd ed.). New York, NY: Free Press.

Simon, H. A. (1957). *Models of man*. New York, NY: Wiley & Sons.

Simon, H. A. (1997). *Models of bounded rationality* (*Vol. 3*). Cambridge, MA: The MIT Press.

Simon, H. A. (1986). Rationality in psychology and economics. In Hogarth, R. M., & Reder, M. W. (Eds.), *Rational choice: The contrast between economics and psychology* (pp. 25–40). Chicago, IL: The University of Chicago Press.

Singer, M., Konstantinidis, G., Roubik, R., & Beffermann, E. (2009). Does e-procurement save the state money? *Journal of Public Procurement, 9*(1), 58–78.

Smeltzer, L. R. (1997). The meaning and origin of trust in buyer-supplier relationships. *International Journal of Purchasing and Materials Management, 33*(1), 40–48.

Smeltzer, L., & Carr, A. (2003). Electronic reverse auctions: Promises, risks, and conditions for success. *Industrial Marketing Management, 32*(6), 481–488. doi:10.1016/S0019-8501(02)00257-2

Smith, D. (2000). *The measure nightmare: How the theory of constraints can resolve conflicting strategies, policies and measures*. Boca Raton, FL: St. Lucie Press.

Smith, S. P., Johnston, R. B., Shanks, G., & Rahim, M. M. (2007). *From intention to motivation: Developing a motivation-based model of IOS implementation.* Paper presented on the Twenty Eighth International Conference on Information Systems, Montreal, Canada.

Smithies, A. (1955). *The budgetary process in the United States*. New York, NY: McGraw-Hill.

Soete, L., & Weehuizen, R. (2004). The economics of e-government: A bird's eye view. *International Journal of Communications Law and Policy, 8*(Winter).

Sok, C., Sia, S. K., Boh, W. F., & Tang, M. (2003). Misalignments in ERP implementation: A dialectic perspective. *International Journal of Human-Computer Interaction, 16*(3), 81–100.

Southon, F., Sauer, C., & Dampney, C. (1997). Information technology in complex health services: organizational impediments to successful technology transfer and diffusion. *Journal of the American Medical Informatics Association, 4*(2), 112. doi:10.1136/jamia.1997.0040112

Srinivasan, M. M. (2004). *Streamlined – 14 principles for building and managing the lean supply chain*. Cincinnati, OH: Thomson.

Stacey, R. (2003). Learning as an activity of interdependent people. *The Learning Organization, 10*(6), 323–331. doi:10.1108/09696470310497159

Stalk, G., & Hout, T. (1990). *Competing against time*. London, UK: Free Press.

Star, S. L., & Griesemer, J. R. (1989). Institutional ecology, translations and boundary objects: Amateurs and professionals in Berkeley's Museum of Vertebrate Zoology, 1907-39. *Social Studies of Science, 19*(3), 387–420. doi:10.1177/030631289019003001

Statistics Korea. (2010). *E-commerce and cyber shopping survey in 2009 and in the fourth quarter 2009.* Retrieved from http://kostat.go.kr

Steenkamp, J. B., Hofstede, F., & Wedel, M. (1999). A cross-national investigation into the individual and national cultural antecedents of consumer innovativeness. *Journal of Marketing, 63*(2), 55–69. doi:10.2307/1251945

Steinfield, C. W., Markus, M. L., & Wigand, R. T. (2005). Exploring interorganizational systems at the industry level of analysis: Evidence from the US home mortgage industry. *Journal of Information Technology, 20*(4), 224–233. doi:10.1057/palgrave.jit.2000051

Stemp, S. D., Minkin, J. E., Thomopoulos, J., & Stemp, M. W. (1985). *Decision support system*. Montvale, NJ: National Association of Accountants.

Straub, D., Keil, M., & Brenner, W. (1997). Testing the technology acceptance model across cultures: A three country study. *Information & Management*, *33*, 1–11. doi:10.1016/S0378-7206(97)00026-8

Stylianou, A. C., & Jeffries, C. J. (1996). Corporate mergers and the problems of IS integration. *Information & Management*, *31*(4), 203. doi:10.1016/S0378-7206(96)01082-8

Subramaniam, C., & Shaw, M. (2002). A study of the value of B2B e-commerce: The case of Web-based procurement. *International Journal of Electronic Commerce*, *6*(6), 19–40.

Suh, T., Xie, H., & Kwon, I.-W. (2005). The effect of total and asymemetric specific asset investment on supplier-buyer relationship: A structural model. *Proceeding of the 2005 Winter American Marketing Association Conference*, San Antonio, Texas, February, (pp. 298-299).

Swanson, E. B. (1974). Management Information Systems: Appreciation and involvement. *Management Science*, *21*(2), 178–188. doi:10.1287/mnsc.21.2.178

Synodinos, N. E. (2001). Understanding Japanese consumers: Some important underlying factors. *The Japanese Psychological Research*, *43*(4), 235–248. doi:10.1111/1468-5884.00181

Szajna, B. (1996). Empirical Evaluation of the revised technology acceptance model. *Management Science*, *42*(1), 85–92. doi:10.1287/mnsc.42.1.85

Szajna, B., & Scamell, R. W. (1993). The effects of Information System user expectations on their performance and perceptions. *Management Information Systems Quarterly*, *17*(4), 493–516. doi:10.2307/249589

Tabak, E. (2010). Opportunistic translation in development and managment of an organisational intranet. In A. M. Rawani, H. Kettani & L. Zhang (Eds.), *International Conference on Innovation, Management and Service (ICIMS 2010)* (pp. 47-52). Singapore: World Academic Press.

Tadelis, S. (2007). The innovative organization: Creating value through outsourcing. *California Management Review*, *50*(1), 261–277.

Taylor, S., & Todd, P. (1995). Assessing IT usage: The role of prior experience. *Management Information Systems Quarterly*, *19*(4), 561–570. doi:10.2307/249633

Taylor, G. M. (1977). Introduction to zero-based budgeting. *The Bureaucrat*, *6*(1), 33–55.

Telgen, J. (1998). Revolution through electronic purchasing. *7th International Annual IPSERA Conference Proceedings*, London, (pp. 499-504).

Teo, T. S. H., Lin, S., & Lai, K.-H. (2009). Adopters and non-adopters of e-procurement in Singapore: An empirical study. *Omega*, *37*, 972–987. doi:10.1016/j.omega.2008.11.001

Thai, K. V. (2001). Public procurement re-examined. *Journal of Public Procurement*, *1*(1), 9–50.

Themistcloeous, M., Irani, Z., & Love, P. E. D. (2004). Evaluating the integration of supply chain Information Systems: A case study. *European Journal of Operational Research*, *159*(2), 393–405. doi:10.1016/j.ejor.2003.08.023

Thomas, K. (1992). Overview of conflict and conflict management. *Journal of Organizational Behavior*, *13*(3), 263–264. doi:10.1002/job.4030130306

Thompson, J. D. (1967). *Organizations in action - Social science bases of administrative theory*. New York, NY: McGraw-Hill.

Thompson, F., & Sumeta, W. (1981). Control and controls: A reexamination of control patterns in budget execution. *Policy Sciences*, *13*(1), 25–50. doi:10.1007/BF00155931

Tornatzky, L. G., & Klein, R. J. (1982). Innovation characteristics and innovation adoption-implementation: A meta-analysis of findings. *IEEE Transactions on Engineering Management*, *29*, 28–45.

Transparencies International. (2009). *Corruption perception index 2009*. Retrieved from http://www.transparency.org/policy_research/surveys_indices/cpi/2009

Trauth, E. M. (2001). The choice of qualitative methods in IS research. In Trauth, E. M. (Ed.), *Qualitative research in IS: Issues and trends* (pp. 1–19). Hershey, PA: Idea Group Publishing.

Trist, E., & Bamforth, K. (1951). Some social and psychological consequences of the longwall method of coal-getting: An examination of the psychological situation and defences of a work group in relation to the social structure and technological content of the work system. *Human Relations*, *4*(1), 3–38. doi:10.1177/001872675100400101

True, J. L. (2000). Avalanches and incrementalism: Making policy and budgets in the United States. *American Review of Public Administration*, *30*(1), 3–18. doi:10.1177/02750740022064524

True, J. L., Jones, B. D., & Baumgartner, F. R. (1999). Punctuated equilibrium theory: Explaining stability and changes in American policymaking. In Sabatier, P. (Ed.), *Theories of the policy process*. Boulder, CO: Westview.

Turban, E., King, D., Lee, J., Warkentin, M., & Chung, H. M. (2002). *Electronic commerce 2002: A managerial perspective*. New Jersey: Prentice-Hall.

Tyler, C., & Willand, J. (1997). Public budgeting in America: A twentieth century retrospective. *Journal of Public Budgeting, Accounting, &. Financial Management*, *9*(2), 189–219.

Umble, M., & Srikanth, M. L. (1990). *Synchronous manufacturing: Principles for world class excellence*. Cincinnati, OH: South-Western Publishing.

Underwood, J. (2001b). Translation, betrayal and ambiguity in IS development. In Liu, K., Clark, R. J., Andersen, P. B., & Stamper, R. (Eds.), *Organizational semiotics: Evolving a science of information systems* (pp. 91–108). Boston, MA: Kluwer.

Underwood, J. (1992). *Information systems work: Contradictions in practice and theory.* Paper presented at the Third Australian Conference on Information Systems, Wollongong.

Underwood, J. (2001a). *Meaning in IS development.* Unpublished PhD thesis, University of Wollongong.

United Nations. (2006). *E-procurement. Economic and social commission for Asia and the Pacific Asian*. Thailand: Development Bank Institute.

Urbach, N., Smolnik, S., & Riempp, G. (2009). The state of research on information systems success – A review of existing multidimensional approaches. *Business & Information Systems Engineering*, *1*(4), 315–325. doi:10.1007/s12599-009-0059-y

US Congress. (2001). *E-Government Bill of 2001*. Bill introduced into the US Senate by Joseph Lieberman, May 1.

Uzal, R., Debnath, N. C., Montejano, G., & Riesco, D. (2005). *Software engineer first duty: The preliminary financial feasibility analysis of real world software projects*. IEEE International Symposium on Signal Processing and Information Technology. Retrieved from http://www.computer.org/portal/web/csdl/doi/10.1109/ISSPIT.2005.1577185

Uzzi, B. (1997). Social structure and competition in interfirm networks: The paradox of embeddedness. *Administrative Science Quarterly*, *42*(1), 35–67. doi:10.2307/2393808

Uzzi, B. (1997). Social structure and competition in interfirm networks: The paradox of embeddedness. *Administrative Science Quarterly*, *42*, 35–67. doi:10.2307/2393808

Vaidya, K., Sajeev, A. S. M., & Callender, G. (2006). e-Procurement initiatives in the public sector: Critical success factors that influence implementation success. *Journal of Public Procurement*, *4*(4/5), 70–99.

Vaidya, K., & Hyde, M. (2011). Inter-organisational information systems assimilation: An empirical evaluation in light of the diffusion of innovation theory. *International Journal of Business Information Systems*, *7*(3), 247–258. doi:10.1504/IJBIS.2011.039330

Vaidya, K., Sajeev, A. S. M., & Callender, G. (2006). Critical factors that influence e-procurement implementation success in the public sector. *Journal of Public Procurement*, *6*(1&3), 70–99.

Vaidya, K. (2007). *Electronic procurement in the Australian public sector: Organisational assimilation and its impacts on public procurement performance*. PhD thesis, The Univesity of New England, NSW Australia.

Vaidya, K., & Hopkins, P. (2006). The case of Smartbuy® e-Marketplace in the NSW public sector: Constraints and lessons learnt. *Proceedings of the 8th Collaborative Electronic Commerce Technology and Research International Conference*, December 8-9, Adelaide, Australia.

Vaidya, K., Sajeev, A. S. M., Johnston, J., & Cox, M. A. (2008). *Assimilation of public procurement innovation: an empirical; analysis in the light of transaction cost theory*. In Annual Conference of International Purchasing and Supply Education and Research Association, 9-12 March, Perth, Australia.

Vallerand, R. J. (1997). Toward a hierarchical model of intrinsic and extrinsic motivation. *Advances in Experimental Social Psychology*, 271–360. doi:10.1016/S0065-2601(08)60019-2

Van Manen, M. (1990). *Researching lived experience: Human science for an action sensitive pedagogy*. Albany, NY: State University of New York.

Vaughan, P. J. (2000). *System implementation success factors: It's not just the technology*. University of Colorado at Boulder.

Vaughan, E. J. (1997). *Risk management*. UK: Wiley.

Venkatash, V., & Morris, M. (2000). Why don't men ever stop to ask for directions? Gender, social influence, and their role in technology acceptance and usage. *Management Information Systems Quarterly*, *24*, 115–139. doi:10.2307/3250981

Venkatesh, V. (2000). Determinants of perceived ease of use: Integrating control, intrinsic motivation, and emotion into the technology acceptance model. *Information Systems Research*, *11*(4), 342–365. doi:10.1287/isre.11.4.342.11872

Venkatesh, V., & Davis, F. D. (1996). A model of the antecedents of perceived ease of use: Development and test. *Decision Sciences*, *27*(3), 451–481. doi:10.1111/j.1540-5915.1996.tb01822.x

Venkatesh, V., & Davis, F. D. (2000). A theoretical extension of the technology acceptance model: Four longitudinal field studies. *Management Science*, *46*(2), 186–204. doi:10.1287/mnsc.46.2.186.11926

Venkatesh, V., & Morris, M. G. (2000). Why don't men ever stop to ask for directions? Gender, social influence, and their role in technology acceptance and usage behaviour. *Management Information Systems Quarterly*, *24*(1), 115–139. doi:10.2307/3250981

Venkatesh, V., Morris, M. G., Davis, G. B., & Davis, F. D. (2003). User acceptance of Information Technology: Toward a unified view. *Management Information Systems Quarterly*, *27*(3), 425–478.

Venkatesh, V., & Bala, H. (2008). Technology acceptance model 3 and a research agenda on interventions. *Decision Sciences*, *39*(2), 273–315. doi:10.1111/j.1540-5915.2008.00192.x

Venkatesh, V. (1999). Creation of favorable user perceptions: Exploring the role of intrinsic motivation. *Management Information Systems Quarterly*, *23*, 239–260. doi:10.2307/249753

Verhoef, P. C., & Langerak, F. (2001). Possible determinants of consumers' adoption of electronic grocery shopping in the Netherlands. *Journal of Retailing and Consumer Services*, *8*, 275–285. doi:10.1016/S0969-6989(00)00033-3

Verner, J. C.ox, K., & Bleistein, S. J. (2006). Predicting good requirements for in-house development projects. In *Proceedings of the 2006 ACM/IEEE International Symposium on Empirical Software Engineering*, Rio de Janeiro, (pp. 154–163).

Visich, J. K., Li, S., Khumawala, B. M., & Reyes, P. M. (2010). Empirical evidence of RFID impacts on supply chain performance. *International Journal of Operations & Production Management*, *29*(12).

Volkoff, O., Strong, D. M., & Elmes, M. B. (2007). Technological embeddedness and organizational change. *Organization Science*, *18*(5), 832–848. doi:10.1287/orsc.1070.0288

Volkow, N. (2003). *Interaction between Information Systems and organizational change: Case study of Petroleos Mexicanos*. London: Unpublished PhD, University of London.

Waddell, D. M., Cummings, T. G., & Worley, C. G. (2011). *Organisational change, development and transformation. Asia Pacific* (4th ed.). Cengage Learning Australia.

Wade, M. R., & Hulland, J. (2004). The resource-based view and information systems research: Review, extension, and suggestions for future research. *Management Information Systems Quarterly*, *28*(1), 107–142.

Waldman, S. (2010). *Creative disruption: What you need to do to shake up your business in a digital world.* Prentice Hall, Financial Times, UK.

Walker, H., & Harland, C. (2008). E-procurement in the United Nations: Influences, issues, and impact. *International Journal of Operations & Production Management*, *28*(9), 831–857. doi:10.1108/01443570810895276

Walstrom, K. A., & Wilson, R. L. (1997). An examination of executive information systems (EIS) users. *Information & Management, 32*(2), 75–83. doi:10.1016/S0378-7206(97)00010-4

Wang, J., Gwebu, K., Shanker, M., & Troutt, M. D. (2009). An application of agent-based simulation to knowledge sharing. *Decision Support Systems, 46*(2), 532–541. doi:10.1016/j.dss.2008.09.006

Watson, K. J., Blackstone, J. H., & Gardiner, S. C. (2007). The evolution of a management philosophy: The theory of constraints. *Journal of Management, 25*, 387–402.

Wears, R. L., & Berg, M. (2005). Computer technology and clinical work: Still waiting for Godot. *Journal of the American Medical Association, 293*(10), 1261–1263. doi:10.1001/jama.293.10.1261

Weber, M. (1964). *The theory of social and economic organization (Trans. A.M. Henderson & T. Parsons)*. New York, NY: Free Press.

Weber, Y., & Pliskin, N. (1996). The effects of information systems integration and organizational culture on a firm's effectiveness. *Information & Management, 30*(2), 81–90. doi:10.1016/0378-7206(95)00046-1

Weiber, R., & Adler, J. (1995). Informationsökonomisch begründete Typologisierung von Kaufprozessen. *Zeitschrift fuer betriebswirtschaftliche. Forschung, 47*(1), 43–65.

Weinberg, G. (1975). *An introduction to general systems thinking*. New York, NY: Wiley.

Weiss, G. (1999). *Multiagent systems, a modern approach to distributed artificial intelligence*. Cambridge, MA: MIT Press.

Wells, M. A. (2009). *Perceptions of knowledge gatekeepers: Social aspects of information exchange in an organisation undergoing change*. Sydney: University of Western Sydney.

Wells, M. A., & Fisher, M. D. (2007). *The phenomena of uncontrolled communication as resistance during the implementation of an enterprise resource planning system*. Paper presented at the ANZAM 2007, Sydney, NSW, Australia.

Wenger, E. (2002). *Communities of practice - Learning, meaning, and identity*. Cambridge, UK: Cambridge University Press.

Wenger, E. (2004). Knowledge management as a doughnut: Shaping your knowledge strategy through communities of practice. *Ivey Business Journal Online*, January/February 2004.

Westbrook, J. I., Braithwaite, J., Georgiou, A., Ampt, A., Creswick, N., & Coiera, E. (2007). Multimethod evaluation of information and communication technologies in health in the context of wicked problems and sociotechnical theory. *Journal of the American Medical Informatics Association, 14*(6), 746–755. doi:10.1197/jamia.M2462

Whetton, S. (2005). *Health informatics: A socio-technical perspective*. Oxford University Press.

Whiteley, A. (1995). *Managing change: A core values approach*. South Melbourne, Australia: Macmillan Education Australia Pty Ltd.

Wijnhoven, F., Spil, T., Stegwee, R., & Fa, R. T. (2006). Post-merger IT integration strategies: An IT alignment perspective. *The Journal of Strategic Information Systems, 15*(1), 5–28. doi:10.1016/j.jsis.2005.07.002

Wildavsky, A. (1961). Political implications of budgetary reform. *Public Administration Review, 21*(3), 183–190. doi:10.2307/973628

Wildavsky, A. (1964). *The politics of the budget process*. Boston, MA: Little Brown.

Wildavsky, A. (1992). Political implications of budget reform: A retrospective. *Public Administration Review, 52*(3), 594–599. doi:10.2307/977170

Willcocks, L. P., & Kern, T. (2001). *The relationship advantage: Information technologies, sourcing and management*. Oxford, UK: Oxford University Press.

Willcocks, L. P., Kern, T., & Van Heck, E. (2002). The winner's curse in IT outsourcing: Strategies for avoiding relational trauma. *California Management Review, 44*(2), 47–69.

Williams, R., & Edge, D. (1996). The social shaping of technology. *Research Policy, 25*(5), 865–899. doi:10.1016/0048-7333(96)00885-2

Williamson, O. E. (1975). *Markets and hierarchies: Analysis and antitrust implications. A study in the economics of internal organization*. New York, NY: The Free Press.

Williamson, O. E. (1985). *The economic institutions of capitalism*. New York, NY: Free Press.

Williamson, O. (1981). The economics of organizations: The transaction cost approach. *American Journal of Sociology, 87*(3), 548–577. doi:10.1086/227496

Williamson, O. (2008). Outsourcing: Transaction cost economics and supply chain management. *Journal of Supply Chain Management, 44*(2), 5–16. doi:10.1111/j.1745-493X.2008.00051.x

Williamson, O. E. (1985). *The economic institutions of capitalism*. New York, NY: The Free Press.

Williamson, O. E. (1999). Public and Private Bureaucracies: A transaction cost economics perspective. *Journal of Law Economics and Organization, 15*, 306–342. doi:10.1093/jleo/15.1.306

Williamson, O. E. (1991). Comparative economic organization: Vergleichende ökonomische Organisationstheorie: Die Analyse diskreter Strukturalternativen. In Ordelheide, D., Rudolph, B., & Büsselmann, E. (Eds.), *Betriebswirtschaftslehre und ökonomische Theorie* (pp. 13–49). Stuttgart, Germany: Schaeffer-Poeschel.

Williamson, O. E. (1989). *Operationalizing the new institutional economics: The transaction cost economics perspective*. Working Paper, Berkeley.

Williamson, O. E. (1990). *Comparative economic organization: The analysis of discrete structural alternatives*. Walter A. Haas School of Business Working Paper, Berkeley.

Williamson, O. E. (1989). *Operationalizing the new institutional economics: The transaction cost economics perspective*. Walter A. Haas School of Business Working Paper. University of California, Berkeley.

Willoughby, W. F. (2002). The movement for budgetary reform in the states. In A. C. Hyde (Ed.), *Government budgeting: Theory, process, and politics* (pp. 20-23). Thomson Learning. Wu, F. H. (1981). Incrementalism in financial strategic planning. *Academy of Management Review, 6*(1), 133-143.

Wilson, T. (1997). Information behaviour: An interdisciplinary approach. *Information Processing & Management, 33*, 551–572. doi:10.1016/S0306-4573(97)00028-9

Winkler, J., Dibbern, J., & Heinzl, A. (2008). The impact of cultural differences in offshore outsourcing: Case study results from German-Indian application development projects. *Information Systems Frontiers, 10*(2), 243–258. doi:10.1007/s10796-008-9068-5

Wirtz, B. (2010). An empirical analysis of the acceptance of e-procurement in the German public sector. *International Journal of Public Administration, 33*, 26–42. doi:10.1080/01900690903188768

Wixom, B. H., & Todd, P. A. (2005). A theoretical integration of user satisfaction and technology acceptance. *Information Systems Research, 16*(1), 85–102. doi:10.1287/isre.1050.0042

Wolfe, R. A. (1994). Organizational innovation: Review, critique and suggested research directions. *Organizational Dynamics, 31*(3), 403.

Woods, D. (1998). Designs are hypotheses about how artifacts shape cognition and collaboration. *Ergonomics, 41*(2), 168–173. doi:10.1080/001401398187215

Wooldridge, M. (2002). *An introduction to multiagent systems*. New York, NY: John Wiley and Sons.

Woolhandler, S., Campbell, T., & Himmelstein, D. (2003). Costs of health care administration in the United States and Canada. *The New England Journal of Medicine*, 349.

World Bank. (2003). *Electronic government procurement (e-GP): World Bank draft strategy*. Washington, DC: Author.

Xie, Y. H., Suh, T., & Kwon, I.-W. (2010). Do magnitude and asymmetry of specific asset investment matter in supplier-buyer relationship? *Journal of Marketing Management, 26*(9).

Yang, K. C. C. (2005). Exploring factors affecting the adoption of mobile commerce in Singapore. *Telematics and Informatics, 22*, 257–277. doi:10.1016/j.tele.2004.11.003

Yang, C., & Wu, C.-Y. (2003, October). *Perception difference between users and information professionals: A case study of TaiPower*. Paper presented at the ASIST Annual Meeting, Washington, DC.

Yen, G., & Ng, E. (2002). Migrating procurement onto the internet. *Electronic Commerce Research, 2*(1-2), 113–134. doi:10.1023/A:1013348303943

Yin, R. K. (2003). *Case study research: Design and methods*. Newbury Park, CA: Sage Publications Inc.

Yoshino, M., & Rangan, S. (1995). *Strategic alliances: An entrepreneurial approach to globalization*. Boston, MA: Harvard Business School Press.

Young-Ybarra, C., & Wiersema, M. (1999). Strategic flexibility in Information Technology alliances: The influence of transaction cost economics and social exchange theory. *Organization Science, 10*(4), 439–459. doi:10.1287/orsc.10.4.439

Zaheer, A., McEvily, B., & Perrone, V. (1998). Does trust matter? Exploring the effects of inter-organizational and interpersonal trust on performance. *Organization Science, 9*(2), 141–159. doi:10.1287/orsc.9.2.141

Zahn, E., Barth, T., & Hertweck, A. (1998). Outsourcing unternehmensnaher Dienstleistungen in der Region Stuttgart: Ergebnisse einer empirischen Untersuchung. In Gassert, H., Prechtl, M., & Zahn, E. (Eds.), *Innovative Dienstleistungspartnerschaften: Neue Formen der Zusammenarbeit zwischen Industrie und Dienstleistern* (pp. 109–137). Stuttgart, Germany: Schaeffer-Poeschel.

Zajac, E. J., & Olsen, C. P. (1993). From transaction cost to transaction value analysis: Implications for the study of interorganizational strategies. *Journal of Management Studies, 30*(1), 131–145. doi:10.1111/j.1467-6486.1993.tb00298.x

Zey, M. (Ed.). (1992). *Decision making: Alternatives to rational choice models*. Newbury Park, CA: Sage.

About the Contributors

Kishor Vaidya is Adjunct Senior Lecturer at the University of Southern Queensland, and Honorary Professional Associate at the Faculty of Information Sciences and Engineering of the University of Canberra. Dr Vaidya has a Master's degree in Information Systems from Central Queensland University and a PhD from the University of New England. He is the author of the book *Electronic Procurement: Impact on Procurement Performance*. He has published over 30 peer reviewed articles in various journals, book chapters, and international conference proceedings. His current research interests include adoption and assimilation of inter-organisational information systems, organizational theories, and theory-based evaluation of e-Business/e-Government initiatives. More recently, he has developed his research interests in issues relating to ICT for developing countries, including using ICT to combat corruption in public procurement.

* * *

Kanokwan Atchariyachanvanich is Lecturer at Thai-Nichi Institute of Technology, Thailand after completing a postdoctoral fellowship program from National Institute of Informatics, Japan. She received a Ph.D. in Informatics from the Graduate University for Advanced Studies, Japan in 2007, a M.S. in Information Management from the Asian Institute of Technology, Thailand in 2001, and a B.S. in Information Technology from Assumption University, Thailand in 1999. Her research interests include critical success factors in electronic commerce (EC), business models for EC and consumer behavior in EC market. Her prior research has been published in international journals and international proceedings such as International Journal of Electronic Customer Relationship Management, International Conference on Electronic Commerce, Information Processing Society of Japan (IPSJ) Journal, IEEE/IPSJ International Symposium on Applications and the Internet (SAINT), and ACM SIGecom Exchanges.

Joanne Callen is Associate Professor and works as a Senior Research Fellow in the Centre for Health Systems and Safety Research at the University of New South Wales. Previously she was Head of the Discipline of Health Informatics at the University of Sydney. Her research centres on exploring how information and communication technologies (ICT) can improve health outcomes for patients and support health professionals in the delivery of high quality, safe, and efficient patient care. She has published a considerable body of research on the use of clinical information systems and published the first international study which quantitatively linked organisational culture with the use of information systems. Recently her research has focused on how to use information technology and other systems strategies to improve the safety of test result follow-up.

John Campbell is Professor of Information Systems in the Faculty of Information Sciences and Engineering at the University of Canberra. A major theme throughout his research is how users interact through information systems in the social world and, in particular, the ways in which organizational decision-making and community interaction are enacted through collaborative technologies. He has published in *Information systems Journal*, *Information & Management*, *Data Base for Advances in Information Systems*, *Behaviour & Information Technology*, *Journal of Organizational Computing and Electronic Commerce*, and *Australasian Journal of Information Systems*.

Michael Essig is Professor and Chair for Materials Management & Distribution at Bundeswehr University Munich and is Co-Director of the Research Center for Law and Management of Public Procurement as well as the Transfer Center for Defence Supply Chain Management. Professor Essig acts on the review board of the "Journal of Supply Chain Management", the "Journal of Purchasing and Supply Management", "Supply Chain Management: An International Journal" and for the Research College of the Chartered Institute of Purchasing and Supply (CIPS). He is member of the Scientific Board of the German Purchasing Association, member of the Scientific Advisory Board of the Austrian Minister of Defence, member of the Scientific Board of the European Defence Public Private Partnership Association, and a former member of the advisory board of the European Research Center of Purchasing and Supply (ERPS) and of the management committee of the International Purchasing & Supply Education & Research Association (IPSERA).

Scott Gardner is Associate Professor and the Foundation Director of the Master Class Program at Murdoch University. Dr Gardner has fifteen years experience as an academic educator and manager, consultant and facilitator working in Australia, the United Kingdom (UK) and South East Asia. As a specialist in change management, strategic management and stakeholder communications he has published widely in academic and professional journals. His professional portfolio includes training or consulting for major public and private sector clients spanning Western Australia, (WA), New South Wales (NSW), the UK and Indonesia and acting as an internal strategy advisor for senior executive teams at two WA Universities.

Andrea Genovese is Lecturer at the University of Sheffield Management School. Dr Genovese received an MSc degree in Engineering and Technology Management from the University of Naples "Federico II" (Italy) and a PhD in Science and Technology Management from the same institution. He also holds a MBA from Whittemore School of Business and Economics at University of New Hampshire (USA). Since 2010, he has been working at the Logistics and Supply Chain Research Centre at the University of Sheffield Management School (UK), first as a post-doctoral researcher and then as a Lecturer. His research interests include the design of decision support systems for solving logistic problems and low carbon innovation management for supply chains.

Andrew Georgiou is Senior Research Fellow at the Centre for Health Systems and Safety Research, part of the Australian Institute of Health Innovation, University of New South Wales. He has worked in a number of senior research and executive positions including as the United Kingdome NHS Assistant Director of Classifications (1995-1997) and Co-coordinator for the Coronary Heart Disease Programme for the Royal College of Physicians in London (1999–2002) and Senior Research Fellow at the Centre for General Practice Integration Studies (2002-2004). Andrew is currently an Editorial Board member of the Open Medical Informatics Journal, the Journal of Pathology Informatics, Health Care Informatics Review and the International Journal of Medical Informatics.

Kholekile L. Gwebu is Assistant Professor of Decision Sciences at the University of New Hampshire. He earned his Ph.D. in Management and Information Systems from Kent State University. His research interests are in agent-based simulation, decision support, Open-Source Software and IT Outsourcing. His papers have appeared in Decision Support Systems, Journal of Information Systems, Journal of Strategic Information Systems, and Journal of Systems and Software.

John W. Hamilton is the Associate Director of the Consortium for Supply Chain Management Studies and Assistant Professor of Management at St. Louis University. He has an undergraduate degree from Washington University in St. Louis and MBA and doctoral degrees from St. Louis University. He retired from UniGroup, Inc., a private multi-billion dollar transportation company, as Senior Vice President and Chief Information Officer in 2002. He is and has been active in professional and community organizations including; the Center for the Advancement of Information Technology, Washington University; Academy of Management; and the National Defense Transportation Association. He is on the board of several local community and service organizations. He has published papers and presented on topics including *Trust and Transaction Cost in Supply Chain Optimization: An Exploratory Study, The Turnaround ERP Project: Strategies and Issues* to *'Wireless Communication Systems: A Satellite Based Approach for Competitive Advantage in Logistic and Transportation Support Services.'*

Seock-Jin Hong is a Professor at the Bordeaux Management School (BEM) in Bordeaux, France. Prior to joining BEM, Prof. Hong was a Associate Professor and Director at the Graduate School of Logistics at the University of Incheon. Prof Hong was a Research associate at the air transport department of the Korea Transport Institute (KOTI) and an Assistant general manager in Korean Airlines Seoul from 1988. During his stay in Korean Airline, he acted as a key person on global alliance with Air France and Delta and preparation of open-up the Incheon International Airport. And also, He has acted as a Researcher of ITA (Institute of Air Transport – Institut du Transport Aérien) in Paris, France. His research interests include supply chain and transport, supply chain risk managements, air transport and cargo and lean logistics. His papers have appeared in various journals such as *World Review of Intermodal Transportation Research, Transport Policy Studies, International Journal Electronic Customer Relationship Management and Korea Logistics Review*. He serves as a referee for *World Review of Intermodal Transportation Research, Journal of Korean Society of Transportation and Eastern Asia Society for Transportation Studies.*

Luke Houghton is lecturer in Information Systems and Management, in the Griffith Business School, Griffith University. He has worked in higher education fields since 2002 and completed his doctoral thesis in 2008 on the topic of cognitive engagement and unstructured problems. In his current role Luke acts as a Lecturer in Management, Logistics and Information Systems related courses. He also provides academic and service leadership to the Logistics and Management groups. His main interests lie in the role cognition and learning play in complex problem solving in business, organisations, information systems and higher education environments. He has been published in: *the Journal of the Operational Research Society, Australian Journal of Information Systems, Australasian Journal of Educational Technology, Systems Research and Behaviorial Science* and *the Journal of Information Technology Education.*

Robert Johnston is Professor and John Sharkey Chair of Information Systems and Organisation at University College Dublin. His main research areas are electronic commerce, supply chain management, inter-organisational information systems and theoretical foundations of Information Systems. He has over 130 refereed publications, many in leading international journals, including *Information Systems Research, Management Science, European Journal of Information Systems, Communications of the ACM, International Journal of Electronic Commerce, Elecronic Markets, Journal of the Operational Research Society, International Journal of Production Economics, Journal of Stategic Information Systems,* and *Supply Chain Management.* Prior to becoming an academic he spent 13 years as a freelance consulting analyst / project manager, designing and implementing about 25 large computer systems for inventory and production planning in a number of leading manufacturing companies in Australia.

Stefan Klein is Professor for Interorganizational Systems and a Director of the European Research Center for Informations Systems (ERCIS) at the Department of Information Systems, University of Münster. He has held teaching or research positions at University College Dublin, Ireland, University of Linz, Austria, University of Koblenz-Landau, Germany, University St. Gallen, Switzerland, Harvard University, German National Research Center for Computer Science (GMD), and University of Cologne. His current research areas are Information Infrastructures, Network Economy, Information Management, Social Media and the transformation of work.

Ik-Whan G. Kwon is Professor of Decision Sciences and MIS at the John Cook School of Business, St. Louis University. He is also a Director of the Center for Supply Chain Management Studies at the John Cook School of Business since 1998. Dr. Kwon is one of the founding members of the Center for Supply Chain Management Studies in 1998 and assumed the role of Directorship of the Center since its inception. Dr. Kwon has published more than 125 academic articles and professional papers in numerous journals including Journal of Supply Chain Management, Supply Chain Management: An International Journal, International Journal of Physical Distribution and Logistics Management, New England Journal of Medicine, American Journal of Medical Association, American Journal of Public Health and others. He serves on the Editorial Board of *Information Systems and Supply Chain Management*, Member of Editorial Board of *International Journal of Business Innovation and Research, Member of Editorial Board of International Journal of Procurement Management, Member of the Review Board of Supply Chain Management: An International Journal*, Member of the Review Board of *Managerial Issues*, and Member of Advisory Board at Business Innovative Research Center (BIRC) at University of Mass at Dartmouth.

Julie Li is a Research Assistant and PhD Candidate in the Centre for Health Systems and Safety Research within the Australian Institute of Health Innovation at the University of New South Wales. Julie has a background in health information management and is interested in the broader social implications of electronic information systems implementation with emphasis on innovations in clinical work practice. Prior to commencing her PhD, Julie completed an Honours project focussing on the impact of Computerised Provider Order Entry on the test management work practices of Emergency clinicians. She is currently undertaking a PhD exploring the influence of information communication technology on the clinical work practices and role of Nurse Practitioners in emergency departments. She also sits as a student member on the editorial board of the Methods of Information in Medicine journal.

Yaotai Lu is Adjunct faculty in the School of Public Administration, Florida Atlantic University. His major research areas include public budgeting and finance, public asset management, public procurement, and public safety management.

Maria Madlberger is Professor at the Department of Business and Management at Webster Vienna Private University. Her research is focused on the interdisciplinary links between information systems, supply chain management, and marketing. Current research interests are related to information systems-based inter-organizational collaboration, such as electronic data interchange, information sharing, supply chain collaboration in the context of efficient consumer response (ECR), and electronic commerce B2B and B2C. Dr. Madlberger published her research in journals such as the International Journal of e-Collaboration, Journal of Electronic Commerce in Organizations, Electronic Markets, and International Journal of Physical Distribution and Logistics Management, among others. She is an Associate Editor of the Electronic Commerce Research Journal and serves as a session and minitrack chair at various conferences (e.g., AMCIS, ECIS, Conf-IRM). She received her Ph.D. from the Vienna University of Economics and Business where she was an Assistant Professor at the Department of Management Information Systems and the Department of Retailing and Marketing.

Bruce McCabe works at the intersection of technology, innovation and business. He began his career at IBM in 1988 and has held senior roles at IBM, WordPerfect, Novell and Gartner. In 2002 he founded S2 Intelligence, a think tank to support organisational innovation through grounded research. In 2009 he started an Innovation Advisory practice for KPMG, to help organisations create value through innovative new products, services and processes. He is currently working with National ICT Australia, the nation's peak computer science organisation, to help them spin-off new commercial enterprises. Bruce is widely recognised for his pioneering research into how new technologies are adopted and applied in business. He has authored more than 300 essays, columns and research papers. Over the past 16 years has supplied independent analysis to most companies on the ASX-100, and to agencies in every State and Federal government. He has acted as an advisor to the Commonwealth Scientific and Industrial Research Organisation (CSIRO) and maintains relationships with a variety of universities, science organisations and commercial R & D labs.

Flávio Perazzo Barbosa Mota is Assistant Professor of Public Administration at Universidade Federal da Paraíba, Brazil. He completed his graduated studies at Universidade Federal do Ceara and his Master at Universidade Federal da Paraíba. His areas of interests include management information systems, organizational theory and e-government.

Hitoshi Okada is an Associate Professor of the Information and Society Research Division, at the National Institute of Informatics (NII), Japan. Dr Okada got his Bachelor of Public Law (LLB) and Bachelor of Private Law (LLB) from the University of Tokyo, Japan. He completed his MA at the Osaka School of International Public Policy (OSIPP) at Osaka University, Japan. He got his Ph.D. in International Public Policy from Osaka University, Japan. His current research topic is law and economics of e-money and e-commerce. He published a book titled 'Understanding E-Money (in Japanese)' from the Nikkei Newspaper Publisher in Japan. He is a co-organizer of the Workshop of IT-enabled Service (ITeS) at the Symposium of IEEE/IPSJ International Symposium on Applications and the Internet (SAINT). He was selected as a Member of the Committee for Convergence of Communications and Broadcasting at the

Ministry of Internal Affairs and Communications (MIC) in Japan, a Member of the Information Frontier Research Committee at MIC in Japan, and a Member of the Information Exploration Era Research Committee at the Ministry of Economy, Trade and Industry (METI) in Japan. He is a Special Senior Research Fellow of the Institute for Information and Communications Policy (IICP) at MIC in Japan.

Md Mahbubur Rahim is Senior Lecturer at the Caulfield School of Information Technology, Faculty of IT, MONASH University, Australia. He has research and teaching interests in the areas of e-business, e-governance, adoption and impact of IT-enabled systems in organisations, and formulation and implementation of IT strategies in organisations. Rahim has published the outcomes of his research in about 70 refereed journals and conference proceedings. He is also the recipient of the BEST PAPER AWARD at the International Conference on e-Commerce, e-Administration, e-Society and e-Education (e-CASE2008), Thailand, and IT and Its Applications (ITA94) conference, UK, 1994. Rahim has received over a quarter million in research funding from the Australian Research Council. Currently, Rahim is serving as the Chief Editor, IBIMA Journal of Innovations Management in SMEs. He is also an editorial board member for the Journal of Administration & Governance.

Shams Rahman is Professor of Supply Chain Management, at the School of Business IT and Logistics, RMIT University. Professor Rahman, a former British Commonwealth scholar, has worked in various Universities in Australia, United Kingdom, and Thailand. He is on the editorial board of ten international journals and a foundation member of the International Advisory Committee of the Asia-Pacific Federation of Logistics & Supply Chain Systems. Professor Shams Rahman has published over 120 scholarly papers which include articles in international journals, book chapters, and referred papers in international conference proceedings. He is frequently called upon to make presentations for professional bodies and senior executives on issues such as supply chain management, cold logistics, six sigma and quality management, reverse logistics, and theory of constraints. Professor Rahman holds masters degrees in Industrial Engineering and in Mechanical Engineering and a PhD in Operations Research from the University of Exeter, UK.

Kai Reimers is Professor of Information Systems at RWTH Aachen University in the Faculty of Business and Economics. Trained in economics and business administration in Germany, Professor Reimers works at the interface between information systems and organization theory. He received a doctorate in economics and business administration from the University of Wuppertal with a thesis on the economic analysis of standardization processes and earned a post-doctorate degree ("venia legendi") at the University of Bremen with a thesis on IT Management. From September 1998 to August 2003 he worked as a Visiting Professor at the School of Economics and Management, Tsinghua University, Beijing, sponsored by the German Academic Exchange Service (DAAD). Since September 2003 he works as a Full Professor of Information Systems at RWTH Aachen University in the Faculty of Business and Economics where he heads the Research Group on Electronic Business. His fields of interest cover inter-organizational information systems (electronic data interchange, electronic markets), enterprise systems implementation, and issues of information systems standardization.

José Rodrigues Filho is an associate professor of Management Information Systems at the Universidade Federal da Paraíba, Brazil. He was Takemi Fellow at Harvard University and completed his postdoctoral studies at the Johns Hopkins University School of Public Health, and his doctoral studies at the University of Manchester, England. He was visiting professor at Acadia University (Canada), and associate professor at the Universidade Federal de Pernambuco, Brazil. His areas of interests include management information systems, information management, specially, health information, nursing information and hospital information systems, in addition to e-government and e-voting.

Anne Rouse is Associate Professor of Innovation and Business Strategy and an organizational psychologist at the Deakin Graduate School of Business. There she teaches innovation management, IT strategy, and business consulting. She joined Deakin after several decades in industry, working as a project management and business process specialist. Dr Rouse's PhD, from the University of Melbourne, investigated outsourcing risks and benefits. As a result of this research she became co-author of the first Federal Government's guide to sourcing, published in 2004. This guide continues to be adapted and used by Australian Federal and State governments as a blueprint for managing outsourced arrangements. Dr Rouse publishes on innovation and outsourcing-related topics.

Barry Shore, Professor of Management Sciences at the University of New Hampshire, received his undergraduate degree in engineering from Tufts University and his PhD from the University of Wisconsin. He has authored over 100 peer-reviewed research articles and presentations and four books published by McGraw-Hill and Holt Rinehart and Winston. Previous to receiving his PhD he worked for Boeing Company, General Electric and Hewlett-Packard. He is a fellow of the Global Information Technology Association, has served as Chairman of the Board and was elected in 2010 to the Cosmos Club in Washington, D.C.

Jeffrey Soar is Professor and Chair in Intelligent Domestic Healthcare Infrastructure at the University of Southern Queensland. He is internationally recognised for his research leadership in eHealth and specifically the field of technology to support seniors in independent living and access to healthcare. He came into research leadership roles in academia following a long career as a senior industry executive with strategic responsibilities in Australian state and federal government agencies as well as national and regional agencies in New Zealand. Prof Soar is the founder and Convenor of the Queensland Smart Home Initiative and the SAIL (Smart Ageing & Independent Living) research consortium. Jeffrey has over 100 peer-reviewed publications and has attracted over 30 grants and commissions for research projects including national strategy papers. He has been engaged by governments and international development agencies for projects and strategic advice in the Asia-Pacific and Middle East regions.

Khi V. Thai is Professor, and Director, School of Public Administration, and also Interim Director, School of Criminology and Criminal Justice, Florida Atlantic University. His expertise is in public budgeting, financial management and public procurement. He authored or co-authored to over 100 refereed journal articles, book chapters, books, technical reports, and has been editing three academic journals. Most recently, he has provided technical assistance to the South Florida Water Management District, the Government of Sierra Leone, Uganda, Bulgaria, Columbia, United Nations, USAID, and the Federal Government of Canada in the area of procurement reforms, procurement integrity and international procurement He is the founder of the Public Procurement Research Center in 1999, and served as its director until 2007. In 2004, Professor Thai initiated the International Public Procurement Conference, which has become the largest international conference in the field of government procurement in the world.

Sebastian Titz studied industrial engineering and management at a the TU Ilmenau, Germany and received an MBA at the Unibesity oh New Hampshire, USA. He completed his PhD at the University of Naples, Italy, his research focusing on the social interaction of employees after corporate mergers.

Shiro Uesugi is Professor of Management Information System (MIS) at Matsuyama University in Shikoku Island, Japan since 2001. He teaches such courses as "Social Business," and MIS for graduate students at Graduate School of Business Administration, and MIS, and "Information Society and Ethics" for undergraduate students of Business Administration major. His research interests include Electronic Commerce, Digital Business, Privacy Protection in e-Business, Information Ethics, IT-enabled Services, Digital Divide, and Social Entrepreneurship. Born in Kyoto 1965, he was educated at Osaka University, where he graduated with the degree of Bachelor of Economics. He worked at Japanese Commercial Megabank and Japan's Ministry of Foreign Affairs before joining academia. He was an Adjunct lecture at Kobe City University of Foreign Studies (2000-01), Ehime University (2006-07) while he teaches at Matsuyama University. He published articles in such journal as "info" and "Journal of Entrepreneurship Research," and various conference papers of IEEE, ITS, IEICE, JSIM. He is the executive editor of "Journal of Informatics and Regional Studies." He has been served as a board member of Japan Society for Information and Management (JSIM), he is also a member of IEEE, ITS, ISTR, JANPORA, IEICE, JASMIN. He has MPA from Harvard University, Ph.D. from Osaka University.

Jim Underwood is Senior Lecturer at the University of Technology, Sydney. Dr Underwood has been teaching and researching the social aspects of IS development for more than 40 years, mostly in Canberra and Sydney. He was originally a mathematician and has worked for several IT consulting companies. His interests include the politics of information systems development, the dynamics of learning, and the meaning of knowledge and self in a virtual society, approached through the philosophical lenses of Foucault, Latour and Deleuze (amongst others).

Venky Venkatachalam is Professor and Co-Project Leader for the Green Launching Pad project at the University of New Hampshire. He is the Chair of the Decision Sciences department and Professor of Information Systems in the Whittemore School of Business and Economics at the University of New Hampshire. Since August 2005 he has been Director of the Enterprise Integration Research Center at the University of New Hampshire. He received his bachelors degree with honors in mechanical engineering from the University of Madras, India, MBA from the Indian Institute of Management, Calcutta, and Ph.D. from the University of Alabama.

Jing Wang is assistant professor of Decision Sciences at the Whittemore School of Business and Economics, University of New Hampshire. Her research focuses on the area of IT Outsourcing, Open Source Software, and Agent-based Decision Support Systems. Her work has been published in the *Decision Support Systems, Journal of Business Research, Journal of Information Systems, Journal of Strategic Information Systems*, and *Journal of Systems and Software*.

Marilyn Wells is Lecturer in the School of Information and Communications Technology (SICT) at CQUniversity (CQUni), and previously worked at University of Western Sydney (UWS) for five years before joining CQUni. Marilyn joined UWS after holding senior management positions in various organisations as well as implementing information systems in SMEs. Marilyn has experience in teaching at postgraduate and undergraduate levels, and her research interests include the power/knowledge nexus, resistance to change, perceptions of implementing new information systems and student educational experience. Marilyn holds a PhD and Masters of Commerce (IS) from UWS.

Johanna Westbrook is Professor and Director of the Centre for Health Systems and Safety Research (CHSSR), Australian Institute of Health Innovation (AIHI), Faculty of Medicine, University of New South Wales. Her research expertise centres on the design and execution of complex multi-method evaluations in the health sector with a particular focus on the effective use of information and communication technologies. She has undertaken leading research on medication safety, the effectiveness of electronic medication management systems to reduce errors and safe work and communication practices in hospitals. Professor Westbrook has an extensive publication record which includes over 200 refereed publications and has won several awards for her research.

Index

A

B

C

D

E

F

G

H

I

J

K

L

M

N

O

P

R

S

CPSIA information can be obtained at www.ICGtesting.com
Printed in the USA
BVOW050744011211

276863BV00002B/3/P

9 781609 607685